ALL WE ASK IS TO BE LET ALONE

THE LOCHLAINN SEABROOK COLLECTION

Everything You Were Taught About the Civil War is Wrong, Ask a Southerner!
Everything You Were Taught About American Slavery is Wrong, Ask a Southerner!
Everything You Were Taught About African-Americans and the Civil War is Wrong, Ask a Southerner!
Lincoln's War: The Real Cause, the Real Winner, the Real Loser
Abraham Lincoln Was a Liberal, Jefferson Davis Was a Conservative: The Missing Key to Understanding the American Civil War
Confederate Flag Facts: What Every American Should Know About Dixie's Southern Cross
Give This Book to a Yankee! A Southern Guide to the Civil War For Northerners
Women in Gray: A Tribute to the Ladies Who Supported the Southern Confederacy
The Unholy Crusade: Lincoln's Legacy of Destruction in the American South
Honest Jeff and Dishonest Abe: A Southern Children's Guide to the Civil War
Confederacy 101: Amazing Facts You Never Knew About America's Oldest Political Tradition
Slavery 101: Amazing Facts You Never Knew About America's "Peculiar Institution"
The Great Yankee Coverup: What the North Doesn't Want You to Know About Lincoln's War!
All We Ask Is To Be Let Alone: The Southern Secession Fact Book
Confederate Blood and Treasure: An Interview With Lochlainn Seabrook
The Ultimate Civil War Quiz Book: Test Your Knowledge of America's Most Misunderstood Conflict
A Rebel Born: A Defense of Nathan Bedford Forrest - Confederate General, American Legend (winner of the 2011 Jefferson Davis Historical Gold Medal)
A Rebel Born: The Screenplay
Nathan Bedford Forrest: Southern Hero, American Patriot - Honoring a Confederate Icon and the Old South
The Quotable Nathan Bedford Forrest: Selections From the Writings and Speeches of the Confederacy's Most Brilliant Cavalryman
Give 'Em Hell Boys! The Complete Military Correspondence of Nathan Bedford Forrest
Forrest! 99 Reasons to Love Nathan Bedford Forrest
Saddle, Sword, and Gun: A Biography of Nathan Bedford Forrest For Teens
Nathan Bedford Forrest and the Battle of Fort Pillow: Yankee Myth, Confederate Fact
Nathan Bedford Forrest and the Ku Klux Klan: Yankee Myth, Confederate Fact
Nathan Bedford Forrest and African-Americans: Yankee Myth, Confederate Fact
The Quotable Jefferson Davis: Selections From the Writings and Speeches of the Confederacy's First President
The Quotable Alexander H. Stephens: Selections From the Writings and Speeches of the Confederacy's First Vice President
The Alexander H. Stephens Reader: Excerpts From the Works of a Confederate Founding Father
The Quotable Robert E. Lee: Selections From the Writings and Speeches of the South's Most Beloved Civil War General
The Old Rebel: Robert E. Lee As He Was Seen By His Contemporaries
The Articles of Confederation Explained: A Clause-by-Clause Study of America's First Constitution
The Constitution of the Confederate States of America Explained: A Clause-by-Clause Study of the South's Magna Carta
The Quotable Stonewall Jackson: Selections From the Writings and Speeches of the South's Most Famous General
Abraham Lincoln: The Southern View - Demythologizing America's Sixteenth President
The Unquotable Abraham Lincoln: The President's Quotes They Don't Want You To Know!
Lincolnology: The Real Abraham Lincoln Revealed in His Own Words - A Study of Lincoln's Suppressed, Misinterpreted, and Forgotten Writings and Speeches
The Great Impersonator! 99 Reasons to Dislike Abraham Lincoln
Encyclopedia of the Battle of Franklin - A Comprehensive Guide to the Conflict that Changed the Civil War
Carnton Plantation Ghost Stories: True Tales of the Unexplained from Tennessee's Most Haunted Civil War House!
The McGavocks of Carnton Plantation: A Southern History - Celebrating One of Dixie's Most Noble Confederate Families and Their Tennessee Home
Jesus and the Law of Attraction: The Bible-Based Guide to Creating Perfect Health, Wealth, and Happiness Following Christ's Simple Formula
The Bible and the Law of Attraction: 99 Teachings of Jesus, the Apostles, and the Prophets
Christ Is All and In All: Rediscovering Your Divine Nature and the Kingdom Within
Jesus and the Gospel of Q: Christ's Pre-Christian Teachings As Recorded in the New Testament
Seabrook's Bible Dictionary of Traditional and Mystical Christian Doctrines
The Way of Holiness: The Story of Religion and Myth From the Cave Bear Cult to Christianity
Christmas Before Christianity: How the Birthday of the "Sun" Became the Birthday of the "Son"
Britannia Rules: Goddess-Worship in Ancient Anglo-Celtic Society - An Academic Look at the United Kingdom's Matricentric Spiritual Past
The Book of Kelle: An Introduction to Goddess-Worship and the Great Celtic Mother-Goddess Kelle, Original Blessed Lady of Ireland
The Goddess Dictionary of Words and Phrases: Introducing a New Core Vocabulary for the Women's Spirituality Movement
Aphrodite's Trade: The Hidden History of Prostitution Unveiled
UFOs and Aliens: The Complete Guidebook
The Caudills: An Etymological, Ethnological, and Genealogical Study - Exploring the Name and National Origins of a European-American Family
The Blakeneys: An Etymological, Ethnological, and Genealogical Study - Uncovering the Mysterious Origins of the Blakeney Family and Name
Princess Diana: Modern Day Moon-Goddess - A Psychoanalytical and Mythological Look at Diana Spencer's Life, Marriage, and Death (with Dr. Jane Goldberg)
Autobiography of a Non-Yogi: A Scientist's Journey From Hinduism to Christianity (with Dr. Amitava Dasgupta)

Five-Star Books & Gifts From the Heart of the American South

SeaRavenPress.com

LINCOLN ON SECESSION

Any people anywhere, being inclined and having the power, have the right to rise up, and shake off the existing government, and form a new one that suits them better. This is a most valuable, a most sacred right—a right which, we hope and believe, is to liberate the world. Nor is this right confined to cases in which the whole people of an existing government may choose to exercise it. Any portion of such people that can may revolutionize, and make their own of so much of the territory as they inhabit.[1]

> Abraham Lincoln, January 12, 1848, in a speech before the U.S. House of Representatives

DAVIS ON SECESSION

The Right of Secession—that subject which, beyond all others, ignorance, prejudice, and political rancor have combined to cloud with misstatements and misapprehensions—is a question easily to be determined in the light of . . . the history and principles of the Constitution. It is not something standing apart by itself—a factious creation, outside of and antagonistic to the Constitution—as might be imagined by one deriving his ideas from the [Northern] political literature most current of late years. So far from being against the Constitution or incompatible with it, we contend that, if the right to secede is not prohibited to the States, and no power to prevent it expressly delegated to the United States, it remains as reserved to the States or the people, from whom all the powers of the General Government were derived.[2]

> Jefferson Davis, from *The Rise and Fall of the Confederate Government*, 1881

ALL WE ASK IS TO BE LET ALONE

THE SOUTHERN SECESSION FACT BOOK

GENEROUSLY ILLUSTRATED BY THE AUTHOR, "THE VOICE OF THE TRADITIONAL SOUTH," COLONEL

LOCHLAINN SEABROOK

JEFFERSON DAVIS HISTORICAL GOLD MEDAL WINNER

Diligently Researched for the
Elucidation of the Reader

2017
Sea Raven Press, Nashville, Tennessee, USA

ALL WE ASK IS TO BE LET ALONE

Published by
Sea Raven Press, Cassidy Ravensdale, President
The Literary Wing of the Pro-South Movement
PO Box 1484, Spring Hill, Tennessee 37174-1484 USA
SeaRavenPress.com • searavenpress@gmail.com

Copyright © 2017 Lochlainn Seabrook
in accordance with U.S. and international copyright laws and regulations, as stated and protected under the Berne Union for the Protection of Literary and Artistic Property (Berne Convention), and the Universal Copyright Convention (the UCC). All rights reserved under the Pan-American and International Copyright Conventions.

1st SRP paperback edition, 1st printing: June 2017, ISBN: 978-1-943737-46-8
1st SRP hardcover edition, 1st printing: June 2017, ISBN: 978-1-943737-47-5

ISBN: 978-1-943737-46-8 (paperback)
Library of Congress Control Number: 2017937645

This work is the copyrighted intellectual property of Lochlainn Seabrook and has been registered with the Copyright Office at the Library of Congress in Washington, D.C., USA. No part of this work (including text, covers, drawings, photos, illustrations, maps, images, diagrams, etc.), in whole or in part, may be used, reproduced, stored in a retrieval system, or transmitted, in any form or by any means now known or hereafter invented, without written permission from the publisher. The sale, duplication, hire, lending, copying, digitalization, or reproduction of this material, in any manner or form whatsoever, is also prohibited, and is a violation of federal, civil, and digital copyright law, which provides severe civil and criminal penalties for any violations.

All We Ask Is To Be Let Alone: The Southern Secession Fact Book, by Lochlainn Seabrook. Includes an index, endnotes, and bibliographical references.

Front and back cover design and art, book design, layout, and interior art by Lochlainn Seabrook
All images, graphic design, graphic art, and illustrations copyright © Lochlainn Seabrook
Cover images & design copyright © Lochlainn Seabrook
Portions of this book have been adapted from the author's other works

The views on the American "Civil War" documented in this book are those of the publisher.

The paper used in this book is acid-free and lignin-free. It has been certified by the Sustainable Forestry Initiative and the Forest Stewardship Council and meets all ANSI standards for archival quality paper.

PRINTED & MANUFACTURED IN OCCUPIED TENNESSEE, FORMER CONFEDERATE STATES OF AMERICA

DEDICATION

To my secessionist ancestors, from both the first American Revolution and the second American Revolution.

EPIGRAPH

All we ask is to be let alone—that those who never held power over us shall not now attempt our subjugation by arms. This we will, we must, resist to the direst extremity. The moment that this pretension is abandoned, the sword will drop from our grasp, and we shall be ready to enter into treaties of amity and commerce that can not but be mutually beneficial. So long as this pretension is maintained, with a firm reliance on that Divine Power which covers with its protection the just cause, we must continue to struggle for our inherent right to freedom, independence, and self-government.

C.S. President Jefferson Davis

BEFORE THE CONFEDERATE CONGRESS
MONTGOMERY, ALABAMA, APRIL 29, 1861
TWO WEEKS AFTER THE START OF LINCOLN'S WAR

CONTENTS

Notes to the Reader - 11
Introduction, by Lochlainn Seabrook - 17

1 SECESSION: CONSTITUTIONAL OR UNCONSTITUTIONAL? - 21
2 THE SOUTHERN RESPONSE TO THE IDEA OF SECESSION - 89
3 THE THIRTEEN SOUTHERN SECESSION ORDINANCES - 114
4 THE HISTORY BEHIND THE SECESSION ORDINANCES - 136
5 THE MOTIVATIONS BEHIND THE SECESSION ORDINANCES - 152
6 THE SOUTHERN DEFENSE OF SECESSION - 169
7 THE PRO-SLAVERY SECESSIONISTS - 215
8 BOTH SIDES SAID THAT THE WAR WAS NOT OVER SLAVERY - 244
9 WHY YANKEES HAVE NO RIGHT TO CRITICIZE THE SOUTH FOR SECEDING FROM THE UNION - 269
10 ECONOMICS: THE MAIN REASON THE NORTH DID NOT WANT THE SOUTH TO SECEDE - 301
11 SECESSION & THE UNITED STATES ARE SYNONYMOUS - 315

Appendix A: The Day South Carolina Seceded - 353
Appendix B: The Kentucky and Virginia Resolutions - 356
Appendix C: The Virginia Report of 1799 - 363
Appendix D: The Growth of Sectional Antagonism - 399
Appendix E: Secession A Legal Right - 405
Appendix F: Reasons for Secession - 406
Appendix G: Averments of Fact or, Why Jefferson Davis Was Not a Traitor - 408
Notes - 410
Bibliography - 428
Index - 443
Meet the Author - 449

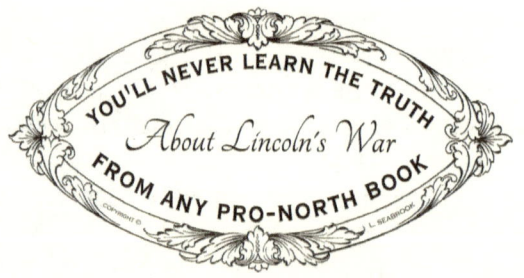

NOTES TO THE READER

"NOTHING IN THE PAST IS DEAD TO THE MAN WHO WOULD
LEARN HOW THE PRESENT CAME TO BE WHAT IT IS."

WILLIAM STUBBS, VICTORIAN ENGLISH HISTORIAN

THE TWO MAIN POLITICAL PARTIES IN 1860
☛ In any study of America's antebellum, bellum, and postbellum periods, it is vitally important to understand that in 1860 the two major political parties—the Democrats and the newly formed Republicans—were the opposite of what they are today. In other words, the Democrats of the mid 19th Century were Conservatives, akin to the Republican Party of today, while the Republicans of the mid 19th Century were Liberals, akin to the Democratic Party of today.[3]

Thus the Confederacy's Democratic president, Jefferson Davis, was a Conservative (with libertarian leanings); the Union's Republican president, Abraham Lincoln, was a Liberal (with socialistic leanings).[4]

The author's cousin, Confederate Vice President and Democrat Alexander H. Stephens: a Southern Conservative.

This is why, in the mid 1800s, the conservative wing of the Democratic Party was known as "the States' Rights Party."[5]

Hence, the Democrats of the Civil War period referred to themselves as "conservatives," "confederates," "anti-centralists," or "constitutionalists" (the latter because they favored strict adherence to the original Constitution—which tacitly guaranteed states' rights—as created by the Founding Fathers), while the Republicans called themselves "liberals," "nationalists," "centralists," or "consolidationists" (the latter three because they wanted to nationalize the central government and consolidate political power in Washington, D.C.).[6]

Since this idea is new to most of my readers, let us further demystify it by viewing it from the perspective of the American Revolutionary War. If Davis and his conservative Southern constituents (the Democrats of 1861) had been alive in 1775, they would have sided with George Washington and the American colonists, who sought to secede from the tyrannical government of Great Britain; if Lincoln and his Liberal Northern constituents (the Republicans of 1861) had been alive at that time, they would have sided with King George III and the English monarchy, who sought to maintain the American colonies as possessions of the British Empire. It is due to this very comparison that Southerners often refer to their secession as the Second Declaration of Independence and the "Civil War" as the Second American Revolutionary War.

Without a basic understanding of these facts, the American "Civil War" will forever remain incomprehensible. For a full discussion of this topic see my book, *Abraham Lincoln Was a Liberal, Jefferson Davis Was a Conservative: The Missing Key to Understanding the American Civil War.*

THE TERM "CIVIL WAR"

☛ As I heartily dislike the phrase "Civil War," its use throughout this book (as well as in my other works) is worthy of explanation.

Today America's entire literary system refers to the conflict of 1861 using the Northern term the "Civil War," whether we in the South like it or not. Thus, all book searches by readers, libraries, and retail outlets are now performed online, and as all bookstores categorize works from this period under the heading "Civil War," book publishers and authors who deal with this particular topic have little choice but to use this term themselves. If I were to refuse to use it, as some of my Southern colleagues have suggested, few people would ever find or read my books.

The American "Civil War" was not a true civil war as Webster defines it: "A conflict between opposing groups of citizens of the *same* country." It was a fight between two individual countries; or to be more specific, two separate and constitutionally formed confederacies: the U.S.A. and the C.S.A.

Add to this the fact that scarcely any non-Southerners have ever heard of the names we in the South use for the conflict, such as the "War for Southern Independence"—or my personal preference, "Lincoln's War." It only makes sense then to use the term "Civil War" in most commercial situations, distasteful though it is.

We should also bear in mind that while today educated persons, particularly educated Southerners, all share an abhorrence for the phrase "Civil War," it was not always so. Confederates who lived through and even fought in the conflict regularly used the term throughout the 1860s, and even long after. Among them were Confederate generals such as Nathan Bedford Forrest, Richard Taylor, and Joseph E. Johnston, not to mention the Confederacy's vice president, Alexander H. Stephens.

Confederate General James Longstreet was just one of many Southern officials who referred to the conflict of 1861 as the "Civil War."

In 1895 Confederate General James Longstreet wrote about his military experiences in a work subtitled, *Memoirs of the Civil War in America*. Even the Confederacy's highest leader, President Jefferson Davis, used the term "Civil War,"[7] and in one case at least, as late as 1881—the year he wrote his brilliant exposition, *The Rise and Fall of the Confederate Government*.[8] Authors writing for *Confederate Veteran* magazine sometimes used the phrase well into the early 1900s,[9] and in 1898, at the Eighth Annual Meeting and Reunion of the United Confederate Veterans (the forerunner of today's Sons of Confederate Veterans), the following resolution was proposed: that from then on the Great War of 1861 was to be designated "the Civil War Between the States."[10]

A WORD ON EARLY AMERICAN MATERIAL

☞ In order to preserve the authentic historicity of the Revolutionary and Civil War periods, I have retained the original spellings, formatting, and punctuation of the early Americans I quote. These include such items as British-English spellings, long-running paragraphs, obsolete words, and various literary devices peculiar to the time. Bracketed words within quotes are my additions and clarifications, while italicized words within quotes are (where indicated) my emphasis.

PRESENTISM

☛ As a historian I view *presentism* (judging the past according to present day mores and customs) as the enemy of authentic history. And this is precisely why the Left employs it in its ongoing war against traditional American, conservative, and Christian values. By looking at history through the lens of modern day beliefs, they are

Judging our ancestors by our own standards is unfair, unjust, misleading, and unethical.

able to distort, revise, and reshape the past into a false narrative that fits their ideological agenda: the liberalization *and* Northernization of America, the enlargement and further centralization of the national government, and total control of American political, economic, and social power, the same agenda that Lincoln championed.

This book rejects presentism and replaces it with what I call *historicalism*: judging our ancestors based on the values of their own time. To get the most from this work the reader is invited to reject presentism as well. In this way—along with casting aside preconceived notions and the fake "history" churned out by our left-wing education system—the truth in this work will be most readily ascertained and absorbed.

LEARN MORE

☛ Lincoln's War on the American people and the Constitution can never be fully understood without a thorough knowledge of the South's perspective. As this book is only meant to be a brief introductory guide to these topics, one cannot hope to learn the complete story here. For those who are interested in additional material from the South's perspective, please see my comprehensive histories listed on page 2.

Keep Your Body, Mind, & Spirit Vibrating at Their Highest Level

YOU CAN DO SO BY READING THE BOOKS OF

SEA RAVEN PRESS

There is nothing that will so perfectly keep your body, mind, and spirit in a healthy condition as to think wisely and positively. Hence you should not only read this book, but also the other books that we offer. They will quicken your physical, mental, and spiritual vibrations, enabling you to maintain a position in society as a healthy erudite person.

KEEP YOURSELF WELL-INFORMED!

The well-informed person is always at the head of the procession, while the ignorant, the lazy, and the unthoughtful hang onto the rear. If you are a Spiritual man or woman, do yourself a great favor: read Sea Raven Press books and stay well posted on the Truth. It is almost criminal for one to remain in ignorance while the opportunity to gain knowledge is open to all at a nominal price.

We invite you to visit our Webstore for a wide selection of wholesome, family-friendly, well-researched, educational books for all ages. You will be glad you did!

Five-Star Books & Gifts From the Heart of the American South

SeaRavenPress.com

To live under the American Constitution is the greatest privilege that was ever accorded the human race.

CONSERVATIVE U.S. PRESIDENT
CALVIN COOLIDGE

INTRODUCTION

In my experience as an unreconstructed Southern historian, one of the greatest barriers to truly understanding Lincoln's War is the concept of secession. Our mainstream education system, along with its aggressive army of South-hating, South-shaming Liberal teachers, writers, and academics, has made this topic even more difficult than it already was due to their fabrication of thousands of fictions, meant to sow both misinformation and disinformation into the public domain. Sage writes that shortly after the formation of the U.S.A. in 1776,

> political tricksters, perverters of constitutions, corrupters of public sentiment, and violators alike of sacred faith and common decency, have compelled the patriots and statesmen of the country to retire, and have, for selfish and partisan purposes, introduced a false worship, which may be called unionolatry... [11]

Yes, progressive enemies of the Conservative South place the Union, which they incorrectly consider "sacred" and "perpetual," above everything, including the Constitution. The problem here is one of ignorance, for those who view the Constitution as an inferior document are generally those who know the least about it. And what they do know they misunderstand and therefore misinterpret.

Not surprisingly, the primary "political tricksters, perverters of constitutions, and corrupters of public sentiment" today are Liberals; though uneducated Conservatives are often responsible as well. Nowhere are their tricks, perversions, and corruptions more evident than on the topic of the American "Civil War." Because they operate from emotion rather than reason, from ideology rather than fact, from opinion rather than history, nothing is too illogical, too bizarre. In the Liberal world of fake Civil War history, inventions, sophistry, lies, editorializing, and absurdities abound, most which, sadly, have been accepted wholesale by an unwitting public.

At the top of the list of these insidious and incongruous falsehoods is the myth that "secession was illegal in the 1860s." To the uninformed, if it was illegal then this means, in turn, that the Southern states committed a heinous crime by separating from the Union, and therefore "deserved everything they got"—a statement I have heard more than once from the naive, the unenlightened, the anti-intellectual, the malevolent, and the primitive.

Another vacuous contrivance of the anti-South movement is that "Abraham Lincoln was a lifelong anti-secessionist," a stupendous fraud that rates alongside such old fables as "Lincoln preserved the Union," "Lincoln freed the slaves," "Lincoln was a lifelong abolitionist," and "Lincoln loved the black race," all pieces of fake history, arrogantly served up to the unwary masses by the fact-hating Left.

Under the overt double standard practiced by Liberals, they freely reverse reality in order to present themselves in a good light and their conservative foes in a bad one. Thus was manufactured the canard that early Americans who supported secession were "unpatriotic," "nullifiers," "disunionists," and "traitors," guilty of "high crimes and treason." As my book will show, the opposite is true. Those who believed in the right of secession were authentic patriots following American law, history, custom, and tradition. It is those who opposed it who were violating the foundational underpinnings of the U.S., the wishes of the Founding Fathers, and indeed the very spirit of the Constitution itself.

One secession myth that has always been both particularly contentious and ludicrous declares that the 13 Southern Secession Ordinances prove that "the South only seceded in order to preserve slavery." This demonstrable misrepresentation was being used against the South from even before the start of Lincoln's War, and it is still being used to tarnish Dixie's legacy today.

Throughout this book I will dismantle these and a host of other Liberal and Yankee fantasies related to secession, the Confederacy, Davis, the Union, and Lincoln. Unlike mainstream "educators," who target the ignorant and uneducated for indoctrination using feelings, anecdotes, and persuasion, I will use the scientific method by relying on proven facts, genuine knowledge, verified history, hard evidence, and professional and eyewitness testimony to illustrate and document the truth. This is, after all, why I subtitled this work, *The Southern Secession Fact Book*.

Along the way it will become clear that the Liberal yarns created to negate, obscure, and blemish the American right of secession are only accepted today due to a lack of familiarity with the Constitution, with constitutional law, and with constitutional history.

As we will see, secession, which naturally flows from the rights possessed by sovereign entities, was the literal founding principle of the United States of America, and thousands of our Revolutionary ancestors died in order to preserve it for future generations. How tragic then that the uniformed, the spiteful, and the megalomaniacal have worked so hard to suppress and even obliterate the truth about this all-important ancient political idea; one, in fact, that the Founding Generation considered one of the most sacred and defining characteristics of our republic; one at the very root of Americanism: the right of secession.

Lochlainn Seabrook, secessionist
Nashville, Tennessee, U.S.A.
June 2017

1

SECESSION: CONSTITUTIONAL OR UNCONSTITUTIONAL?

WHAT IS SECESSION? IT IS** defined by Webster as the "formal withdrawal from an organization or political body."[12] It is not a Northern word, as some maintain, nor a Southern one, as others think (it has long been regularly used by both regions).[13] It is an English word that was coined in 1604 from the Latin word *secessio* or *secessus*, the past participle of *secedere*[14]: an intransitive verb meaning "go outside," "withdraw," or "to rebel."[15] The Latin elements themselves break down as follows: *se*, "apart" and *cedere*, "to go."[16] This gives *secedere* or secession the meaning "to go apart" or to "withdraw into solitude," which is precisely what America's Southern states did in 1860.

★ FACT: SECESSION IS ALL-AMERICAN!
Secession is not a "dirty word," though the anti-South movement would like you to believe it is. It is an all-American word! And neither is it directly or specifically connected to the South, treason, racism, or slavery. Secession is actually a universal term, one found in the writings and speeches of both countless Americans and Europeans, from colonial times up to Lincoln's War, including such individuals as Samuel Johnson (1775), Edmund Burke (1777), Thomas Jefferson (1825), William M. Thackeray (1848), and Jefferson Davis (1861).[17]

★ **FACT: THE SOUTH WAS RIGHT TO SECEDE**
The South has long maintained that secession was legal from the very formation of the confederate republic we know as the U.S.A., and we modern traditional Southerners maintain that it is still legal to this day. In this chapter we will study the history of American secession, which proves over and over again, as Samuel Augustus Steel of South Carolina declared in 1914, that "the South was right." Why was she right?

★ **FACT: THE FOUNDERS INTENDED OUR GOVERNMENT TO BE BASED ON CONSERVATIVE VALUES**
Because of two basic facts, both which are vital to a true understanding of Lincoln's War: 1) all governments are, by nature, innately conservative, and 2) a perfectly equalitarian government, one of the primary goals of liberalism, is a utopian fantasy. These are the main reasons the Founding Fathers established the U.S.A. on *conservative* principles rather than on *liberal* ones.[18]

English intellectual Dr. Samuel Johnson was writing about secession prior to the formation of the U.S.A.

★ **FACT: BECAUSE THE NORTH WAS WRONG, THE SOUTH'S POSITION NEEDS TO BE CORRECTLY UNDERSTOOD**
What this means for our understanding of the Civil War is that a conservative not a liberal government is the only proper one for America—most of whose citizens cherish personal freedom above all else (the U.S.A. is predominately conservative, with Liberals making up only a minority—less than 25 percent). This is why the South fought, and it is why the conservative South was right and the liberal North was wrong.[19] Wrote Steel in 1914:

> I believed in the beginning of the war, though only a child, that the South was right, and I believe it now. And I believe further that if this government lasts a hundred years longer, and continues to be a nation of free people, it will be because the principles of political liberty, for which the South contended, survive the shock of that tremendous revolution. For this reason, if for no other, the position of the South should be understood.[20]

★ FACT: THE U.S.A. WAS FOUNDED ON SECESSION
The United States of America is the literal offspring of secession: born in the cauldron of discontent, she was forged on the anvil of separation from the Mother Country (Britain), an act of political withdrawal (the American Revolutionary War) without which she would not exist today.

★ FACT: SECESSION WAS ONE OF OUR FIRST STATES' RIGHTS
This is why secession is one of the original rights of states, and it is why states' rights are assured and openly declared in the Declaration of Independence, penned by Southern hero and Founding Father Thomas Jefferson. Indeed, the Declaration of Independence, issued by the U.S. Congress on July 4, 1776, could rightly be called a "states' rights document," for from beginning to end it speaks of almost nothing else, as the following excerpts illustrate:

> When, in the course of human events, *it becomes necessary for one people to dissolve the political bands which have connected them with another* . . . a decent respect to the opinions of mankind requires that they should declare the causes which impel them to the separation.
> We hold these truths to be self-evident, that all men are created equal, that they are endowed by their Creator with certain *unalienable rights*, that among these are life, liberty and the pursuit of happiness. That, *to secure these rights, Governments are instituted among men, deriving their just powers from the consent of the governed*; that, *whenever any form of government becomes destructive of these ends, it is the right of the people to alter or to abolish it, and to institute new government, laying its foundation on such principles, and organizing its powers in such form, as to them shall seem most likely to effect their safety and happiness*.
> . . . We, therefore, the representatives of the United States of America, in general Congress assembled . . . do, in the name, and *by the authority of the good people* of these colonies, solemnly publish and declare, that these united colonies are, and of right ought to be, *free and independent states* . . . and that *as free and independent states, they have full power to* levy war, conclude peace, contract alliances, establish commerce, and to *do all other acts and things which independent states may of right do*.[21]

It is true that the Declaration of Independence was meant as a document officially separating the American colonies from Britain. However, its focus on states' rights, and the concomitant right of secession, was carried forward into the formulation of America's first constitution: the Articles of Confederation—proposed by Congress

November 15, 1777, and ratified March 1, 1781.

★ **FACT: OUR FIRST CONSTITUTION IMPLIED THE RIGHT OF SECESSION**
In the Articles of Confederation the central government was given explicit limited powers, while the states retained all other powers.[22] This, the essence of states' rights, is plainly laid out in Article 2:

> *Each state retains its sovereignty, freedom, and independence*, and every power, jurisdiction, and right, which is not by this Confederation expressly delegated to the United States, in Congress assembled.[23]

★ **FACT: IN OUR SECOND CONSTITUTION THE TENTH AMENDMENT CONNOTES THE RIGHT OF SECESSION**
For various reasons the first American Confederacy (i.e., the original 13 colonies) eventually found the Articles of Confederation wanting,[24] which led to the creation of the Constitution of the United States of America—proposed by convention (at Philadelphia), September 17, 1787, and made effective March 4, 1789.

Again the Founders did not neglect states' rights. In fact, they considered them so important that they were included as a separate amendment in the Bill of Rights (the first ten Amendments), which went into effect in 1791. The Tenth Amendment is, in its entirety, solely devoted to states' rights[25]:

> The powers not delegated to the United States by the Constitution, nor prohibited by it to the States, *are reserved to the States respectively, or to the people*.[26]

In other words—based on John Locke's view that government is created by the people merely to protect already existing rights[27]—our federal government was only allowed to

John Locke's idea of "God-given natural rights"—which by definition includes the right of secession—had a profound effect on the Founding Fathers, who incorporated it into our Constitution.

exercise those powers bestowed on it by the people. What are these powers? They are explicitly defined in Article 4, Section 4:

> The United States shall guarantee to every state in this Union a *republican form of government*, and shall protect each of them against *invasion*; and on application of the Legislature, or of the executive (when the Legislature cannot be convened), against *domestic violence*.[28]

★ FACT: THE U.S. CONSTITUTION DOES NOT GIVE THE GOVERNMENT THE POWER TO CURB SECESSION

As laid out here, in essence, the only power originally granted to the federal government by the people was to protect them against the formation of state dictatorships, foreign invasion, and internal disturbances (e.g., riots). Outside of these three obligations (basically, the defense of lives, rights, and property), all sovereign power was to remain in the hands of the people.[29] President James Madison put it this way:

James Madison declared that the powers of the states are "numerous and indefinite," leaving the door open for secession.

> The powers delegated by the proposed constitution to the Federal Government are *few and defined*; those which are to remain in the State governments [the people] are *numerous and indefinite*; the former will be exercised *principally on external objects*, as war, peace, negotiation, and foreign commerce—with which last the powers of taxation will, for the most part, be connected. *The powers reserved to the several States, will extend to all the objects which, in the ordinary course of affairs, concern the lives, liberties, and properties of the people, and the internal order, improvement, and prosperity of the State.*[30]

★ FACT: THE NINTH AMENDMENT PROTECTS THE TENTH AMENDMENT

Because every states' right could not be listed in the Constitution, James Madison had the Ninth Amendment added to the Bill of Rights. It protects against the federal government trying to restrict any of the rights of the states simply because they are not mentioned.[31] It reads:

> The enumeration in the Constitution, of certain rights, shall not be construed to deny or disparage others retained by the people.[32]

★ FACT: VATTEL PENNED THE ULTIMATE ARTICLE OF FAITH REGARDING STATES' RIGHTS

In our discussion of secession the Ninth and Tenth Amendments are highly significant, for they reaffirm the fact that the states did not lose their sovereignty when they joined the Union. The famous Swiss judicial authority Emer de Vattel enshrined this principle in the 18th Century, writing:

> *Several sovereign and independent States* may unite themselves together by a *perpetual confederacy [such as the U.S.A.]*, without ceasing to be, each individually, *a perfect State.* They will together constitute a *federal [that is, confederate] republic*: their joint deliberations will not impair the sovereignty of each member, though they may, in certain respects, put some restraint on the exercise of it, in virtue of voluntary engagements.[33]

★ FACT: ALEXANDER HAMILTON SAID THE FEDERAL GOVERNMENT IS LIMITED TO "SPECIFIC POWERS"

In arguing for the constitutionality of forming a national bank, early American Liberal, Federalist Alexander Hamilton, wrote the following to President George Washington on February 23, 1791. Some have interpreted these words to include the right of secession. In regards to the "specified powers of the government," Hamilton notes, it is said that only "necessary and proper means are to be employed"—which gives wide latitude depending on how one defines "necessary." Yet, he continues,

Alexander Hamilton did not like the idea of secession, but accepted that it was a legitimate right of sovereigns.

> the doctrine which is contended for is not chargeable with the consequences imputed to it. It does not affirm that the national government is sovereign in all respects, but that it is sovereign to a certain extent; that is, to the extent of the objects of its specified powers.

It leaves, therefore, a criterion of what is constitutional, and of what is not so. This criterion is the end, to which the measure relates as a mean. If the end be clearly comprehended within any of the specified powers, and if the measure have an obvious relation to that end, and is not forbidden by any particular provision of the Constitution, it may safely be deemed to come within the compass of the national authority.

There is also this further criterion, which may materially assist the decision: Does the proposed measure abridge a pre-existing right of any State or of any individual? If it does not, there is a strong presumption in favor of its constitutionality, and slighter relations to any declared object of the Constitution may be permitted to turn the scale.[34]

★ FACT: BY INFERENCE HAMILTON SUPPORTED SECESSION

Even if Liberal Hamilton did not openly or even tacitly support the idea of secession, unlike Liberal Lincoln and his left-wing Yankee constituents, he was against the idea of using physical force to hold the Union together—which infers that he sanctioned the right of secession. Wrote Hamilton:

It has been observed, *to coerce the States is one of the maddest projects that was ever devised*. A failure of compliance will never be confined to a single State; this being the case, can we suppose it wise to hazard a civil war? Suppose Massachusetts, or any larger State should refuse, and Congress should attempt to compel them, would they not have influence to procure assistance, especially from those States that are in the same situation as themselves? What a picture does this idea present to our view? A complying State at war with a non-complying State; Congress marching the troops of one State into the bosom of another; the State collecting auxiliaries, and forming, perhaps, a majority against its Federal head. Here is a nation at war with itself. *Can any reasonable man be well disposed towards a Government which makes war and carnage the only means of supporting itself?—a Government that can exist only by the sword?* Every such war must involve the innocent with the guilty. *This single consideration should be sufficient to dispose every peaceable citizen against such a Government.*[35]

★ FACT: PHYSICAL COERCION OF THE STATES GOES AGAINST THE IDEALS OF THE FOUNDING FATHERS & THE CONSTITUTION

If physical, violent, or military coercion of the states was not condoned by the Founding Fathers, then by inference secession is legal. For those who claim it is not, there is only one remedy then for trying to block a seceding state: *legal* coercion. Fowler writes:

> The founders of the Federal Government did not rely for its preservation, mainly upon physical force, as if it were a military despotism, but upon mutual confidence and "conciliated interests." We have no evidence that it was the intention of the [Philadelphia] Convention that formed the Constitution, or of the States that were parties to the compact, to clothe the Government with power to use military coercion against a State that had placed itself on its reserved rights. *If there was such an intention, where is it recorded?* What they did rely upon was *legal coercion*, acting through the forms of law upon individuals. Mr. [George T.] Curtis, in his excellent history of the Constitution, says: *"One of the leading objects in forming the Constitution, was to obtain for the United States the means of coercion, without a resort to force against the people of the States collectively....* The introduction, therefore, of the judicial department [basically the Supreme Court] into the new plan of Government, of itself evinces an intention to clothe that Government with powers that could be executed peacefully, and without the necessity of putting down the organized opposition of subordinate communities."
>
> Washington, in a letter addressed to Alexander Hamilton, August 26, 1792, having spoken of "mutual forbearance and yielding on all sides," adds, "without these, I do not see how the reins of Government are to be managed, or how the Union of the States can much longer be preserved."[36]

Andrew Jackson too was repulsed by the idea of secession; but at the same time he acknowledged that governmental coercion was unconstitutional.

Bledsoe writes:

> But *if the Constitution does not authorize coercion, then it permits secession*; or, in other words, secession is a Constitutional right, which every power on earth is bound to respect as existing under the supreme law of the land; a Constitutional right, which the Federal Government could deny only by an act of usurpation.
>
> *Coercion is unconstitutional. Coercion is wrong.* Coercion strikes down and demolishes the great fundamental principle of the Declaration of Independence,—*the sacred right of self-government itself.* Coercion wages war on the autonomy of free States. Secession, on the other hand, asserts the right of self-government for every free, sovereign, and independent State in existence.[37]

Though President Andrew Jackson was against the idea of secession, even once declaring that "the Union must and shall be preserved," he recognized that physical coercion was far worse. On March 3, 1837, he issued his farewell address, which included the following words:

> But the Constitution cannot be maintained, nor the Union preserved in opposition to public feeling by the mere exertion of coercive powers of the Government. The foundations must be laid in the affections *of the people*, in the security it gives to life, liberty, and property in every quarter of the country; and in the fraternal attachments which the citizens of the several States bear to one another, as members of one political family, materially contributing to promote the happiness of each other.[38]

★ FACT: HAMILTON EXPECTED THE DISSOLUTION OF THE UNION

If Hamilton did not sanction secession, one must wonder why he fully expected the Union to break apart at some point, even referring to the U.S. Constitution as a "temporary bond."[39] Just prior to the adoption of the new Constitution in 1789, he made these interesting remarks:

> If the Government be adopted, it is probable General Washington will be the President of the United States. This will insure a wise choice of men to administer the Government, and a good administration. A good administration will conciliate the confidence and affections of the people, and perhaps enable the Government to acquire more consistency than the proposed Constitution seems to promise for so great a country. *It may thus triumph, altogether over the State Governments, and reduce them to an entire subordination, dividing the larger States into smaller districts.* The organs of the General Government may also acquire additional strength.
>
> If this should not be the case, in the course of a few years, it is probable that the contests about the boundaries of power between the particular Governments and the General Government and *the momentum of the larger States, will produce a dissolution of the Union.* This, after all, seems to be the most likely result.[40]

★ FACT: U.S. PRESIDENT JOHN ADAMS ALSO ANTICIPATED AN EVENTUAL END TO THE UNION

Like Jefferson and Hamilton, President John Adams expected the Union to break asunder in the future as well. Though a Liberal (then known as a Federalist), this would again seem to indicate that he acknowledged the right of secession. Fowler comments:

The Rev. Mr. Coffin of New England, who is now here soliciting donations for a College in Greene County, Tennessee, . . . [says] that when he first determined to engage in this enterprise, he wrote a letter recommendatory of the enterprise, which he meant to get signed by clergymen, and a similar one for persons of a civil character, at the head of which he wished to have Mr. Adams to put his name, he being the President of the United States, and the application going only for his name, and not for a donation. *Mr. Adams, after reading the paper, and considering, said he saw no possibility of continuing the Union of the States; that their dissolution must necessarily take place; that he therefore saw no propriety in recommending to New England men to promote an institution in the South; that it was, in fact, giving strength to those who were to be their enemies,* and therefore he would have nothing to do with it.[41]

John Adams did not expect the Union to hold together, indicating that he accepted the right of secession.

The difficulty of holding together a Union made up of two different "civilizations," with conflicting views and completely opposing interpretations of the Constitution, was highlighted in 1849 by Ohio Congressman Robert C. Schenck, a future Union general:

If we of the Northern States will not vote for a Southern man, merely because he is a Southern man, and men of the South will not vote for a Northern man, merely because he is a Northern man, and if that principle is to be carried out in all our national politics and elections, what must be the result? *Disunion.* That itself is disunion. You may disguise and cover it up as you please, but that it will be. It may be regarded, as but the first step in disunion, but its consequences follow as inevitably as fate. One section—the North or the South—must always have the majority. Disfranchise all upon the other side, and the Union could not hold together a day; *it ought not to hold together upon such conditions a day.*[42]

★ **FACT: THE SOUTH INTERPRETED THE CONSTITUTION STRICTLY, THE NORTH BROADLY**
This stark dichotomy between the Conservative South's strict interpretation and the Liberal North's broad interpretation of the Constitution was, without question, at the very root of the American Civil War, as I discuss in detail in my book *Lincoln's War: The Real Cause, the Real Winner, the Real Loser*. Conservative President James Madison's political conflicts with Liberal Alexander Hamilton prompted the following remarks from the former. Said Madison:

A decade before Lincoln's War Ohio Congressman Robert C. Schenck predicted the breakup of the Union over sectional animosity.

> In a word, the divergence between Colonel Hamilton and myself took place from his wishing to administration, or rather *to administer the Government into what he thought it ought to be*; while, on my part, I endeavored *to make it conform to the Constitution*, as understood by the Convention that produced and recommended it, and particularly by the State Conventions that adopted it.[43]

Fowler touches on this topic in his 1864 book *The Sectional Controversy*, making the following excellent points:

> . . . sectional views of the Constitution had an influence in producing a sectional policy in the administration of the Government. *The South, from the start, favored a strict construction of the Constitution*. The leading statesmen of that section, from [Conservatives] Thomas Jefferson to Jefferson Davis, generally inquired for the "enumerated powers," and the "delegated powers "contained in the Constitution, and insisted that federal action must be carefully limited by these powers. And if, in any case, the action of the Federal Government, in any of its branches, should go outside of these "granted powers," to usurp the powers reserved to the States, it is then null and void, because unconstitutional.
> On the other hand, *the North has been inclined to a broad construction of the Constitution*. The leading statesmen of that section, from [Liberals] Alexander Hamilton to Daniel Webster, generally were disposed to magnify the "granted powers," though at the expense of the powers reserved to the States.

To these general statements there are many exceptions, both in the North and the South.

Is a national bank constitutional? The Southern statesman examines the Constitution, and finding no grant of power to Congress to establish such a bank, therefore pronounces the establishment of a bank unconstitutional. A Northern states man, on the other hand, while he acknowledges that the Constitution contains no express grant of power to Congress to establish a bank or any corporation, says that, inasmuch as a bank would be convenient or appropriate for carrying into operation other grants of power, it is therefore constitutional.

Are internal improvements constitutional? On the same grounds as in the other case, the Southern statesman says no, the Northern yes.

Are high tariffs for protection constitutional? On the same ground as before the Southern statesmen say no, inasmuch as the Constitution empowers Congress to lay duties for revenue, but not for protection or prohibition. The Northern statesmen say yes; because, as they judge, they are "necessary" in order to promote the "general welfare," or at least the welfare of their section of the country.[44]

Here we see the source of the existential conflict between South and North that emerged even as our country was forming: *conservatism*, which was predominant (and still is) in the South, versus *liberalism*, which was predominant (and still is) in the North. The U.S.A. has thus, from the start, hung together by the thinnest of cords, any one which could snap at a moment's notice.

In short, the fragile nature of our voluntary American Union, with its two highly sectional, conflicting, and irreconcilable regions, means that disunion is always only a breath away. This is one of the main reasons the Founders, in their wisdom, did not make secession illegal in the Constitution, but left it to the states—as small "free and independent nations"—to decide for themselves. As Fowler notes, "the States retained their sovereignty for the reason that it was not delegated to the Constitution."[45]

★ FACT: THE VIRGINIA & KENTUCKY RESOLUTIONS PERMANENTLY ESTABLISHED THE RIGHT OF SECESSION
The Alien and Sedition Laws, which passed in the Summer of 1798, were disliked by early American Conservatives, one of whom was Thomas Jefferson. In response he helped put together the Virginia and Kentucky Resolutions of 1798 to 1799 (for the full text see Appendix B), from

which the following pertinent excerpts are taken:

> That the several States composing the United States of America are not united on the principle of unlimited submission to their general government, but that by a compact under the style and title of the Constitution for the United States, and of amendments thereto, they constituted a general government for special purposes; delegated to that government certain definite powers; *reserving, each State to itself, the residuary measure of right to their own self-government*; and that, *whensoever the general government assumes undelegated powers, its acts are unauthoritative, void, and of no force; that to this compact each State acceded as a State, and is an integral party; that the government created by this compact was not made the exclusive or final judge of the extent of the powers delegated to itself, since that would have made its discretion, and not the Constitution, the measure of its powers*; but that, *as in all other cases of compact among parties having no common judge, each party has an equal right to judge for itself*; as well of infractions as of the mode and measure of redress, . . . and that a *nullification by those sovereignties of all unauthorized acts done under the color of that instrument is the rightful remedy*.⁴⁶

Thomas Jefferson's Declaration of Independence and his Kentucky Resolutions formed the basis of a long tradition of secession movements, including the one that emerged in the South in 1860. This earns him the title "The Father of Southern Secession."

★ **FACT: JAMES MADISON'S REPORT ON THE VIRGINIA & KENTUCKY RESOLUTIONS FURTHER STRENGTHENED THE RIGHT OF SECESSION**

James Madison, who drew up the resolutions of Virginia (Jefferson "sketched" out those of Kentucky),[47] filed a white paper on the Virginia and Kentucky Resolutions known as "The Virginia Report of 1799" (for the full text, see Appendix C), stating, in part:

> It appears to your committee to be a plain principle founded in common sense, illustrated by common practice, and *essential to the nature of compacts, that, where resort can be had to no tribunal superior to the authority of the parties, the parties themselves must be the rightful judges*, in the last resort, whether the bargain made has been pursued or violated. The Constitution of the United States was formed by the sanction of the States given by each in its *sovereign capacity*. The States, then, being parties to the constitutional compact, and in their *sovereign capacity*, it follows of necessity that *there can be no tribunal above their authority* to decide on the last resort whether the compact made by them be violated; and, consequently, that, as parties to it, *they must themselves decide* in the last resort such questions as may be of sufficient magnitude to require their interposition.[48]

Such words flowed from the Southern belief that "under the guidance of Northern men," the administration of Liberal President John Adams "had assumed powers not enumerated in the Constitution, and in this way had usurped the powers belonging to the states."[49]

★ **FACT: CONSERVATIVE U.S. PRESIDENT THOMAS JEFFERSON REGARDED SECESSION AS A LEGITIMATE RIGHT OF THE STATES**

In his First Inaugural Address, March 4, 1801, President Thomas Jefferson spoke plainly about the states' right of secession:

> If there be any among us who would wish to *dissolve the Union or to change its republican form*, let them stand undisturbed as monuments of the safety with which error of opinion may be tolerated where reason is left free to combat it.[50]

★ **FACT: SOUTHERN JUDGE ST. GEORGE TUCKER UPHELD THE RIGHT OF SECESSION**

In 1803, Southern abolitionist, lawyer, and judge, St. George Tucker of

Virginia, gave one of the most concise and accurate interpretations of the constitutional power of disunionization:

Yankee Founding Father Gouverneur Morris held that the states "enjoy sovereign power."

The Constitution of the United States, then, being that instrument by which the Federal Government hath been created, its powers defined and limited, and the duties and functions of its several departments prescribed, the Government, thus established, may be pronounced to be a *Confederate Republic*, composed of several *Independent and Sovereign Democratic States*, united for their common defence and security against foreign Nations, and for the purposes of harmony and mutual intercourse between each other; *each State retaining an entire liberty of exercising, as it thinks proper, all those parts of its Sovereignty which are not mentioned in the Constitution, or Act of Union, as parts that ought to be exercised in common.*

In becoming a member of the Federal Alliance, established between the American States by the Articles of Confederation, she expressly retained her Sovereignty and Independence. The constraints, put upon the exercise of that Sovereignty by those Articles, did not destroy its existence.

The Federal Government, then, appears to be the organ through which the united Republics communicate with foreign Nations, and with each other. Their submission to its operation is *voluntary*; its councils, its engagements, its authority, are theirs, modified and united. *Its Sovereignty is an emanation from theirs, not a flame, in which they have been consumed, nor a vortex, in which they are swallowed up. Each is still a perfect State, still Sovereign, still independent, and still capable, should the occasion require, to resume the exercise of its functions, as such, in the most unlimited extent.*

But, until the time shall arrive, when the occasion requires a resumption of the rights of Sovereignty by the several States (and far be that period removed, when it shall happen), the exercise of the rights of Sovereignty by the States, individually, is wholly suspended or discontinued in the cases before mentioned; nor can that suspension ever be removed, so long as the present Constitution remains unchanged, but by the dissolution of the bonds of union; an event which no good citizen can wish, and which no good or wise administration will ever hazard.[51]

★ FACT: FOUNDING FATHER GOUVERNEUR MORRIS BELIEVED IN THE RIGHT OF SECESSION

One of our more popular Founding Fathers was Gouverneur Morris of New York, also a noted politician and diplomat. He made his views on secession clear when he uttered the following remarks in 1814, during the rise of the *Northern* secession movement and its efforts to leave the Union in order to establish a "New England Confederacy":

> That the Constitution was a compact, not between solitary individuals, but between political societies, the people, not of America, but of the United States—each (State) enjoying *sovereign power*, and of course equal rights.[52]

Like many other Civil War officers Confederate General George E. Pickett was taught about the right of secession at West Point—by Yankees.

★ FACT: THE RIGHT OF SECESSION WAS ONCE TAUGHT AT WEST POINT, BY A YANKEE

While these facts would later be purposefully distorted by Lincoln for political gain, before 1861 the right of secession was once so well understood and accepted by all Americans that it was taught for years at New York's West Point Military Academy—*by Northerners*.[53]

The primary textbook used, *A View of the Constitution of the United States of America*, was penned in 1829 by William Rawle of Pennsylvania, appointed by President George Washington as U.S. District Attorney for Pennsylvania. In fact, many of both the North's and the South's future "Civil War" officers were taught Constitutional law, and the right of secession, from this very book. In a letter to his wife, one of these men, Confederate General George E. Pickett, wrote:

> I, of course, have always strenuously opposed disunion, not as doubting the right of secession, which was taught in our textbook at West Point, but as gravely questioning its expediency.[54]

Rawle's statements, such as the following, were memorized by thousands of Northern and Southern military men like Pickett, and, handed down from generation to generation as an American tradition, were thus "mutually understood." For a state, Rawle wrote in his textbook, to withdraw from the Union is a solemn, serious act. Whenever it may appear expedient to the people of a state, it must be manifested in a direct and unequivocal manner. If it is ever done indirectly, the people must refuse to elect representatives, as well as to suffer their legislature to re-appoint senators.

. . . But without plain, decisive measures of this nature, proceeding from the only legitimate source, the people, the United States cannot consider their legislative powers over such states suspended, nor their executive or judicial powers any way impaired . . .

. . . *This right [of secession] must be considered as an ingredient in the original composition of the general government, which, though not expressed, was mutually understood . . . The states, then, may wholly withdraw from the Union* . . .[55]

District Attorney Rawle went on to write:

It depends on the State itself whether to retain or to abolish the principle of representation, because it depends on itself whether it will remain a member of the Union. To deny this right, would be inconsistent with *the principle on which all our political systems are founded*; which is, that *the people have in all cases a right to determine how they will be governed.*

. . . *The secession of a State from the Union depends on the will of the people of such State. The people alone . . . have the power to alter the Constitution.*[56]

★ **FACT: CONSERVATIVE U.S. VICE PRESIDENT JOHN C. CALHOUN SUPPORTED THE RIGHT OF SECESSION**
On February 16, 1833, (now former) Vice President John C. Calhoun of South Carolina delivered an address in the U.S. Senate which included the following comments:

If *a league between sovereign powers* have no limitation as to the time of its duration, and contain nothing making it perpetual, *it subsists only during the good pleasure of the parties*, although no violation be complained of. If, in the opinion of either party, it be violated, such party may say that he will no longer fulfil its obligations on his part, but will consider the whole league or compact at an end, although it might be one of its stipulations that it should be perpetual.[57]

Southern statesman John C. Calhoun asserted that a union between sovereign powers exists at "the good pleasure of the parties."

★ **FACT: SUPREME COURT OFFICIAL JOSEPH STORY DEFENDED THE RIGHT OF SECESSION**
That same year, 1833, Associate Justice of the Supreme Court Joseph Story of Massachusetts wrote:

> The obvious deductions which may be, and indeed, have been, drawn from considering *the Constitution* a compact between States, are, that *it operates as a mere treaty, or convention between them, and has an obligatory force upon each state no longer than suits its pleasure, or its consent continues*; that *each state has a right to judge for itself in relation to the nature, extent, and obligations of the instrument, without being at all bound by the interpretation of the federal government, or by that of any other state*; and that *each retains the power to withdraw from the confederacy and to dissolve the connexion, when such shall be its choice*; and *may suspend the operations of the federal government, and nullify its acts within its own territorial limits, whenever, in its own opinion, the exigency of the case may require*. These conclusions may not always be avowed; but they flow naturally from the doctrines [of constitutional law and theory].[58]

★ **FACT: LIBERAL U.S. PRESIDENT JOHN QUINCY ADAMS BELIEVED IN THE RIGHT OF SECESSION**
In 1839 President John Quincy Adams of Massachusetts, though an anti-Jeffersonian Federalist (that is, a Liberal), gave a passionate speech at the fiftieth anniversary celebration of George Washington's inauguration, in which he touched positively on secession. According to Adams:

> *To the people alone is then reserved, as well the dissolving as the constituent power*; and that power can be exercised by them only under the tie of conscience, binding them to the retributive justice of heaven. With these qualifications, we may admit the same right to be vested in the people of every State in the Union, with reference to the general government, which was exercised by the people of the United colonies with reference to the supreme head of the British Empire, of which they formed a part; and, under these limitations, *have the people of each State in the Union a right to secede from the Confederated Union itself*. Thus stands the right. But the indissoluble link of union between the people of the several States of *this confederated nation* is, after all, *not in the right, but in the heart*. If the day should ever come (may heaven avert it!) when the affections of the people of these States shall be alienated from each other—when the fraternal spirit shall give way to cold indifference, or collisions of interest shall fester into hatred—the bands of political association will not long hold together parties no longer attracted by the magnetism of conciliated interests and kindly sympathies; and *far better will it be for the people of the disunited States to part in friendship from each other, than to be held together*

by constraint.⁵⁹

★ FACT: IN HIS MEMOIR JOHN QUINCY ADAMS OPENLY SUPPORTED SECESSION

In Josiah Quincy's *Memoir of John Quincy Adams*, we find Adams backing the idea of the secession of the Northern states in order to form a "New England Confederacy":

> ... I have favored this Missouri Compromise, believing it to be all that could be effected under the present Constitution, and from extreme unwillingness to put the Union at hazard. But perhaps it would have been a wiser and a bolder cause to have persisted in the restriction on Missouri, until it should have terminated in a Convention of the States to revise and amend the Constitution. *This would have produced a new [Northern] Union of thirteen or fourteen States*, unpolluted with slavery, with a great and glorious object, that of rallying to their standard the other States, by the universal emancipation of their slaves. *If the Union must be dissolved, slavery is precisely the question upon which it ought to break.*⁶⁰

U.S. President John Quincy Adams accepted the ideas of disunion and secession.

★ FACT: IN 1840 LIBERAL JUDGE ABEL P. UPSHUR SUPPORTED THE RIGHT OF SECESSION

In 1840 Abel Parker Upshur, a Liberal (Whig) Virginia judge, lawyer, politician, and both the secretary of the navy and secretary of state under U.S. President John Tyler, wrote the following concerning secession:

But whether this check [secession] be the best or the worst in its nature, it is at least one which our system allows. *It is not found within the Constitution but exists independent of it. As that Constitution was formed by sovereign States, they alone are authorized, whenever the question arises between them and their common government, to determine, in the last resort, what powers they intended to confer on it. This is an inseparable incident of sovereignty; a right which belongs to the States, simply because they have never surrendered it to any other power.* But to render this right available for any good purpose, it is indispensably necessary to maintain the States in their proper position. If their people suffer them to sink into the insignificance of mere municipal corporations, it will be vain to invoke their protection against the gigantic power of the federal government. This is the point to which the vigilance of the people should be chiefly directed. *Their highest interest is at home; their palladium is their own State governments. They ought to know that they can look nowhere else with perfect assurance of safety and protection.* Let them then maintain those governments, not only in their rights, but in their dignity and influence. Make it the interest of their people to serve them; an interest strong enough to resist all the temptations of federal office and patronage. Then alone will their voice be heard with respect at Washington; then alone will their interposition avail to protect their own people against the usurpations of the great central power. It is vain to hope that the federative principle of our government can be preserved, or that anything can prevent it from running into the absolutism of consolidation, if we suffer the rights of the States to be filched away, and their dignity and influence to be lost, through our carelessness or neglect.[61]

★ **FACT: FROM THE BEGINNING AMERICAN CONSERVATIVES HAVE FOLLOWED THE LEAD OF THE KENTUCKY & VIRGINIA RESOLUTIONS REGARDING THE INFERRED RIGHT OF SECESSION**

During the presidential matchup between Liberal William Henry Harrison and Conservative Martin Van Buren, "The Secession Resolution of 1840" was adopted by the Democratic Party, then the Conservative party. It stated, in part:

> That the Federal Government is one of limited powers, derived solely from the Constitution, and the grants of power shown therein ought to be strictly construed by all the departments and agents of the Government; and that it is inexpedient and dangerous to exercise doubtful constitutional powers.[62]

This declaration was again supported by the Democrats (Conservatives) in the elections of 1844 and 1848. In 1852 the Democratic Party (the Conservative party) proposed and adopted a new resolution, which asserted:

> That the Democratic Party will faithfully abide by and uphold the principles laid down in the Kentucky and Virginia Resolutions of 1798 and 1799, and in the Report of Mr. [James] Madison to the Virginia Legislature in 1799; that it adopts those principles as constituting one of the main foundations of its political creed; and is resolved to carry them out in their obvious meaning and import.[63]

We will note here that though the Kentucky and Virginia Resolutions did not discuss secession specifically, they asserted in plain terms, for the first time, the sovereignty of the states[64]—which includes the rights of both accession and secession.[65] Writes Johnston:

> The two sets of resolutions agreed in the assertion that the Constitution was a "compact," and that the States were the "parties" which had formed it. In these two propositions lies the gist of State sovereignty, of which all its remotest consequences are only natural developments. If it were true that the States, of their sovereign will, had formed such a compact; if it were not true that the adoption of the [U.S.] Constitution [in 1789] was a mere alteration of the form of a political state already in existence; it would follow, as the Kentucky resolutions asserted, that *each State had the exclusive right to decide for itself when the compact had been broken, and the mode and measure of redress*. It followed, also, that, if the existence and force of the Constitution in a State were due solely to the sovereign will of the State, the sovereign will of the State was competent, on occasion, to oust the Constitution from the jurisdiction covered by the State. In brief, *the Union was wholly voluntary in its formation and in its continuance; and each State reserved the unquestionable right to secede, to abandon the Union, and assume an independent existence whenever due reason, in the exclusive judgment of the State, should arise.* These latter consequences, not stated in the Kentucky resolutions, and apparently not contemplated by the Virginia resolutions, were put into complete form by Professor [St. George] Tucker, of the University of Virginia, in 1803, in the notes to his edition of [William] "Blackstone's Commentaries." Thereafter *its statements of American constitutional law controlled the political training of the South.*[66]

★ FACT: THE DEMOCRATS' SECESSION RESOLUTION OF 1840 WAS UPHELD BY FELLOW CONSERVATIVES THROUGHOUT THE ELECTIONS OF 1852, 1856, & 1860
This, the Democratic (then Conservative) Secession Resolution, was again repeated and upheld during the elections of 1852, 1856, and

during the all important 1860 election as well.

★ FACT: IN 1860 YANKEE CONSERVATIVE SAMUEL J. TILDEN STOOD FOR THE RIGHT OF SECESSION

Around the time of the 1860 presidential campaign, Democrat (Conservative) politician Samuel J. Tilden of New York came forward and reasserted the right of secession as laid down by Thomas Jefferson and James Madison. In a letter to the Honorable William Kent, Tilden writes:

An 1876 Democratic Party presidential campaign banner showing Samuel J. Tilden, a supporter of the right of secession, and his vice presidential running mate Thomas A. Hendricks. At the time the Democratic Party was the Conservative party.

Each section is organized into States with complete governments, holding the power and wielding the sword. They are held together only by a compact of confederation. . . . The single, slender, conventional tie which holds the States in confederation has no strength compared with the compacted intertwining fibres which bind the atoms of human society into one formation of natural growth. . . . *The masters in political science who constructed our system preserved the State Governments as bulwarks of the freedom of individuals and localities against oppression from centralized power. They recognized no right of constitutional secession; but they left revolution organized whenever it should be demanded by the public opinion of a state,—left it, with the power to snap the tie of confederation as a Nation might break a treaty, and to repel coercion as a nation might repel invasion. They caused us to depend in great measure upon the public opinion of the States, in order to maintain a confederated union. . . .*

As a rule of right and duty, for the construction and execution of the Constitution, the theory maintained by Mr. [William H.] Seward, and too exclusively accepted (that the Government could exclude slavery from the Territories), is *entirely fallacious. No contract governing complicated transactions or relations between men, and applying permanently through the changes inevitable in human affairs can be effectual if either party intended to be bound by it is at liberty to construe or execute its provisions in a spirit of hostility to the substantial objects of those provisions, especially is this true of a compact of confederation between, the States, where there can be no common arbiter invested with authorities and powers equally capable with those which courts possess between individuals for determining and enforcing a just construction and execution of the instrument.*[67]

★ **FACT: NOVEMBER 6, 1860, THE DAY OF LINCOLN'S ELECTION, THE SOUTHERN STATES WERE ALREADY PREPARING FOR LEGAL SECESSION**
Of this tumultuous and revolutionary period in American history Rogers comments:

> These words of encouragement and instruction for the Southern States had hardly fallen from Mr. Tilden's lips than they proceeded to put them in practice. At that time [Andrew] Jackson no longer stood with flaming sword to bar the way. On the sixth day of November, 1860, before the election of Mr. Lincoln, the Legislature of the State of *South Carolina* assembled, and received a message from the Governor, in which he expressed his opinion that the only alternative left to it was secession from the Federal Union. On the 7th of November, the Postmaster, Collector, and other Federal officers in Charleston resigned their respective positions. On the 10th of November, the Senators from that State, in Congress, resigned. On the 13th of November, the collection of debts due to citizens of non-slaveholding States was prohibited. On the same day, Francis W. Pickens was elected Governor, and appointed, as a Cabinet, Andrew G. McGrath, Secretary of State; David F. Jamison, Secretary of War; Christopher G. Memminger, Secretary of the Treasury; William W. Harllee, Postmaster General; and Albert C. Garlington, Secretary of the Interior. On the 17th of the same month, the ordinance of secession was unanimously adopted by a convention of delegates called for that purpose. On the 21st of November, commissioners were appointed to proceed to Washington to treat for the delivery to the State of the property of the United States within its limits. On the 24th of November, the Representatives of the State in Congress resigned their seats. And, on the 20th of December, 1860, the Governor of the State announced the repeal, by the people of South Carolina, of the ordinance (of the adoption of the Constitution) of May 23, 1788, and the dissolution of the Union between the State of South Carolina and other States, under the name of the United States of America; and proclaimed to the world that *"the State of South Carolina is, as she has a right to be, a separate, sovereign, free, and independent State; and, as such, has the right to levy war, to conclude peace, to negotiate treaties, leagues, or covenants, and to do all acts whatsoever right fully appertaining to a free and independent State."*
>
> The history of one seceding State will do for all. All the Southern States, as speedily as possible, followed the example of South Carolina, adopting her language and acts as precedents for theirs; so that, before Mr. Lincoln came to the Presidential Chair, nearly all of the Southern States had asserted, and apparently effected, the right of secession which Mr. Tilden proclaimed for them on every stump, and which he did all that lay in his power to forward.[68]

★ **FACT: U.S. PRESIDENT FRANKLIN PIERCE SUSTAINED THE SOUTH'S RIGHT TO SECEDE**
In the following letter, dated January 6, 1860, Conservative Yankee and former U.S. President Franklin Pierce of New Hampshire, addresses his friend and former U.S. Secretary of War Jefferson Davis, acknowledging the right of secession:

> I have just had a pleasant interview with Mr. ____, whose courage and fidelity are equal to his learning and talents. He says he would rather fight the battle under you as a standard bearer in 1860, than under the auspices of any other leader. The feeling and judgment of Mr. ____ is, I am confident, rapidly gaining ground.
>
> Our people are looking for the "Coming Man," one who is raised by all the elements of his character above the atmosphere ordinarily breathed by politicians; a man really formed for this exigency, by his ability, courage, broad statesmanship, and patriotism. Colonel Thomas H. Seymour arrived here this morning, and expressed his views in this relation in almost the identical language used by Mr. ____ . . . . .
>
> I do not believe that our friends at the South have any just idea of the state of feeling, hurrying at this moment to the pitch of intense exasperation, between those who respect their political obligations and those who have apparently no impelling power but that which the fanatical passion on the subject of slavery imparts. *Without discussing the question of right, of abstract power to secede, I have never believed that actual disruption of the Union can occur without blood; and if through the madness of northern abolitionism, that dire calamity must come, the fighting will not be along Mason and Dixon's Line merely. It will be within our own borders, in our own streets, between the two classes of citizens to whom I have referred. Those who defy law, and scout constitutional obligations, will, if we ever reach the arbitrament of arms, find occupation enough at home.*[69]

★ **FACT: YANKEE SOCIALIST HORACE GREELEY DECLARED SECESSION A LEGITIMATE POLITICAL RIGHT**
Though at the time (1860) Lincoln was not among them, a truly stunning number of Northerners agreed with both the Confederate Constitution and the "Cotton States" (i.e., the South) that secession was indeed lawful, and that, under the circumstances, it was entirely appropriate. One of these was left-wing Yankee abolitionist and New York *Tribune* owner Horace Greeley,[70] who, in the November 10, 1860 issue, wrote:

> And now, if the Cotton States consider the value of the Union debatable, we maintain their perfect right to discuss it. Nay, *we hold with Jefferson to the*

inalienable right of communities to alter or abolish forms of government that have become oppressive or injurious; and if the Cotton States shall decide that they can do better out of the Union than in it, we insist on letting them go in peace. The right to secede may be a revolutionary one, but it exists nevertheless; and we do not see how one party can have a right to do what another party has a right to prevent. We must ever resist the asserted right of any State to remain in the Union and nullify or defy the laws thereof; to withdraw from the Union is quite another matter. *And whenever a considerable section of our Union shall deliberately resolve to go out, we shall resist all coercive measures designed to keep it in. We hope never to live in a republic, whereof one section is pinned to the residue with bayonets.*[71]

Though a radical left-wing socialist and abolitionist, Yankee newspaper owner Horace Greeley believed in the right of secession. "Let the Southern states go in peace," he declared.

Clearly, many people—that is, Liberals like Lincoln—actually *wanted* to live in a republic "pinned to the residue with bayonets." Yet revealingly, as we will see, his predecessor President James Buchanan also understood the legal nature of secession, citing Southern Founding Father President James Madison as confirmation of his views.

★ FACT: THE CONSTITUTION OF THE CONFEDERATE STATES OF AMERICA GAVE TACIT APPROVAL TO SECESSION
On March 11, 1861, seventy years after the Bill of Rights went into effect, the Southern states—now a sovereign republic called the Confederate States of America (C.S.A.)—issued its own the national charter. The C.S. Constitution, closely patterned on the U.S. Constitution, began with the following preamble:

> We, the people of the Confederate States, *each State acting in its sovereign and independent character*, in order to form a permanent federal government, establish justice, insure domestic tranquillity, and secure the blessings of liberty to ourselves and our posterity—invoking the favor and guidance of Almighty God do ordain and establish this Constitution for the Confederate States of America.[72]

Then, in Article 6, the C.S. Constitution uses the exact wording of the Tenth Amendment in its proclamation of states' rights, only substituting the words United States with Confederate States:

> The powers not delegated to the Confederate States by the Constitution, nor prohibited by it to the States, are reserved to the States, respectively, or to the people thereof.[73]

★ FACT: SECESSION WAS & STILL IS CONSTITUTIONAL

Based on the preceding, if the individual states of the U.S. were intended to be *sovereign nation-states*,[74] as all of the official early American documents clearly assert they were, and are, then the rights of both accession (joining) and secession (leaving) are legal.[75]

Lincoln ardently supported secession before becoming president but repudiated it afterward. Why? This book answers the question.

Since the original function of the federal government was merely "protection" (from invasion, domestic violence, and threats to republicanism), it is obvious that all other powers were to remain with the states. This system, part of what was known as the "separation of powers," was intentionally built into the Constitution to prevent the very type of tyranny that Lincoln would later institute in 1861.[76]

States' rights then, which include secession, were legal across the U.S.A. in the mid-1800s, for they are clearly elucidated in the Declaration of Independence and implicitly in the Articles of Confederation and the United States Constitution. These rights rest, not on the authority of the federal government, or even on the Constitution, but on *the God-given authority derived from the will of the people*—as noted in the following statements in the Constitution.[77] The Preamble reads:

> We the people of the United States, in order to form a more perfect Union, establish justice, insure domestic tranquility, provide for the common defence, promote the general welfare, and secure the blessings of liberty to ourselves and our posterity, do ordain and establish this Constitution for the United States of America.[78]

And Article 7 reads:

> The ratification of the Conventions of nine states shall be sufficient for the Establishment of this Constitution between the States so ratifying the same.[79]

★ FACT: LINCOLN WAS CONSTITUTION-ILLITERATE

Lincoln apparently never read any of the Founding Fathers' writings, letters, or speeches; or if he did, like Liberals today he disregarded them because they did not conform to his political views and agenda. In 1911, Confederate Captain Samuel A. Ashe, of Raleigh, North Carolina—the "last surviving commissioned officer of the Confederate States Army"—commented on the Illinois rail-splitter's level of knowledge pertaining to American history:

> . . . Lincoln says that no state ever was a state out of the Union; and that the Union was made in 1774. All untrue! He did not know what he was talking about![80]

★ FACT: COUNTLESS FOREIGNERS RECOGNIZED THE AMERICAN RIGHT OF SECESSION

The depth of Lincoln's ignorance (or more likely, pretended ignorance) pertaining to secession is highlighted by the fact that even many foreigners had a far better grasp of the Founding documents than he did. For instance, in his two-volume book *Democracy in America*, published consecutively in 1835 and 1840, French aristocrat, Alexis de Tocqueville, displayed a clear understanding of the legal right of secession in America:

> The [American] Union was formed by the *voluntary* agreement of States; and, in uniting together, *they have not forfeited their nationality* [that is, sovereignty], nor have they been reduced to the condition of one and the same people. *If one of the States chose to withdraw its name from the contract, it would be difficult to disprove its right of doing so; and the Federal Government would have no means of maintaining its claims directly either by force or by right*.[81]

Irish author Thomas Colley Grattan noted of the American right of secession:

> Any State may, at any time, constitutionally withdraw from the Union, and thus

virtually dissolve it. It was not certainly created with the idea that the States, or several of them, would desire a separation. But *whenever they chose to do it, they have no obstacle in the way.*[82]

Scottish journalist Dr. Alexander Mackay said:

> The Federal Government exists on sufferance only. *Any State may, at any time, Constitutionally withdraw from the Union, and thus virtually dissolve it.* It was not certainly created with the idea that the States, or several of them, would desire a separation; but *whenever they choose to do it, they have no obstacle in the Constitution.*[83]

★ **FACT: NOWHERE DOES THE U.S. CONSTITUTION PROHIBIT SECESSION**
As some have argued, it is true that, despite the inclusion of the Tenth Amendment, the Constitution of the United States does not refer directly to the right of secession. At the same time, however, it should be pointed out that it makes no mention of any governmental power to prohibit it.

★ **FACT: THE FOUNDERS PURPOSEFULLY LEFT ANY REFERENCE TO SECESSION OUT OF THE CONSTITUTION**
The question is, why did the Founders not speak clearly about secession in the Constitution? It was, in part, because they took this very important right so for granted that they did not feel it was necessary. After all, said Rawle, it was "an ingredient in the original composition of the general government," and thus, "though not expressed, was mutually understood."[84] Alexander H. Stephens too noted that the right of secession "was generally recognized in all parts of the Union during the earlier days of the Republic."[85]

Actually, up until 1865 secession was the most frequently discussed political issue in both the United States and the Confederate States.[86] Thus to both the Framers and the general populace it was just another common law that was universally recognized and accepted by every American citizen. Why belabor the point by spelling it out in the Constitution? Sage writes that the "right of secession was considered by the fathers unquestionable—too much so, indeed, for discussion." Cooper, Estill, and Lemmon comment:

> *The right of a state to secede was not questioned during the time while the Constitution was being formed and while the states were entering into the Union. It is safe to say that the Union could not have been formed had the right to secede been denied. Virginia, New York, and Rhode Island, in adopting the Constitution, expressly affirmed the right of the people of the states to resume the powers delegated to the Union if they should find cause to do so afterwards. Innumerable instances of the assertion of this right by statesmen, jurists, political writers, state legislatures, and conventions may be cited.*[87]

Confederate Founding Father Robert A. Toombs put the matter to the U.S. Senate this way:

> [One of the senators has come forward claiming] he can find no constitutional right of secession. Perhaps not; but *the Constitution is not the place to look for State rights. If that right belongs to independent States, and they did not cede it to the Federal Government, it is reserved to the States, or to the people.*[88]

Likewise, Confederate President Jefferson Davis held that:

> It was not necessary in the Constitution to affirm the right of secession, because it was an attribute of sovereignty, and the states had reserved all which they had not delegated [to the central government].[89]

★ **FACT: THE FOUNDERS' INTENT REGARDING SECESSION IS CLEAR: IT IS AN INHERENT RIGHT OF SOVEREIGN STATES**
No matter how we choose to interpret the Constitution, it is patently obvious what the Founders' intentions were concerning this issue 225 years ago. In June 1816, the man who authored the Declaration of Independence, now former U.S. President Thomas Jefferson, wrote a letter to William Crawford that read in part:

> If any state in the Union will declare that it prefers separation to a continuance in the Union, *I have no hesitation in saying, 'Let us separate.'*[90]

★ **FACT: C.S. PRESIDENT JEFFERSON DAVIS GAVE LIFELONG SUPPORT TO THE RIGHT OF SECESSION**
President Jefferson Davis, a brilliant scholar and an accomplished student of the U.S. Constitution, noted that in addition to the Tenth Amendment, several state Constitutions openly refer to the right of secession. Virginia's Constitution, for example, affirms that

the powers granted under the [U.S.] Constitution, *being derived from the people of the United States, may be resumed by them, whensoever the same shall be perverted to their injury or oppression*, and that every power not granted thereby remains with them and at their will.[91]

The Constitutions of New York and Rhode Island also include clauses regarding secession, stating that

the powers of government may be resumed by the people whenever it shall become necessary to their happiness.[92]

In 1881 Davis wrote a brilliant exposition on secession that is still used as a reference by Southerners to this day.

As Davis points out in his brilliant pro-South book, *The Rise and Fall of the Confederate Government*:

By inserting these declarations in their ordinances, Virginia, New York, and Rhode Island *formally, officially, and permanently declared their interpretation of the [U.S.] Constitution as recognizing the right of secession by the resumption of their grants*. By accepting the ratifications with this declaration incorporated, *the other states as formally accepted the principle which it asserted*.[93]

One of Davis' postwar attorneys, Bernard J. Sage, noted importantly that

all the states were co-equal republics, federating and delegating power; [thus] . . . any general principle, though uttered by but one, was equally applicable to all.[94]

★ **FACT: THE FOUNDERS REGARDED SECESSION AS A POLITICAL NECESSITY**
When, beginning in 1860, the South began acting on the principal of legal, peaceful "separation" and the resumption of "the powers of government," it was derogatorily called a "rebellion" by Lincoln, as if it were a great political sin.[95] However, here is what Thomas Jefferson, writing from Paris, France, to James Madison on January 30, 1787, said on this subject:

> The spirit of resistance to government is so valuable on certain occasions, that I wish it always to be kept alive. It will often be exercised when wrong, but better so than not to be exercised at all. *I like a little rebellion now and then. It is like a storm in the atmosphere.*[96]

After decades of interference from the Northern states, the South finally decided to exercise her Constitutional right to foment "a little rebellion," a Jeffersonian act of secession that was both correct and legal according to every important official document created by the U.S. government up to that time. Again, let us recall President Jefferson's words from his First Inaugural Address in 1801:

> If there be any among us who would wish to *dissolve this union* or to change its republican form, let them stand undisturbed as monuments of the safety with which error of opinion may be tolerated where reason is left free to combat it.[97]

If any states want to secede, Jefferson noted further:

> It is the elder and the younger son differing. God bless them both, and keep them in the union, if it be for their good, *but separate them, if it be better.*[98]

★ **FACT: PRESIDENT JAMES MADISON WAS ONCE A STRONG ADVOCATE OF STATE SOVEREIGNTY & THE RIGHT OF SECESSION**
Our fourth president, Conservative James Madison, had much to say about the U.S. Constitution, our government, and state sovereignty. In speaking of "the parties to the compact of the Constitution," he made the following pertinent remarks:

On examining the first relation, it appears, on one hand that the Constitution is to be founded on the assent and ratification of the people of America, given by deputies elected for the special purpose; but on the other, that this assent and ratification is given by the people, not as individuals composing one entire nation, *but as composing the distinct and independent States to which they respectively belong.*

President James Madison and his private residence "Montpelier," in Orange County, Virginia.

It is to be the assent and ratification of the several States, derived from the supreme authority in each State—*the authority of the people themselves. The act, therefore, establishing the Constitution, will not be a national, but a Federal [that is, Confederal or Confederate] act.*

That it will be a Federal and not a national act, as these terms are understood by the objectors, the act of the people, as forming so many independent States, not as forming an aggregate nation, is obvious from this single consideration, that it is to result neither from the decision of a majority of the people, nor from a majority of the States. It must result from the unanimous assent of the several States that are parties to it, differing no otherwise from their ordinary consent than in its being expressed, not by the legislative authority, but by that of the people themselves.

. . . If we [that is, the state of Virginia] be dissatisfied with the National Government, if we should choose to renounce it [that is, secede], this is an additional safeguard to our defence.[99]

★ FACT: PRESIDENT MADISON ONCE HELD THE RIGHT OF SECESSION TO BE SACRED

Though Madison's views on secession softened later in life,[100] he began his political career as a strong supporter. In 1787, for instance, he said:

It has been alleged that *the confederation* [that is, the U.S.A.], having been formed by unanimous consent, could be dissolved by unanimous consent only. Does this doctrine result from the nature of compacts? Does it arise from any particular stipulation on the articles of *confederation*? If we consider the Federal [Confederate] Union as analogous to the fundamental compact by which individuals compose our society, and which must, in its theoretic origin at least, have been the unanimous act of the component members, *it cannot be said that no dissolution of the compact can be effected without unanimous consent. A breach of the fundamental principles of the compact by a part of the society would certainly absolve the other part from their obligations to it.*[101]

★ FACT: PRESIDENT MADISON DECLARED THE POWERS OF THE STATES TO BE "NUMEROUS & INDEFINITE"
We will remember the words of Madison pertaining to the federal (central) government and its powers and purposes. He was emphatic that the states were to retain their sovereign powers:

The powers delegated to the Federal Government are few and defined. Those which are to remain to the State Government are numerous and indefinite. The former [the Federal Government] will be exercised principally on external objects, as war, peace, negotiation, and foreign commerce; with which last the power of taxation will for the most part be connected. The powers reserved to the several States will extend to all the objects which, in the ordinary course of affairs, concern the lives, the liberties, and the properties of the people, and the internal order, improvement, and prosperity of the State.[102]

★ FACT: SOUTHERN STATESMEN VIEWED SECESSION AS THE BEST GUARD OF PERSONAL LIBERTY & PUBLIC JUSTICE
In February 1833 well-respected North Carolina statesman Nathaniel Macon spoke for nearly all Southerners when he said:

I have never believed that a State could nullify, and remain in the Union; but *I have always believed that a State might secede when it pleased*, provided she would pay her proportion of the public debt; and this right *I have considered the best guard to public liberty and to public justice that could be devised, and it ought to have prevented what is now felt in the South—oppression.*[103]

It was from these very same sentiments that America's first and second Confederacies were created: the former, the U.S.A. in 1776, to "throw off" the despotic government of Britain's King George; the latter, the C.S.A. in 1861, to "throw off" the despotic government of America's "King Abraham."

★ FACT: THE FOUNDERS PLACED STATE SOVEREIGNTY OVER NATIONAL SOVEREIGNTY
In both cases the Founders' intention was to form a government in which the Union was subservient to the individual states. In 1776 this

succeeded because the colonies, which were considered individual "nation-states"[104]—a loose union of sovereign and independent "little republics," as Jefferson styled them,[105] or "distinct nations," as Jay referred to them[106]—did indeed create the Union. This is why, in 1781, Jefferson spoke of Virginia as "but one of thirteen nations, who have agreed to act and speak together."[107] It is because of this concept, state sovereignty, that there *cannot* be a Union without states. And it is why there *can* be states without a Union—contrary to Lincoln's absurd and unhistorical belief that "the Union created the states."[108]

★ FACT: THE AMERICAN COLONIES SECEDED FROM ENGLAND AS SEPARATE SOVEREIGNS, NOT AS A SINGLE COUNTRY

This is also why, during the First American War of Independence, the American colonies did not secede from Britain as a unified body. While independence was declared jointly, each state, a nation in its own right, declared itself independent *individually*.[109] Hence, when King George III signed an agreement recognizing the nation-states known as the "original thirteen colonies" as sovereign,[110] he addressed each one individually, by name.[111] In Article 1 of the *Treaty With Great Britain* we find the following passage:

> His Britannic Majesty acknowledges the said United States, viz., New Hampshire, Massachusetts Bay, Rhode Island and Providence Plantations, Connecticut, New York, New Jersey, Pennsylvania, Delaware, Maryland, Virginia, North Carolina, South Carolina, and Georgia, *to be free, sovereign and independent States; that he treats with them as such*, and for himself, his heirs and successors, relinquishes all claims to the Government, propriety and territorial rights of the same, and every part thereof.[112]

Like other Southerners, Lee pledged his allegiance to his home state, not the U.S.A.

★ FACT: EARLY SOUTHERNERS PLEDGED ALLEGIANCE TO THEIR INDIVIDUAL STATES, NOT THE U.S.A.

That the original thirteen American colonies began life as separate nation-states[113] is the same reason early Southerners pledged their allegiance to their native states rather than to the U.S.A.[114] Hence Conservative Southerners, like Robert E. Lee, literally referred to their home states as "my country." Though admitting that he was a citizen of the United States, Jefferson Davis observed that "my allegiance is first due to the State I represent."[115] Thomas Jefferson too called Virginia "my country."[116] John Randolph of Virginia took note of the North's desire to exact allegiance from the Southern states, saying:

> When I speak of my country, I mean the Commonwealth of Virginia. I was born in allegiance to [the English King] George III. . . . My ancestors threw off the oppressive yoke of the mother country, but they never made me subject to New England in matters spiritual or temporal; neither do I mean to become so voluntarily.[117]

Thus in the Old South one would refer to himself as a Tennessean, a South Carolinian, a Floridian, a Virginian, or a Texan, while a Northerner would refer to himself as a "citizen of the United States."[118]

★ FACT: THE DECLARATION OF INDEPENDENCE PROVES THE POLITICAL AUTONOMY OF THE STATES

If any doubts remain as to these facts, we need only reexamine the last paragraph of the Declaration of Independence. We will recall that in breaking their ties with Great Britain, the leaders of the 13 American colonies, or "little republics," repeatedly refer to themselves as "Free and Independent States,"[119] each endowed with all the powers of a sovereign nation:

> We, therefore, the Representatives of the United States of America, in General Congress, Assembled, appealing to the Supreme Judge of the world for the rectitude of our intentions, do, in the Name, and by Authority of the good People of these Colonies, solemnly publish and declare, That *these united Colonies are, and of Right ought to be Free and Independent States*, that they are Absolved from all Allegiance to the British Crown, and that all political connection between them and the State of Great Britain, is and ought to be totally dissolved; and that *as Free and Independent States*, they have full Power to levy War, conclude Peace, contract Alliances, establish Commerce, and to do all other Acts and Things which *Independent States* may of right do. And for the support of this Declaration, with a firm reliance on the protection of Divine Providence, we mutually pledge to each other our Lives, our Fortunes, and our sacred Honor.[120]

Beneath these words, at the bottom of the Declaration of Independence, each nation-state was itemized, along with the signers from that particular colony. Importantly, the states were listed not as a single nationalized people, as the "United States of America," but separately, as individual political bodies—each an autonomous nation unto itself. Here is the actual text showing the names of the signatories along with their home-countries (states):

> New Hampshire: Josiah Bartlett, William Whipple, Matthew Thornton
> Massachusetts: John Hancock, Samuel Adams, John Adams, Robert Treat Paine, Elbridge Gerry
> Rhode Island: Stephen Hopkins, William Ellery
> Connecticut: Roger Sherman, Samuel Huntington, William Williams, Oliver Wolcott
> New York: William Floyd, Philip Livingston, Francis Lewis, Lewis Morris
> New Jersey: Richard Stockton, John Witherspoon, Francis Hopkinson, John Hart, Abraham Clark
> Pennsylvania: Robert Morris, Benjamin Rush, Benjamin Franklin, John Morton, George Clymer, James Smith, George Taylor, James Wilson, George Ross
> Delaware: Caesar Rodney, George Read, Thomas McKean
> Maryland: Samuel Chase, William Paca, Thomas Stone, Charles Carroll of Carrollton
> Virginia: George Wythe, Richard Henry Lee, Thomas Jefferson, Benjamin Harrison, Thomas Nelson, Jr., Francis Lightfoot Lee, Carter Braxton
> North Carolina: William Hooper, Joseph Hewes, John Penn
> South Carolina: Edward Rutledge, Thomas Heyward, Jr., Thomas Lynch, Jr., Arthur Middleton
> Georgia: Button Gwinnett, Lyman Hall, George Walton[121]

★ **FACT: JUDICIAL EXPERTS AGREE THAT THE DECLARATION OF INDEPENDENCE ASSERTS THE SOVEREIGNTY OF THE COLONIES OR STATES**
Judicial authorities from around the world concur that the Declaration of Independence affirmed "the individual independence, freedom, and sovereignty of each of the thirteen states."[122] Once of these, Judge Salmon P. Chase of the Superior Court of the United States, writes:

> I consider the Declaration of Independence as a declaration, not that the United Colonies jointly, in a collective capacity, were independent States, but that *each of them was an independent State*.[123]

★ **FACT: STATE SOVEREIGNTY HAS NEVER BEEN CONSTITUTIONALLY PROHIBITED**
Although the concept of state sovereignty was severely damaged by Lincoln's War, and although amendments like the Fourteenth weakened it, it did not disappear. The original Constitution guarantees the rights of states (Ninth and Tenth Amendments), while simultaneously no amendment has ever been added to the Constitution that specifically cancels the sovereign independence of the individual states. Therefore state sovereignty is still active, legal, and operable—despite the resistance to this fact by big government Liberals, socialists, communists, and uninformed Conservatives. And state sovereignty, *by definition*, includes the rights of both accession and secession.[124]

England's King George III recognized the seceding American colonies as "free, sovereign, and independent states."

★ **FACT: BECAUSE OF THE RIGHT OF SECESSION THE U.S.A. WAS ONCE CALLED "THE CONFEDERATE STATES OF AMERICA"**
From such documents the conclusion is clear: the United States of America began as a confederation of 13 individual nations with a weak central government, a Union that was subordinate to those states. After the Constitutional Convention of 1787 at Philadelphia, the Articles of Confederation were replaced by the U.S. Constitution. But our government remained a confederate republic,[125] and each of the states retained all of the rights originally accorded to them as individual nation-states by the Declaration of Independence, the Articles of Confederation, the U.S. Constitution, and finally the Bill of Rights. And what was one of the more popular 18th- and 19th-century nicknames for the U.S.A.? "The Confederate States of America."[126]

★ **FACT: THE FOUNDERS VIEWED THE U.S. AS THE "STATES UNITED," NOT THE "UNITED STATES"**
In one of the more bizarre incidents in American history, in 1861

Lincoln dismissed all of this, as if none of it were true or had ever even existed. Since his erroneous thinking on this topic helped launch the War, let us examine it in more detail for a moment.

We have established that the U.S. began as a confederacy, with the Union being inferior to the states. As mentioned, this obviously means that the Union *could not* exist without the states, but that the states *could* exist without the Union. Our country at this time was seen then, not as the "United States," but rather as the "States United,"[127] a vitally important distinction.

★ FACT: THE MAJORITY OF THE FOUNDING FATHERS REJECTED THE IDEA OF A NATIONAL GOVERNMENT
On December 3, 1787, in considering the formulation of the new U.S. Constitution, Samuel Adams hesitated, for it seem weighted in favor of a national government rather than the sovereignty of the states:

> I stumble at the threshold. I meet with a *national government*, instead of a *federal [confederate] union of sovereign states*. . . . If the several states are to become one entire nation, under one legislature, its powers to extend to all legislation, and its laws to be supreme, and control the whole, the idea of sovereignty in these states must be lost.[128]

The Founders, ever concerned about governmental consolidation and the subsequent loss of state sovereignty, carefully distinguished between a national government (a nation) and a federal government (a confederacy).[129] At the Philadelphia Convention in 1787—where big government Liberals like Alexander Hamilton had pushed for a "consolidation of the Sovereignties of the several States in[to] one single grand Republic"[130]—one of them, William Patterson of New Jersey, correctly asserted that

> the amendment of the confederacy was the object of all the laws and commissions upon the subject. . . . The commissions under which we act are not only the measure of our power, they denote, also, the sentiments of the states on the subject of our deliberation. The idea of a *national government* [nation], as contradistinguished from a *federal one* [confederacy], never entered into the mind of any of them [the states]; and to the public mind we must accommodate ourselves. . . . *We are met here as deputies of thirteen independent sovereign states, for federal [confederate] purposes.* Can we consolidate their

sovereignty, and form one nation, and *annihilate the sovereignty of our states*, who have sent us here for other purposes? . . . But it is said that this national government is to act on individuals, and not on states; and cannot a federal [confederate] government be so formed as to operate in the same way? It surely may. I therefore declare that I will never consent to the present system, and I shall make all the interest against it, in the state I represent, that I can.[131]

Likewise, Founder Patrick Henry of Virginia noted:

Who authorised them [the members of the Philadelphia Convention] to speak the language of *we, the people*, instead of *we, the states? States are the characteristics and the soul of a confederation [like the U.S.A.].* If the states be not the agents of this compact, it must be one great, consolidated, national government [that is, a nation], of the people of all the states. . . . This is an alarming transition from a confederacy to a consolidated government.[132]

★ FACT: LINCOLN PURPOSEFULLY REINTERPRETED THE CONSTITUTION & REVISED EARLY AMERICAN POLITICAL HISTORY

Some 75 years later Liberal Lincoln took up the banner of the Liberal Founding Fathers, who had preferred a nation (unlimited government) over a confederacy (limited government). Fortunately, in 1787 the Liberals (the "Federalists") were in the minority. But with Lincoln's win in 1860 all of that changed. The next year Victorian Liberals took over the federal government and set about challenging the Constitution and rewriting American history, the same thing Liberals are doing today!

Small government Conservative Patrick Henry fought against the Liberal idea of turning the U.S.A. into a nation, preferring that it remain, as was originally intended, a confederacy.

Lincoln began his efforts to install big government in Washington by *reversing the facts*, the standard Liberal ploy. He did this by insisting, impossibly, that "the Union created the states," that they were indeed the "*United* States,"[133] even declaring, as he did in the Gettysburg Address, that:

Four score and seven years ago our fathers brought forth on this continent, a new *nation* . . .[134]

★ **FACT: THE FOUNDERS REJECTED THE IDEA OF A NATIONAL GOVERNMENT IN FAVOR OF A CONFEDERATE (FEDERAL) ONE**
But by declaring its independence from Britain in 1776 a "new nation" was not "brought forth"—for the U.S. was not then, and has never been, a "nation": a government in which all power is consolidated within it, and its states have virtually no autonomy, sovereignty, or independence.

On May 30, shortly after the start of the Philadelphia Convention on May 25, 1787, "it was resolved, that a *national government* ought to be established, consisting of a supreme legislative, executive and judiciary." Naturally, the more conservative majority was against this idea (one heartily promoted by Alexander Hamilton and other Liberals). The Conservatives (then just beginning to become known as "Anti-Federalists," or more correctly, "Republicans") quite emphatically and intentionally demanded that the new government be styled a "Confederacy of States" (that is, a Federal, Confederal, or Confederate government) rather than a nation. Additionally they asked that the Constitution be styled "the articles of union."[135] Fowler writes:

> So intent were the Conventions upon making a Federal [Confederate] and not a consolidated Government, that, at the motion of Mr. [Oliver] Ellsworth, *the term "national Government" was by an [sic] unanimous vote struck out from the Constitution*, and instead of it the "Government of the United States" was substituted. It is in its origin and nature Federal [Confederate], having been framed by the States as parties, and depending for its existence on the action of the States.
>
> The letter addressed to Congress by General Washington, President of the Convention, and agreed to by that body, by paragraphs, speaks of the "Federal Government of *these States*," and not of a *national* Government. *The word Federal [Confederate] indicates that the Constitution is a compact between the States. The term "national Government" is used [only] in a popular sense.*[136]

Many others came forward with the same concerns, ultimately leading to the creation of the Bill of Rights, whose Ninth and Tenth Amendments secured the separation of powers and ensured states' rights.

★ **FACT: THE FOUNDING FATHERS CREATED A "CONFEDERATE STATES OF AMERICA" ON THE POLITICAL IDEAS OF BARON DE MONTESQUIE**

Montesquieu's ideas about confederacies and republics deeply influenced the Founding Fathers.

What was eventually created then was not a nation, but a confederacy, the U.S.A., modeled upon the 18th-Century French philosopher Baron de Montesquieu's concept of a "confederate republic,"[137] the name by which George Washington, Alexander Hamilton, St. George Tucker, and many other Founders referred to our type of government;[138] a government made up of 13 sovereign and autonomous nations (today commonly referred to as colonies or states), and widely known as "The Confederate States of America" by 18th- and 19th-Century Americans and foreigners.[139]

★ **FACT: LINCOLN'S VIEWS OF AMERICAN HISTORY & THE CONSTITUTION WERE SILLY, FALSE, & PERILOUS**
Despite these irrefutable facts, from his own twisted mind Lincoln extrapolated that the U.S.A. was a "nation," and that because of this, there could be no states without the national government or Union, and that this Union was meant to be "perpetual." Here, on March 4, 1861, is how he phrased these irrational, confused, and ultimately dangerous ideas in his First Inaugural Address:

> I hold that, in contemplation of universal law, and of the Constitution, the Union of these States is perpetual. Perpetuity is implied, if not expressed, in the fundamental law of all national governments. It is safe to assert that no government proper ever had a provision in its organic law for its own termination. Continue to execute all the express provisions of our national Constitution, and the Union will endure forever—it being impossible to destroy it, except by some action not provided for in the instrument itself.
>
> Again, if the United States be not a government proper, but an association of States in the nature of contract merely, can it, as a contract, be peaceably unmade, by less than all the parties who made it? One party to a contract may violate it—break it, so to speak; but does it not require all to lawfully rescind it?
>
> Descending from these general principles, we find the proposition that, in legal contemplation, the Union is perpetual, confirmed by the history of the Union itself. The Union is much older than the Constitution. It was formed in fact by the Articles of Association in 1774. It was matured and

continued by the Declaration of Independence in 1776. It was further matured, and the faith of all the then thirteen States expressly plighted and engaged that it should be perpetual, by the Articles of Confederation in 1778. And, finally, in 1787, one of the declared objects for ordaining and establishing the Constitution, was "*to form a more perfect Union.*"

But if the destruction of the Union, by one, or by a part only, of the States, be lawfully possible, the Union is *less* perfect than before, the Constitution having lost the vital element of perpetuity.

It follows, from these views, that no State, upon its own mere motion, can lawfully get out of the Union; that *resolves* and *ordinances* to that effect are legally void, and that acts of violence, within any State or States, against the authority of the United States, are insurrectionary or revolutionary, according to circumstances.

I, therefore, consider that, in view of the Constitution and the laws, the Union is unbroken, and, to the extent of my ability, I shall take care, as the Constitution itself expressly enjoins upon me, that the laws of the Union be faithfully executed in all the States.[140]

Spoken like a true uneducated Liberal! As this book will show, nearly every one of these statements is incorrect: many of them are based on stupidity, some on left-wing wishful thinking; the rest are nothing but purposeful falsehoods.

The ignorance and arrogance behind these comments would not be so appalling if they had come from an illiterate, 19th-Century common laborer. What makes them truly shocking is that they came from an intelligent and successful lawyer, a man who should have known better; the man who became our sixteenth president.

★ FACT: SOUTHERNERS WERE WELL AWARE OF LINCOLN'S IGNORANCE OF THE CONSTITUTION

Edward A. Pollard artfully expressed the conservative South's reaction to Lincoln's progressive nonsense:

> In his message, Mr. Lincoln announced a great political discovery. It was that all former statesmen of America had lived, and written, and labored under a great delusion: that the States, instead of having created the Union, were its *creatures*; that they obtained their sovereignty and independence from it, and never possessed either until the Convention of 1787. *This singular doctrine of consolidation was the natural preface to a series of measures to strengthen the Government, to enlarge the Executive power,* and to conduct the war with new decision, and on a most unexpected scale of magnitude.[141]

Pollard was entirely correct. Lincoln went on to use his fictitious ideas to help justify crushing personal liberties across the country, both South and North, severely damaging civil rights, as John C. Breckinridge of Kentucky pointed out:

> *The atrocious doctrine* is announced by the President, and acted upon, that *the States derive their power from the Federal Government*, and may be suppressed on any pretence of military necessity. Everywhere the civil has given way to the military power.[142]

Big government Liberal Lincoln held a myriad of untenable, confused, contradictory, and fallacious ideas about U.S. history and the Constitution. But this did not prevent his Northern constituents from voting him into the Oval Office—twice.

Lincoln's personal beliefs, that the states could not exist without the Union and that the Union was meant to be "perpetual," must certainly rank as two of the most preposterous and historically inaccurate ideas ever put forth. Why? Because as any first-year student of American history knows, *the Union did not exist prior to the states*. It only came afterward as a result of its creation by those states, at which point the 13 original colonies legally and voluntarily joined it.

★ FACT: THE ORIGINAL OPENING OF THE CONSTITUTION WAS "WE, THE PEOPLE OF THE STATES . . ."

Why then, some counter, did the Founding Fathers begin the Preamble of the U.S. Constitution with the words "We the people of the United States . . ." if they did not intend to create a *nation* of one people?

The answer is quite simple: these were not the original opening words of the Preamble.[143] In his *Notes of the Debates in the Federal Convention*, James Madison reveals the introductory text of the Preamble as it was written (about August 1787) in the first draft of the U.S. Constitution. It read:

> *We, the people of the States of* New Hampshire, Massachusetts, Rhode-Island and Providence Plantations, Connecticut, New York, New Jersey,

Pennsylvania, Delaware, Maryland, Virginia, North Carolina, South Carolina, and Georgia, do ordain, declare and establish, the following Constitution, for the government of ourselves and our posterity.[144]

In other words, in the earliest rough outline of the Constitution, the 13 original nation-states were listed individually, as "we, the people of the states of New Hampshire, Massachusetts, Rhode-Island . . ." etc.

★ FACT: "UNITED STATES" WAS ADDED DUE TO THE RESTRICTIONS OF THE RATIFICATION CALENDAR

Why then was this sentence dropped and replaced with the trimmed down phrase, "of the United States"? This question was aptly answered in 1876 by lawyer, author, and legal scholar William O. Bateman:

> The change of this expression of the organic will, to that of "We, the people of the United States," etc., was proposed by a sub-committee on *style*. And wherefore? Because, it could not be foreknown, which of the States would accept and ratify the new constitution. If any *nine* of them should do so, they, at all events, *according to the last article of the instrument*, would thence become the *United States* of America. Hence the committee on style revised the language of the convention, and substituted "the United States," in place of "the States of New Hampshire, Massachusetts, Rhode Island," etc.[145]

The change in wording then occurred due to a simple timing issue.

★ FACT: THE MEANING OF THE CONSTITUTIONAL PHRASES "UNITED STATES" AND "PEOPLE" HAVE BEEN DISTORTED FOR POLITICAL PURPOSES

Though the Founding Generation, being the authors of the Declaration of Independence, the Articles of Confederation, and the U.S. Constitution, understood the original meaning of the phrases "United States" and "people," these meanings have been perverted over time by those seeking to centralize power in Washington, D.C. Let us then reassert the authentic meaning behind them. Fowler did an admirable job of this, so I will cite him:

> United States: This term replaced the term "United Colonies," on the Declaration of Independence. The use of the term United Colonies did not annul the separate distinctive rights of the Colonies. *The use of the term United States does not annul the separate distinctive rights of the States, whether before the*

adoption of the Articles of Confederation, or after the adoption of the Articles of Confederation, or after the adoption of the Federal Constitution. The word "United," used in these four different sets of circumstances, does not imply that the Colonies or the States were one people, in the sense in which a colony or a State is one, but only that the several Colonies before the Declaration of Independence, and the several States before the adoption of the Articles of Confederation, and after their adoption, and after the adoption of the Constitution, united for certain purposes and in certain respects.

In the minds of the framers and friends of the Constitution, the *plural* idea was the ruling idea in the use of the term "United States." *The term was equivalent to the "States of the Union."* Thus General Washington, in his reply to [Native-American Chief] Cornplanter [said]: "The United States desire to be the friends of the Indians. . . . The United States will be true and faithful to their engagements."

But in the minds of foreigners, and those ignorant of the structure of our Government, the *singular* idea is attached to the term. They sometimes say, "the United States is able to take care of itself."

In the Convention of Virginia, which ratified the Constitution, *Patrick Henry objected to the words, "We, the people of the United States," lest it might be supposed that it meant the inhabitants of all the States as one homogeneous mass or aggregate.* But Mr. Madison replied, *"The parties to it are to be the people, but not the people as composing one great society, but the people as composing thirteen sovereignties."* The accession or adoption was the separate act of the people of each State, quite independent of the people of any other State. And the articles at the end are declared to be "done in Convention by the unanimous consent *of the States* present."

People: This term was used in application to the individuals who composed a separate Colony or a separate State. "The good people of these Colonies," meant the good people in the several Colonies. *It meant those for whom the delegates severally acted, and it did not mean those people in the aggregate. The several peoples represented in the Convention acted by their respective delegates.* Thus, the people of Connecticut acted for themselves by their delegates Roger Sherman, Samuel Huntington, William Williams, Oliver Wolcott. In the Articles of Confederation, the following phrases are employed: "among the people of the different States"; "and the people of each State"; "their own people," that is, *the people of the respective States. In the Constitution the word "people" is used only for reference to the inhabitants of the several States, or portions of the same, and in no case for the collective inhabitants of all the States in the aggregate.* It is applied to those who were accustomed to act together under State authority, at a particular time or place, or to portions of them. Thus, "The powers not delegated to the United States by the Constitution, nor prohibited by it to the States, are reserved to the States or to the people" (that is, to the people of the States). In the phrase, "We, the people of the United States," there is an equivalent for we, the people of New Hampshire, and the people of Massachusetts, etc. The articles of the Constitution was a compact "between the States ratifying the same." The "style" of the Federal

[Confederate] Union in the new Constitution was borrowed from the old, namely, the Articles of Confederation, and *has the same meaning.*

The reason why the Constitution was submitted to the people of each State, and not to the several Legislatures, was because it was apprehended that the latter would oppose it. Said Wilson: "I know that they, the Legislatures and the State officers, will oppose it; I am for carrying it to the people of each State." *The ratification was the act of each State, and not of the Federal Government, which then had no existence, or of the aggregate people under that Government.*

Massachusetts, in Convention, in ratifying the "new Constitution," speaks of the "rights of the people," that is, the people of the several States; and also uses the language, "in the name and by the authority of the people of this Commonwealth." *"The freedom of the people," was understood to mean the freedom or the rights of the States, or of the people of the States, in distinction from the granted rights or powers of the Federal Government.*[146]

★ FACT: THE STATES' RIGHT OF ACCESSION INSURES THE STATES' RIGHT OF SECESSION

With these issues settled it is plain to see that the right of *accession*, that is, the right to voluntarily enter a union, gives one the concomitant right of *secession*, that is, the right to voluntarily leave a union as well.[147] This idea, being both the founding principle and the very cornerstone of the original U.S. government, decimates Lincoln's conviction that the Union, and by extension the Constitution, were meant to be "perpetual."[148]

★ FACT: THE FOUNDERS DID NOT INTEND THE AMERICAN UNION TO BE "PERPETUAL"

Eighty years earlier, in his pamphlet *Notes on the State of Virginia* (authored from 1781 to 1782), Thomas Jefferson wrote of the formation of America's first government by the colonies, noting that

> . . . they organized the government by the ordinance entitled a Constitution . . . . *it does not say, that it shall be perpetual; that it shall be unalterable.*[149]

Jefferson goes on to refute those who wrongly declared that both the Constitution and the Union were meant to be everlasting:

> *Not only the silence of the instrument is a proof they [i.e., the legislatures] thought it would be alterable, but their own practice also: for this very convention, meeting as a*

House of Delegates in General Assembly with the new Senate in the autumn of that year, passed acts of assembly in contradiction to their ordinance of government; and every assembly from that time to this has done the same. *I am safe therefore in the position, that the constitution itself is alterable by the ordinary legislature.* Though this opinion seems founded on the first elements of common sense, yet is the contrary maintained by some persons: 1. Because, say they, the conventions were vested with every power necessary to make effectual opposition to Great-Britain. But to complete this argument, they must go on, and say further, that effectual opposition could not be made to Great-Britain, without establishing a form of government perpetual and unalterable by the legislature; *which is not true.* An opposition which at some time or other was to come to an end, *could not need a perpetual institution to carry it on*: and a government, amendable as its defects should be discovered, was as likely to make effectual resistance, as one which should be unalterably wrong. Besides, the assemblies were as much vested with all powers requisite for resistance as the conventions were. If therefore these powers included that of modelling the form of government in the one case, they did so in the other. *The assemblies then as well as the conventions may model the government; that is, they may alter the ordinance of government.*[150]

Founding Father Thomas Jefferson made it clear that it was not the Union or even the Constitution that were meant to be "perpetual." It was the sovereignty of the states—the exact opposite of what Lincoln believed and preached.

Fowler correctly answers the question concerning the alleged "perpetuity" of the Union:

Was the new Confederacy or Union [the U.S.A.] expected to be permanent? *The Union of the Old England Colonies* established in 1643, though solemnly declared in the Constitution to be "perpetual," *was dissolved.* The Union, under the British Constitution, of the Colonies with the mother country, which was supposed to be organic, and claimed to be perpetual, *was dissolved.* The Union formed [in 1781] by the Federal Constitution, or "Articles of Confederation and Perpetual Union," and which was in that instrument solemnly declared to be perpetual, *was dissolved.*

Was the new Union, like those three Unions, expected to be dissolved and pass away?

The States were familiar with the idea, that *"Governments derive their just powers from the consent of the governed,"* and that *"when any form of Government becomes destructive of the ends for which it was established, it is the right of the people to alter or to abolish it, and institute a new Government."* By an article in the new Constitution, "the ratification of the Convention of nine States shall be sufficient for the establishment of this Constitution between the States ratifying the same"; *thus justifying the doctrine, that nine States might secede from the remaining four*, notwithstanding the article in the old Constitution, namely,

> "And the Articles of this Confederation shall be inviolably observed by every State, and the Union shall be perpetual; nor shall any alteration at any time hereafter be made in any of them, unless such alteration be agreed to in a Congress of the United States, and be afterwards confirmed by the Legislatures of every State."

In the new Constitution there is no declaration that the Union shall be perpetual, no promise on the part of the States to abide in it, and no power delegated to the Federal Government to retain them in it by force. Will they stay in it?

Many of the fathers had their fears and misgivings. Even [George] Washington hardly dared to look into the future. "Let experience," said he, "solve the question. To look to speculation in such a case were criminal." He evidently feared to reason on the subject, lest he should be carried to the conclusion, that *the Union could not be preserved*, however much he loved it.[151]

★ FACT: MANY FOREIGNERS DID NOT EXPECT THE AMERICAN UNION TO BE PERMANENT

Foreigners too understood that the U.S.A. could not and would not be a "permanent" or "perpetual" Union. Writing in 1833, English poet Samuel T. Coleridge made these prophetic comments:

> *Can there be any thorough national fusion of the Northern and the Southern States? I think not.* The fact is, the Union will be shaken almost to dislocation, whenever a very serious question between the States arises. *The American Union has no centre, and it is impossible to make one.* The more they extend their borders into the Indian land, the weaker will the national cohesion be. I look upon the States as splendid masses to be used by-and-by in the composition of two or three Governments.[152]

Likewise, in 1856 Russian writer Ivan Golovin said:

> A visit to the United States has the strange property of cooling democrats. Again, I tell you, the manifest destiny of the States is, disunion. I do not give the Union eight years to last.[153]

★ **FACT: THE U.S. CONSTITUTION DOES NOT SAY ANYTHING ABOUT PERPETUITY**
If the American Union is mean to be "perpetual," as Lincoln and other 19th-Century Liberals believed, where does the Constitution state this? I will let Bledsoe answer the question:

> It is a remarkable fact, that, in the Constitution of the United States, there is not a word relating to the perpetuity or continuance of the Government established by it. This momentous question is passed over in profound silence. Nor was this omission an act of forgetfulness. It was, on the contrary, the result of deliberate design. The [earlier] . . . Articles of Confederation [had] expressly provided that the government established by them should be "perpetual," and should never be changed without the unanimous consent of all the States of the Union. This provision was *deliberately struck out, or not permitted to appear in the new Constitution.* In the act of receding from the compact of the Union, which had expressly pronounced itself "perpetual," *the fathers had not the face to declare that the new compact should last forever. Time had demonstrated the futility of such a provision.* The [Philadelphia] Convention of 1787 had been most sadly hampered by it in their design to erect a new form of government, as appears from the Madison Papers, and other accounts of its proceedings. Hence *they wisely determined to leave no such obstacle in the way of the free action of future generations, in case they should wish to new-model their government. It is certain that no such obstacle is found in the Constitution framed by them.*
>
> . . . The truth is, that the new Constitution was designed by its authors to last just as long as it should be faithfully observed by the parties to it, or as it should answer the great ends of its creation, and no longer. On the failure of either of these conditions, then, in their view, the power by which it was ordained possessed the inherent and indefeasible right to withdraw from it. Otherwise there would be no remedy, not even in the sovereign power itself, for the greatest of all political evils or abuses. Otherwise we should have to repudiate and reject the great principle of American freedom, which has never been called in question by any statesman of the New World, or over which the least cloud of suspicion has ever been cast by any American citizen. What, then, is the position assumed by those who deny the right of secession? In asserting that a State has no right to withdraw from the Union, they declare that the Constitution, or Articles of Union, is perpetually binding. That is to say, by a forced construction, *they introduce into the Constitution, the very provision which its framers most deliberately refused to insert therein!* They refused to say, that the new compact should be perpetual; and yet these interpreters declare, that they designed to make it perpetual!
>
> . . . The truth is, that the Convention, in its desire to secede from the old compact, was so greatly embarrassed by the clause declaring that "the Union shall be perpetual," that it deliberately removed that obstacle from the path of future legislation: and, whether it was intended by the Convention or not, the legal effect of this was to establish the right of secession under the new compact between the same

parties.¹⁵⁴

★ FACT: ONLY THE SOVEREIGNTY OF THE STATES WAS MEANT TO BE PERPETUAL
From what we have examined it is evident that because of the right of secession, the Union was not, is not, and could not be perpetual. The same is true of the original Constitution: because of the right of legislative amendments, it was not, is not, and could not be perpetual. And the Constitution now possesses twenty-seven Amendments added to it since its creation to prove it.¹⁵⁵ The only thing that *was* meant to be perpetual was the sovereignty of the states, the very thing that Liberals like Lincoln despised and tried to destroy.

★ FACT: AMERICA'S FIRST OFFICIAL SECESSION MOVEMENT BEGAN IN THE NORTH, NOT IN THE SOUTH
Lincoln liked to pretend that the Southern states were the first to desire secession from the Union, an act of "rebellion" for which he felt they should be punished. But the well-read politician knew full well that long before the formation of the Southern Confederacy in 1861, the New England states had been seriously discussing the idea, and were in fact the first to do so. Indeed, as any knowledgeable historian is aware, "in the early years of our country's history the secession sentiment was strongest in New England."¹⁵⁶

Rufus King of Maine, one of thousands of Liberal Yankees who pushed for the secession of New England in the early 1800s.

★ FACT: PRESIDENT THOMAS JEFFERSON'S POLICIES TRIGGERED THE NEW ENGLAND SECESSION MOVEMENT
Yankee secessionist sentiment was born of infuriation over several legislative actions by then U.S. President Thomas Jefferson (who served from 1801 to 1809). These included the Louisiana Purchase (1803), the Embargo Act—which placed restrictions on Yankee merchants and exporters (1807), and the War of 1812 (caused, in part, by the embargo).¹⁵⁷ These actions, and others that

were felt to negatively impact the North, launched the 14-year New England Secession Movement, led by Massachusetts Senator Timothy Pickering, George Washington's former adjutant general,[158] and later President John Adams' secretary of state.[159]

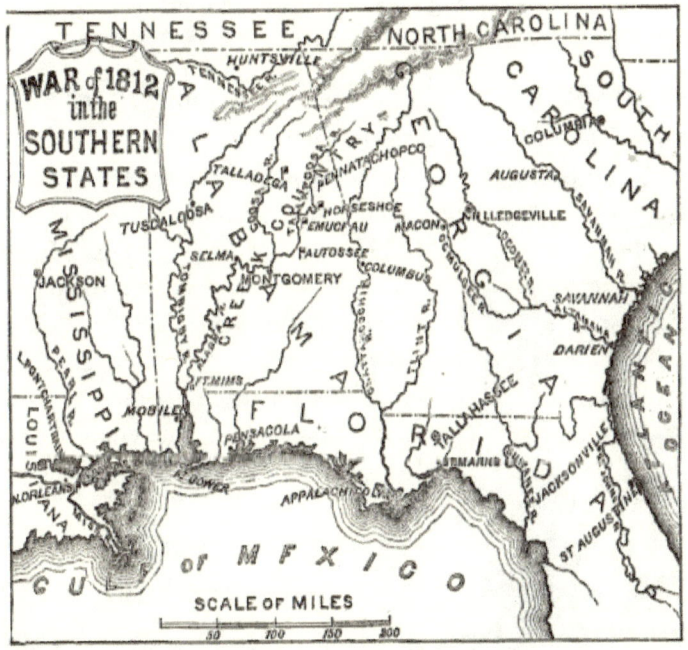

The War of 1812 was one of the issues that triggered the Northern states to begin plans to separate from the Union, our country's first true secession movement.

In a March 4, 1804, letter to fellow Liberal New Englander Rufus King (like most other Yankees, both a Federalist and an advocate of black colonization),[160] Jefferson-hating Pickering discussed the proposed secession plan of the Northern states:

> I am disgusted with the [Southern] men who now rule us and with their measures. At some manifestations of their malignancy I am shocked. . . . I am therefore ready to say "come out from among them and be ye separate.". . . . Were New York detached (as under his [Aaron Burr's] administration it would be) from the Virginian influence, the whole Union would be benefitted. [President] Jefferson would then be forced to observe some caution and forbearance in his measures. And, *if a separation should be deemed*

proper, the five New England States, New York, and New Jersey would naturally be united. Among those seven States, there is a sufficiency of congeniality of character to authorize the expectation of practicable harmony and a permanent union, New York the centre. Without a separation, can those States ever rid themselves of negro Presidents and negro Congresses, and regain their just weight in the political balance? . . . As population is *in fact* no rule of taxation, the negro representation ought to be given up. If refused, it would be a strong ground of separation; tho' perhaps an earlier occasion may occur to declare it.[161]

★ FACT: IN 1814 & 1815 YANKEE LIBERALS DISCUSSED FORMING A "NEW ENGLAND CONFEDERACY"

The brewing issue finally culminated in the Hartford Convention, a Yankee secession conference held in December 1814 and January 1815.[162] Here, twenty-six Federalist (Liberal) delegates met secretly to not only propose amendments that would lessen the influence of the Conservative South,[163] but to discuss leaving the Union in order to form a new and separate confederacy, the "New England Confederacy," as they called it, one they hoped would eventually include New York, Pennsylvania, and even Nova Scotia.[164]

In 1814 South-hater Timothy Pickering of Massachusetts helped lead the Yankee secession effort to form a "Northern Confederacy."

★ FACT: MASSACHUSETTS LIBERAL TIMOTHY PICKERING LED THE NORTHERN CONFEDERACY MOVEMENT

A furious, anti-South Pickering—who once called Southern Conservative Thomas Jefferson a "revolutionary monster," and accused him of cruelty, cowardice, turpitude, corruption, and baseness[165]—spoke for the convention's left-wing members:

I will rather anticipate a new Confederacy, exempt from the corrupt and corrupting influence of the aristocratic Democrats [Conservatives] of the South. There will be—and our children at farthest will see it—a separation. The white and black population will mark the boundary. The British Provinces, even with the assent of Britain, will become members of the [Liberal] Northern confederacy. A continued tyranny of the present ruling sect will precipitate that event.[166]

★ FACT: THE SOUTH DID NOT TRY TO BLOCK THE SECESSION OF THE NORTHERN STATES
With congressional ratification of the Treaty of Ghent on February 15, 1815, the War of 1812 soon came to an end.[167] New England then decided against secession, though only for economic reasons. The important point, however, is that had she desired to do so, New England could have seceded legally and peacefully—and unlike Lincoln's violent, militaristic reaction to Southern secession, the South would not have stood in New England's way.[168] Why?

★ FACT: IN 1860 U.S. PRESIDENT JAMES BUCHANAN UPHELD THE RIGHT OF SECESSION
There was never any doubt among Americans in the early 1800s that the individual states were independent nations, and that secession was therefore a constitutional right, as Southern President Woodrow Wilson would later confirm in his writings.[169] Indeed, this is why Lincoln's predecessor, President James Buchanan, allowed the first seven Southern states to leave the Union in peace in early 1861.[170] Jefferson Davis noted of America's fifteenth president:

> Like all who had intelligently and impartially studied the history of the formation of the Constitution, he held that *the federal government had no rightful power to coerce a state.*[171]

Davis was referring to Buchanan's Final Annual Message, which he gave on December 4, 1860, just before vacating his office to Lincoln. Unfortunately, the latter did not possess the former's firm knowledge of constitutional history, as is evident from the following excerpt from Buchanan's speech. Note that he refers to the U.S. as "the Confederacy" only five months before Lincoln's War:

> The question, fairly stated, is: Has the Constitution delegated to Congress the power to coerce a State into submission which is attempting to withdraw or has actually withdrawn from the Confederacy? If answered in the affirmative, it must be on the principle that the power has been conferred upon Congress to declare and to make war against a State. *After much serious reflection I have arrived at the conclusion that no such power has been delegated to Congress nor to any other department of the Federal Government. It is manifest, upon an inspection of the Constitution, that this is not among the specific and enumerated powers granted to*

President James Buchanan and his private residence "Wheatland," at Lancaster, Pennsylvania.

Congress; and it is equally apparent that its exercise is not "necessary and proper for carrying into execution" any one of these powers. So far from this power having been delegated to Congress, it was expressly refused by the Convention which framed the Constitution. It appears, from the proceedings of that body, that on the 31st May, 1787, the clause "authorizing an exertion of the force of the whole against a delinquent State" came up for consideration. Mr. Madison opposed it in a brief but powerful speech, from which I shall extract but a single sentence. He observed: "The use of force against a State would look more like a declaration of war than an infliction of punishment, and would probably be considered by the party attacked as a dissolution of all previous compacts by which it might be bound." *Upon his motion the clause was unanimously postponed, and was never, I believe, again presented.* Soon afterwards, on the 8th June, 1787, when incidentally adverting to the subject, he said: "Any Government for the United States, formed on the supposed practicability of using force against the unconstitutional proceedings of the States, would prove as visionary and fallacious as the government of Congress," evidently meaning the then existing Congress of the old Confederation [1781-1789].

Without descending to particulars, *it may be safely asserted that the power to make war against a State is at variance with the whole spirit and intent of the Constitution.* Suppose such a war should result in the conquest of a State, how are we to govern it afterwards? Shall we hold it as a province and govern it by despotic power? *In the nature of things we could not, by physical force, control the will of the people,* and compel them to elect Senators and Representatives to Congress, and to perform all the other duties depending upon their own volition, and *required from the free citizens of a free State as a constituent member of the Confederacy.*

But, if we possessed this power, would it be wise to exercise it under existing circumstances? The object would doubtless be to preserve the Union. *War would not only present the most effectual means of destroying it, but would banish all hope of its peaceable reconstruction. Besides, in the fraternal conflict a vast amount of blood and treasure would be expended, rendering future reconciliation between the States impossible.* In the meantime who can foretell what would be the sufferings and privations of the people during its existence?

The fact is, that our Union rests upon public opinion, and can never be cemented by the blood of its citizens shed in civil war. If it cannot live in the affections of the people, it must one day perish. Congress possesses many means of preserving it by conciliation; but the sword was not placed in their hand to preserve it by force.[172]

In this conclusion, I shall merely call attention to the few sentences in Mr. Madison's justly celebrated Report in 1799, to the Legislature of Virginia [see Appendix C]. In this he ably and conclusively defended the [Kentucky and Virginia] Resolutions of the preceding Legislature (of 1798) against the strictures of several other State Legislatures [see Appendix B]. These were mainly founded upon the protest of the Virginia Legislature against the [Liberals'] Alien and Sedition Laws, as palpable and alarming infractions of the Constitution. In pointing out the peaceful and constitutional remedies, and he referred to none other, to which the States were authorized to resort on such occasions, he concludes by saying that the Legislatures of the States might have made direct representation to Congress with a view to obtain a rescinding of the two offending acts; or they might have represented to their respective Senators in Congress their wish that two-thirds thereof would propose an explanatory amendment of the Constitution; or two-thirds of themselves, if such had been their option, might, by an application to Congress, have obtained a Convention for the same object.[173]

These brilliant words spoken by Buchanan, a rank-and-file Northerner,[174] were words that every Southerner could truly appreciate, and hopes were high that when Lincoln—himself originally a Southerner—entered the White House, he would follow in Buchanan's footsteps.[175] We will note here that Buchanan

fully adopted the Resolutions of 1798 and 1799, and the Report of Mr. Madison to the Virginia Legislature in 1799; and that he adopted the principle contained therein [perpetual state sovereignty] as constituting one of the main foundations of political creed of the Democratic [then Conservative] Party, and had resolved to carry them out in their obvious meaning and import.[176]

★ **FACT: YANKEE ATTORNEY GENERAL JEREMIAH S. BLACK SUPPORTED SECESSION**
On November 20, 1860, President Buchanan's famous and well respected U.S. attorney general, Jeremiah S. Black of Pennsylvania, wrote out the following comments concerning whether a U.S. president or the government has the right to force seceding states back into the Union. It was addressed to President Buchanan:

. . . The existing laws put and keep the Federal Government strictly on the defensive. You can use force only to repel an assault on the public property, and aid the courts in the performance of their duty. If the means given you to collect the revenue and execute the other laws be insufficient for that purpose, Congress may extend and make them more effectual to that end.

If one of the States should declare her independence, your action cannot depend upon the rightfulness of the cause upon which such declaration is based. Whether the retirement of a State from the Union be the exercise of a right reserved in the Constitution or a revolutionary movement, it is certain that you have not in either case the authority to recognize her independence or to absolve her from her Federal obligations. Congress or the other States in convention assembled must take such measures as may be necessary and proper. In such an event I see no course for you but to go straight onward in the path you have hitherto trodden, that is, execute the laws to the extent of the defensive means placed in your hands, and act generally upon the assumption that the present constitutional relation between the States and the Federal Government continue to exist until a new order of things shall be established, either by law or force.

Pennsylvania Supreme Court Justice Jeremiah S. Black wrote and spoke extensively on the topic of the right of secession.

Whether Congress has the constitutional right to make war against one or more States, and require the Executive of the Federal Government to carry it on by means of force to be drawn from the other States, is a question for Congress itself to consider. It must be admitted that *no such power is expressly given; nor are there any words in the Constitution which imply it*. Among the powers enumerated in article 1, section 8, is that "to declare war, grant letters of marque and reprisal, and to make rules concerning captures on land and water." This certainly means nothing more than the power to commence and carry on hostilities against the foreign enemies of the nation. Another clause in the same section gives Congress the power "to provide for calling forth the militia," and to use them within the limits of the State. But this power is so restricted by the words which immediately follow, that it can be exercised only for one of the following purposes:

1. To execute the laws of the Union; that is, to aid the Federal officers in the performance of their regular duties.
2. To suppress Insurrections against the States; but this is confined by article 4, section 4, to cases in which the State herself shall apply for assistance against her own people.
3. To repel the invasion of a State by enemies who come from abroad to assail her in her own territory.

All these provisions are made to protect the States, not to authorize an attack by one part of the country upon another; to preserve their peace, and not to plunge them into civil war. Our forefathers do not seem to have thought that war was calculated "to form a more perfect union, establish justice, insure domestic tranquility, provide for the common defence, promote the general welfare, and secure the blessing of liberty to ourselves and our posterity." *There was undoubtedly a strong and universal conviction among the men who framed and ratified the Constitution, that military force would not only be useless, but pernicious as a means of holding the States together.*

If it be true that war cannot be declared nor a system of general hostilities be carried on by the central government against a State, then it seems to follow that an attempt to do so would be *ipso facto* an expulsion of such State from the Union. Being treated as an alien and an enemy, she would be compelled to act accordingly. *If Congress should break up the present Union, by unconstitutionally putting strife, and enmity, and armed hostility, between the different sections of the country, instead of "domestic tranquillity," which the Constitution was meant to insure, will not all the States be absolved from their Federal obligations? Is any portion of the people bound to contribute their money or their blood to carry on a contest like this?*

. . . If this view of the subject be as correct as I think it is, then *the Union must perish, utterly perish, at the moment when Congress shall arm one portion of the people against another*, for any purpose beyond that of merely protecting the General Government in the essence of its proper constitutional functions.[177]

Liberal Henry Cabot Lodge of Massachusetts considered the Union an "experiment" from which each state had the right to "peaceably withdraw."

★ **FACT: LIBERAL NEW ENGLAND SENATOR HENRY CABOT LODGE ADVANCED THE RIGHT OF SECESSION**
Over 100 years ago Republican (then Liberal) Senator Henry Cabot Lodge of Massachusetts made the following comments:

> When the [U.S.] Constitution was adopted [in 1787], it is safe to say that *there was not a man in the country, from Washington and Hamilton on the one side, to George Clinton and George Mason on the other, who regarded the new system as anything but an experiment entered upon by the States, and from which each and every State had the right peaceably to withdraw, a right which was very likely to be exercised.*[178]

★ **FACT: NEW YORK CITY MAYOR FERNANDO WOOD SUPPORTED THE SECESSION OF THE SOUTHERN STATES & WANTED HIS OWN TOWN TO SECEDE WITH THEM**
In the Spring of 1861, as Lincoln's War was just opening on an incredulous world, New York City Mayor Fernando Wood defended Southern secession, emphasizing "the cause of nationality and freedom." In doing so he proclaimed that the allegiance of his constituency was to be dissolved, not only from the U.S., but also from his own state. On May 6, 1861, he sent the following message to the town's council members:

> It would seem the dissolution of the Federal Union is inevitable. Having been formed originally on the basis of general mutual protection, but separate local independence,—*each State reserving the entire and absolute control of its own domestic affairs,*—*it is evidently impossible to keep them together longer than they deem themselves fairly treated by each other, or longer than the interests, honor, and fraternity, of the people of the several States are satisfied. Being a government created by opinion, its continuance is dependent upon the continuance of the sentiments which formed it. It cannot be preserved by coercion, or held together by a resort to this last dreaded alternative would, of itself, destroy not only the government, but the lines and property of the people.*
>
> If these forebodings should be realized, and a separation of the States shall occur, momentous considerations will be presented to the corporate authorities of this city. We must provide for new relations, which will necessarily grow out of the new condition of public affairs.
>
> It will be not only necessary for us to settle the relations which we shall hold to the other cities and States, but to establish new ones, if we can, with a portion of our own State. . . .
>
> California, and her sisters of the Pacific, will no doubt set up an

independent Republic, and husband their own rich mineral resources. The Western States, equally rich in cereals and other agricultural products, will probably do the same. Then it may be said, why should not New York City, instead of supporting by her contributions in revenue two-thirds the expenses of the United States, become also equally independent? As a free city, with but nominal duty on her imports, her local government could be supported without taxation upon her people. Thus we could live free from taxes, and have cheap goods, nearly duty free. In this she would have the whole and united support of the Southern States, as well as all the other States to whose interest and rights under the Constitution she has always been true.[179]

As the Southern states were seceding in 1861, New York City Mayor Fernando Wood campaigned for the secession of his own constituency and the creation of a new state.

★ FACT: NEW JERSEY GOVERNOR RODMAN M. PRICE SUPPORTED SOUTHERN SECESSION

In 1861, as the Southern states were seceding apace, former New Jersey Governor Rodman M. Price was asked, "what ought New Jersey to do?" In a letter addressed to Mr. L. W. Burnett of Newark, he replied:

> I believe the Southern Confederation permanent. The proceeding has taken place with forethought and deliberation; it is no hurried impulse, but *an irrevocable act, based upon the sacred, as was supposed, equality of the States*; and, in my opinion, every slave State will, in a short period of time, be united in one Confederacy. Before that event happens, we cannot act, however much we may suffer in our material interests. It is in that contingency, then, that I answer the second part of your question, "what position for New Jersey will best accord with her interests, honor, and the patriotic instincts of her people?" *I say, emphatically, she would go with the South, from every wise, prudential, and patriotic reason.*[180]

★ FACT: PRIOR TO BECOMING PRESIDENT, LINCOLN SUPPORTED SECESSION, CALLING IT A "SACRED RIGHT"

Secession is lawful, Lincoln himself once asserted. He even called it a "most sacred right." On January 12, 1848, in a speech before the U.S. House of Representatives, he said:

Any people anywhere, being inclined and having the power, have the right to rise up, and shake off the existing government, and form a new one that suits them better. This is a most valuable, a most sacred right—a right which, we hope and believe, is to liberate the world. Nor is this right confined to cases in which the whole people of an existing government may choose to exercise it. Any portion of such people that can may revolutionize, and make their own of so much of the territory as they inhabit.[181]

Liberal Lincoln purposefully introduced historical disinformation into the public forum concerning secession (as well as a host of other subjects), a malicious custom still used by the Left-wing to this day. The purpose? To mislead and confuse in an attempt to more easily control the masses.

★ **FACT: AFTER BECOMING PRESIDENT, LINCOLN DENOUNCED SECESSION FOR POLITICAL REASONS**
When it was politically expedient to change his mind, Lincoln, of course, did just that. Thus, as U.S. president thirteen years later, on July 4, 1861, in his "Message to Congress in Special Session," he called the new Southern Confederacy an "illegal organization,"[182] and the constitutional right of secession an "ingenious sophism," an "insidious debauching of the public mind," and a "sugar-coated invention" of the South.[183] Those who challenged these obviously erroneous views were labeled "traitors" and "rebels." This is how Confederate soldiers got the epithet "Johnny Rebel," and how the name of Lincoln's War, "the War of Rebellion," came about. It is also why, after the War, Confederate officers were charged with "treason": for believing in, and acting on, the legal right of secession. Even the term "Copperhead" (meaning a Northerner who sympathized with the South) was anti-South: ridiculously and incorrectly, it likened such supporters to the deadly venomous snake of the same name.[184]

★ **FACT: IF THE SOUTH WAS "TREASONOUS" FOR SECEDING, THEN SO WERE THE FOUNDING FATHERS**
If Southerners were "traitors," as Lincoln called them, then so were all of the Founding Fathers; true American patriots like James Wilson, Gouverneur Morris, Edmund J. Randolph, Benjamin Franklin, and

Thomas Jefferson. For each one supported the secession of the American colonies from Great Britain. Thus, mid 19th-Century Southerners were merely speaking the language and espousing the beliefs of their revolutionary predecessors.[185] Indeed, it was for this very reason that Southerners referred to the secession of the Southern states as the "Second Declaration of Independence,"[186] and Lincoln's War as "the Second Revolutionary War."[187]

★ FACT: IN BLOCKING THE LEGAL RIGHT OF SECESSION LINCOLN BECAME AMERICA'S GREATEST WAR CRIMINAL
Semantics were just the start of Lincoln's premeditated plan to ignore, alter, and subvert the Constitution, then remake the South in the North's image (i.e., Northernize her), all for personal political gain. To achieve these goals the big government Liberal would go on to commit a litany of crimes unlike anything the Western world had seen since the days of the ancient Roman emperors; men, as it turns out, with whom he had much in common.[188]

Such crimes would include everything from calling himself a "military hero" in the Black Hawk War ("I fought, bled, and came away," Lincoln fibbed to the House of Representatives on July 27, 1848)[189]—even though he actually never saw a single day of combat[190] or even a single Indian in that conflict,[191] to launching the largest and most bloody conflict on U.S. soil without congressional approval, violating Article 1, Section 8, Clause 11 of the U.S. Constitution, which states that only Congress can formally declare war.[192]

If C.S. Founding Father Jefferson Davis was a "traitor," so was Edmund J. Randolph (pictured here), as well as the other conservative U.S. Founding Fathers.

★ FACT: THE SECESSION RESOLUTION WAS CARRIED FORWARD AGAIN AT THE 1864 DEMOCRATIC CONVENTION
While Republican Lincoln (then a Liberal) was preparing for his reelection campaign, during the Democratic Party (Conservative) Convention in Chicago on August 29, 1864, the Secession Resolution inspired by Thomas Jefferson was put forth and upheld once again:

Resolved, That this Convention does explicitly declare, as the sense of the American people, that, after four years of failure to restore the Union by the experiment of war,—during which, under the pretence of military necessity, or war power, [considered by Republicans, the Liberals of the day, to be] higher than the Constitution, the Constitution itself has been disregarded in every part, and public liberty and private life alike trodden down, and the material prosperity of the country essentially impaired,—justice, humanity, liberty, and the public welfare, demand that immediate efforts be made for a cessation of hostilities, with a view to an ultimate convention of the States, or other peaceable means, to the end, that, at the earliest practical moment, peace may be restored on the basis of the Federal States.[193]

★ **FACT: THE FOUNDERS CREATED THE U.S.A. AS A VOLUNTARY UNION**

Despite Lincoln's efforts, which included the illegal arrest, imprisonment, torture, and even murder of countless thousands of both Southerners and Northerners,[194] secession remained a legal right throughout his War, and—for the many reasons already discussed—it remains legal into the present day. Only an amendment to the Constitution prohibiting secession can make it unlawful, and this has not been done, and never will be. Why?

Because, whether Liberals, uninformed Conservatives, and South-loathers like it or not, the Founders intended the United States of America to be a *voluntary* union.[195] Banning secession would make the U.S. an *involuntary* union, transforming our confederate republic[196] into a nation, a type of government, as we have seen, that was never intended by the Founding Fathers. "The United States government was," South Carolina politician Robert Y. Hayne emphasized, "a compact between *independent* sovereign States,"[197] creating a confederate republic.[198] This is why, Sage rightly points out, "none but *voluntary* ties of union can exist among associate republics; for when *involuntariness* supervenes, the republic ceases."[199] And this is why Confederate President Jefferson Davis said:

Such a [U.S.] government as ours had no power to maintain its existence any longer than the contracting parties pleased to cohere, *because it was founded on the great principle of voluntary federation*, and organized "to establish justice and insure domestic tranquillity." *Any departure from this principle by the General Government not only perverts and destroys its nature, but furnishes a just cause to the injured State to withdraw from the union.* A new union might subsequently be formed, but the original one could never by coercion be restored. Any effort on the part of the others to force the seceding State to consent to come back is an attempt at subjugation. It is a wrong which no lapse of time or combination of circumstances can ever make right.[200]

★ FACT: TO THIS DAY A STATE CAN LEGALLY SECEDE, EITHER PEACEFULLY OR FORCEFULLY

With the Constitution lacking any prohibition of secession, and with no official mechanism for withdrawing from the Union, the process of *peaceful* separation must begin with a state petitioning the White House.

According to the First Amendment, the American people have the right to "petition the government for a redress of grievances." Currently the U.S. government requires only 100,000 signatures to review a petition for secession.

If the government's response is negative (which, thanks to the "Civil War," it invariably will be), at that point there is no official law today to prevent a state from simply seceding, and then a *forceful* separation must be resorted to. Force must be used because in 1869 leftist Supreme Court Justice Salmon P. Chase, expressing the aggressive, anti-constitutional, anti-South policies of his former boss, big government Liberal President Lincoln,[201] decided that "the Constitution, in all its provisions, looks to an indestructible Union composed of indestructible States."[202]

Left-leaning Yankee and judicial expert Salmon P. Chase declared the Union "indestructible," another Liberal myth.

The states are indeed "indestructible." But because Chase's comment rejects the idea of state sovereignty while embracing the idea of consolidated government,[203] it is obvious that he was wrong: as any first year history student knows, the Founders never created the Union to be "indestructible." Far from it. From the beginning not only was the Union considered a *voluntary* compact,[204] but they repeatedly referred to the states as "free and independent,"[205] possessing "numerous and indefinite powers"[206]—which included the rights of accession and secession.[207] The federal government, on the other hand, was severely limited in its scope and was given by the people only three powers: the defense of lives, rights, and property.²⁰⁸ Our voluntary Union then was, by its very nature, destructible, not indestructible.

★ FACT: LINCOLN'S WAR DID NOT MAKE SECESSION ILLEGAL
This essentially Liberal Yankee view, that an *involuntary union* was established by Lincoln's defeat of the Southern Confederacy in April 1865, not only contradicts both all that the Founding Fathers stood for, but American history itself (we will recall, for example, the Hartford Convention of 1814 and 1815, at which the secessionist Northern states began planning a "New England Confederacy").

If the U.S. is truly "an indestructible Union composed of indestructible States," as the ill-informed critics of secession enjoy endlessly repeating, why then did Lincoln allow and even encourage the secession of the western portion of Virginia to secede during the middle of his War?

★ FACT: LINCOLN SUPPORTED, AND EVEN ENCOURAGED, SECESSION WHEN IT BENEFITTED HIM
It was on June 20, 1863, to be precise, that in an effort to generate five additional electoral votes for his upcoming reelection campaign (in 1864), Lincoln illegally created our thirty-fifth state, West Virginia.²⁰⁹ This was unlawful, not because secession was unlawful, but because, according to Article 4, Section 3, Clause 1 of the Constitution, a section of a state cannot secede from the parent state without the parent state's approval. This approval was never given by the state of Virginia—which means that West Virginia today does not possess legitimate statehood.²¹⁰

Incredibly, for nothing more than political gain, Lincoln pushed the region that would become West Virginia to secede from Virginia at a time when he was vigorously pronouncing the secession of the Southern states an illegal "rebellion."²¹¹ Though his double standard (a integral aspect of liberalism) did not bother him, he was well aware that his actions were unconstitutional, which is why he pleaded the issue with his cabinet members on December 23, 1862.²¹² It was at this meeting that Lincoln resorted to his usual form of tortured logic to justify his illicit actions, in this case regarding the unconstitutional secession of West Virginia.²¹³

★ FACT: THE WITHDRAWAL OF WEST VIRGINIA FROM VIRGINIA DURING THE CIVIL WAR IS ONE MORE PROOF OF THE LEGALITY OF SECESSION

While Lincoln's act was indeed illegal, it did prove that secession was and is legal, despite his and his followers' public denunciations to the contrary.

It also highlights the rank hypocrisy of self-serving politicians, like our sixteenth president, who condemn a policy if it does not benefit them at the moment, but wholeheartedly support it when it does. It was Lincoln, after all, who was for secession *before* he became president,[214] but who was against it *after* he became president.[215]

Despite the official nature of its seal, West Virginia never achieved true statehood. Why? Because Lincoln created it illegally (on June 20, 1863) by encouraging the region to secede from Virginia without her approval. Hypocritically, at the same time he was bombing the middle and deep South into rubble for seceding from the Union.

★ FACT: GRANT SAID THAT THE UNION WOULD HAVE RECOGNIZED SOUTHERN SECESSION HAD THE CONFEDERACY FOUGHT FOR ONE MORE YEAR

The question that anti-secessionists must ask themselves is this: if secession was legal, and even supported by Lincoln, *before* the Civil War, what made it illegal *afterward*? All the Liberal North proved by "winning" was that it had three times the manpower, funding, and weaponry of the Conservative South. Does might make right, or right make might? Lincoln and his equally liberal followers thought so.[216] But world history has repeatedly disproved this view.

Yankee war hero and slave owner, General Ulysses S. Grant, for instance, our eighteenth president, maintained that if the South had kept up the fight for just one more year, the Union would almost certainly have capitulated to Jefferson Davis' terms, the secession of the South would have been fully recognized, and the Confederate States of America would have been free to go to thrive in peace and prosperity.[217]

★ **FACT: NEARLY EVERY U.S. PRESIDENT, FROM JEFFERSON TO WILSON, HAS ACCEPTED SECESSION AS A LEGAL RIGHT**
If this does not prove that the North, as well as past and future presidents, knew all too well that secession was legal (and understandable) at the time, then nothing can. A list of such chief executives would include everyone from John Quincy Adams, Thomas Jefferson, James Madison, John Tyler, and James K. Polk, to Franklin Pierce, James Buchanan, Abraham Lincoln, Ulysses S. Grant, and Woodrow Wilson.

★ **FACT: YANKEE SCHOLARS & EVEN SOCIALISTS ONCE ACCEPTED THE LEGALITY OF SECESSION**
Yankee historians and constitutional scholars too upheld the right of secession, brilliant academics, as discussed, such as William Rawle of Pennsylvania, whose political doctrines were taught at West Point in the early 1800s. Even many radical progressives, as we have also seen, like socialist Horace Greeley, a friend of Karl Marx and the owner of the left-wing newspaper the *New York Tribune*, accepted the validity of secession, despite their distaste for it.

Northern constitutional scholar William Rawle, hand-selected by President George Washington to be U.S. district attorney for Pennsylvania, taught the legality of secession at West Point.

★ **FACT: MANY EUROPEANS ACCEPTED THE RIGHT OF THE SOUTHERN STATES TO SECEDE**
The right of secession has been upheld by many British politicians; and, even according to some anti-South authors, "that opinion to a great extent prevailed, and to-day prevails, in the English army and navy." Writes Yankee author Caleb W. Loring:

> Mr. John Morley, in his life of Burke, in reference to Burke's speeches denouncing the conduct of Great Britain towards us as [American] colonies, says that *"the current of opinion was then precisely similar in England in the struggle to which the United States owed its existence, as in the great civil war between the Northern and Southern States of the American Union"*; "people in England

convinced themselves, some after careful examination, others on hearsay, that the South had a right to secede.". . . Lord [Garnet J.] Wolseley [an admirer of Nathan Bedford Forrest], in his article in *Macmillan's Magazine* on the life of [Robert E.] Lee, extolling him as the greatest general of his age and the most perfect man, informs us that *each State possessed the right both historically and legally under the Constitution to leave the Union at its will*.[218]

★ FACT: DIXIE REJECTED THE NORTH'S INTERPRETATION OF THE CONSTITUTION, NOT THE CONSTITUTION ITSELF

Though pro-North advocates maintain that the South "rejected" the Constitution by seceding, I have proven that such was not the case. No less an authority than Liberal U.S. President Woodrow Wilson agrees, writing:

> The [Southern] advocates of secession had not rejected the constitution of the United States as it had been in the first days, when read, as they conceived, in its simplicity and original import, *but only the corrupt interpretations which had been put upon it, the leadership of [Liberal] parties which would have wrested its meanings to the South's destruction.*[219]

★ FACT: EARLY AMERICANS FROM ACROSS THE ENTIRE POLITICAL SPECTRUM SUPPORTED THE RIGHT OF SECESSION

It is germane to reemphasize here that both early Americans and Victorians in general upheld the right of secession, including individuals from every point across the political spectrum, from far right Conservatives and traditionalists to far left radicals and progressives, and many in between. Why then do nearly all modern Liberals and Conservatives ignorantly claim that secession is illegal? We will answer this question in succeeding chapters.

★ FACT: IS SECESSION CONSTITUTIONAL? YES & NO!

In fine, was and is secession constitutional? The answer is twofold.

Yes, because under the Constitution our union is a confederacy (or federation—that is, it is "federal," as it is more generally known in political literature), which is defined as *a voluntary alliance of autonomous and free sovereigns, accorded all the rights of small, distinct, independent nations*. This would include the states' right of secession.

No, for basically the same reason: this right is one of the natural rights of sovereigns, and sovereignty is inherent in the people. Thus *the* right of secession existed prior to the Constitution—which is one of the main reasons the Founders left all mention of it out of that compact.[220]

★ FACT: THERE WOULD BE NO U.S.A. TODAY WITHOUT THE PERMANENT & ONGOING RESERVED RIGHT OF SECESSION

Let us bear in mind that without the right of secession the people would be held in the Union against their will. And without political freedom we would not today have the confederate republic intended by the Founders.[221] Clearly we do, for the Constitution's very purpose was to create a *republican* form of government (a small federal government with limited powers), which, in our case, oversees a *confederacy* (a Union of all-powerful sovereign nation-states). In this sense secession is indeed constitutional—though one must read between the lines to uncover this particular meaning.

"Join or Die." The American colonists purposefully imaged the Union as a snake divided into a number of *free, separate, and sovereign* pieces or "nation-states," but which are *voluntarily* part of the whole.

Bledsoe writes that the question of whether accession and secession are constitutional or not betrays a "gross ignorance" of the origins of the states. For

> these rights are not derived from the Constitution at all; on the contrary, *all the rights, powers, or authorities of the Constitution are derived from the States. And all the rights not delegated to the Federal Government by the States, are reserved to the States themselves,—the original fountains of all the powers of "the Constitution of the United States."* This is the doctrine set forth by The Federalist in submitting that instrument or Constitution to the people. "The principles established in a former paper," says *The Federalist*, "teach us, that *the States will retain all preexisting authorities which may not be exclusively delegated to the federal head*." In the former paper here referred to, it is said: "*All authorities, of which the States are not explicitly divested in favor of the Union, remain with them in full vigor.*"[222]

Sculpted from the divinely inspired Doctrine of Reserved Rights, the Ninth and Tenth Amendments are the hallowed constitutional acts that guarantee this. From whatever angle one chooses to look at it then, secession, that great preexistent right of self-governing bodies, was "constitutional" in 1860—and is still "constitutional" today.

2

THE SOUTHERN RESPONSE TO THE IDEA OF SECESSION

ACCORDING TO YANKEE "HISTORY," THE Southern states had been anxiously waiting for a reason to secede for many decades, then used Lincoln's election as an excuse to implement their "enormous conspiracy to deliberately breakup the Union."[223] In this chapter we will examine the facts as they have been handed down to us through *authentic* history. As we go, we will debunk this Liberal tall tale lie by lie.

★ FACT: SOUTHERN SECESSION WAS NOT INTENDED TO HURT THE ALREADY ESTABLISHED UNION, BUT RATHER TO FORM A NEW ONE

Anti-South partisans claim that secession was a "conspiracy," one meant to "destroy the Union and take over the U.S. Federal government."[224] Such a claim is beyond ludicrous, and indeed, nothing could be further from the truth.

Because the Southern states began to separate from the Union in late 1860, their principle dealings were with James Buchanan, who was still in the White House. On December 28, 1860, several Confederate commissioners sent a letter to President Buchanan which included the following words. We are prepared, they wrote, to enter upon this negotiation with the earnest desire to avoid all unnecessary and hostile collision, and so to inaugurate our new relations as to secure mutual respect, general advantage, and a future of good-will and harmony beneficial to all the parties concerned.[225]

★ FACT: AT FIRST NEARLY ALL SOUTHERNERS WERE AGAINST THE IDEA OF SECESSION

Many fans of Confederate General Nathan Bedford Forrest do not realize that he dearly loved the Union and, in the beginning, was wholly against the idea of secession. It was only later, after Lincoln began sending Yankee troops into the South, that "Ol' Bedford" changed his mind. This reaction was nearly universal across Dixie, not atypical, as Yankee myth teaches.

While it is true that Virginia had discussed secession between 1798 and 1799 under Conservative Thomas Jefferson in response to the Liberals' unconstitutional Alien and Sedition Acts, and that South Carolina had seriously considered seceding in 1832 in response to the Yankees' oppressive tariff laws,[226] the South was not "rabidly pursuing secession up till the time of Lincoln," as the fake history books of American Liberals teach.

Indeed, the vast majority of Southerners, including most of the South's political leaders, military leaders, and wealthiest slave owners, were against the idea of secession—even *after* it occurred. In one Alabama county, for example, unionists outnumbered secessionists four to one.[227] Among the more notable anti-secessionists were Jefferson Davis, Alexander H. Stephens, and Nathan Bedford Forrest. All had an ardent love for the Union and the U.S. Flag, and felt that secession should be avoided at all costs if possible. Even anti-South writers have been forced to admit that just before Lincoln's election in November 1860, "the existence of a Union feeling" in the Southern states was "stronger than at any time in a decade."[228]

Four months before the start of Lincoln's War and the secession of his own state, Robert E. Lee, still a U.S. army officer, went as far as to angrily denounce secession, writing to his son on January 23, 1861:

I can anticipate no greater calamity for the country than a dissolution of the Union. It would be an accumulation of all the evils we complain of, and I am willing to sacrifice every thing but honor for its preservation. I hope, therefore, that all constitutional means will be exhausted before there is a resort to force. Secession is nothing but revolution. The framers of our Constitution never exhausted so much labor, wisdom, and forbearance in its formation, and surrounded it with so many guards and securities, if it was intended to be broken by every member of the Confederacy at will. It was intended for "perpetual union," so expressed in the preamble, and for the establishment of a government, not a compact, which *can only be dissolved by revolution, or the consent of all the people in convention assembled.* It is idle to talk of secession. Anarchy would have been established, and not a government, by Washington, Hamilton, Jefferson, Madison, and the other patriots of the Revolution. . . . *Still a Union that can only be maintained by swords and bayonets, and in which strife and civil war are to take the place of brotherly love and kindness, has no charm for me.* I shall mourn for my country and for the welfare and progress of mankind. If the Union is dissolved, and the Government disrupted, I shall return to my native State and share the miseries of my people and save in defense will draw my sword on none.[229]

★ **FACT: EVEN AFTER LINCOLN'S ELECTION ANTI-SECESSION SENTIMENT REMAINED HIGH IN THE SOUTH**

From the beginning in the South, "the popular vote showed a majority for Union." Thus, even after Jefferson Davis' forceful pro-South speech at an assembly held by the Confederacy on March 1, 1861, "the convention voted 39 to 35 *not* to secede from the Union."[230]

Before the outbreak of Lincoln's War, not even fiery anti-North speeches by Confederate leaders like President Jefferson Davis could inspire most Southerners to support the idea of secession.

Proof of the strong Unionist feeling among antebellum Southerners comes from the official legislative secession meetings that were held across the South beginning November 6, 1860, the day of Lincoln's win. Though South Carolina voted unanimously to issue an ordinance of secession,[231] this was the exception. In the rest of the states there was an overt division of sentiment. In Arkansas the ordinance was at first actually defeated by four votes (35 yeas, 39 nays), and only passed two months later (69 yeas, 1 nay). In Georgia the votes were 208 yeas, 89 nays; in Mississippi 84 yeas, 15 nays; in Florida 62 yeas, 7 nays; in Louisiana 113 yeas, 17 nays; in Alabama 61 yeas, 39 nays; in Texas 166 yeas, 7 nays; in Virginia 88 yeas, 55 nays.[232]

In Virginia the public voted 128,884 for secession, 32,134 voted against it.[233] In Texas 34,794 voted in favor of secession, 11,235 against it.[234] At first nearly 40 percent of the citizens of Arkansas voted against even holding a secession convention: 27,412 for, 15,826 against.[235] The same was

Tennessee Governor Isham G. Harris had to work long and diligently to get the people of his state to agree to secession.

true in Tennessee, where an actual majority of the populace voted against meeting to discuss secession: 46,671 for, 47,333 against. After much wrangling, six months later Governor Isham G. Harris simply declared Tennessee "out of the Union," with the vote for separation being 104,913. But there were still many in the Volunteer State who did not agree with secession: 47,238 voted against it at the time.[236]

Clearly the South was not "solidly" behind the idea of secession in November and December 1860. In fact, a large percentage of the population, both official and non-official, were against it, and remained so even after the provisional president of the Confederate Congress, Howell Cobb, announced on February 4, 1861, that secession "is now a fixed and irrevocable fact, and the separation is perfect, complete and perpetual."[237]

It was not until Lincoln tricked the South into firing the first shot at Fort Sumter on April 12, 1861,[238] and then, on April 15, issued his war proclamation calling for 75,000 Union troops to invade Dixie,[239] that a "solid South" formed in favor of leaving the Union—a totally understandable reaction to Liberal Northern chicanery and a menacing and unconstitutional act on the part of our anti-South sixteenth president.

★ FACT: THE ANTI-SOUTH MOVEMENT DECEIVES WHEN IT CLAIMS THAT THE SECESSION CONVENTIONS "OVERRODE THE VOICE OF THE SOUTHERN PEOPLE"
As part of their duplicitous war on the historical facts and constitutional truth, South-loathers have long criticized the Confederate government for "forcing secession on the people, without their consent." One uneducated Liberal, for example, made these comments in 1875:

> The whole secession movement, on the part of the legislature of that State, has been lawless, violent, and tumultuous. The pretense of submitting the ordinance of secession to the vote of the people of the State, after placing her military power and resources at the disposal and under the command of the Confederate States, without any authority from the people, is as bitter and insolent a mockery of popular rights as the human mind could invent.[240]

Another member of the anti-South movement ranted:

> Not the least remarkable facts of all that wild, irrational revolution, were the overriding of the State Constitutions and of a total repudiation of the voice of the people. Not one of the Gulf States, first in revolution, submitted the ordinances of secession to a vote of the people! Not a single State of these which first organized the new "Confederacy" allowed the people one particle of authority or voice in the matter! The Conventions decreed—as summarily, as arbitrarily, as relentlessly as the French Chambers of Deputies, obeying the behests of Napoleon. Napoleon's usurpations received the sanction of the French people just as completely as the usurpations of the State Conventions and the "Confederate Congress" received the sanction of the people of the Slave States.[241]

Such remarks illustrate both the innate malice and the stunning ignorance South-haters possess when it comes to genuine American history, especially in relation to the South.

★ FACT: STATE CONVENTIONS WERE PURPOSEFULLY CHOSEN BY THE SOUTHERN PEOPLE TO REPRESENT THEM REGARDING SECESSION
The truth is that people of the Southern states intentionally operated, as did the early American colonies, through state conventions, that is through their state legislatures. Alexander H. Stephens describes the manner in which the U.S. Constitution, as just one example, was

approved and adopted by the states in the 1780s:

> It was because ultimate, absolute Sovereignty resided with the people of each State respectively. The additional Sovereign powers, which were proposed to be delegated to the States jointly under the Constitution, such as the taxing power, and the power to regulate trade, with the right to pass laws acting directly upon the citizens of the Sovereign States, etc., *could only be delegated by the people in their Sovereign capacity. This delegation could be made only by a Convention of the people for that purpose. These powers, by their then existing Constitutions, were vested in their State Legislatures.* The Legislatures of the several States, at that time, had the sole power to tax, to regulate trade, etc. These powers had to be resumed by the people of each State separately, and taken by them from that set of agents and delegated to another set of agents. No power short of the Sovereignty itself, in each State, could do this; or in other words, as ultimate Sovereignty resided in the people of the States respectively, all new delegations of power, as well as all changes of agents in whom the delegated powers were to be intrusted, could only be made by the people themselves of each state in their Sovereign capacity. This is the whole of it in a nutshell.[242]

Likewise, Fowler writes:

> *In the formation and adoption of the Constitution, the States were the only agents. The State Legislatures appointed the delegates to the Convention. While there, they voted by States. Each delegation made its report to the Legislature or Governor of the States. The Convention which assembled in the several States to ratify or reject the Constitution, was appointed by the people of the several States. The parties to the "Constitutional Compact" were the States.*
>
> . . . The States made the Declaration of Independence, each State acting for itself, and each State becoming "free and independent." The States formed the Articles of Confederation, each State still retaining its sovereignty as to all that was not delegated. The States formed the present Constitution. "*The Convention which formed it, was called by a portion of the States; its members were all appointed by the States; received their authority from the separate States; voted by States in forming the Constitution, transmitted it to Congress to be submitted to the States for their ratification; it was ratified by the people of each State in Convention, each ratifying by itself and for itself, and bound exclusively by its own ratification*; and by express provision it was not to go into operation unless nine out of twelve States should ratify, and then binding only between the States ratifying. Any four States, great or small, could have defeated its adoption."[243]

We see here that the U.S. Constitution was not voted on directly by the people, but through their representatives, the delegates, who were appointed by state legislatures to attend their state conventions. It was this political custom which the Southern states used in 1860 and 1861 in deciding whether to secede or not. It was traditional and constitutional, which is why they employed it. And it was from these very conventions that the 13 Ordinances of Secession were formulated, adopted, and approved by the people. Thus, in 1903 future U.S. President Woodrow Wilson looked back and wrote of the secession movement of 1860:

Though a Southern Liberal, U.S. President Woodrow Wilson stood by his region's earlier decision to secede.

> As in 1788, so now there was no submission of the action of the convention to the vote of the people for ratification. A representative convention was as sovereign in South Carolina in 1860 as in 1788. The other States followed her example as of course. Their theory of constitutional right and practice was identical with hers. Each State in its turn called a convention, as in the old days of the formation of the Union, and committed to it as of course the sovereign determination of the political connections of the commonwealth.
>
> ... [Well educated by either school or life experience] Southern voters were not likely to be made dupes of. They had elected the men who sat in the sovereign conventions which cut their connection with the Union with a full knowledge of the business they were to meet upon, and *did not doubt that the conclusions of those bodies were their own authentic acts.* Political method was not in dispute among them. They accounted themselves disciples of Mr. [John C.] Calhoun in respect of constitutional right and the legal remedy for abuses in the conduct of the federal government. What he had taught them was in their minds the commonplace and matter of course foundation of political theory. *They did not doubt that they had the right to secede, or that sovereign representative conventions were the proper instruments of secession.*
>
> ... Not until the year was out which had been fixed as the term of the provisional government was the direct action of the people asked for, except in Texas, which came to its resolution of secession while the new confederate government was in process of formation, and Virginia, which waited until it had been formed. *In each of those States the ordinance of secession was submitted to the vote of the people and ratified by them.*[244]

While the Secession Conventions did indeed exercise "extraordinary powers," they did not assume more power than was granted or sanctioned by the people. *The Conventions were called to consider the relation of their States to the Federal Government, and were given full power to act in reference to Federal relations.* The revision of the State Constitutions and the passing of certain acts of legislation by the Conventions were incidental but necessary so as to make the political machinery conformable to the new conditions in which the States found themselves.[245]

★ FACT: SHORTLY AFTER LINCOLN'S ELECTION ALEXANDER H. STEPHENS SPOKE VIGOROUSLY AGAINST SECESSION

Another respected Southerner who greatly disliked the idea of leaving the Union was the aforementioned Alexander H. Stephens, soon to become the Confederacy's first vice president. In the following speech, delivered in the hall of the House of Representatives of Georgia on November 14, 1860, just days after Lincoln's election, Stephens provides a fair view of the attitude of the average Southerner at the time. Despite several boisterous pro-secessionists in the audience, he maintains that the idea of secession should only be used as a last resort, admonishes adherence to the Union, defends the U.S.A. against fellow Southern detractors, extends a plea for calm, and cautions patience during a time of great national upheaval and political strain.

Confederate Vice President Alexander H. Stephens was one of the greatest defenders of the Southern Cause; his works are just as relevant today as they were 150 years ago.

Interestingly, Stephens had been on good terms with Lincoln prior to his attaining the White House, and even admired and trusted him to a degree. Thus Stephens assumed that after becoming U.S. president, the "Rail Splitter" from Illinois would follow the Constitution and honor its clauses in dealing with the South—or would at least be hemmed in by the Constitution's many restrictions on the executive.

As we know all too well, this was not to be the case: Stephens grossly underestimated Liberal Lincoln's cunning, lawlessness, and aggressiveness, and he eventually came, though still reluctantly, to support secession.

Because Stephens covers this ground so thoroughly, I need not present any other Southern views on the matter in this chapter. In fact, as noted, though aimed at his fellow Georgians, this early speech aptly captures the mood of the typical Southerner shortly after Lincoln's election, and six months before the start of his war:

> Fellow-Citizens: I appear before you to-night at the request of members of the Legislature and others to speak of matters of the deepest interest that can possibly concern us all of an earthly character. There is nothing—no question or subject connected with this life—that concerns a free people so intimately as that of the Government under which they live. We are now, indeed, surrounded by evils. Never since I entered upon the public stage has the country been so environed with difficulties and dangers that threatened the public peace and the very existence of society as now. I do not now appear before you at my own instance. It is not to gratify desire of my own that I am here. Had I consulted my own ease and pleasure I should not be before you; but, believing that it is the duty of every good citizen to give his counsels and views whenever the country is in danger, as to the best policy to be pursued, I am here. For these reasons, and these only, do I bespeak a calm, patient, and attentive hearing.
>
> My object is not to stir up strife, but to allay it; not to appeal to your passions, but to your reason. Good governments can never be built up or sustained by the impulse of passion. I wish to address myself to your good sense, to your good judgment, and if after hearing you disagree, let us agree to disagree, and part as we met, friends. We all have the same object, the same interest. That people should disagree in republican governments, upon questions of public policy, is natural. That men should disagree upon all matters connected with human investigation, whether relating to science or human conduct, is natural. Hence, in free governments, parties will arise. But a free people should express their different opinions with liberality and charity, with no acrimony towards those of their fellows, when honestly and sincerely given. These are my feelings to-night.
>
> Let us, therefore, reason together. It is not my purpose to say aught to wound the feelings of any individual who may be present; and if in the ardency with which I shall express my opinions, I shall say anything which may be deemed too strong, let it be set down to the zeal with which I advocate my own convictions. There is with me no intention to irritate or offend.
>
> The first question that presents itself is, *shall the people of the South secede from the Union in consequence of the election of Mr. Lincoln to the presidency of the United States? My countrymen, I tell you frankly, candidly, and earnestly, that I do not think that they ought.* In my judgment, the election of no man, constitutionally chosen to that high office, is sufficient cause for any State to separate from the Union. It ought to stand by and aid still in maintaining the constitution of the country. *To make a point of resistance to the Government, to*

withdraw from it because a man has been constitutionally elected, puts us in the wrong. We are pledged to maintain the Constitution. Many of us have sworn to support it. Can we, therefore, for the mere election of a man to the Presidency, and that, too, in accordance with the prescribed forms of the Constitution, make a point of resistance to the Government without becoming the breakers of that sacred instrument ourselves, withdraw ourselves from it? *Would we not be in the wrong? What ever fate is to befall this country, let it never be laid to the charge of the people of the South, and especially to the people of Georgia, that we were untrue to our national engagements. Let the fault and the wrong rest upon others. If all our hopes are to be blasted, if the Republic is to go down, let us be found to the last moment standing on the deck, with the Constitution of the United States waving over our heads.* (Applause.) Let the fanatics [Liberals] of the North break the Constitution, if such is their fell purpose. Let the responsibility be upon them. I shall speak presently more of their acts; but let not the [Conservative] South, let us not be the ones to commit the aggression. We went into the election with this people [Yankee Liberals]. The result was different from what we wished; but the election has been constitutionally held. Were we to make a point of resistance to the Government and go out of the Union on that account, the record would be made up hereafter against us.

Stephens later correctly pointed out that Lincoln's policies were unconstitutional, and as such were a threat to the sovereign rights of the states.

But it is said Mr. Lincoln's policy and principles are against the Constitution, and that if he carries them out it will be destructive of our rights. Let us not anticipate a threatened evil. If he violates the Constitution then will come our time to act. Do not let us break it because, forsooth, he may. If he does, that is the time for us to strike. (Applause.) I think it would be injudicious and unwise to do this sooner. I do not anticipate that Mr. Lincoln will do anything to jeopardize our safety or security, whatever may be his spirit to do it; for he is bound by the constitutional checks which are thrown around him, which at this time renders him powerless to do any great mischief. This shows the wisdom of our system. The President of the United States is no emperor, no dictator—he is clothed with no absolute power. He can do nothing unless he is backed by power in Congress. The House of Representatives is largely in the majority against him.

In the Senate he will also be powerless. There will be a majority of four against him. This, after the loss of [William] Bigler, [John] Fitch, and others, by the unfortunate dissensions of the National Democratic party [Conservative] in their States. Mr. Lincoln cannot appoint an officer without the consent of the Senate—he cannot form a Cabinet without the same consent. He will be in the condition of [King] George III, (the embodiment of Toryism,)[246] who had to ask the Whigs to appoint his ministers, and was compelled to receive a cabinet utterly opposed to his views; and so Mr. Lincoln will be compelled to ask of the Senate to choose for him a cabinet, if the Democracy of that body choose to put him on such terms. He will be compelled to do this or let the Government stop, if the National Democratic men [Conservatives]—for that is their name at the North—the *conservative* men in the Senate, should so determine. Then, how can Mr. Lincoln obtain a cabinet which would aid him, or allow him to violate the Constitution?

Why then, I say, should we disrupt the ties of this Union when his hands are tied, when he can do nothing against us? I have heard it mooted that no man in the State of Georgia, who is true to her interests, could hold office under Mr. Lincoln. But, I ask, who appoints to office? Not the President alone; the Senate has to concur. No man can be appointed without the consent of the Senate. Should any man then refuse to hold office that was given to him by a Democratic Senate?

[Southern Conservative Robert A. Toombs interrupts here, saying that "if the Senate was Democratic, that is, Conservative, it was for John C. Breckinridge."]

Well, then, I apprehend no man could be justly considered untrue to the interests of Georgia, or incur any disgrace, if the interests of Georgia required it, to hold an office which a Breckinridge Senate had given him, even though Mr. Lincoln should be President. (Prolonged applause, mingled with interruptions.)

I trust, my countrymen, you will be still and silent. I am addressing your good sense. I am giving you my views in a calm and dispassionate manner, and if any of you differ with me, you can, on any other occasion, give your views as I am doing now, and let reason and true patriotism decide between us. In my judgment, I say, under such circumstances, there would be no possible disgrace for a Southern man to hold office. No man will be suffered to be appointed, I have no doubt, who is not true to the Constitution, if Southern Senators are true to their trusts, as I cannot permit myself to doubt that they will be.

My honorable friend who addressed you last night, (Mr. Toombs,) and to whom I listened with the profoundest attention, asks if we would submit to Black Republican [Liberal abolitionist] rule? I say to you and to him, as a Georgian, I never would submit to any Black Republican aggression upon our constitutional rights. I will never consent myself, as much as I admire this Union for the glories of the past, or the blessings of the present, as much as it has done for the people of all these States, as much as it has done for civilization, as much as the hopes of the world hang upon it, I would never submit to aggression upon my rights to maintain it longer; and *if they cannot be maintained in the Union*, standing on the Georgia platform, where I have stood from the time of its adoption, *I would be in favor of disrupting every tie which binds the States together.*

I will have equality for Georgia and for the citizens of Georgia in this Union, or I will look for new safeguards elsewhere. This is my position. The only question now is, can they be secured in the Union? That is what I am counselling with you to-night about. Can it be secured? In my judgment it may be, but it may not be; but let us do all we can, so that in the future, if the worst come, it may never be said we were negligent in doing our duty to the last.

My countrymen, I am not of those who believe this Union has been a curse up to this time. True men, men of integrity, entertain different views from me on this subject. I do not question their right to do so; I would not impugn their motives in so doing. Nor will I undertake to say that this Government of our fathers is perfect. There is nothing perfect in this world of a human origin. Nothing connected with human nature, from man himself to any of his works. You may select the wisest and best men for your judges, and yet how many defects are there in the administration of justice? You may select the wisest and best men for your legislators, and yet how many defects are apparent in your laws? And it is so in our Government.

But that this Government of our fathers, with all its defects, comes nearer the objects of all good Governments than any other on the face of the earth is my settled conviction. Contrast it now with any on the face of the earth.

["England," says Mr. Toombs.]

England, my friend says. Well, that is the next best, I grant; but I think we have improved upon England. Statesmen tried their apprentice hand on the Government of England, and then ours was made. Ours sprung from that, avoiding many of its defects, taking most of the good and leaving out many of its errors, and from the whole constructing and building up this model Republic—the best which the history of the world gives an account of.

Compare, my friends, this Government with that of Spain, Mexico, and South American Republics, Germany, Ireland—are there any sons of that downtrodden nation here to-night?—Prussia, or if you travel further East, to Turkey or China. Where will you go, following the sun in its circuit round our globe, to find a Government that better protects the liberties of its people, and secures to them the blessings we enjoy? (Applause.) I think that one of the evils that beset us is a surfeit of liberty, an exuberance of the priceless blessings for which we are ungrateful. We listened to my honorable friend who addressed you last night, (Mr. Toombs,) as he recounted the evils of this Government.

The first was the fishing bounties, paid mostly to the sailors of New England. Our friend stated that forty-eight years of our Government was under the administration of Southern Presidents. Well, these fishing bounties began under the rule of a Southern President, I believe. No one of them during the whole forty-eight years ever set his Administration against the principle or policy of them. It is not for me to say whether it was a wise policy in the beginning; it probably was not, and I have nothing to say in its defence. But the reason given for it was to encourage our young men to go to sea and learn to manage ships. We had at the time but a small navy. It was thought best to encourage a class of our people to become acquainted with seafaring life; to become sailors: to man our naval ships. It requires practice to walk the deck of a ship, to pull the ropes, to furl the sails, to go aloft, to climb the mast; and it was thought, by offering this bounty, a nursery might be formed in which young men would become perfected in these arts, and it applied to one section of the country as well as to any other.

The result of this was, that in the war of 1812 our sailors, many of whom came from this nursery, were equal to any that England brought against us. At any rate, no small part of the glories of that war were gained by the veteran tars of America, and the object of these bounties was to foster that branch of the national defence. My opinion is, that whatever may have been the reason at first, this bounty ought to be discontinued—the reason for it at first no longer exists. A bill for this object did pass the Senate the last Congress I was in, to which my honorable friend contributed greatly, but it was not reached in the House of Representatives. I trust that he will yet see that he may with honor continue his connection with the Government, and that his eloquence, unrivalled in the Senate, may hereafter, as heretofore, be displayed in having this bounty, so obnoxious to him, repealed and wiped off from the statute book.

Due to his many left-wing ideas and policies, Lincoln has long been idolized by communists, as the cover from this 1936 book by communist Earl Browder reveals.

The next evil that my friend complained of was the Tariff. Well, let us look at that for a moment. About the time I commenced noticing public matters, this question was agitating the country almost as fearfully as the slave question now is. In 1832, when I was in college, South Carolina was ready to nullify or secede from the Union on this account. And what have we seen? The Tariff no longer distracts the public councils. Reason has triumphed! The present Tariff was voted for by Massachusetts and South Carolina. The lion and the lamb lay down together—every man in the Senate and House from Massachusetts and South Carolina, I think, voted for it, as did my honorable friend himself. And if it be true, to use the figure of speech of my honorable friend, that every man in the North that works in iron and brass and wood has his muscle strengthened by the protection of the Government, that stimulant was given by his vote, and I believe every other Southern man.

So we ought not to complain of that.

[Mr. Toombs states that "the tariff assessed the duties."]

Yes, and Massachusetts with unanimity voted with the South to lessen them, and they were made just as low as Southern men asked them to be, and that is the rates they are now at. If reason and argument, with experience, produced such changes in the sentiments of Massachusetts from 1832 to 1857, on the subject of the Tariff, may not like changes be effected there by the same means—reason and argument, and appeals to patriotism on the present vexed question; and who can say that by 1875 or 1890 Massachusetts may not vote with South Carolina and Georgia upon all those questions that now distract the country, and threaten its peace and existence. I believe in the power and efficiency of truth, in the omnipotence of truth, and its ultimate triumph when properly wielded. (Applause.)

Another matter of grievance alluded to by my honorable friend was the navigation laws. This policy was also commenced under the Administration of one of these Southern Presidents who ruled so well, and has been continued through all of them since. The gentleman's views of the policy of these laws and my own do not disagree. We occupied the same ground in relation to them in Congress. It is not my purpose to defend them now. But it is proper to state some matters connected with their origin.

One of the objects was to build up a commercial American marine by giving American bottoms the exclusive carrying trade between our own ports. This is a great arm of national power. This object was accomplished. We have now an amount of shipping, not only coastwise, but to foreign countries, which puts us in the front rank of the nations of the world. England can no longer be styled the Mistress of the Seas. What American is not proud of the result? Whether those laws should be continued is another question. But one thing is certain: no President, Northern or Southern, has ever yet recommended their repeal. And my friend's efforts to get them repealed were met with but little favor, North or South.

These, then, were the true main grievances or grounds of complaint against the general system of our Government and its workings—I mean the administration of the Federal Government. As to the acts of the Federal States, I shall speak presently, but these three were the main ones used against the common head. Now, suppose it be admitted that all of these are evils in the system, do they overbalance and outweigh the advantages and great good which this same Government affords in a thousand innumerable ways that cannot be estimated? Have we not at the South, as well as at the North, grown great, prosperous, and happy under its operation? Has any part of the world ever shown such rapid progress in the development of wealth, and all the material resources of national power and greatness, as the Southern States have under the General Government, notwithstanding all its defects?

[Mr. Toombs says, "in spite of it."]

My honorable friends says we have, in spite of the General Government; that without it I suppose he thinks we might have done as well, or perhaps, than we have done this in spite of it. That may be, and it may not be; but the great fact that we have grown great and powerful under the Government as it exists, there is no conjecture or speculation about that; it stands out bold, high, and prominent like your Stone Mountain, to which the gentleman alluded in illustrating home facts in his record—this great fact of our unrivalled prosperity in the Union as it is admitted; whether all this in spite of the Government—whether we of the South would have been better off without the Government—is, to say the least, problematical. On the one side we can only put the fact against speculation and conjecture on the other. But even as a question of speculation I differ with my distinguished friend.

What we would have lost in border wars without the Union, or what we have gained simply by the peace it has secured, no estimate can be made of. Our foreign trade, which is the foundation of all our prosperity, has the protection of the navy, which drove the pirates from the waters near our coast, where they had been buccaneering for centuries before, and might have been still had it not been for the American Navy under the command of such spirits as Commodore [David] Porter. Now that the coast is clear, that our commerce flows freely outwardly, we cannot well estimate how it would have been under other circumstances. The influence of the Government on us is like that of the atmosphere around us. Its benefits are so silent and unseen that they are seldom thought of or appreciated.

Though one of the most ardent pro-South statesmen, at first Stephens argued vehemently against secession, touting the many benefits and blessings of remaining in the Union.

We seldom think of the single element of oxygen in the air we breathe, and yet let this simple, unseen, and unfelt agent be withdrawn, this life-giving element be taken away from this all-pervading fluid around us, and what instant and appalling changes would take place in all organic creation.

It may be that we are all that we are in "spite of the General Government," but it may be that without it we should have been far different from what we are now. It is true there is no equal part of the earth with natural resources superior perhaps to ours. That portion of this country known as the Southern States, stretching from the Chesapeake to the Rio Grande, is fully equal to the picture drawn by the honorable and eloquent Senator last night, in all natural capacities. But how many ages and centuries passed before these capacities were developed to reach this advanced age of civilization? There these same hills, rich in ore, same rivers, same valleys and plains, are as they have been since they came from the hand of the Creator; uneducated and uncivilized man roamed over them for how long no history informs us.

It was only under our institutions that they could be developed. Their development is the result of the enterprise of our people under operations of the Government and institutions under which we have lived. Even our people without these never would have done it. The organization of society has much to do with the development of the natural resources of any country or any land. The institutions of a people, political and moral, are the matrix in which the germ of their organic structure quickens into life takes root and develops in form, nature and character. Our institutions constitute the basis, the matrix, from which spring all our characteristics of development and greatness. Look at Greece. There is the same fertile soil, the same blue sky, the same inlets and harbors, the same Aegean, the same Olympus; there is the same land where Homer sung, where Pericles spoke; it is in nature the same old Greece—but it is living Greece no more. (Applause.)

Descendants of the same people inhabit the country; yet what is the reason of this mighty difference? In the midst of present degradation we see the glorious fragments of ancient works of art—temples with ornaments and inscriptions that excite wonder and admiration—the remains of a once high order of civilization which have outlived the language they spoke—upon them all Ichabod is written—their glory has departed. Why is this so? I answer, their institutions have been destroyed. These were but the fruits of their forms of government, the matrix from which their grand development sprung, and when once the institutions of a people have been destroyed, there is no earthly power that can bring back the Promethean spark to kindle them here again, any more than in that ancient land of eloquence, poetry, and song. (Applause.)

The same may be said of Italy. Where is Rome, once the mistress of the world? There are the same seven hills now, the same soil, the same natural resources; nature is the same, but what a ruin of human greatness meets the eye of the traveller throughout the length and breadth of that most downtrodden land! Why have not the people of that Heaven-favored clime the spirit that animated their fathers? Why this sad difference?

It is the destruction of her institutions that has caused it; and, my countrymen, if we shall in an evil hour rashly pull down and destroy those institutions which the patriotic band of our fathers labored so long and so hard to build up, and which have done so much for us and the world, who can venture the prediction that similar results will not ensue? Let us avoid it if we can. I trust the spirit is among us that will enable us to do it. Let us not rashly try the experiment, for if it fails as it did in Greece and Italy, and in the South American Republics, and in every other place, wherever liberty is once destroyed, it may never be restored to us again. (Applause.)

There are defects in our Government, errors in administration, and shortcomings of many kinds, but in spite of these defects and errors, Georgia has grown to be a great State. Let us pause here a moment. In 1850 there was a great crisis [the Missouri Compromise], but not so fearful as this, for of all I ever passed through, this is the most perilous, and requires to be met with the greatest calmness and deliberation.

There were many amongst us in 1850 zealous to go at once out of the Union, to disrupt every tie that binds us together. Now do you believe, had that policy been carried out at that time, we would have been the same great people that we are to-day? It may be that we would, but have you any assurance of that fact? Would you have made the same advancement, improvement, and progress in all that constitutes material wealth and prosperity that we have?

I notice in the Comptroller-General's report, that the taxable property of Georgia is $670,000,000 and upwards, an amount not far from double that it was in 1850. I think I may venture to say that for the last ten years the material wealth of the people of Georgia has been nearly if not quite doubled. The same may be said of our advance in education, and everything that marks our civilization. Have we any assurance that had we regarded the earnest but misguided patriotic advice, as I think, of some of that day, and disrupted the ties which bind us to the Union, we would have advanced as we have? I think not. Well, then, let us be careful now before we attempt any rash experiment of this sort. I know that there are friends whose patriotism I do not intend to question, who think this Union a curse, and that we would be better off without it. I do not so think; if we can bring about a correction of these evils which threaten—and I am not without hope that this may not yet be done—this appeal to go out, with all the provisions for good that accompany it, I look upon as a great and I fear a fatal temptation.

When I look around and see our prosperity in every thing, agriculture, commerce, art, science, and every department of education, physical and mental, as well as moral advancement, and our colleges, I think, in the face of such an exhibition, *if we can without the loss of power, or any essential right or interest, remain in the Union, it is our duty to ourselves and to posterity to*—let us not too readily yield to this temptation—do so. Our first parents, the great progenitors of the human race, were not without a like temptation when in the Garden of Eden. They were led to believe that their condition would be bettered—that their eyes would be opened—and that they would become as gods. They in an evil hour yielded—instead of becoming gods they only saw their own nakedness.

I look upon this country with our institutions as the Eden of the world, the paradise of the universe. It may be that out of it we may become greater and more prosperous, but I am candid and sincere in telling you that I fear if we rashly evince passion and without sufficient cause shall take that step, that instead of becoming greater or more peaceful, prosperous, and happy—instead of becoming gods, we will become demons, and at no distant day commence cutting one another's throats. This is my apprehension. Let us, therefore, whatever we do, meet these difficulties, great as they are, like wise and sensible men, and consider them in the light of all the consequences which may attend our action. Let us see first clearly where the path of duty leads, and then we may not fear to tread therein.

I come now to the main question put to me, and on which my counsel has been asked. That is, what the present Legislature should do in view of the dangers that threaten us, and the wrongs that have been done us by several of our Confederate [that is, brotherly Northern] States in the Union, by the acts of their legislatures nullifying the fugitive slave law, and in direct disregard of their constitutional obligations. What I shall say will not be in the spirit of dictation. It will be simply my own judgment for what it is worth. It proceeds from a strong conviction that according to it our rights, interests, and honor—our present safety and future security can be maintained without yet looking to the last resort, the *ultima ratio regum* ["a resort to arms"]. That should not be looked to until all else fails. That may come. On this point I am hopeful, but not sanguine. But let us use every patriotic effort to prevent it while there is ground for hope.

Liberal Lincoln (seated center) and his Liberal cabinet. Before Lincoln decided to illegally invade the South, he and Stephens, a dyed-in-the-wool Southern Conservative, had been political friends of sorts. Stephens, assuming that he knew Lincoln, believed that our sixteenth president would obey the Constitution, making secession not only unnecessary, but an irrevocable mistake. The Confederate vice president lived to regret his trusting nature.

If any view that I may present, in your judgment, be inconsistent with the best interests of Georgia, I ask you, as patriots, not to regard it. After hearing me and others whom you have advised with, act in the premises according to your own conviction of duty as patriots. I speak now particularly to the members of the Legislature present. There are, as I have said, great dangers ahead. Great dangers may come from the election I have spoken of. If the policy of Mr. Lincoln and his Republican [Liberal] associates shall be carried out, or attempted to be carried out, no man in Georgia will be more willing or ready than myself to defend our rights, interest, and honor at every hazard, and to the last extremity [war and secession]. (Applause.)

What is this policy? It is in the first place to exclude us by an act of Congress from the Territories with our slave property. He is for using the power of the General Government against the extension of our institutions. Our position on this point is and ought to be, at all hazards, for perfect equality between all the States, and the citizens of all the States, in the Territories, under the Constitution of the United States. If Congress should exercise its power against this, then I am for standing where Georgia planted herself in 1850. These were plain propositions which were then laid down in her celebrated platform as sufficient for the disruption of the Union if the occasion should ever come; on these Georgia has declared that she will go out of the Union; and for these she would be justified by the nations of the earth in so doing.

I say the same; I said it then; I say it now, if Mr. Lincoln's policy should be carried out. I have told you that I do not think his bare election sufficient cause: but if his policy should be carried out in violation of any of the principles set forth in the Georgia Platform, that would be such an act of aggression which ought to be met as therein provided for. If his policy shall be carried out in repealing or modifying the Fugitive Slave law so as to weaken its efficacy, Georgia has declared that she will in the last resort disrupt the ties of the Union, and I say so too. I stand upon the Georgia Platform, and upon every plank, and say if those aggressions therein provided for take place, I say to you and the people of Georgia, keep your powder dry, and let your assailants then have lead, if need be. (Applause.) I would wait for an act of aggression. This is my position.

Now, upon another point, and that the most difficult and deserving your most serious consideration, I will speak. That is the course which this State should pursue towards these [Liberal] Northern States, which by their legislative acts have attempted to [illegally] nullify the Fugitive Slave law. I know that in some of these States their acts pretend to be based upon the principles set forth in the case of Prigg against Pennsylvania; that decision did proclaim the doctrine that the State officers are not bound to carry out the provisions of a law of Congress—that the Federal Government cannot impose duties upon State officials; that they must execute their own laws by their own officers. And this may be true. But still it is the [constitutional] duty of the States to deliver fugitive slaves, as well as the duty of the General Government to see that it is done.

Northern States, on entering into the Federal compact, pledged themselves to surrender such fugitives; and *it is in disregard of their [constitutional] obligations that they have passed laws which even tend to hinder or obstruct the fulfilment of that obligation.* They have violated their plighted faith; what ought we to do in view of this? That is the question. What is to be done? By the law of nations you would have a right to demand the carrying out of this article of agreement, and I do not see that it should be otherwise with respect to the States of this Union; and in case it be not done, we would, by these principles, have the right to commit acts of reprisal on these faithless

Governments, and seize upon their property, or that of their citizens, wherever found. The States of this Union stand upon the same footing with foreign nations in this respect. But by the law of nations we are equally bound, before proceeding to violent measures, to set forth our grievances before the offending Government, to give them an opportunity to redress the wrong. Has our State yet done this? I think not.

Suppose it were Great Britain that had violated some compact of agreement with the General Government, what would be first done? In that case our Minister would be directed in the first instance to bring the matter to the attention of that Government, or a Commissioner be sent to that country to open negotiations with her, ask for redress, and it would only be when argument and reason had been exhausted that we should take the last resort of nations. That would be the course towards a foreign Government, and towards a member of this Confederacy I would recommend the same course.

Let us, therefore, not act hastily in this matter. Let your Committee on the State of the Republic make out a bill of grievances; let it be sent by the Governor to those faithless [Liberal] States, and if reason and argument shall be tried in vain—all shall fail to induce them to return to *their constitutional obligations*, I would be for retaliatory measures, such as the Governor has suggested to you. This mode of resistance to the Union is in our power. It might be effectual, and if in the last resort, we would be justified in the eyes of nations, not only in separating from them, but by using force.

[Someone in the audience says that "the argument was already exhausted."]

Some friend says that the argument is already exhausted. No, my friend, it is not. You have never called the attention of the Legislatures of those States to this subject, that I am aware of., Nothing has ever been done before this year. The attention of our own people has been called to this subject lately.

Now, then, my recommendation to you would be this: In view of all these questions of difficulty, let a convention of the people of Georgia be called, to which they may be all referred. Let the sovereignty of the people speak. Some think that the election of Mr. Lincoln is cause sufficient to dissolve the Union. Some think those other grievances are sufficient to dissolve the same, and that the Legislature has the power thus to act, and ought thus to act. I have no hesitancy in saying that the Legislature is not the proper body to sever our Federal relations, if that necessity should arise. An honorable and distinguished gentleman, the other night, (Mr. Thomas R. R. Cobb,) advised you to take this course—not to wait to hear from the cross-roads and groceries. I say to you, you have no power so to act. You must refer this question to the people and you must wait to hear from the men at the cross-roads and even the groceries; for the people in this country, whether at the cross-roads or the groceries, whether in cottages or palaces, are all equal, and they are the sovereigns in this country. Sovereignty is not in the Legislature. We, the people, are the sovereigns. I am one of them and have a right to be heard, and so has any other citizen of the State. You legislators, I speak it respectfully, are but our servants. You are the servants of the people, and not their masters. Power resides with the people in this country.

The great difference between our country and all others, such as France and England and Ireland, is, that here there is popular sovereignty, while there sovereignty is exercised by kings and favored classes. This principle of popular sovereignty, however much derided lately, is the foundation of our institutions. Constitutions are but the channels through which the popular will may be expressed. Our Constitution came from the people. They made it, and they alone can rightfully unmake it.

[Mr. Toombs says "I am afraid of conventions."]

I am not afraid of any convention legally chosen by the people. *I know no way to decide great questions affecting fundamental laws except by representatives of the people. The Constitution of the United States was made by the representatives of the people. The Constitution of the State of Georgia was made by representatives of the people chosen at the ballot-box.* But do not let the question which comes before the people be put to them in the language of my honorable friend who addressed you last night. Will you submit to abolition rule or resist?

In early 1861 Stephens maintained that Lincoln's election did not warrant the secession of the Southern states. He later admitted that he had been wrong.

[Mr. Toombs says "I do not wish the people to be cheated."]

Now, my friends, how are we going to cheat the people by calling on them to elect delegates to a convention to decide all these questions without any dictation or direction? Who proposes to cheat the people by letting them speak their own untrammelled views in the choice of their ablest and best men, to determine upon all these matters, involving their peace.

I think the proposition of my honorable friend had a considerable smack of unfairness, not to say cheat. He wished to have no convention, but for the Legislature to submit their vote to the people—submission to abolition rule or resistance? Now, who in Georgia would vote "submission to abolition rule" [that is, rule by radical Yankee Liberals]? (Laughter.)

Is putting such a question to the people to vote on, a fair way of getting an expression of the popular will on all these, questions? I think not. Now, who in Georgia is going to submit to abolition rule?

[Mr. Toombs says "the convention will."]

No, my friend, Georgia will never do it. The convention will never secede from the Georgia Platform. Under that there can be no abolition rule under the General Government. I am not afraid to trust the people in convention upon this and all questions. Besides, the Legislature were not elected for such a purpose. They came here to do their duty as legislators. They have sworn to support the Constitution of the United States. They did not come here to disrupt this Government. I am, therefore, for submitting all these questions to a convention of the people. Submit this question to the people, whether they would submit to abolition rule or resist, and then let the Legislature act upon that vote! Such a course would be an insult to the people. They would have to eat their platform, ignore their past history, blot out their records, and take steps backwards, if they should do this. I have never eaten my record or words, and never will.

But how will it be under this arrangement if they should vote to resist, and the Legislature should reassemble with this vote as their instruction? Can any man tell me what sort of resistance will be meant? One man would say secede; another pass retaliatory measures; these are measures of resistance against wrong—legitimate and right—and there would be as many different ideas as there are members on this floor. Resistance don't mean secession—that in no proper sense of the term is resistance. Believing that the times require action, I am for presenting the question fairly to the people, for calling together an untrammelled convention, and presenting all the questions to them whether they will go out of the Union, or what course of resistance in the Union they may think best, and then let the Legislature act, when the people in their majesty are heard, and I tell you now, whatever that convention does, I hope and trust our people will abide by. I advise the calling of a convention with the earnest desire to preserve the peace and harmony of the State. I should dislike above all things to see violent measures adopted, or a disposition to take the sword in hand, by individuals, without the authority of law.

My honorable friend said last night, "I ask you to give me the sword, for if you do not give it to me, as God lives, I will take it myself."

(Mr. Toombs says "I will." Applause on the other side.)

I have no doubt that my honorable friend feels as he says. It is only his excessive ardor that makes him use such an expression; but this will pass off with the excitement of the hour. When the people in their majesty shall speak, I have no doubt that he will bow to their will, whatever it may be, upon the "sober second thought." (Applause.)

Should Georgia determine to go out of the Union, I speak for one, though my views might not agree with them, whatever the result may be, I shall bow to the will of her people. Their cause is my cause, and their destiny is my destiny; and I trust this will be the ultimate course of all. The greatest curse that can befall a free people is civil war.

But, as I said, let us call a convention of the people; let all these matters be submitted to it, and when the will of the majority of the people has thus been expressed, the whole State will present one unanimous voice in favor of whatever may be demanded; for I believe in the power of the people to govern themselves when wisdom prevails and passion is silent.

Look at what has already been done by them for their advancement in all that ennobles man. There is nothing like it in the history of the world. Look abroad, from one extent of the country to the other, contemplate our greatness. We are now among the first nations of the earth. Shall it be said, then, that our institutions, founded upon principles of self-government, are a failure?

Thus far it is a noble example, worthy of imitation. The gentleman, Mr. Cobb, the other night said it had proven a failure. A failure in what? In growth? Look at our expanse in national power. Look at our population and increase in all that makes a people great. A failure? Why are we the admiration of the civilized world, and present the brightest hopes of mankind.

Some of our public men have failed in their aspirations; that is true, and from that comes a great part of our troubles. (Prolonged applause.)

No, there is no failure of this Government yet. We have made great advancement under the Constitution, and I cannot but hope that we shall advance higher yet. Let us be true to our cause.

Now, when this convention assembles, if it shall be called, as I hope it may, I would say in my judgment, without dictation, for I am conferring with you freely and frankly, and it is thus that I give my views, I should take into consideration all those questions which distract the public mind; should view all the grounds of secession so far as the election of Mr. Lincoln is concerned, and I have no doubt they would say that the constitutional election of no man is a sufficient cause to break up the Union, but that the State should wait until he at least does some unconstitutional act.

[Mr. Toombs says "commit some overt act."]

No, I did not say that. The word overt is a sort of technical term connected with treason, which has come to us from the mother country [England], and it means an open act of rebellion. I do not see how Mr. Lincoln can do this unless he should levy war upon us. I do not, therefore, use the word overt. I do not intend to wait for that. But I use the word *unconstitutional* act, which our people understand much better, and which expresses just what I mean. But as long as he conforms to the Constitution he should be left to exercise the duties of his office.

In giving this advice I am but sustaining the Constitution of my country, and I do not thereby become a Lincoln aid man either, (applause) but a Constitutional aid man. But this matter the convention can determine.

As to the other matter, I think we have a right to pass retaliatory measures, provided they be in accordance with the Constitution of the United States, and I think they can be made such. But whether it would be wise for this Legislature to do this now is the question. To the convention, in my judgment, this matter ought to be referred. Before we commit reprisals on New England we should exhaust every means of bringing about a peaceful solution of the question.

One of Lincoln's greatest admirers was the founder of modern communism, Russian revolutionary Karl Marx. The founders of Lincoln's Republican Party (in 1854) included many of Marx's American socialist followers, as well as European radicals like the Forty-Eighters.

Thus did General [Andrew] Jackson in the case of the French. He did not recommend reprisals until he had treated with France, and got her to promise to make indemnification, and it was only on her refusal to pay the money which she had promised, that he recommended reprisals. It was after negotiation had failed. I do think, therefore, that it would be best, before going to extreme measures with our confederate States [to the North], to make presentation of our demands, to appeal to their reason and judgment to give us our rights. Then, if reason should not triumph, it will be time enough to commit reprisals, and we should be justified in the eyes of a civilized world. At least let the States know what your grievances are, and *if they refuse, as I said, to give us our rights under the Constitution of our country, I should be willing, as a last resort, to sever the ties of this Union.* (Applause.)

My own opinion is, that if this course be pursued, and they are informed of the consequences of refusal, these States will secede; but if they should not, then let the consequences be with them, and let the responsibility of the consequences rest upon them. Another thing I would have that convention to do. Reaffirm the Georgia Platform with an additional plank in it. Let that plank be the fulfilment of the obligation on the part of those States to repeal these obnoxious laws as a condition of our remaining in the Union. Give them time to consider it, and I would ask all States south to do the same thing.

I am for exhausting all that patriotism can demand before taking the last step. I would invite, therefore, South Carolina to a conference. I would ask the same of all the other Southern States, so that if the evil has got beyond our control, which God, in his mercy, grant may not be the case, let us not be divided among ourselves—(cheers,)—but, if possible, secure the united cooperation of all the Southern States; and then, in the face of the civilized world, we may justify our action; and, with the wrong all on the other side, we can appeal to the God of battles to aid us in our cause. (Loud applause.) But *let us not do anything in which any portion of our people may charge us with rash or hasty action. It is certainly a matter of great importance to tear this Government asunder. You were not sent here for that purpose.* I would wish the whole South to be united if this is to be done; and I believe if we pursue the policy which I have indicated, this can be effected.

In this way our sister Southern States can be induced to act with us, and I have but little doubt that the States of New York and Pennsylvania and Ohio, and the other Western States, will compel their Legislatures to recede from their hostile attitude if the others do not. Then with these we would go on without New England if she chose to stay out.

[A voice in the assembly says, "we will kick them out."]

I would not kick them out. But if they chose to stay out they might. I think, moreover, that these [Liberal] Northern States being principally engaged in manufactures, would find that they had as much interest in the Union under the Constitution as we, and that *they would return to their constitutional duty*—this would be my hope. If they should not, and if the Middle States and Western States do not join us, we should at least have an undivided South. *I am, as you clearly perceive, for maintaining the Union as it is, if possible. I will exhaust every means thus to maintain it with an equality in it.* My principles are these:

First, the maintenance of the honor, the rights, the equality, the security, and the glory of my native State in the Union; but *if these cannot be maintained in the Union, then I am for their maintenance, at all hazards, out of it.* Next to the honor and glory of Georgia, the land of my birth, I hold the honor and glory of our common country. In Savannah I was made to say by the reporters, who very often make me say things which I never did, that I was first for the glory of the whole country, and next for that of Georgia.

I said the exact reverse of this. I am proud of her history, of her present standing. I am proud even of her motto, which I would have duly respected at the present time by all her sons—Wisdom, Justice, and Moderation. I would have her rights and that of the Southern States maintained now upon these principles. Her position now is just what it was in 1850, with respect to the Southern States. Her platform then has been adopted by most, if not all, the other Southern States. Now I would add but one additional plank to that platform, which I have stated, and one which time has shown to be necessary.

If all this fails, we shall at least have the satisfaction of knowing that we have done our duty and all that patriotism could require.

[Mr. Stephens continued for some time on other matters, which are omitted, and then took his seat amidst great applause.][247]

3

THE THIRTEEN SOUTHERN SECESSION ORDINANCES

HAVING ESTABLISHED THE TRUE MEANING, history, authority, and legality of American secession, as well as the generally negative view most Southerners at first had toward it, we now turn to the Southern Ordinances of Secession themselves, those so-called "controversial" documents which the Left routinely misunderstands and therefore misinterprets. This misinterpretation, of course, only intensifies the already widespread unwarranted ignorance and incrimination of secession, while disseminating more slander, myth, and fraud about the Confederacy—part of the anti-South movement's war on anything and everything Southern and Conservative. South-shaming is, after all, the name of the game among progressives, and among many uneducated Conservatives as well.

★ FACT: SOUTH-HATERS ARE TRADITIONALLY CLOSE-MINDED, UNIFORMED, & INTOLERANT OF OPPOSING VIEWS
When it comes to American Civil War history, most South-haters are innately ahistoric; that is, they have no interest in authentic history, for it contradicts their anti-South mindset; a mindset that will not tolerate opposing views. Thus, they choose to embrace the fake Civil War history invented by the Left, a false narrative that supports their bizarre and untenable liberal ideologies—the primary one being that "the

Confederacy was made up of white racists who were fighting only to preserve slavery." It does not matter that there is no evidence to support this myth and plenty that contradicts it.

★ FACT: SOUTH-HATERS TEND TO BE GENERALISTS WHO PRACTICE PRESENTISM & INTERPRET HISTORY OUT OF CONTEXT
Another significant problem with anti-Southers is that they tend to be extreme generalists, with little or no interest in the nuanced gray areas that make up true history. For them, our "Civil War" history is a simple black and white schematic, with Southerners portrayed as the villains and Northerners as the heroes. Because of this, their view of history is always taken out of context, one of the worst sins one can commit when studying the world of our ancestors. Add to this the distorting practice of presentism: viewing the past through the lens of the present, which unfairly overlays modern values, ethics, and mores on those who lived before us—usually in a world completely different than our own.

★ FACT: WITH NO UNDERSTANDING OF GENUINE SOUTHERN HISTORY & CULTURE, SOUTH-HATERS ARE INCAPABLE OF UNDERSTANDING THE SECESSION ORDINANCES
Nowhere do these conventional but wholly unscientific practices cause more problems than with the 13 Southern Secession Ordinances. Though they have been available for all to read for 150 years, few take the time to do so, and most of those who do are presentism-practicing generalists, which makes them incapable of truly understanding these very important all-American documents.

★ FACT: THE SOUTHERN SECESSION ORDINANCES MUST BE STUDIED CAREFULLY & IN THE CONTEXT OF REAL SOUTHERN HISTORY, AS OPPOSED TO FAKE NORTHERN HISTORY
In this chapter I present all 13 of the Secession Ordinances. Not just to preserve them for future generations, but so that the reader can take the time to study them in depth and reflect on them in order to gain a deeper appreciation of what occurred in the nine months between December 20, 1860 (the date of the first Southern state secession) and November 20, 1861 (the date of the last Southern state secession).

★ **FACT: THE OLD NORTH & OLD SOUTH WERE ANALOGOUS TO AN OVERLY STRICT OLDER BROTHER & AN INDIVIDUALISTIC YOUNGER BROTHER**
To insure that the history behind the Ordinances will not be distorted, nor the meaning and motivation behind them taken out of context, in the following chapters I provide thousands of facts that help clarify and explain them. In the process, I set the Ordinances in their proper perspective within the larger framework of American history, from the Revolutionary Period to the 21st Century.

Only then can they be understood for what they really were: an independent-minded younger brother (the South) telling his nosey, overbearing, authoritarian older brother (the North) to back off and allow him to grow up in his own time and way. Those who view or describe the Ordinances any other way are either lying, illiterate, or ignorant of the facts. For, as this book will show in distilling the facts down to their lowest common denominator, the evidence is simple and clear:

Charles A. Dana of New Hampshire, one of the many radical socialists who worked in the Lincoln administration, fabricating false, slanderous, anti-South propaganda—such as "secession was illegal"—that is taught in our schools to this day.

1. Secession is a historic and legal right of the states.
2. The Southern states had more than sufficient reason for withdrawing from the Union.[248]

Let us begin with the Ordinance of the first state that seceded, and proceed through the remaining 12 in chronological order. As we progress note how, after the War begins (April 12, 1861) and its violent, unconstitutional, and malevolent purposes (to crush states' rights, consolidate *Liberal* political power at Washington, and Northernize the conservative South) becomes more evident across Dixie, the ordinances become more detailed, emphatic, and final.

SOUTH CAROLINA
First State: December 20, 1860—South Carolina's Ordinance of Secession

An Ordinance to dissolve the Union between the State of South Carolina and other States united with her under the compact entitled "the Constitution of the United States of America."

We, the People of the State of South Carolina, in Convention assembled, do declare and ordain, and it is hereby declared and ordained.

That the Ordinance adopted by us in Convention, on the twenty-third day of May, in the year of our Lord one thousand seven hundred and eighty-eight [1788], whereby the Constitution of the United States of America was ratified, and also, all Acts and parts of Acts of the General Assembly of this State, ratifying amendments of the said Constitution, are hereby repealed; and that the union now subsisting between South Carolina and other States, under the name of "The United States of America," is hereby dissolved.[249]

MISSISSIPPI

Second State: January 9, 1861—Mississippi's Ordinance of Secession

An Ordinance to dissolve the union between the State of Mississippi and other States united with her under the compact, entitled, "the constitution of the United States of America."

The people of the State of Mississippi, in convention assembled, do ordain and it is hereby ordained and declared, as follows, to wit:

Sec. 1. That all the laws and ordinances by which the said State of Mississippi became a member of the Federal Union of the United States of America be, and the same are hereby repealed, and that all obligations on the part of the said State, or the people thereof to observe the same, be withdrawn, and that the said State doth hereby resume all the rights, functions, and powers which by any of said laws or ordinances were conveyed to the Government of the said United States, and is absolved from all the obligations, restraints, and duties incurred to the said Federal Union, and shall henceforth be *a free, sovereign, and independent State.*

Sec. 2. That so much of the first section of the seventh article of the Constitution of this State, as requires members of the Legislature and all officers, executive and judicial, to take an oath or affirmation to support the Constitution of the United States be, and the same is hereby abrogated and annulled.

Sec. 3. That all rights acquired and vested under the Constitution of the United States, or under any act of Congress passed or treaty made in pursuance thereof, or under any law of this State, and not incompatible with this Ordinance, shall remain in force, and have the same effect as if this Ordinance had not been passed.

Sec. 4. That the people of the State of Mississippi hereby consent to form a Federal Union with such of the States as may have seceded or as may secede from the Union of the United States of America, upon the basis of the present Constitution of the said United States, except such parts thereof as embrace other portions than such seceding States.

Thus ordained and declared in convention the 9th day of Jan., in the year of our Lord One Thousand Eight Hundred Sixty-one.[250]

FLORIDA

Third State: January 10, 1861—Florida's Ordinance of Secession

Whereas, all hope of preserving the Union upon terms consistent with the safety and honor of the slaveholding [read "Conservative"] States, has been fully dissipated by the recent indications of the strength of the anti-slavery [read "Liberal"] sentiment of the free States; therefore, be it enacted by the people of Florida, in convention assembled, that it is undoubtedly the right of the several States of the Union, at such time and for such cause as in the opinion of the people of such States, acting in their sovereign capacity, may be just and proper, to withdraw from the Union, and, in the opinion of this Convention, the existing causes are such as to compel Florida to proceed to exercise this right.

We, the people of the State of Florida, in Convention assembled, do solemnly ordain, publish, and declare, That the State of Florida hereby withdraws herself from the Confederacy of States existing under the name of the United States of America, and from the existing Government of the said States; and that all political connection between her and the Government of said States ought to be, and the same is hereby totally annulled, and said Union of States dissolved; and the State of Florida is hereby *declared a sovereign and independent nation*; and that all ordinances heretofore adopted, in so far as they create or recognize said Union, are rescinded; and all laws, or parts of laws, in force in this State, in so far as they recognize or assent to said Union, be and they are hereby repealed.[251]

ALABAMA
Fourth State: January 11, 1861—Alabama's Ordinance of Secession

An ordinance to dissolve the Union between the State of Alabama and other States united under the compact styled "the Constitution of the United States of America."

Whereas, the election of Abraham Lincoln and Hannibal Hamlin to the offices of President and Vice-President of the United States of America, by *a sectional party, avowedly hostile to the domestic institutions and to the peace and security of the people of the State of Alabama*, preceded by *many and dangerous infractions of the Constitution of the United States by many of the States and people of the Northern section*, is a political wrong of so insulting and menacing a character as to justify the people of the State of Alabama in the adoption of prompt and decided measures for their future peace and security: Therefore,

Sec. 1. Be it declared and ordained by the people of the State of Alabama in convention assembled, that the State of Alabama now withdraws, and is hereby withdrawn, from the Union known as "the United States of America," and henceforth ceases to be one of said United States, and *is, and of right ought to be, a sovereign and independent State*.

Sec. 2. Be it further declared and ordained by the people of the State of Alabama in convention assembled, that all the powers over the territory of said State, and over the people thereof, heretofore delegated to the Government of the United States of America be, and they are hereby, withdrawn from said Government, and are hereby resumed and vested in the people of the State of Alabama.

And as it is the desire and purpose of the State of Alabama to meet the slaveholding [read "Conservative"] States of the South who may approve such purpose, in order to frame a provisional as well as permanent government, upon the principles of the Constitution of the United States.

Be it resolved by the people of Alabama in convention assembled, that the people of the States of Delaware, Maryland, Virginia, North Carolina, South Carolina, Florida, Georgia, Mississippi, Louisiana, Texas, Arkansas, Tennessee, Kentucky, and Missouri, be, and are hereby, invited to meet the people of the State of Alabama, by their delegates, in convention, on the 4th day of February, A. D. 1861, at the city of Montgomery, in the State of Alabama, for the purpose of consulting with each other as to the most effectual mode of securing concerted and harmonious action in whatever measures may be deemed most desirable for our common peace and security.

And be it further resolved, that the President of this convention be, and is hereby, instructed to transmit forthwith a copy of the foregoing preamble, ordinance, and resolutions, to the Governors of the several States named in said resolutions.

Done by the people of the State of Alabama in convention assembled, at Montgomery, on this, the 11th day of January, A.D. 1861.[252]

GEORGIA
Fifth State: January 19, 1861—Georgia's Ordinance of Secession

An Ordinance to dissolve the union between the State of Georgia and other States united with her under the compact of Government entitled "the Constitution of the United States."

We the people of the State of Georgia, in Convention assembled, do declare and ordain, and it is hereby declared and ordained, that the ordinance adopted by the people of the State of Georgia in Convention on the second day of January, in the year of our Lord seventeen hundred and eighty-eight, whereby the Constitution of the United States of America was assented to, ratified, and adopted, and also all acts and parts of acts of the General Assembly of this State ratifying and adopting amendments of the said Constitution, are here by repealed, rescinded, and abrogated; We do further declare and ordain, that the Union now subsisting between the State of Georgia and other States, under the name of the "United States of America," is hereby dissolved; and that the State of Georgia is in *full possession and exercise of all those rights of sovereignty which belong and appertain to a free and independent State.*[253]

LOUISIANA
Sixth State: January 26, 1861—Louisiana's Ordinance of Secession

An Ordinance to dissolve the Union between the State of Louisiana and other States united with her, under the compact entitled: "The Constitution of the United States of America."

We, the people of the State of Louisiana, in Convention assembled, do declare and ordain, and it is hereby declared and ordained, that the Ordinance passed by us in Convention on the 22nd day of November, in the year eighteen hundred & eleven, whereby the Constitution of the United States of America, and the amendments of the said Constitution, were adopted, and all laws and ordinances by which the State of Louisiana became a member of the Federal Union, be and the same are hereby repealed and abrogated; and that the union now subsisting between Louisiana and other States, under the name of "The United States of America" is hereby dissolved.

We do further declare and ordain, that the State of Louisiana hereby resumes all rights and powers heretofore delegated to the Government of the United States of America; That her citizens are absolved from all allegiance to said Government; and that she is in *full possession and exercise of all those rights of sovereignty which appertain to a free and independent State.*

We do further declare and ordain, that all rights acquired and vested under the Constitution of the United States, or any acts of Congress, or treaty, or under any law of this State, and not incompatible with the Ordinance, shall remain in force, and have the same effect as if this Ordinance had not been passed.

Adopted in Convention at Baton Rouge the 26th of January, 1861.[254]

TEXAS

Seventh State: February 1, 1861—Texas' Ordinance of Secession

An Ordinance to dissolve the Union between the State of Texas and the other States under the compact styled "The Constitution of the United States of America."

Sec. 1. Whereas the Federal Government has failed to accomplish the purposes of the compact of union between these States, in giving protection either to the persons of our people upon an exposed frontier, or to the property of our citizens; and whereas, *the action of the Northern States is violative of the compact between the States and the guarantees of the Constitution*; and whereas, the recent developments in Federal affairs make it evident that *the power of the Federal Government is sought to be made a weapon with which to strike down the interests and property of the people of Texas and her sister slave-holding [read "Conservative"] States, instead of permitting it to be, as was intended—our shield against outrage and aggression*—therefore, "We, the people of the State of Texas, by delegates in the Convention assembled, do declare and ordain that the ordinance adopted by our Convention of delegates on the fourth (4th) day of July, A.D. 1845, and afterwards ratified by us, under which the Republic of Texas was admitted into the Union with other States, and became a party to the compact styled 'The Constitution of the United States of America,' be, and is hereby repealed and annulled."

That all the powers which, by the said compact, were delegated by Texas to the Federal Government are resumed. That Texas is of right absolved from all restraints and obligations incurred by said compact, and is a separate sovereign State, and that her citizens and people are absolved from all allegiance to the United States or the Government thereof.

Sec. 2. The ordinance shall be submitted to the people of Texas for their ratification or rejection, by the qualified voters, on the 23rd day of February, 1861; and unless rejected by a majority of the votes cast, shall take effect and be in force on and after the 2nd day of March, A.D. 1861. Provided that in the representative district of El Paso said election may be held on the 18th day of February, 1861. Done by the people of the State of Texas, in convention assembled, at Austin, the 18th day of February, A.D. 1861.[255]

VIRGINIA

Eighth State: April 17, 1861—Virginia's Ordinance of Secession

An Ordinance to repeal the ratification of the Constitution of the United States of America, by the State of Virginia, and to resume all the rights and powers granted under said Constitution.

The people of Virginia, in the ratification of the Constitution of the United States of America, adopted by them in Convention, on the 25th day of June, in the year of our Lord one thousand seven hundred and eighty-eight, having declared that *the powers granted under the said Constitution were derived from the people of the United States, and might be resumed whensoever the same should be perverted to the injury and oppression,* and the Federal Government having perverted said powers, not only to the injury of the people of Virginia, but to the oppression of the Southern slaveholding [read "Conservative"] States.

Now, therefore, the people of Virginia, do declare and ordain, that the Ordinance adopted by the people of this State in Convention on the twenty-fifth day of June, in the year of our Lord one thousand seven hundred and eighty-eight, whereby the Constitution of the United States of America was ratified, and all acts of the General Assembly of this State ratifying or adopting amendments to said Constitution, are hereby repealed and abrogated; that the union between the State of Virginia and the other States under the Constitution aforesaid is hereby dissolved, and that the State of Virginia is in the *full possession and exercise of all the rights of sovereignty which belong and appertain to a free and independent State*. And they do further declare that said Constitution of the United States of America is no longer binding on any of the citizens of this State.

This Ordinance shall take effect and be an Act of this day, when ratified by a majority of the votes of the people of this State, cast at a poll to be taken thereon, on the fourth Thursday in May next, in pursuance of a schedule hereafter to be enacted.

Done in Convention in the City of Richmond, on the seventeenth day of April, in the year of our Lord one thousand eight hundred and sixty-one, and in the eighty-fifth year of the Commonwealth of Virginia.[256]

ARKANSAS
Ninth State: May 6, 1861—Arkansas' Ordinance of Secession

An Ordinance to dissolve the Union now existing between the State of Arkansas and the other States united with her under the compact entitled "The Constitution of the United States of America."

Whereas, in addition to the well-founded cause of complaint set forth by this Convention in resolutions adopted on the 11th March, A.D., 1861, against *the sectional [Republican] party [then the Liberal party] now in power at Washington City, headed by Abraham Lincoln, he has, in the face of the resolutions passed by this Convention, pledging the State of Arkansas to resist to the last extremity any attempt on the part of such power to coerce any State that seceded from the old Union, proclaimed to the world that war should be waged against such States, until they should be compelled to submit to their rule, and large forces to accomplish this have by this same power been called out, and are now being marshalled to carry out this inhuman design, and longer to submit to such rule or remain in the old Union of the United States would be disgraceful and ruinous to the State of Arkansas:*

Therefore, we, the people of the State of Arkansas, in Convention assembled, do hereby declare and ordain, and it is hereby declared and ordained, that the "ordinance and acceptance of compact," passed and approved by the General Assembly of the State of Arkansas on the 18th day of October, A.D. 1836, whereby it was by said General Assembly ordained that, by virtue of the authority vested in said General Assembly, by the provisions of the ordinance adopted by the Convention of delegates assembled at Little Rock, for the purpose of forming a Constitution and system of Government for said State, the propositions set forth in "an act supplementary to an act entitled an act for the admission of the State of Arkansas into the Union, and to provide for the due execution of the laws of the United States within the same, and for other purposes," were freely accepted, ratified, and irrevocably confirmed articles of compact and union between the State of Arkansas and the United States, and all other laws, and every other law and ordinance, whereby the State of Arkansas became a member of the Federal Union, be, and the same are hereby in all respects, and for every purpose herewith consistent, repealed, abrogated, and fully set aside;

and the union now subsisting between the State of Arkansas and the other States under the name of the United States of America, is hereby forever dissolved.

And we do further hereby declare and ordain that the State of Arkansas hereby *resumes to herself all rights and powers heretofore delegated to the Government of the United States of America*—that her citizens are absolved from all allegiance to said Government of the United States, and that she is *in full possession and exercise of all the rights and sovereignty which appertain to a free and independent State.*

We do further ordain and declare that all rights acquired and vested under the Constitution of the United States of America, or of any act or acts of Congress, or treaty, or under any law of this State, and not incompatible with this ordinance, shall remain in full force and effect, in no wise altered or impaired, and have the same effect as if this ordinance had not been passed. Adopted and passed in open Convention on the 6th day of May, *Anno Domini* 1861.[257]

TENNESSEE

Tenth State: May 7, 1861—Tennessee's Ordinance of Secession

Declaration of Independence and Ordinance dissolving the Federal relations between the State of Tennessee and the United States of America.

1st. We, the people of the State of Tennessee, waiving an expression of opinion as to *the abstract doctrine of secession,* but *asserting the right as a free and independent people to alter, reform, or abolish our form of Government in such manner as we think proper,* do ordain and declare that all the laws and ordinances by which the State of Tennessee became a member of the Federal Union of the United States of America; are hereby abrogated and annulled, and that all obligations on our part be withdrawn therefrom; and we do hereby resume all the rights, functions, and powers which by any of said laws and ordinances were conveyed to the Government of the United States, and absolve ourselves from all the obligations, restraints, and duties incurred there to; and do hereby henceforth become a free, sovereign, and independent State.

2nd. We furthermore declare and ordain, that Article 10, Sections 1 and 2 of the Constitution of the State of Tennessee, which requires members of the General Assembly, and all officers, civil and military, to take an oath to support the Constitution of the United States, be and the same are hereby abrogated and annulled, and all parts of the Constitution of the State of Tennessee, making citizenship of the United States a qualification for office, and recognizing the Constitution of the United States as the supreme law of this State, are in like manner abrogated and annulled.

3rd. We furthermore ordain and declare that all rights acquired and vested under the Constitution of the United States, or under any act of Congress passed in pursuance thereof, or under any law of this State, and not incompatible with this ordinance, shall remain in force and have the same effect as if this ordinance had not been passed.[258]

NORTH CAROLINA

Eleventh State: May 20, 1861—North Carolina's Ordinance of Secession

An Ordinance dissolving the union between the State of North Carolina and the other States united with her under the compact of Government entitled, "the Constitution of the United States.'"

We, the people of the State of North Carolina, in Convention assembled, do declare and ordain, and it is hereby declared and ordained, that the ordinance adopted by the State of North Carolina, in the Convention of 1789, where by the Constitution of the United States was ratified and adopted, and also all acts and parts of acts of the General Assembly, ratifying and adopting amendments to the said Constitution, are hereby repealed, rescinded, and abrogated.

We do therefore declare and ordain, that the Union now subsisting between the State of North Carolina and the other States, under the title of the "United States of America," is hereby dissolved, and that the State of North Carolina is in the *full possession and exercise of all those rights of sovereignty which belong and appertain to a free and independent State.* Done at Raleigh, 20th day of May, in the year of our Lord 1861.[259]

MISSOURI

Twelfth State: October 31, 1861—Missouri's Ordinance of Secession
(Note: only a portion of Missouri seceded)

Whereas it is the common desire of the State of Missouri and the Confederate States of America, that said State should become a member of the confederacy; and whereas, the accomplishment of their purpose is now prevented by an armed invasion of the territory of said State by the United States; and whereas, the interests of both demand that they should make common cause in the war waged by the United States against the liberties of both; now, therefore, for those most desirable objects, the Executive power of the State of Missouri has conferred full powers of Edward Carrington Cabell and Thomas L. Snead, and the President of the Confederate States of America on R. M. T. Hunter, their Secretary of State, who, after having exchanged their said full powers in due and proper form, have agreed to the following articles:

Article 1. The State of Missouri shall be admitted into the Confederacy on an equal footing with the other States composing the same, on the fulfilment of the conditions set forth in the second section of the act of the Congress of the Confederate States, entitled "An act to aid the State of Missouri in repelling invasion by the United States, and to authorize the admission of said State as a member of the Confederate States of America, and for other purposes," approved August 20th, 1861.

Article 2. Until said State of Missouri shall become a member of said Confederacy, the whole military force, material of war and military operations, offensive and defensive, of said State shall be under the chief control and direction of the President of the Confederate States, upon the same basis, principles and footing as if said State were now and during the interval, a member of said Confederacy, the said force, together with that of the Confederate States, to be employed for their common defense.

Article 3. The State of Missouri will, whenever she becomes a member of said Confederacy, turn over to said Confederate States all the public property, naval stores and munitions of war, of which she may then be in possession, acquired from the United States (excepting the public lands) on the same terms and in the same manner as the other

States of said Confederacy have done in like cases.

Article 4. All expenditures for the prosecution of the existing war incurred by the State of Missouri, from and after the date of the signing of this convention, shall be met and provided for by the Confederate States.

Article 5. The alliance hereby made between the said State of Missouri and the Confederate States shall be offensive and defensive, and shall be and remain in force during the continuance of the existing war with the United States, or until superseded by the admission of said State into the Confederacy, and shall take effect from the date thereof, according to the provisions of the third section of the aforesaid act, approved August 20th, 1861.

In faith whereof, we, the Commissioners of the State of Missouri, and of the Confederate States of America, have signed and sealed these presents.

Done, in duplicate, at the city of Richmond, on the 31st day of October, in the year of our Lord one thousand eight hundred and sixty-one.[260]

KENTUCKY

Thirteenth State: November 20, 1861—Kentucky's Ordinance of Secession
(Note: only a portion of Kentucky seceded)

Whereas, the Federal Constitution, which created the Government of the United States, was declared by the framers thereof to be the supreme law of the land, and was intended to limit, and did expressly limit, the powers of said Government to certain general specified purposes, and did expressly reserve to the States and people all other powers whatever, and *the President [Lincoln] and Congress have treated the supreme law of the Union with contempt, and usurped to themselves the power to interfere with the rights and liberties of the States and the people, against the express provisions of the Constitution, and have thus substituted for the highest forms of rational liberty and Constitutional Government a central despotism, founded upon the ignorant prejudices of the masses of Northern society, and instead of giving protection, with the Constitution, to the people of fifteen States of the Union, have turned loose upon them the unrestrained and raging passions of mobs and fanatics; and because we now seek to hold our liberties, our property, our homes and our families, under the protection of the reserved powers of the States, have blockaded our ports, invaded our soil and waged war upon our people, for the purpose of subjugating us to their will.*

And whereas, our own honor and our duty to posterity demand that we shall not relinquish our own liberty, and shall not abandon the rights of our descendants and the world to the inestimable blessings of Constitutional Government; therefore,

Be it ordained, that we do hereby forever sever our connection with the Government of the United States, and in the name of the people we do hereby declare Kentucky to be *a free and independent State, clothed with all the power to fix her own destiny and to secure her own rights and liberties.*

And whereas, *the majority of the Legislature of Kentucky have violated their most solemn pledges made before the election, and deceived and betrayed the people; have abandoned the position of neutrality assumed by themselves and the people, and invited into the State the organized armies of Lincoln; have abdicated the Government in favor of the military despotism which they have placed around themselves, but cannot control, and have abandoned the duty of shielding the citizen with their protection; have thrown upon our people and the State the* horrors and ravages of war, instead of attempting to preserve the peace; and have voted men and money for the war waged by the North for the destruction of our constitutional rights; have violated the express words of the Constitution by borrowing five millions of money for the support of the war without a vote of the people; have permitted the arrest and imprisonment of our citizens, and transferred the constitutional prerogatives of the Executive to a military commission of partisans; have seen the writ of habeas corpus suspended without an effort for its preservation, and permitted our people to be driven in exile from their homes; have subjected our property to confiscation, and our persons to confinement in the penitentiary as felons, because we may choose to take part in a contest for civil liberty and Constitutional Government, against a sectional majority waging war against the people and institutions of fifteen States of the old Federal Union, and have done all these things deliberately, against the warnings and voices of the Governor and the solemn remonstrances of the minority in the Senate and House of Representatives; therefore,

Be it further ordained, that *the unconstitutional edicts of a factious majority of a Legislature, thus false to their pledges, their honor and their interests, are not law, and that such a Government is unworthy of the support of a brave and free people*, and we do hereby declare that the people are absolved from all allegiance to said Government, and have the right to establish any Government, which to them may seem best adapted to the preservation of their rights and liberties.

PLAN OF PROVISIONAL [KENTUCKY] GOVERNMENT

Section 1. The supreme Executive and Legislative power of the Provisional Government of this Commonwealth hereby established, shall be vested in a Governor and ten Councilmen, one from each of the present Congressional districts, a majority of whom shall constitute a quorum to transact business; the Governor and Councilmen to be elected by the members of this Convention, in such manner as this Convention may prescribe.

Sec. 2. The Governor and Council are hereby in vested with full power to pass all laws necessary to effect the object contemplated by the formation of the Government. They shall have full control of the army and navy of this Commonwealth, and the militia thereof.

Sec. 3. No law shall be passed, or act done, or appointment made, either civil or military, by the Provisional Government, except with the concurrence of a majority of the Council and approval of the Governor, except as hereinafter specially provided.

Sec. 4. In the case of a vacancy in the gubernatorial office, occasioned by death, resignation or any other cause, the Council shall have power to elect a Governor, and his successor, who shall not, however, be a member of their body.

Sec. 5. The Council hereby established shall consist of one person selected from each Congressional district in the State, to be chosen by this Convention, who shall have power to fill all vacancies from any cause from the district in which such vacancy shall occur.

Sec. 6. The Council shall have power to pass any acts which they may deem essential to the preservation of our liberty and the protection of our rights, and such acts, when approved by the Governor, shall become law, and as such, shall be sustained by the courts and other departments of the Government.

Sec. 7. The Governor shall nominate and, by and with the advice and consent of the Council, appoint all judicial and executive and other officers necessary for the enforcement of law and the protection of society, under the extraordinary circumstances now existing, who shall continue in office during the pleasure of the Governor and Council, or until the establishment of a Permanent Government.

Sec. 8. The Governor shall have power, by and with the consent and advice of the Council, to conclude a treaty with the Confederate States of America, by which the State of Kentucky may be admitted as one of said Confederate States, upon an equal footing in all respects with the other States of said Confederacy.

Sec 9. Three Commissioners shall be appointed by this Convention to the Government of the Confederate States of America, with power to negotiate and treat with said Confederate States for the earliest practicable admission of Kentucky into the Government of said Confederate States of America, who shall report the result of their mission to the Governor and Council of this Provisional Government, for such future action as may be deemed advisable; and should less than the full number attend, such as may attend may conduct such negotiation.

Sec. 10. So soon as an election can be held, *free from the influence of the armies of the United States*, the Provisional Government shall provide for the assembling of a Convention to adopt such measures as may be necessary and expedient for the restoration of a Permanent Government. Said Convention shall consist of one hundred delegates, one from each representative district in the State, except the counties of Mason and Kenton, each of which shall be entitled to two delegates.

Sec. 11. An Auditor and Treasurer shall be appointed by the Provisional Government, whose duties shall be prescribed by law, and who shall give bond, with sufficient security, for the faithful discharge of the duties of their respective offices, to be approved by the Governor and Council.

Sec. 12. The following oath shall be taken by the Governor, members of the council, judges and all other officers, civil and military, who may be commissioned and appointed by this Provisional Government:

> I, _____, do solemnly swear, or affirm, in the presence of Almighty God and upon my honor, that I will observe and obey all the laws passed by the Provisional Government of Kentucky, so help me God.

Sec. 13. The Governor shall receive as his salary, two thousand dollars per annum, and the Councilmen five dollars per diem while in session, and the salary of the other officers shall be fixed by law.

Sec. 14. The Constitution and laws of Kentucky not inconsistent with the act of this Convention and the establishment of this Government, and the laws which may be enacted by the Governor and Council, shall be the laws of this State.

Sec. 15. Whenever the Governor and Council shall have concluded a treaty with the Confederate States for the admission of this State into the Confederate Government, the Governor and Council shall elect two Senators and provide by law for the election of members of the House of Representatives in Congress.

Sec. 16. The Provisional Government, hereby established, shall be located at Bowling Green, Kentucky, but the Governor and Council shall have power to meet at any other place that they may consider appropriate. Done at Russelville, in the State of Kentucky, this 20th day of November, in the year of our Lord, 1861.[261]

4

THE HISTORY BEHIND THE SECESSION ORDINANCES

ONE OF THE MAIN REASONS the Secession Ordinances and their associated documents are so widely misunderstood is, as we have seen, because the average person has no awareness of the long and complex history behind them. Instead, they are read literally and in isolation, and thus out of context. Worse still, they are viewed through the lens of presentism (judging the past based on today's values), as if they were written by 21st-Century Southerners. Those who promote this fault-ridden interpretation do not understand how dissimilar the world was in the 1860s, or how differently our Victorian ancestors viewed the government, the Constitution, secession, and slavery.

Thanks to the willful misrepresentations of the agenda-driven Left-wing, which has thoroughly rewritten, bowdlerized, refashioned, and edited American Civil War history to fit its progressive ideology, the sin of presentism is today nearly universal. Those who knowingly engage in presentism are beyond redemption. The unwitting victims of presentism, however, are a different matter. Such individuals are not entirely at fault for misunderstanding Lincoln's War, for our Liberal-run education system and media have suppressed the truth and replaced it with their own revisionist fake history.

In this chapter I will bring back the buried facts so that the intelligent, open-minded, intellectually curious reader can reeducate himself or herself on one of the most significant facets of American history: the Southern Secession Ordinances. To accomplish this we must first understand the history behind them.

★ FACT: NONE OF THE 13 ORDINANCES MENTION THE WORD "SLAVERY"

If one is to believe the fake history of Liberal historians, "slavery is the only issue discussed" in the 13 Secession Ordinances, and their authors give this as "the sole justification" for leaving the Union.

Contrary to this overt disinformation, however, the word "slavery" does not appear in any of the ordinances. Why? Because, as I make quite clear throughout this book, neither Lincoln's War or the secession of the Southern states had anything directly to do with slavery.

★ FACT: THE NORTH INVENTED FALSE TERMS FOR DIXIE IN ORDER TO MISLEAD THE PUBLIC & BESMIRCH THE SOUTH

The ordinances do make reference to the "slaveholding states" and to "anti-slavery sentiment." However, in the 1860s the term "slaveholding states" was merely a euphemism for the conservative South, while "anti-slavery sentiment" was a euphemism for the anti-South views held by Yankee Liberals. Thus these terms, in the context of their 19th-Century *Southern* milieu, were innocent enough.

Yankee slave owners visiting the slaves on their Rhode Island plantation. In the Old North slaves were made slaves for life. In the Old South slaves, known more accurately as servants, could purchase their freedom at any time—just one of the many differences between Southern servitude and Northern slavery.

Modern South-loathing Liberals, however, have literalized them, altering the meaning of "slave states" (or "slaveholding states") and "free states" (or "non-slaveholding states"), an effort to cast aspersion on the kind and noble people of Dixie. Indeed, the *modern Left-wing* use of the anti-South term "slaveholding states" must rank as one of the greatest scams in history, for up until the late 1700s, the North, the veritable birthplace of American slavery,[262] had far more slaves than the South.[263] It was at this time that the racist Yankee began to find the presence of Africans in his midst "disgusting"[264] and slavery itself unprofitable,[265] and so he began pushing the institution southward—on, it should be emphasized, a largely uninterested populace.[266]

By the time of the Civil War there were still an estimated 500,000 to 1 million black slaves in the North.[267] The Union army itself possessed some 315,000 slave owners, as opposed to only 200,000 in the Confederate military.[268] More important facts you will not find in any mainstream history book.

★ FACT: THE SOUTH WAS NOT "PRO-SLAVERY" BUT "PRO-CHOICE" CONCERNING SLAVERY
The truth is that the South was not "pro-slavery," but rather "pro-choice" when it came to the institution. What she really desired was for the individual states, not the federal government, to be able to decide whether to allow or prohibit slavery within their own borders.

Put another way, Southern Conservatives (the Democrats in the 1860s) were never interested in trying to "extend" slavery, as Northern Liberals (the Republicans in the 1860s) have always charged. *They were states' righters seeking to have a law put in place that would leave the decision up to the people of each individual state.*[269]

For example, under the administration of Conservative U.S. President Franklin Pierce the government's policy toward the states and slavery remained not pro-slavery, but pro-choice. The Kansas-Nebraska Act, which passed on May 30, 1854, admitted these territories as states with or without slavery, "as their constitutions might prescribe, at the time of admission, and repealed the Missouri Compromise of 1850, by declaring it"

> inconsistent with the principle of non-intervention by Congress with slavery in the States and Territories, as recognized by the legislation of 1850, commonly called The Compromise Measures, it being the true intent and meaning of this act, not to legislate slavery into any State or Territory nor to exclude it therefrom, but to *leave the people thereof perfectly free to form and regulate their domestic institutions in their own way, subject only to the Constitution of the United States.*[270]

Right up to the War period the South was still voting against doing anything to try and "preserve slavery," including attempting to force it on the states. Indeed, they went in the opposite direction. "Take slavery or leave it. It is a pro-choice, individual state issue," they consistently asserted. Two instances from this time period are instructive.

The first occurred during the South Carolina State Convention in April 1860, at Columbia. Here, after reaffirming several earlier Democratic (Conservative) platforms, the convention added that

> prior to the formation of a state constitution and admission to the Union, *a territorial government had no power to abolish or exclude slavery either by direct or unfriendly legislation.*[271]

That same month the National Democratic (Conservative) Convention met at Charleston, South Carolina, where

> the majority report of the platform committee, satisfactory to the South—providing for the protection of slavery in the territories by Congress—had been rejected, by vote of the Convention, for the minority, Douglas, or northern platform—*leaving the slavery question to the people of the territories.*[272]

This "non-interventionist" doctrine was

> interpreted to mean that *Congress could not legislate slavery out of the territories, and it would be folly to insist on positive protection of slavery in the territories by Congress* in view of the fact that if the territory were suited to slavery, slavery would live and nourish, while if the territory were not suited to slavery it was folly to quibble over the abstract right to carry slaves there.[273]

Long after the War, Jefferson Davis confirmed the South's pro-choice position on slavery, saying:

> One of the incidents that led to our withdrawal from the Union was the apprehension that it was the intention of the United States Government to violate *the constitutional right of each State* to adopt and maintain, *to reject or abolish slavery, as it pleased.*[274]

From these examples alone it is obvious that the Old South's focus was always primarily on state sovereignty and states' rights, not slavery—either spreading it or saving it. This is why Georgia statesman Robert A. Toombs declared that "if the South cannot find security for our constitutional rights in the Union, then the only course of action is to leave the Union."²⁷⁵

Typical Northern-slanted, historically inaccurate map showing the "Free States" in the North and the "Slave States" in the South. Such Yankee terminology, meant to turn public opinion against the South, was, unfortunately picked up by unwary Southern writers, reinforcing the falsehoods behind these terms. The so-called "free states" were actually *slavery prohibited states*, while the so-called "slave states" were actually *slavery optional states*. In other words, they were opposite in meaning from what their falsified names suggest.

★ FACT: SOUTH CAROLINA'S "DECLARATION OF CAUSES" MENTIONS "SLAVES" & "SLAVERY," BUT *ONLY* IN THEIR RELATIONSHIP TO THE CONSTITUTION

It is true that South Carolina's "Declaration of Causes Which Induced Her Secession from the Federal Union"—written on December 24, 1860, four days after her Secession Ordinance—makes a number of references to slaves and slavery. These are always in relation to the law, however, and more specifically constitutional law, which, let us remember, permitted slavery in every state of the Union at the time.

The main concern here was not whether the South would be able to continue practicing slavery or not. The home of the American abolition movement, she had been trying to rid herself of the institution for centuries.²⁷⁶ Rather, as the document itself says, the South's concern was over "the subversion of the Constitution" by those Liberals who were using blacks as little more than unwitting pawns in a cruel political game that was meant to inflict slander and suffering on the South; the same method used by radical Liberals on the South today.

As further evidence that slavery was never the focus of the seceding states, consider the massive *Journal of the Convention of the People of South Carolina*, which covers a three year period, from 1860 to 1862. It is nearly 900 pages long, and yet it only mentions the word "slavery" 14 times and the word "slave" 20 times; and in each of these cases these words are only used in relation to the Constitution, states' rights, constitutional law, and the many difficulties that arise when a pro-choice slavery region (in this case the South) and a no-choice abolition region (the North) are forced to live together under a government that favors the no-choice option.[277]

Southern Senator Thomas L. Clingman wisely advised resisting the policies of Abraham Lincoln, one of the most ardent anti-American Liberals to ever occupy the Oval Office.

As with the *Journal*, the entire point of South Carolina's "Declaration of Causes" was straightforward: if Liberal Lincoln and his left-wing followers were willing to ignore the Constitution on the matter of slavery, they might be willing to ignore it on other issues as well, including the rights of the individual states and the limited rights granted to the central government under Amendments Nine and Ten. In short, *the chief concern in Dixie was self-government, the sovereignty of each state*, which, in turn, automatically prohibited the national government from interfering in state, county, and city issues that are already covered by the Constitution. As nullification (in which a state may repeal or counteract a federal law) had been earlier tried by the Southern states (primarily under John C. Calhoun) without success, the only recourse left was secession.[278] (Let us note here that while, in 1833, President Andrew Jackson managed to overturn the idea of nullification before it could become law,[279] Northern Liberals continued to practice nullification right into the Civil War period by ignoring and even overturning constitutional laws regarding slavery.)[280] Thus on December

4, 1860, North Carolina Senator Thomas L. Clingman made these statements before the U.S. Senate:

> My purpose was not so much to make a speech as to state what I think is *the great difficulty*; and that is that *a man has been elected because he has been and is hostile to the South.* It is this that alarms our people; and I am free to say, as I have said on the stump this summer repeatedly, that if an election were not resisted, either now or at some day not far distant the Abolitionists would succeed in abolishing slavery all over the South.
>
> Now, as to this idea of gentlemen waiting for overt acts. Why, sir, if the fugitive-slave law had been repealed without these occurrences it could not have produced half the excitement in the country. Men would have said: "We have gotten back very few negroes under it; its repeal merely puts us where we were ten years ago." Again, if you were to abolish slavery in this District it would be said: "There are only a few thousand slaves here; that is a small matter; are you going to disturb this great Union just for the sake of a few thousand slaves?" It is said, however, by some persons, that we are to submit until revolution is more tolerable than the acts of which we complain. *That was not the policy of our revolutionary fathers. Nobody supposes that the tea tax or the stamp tax was an oppressive measure in itself. They saw, however, that if they were submitted to, in time oppression would be practised, and they wisely resisted at the start.*[281]

The South's fears concerning the North's potential for lawlessness turned out to be absolutely correct. Liberal Lincoln and his left-wing cronies went on to commit a record number of war crimes, the likes which America has never seen before or since.

★ **FACT: SLAVERY WAS ONLY AN ISSUE BECAUSE NORTHERN RADICALS (EXTREME LIBERAL YANKEE ABOLITIONISTS) INTENTIONALLY MADE IT INTO ONE**
Slavery was clearly *not* the focal point of either the Secession Ordinances or the War. We will recall the words of the highest leader in the Union, President Abraham Lincoln:

> My paramount object in this struggle is to save the Union, and is not either to save or to *destroy slavery. If I could save the Union without freeing any slave I would do it.*[282]

The Confederacy's highest leader, President Jefferson Davis, echoed this, saying:

We are not fighting for slavery. *We are fighting for independence.*[283]

Why then do our mainstream history books claim that slavery was the foundation of both Southern secession and the War? Because the ideological Republicans (the Liberals at the time) decided that this would be the perfect issue by which to justify their war. They believed, wrongly as it turned out, that the majority of Americans would be more sympathetic to a war on the South if it was presented as a *moral* conflict rather than a *political* one. This is why halfway through the conflict Lincoln pretended to switch its character (though not its purpose) from "preserving the Union" to abolishing slavery.[284]

The truth came out later, however, when, in 1862, during a private conversation, Lincoln told U.S. Interior Department official T. J. Barnett that his secret motivation for invading the South was "subjugation."[285] The word slavery never came up.

During Lincoln's First Inaugural Address, shown here, he promised not to interfere with slavery, adding that he had no right or desire to do so. Nevertheless, the ignorant, the deceptive, and the puerile continue to tell us that Lincoln's War was "fought over slavery."

★ FACT: IN HIS FIRST INAUGURAL ADDRESS LINCOLN PROMISED NOT TO INTERFERE WITH SOUTHERN SLAVERY

But the South did not fall for this charade, and neither did Europe—and neither did many Northerners. For one thing, as we have seen, Lincoln had promised not to disturb slavery in his First Inaugural Address on March 4, 1861. Only the president himself assumed that by 1863 no one would remember these infamous words of his:

> *I have no purpose, directly or indirectly, to interfere with the institution of slavery* in the States where it exists. *I believe I have no lawful right to do so, and I have no inclination to do so.* Those who nominated and elected me did so with *full knowledge that I had made this and many similar declarations, and had never recanted them.*[286]

144 ALL WE ASK IS TO BE LET ALONE

On December 18, 1860, in an attempt to stave off the secession of the Southern states, a proposal was offered to Dixie by politically moderate Kentucky Senator John J. Crittenden (above). The "Crittenden Resolutions" or "Crittenden Compromise," as it was variously called, suggested adding several amendments to the Constitution which would allow slavery to remain permanently untouched in the South, permit its extension beyond the Missouri Compromise of 1850, and enable further strengthening of the Fugitive Slave Laws. Many in Washington genuinely disliked the Crittenden Compromise, and for good reason. Lincoln and his Republican Party (the Liberal party of the day, and in no way connected to today's Republican Party) could not fully support it, as I will discuss in detail, for both self-serving political and racist reasons. The Democrats (the Conservative party of the day) were not tempted to sign it because the South's primary grievance had nothing to do with slavery, but with the Liberal North's numerous constitutional violations, as I also discuss. Due to this general animosity, the Compromise was tabled and defeated in Congress—only to be followed up a few months later by a second attempt known as the "Crittenden-Johnson Resolution," which this time wisely took care to avoid any mention of "slavery" (see following page). What is pertinent to our understanding of the history of Southern secession is that those Yankees who responded negatively to the Senator's first proposal were in the minority. In reality there was a large group of Northerners who supported it; thousands who were fervently "praying for the adoption of the Crittenden Compromise"; Yankees, both politicians and everyday citizens, who were more than willing to permit slavery to continue in order to avoid both secession and war. Among the former group there was William Bigler of Pennsylvania, James A. Bayard of Delaware, John P. Kennedy of Maryland, Henry Wilson of Massachusetts, and most noteworthy, William H. Seward of New York, soon to become Lincoln's secretary of state. The latter group, the public, sent in thousands of petitions supporting the adoption of the Compromise from such states as Vermont, Massachusetts, New York, Indiana, Pennsylvania, Illinois, Wisconsin, New Jersey, Delaware, Maryland, Michigan, Ohio, Minnesota, Iowa, New Hampshire, and Maine, and also Washington, D.C. What we see here, in short, is *the North offering to permanently protect slavery in the South and the South rejecting the offer!* How could this be if the North took up arms to "end slavery," and if "slavery was at the root of Southern secession," as our mainstream history books tell us? The answer is that neither the North or the South were particularly interested in slavery in December 1860, nearly a half year before the start of the War. It only became an "issue" much later, near the end of 1862, when it appeared that the Union was losing ground. It was at this time that Lincoln and his Liberal constituents realized that slavery could be used as an effective political tool and a "moral" weapon to influence public opinion, maintain Union (Liberal) support for the War, and violate the Constitution—by which they hoped to destabilize, divide, and conquer the South. Another Yankee myth exposed.[287]

★ FACT: THE PRO-NORTH 1861 CRITTENDEN-JOHNSON RESOLUTION DOES NOT MENTION SLAVERY
On July 25, 1861, the 37th U.S. Congress unanimously passed the pro-North Crittenden-Johnson Resolution (named after John J. Crittenden and Andrew Johnson).[288] Revealingly, the document does not refer to slavery directly, indicating that in the North the institution had no bearing on the War either way at the time.

Though the resolution was later defeated, it plainly illustrates that Northern Liberals (Yankee Republicans) were largely apathetic toward slavery shortly after the start of the War. The pertinent clause resolves

> that this war is not prosecuted on our part in any spirit of oppression nor for any purpose of conquest or subjugation, nor purpose of overthrowing or interfering with the rights or *established institutions* of those States, but to defend and maintain the supremacy of the Constitution and all laws made in pursuance thereof, and to preserve the Union with all the dignity, equality, and rights of the several States unimpaired; that as soon as these objects are accomplished, the war ought to cease.[289]

In other words, as far as Lincoln and the Union were concerned the War had nothing to do with slavery, inferring that after the conflict ended and the Southern states had returned to the Union, slavery could and would continue to be constitutionally legal across the U.S. As we will see, Lincoln himself would later present this very idea to the South.

★ FACT: NORTHERN LIBERALS WERE TRYING TO INJURE THE CONSERVATIVE SOUTH LONG BEFORE THE CIVIL WAR
Despite such promising declarations as were uttered in the Crittenden-Johnson Resolution, the left-wing plan to cast the Civil War as a fight between "tolerant" Northern abolitionists and "racist" Southern slaveholders was established. It was not a new idea. It was merely a continuation of a far older Liberal Northern movement to defame, humiliate, and economically dominate the Conservative South.

★ FACT: "THE WAR WAS OVER SLAVERY" MYTH WAS INVENTED TO CONCEAL THE TRUTH ABOUT THE CONFLICT
On October 25, 1858, for example, during his "The Irrepressible Conflict" speech, Lincoln's future secretary of state, Liberal William H.

Seward, made the following notorious comment:

> Our country is a theatre, which exhibits, in full operation, two radically different political systems: the one [in the South] resting on the basis of servile or slave labor, the other [in the North] on voluntary labor of free men.[290]

That this is an outrageous misrepresentation of reality can be seen from the above quotes by Davis and Lincoln alone. Indeed, this entire argument is nothing but a straw man, purposefully invented by early American Liberals to divert attention away from the real issue: the South's desire to maintain the original sovereignty of the states (states' rights) and the North's desire to crush that sovereignty into dust.[291]

William H. Seward, another Yankee Liberal who spread disinformation about the South.

★ FACT: THE REPUBLICAN PARTY OF 1860 WAS FOUNDED TO STOP THE SPREAD OF SLAVERY, NOT SLAVERY ITSELF

The Republican Party (Liberal) to which Lincoln belonged (and which is in no way connected to the Conservative Republican Party of Thomas Jefferson or Ronald Reagan)[292] was founded in 1854 for one primary purpose: to stop the spread of slavery. It was never the party's intention to completely abolish slavery, as Lincoln himself testified in his First Inaugural Address. At the time its founders, Liberals, socialists, and communists, were mainly concerned with preventing the extension of American slavery outside where it already existed;[293] and this was only because, being Yankee bigots, they did not want freed Southern blacks moving North, not over concern for black civil rights.[294]

★ FACT: LINCOLN SUPPORTED THE IDEA OF AMERICAN APARTHEID

Nowhere was this white Northern racist attitude more evident than with Lincoln himself. A dyed-in-the-wool white separatist, he was literally obsessed with the idea of American apartheid (the geographical segregation of the races), which is one reason why, when he was a member of the Illinois legislature, he asked for funds to expel all free blacks from the state.[295] This was also the reason he became a manager of the Illinois chapter of the anti-black American Colonization Society—at one time headed by his "beau ideal," Kentucky slave owner Henry Clay.[296]

On September 16, 1859, in a speech at Columbus, Ohio, Lincoln voiced his specific concerns on this subject. If slavery is allowed to spread across the U.S., he said fearfully:

> They will be ready for Jeff Davis and [Alexander H.] Stephens and other leaders of that company, to sound the bugle for the revival of the slave-trade, for the second Dred Scott decision, for the flood of slavery to be poured over the Free States, while we shall be here tied down and helpless, and run over like sheep.[297]

We will note here that none of these statements are true: neither Jefferson or Stephens wanted to "revive the slave trade"; indeed, after forming the Confederacy two years later, one of the first new clauses they added to the C.S. Constitution was a ban on the foreign slave trade.[298] Secondly, Lincoln and his prejudiced Yankee constituents need not have feared a "flood" of freed Southern blacks coming North, for the majority of them had no desire to move to a region known for possessing the most extreme white racism in the country.[299]

★ FACT: WHITE SEPARATIST LINCOLN SUPPORTED THE IDEA OF FORCING AFRICAN-AMERICANS INTO THEIR OWN ALL-BLACK STATE
With visions of millions of freed Southern blacks migrating North to "run over" whites "like sheep," it is not surprising that just two years before he was elected president of the U.S., racist Lincoln began publicly supporting the idea of corralling all African-Americans in their own all-black state—but only if the American Colonization Society's plan for nationwide black deportation proved unworkable.[300]

★ FACT: LINCOLN FOLLOWED A "CONTAINMENT" POLICY IN AN EFFORT TO FORCE BLACKS TO REMAIN IN THE SOUTH
Some from Lincoln's party, trying to stem the panic and reassure fearful Northern whites, turned the situation around, claiming hopefully that a

Southern emancipation would actually create a "mass migration" of Northern blacks *southward* into Dixie. No one believed this, of course, and the North-wide scare continued. Thus, after issuing his fake and illegal Final Emancipation Proclamation (on January 1, 1863), Lincoln tried following a "containment" policy, a method by which he hoped to keep freed slaves "hemmed in," as Stephen A. Douglas put it, across the South.[301] But this, like his so-called "emancipation" itself, turned out to be nothing more than a transparent political maneuver meant to garner support and votes for his reelection in 1864.[302]

★ **FACT: NORTHERN ABOLITIONISTS (RADICAL LIBERALS) WERE A SMALL & BUMPTIOUS MINORITY**

The truth of the matter is that the so-called "antislavery" men and women of the North made up only a loud but tiny fraction of the populace of the region.[303] Abolitionists were, in general, disliked and distrusted in the antebellum North,[304] and the stories of hatred and mob violence against such abolitionists as William Lloyd Garrison of Massachusetts, Prudence Crandall of Rhode Island, and Theodore Weld of Connecticut, not to mention Elijah Lovejoy of Maine (who was murdered by a Yankee anti-abolition mob), are well-known. In truth, the average Yankee did not care about slavery either way, especially *Southern* slavery, and was content to let Dixie handle her own concerns.[305] One group of historians put it this way:

Nosey, trouble-making, Yankee propagandist William Lloyd Garrison was disliked just as much by fellow Northerners for his abolitionist activities as he was by Southerners. Not because he wanted to destroy slavery, but because he was willing to violate the law, including the Constitution, to do it.

> The great majority of the people were opposed to the agitation and strife [abolition] engendered. . . . *The great mass of the people were for preserving the Union as it stood [that is, with slavery as a legal and protected institution]*, and were in favor of suppressing in a lawful way all disorganizing violence, whether North or South.[306]

★ FACT: NORTHERN ABOLITION WAS BASED ON A HATRED & JEALOUSY OF WHITE SOUTHERNERS, NOT A DESIRE TO FORWARD BLACK CIVIL RIGHTS

If Northern abolitionary sentiment was both widespread and based on political or religious conviction, as today's pro-North writers assert, why did a massive antebellum, anti-abolition movement emerge in the North in which anti-slavery advocates were routinely tormented, arrested, beaten, and even killed? It is because abolitionists were seen as troublemakers, dissidents, and agitators working against the ideals of mainstream America, hence the nickname they were given: "Radicals."

That the "Northern abolition movement" was small, unpopular, and generally detested up until 1860 was only natural then, since it

> was mainly the result of social spite, springing from antipathy to the slaves as a race, and antipathy to the masters because they enjoyed a position impossible among northerners. It was because of this basis in social sentiment, rather than in party creeds, that the antislavery movement had such indestructible vitality. This feeling was what made the [Liberal] North now profess to believe in the sacredness of a compromise when the Missouri Compromise was repealed, though they had said nothing of the kind when they broke the Tariff Compromise of 1833. *This was what caused them* with much self-confidence to declare that never again would a slave state be admitted into the Union, and *to believe that they could indirectly practice state interposition against the fugitive slave law, and yet denounce it as treason and rebellion when tried openly by the South.*[307]

★ FACT: THE NORTH TRIED TO STOP SOUTHERN SECESSION OUT OF MALICE & VENGEANCE

Why had Northern Liberals been trying for decades to break apart the Union (e.g., witness the Hartford Convention of 1814-1815), even slandering the Constitution, then pretending to adore it as soon as the Southern states began to leave in 1860? The truth is that

> secession offered a splendid opportunity, or occasion, on which to wreak a little wrath on the slave-holders of the South, on those "incorrigible men-stealers, merciless tyrants, and blood-thirsty assassins," who so richly deserved to die. But it would, of course, be much more respectable to kill them as "rebels and traitors," than merely as slave-holders. Hence, the very [Northern] men who had been foremost and fiercest in preaching the duty of secession and disunion [in the early 1800s], became, all on a sudden, the most clamorous for the blood of secessionists as traitors to "the glorious Union." As the cynic, Diogenes, trampled on the robe of Plato's pride with

a still greater pride; so the abolitionists panted for the blood of "blood thirsty assassins" with a still greater thirst. Hence, more than any other class of men, they insisted that Mr. Lincoln, however reluctant, should "cry havoc, and let slip the dogs of war."

Secession furnished a fine pretext, a glorious occasion, for the forced emancipation of the slaves at the South. Hence, just before Mr. Lincoln publicly declared that he had neither the wish, nor the power, to interfere with slavery in the States, the word privately went forth from a member of his Cabinet, that secession should be punished with the emancipation of the blacks, and with the utter devastation of the South, by fire and sword. This word was, of course, intended for "the faithful." For if, at that early day, such a design had been publicly avowed, it would have filled the North with amazement, horror, and disgust. But has it not been accomplished to the very letter?[308]

★ FACT: MANY NORTHERNERS AGREED WITH THE SOUTH REGARDING THE CONSTITUTION & SLAVERY

Though enemies of the South would rather you not know it, the fact is that a large percentage of Yankees were in agreement with Southerners when it came to obeying constitutional laws concerning slavery. They believed that such rules should be followed, enforced, and even strengthened, whatever one personally felt about the institution.

One of these individuals was Representative Thomas B. Florence of Pennsylvania, who, during a meeting of the House of Representatives on December 4, 1860, recommended a number of amendments be added to the Constitution. Among them were:

Like the majority of Yankees, when it came to slavery Congressman Thomas B. Florence believed that the Constitution should be obeyed until it was changed through the amendment process. Contrary to Northern myth, this view was not "racist" or "pro-slavery." It was the opposite. Practical and compassionate, gradual emancipation would have lessened the economic impact on slave owners, while giving slaves themselves time to adjust to their new lives of freedom.

- Granting the right to hold slaves in all territory south of 36° 30', and prohibiting Congress and the Territorial Legislature from interfering with it therein, or in any other place within the jurisdiction of the United States, without the consent of all the slave States.

- Admitting States into the Union with a population equal to the ratio of representation, *with or without slavery, as their Constitution shall prescribe.*
- Prohibiting any alteration of the present basis of representation—*declaring the slavery question to be one exclusively for each State*; but with proviso that this amendment shall not be construed so as to release the General Government from its obligations to suppress domestic insurrection in any State.
- Giving the right to abolish slavery in the District of Columbia *exclusively to the State of Maryland.*
- Prohibiting any State from passing laws to obstruct the rendition of fugitive slaves.
- Granting the right of transit with slaves through all the States.
- Declaring all slaves brought into any State by permission thereof, and escaping, to be fugitives from labor.
- Prohibiting the African slave-trade, and also prohibiting persons of African descent from becoming citizens.
- Making all acts of any inhabitants of the United States tending to incite slaves to insurrection, penal offences.
- Making the county in which any fugitive slave shall be rescued, liable to pay the value thereof.
- Prohibiting slavery in territory north of 36° 30'.
- Giving returned fugitive slaves a trial by a jury in the place to which they shall have been returned.
- Provides for rendition of fugitives from justice.
- Declaring inviolable the rights of the citizens of any State sojourning in another State.[309]

Hundreds of other South-sympathizing Northern politicians could be added to this list, a list that could just as easily have been written by a Southerner.

In this chapter the incontrovertible truth has been established: reading the 13 Secession Ordinances literally, as well as out of the context of authentic American history, is a fool's errand: dangerous, inaccurate, unethical, and unscientific. Those who continue to do so only put their reputations in peril, while furthering the pandemic view of South-haters as unwholesome anti-intellectuals who fall somewhere between illiteracy and imbecility.

5

THE MOTIVATIONS BEHIND THE SECESSION ORDINANCES

WE HAVE RECORDED THE 13 Southern Secession Ordinances for posterity, and in studying the history behind them we have come one step closer to understanding the forces that drove the Southern states from the Union. We have also examined the initial negative response the South had toward secession prior to Lincoln's immoral, unnecessary, and illegal invasion of Dixie.

In this chapter we will tackle the anti-South movement's claim that "the Secession Ordinances prove that the South seceded for the sole purpose of preserving slavery."

★ FACT: ENEMIES OF THE SOUTH IGNORE AUTHENTIC HISTORY IN ORDER TO PRESENT A NEGATIVE VIEW OF DIXIE
As we have seen, it is the usual practice among South-haters to read and interpret the Secession Ordinances literally, without the slightest bit of knowledge of the many historical, political, and social nuances behind and within them. They are also routinely taken out of context, removed from their time, place, and authors so as to create a false picture; one that portrays the Confederacy in a poor light, as an "inhumane and racist slavocracy." Though there is no proof for this charge, and mountains of evidence against it, this tired old myth continues to circulate among the uneducated—in great part due to Victorian Yankees like Thaddeus

Stevens, a radical South-hater who once arrogantly and ignorantly pronounced that all the South wants is "to have a slave empire."³¹⁰ Pure anti-South propaganda; unfounded, absurd, and demonstrably false.

To correct the numerous Yankee myths surrounding secession, we will now examine the authentic motivations behind the cascade of secessions that occurred across the South in 1860 and 1861. And we will do so using a scientific and wholistic approach to get to the bottom of what the Secession Ordinances actually mean, not what South-haters want them to mean. It is impossible to fully understand why eleven of the Southern states, as well as portions of two others, chose to separate from a Union they had revered up to Lincoln's election without seeing the entire picture.

The number one South-hater of all time, mean-spirited Victorian radical Liberal Thaddeus Stevens of Vermont, did more damage to Dixie's reputation than any other single person, principally through overt slander, erroneous charges, perverse Yankee myths, and outright lies.

★ FACT: AUTHENTIC AMERICAN HISTORY SHOWS THAT SLAVERY WAS NEVER AT THE ROOT OF ANY OF OUR SECESSION MOVEMENTS

An analysis of the many Northern and Southern secession movements during America's 250 history reveals that the root cause was never slavery. Instead, impartial historians have found them all to be solely based on *conflicting economic interests between the South and the North*.³¹¹

For example, we have the New England secession movement of 1814 to 1815, and the Southern secession movement of 1832, neither which were related in any way to slavery, but which were founded on what each side believed to be economic injustices.³¹²

The Southern secession movement of 1860-1861 was no different, but was in fact a continuation of the 1832 movement. Indeed, it derived from a long history of Northern economic abuse, arrogance, and meddling, culminating in the election of a man who promised to be the most abusive, the most arrogant, and most meddlesome Yankee of all: Abraham Lincoln. What this means, in short, is that the secession of the

Southern states and the launching of the Civil War would have occurred whether slavery existed or not—and antebellum Americans predicted this exact scenario.

In 1847 a Southern writer in *De Bow's Commercial Review of the South and West* made the following sagacious comments, accurately prognosticating the foundation of Lincoln's War 14 years later:

> A contest has been going on between the North and South, not limited to slavery or no slavery—to abolition or no abolition, nor to the politics of either Whigs [Liberals] or Democrats [then Conservatives], as such, but a contest for the wealth and commerce of the great valley of the Mississippi—a battle for no principle of government, no right of human freedom in the abstract; but a contest tendered by our Northern brethren, whether the growing commerce of the great West, shall be thrown upon New Orleans, or given to the Atlantic cities. Which shall receive, store, sell and ship the immense products, of that great country, lying between the Appalachian and Rocky Mountains? Shall Boston, New York, Philadelphia and Baltimore do it, or shall our own New Orleans?[313]

★ **FACT: THE SOUTH SECEDED TO HELP RETAIN THE BALANCE OF POLITICAL POWER BETWEEN HERSELF & THE NORTH**

Even anti-South historians have not been able to ignore the obvious economic underpinnings of the War for Southern Independence. In his 1937 book, *American Political and Social History*, Harold U. Faulkner admits that in 1860, with the election of big government, anti-South Liberal Lincoln, the South realized that her political power was shattered, and that now "only secession could save her economic system."[314] Many Yankees in general understood the South's economic concerns, including Liberal U.S. Representative Horace Mann of Massachusetts, who, in March 1850, stated that it is not the fear of losing slavery that worries the South in her dealings with the North. "It is a fear," he noted, "of losing the balance of power, as they call it."[315]

Intelligent Liberal Yankees, like Congressman Horace Mann, were well aware that it was not the proposition of abolition that worried the South, it was the "balance of political power."

This is, of course, precisely the point behind Jefferson Davis' comments before the U.S. Senate in the late 1850s:

Long before Lincoln's War Jefferson Davis and thousands of other Southern statesmen were expressing displeasure over the North's ceaseless and aggressive attempts to "weaken the political power of the Southern states."

What do you propose, gentlemen of the [Liberal] Free-Soil party? Do you propose to better the condition of the slave? Not at all. What then do you propose? You say you are opposed to the expansion of slavery. . . . Is the slave to be benefitted by it? Not at all. It is not humanity [that is, black civil rights] that influence you in the [abolitionist] position which you now occupy before the country.

. . . It is that you may have an opportunity of cheating us that you want to limit slave territory within circumscribed bounds. It is that you may have a majority in the Congress of the United States and convert the Government into an engine of northern aggrandizement. It is that your section may grow in power and prosperity upon treasures unjustly taken from the South, like the vampire bloated and gorged with the blood which it has secretly sucked from its victim.

. . . You desire to weaken the political power of the southern states; and why? Because you want, by an unjust system of legislation, to promote the industry of the New England states, at the expense of the people of the South and industry.[316]

★ **FACT: THE NORTHERN-IMPOSED TARIFF WAS THE MAIN REASON FOR SOUTHERN SECESSION**
Though South-loathers will not admit it, the North's burdensome tariffs, which Yankees had been unfairly imposing on the South for decades, had long been the chief grievance in Dixie. As such, the North's dishonest, inequitable, biased treatment of the South, as shown by her exceptionally high taxes on Southern imports and exports, was one of Dixie's chief motivations for secession. South Carolina Conservative Robert B. Rhett, in fact, made this exact declaration on December 24, 1860, the same day his state published its manifesto justifying its departure from the Union.[317]

This fact was well-known at the time, not only in the South but across the Atlantic Ocean as well. In 1862, during a session in the British

House of Commons, for example, when uninformed Liberal statesman William E. Forster charged that "there is no question that slavery was the cause of the American Civil War," he was rightfully shouted down by cries of "no, no, it was the tariff!"[318]

★ **FACT: THE LIBERALS' "AMERICAN SYSTEM" JUSTIFIED HIGHER TAXES ON THE CONSERVATIVE SOUTH**
Another impetus for Southern secession was the wrongly and deceptively named "American System," elaborated and promoted by Liberal Kentuckian and slave owner Henry Clay. Known today as "crony capitalism," the American System was the Victorian Liberal's effort to install big government at Washington, an industrial empire that would economically benefit the industrial North but economically injure the agricultural South.[319] Naturally, as Fowler notes, the Southern states

Liberal Southerner Henry Clay was the great instigator behind the wholly un-American "American System," a big government plan to stifle conservatism and install the Left in the seat of power at Washington, D.C.

became very hostile to the strangely so-called "American system," which they viewed as *adopted to enrich Northern manufacturers, and exalt to office its patrons*. From the increasing demands of manufacturers, they came to regard the tariff for protection as a "daughter of the horse-leech which cries 'Give, give.'"

It was not strange that the Southern States should have the same repugnance to Federal legislation in 1828, which imposed ruinous burdens upon their agricultural industry, which the Northern States manifested during and some years before the war of 1812, towards Federal legislation, which imposed severe restrictions upon their commerce. However injudicious, *it is not strange that they should look to nullification or secession as a relief from what they deemed unconstitutional burdens, just as some of the Northern States then did*.

Northern manufacturers, like Northern men generally, were not acquainted with the agricultural interests of the South; just as Southern planters were not acquainted with Northern interests. *They did not apprehend the real operation of the tariff upon the planting States. Politicians and manufacturers persuaded themselves that they understood the interests of the South better than Southern men did. They seriously attempted in Congress, in editorials, and in conversation, to show that it was for the benefit of Southern planters that they should pay high duties to the Government, or high prices to Northern manufacturers. They wrote or talked as if the Northern States were justified in forcing upon the South a high tariff for its benefit.*[320]

★ FACT: SOUTHERN SECESSION WAS A FORM OF RESISTANCE TO YANKEE BULLYING

No one likes to be harassed or tormented by a bully. The immediate response is resistance, and this is what the Southern Secession Ordinances represent: the resistance of the Southern states to a Northern bully trying to force Northern ideas on them. U.S. President Woodrow Wilson put the matter this way:

Before Mr. Lincoln was inaugurated seven southern States had withdrawn from the Union, and revolution was upon the country. The southern leaders of the extreme school of state rights and the doctrine of the Dred Scott case had consciously, avowedly staked everything upon the election, and accepted the result as conclusive of what self-respect and political exigency demanded of them. *They looked upon this coming into power of the men of a minority which had set itself to check slavery and to shut the slave-holding States in, in order that they might be thrust from their place in the politics of the nation, as a thing fatal to the very principles of the partnership formed in those first days when the constitution had been framed, and accepted as a pledge of equality between the States. The Republican party [the Liberal party of the day] had, indeed, always and with all proper emphasis disavowed any wish or intention to lay any hand of molestation or change upon the domestic institutions of the South itself.* The anti-slavery men who were abolitionists were little more numerous in 1860 than they had been in 1840, and those who spoke for the Republicans vehemently disclaimed all alliance or sympathy with them. But, though they did not mean to lay the axe to the root of the tree, the partisans of Mr. Lincoln did mean to gird it about and let it die where it stood, as one of the senators from Louisiana passionately told them. They meant by law and force to keep slavery from getting any growth or outlet whatever. They meant also to nullify, if they could not repeal, the laws whose adoption the constitution commanded for the apprehension and return of runaway slaves, and put the whole system of slavery, so far as they might within the formal limits of the fundamental law, beyond the recognition or countenance

Liberal Southerner U.S. President Woodrow Wilson sympathized with his region, readily acknowledging that secession was not about slavery, but rather Northern political and social "hostility towards the South."

of federal statute. *Their creed and their actions alike were compounded of hostility towards the South; and the challenge of their success was direct and unmistakable. Men of southern mettle could not disregard or decline it.*[321]

★ FACT: SECESSION WAS SEEN BY SOUTHERNERS AS A WAY TO RESOLVE THE MANY EXTREME DIFFERENCES THEY HAD WITH THE NORTH

It is a well established fact that culturally, politically, socially, spiritually, and psychologically, the South and the North have always been overtly dissimilar. Certainly by the time of the founding of the U.S.A. in 1776 the two regions were manifesting sharp cultural, religious, social, and political differences. They were by then like two distinct nations, two nations that some believe would have been better off not uniting to begin with.

As early as the Revolutionary period Americans like Charles C. Pinckney were already commenting on the "strong marks of distinction" between the Conservative religious South and the Liberal atheistic North, sharp contrasts that remain to this day.

Indeed, these differences only became more evident when the Southern and the Northern colonies combined, forming Jefferson's American Confederacy in 1781, later to be known as the United States of America.[322] Southern historian Frank Lawrence Owsley rightly called this merger the union of two completely different business and societal models, two opposing civilizations, in fact.[323] In fact, many believe, myself among them, that the main underlying concern of the Constitutional Convention at Philadelphia in 1787 was not to "improve" on the Articles of Confederation, but to reconcile the enormous social gap between the two sections.[324] In 1788 General Charles C. Pinckney of South Carolina said:

> But striking as this difference is, it is not to be compared to the difference that there is between *the inhabitants* of the Northern and Southern states; when I say Southern, I mean Maryland, and the states southward of her. There we may truly observe that *nature has drawn as strong marks of distinction in the habits and manners of the people, as she has in her climates and productions*. The Southern citizen beholds with a kind of surprise the simple manners of the East, and is too often induced to entertain undeserved opinions of the purity of the

[Yankee] Quaker, while they, in their turn, seem concerned at what they term the extravagance and dissipation of their Southern friends, and reprobate, as an unpardonable moral and political evil, the dominion they hold over a part of the human race.[325]

Far from the Yankee myth that the South and North were equals, homogenous, compatible, even interchangeable, the two were actually separated by a deep cultural chasm that few today, particularly in the North, appreciate. Many modern Southerners too, now accustomed to Northern accents (thanks to the contemporary "Second Yankee Invasion" of the South) have forgotten how divergent the two regions once were.

Prior to the "Civil War" the North was primarily industrial, institutional, urban, nationalistic, liberal, radical, conformist, agnostic, Catholic, progressive, business oriented, and publicly schooled. To the Yankee mind the Union was a purely commercial entity, a single monolithic democracy by which that region could profit through tariffs, bounties, and "sectional aggrandizement."[326]

In contrast to this worldview, known as "Yankeeism" in the South, Dixie was mainly agricultural, personal, rural, localistic, conservative, Constitutional, individualistic, highly religious, Protestant, traditional, family oriented, and home-schooled.[327] To the Southern mind the Union was a moral social order, a "voluntary and a happy union,"[328] a "friendly association" of states held together by "good faith," the "exchanges of equity and comity," and the concept of states' rights.[329]

There were a number of other social and cultural differences, however. As the South saw it, Northerners were discourteous and reserved, while they themselves were well mannered and emotional. Northerners were greedy, shrewd, and materialistic, while Southerners were generous, hospitable, and spiritual. Northern society was prim, proper, and fast-paced, Southern society was relaxed, informal, and leisurely.[330]

Pro tem president of South Carolina's secession convention, David F. Jamison, spoke for most Southerners when, in 1861, he referred to what he saw as the "jealousy," "aggressions," "cupidity," and "avarice of the Northern people . . ." Tired of Yankee meddling, overtaxation, and annoying insults, and violently resenting the North's constant attempt to interfere with local and state affairs, Jamison said: "As there is no common bond between us, all attempts to continue as united will only prove futile."³³¹

Thomas Jefferson was of the same mind. In a letter dated April 22, 1820, he spoke of the Mason-Dixon Line, revealing what few dared consider at the time: one day in the future the South and the North would split apart along this line, severing the Union in a bloodbath of unprecedented and tragic proportions:

In December 1860, as the Southern states were preparing to secede, Georgia Senator Alfred Iverson Sr. remarked on the reason why. "The enmity between the Northern and Southern people," he declared, "is deep and enduring, and you can never eradicate it—never!"

*A geographical line coinciding with a marked principle, moral and political, and conceived and held up by the angry passions of men, will never be obliterated, and every new irritation will make it deeper and deeper. . . . I regret, now, to die in the belief that the useless sacrifice of themselves by the generation of 1776, to acquire self-government and happiness to their country, is to be thrown away by the unwise passions of their sons, and that my only consolation is to be, that I do not live to weep over it.*³³²

Thus it was that many Southerners justified secession as a means to finally escape the centuries-long interference and economic injustices of the arrogant and rigid Yankee, to the Southerner—then and now—as alien as a being from another planet. One of these was Georgia Senator Alfred Iverson Sr., who, in December 1860, made the following statements before the U.S. Senate:

But, sir, I apprehend that when we go out and form our confederacy—as I think and hope we shall do very shortly—the Northern States, or the Federal Government, will see its true policy to be to let us go in peace and make treaties of commerce and amity with us, from which they will derive more advantages than from any attempt to coerce us. They cannot succeed in coercing us. If they allow us to form our government without difficulty, we shall be very willing to look upon them as a favored nation and give them all the advantages of commercial and amicable treaties. *I have no doubt that both of us—certainly the Southern States—would live better, more happily, more prosperously, and with greater friendship, than we live now in this Union.*

> Sir, disguise the fact as you will, there is an enmity between the Northern and Southern people that is deep and enduring, and you never can eradicate it—never! Look at the spectacle exhibited on this floor. How is it? There are the Republican [then Liberal] Northern Senators upon that side. Here are the Southern [Conservative] Senators on this side. How much social intercourse is there between us? *You sit upon your side, silent and gloomy; we sit upon ours with knit brows and portentous scowls.* Yesterday I observed that there was not a solitary man on that side of the Chamber came over here even to extend the civilities and courtesies of life; nor did any of us go over there. Here are two hostile bodies on this floor; and it is but a type of the feeling that exists between the two sections. *We are enemies as much as if we were hostile States.* I believe that the Northern people hate the South worse than ever the English people hated France; and I can tell my brethren over there that there is no love lost upon the part of the South.
>
> In this state of feeling, divided as we are by interest, by a geographical feeling, by every thing that makes two people separate and distinct, I ask *why we should remain in the same Union together? We have not lived in peace; we are not now living in peace. It is not expected or hoped that we shall ever live in peace.* My doctrine is that whenever even man and wife find that they must quarrel, and cannot live in peace, they ought to separate; and these two sections—*the North and South*—manifesting, as they have done and do now, and probably will ever manifest, feelings of hostility, separated as they are in interests and objects, my own opinion is they can never live in peace; and the sooner they separate the better.[333]

Fowler aptly captured the violent animus that existed between South and North during the Victorian period:

> In the progress of years, a thorough alienation of feeling had grown up between large masses at the North, and large masses at the South. Men hate those whom they injure as well as those who injure them. *In the North there was the feeling of contempt mingled with the hatred*, namely contempt for the supposed imbecility and poverty of the South, and its dependence on the North for conveniences and necessaries of life manufactured at the North. There was also a deep moral abhorrence of Southern men as slaveholders, inasmuch as slavery was supposed to include in it "the sum of all villainies." The supposed "barbarism of the South" furnished the staple for speeches, and newspaper articles, and local conversation. There were those, and not a few, who felt that those Southern barbarians were not any better entitled to equal rights in the territories, according to the guarantees of the Constitution, than were the children of Ishmael to the promises made exclusively to the seed of Isaac, or than were the descendants of Esau to a share with the children of Israel in the territories of the Promised Land. In short, *they felt that, as "Saints," Northern men should "inherit the North"; that they should take possession of the common territories by a direct grant from Congress, overriding the Constitution; and that, in due time, under a patent from the Almighty, they should take possession*

of the Southern States, as fast as they could expel the Canaanites from the land.

And, on the other hand, *Southern men repaid, if possible, this Northern hatred with interest; for their hatred was intensified by the fear of those who politically had power to injure them. They distrusted men who claimed to have large powers from the Constitution to injure the South, while in cases in which the Constitution expressly protects the interests of the South, they would place themselves under the subterfuge of a "higher law"* [that is, the eternal cry of the Liberal: "social justice"], *in order to violate their constitutional obligations. They feared and distrusted men who would thus act under the Constitution with their own construction of it, or the higher law with their own construction of it, according as the one or the other would help to enlarge the rights of the North, and lessen the rights of the South. They distrusted, and feared, and hated men, who, under a pretence of the right of petition, and of the freedom of the press, and liberty of speech, would deluge the floor of Congress with insults and slanders, and fill the mail bags with incendiary publications; and send insurrectionary apostles of abolitionism, to kindle the flames of rebellion in the South. They distrusted, and feared, and hated men, sixty-eight of whose representatives had recommended a book* [by Hinton R. Helper], *written to injure Southern institutions protected by the Constitution—men who sympathized with a convict [*John Brown*], and crowned him with sepulchral honors, because he hated slavery; who, thirty years ago, would have been "hung like a felon, and buried like a dog." They distrusted, and feared, and hated men, who ostracized and excluded from office some of the ablest and best men in the Northern States, and put abolitionists in their place, simply upon the suspicion that the former were national and not sectional in their politics*; who had let loose their war dogs to pursue their great man, Daniel Webster, even into his grave; and who, for a season, instead of allowing ministers of the Gospel to preach Christ and him crucified, demanded that they "should preach [Stephen A.] Douglas and him damned"; all because they suspected these two men of favoring the South. They distrusted, and feared, and hated men, *who could aid in passing personal liberty bills, which violate and nullify the Constitution in one of its clauses, and who can vilify and set at nought the decision of the Supreme Court of the United States, which many of them had never even read.*[334]

The anti-South book *The Impending Crisis of the South: How to Meet It*, by South-loathing Southerner Hinton R. Helper, was used by radical Liberals to undermine the Constitution.

★ FACT: SECESSION WAS MEANT TO GIVE THE SOUTH TIME TO FIGURE OUT A WORKABLE SOLUTION TO ENDING SLAVERY
Thanks to meddlesome Yankee, anti-slavery advocate William Lloyd Garrison of Massachusetts, from 1831 on, Northern abolitionists began demanding immediate, complete, and uncompensated emancipation across the South—this coming from New England, the very section of the country that gave birth to both the American slave trade and American slavery, and gave itself over 200 years to finally abolish both![335]

No one likes to be ordered around, including Southerners; especially not by self-righteous, liberal do-gooders such as Garrison, who have no respect for the rights, ways, and mannerisms of other people, but simply want to antagonize and impose their views on those who do not agree with them.[336] North Carolina politician J. Taylor once said:

> We plainly see that men that come from New England are different from us; they are ignorant of our situation; they do not know the state of our country. They cannot legislate for us.[337]

Though the South had been the center of American abolitionism for a half century by this time, she understood that one could not rush the operation. Complete abolition was a complex procedure that had taken other countries years, decades, centuries, to complete, and it would take Dixie just as long, or longer. Thomas Jefferson rightfully likened the delicate process to holding a wolf by the ear. Time was needed to prepare, from designing laws and rules to regulate the process of readying 3.5 million former slaves for a life of freedom, to finding the capital ($4 billion, or $120 billion in today's currency) to compensate former Southern slave owners and establish housing and jobs for Southern freedmen and women.[338]

Thomas Jefferson compared abolition to holding a wolf by the ear. "We can neither hold him, nor safely let him go," he wisely noted. In other words, time would be needed to plan out the hazardous process of Southern emancipation; time the North gave itself, but refused to grant Dixie.

Liberal Yankees demanded "complete, immediate, and uncompensated abolition" across Dixie. But suddenly turning 3.5 million largely uneducated black servants free—after a lifetime of having all their needs taken care of by their owners—would have been a social catastrophe of unprecedented proportions. This is precisely what Northern Radicals wanted, however, which is why they pushed sudden and violent abolition on the South. The result was that by 1867, just four years after the Emancipation Proclamation, some 1 million Southern blacks had perished from starvation, disease, and neglect.

Dixie only asked the North for the same amount of time to develop a functional emancipation program that it had given itself. But this the North would not do. The slavery issue was never purely about slavery or even black civil rights in the North—where white racism has always been far more severe and entrenched than in the South.[339] In truth, Northern Liberals were using slavery as a Yankee sledgehammer to force their progressive ideas on the South. The South resisted, claiming states' rights under the U.S. Constitution. The result was secession; in short, an attempt by the South to buy herself more time to figure out how to abolish the institution in such a way that it would not hurt the Confederacy or her people (both white and black) socially and economically.[340]

This topic was front and center across the South from the 1700s onward, and was discussed by commentators from every part of the globe, not just the U.S. Besides the pure economics of the situation (as mentioned, Southerners had $120 billion in today's currency invested in slavery), Tocqueville, for example,

> demonstrated beyond a doubt, that *the abolition of slavery in the South was a far different problem from, and a far graver problem than, its abolition in the North*. This was true (1) because the climate of the South was far more favorable to slave labor than the climate of the North; (2) because of the nature of the Northern and of the Southern crops, the former requiring attention only at intervals, the latter requiring almost constant attention; (3) because of *the tendency of slavery to move toward the South*.

He pointed out the fact that in 1830 there was in Maine only one negro for every three hundred of the whites; in Massachusetts one negro for every one hundred; in Virginia forty-two for every one hundred; in South Carolina fifty-five for every one hundred. And his conclusion was that *"the most Southern States of the Union cannot abolish slavery without incurring very great danger, which the North had no reason to apprehend when it emancipated its black population. . . . The Northern States had nothing to fear from the contrast, because in them the blacks were few in number, and the white population was very considerable. But if this faint dawn of freedom were to show two millions of men their true position, the oppressors would have reason to tremble."* He disclaimed any sympathy with the principle of negro slavery, but said . . . *"The question of slavery was a question of commerce and manufacture for the slave-owners in the North; for those of the South, it is a question of life and death."*[341]

★ FACT: UNDER THE CONSTITUTION SLAVERY WAS LEGAL IN EVERY STATE IN 1860

At the time of the South's secession, slavery was still legal nationally under the Constitution—and it was confirmed as such by our highest judicial body, the Supreme Court. This fact was spotlighted by the landmark 1857 Dred Scott case in which a black Southern slave unsuccessfully sued for his freedom. In ruling against Scott, the Court

Southern servant ("slave" to Yankees) Dred Scott lost his bid for freedom, not because of white racism, but because, as the Supreme Court reminded the world in 1857, slavery was still legal under the Constitution at the time. The Conservative South defended slavery for the very same reason.

fully sustained every point of the . . . Southern claims as to the status of slavery in the Territories; *it had held that slaves were property in the view of the Constitution; that Congress was bound to protect slave-holders in this property right in the Territories, and, still more, bound not to prohibit slavery or allow a Territorial Legislature to prohibit slavery in the Territories*, and that the Missouri compromise of 1820 was unconstitutional and void. *The Southern Democrats [the Conservatives at the time] entered the election of 1860 with this distinct decision of the highest judicial body of the country to back them.*[342]

Unfortunately, Northern Liberals (then the Republican party) refused to accept the decision of the Dred Scott case as lawful or binding.[343]

166 ～ALL WE ASK IS TO BE LET ALONE

Abraham Lincoln: The left-wing "might is right" president who divided the country, stirred up racism, trampled the Constitution, and sought to destroy the Union.

★ FACT: THE ANTI-CONSTITUTION NORTH VIRTUALLY PUSHED THE PRO-CONSTITUTION SOUTH OUT OF THE UNION

By seceding, the South was merely reasserting the constitutional authority of the states under the Ninth and Tenth Amendments, which tacitly guarantee states rights. By trying to push the South into complete, immediate, and uncompensated abolition, the North was forcing the South to make a choice between staying in the Union and losing states' rights, or seceding and retaining states' rights, which included the power to keep or destroy slavery in the Southern states.

As I have demonstrated, slavery was in no way the cause of the War.[344] However, it helped force the debate over states' rights to the foreground. When the North began violating the Constitution (by, for example, declaring war without congressional approval), and disregarded all attempts at a diplomatic resolution and instead threatened invasion, the South had little choice but to secede; an effort to preserve her land, her people, and America's unique conservative political heritage: state sovereignty, self-government, and personal freedom.

★ FACT: THE SOUTH WISHED TO PRESERVE THE CONSTITUTION, NOT SLAVERY

Self-evidently it was not slavery the independent-minded South was trying to preserve, but the original Constitution of the Founding Fathers, with its implied guarantee of states' rights and self-government, rights that are innate to "free and independent" sovereigns—which is how the states were defined by the Founding Fathers.[345]

This makes abolition merely one of the many accidental results of the War, not the direct or even indirect cause.[346] As we will see, Yankee abolitionism was never the end goal. It was just a political tool by which big government Liberal Lincoln hoped to achieve his own end goal:

enlarging the federal government.³⁴⁷

★ FACT: EVEN AFTER THE SOUTH BEGAN EMANCIPATING HER SERVANTS THE CIVIL WAR CONTINUED
Evidence of this fact took place at the Hampton Roads Conference on February 3, 1865. Here, Lincoln demanded restoration of the Union, while the Southern peace commissioners demanded independence. Neither side would budge and the War continued for another two months. If the conflict had been over slavery, as Northern mythology repeatedly tells us, then it would have ended that day,³⁴⁸ for Davis had already decided to emancipate Southern slaves and enlist them in the Confederate army (this decision was made official by the Confederate Congress just a few weeks later, in March 1865).³⁴⁹

★ FACT: LINCOLN'S ATTACK ON THE SOUTH COULD NOT HAVE BEEN AN ATTACK ON SLAVERY
Patrick J. Buchanan points out that at the time Lincoln declared war on the South, the vast majority of slave owners and their slaves were still part of the U.S. On April 12, 1861, the day the Battle of Fort Sumter began, Virginia, for example, one of the largest slave-holding states, had not yet seceded and was still in the Union. Obviously then, *Lincoln's attack on the South was not an attack on slavery*.³⁵⁰

★ FACT: THE CIVIL WAR WAS A CRISIS OF CONSTITUTIONALISM, NOT A CRISIS OF ABOLITION
In short, the Civil War was not a "crisis of abolition." It was what objective historians call a "crisis of constitutionalism"—which is precisely why the South seceded.³⁵¹ Thus President Woodrow Wilson writes:

> The time came when, early in April, 1861, word was sent from Washington to the governor of South Carolina that Fort Sumter would be reinforced and provisioned against seizure. The message was sent on April 8ᵗʰ. On the 12ᵗʰ fire was opened upon the fort; on the 14ᵗʰ, ere [that is, before] reinforcements could reach them, its little garrison surrendered. On the 15ᵗʰ Mr. Lincoln called, by proclamation, for seventy-five thousand volunteers. Upon that signal, four more southern States seceded: Arkansas on the 6ᵗʰ of May, North Carolina on the 20ᵗʰ, Virginia on the 23ʳᵈ, and Tennessee on the 8ᵗʰ of June. Issue was made up, and all men knew what it meant,—not compromise, but war.

The southern leaders had not at first expected this. They had thought to bring on a constitutional crisis, but not a civil war. They had meant at any hazard to make good their rights under the federal arrangement, and had deliberately resorted to secession because they thought that better terms could be made out of the Union than in it; but they had expected their opponents at the North to come to terms. Their people had followed and upheld them upon that expectation, and would not willingly have followed them on any other. But when the sound of the guns at Sumter was heard it became at once another matter. The thrill of a new purpose and passion shot through the country, north and south. It was with the one side as with the other. The southern people would not at the first choice have deliberately set themselves with open eyes to bring a war of revolution on . . .[352]

If early American Southern Conservative Thomas Jefferson were alive today we can be quite sure that not only would he agree with the secession of the Southern states in 1860 and 1861, he would be spearheading a second Southern secession movement to separate Dixie from the Liberal North once and for all.

6

THE SOUTHERN DEFENSE OF SECESSION

THOUGH ENEMIES OF THE SOUTH like to pretend that there is no evidence justifying the secession of the Southern states in 1860 and 1861, they are, as usual, in error. In fact, volumes of testimony were written, before, during, and after Lincoln's War, all of it carefully penned by those living at the time, most of them highly educated academics and brilliant constitutional, judicial, and legal scholars—from both the South and the North.

In this chapter we will examine a mere handful of these passionate defenses, and in doing so draw that much closer to the truth about Southern secession. Let us begin with the first state to secede.

★ FACT: SOUTH CAROLINA, LIKE THE OTHER SOUTHERN STATES, IDENTIFIED WITH THE AMERICAN COLONIES & THEIR SECESSION FROM GREAT BRITAIN
From the beginning of the formation of the U.S.A., South Carolinians had been among the most ardent leaders when it came to American conservatism, with a strong affinity for rugged individualism, independent thinking, the Constitution, and self-government. After decades of meddling, over-taxation, and general persecution by the North, it is little wonder they were the first to go out of the Union.

What follows is South Carolina's explanation for why she did so.

Clearly and convincingly articulated, it was written on December 24, 1860, just four days after the Palmetto State seceded. It was reported by one of the Confederate Founding Fathers, Christopher G. Memminger.

SOUTH CAROLINA'S DECLARATION OF CAUSES WHICH INDUCED HER SECESSION FROM THE FEDERAL UNION December 24, 1860

Declaration of the Immediate Causes Which Induce and Justify the Secession of South Carolina from the Federal Union.

The People of the State of South Carolina, in Convention assembled, on the 26th day of April, A.D., 1852, declared that *the frequent violations of the Constitution of the United States, by the Federal Government, and its encroachments upon the reserved rights of the States,* fully justified this State in then withdrawing from the Federal Union; but in deference to the opinions and wishes of the other slaveholding States, she forbore at that time to exercise this right. Since that time, these encroachments have continued to increase, and further forbearance ceases to be a virtue.

And now the State of South Carolina having resumed her separate and equal place among *nations,* deems it due to herself, to the remaining United States of America, and to the nations of the world, that she should *declare the immediate causes which have led to this act.*

Another Conservative hero: German-American Christopher G. Memminger of South Carolina, Confederate Founding Father and C.S. secretary of the Treasury.

In the year 1765, that portion of the British Empire embracing Great Britain, undertook to make laws for the government of that portion composed of the thirteen American Colonies. A struggle for the right of self-government ensued, which resulted, on the 4th July, 1776, in a Declaration, by the Colonies, "that *they are, and of right ought to be, free and independent states*; and that, as free and independent States, they have full power to levy war, conclude peace, contract alliances, establish commerce, and to do all other acts and things which independent States may of right do."

They further solemnly declared that whenever any *"form of government becomes destructive of the ends for which it was established, it is the right of the people to alter or abolish it, and to institute a new government."* Deeming the Government of Great Britain to have become destructive of these ends, they declared that the Colonies "are absolved from all allegiance to the British

Crown, and that all political connection between them and the State of Great Britain is, and ought to be, totally dissolved."

In pursuance of this Declaration of Independence, *each of the thirteen States proceeded to exercise its separate sovereignty*; adopted for itself a Constitution, and appointed officers for the administration of government in all its departments—Legislative, Executive and Judicial. For purposes of defence, they united their arms and their counsels; and, in 1778, they entered into a League known as the Articles of Confederation, whereby they agreed to entrust the administration of their external relations to a common agent, known as the Congress of the United States, expressly declaring, in the first article, *"that each State retains its sovereignty, freedom and independence, and every power, jurisdiction and right which is not, by this Confederation, expressly delegated to the United States in Congress assembled."*

South Carolina has a long history of freedom-loving patriotism, as this Revolutionary War painting of the 1780 Battle of Camden shows.

Under this *Confederation* the War of the Revolution was carried on, and on the 3rd September, 1783, the contest ended, and a definitive Treaty was signed by Great Britain, in which she acknowledged the Independence of the Colonies in the following terms:

> "Article 1.—His Britannic Majesty acknowledges the said United States, viz: New Hampshire, Massachusetts Bay, Rhode Island and Providence Plantations, Connecticut, New York, New Jersey, Pennsylvania, Delaware, Maryland, Virginia, North Carolina, South Carolina and Georgia, to be *free, sovereign and independent states; that he treats with them as such*; and for himself, his heirs and successors, relinquishes all claims to the government, propriety and territorial rights of the same and every part thereof."

Thus were established the two great principles asserted by the Colonies, namely: the right of a State to govern itself; and the right of a people to abolish a Government when it becomes destructive of the ends for which it was instituted. And concurrent with the establishment of these principles, was the fact, that each Colony became and was recognized by the mother Country as a free, sovereign and independent state.

In 1787 [at the Philadelphia Convention], Deputies were appointed by the States to revise the Articles of Confederation, and on 17th September, 1787, these Deputies recommended, for the adoption of the States, the Articles of Union, known as the Constitution of the United States.

The parties to whom this Constitution was submitted, were the several sovereign States; they were to agree or disagree, and when nine of them agreed, the compact was to take effect among those concurring; and the General Government, as the common agent, was then to be invested with their authority.

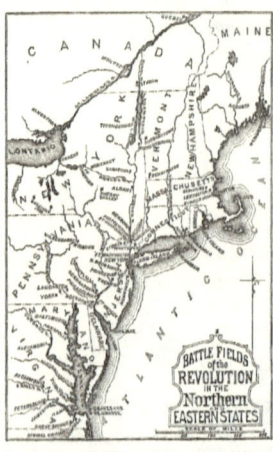

A map of Revolutionary War battlefields in the Northeast. After seceding from England the American Founding Fathers constructed the Constitution as a *mutually obligatory* compact. Thus, if one of the parties to the compact fails to fulfill its constitutional responsibilities (as the North did), it releases the others from any further obligations to that compact. As independent sovereigns they are then remitted to their own judgement as to what course to pursue, including the possibility of secession. This was the correct and legal constitutional reasoning of the South in 1860.

If only nine of the thirteen States had concurred, the other four would have remained as they were—separate sovereign States, independent of any of the provisions of the Constitution. In fact, two of the States did not accede to the Constitution until long after it had gone into operation among the other eleven, and during that interval, they each exercised the functions of an independent nation.

By this Constitution, certain duties were imposed upon the several States, and the exercise of certain of their powers was restrained, which necessarily implied their continued existence as sovereign States. But, to remove all doubt, an amendment [the Tenth] was added, which declared that the powers not delegated to the United States by the Constitution, nor prohibited by it to the States, are reserved to the States, respectively, or to the people. On 23rd May, 1788, South Carolina, by a Convention of her people, passed an Ordinance assenting to this Constitution, and afterwards altered her own Constitution, to conform herself to the obligations she had undertaken.

Thus was established, by compact between the States, a Government, with defined objects and powers, limited to the express words of the grant. *This limitation left the whole remaining mass of power subject to the clause reserving* it to the States or to the people, and rendered unnecessary any specification of reserved rights.

We hold that the Government thus established is subject to the two great principles asserted in the Declaration of Independence; and we hold further, that the mode of its formation subjects it to a third fundamental principle, namely: the law of compact. We maintain that in every compact between two or more parties, the obligation is mutual; that the failure of one of the contracting parties to perform a material part of the agreement, entirely releases the obligation of the other; and that where no arbiter is provided, each party is remitted to his own judgment to determine the fact of failure, with all its consequences.

South Carolina's "Liberty Flag," from 1775.

In the present case, that fact is established with certainty. We assert, that fourteen of the States have deliberately refused for years past to fulfil their constitutional obligations, and we refer to their own Statutes for the proof.

The Constitution of the United States, in its 4th Article, provides as follows:

> "No person held to service or labor in one State, under the laws thereof, escaping into another, shall, in consequence of any law or regulation therein, be discharged from such service or labor, but shall be delivered up, on claim of the party to whom such service or labor may be due."

This stipulation [the Fugitive Slave Law] was so material to the compact, that without it that compact would not have been made. The greater number of the contracting parties held slaves, and they had previously evinced their estimate of the value of such a stipulation by making it a condition in the Ordinance for the government of the territory ceded by Virginia, which now composes the States north of the Ohio river.

The same article of the Constitution stipulates also for rendition by the several States of fugitives from justice from the other States.

The General Government, as the common agent, passed laws to carry into effect these stipulations of the States. For many years these laws were executed. But an increasing hostility on the part of the non-slaveholding States to the Institution of Slavery has led to a disregard of their obligations, and the laws of the General Government have ceased to effect the objects of the Constitution. The States of Maine, New Hampshire, Vermont, Massachusetts, Connecticut, Rhode Island, New York, Pennsylvania, Illinois, Indiana, Michigan, Wisconsin and Iowa, have enacted laws which either nullify the Acts of Congress or render useless any attempt to execute them. In many of these States the fugitive is discharged from the service or labor claimed, and in none of them has the State Government complied with the stipulation made in the Constitution. The State of New Jersey, at an early day, passed a law in conformity with her constitutional obligation; but the current of anti-slavery feeling has led her more recently to enact laws which render inoperative the remedies provided by her own law and by the laws of Congress. In the State of New York even the right of transit for a slave has been denied by her tribunals; and the States of Ohio and Iowa have refused to surrender to justice fugitives charged with murder, and with inciting servile insurrection in the State of Virginia. Thus the constitutional compact has been deliberately broken and disregarded by the non-slaveholding States, and the consequence follows that South Carolina is released from her obligation.

The ends for which this Constitution was framed are declared by itself to be "to form a more perfect union, establish justice, insure domestic tranquility, provide for the common defence, promote the general welfare, and secure the blessings of liberty to ourselves and our posterity."

These ends it endeavored to accomplish by a Federal Government, in which *each State was recognized as an equal, and had separate control over its own institutions.* The right of property in slaves was recognized by giving to free persons distinct political rights, by giving them the right to represent, and burthening them with direct taxes for three-fifths of their slaves; by authorizing the importation of slaves for twenty years; and by stipulating for the rendition of fugitives from labor.

Lincoln literally promised to subvert the Constitution, split the country in half, and northernize Dixie, leaving no question as to the rightness of South Carolina's decision to secede December 20, 1860.

We affirm that *these ends for which this Government was instituted have been defeated, and the Government itself has been made destructive of them by the action of the non-slaveholding States.* Those States have assumed the right of deciding upon the propriety of our domestic institutions; and have denied the rights of property established in fifteen of the States and recognized by the Constitution; they have denounced as sinful the institution of Slavery; they have permitted the open establishment among them of societies, whose avowed object is to disturb the peace and to eloign the property of the citizens of other States. They have encouraged and assisted thousands of our slaves to leave their homes; and those who remain, have been incited by emissaries, books and pictures to servile insurrection.

For twenty-five years this agitation has been steadily increasing, until it has now secured to its aid the power of the Common Government. Observing the forms of the Constitution, *a sectional party [that is, the Republican Party, the Liberal party of that day] has found within that article establishing the Executive Department, the means of subverting the Constitution itself.*

A geographical line has been drawn across the Union, and all the States north of that line have united in the election of a man to the high office of the President of the United States [Lincoln] whose opinions and purposes are hostile to slavery. He is to be entrusted with the administration of the Common Government, because he has declared that that "Government cannot endure permanently half slave, half free," and that the public mind must rest in the belief that Slavery is in the course of ultimate extinction.

This sectional combination for the subversion of the Constitution, has been aided in some of the States by elevating to citizenship, persons, who, by the Supreme Law of the land, are incapable of becoming citizens; and their votes have been used to inaugurate a new policy, hostile to the South, and destructive of its peace and safety. [Note: Liberals have continued this illegal practice into the present day.]

Confederate monument, Magnolia Cemetery, Charleston, South Carolina.

On the 4th March next, this party [again, the Republican Party, the Liberal party at that time] will take possession of the Government. It has announced, that the South shall be excluded from the common Territory; that the Judicial Tribunals shall be made sectional, and that a war must be waged against slavery until it shall cease throughout the United States.

The Guaranties of the Constitution will then no longer exist; the equal rights of the States will be lost. The slaveholding States will no longer have the power of self-government, or self-protection, and the Federal Government will have become their enemy.

Sectional interest and animosity will deepen the irritation, and all hope of remedy is rendered vain, by the fact that *public opinion at the North has invested a great political error with the sanctions of a more erroneous religious belief.*

We, therefore, the people of South Carolina, by our delegates, in Convention assembled, appealing to the Supreme Judge of the world for the rectitude of our intentions, have solemnly declared that the Union heretofore existing between this State and the other States of North America, is dissolved, and that the State of *South Carolina has resumed her position among the nations of the world, as a separate and independent State; with full power to levy war, conclude peace, contract alliances, establish commerce, and to do all other acts and things which independent States may of right do.*[353]

★ **FACT: SOUTH CAROLINA'S "DECLARATION" WAS UNPOPULAR ACROSS THE SOUTH DUE TO ITS EMPHASIS ON SLAVERY**

It is true that this document, "South Carolina's Declaration of Causes Which Induced Her Secession," focuses some of its attention on slaves and slavery.

But this focus was mainly for the benefit of the few large and wealthy slaveholders in the state, the so-called "Aristocratic Planters," a tiny minority of Caucasian males who, in 1860, made up just 0.03 percent of the total white population,[354] and who had neither the real support or the respect of the general Southern population (slave owning had always been viewed as a disreputable though sometimes necessary evil in the South).[355]

In any event, the entire "slavery issue" was nothing but a Liberal Yankee red herring, one meant to distract the world from the North's true ambition: to be "united in its power; and thus carry out its measures of sectional ambition, encroachment and aggrandizement."[356] Though the majority of Southerners and Northerners did not truly care about slavery, Yankee Radicals saw it as the ideal unifying issue to help achieve their goal of consolidating political power at Washington, D.C. and stripping the states of their sovereignty and rights. Confederate General Patrick R. Cleburne correctly noted in early 1865, that slavery

is merely the pretense to establish sectional superiority and a more centralized form of government, and to deprive us of our rights and liberties.[357]

Thus the South Carolina Declaration's emphasis on slavery was greatly misplaced, and was not appreciated by the public, or even by other Southern politicians. Indeed, as we are about to see, when "The People of South Carolina" issued their own "Declaration of Causes," they put the focus squarely back on where it belonged: the North's long history of constitutional violations, its "reckless lust for power," and its outlandish train of abuses and sectional mistreatment of the South.

★ **FACT: MANY CONVENTION MEMBERS THEMSELVES OBJECTED TO SOUTH CAROLINA'S SECESSION DECLARATION FOR PLACING TOO MUCH IMPORTANCE ON SLAVERY**
Though one convention delegate, South Carolina Congressman Laurence M. Keitt (soon to become a Confederate general), admired the speech, saying that slavery "is the great central point from which we are now proceeding," this was, and remained, the minority opinion. This is only logical since less than 5 percent of white Southerners owned slaves.[358] (Compare this figure to that of free Southern blacks, 25 percent of whom were slave owners.)[359]

The majority view was enunciated by convention member and states' righter Maxcy Gregg (also a future Confederate general), who disapproved of the Declaration's emphasis on fugitive slaves:

Like the majority of Southerners, Maxcy Gregg was opposed to any emphasis on slavery as a reason for secession. It was "about the North's violations of the Constitution," he rightly noted.

. . . my objection to the paper is . . . this, . . . that, as a State paper, to go out as a new Declaration of Independence, it is entirely defective and imperfect. It purports to be a declaration of the causes which justify the Secession of South Carolina from the Federal Union. The causes! And yet *in all this declaration not one word is said about the tariff, which for so many years caused a contest in this State against the Federal Government. Not one word is said about the violations of the Constitution in expenditures not authorized by that instrument; but the main stress is laid upon an incomparably unimportant point relative to fugitive slaves, and the laws passed by Northern States obstructing the recovery of fugitive slaves.* Mr. President, if we undertake to set forth a declaration of the causes which justify our Secession, we ought to publish a complete document—a document which might vie in its completeness with that which was adopted in 1776—not that I mean to say that that is a model cause!—that would be to say a good deal too much. This declaration might be put forth by gentlemen who had no objection whatever to *the lavish and unconstitutional expenditures which have been made by the Federal Government for forty years past.* This is not the sort of paper which, in my opinion, ought to go forth to justify our action. A correct designation of this paper would be a declaration of some of the causes which justify the secession of South Carolina from the Federal Union. If it is proper to set forth in a solemn declaration some of the causes, why let the title be altered, and, if the Convention think proper, let it go forth; but if we undertake to set forth all the causes, do we not dishonor the memory of all the statesmen of South Carolina, now departed, who commenced forty years ago *a war against the tariff and against internal improvements, saying nothing of the United States Bank and other measures* which may now be regarded as obsolete. Many of the acts of the non-slaveholding States obstructing the recovery of fugitive slaves have been passed since 1852—I think the majority of them; but *I do not regard it as a matter of any importance.* But when the people of South Carolina, eight years since, declared that the causes then existing fully justified the State in seceding, did they confine themselves to these miserable fugitive slave laws? No! Sir, *I regard it as unworthy of the State of South Carolina to send forth a new declaration now, and in it to say nothing about any other cause justifying their action but fugitive slaves.* I am in favor of laying this report on the table, or recommitting it.[360]

Another convention member, Edmund S. Dargan, was also unhappy with the Declaration's focus on slavery, affirming the real reason the Southern states intended to secede from the Union:

Courtesy to our late Confederates [Yankee Liberals], whether enemies or not, calls for the reasons that have actuated us. *It is not true, in point of fact, that all the Northern people are hostile to the rights of the South.* We have a Spartan [Conservative] band in every Northern State. It is due to them they should know the reasons which influence us. According to our apprehensions *the necessity which exists for our immediate withdrawal from association with the Northern States is that this hostile Abolition party [that is, radical Yankee Leftists] have the control of the Government, and [thus] there is no hope of redress for our grievances.*[361]

★ FACT: OFFICIALLY SOUTH CAROLINA JUSTIFIED SECESSION ON THE NORTH'S CONSTITUTIONAL VIOLATIONS, NOT ON SLAVERY

In the following document, reported by Robert B. Rhett and presented before the Southern Congress, South Carolina addresses her fellow states, entreating them to leave the Union as a unified confederacy.

From the reference to "Slaveholding States" in the title alone, it is clear that there is a concern over the "peculiar institution," and the topic of slavery comes up numerous times. As I devote several chapters to slavery and its relation to secession, I need not go into detail here.

What is important to emphasize is that nowhere in this public paper do "the people of South Carolina" argue that slavery is the sole reason, or even a good reason to secede. *The justification for secession, as was universal across the South, is based on the Liberal North's lack of respect for both the U.S. Constitution and her Southern compatriots:*

> The Address of the People of South Carolina, assembled in Convention, to the People of the Slaveholding States of the United States.
>
> It is seventy-three years since the Union between the United States was made by the Constitution of the United States. During this time, their advance in wealth, prosperity and power has been with scarcely a parallel in the history of the world. The great object of their Union was defence against external aggression; which object is now attained, from their mere progress in power. Thirty-one millions of people, with a commerce and navigation which explore every sea, and with agricultural productions which are necessary to every civilized people, command the friendship of the world. But unfortunately, our internal peace has not grown with our external prosperity. Discontent and contention have moved in the bosom of the Confederacy [the U.S.A.] for the last thirty-five years. During this time, South Carolina has twice called her people together in solemn Convention, to take into consideration the aggressions and unconstitutional wrongs perpetrated by the people of the North on the people of the South.

The house of Southern icon Robert B. Rhett, Beaufort, South Carolina.

> These wrongs were submitted to by the people of the South, under the hope and expectation that they would be final. But such hope and expectation have proved to be vain. Instead of producing forbearance, our acquiescence has only instigated to new forms of aggression and outrage; and South Carolina, having again assembled her people in Convention, has this day dissolved her connection with the States constituting the United States.

The one great evil, from which all other evils have flowed, is the overthrow of the Constitution of the United States. The Government of the United States is no longer the Government of Confederated Republics, but of a consolidated Democracy. It is no longer a free Government, but a despotism. It is, in fact, such a Government as Great Britain attempted to set over our fathers; and which was resisted and defeated by a seven years' struggle for independence.

The Revolution of 1776 turned upon one great principle, *self-government*—and *self-taxation*, the criterion of self-government. Where the interests of two people united together under one Government, are different, each must have the power to protect its interests by the organization of the Government, or they cannot be free. The interests of Great Britain and of the Colonies were different and antagonistic. Great Britain was desirous of carrying out the policy of all nations towards their Colonies, of making them tributary to her wealth and power. She had vast and complicated relations with the whole world. Her policy towards her North American Colonies was to identify them with her in all these complicated relations; and to make them bear, in common with the rest of the Empire, the full burden of her obligations and necessities. She had a vast public debt; she had a European policy and an Asiatic policy, which had occasioned the accumulation of her public debt; and which kept her in continual wars. The North American Colonies saw their interests, political and commercial, sacrificed by such a policy. Their interests required that they should not be identified with the burdens and wars of the mother country. They had been settled under charters, which gave them *self-government*; at least so far as their property was concerned. They had taxed themselves, and had never been taxed by the Government of Great Britain. To make them a part of a *consolidated Empire*, the Parliament of Great Britain determined to assume the power of legislating for the Colonies in all cases whatsoever. *Our ancestors resisted the pretension. They refused to be a part of the consolidated Government of Great Britain.*

The Southern States now stand exactly in the same position towards the Northern States that the Colonies did towards Great Britain. The Northern States, having the majority in Congress, claim the same power of omnipotence in legislation as the British Parliament. "The General Welfare," *is the only limit to the legislation of either; and the majority in Congress, as in the British Parliament, are the sole judges of the expediency of the legislation this "General Welfare" requires. Thus, the Government of the United States has become a consolidated Government; and the people of the Southern States are compelled to meet the very despotism their fathers threw off in the Revolution of, 1776.*

The consolidation of the Government of Great Britain over the Colonies, was attempted to be carried out by the taxes. The British Parliament undertook to tax the Colonies, to promote British interests. Our fathers resisted this pretension. They claimed *the right of self-taxation through their Colonial Legislatures. They were not represented in the British Parliament*, and, therefore, could not rightly be taxed by its legislation. The British

Government, however, offered them a representation in Parliament; but it was not sufficient to enable them to protect themselves from the majority, and they refused the offer. Between *taxation without any representation*, and taxation without a representation adequate to protection, there was no difference. In neither case would the Colonies tax themselves. Hence, they refused to pay the taxes laid by the British Parliament.

And so with the Southern States, towards the Northern States, in the vital matter of taxation. They are in a minority in Congress. Their representation in Congress is useless to protect them against unjust taxation; and they are taxed by the people of the North for their benefit, exactly as the people of Great Britain taxed our ancestors in the British Parliament for their benefit. For the last forty years, the taxes laid by the Congress of the United States, have been laid with a view of subserving the interests of the North. The people of the South have been taxed by duties on imports, not for revenue, but for an object inconsistent with revenue—to promote, by prohibitions, Northern interests in the productions of their mines and manufactures.

There is another evil, in the condition of the Southern towards the Northern States, which our ancestors refused to bear towards Great Britain. Our ancestors not only taxed themselves, but all the taxes collected from them, were expended amongst them. Had they submitted to the pretensions of the British Government, the taxes collected from them would have been expended in other parts of the British Empire. They were fully aware of the effect of such a policy in impoverishing the people from whom taxes are collected, and in enriching those who receive the benefit of their expenditure. *To prevent the evils of such a policy, was one of the motives which drove them on to revolution. Yet this British policy has been fully realized towards the Southern States by the Northern States. The people of the Southern States are not only taxed for the benefit of the Northern States, but after the taxes are collected, three-fourths of them are expended at the North.* This cause, with others, connected with the operation of the General Government, has made the cities of the South provincial. Their growth is paralyzed; they are mere suburbs of Northern cities. The agricultural productions of the South are the basis of the foreign commerce of the United States; yet Southern cities do not carry it on. Our foreign trade is almost annihilated. In 1740, there were five shipyards in South Carolina, to build ships to carry on our direct trade with Europe. Between 1740 and 1779, there were built in these yards, twenty-five square rigged vessels, besides a great number of sloops and schooners, to carry on our coast and West India trade. In the half century immediately preceding the Revolutions from 1725 to 1775, the population of South Carolina increased seven fold.

Early Charleston, South Carolina.

No man can, for a moment, believe that our ancestors intended to establish over their posterity, exactly the same sort of Government they had overthrown. *The great object of the Constitution of the United States, in its internal operation, was, doubtless, to secure the great end of the Revolution—a limited free Government—a Government limited to those matters only, which were general and common to all portions of the United States. All sectional or local interests were to be left to the States. By no other arrangement would they obtain free Government, by a Constitution common to so vast a Confederacy [that is, the U.S.A.]. Yet, by gradual and steady encroachments on the part of the people of the North, and acquiescence on the part of the South, the limitations in the Constitution have been swept away; and the Government of the United States has become consolidated, with a claim of limitless powers in its operations.*

It is not at all surprising, such being the character of the Government of the United States, that it should assume to possess power over all the institutions of the country. *The agitations on the subject of slavery are the natural results of the consolidation of the Government.* Responsibility follows power; and if the people of the North have the power by Congress "to promote the general welfare of the United States," by any means they deem expedient—why should they not assail and overthrow the institution of slavery in the South? They are responsible for its continuance or existence, in proportion to their power. A majority in Congress, according to their interested and perverted views, is omnipotent. *The inducements to act upon the subject of slavery, under such circumstances, were so imperious, as to amount almost to a moral necessity. To make, however, their numerical power available to rule the Union, the North must consolidate their power. It would not be united, on any matter common to the whole Union—in other words, on any constitutional subject—for on such subjects divisions are as likely to exist in the North as in the South. Slavery was strictly a sectional interest. If this could be made the criterion of parties at the North, the North could be united in its power; and thus carry out its measures of sectional ambition, encroachment and aggrandizement.* To build up their sectional predominance in the Union, the Constitution must be first abolished by constructions; but that being done, the consolidation of the North, to rule the South, by the tariff and slavery issues, was in the obvious course of things.

The Constitution of the United States was an experiment. The experiment consisted in uniting under one Government, peoples living in different climates, and having different pursuits and institutions. It matters not how carefully the limitations of such a Government be laid down in the Constitution—its success must, at least, depend upon the good faith of the parties to the constitutional compact, in enforcing them. It is not in the power of human language to exclude false inferences, constructions and perversions, in any Constitution; and *when vast sectional interests are to be subserved, involving the appropriation of countless millions of money, it has not been the usual experience of mankind, that words on parchments can arrest power.* The Constitution of the United States, irrespective of the interposition of the States, rested on the assumption that power would yield to faith—that

The Confederate First National Flag floating over Fort Sumter, Charleston Harbor, South Carolina.

integrity would be stronger than interest; and that thus, the limitations of the Constitution would be observed. The experiment has been fairly made. *The Southern States, from the commencement of the Government, have striven to keep it within the orbit prescribed by the Constitution. The experiment has failed. The whole Constitution, by the constructions of the Northern people, has been absorbed by its preamble. In their reckless lust for power, they seem unable to comprehend that seeming paradox—that the more power is given to the General Government, the weaker it becomes. Its strength consists in the limitation of its agency to objects of common interests to all sections. To extend the scope of its power over sectional or local interests, is to raise up against it opposition and resistance. In all such matters, the General Government must necessarily be a despotism, because all sectional or local interests must ever be represented by a minority in the councils of the General Government—having no power to protect itself against the rule of the majority. The majority, constituted from those who do not represent these sectional or local interests, will control and govern them. A free people cannot submit to such a Government. And the more it enlarges the sphere of its power, the greater must be the dissatisfaction it must produce, and the weaker it must become.* On the contrary, the more it abstains from usurped powers, and the more faithfully it adheres to the limitations of the Constitution, the stronger it is made. *The Northern people have had neither the wisdom nor the faith to perceive, that to observe the limitations of the Constitution was the only way to its perpetuity.*

Under such a Government, there must, of course, be many and endless "irrepressible conflicts," between the two great sections of the Union. The same faithlessness which has abolished the Constitution of the United States, will not fail to carry out the sectional purposes for which it has been abolished. *There must be conflict; and the weaker section of the Union can only find peace and liberty in an independence of the North. The repeated efforts made by South Carolina, in a wise conservatism, to arrest the progress of the General Government in its fatal progress to consolidation, have been unsupported, and she has been denounced as faithless to the obligations of the Constitution, by the very men and States, who were destroying it by their usurpations.* It is now too late to reform or restore the Government of the United States. All confidence in the North is lost by the South. *The faithlessness of the North for half a century, has opened a gulf of separation between the North and the South which no promises nor engagements can fill.*

It cannot be believed, that our ancestors would have assented to any union whatever with the people of the North, if the feelings and opinions now existing amongst them, had existed when the Constitution was framed. There was then no tariff—no fanaticism concerning negroes. It was the delegates from New England who proposed in the Convention which framed the Constitution, to the delegates from South Carolina and Georgia, that if they would agree to give Congress the power of regulating commerce by a majority, that they would support the extension of the African Slave Trade for twenty years. African slavery existed in all the States but one. The idea that the Southern States would be made to pay that tribute to their northern confederates which they had refused to pay to Great Britain; or that *the institution of African slavery would be made the grand basis of a sectional organization of the North to rule the South*, never crossed the imaginations of our ancestors. *The Union of the Constitution was a Union of slaveholding States. It rests on slavery, by prescribing a representation in Congress for three-fifths of our slaves. There is nothing in the proceedings of the Convention which framed the Constitution, to show that the Southern States would have formed any other Union; and still less, that they would have formed a Union with more powerful non-slaveholding States, having majority in both branches of the Legislature of the Government. They were guilty of no such folly. Time and the progress of things have totally altered the relations between the Northern and Southern States, since the Union was established. That identity of feelings, interests and institutions which once existed, is gone. They are now divided, between agricultural and manufacturing, and commercial States; between slaveholding and non-slaveholding States. Their institutions and industrial pursuits have made them totally different peoples. That equality in the Government between the two sections of the Union which once existed, no longer exists.* We but imitate the policy of our fathers in dissolving a union with non-slaveholding confederates, and seeking a confederation with slaveholding States.

Experience has proved that slaveholding States cannot be safe in subjection to non-slaveholding States. Indeed, no people can ever expect to preserve its rights and liberties, unless these be in its own custody. To plunder and oppress, where plunder and oppression can be practiced with impunity, seems to be the natural order of things. The fairest portions of the world elsewhere, have been turned into wildernesses, and the most civilized and prosperous communities have been impoverished and ruined by anti-slavery fanaticism. The people of the North have not left us in doubt as to their designs and policy. United as a section in the late Presidential election, they have elected as the exponent of their policy, one who has openly declared that all the States of the United States must be made free States or slave States. It is true, that amongst those who aided in his election, there are various shades of anti-slavery hostility. *But if African slavery in the Southern States be the evil their political combination affirms it to be, the requisitions of an inexorable logic must lead them to emancipation. If it is right to preclude or abolish slavery in a Territory, why should it be allowed to remain in the States? The one is not at all more unconstitutional than the other, according to the decisions of the Supreme Court of the United States.* And when it is considered that *the Northern States* will soon have the power to make that Court what they please, and that *the Constitution never has been any barrier whatever to their exercise of power*, what check can there be, in the unrestrained counsels of the North, to emancipation? There is sympathy in association, which carries men along without principle; but when there is principle, and that principle is fortified by long existing prejudices and feelings, association is omnipotent in party influences. In spite of all disclaimers and professions, there can be but one end by the submission of the South to the rule of a sectional anti-slavery government at Washington; and that end, directly or indirectly, must be—the emancipation of the slaves of the South. The hypocrisy of thirty years—the faithlessness of their whole course from the commencement of our union with them, show that the people of the non-slaveholding North are not and cannot be safe associates of the slaveholding South, under a common Government. *Not only their fanaticism, but their erroneous views of the principles of free Governments, render it doubtful whether, if separated from the South, they can maintain a free Government amongst themselves. Numbers, with them, is the great element of free Government. A majority, is infallible and omnipotent. "The right divine to rule in kings," is only transferred to their majority. The very object of all Constitutions, in free popular Government, is to restrain the majority. Constitutions, therefore, according to their theory, must be most unrighteous inventions, restricting liberty.* None ought to exist; but the body politic ought simply to have political organization, to bring out and enforce the will of the majority. This theory may be harmless in a small community, having identity of interests and pursuits; but over a vast State—still more, over a vast Confederacy, having various and conflicting interests and pursuits, it is a *remorseless despotism.* In resisting

As proven by his own statements, Lincoln used the slavery issue to consolidate Liberal political power in Washington, D.C., not to help African-Americans.

it, as applicable to ourselves, *we are vindicating the great cause of free Government,* more important, perhaps, to the world, than the existence of all the United States. Nor, in resisting it, do we intend to depart from the safe instrumentality, the system of Government we have established with them, requires. *In separating from them, we invade no rights—no interest of theirs. We violate no obligation or duty to them. As separate, independent States in Convention, we made the Constitution of the United States with them; and as separate independent States, each State acting for itself, we adopted it. South Carolina, acting in her sovereign capacity, now thinks proper to secede from the Union. She did not part with her Sovereignty in adopting the Constitution. The last thing a State can be presumed to have surrendered, is her Sovereignty. Her Sovereignty is her life. Nothing but a clear express grant can alienate it. Inference is inadmissible. Yet it is not at all surprising that those who have construed away all the limitations of the Constitution, should also by construction, claim the annihilation of the Sovereignty of the States. Having abolished all barriers to their omnipotence, by their faithless constructions in* the operations of the General Government, it is most natural that they should endeavor to do the same towards us in the States. The truth is, they having violated the express provisions of the Constitution, it is at an end, as a compact. It is morally obligatory only on those who choose to accept its perverted terms. South Carolina, deeming the compact not only violated in particular features, but virtually abolished by her Northern confederates, withdraws herself as a party from its obligations. The right to do so is denied by her Northern confederates. *They desire to establish a sectional despotism, not only omnipotent in Congress, but omnipotent over the States; and as if to manifest the imperious necessity of our secession, they threaten us with the sword, to coerce submission to their rule.*

Citizens of the slaveholding States of the United States! Circumstances beyond our control have placed us in the van of the great controversy between the Northern and Southern States. We would have preferred that other States should have assumed the position we now occupy. Independent ourselves, we disclaim any design or desire to lead the counsels of the other Southern States. Providence has cast our lot together, by extending over us an identity of pursuits, interests and institutions. South Carolina desires no destiny separated from yours. To be one of a great Slaveholding Confederacy, stretching its arms over a territory larger than any power in Europe possesses—with a population four times greater than that of the whole United States when they achieved their independence of the British Empire—with productions which make our existence more important to the world than that of any other people inhabiting it—with common institutions to defend, and common dangers to encounter—we ask your sympathy and confederation. Whilst constituting a portion of the United States, it has been your statesmanship which has guided it, in its mighty strides to power and expansion. In the field, as in the cabinet, you have led the way to its renown and grandeur. You have loved the Union, in whose service your great statesmen have labored, and your great soldiers have fought and conquered—not for the material benefits it conferred, but with the faith of a generous and devoted chivalry. *You have long lingered in hope over the shattered remains of a broken Constitution. Compromise after compromise, formed by your concessions, has been trampled under foot by your Northern confederates. All fraternity of feeling between the North and the South is lost, or has been converted into hate; and we, of the South, are at last driven together by the stern destiny which controls the existence of nations.* Your bitter experience of the faithlessness and rapacity of your Northern confederates may have been necessary to evolve those great principles of free Government, upon which the liberties of the world depend, and to prepare you for the grand mission of vindicating and reestablishing them: We rejoice that other nations should be satisfied with their institutions. Contentment is a great element of happiness, with nations as with individuals. We are satisfied with ours. If they prefer a system of industry, in which capital and labor are in perpetual conflict—and chronic starvation keeps down the natural increase of population—and a man is worked out in eight years—and the law ordains that children shall be worked only ten hours a day—and the sabre and the bayonet are the instruments of order—be it so. It is their affair, not ours. We prefer, however, our system of industry, by which labor and capital are identified in interest, and capital, therefore, protects labor—by which our population doubles every twenty years—by which starvation is unknown, and abundance crowns the land—by which order is preserved by an unpaid police, and many fertile regions of the world, where the white man cannot labor, are brought into usefulness by the labor of the African, and the whole world is blessed by our productions. *All we demand of other peoples is to be left alone, to work out our own high destinies.* United together, and we must be the most independent, as we are among the most important, of the nations of the world. United together, and we require no other instrument to conquer peace, than our beneficent productions. United together, and we must be a great, free and prosperous people, whose renown must spread throughout the civilized world, and pass down, we trust, to the remotest ages. We ask you to join us in forming a Confederacy of Slaveholding [that is, slavery-optional] States.[362]

★ **FACT: JEFFERSON DAVIS WAS NOT THE FOUNDER OR LEADER OF THE SOUTHERN SECESSION MOVEMENT**
Like America's many other Southern heroes, Lee, Jackson, Forrest, Ashby, Mosby, Stuart, Morgan, Gordon, and Longstreet, to name but a few, Liberals and uneducated Conservatives long ago relegated Confederate President Jefferson Davis to the trash bin of history, causing him to be all but ignored for the past 150 years.

Not only will we traditional Southerners not allow his name to be besmirched, we will continue to proudly preserve his reputation and service as one of America's greatest Conservatives, an honorable statesman we lovingly refer to here in Dixie as "the Patriot of Patriots."

As the C.S.A.'s top leader, and one of America's most intelligent, experienced, and educated individuals, there is no higher authority on the topic of Southern secession than President Davis.

Contrary to Yankee myth, Davis, though a secessionist, was against it without due and urgent cause, just one reason he could not have been the *founder* of the Southern secession movement (which actually began in the 18th Century with Thomas Jefferson). In fact, Davis was chosen to be the Confederacy's first chief executive because he was *not* a radical fire-eater, but was instead well-known for his reasoned and balanced approach to South-North relations. And neither could Davis have been the *leader* of the Southern secession movement of 1860, for it began months before he quit his position as a U.S. Mississippi senator.

★ FACT: JEFFERSON DAVIS DID NOT QUIT THE U.S. SENATE UNTIL AFTER HIS STATE SECEDED

Like nearly every other Confederate citizen, Senator Davis accepted separation when it came, though only as a last and distasteful resort to a hopeless situation: the Northern Liberal's refusal to obey the Constitution or recognize its guarantee of state sovereignty. What follows is his brief but thoughtful speech "on leaving the U.S. Senate," which he gave before his fellow members in January 1861:

Though an advocate of secession Jefferson Davis was no fire-eater. Indeed, he did not leave the U.S. Senate until *after* his home state, Mississippi, seceded a few days earlier on January 9, 1861.

I rise for the purpose of announcing to the Senate that I have satisfactory evidence that the State of Mississippi, by solemn ordinance in convention assembled, has declared her separation from the United States. Under these circumstances, of course, my functions terminate here. It has seemed to be proper that I should appear in the Senate and announce that act, and to say something, though very little, upon it. The occasion does not invite me to go into the argument, and my physical condition will not permit it, yet something would seem to be necessary on the part of the State I here represent, on an occasion like this. It is known to Senators who have served here, that I have for many years advocated, as an essential attribute of State sovereignty, the right of a State to secede from the Union. If, therefore, I had not believed there was justifiable cause—if I had thought the State was acting without sufficient provocation—still, under my theory of government, I should have felt bound by her action. I, however, may say I think she had justifiable cause, and I approve of her acts.

I conferred with the people before that act was taken, and counselled them that if they could not remain, that they should take the act. I hope none will confound this expression of opinion with the advocacy of the right of a State to remain in the Union, and disregard its constitutional obligations by nullification. Nullification and secession are indeed antagonistic principles. Nullification is the remedy which is to be sought and applied, within the Union, against an agent of the United States, when the agent has violated constitutional obligations, and the State assumes for itself, and appeals to other States to support it.

But *when the States themselves, and the people of the States, have so acted as to convince us that they will not regard our constitutional rights, then, and then for the first time, arises the question of secession in its practical application.* That great man who now reposes with his fathers, who has been so often arraigned for want of fealty to the Union, advocated the doctrine of nullification, because it preserved the Union. It was because of his deep-seated attachment to the Union that Mr. [John C.] Calhoun advocated the doctrine of nullification, which he claimed would give peace within the limits of the Union, and not disturb it, and only be the means of bringing the agent before the proper tribunal of the States for judgment. Secession belongs to a different class of rights, and is to be justified upon the basis that the States are sovereign.

The time has been, and I hope the time will come again, when a better appreciation of our Union will prevent any one denying that *each State is a sovereign in its own right*. Therefore, I say I concur in the act of my State, and feel bound by it. It is by this confounding of nullification and secession that the name of another great man has been invoked to justify the coercion of a seceding State. The phrase "to execute the law," as used by General [Andrew] Jackson, was applied to a State refusing to obey the laws and still remaining in the Union.

I remember well when Massachusetts was arraigned before the Senate. The record of that occasion will show that I said, if Massachusetts, in pursuing the line of steps, takes the last step which separates her from the Union, the right is hers, and I will neither vote one dollar nor one man to coerce her, but I will say to her, "God speed!" (Mr. Davis then proceeded to argue that *the equality spoken of in the Declaration of Independence was the equality of a class in political [not social] rights*, referring to the charge against George III for inciting insurrection, as proof that it had no reference to the slaves.)

But we have proclaimed our independence. This is done with no hostility or any desire to injure any section of the country, nor even for our pecuniary benefit, but from *the high and solid foundation of defending and protecting the rights we inherited, and transmitting them unshorn to our posterity*. I know no hostility to you Senators here, and am sure there is not one of you, whatever may have been the sharp discussion between us, to whom I cannot now say, in the presence of my God, I wish you well.

And such is the feeling, I am sure, the people I represent feel towards those whom you represent. I, therefore, feel I but express their desire, when I say I hope and they hope for those peaceful relations with you, though we must part, that may be mutually beneficial to us in the future. There will be peace if you so will it, and you may bring disaster of every part of the country, if you thus will have it. And if you will have it thus, we will invoke the God of our fathers, who delivered them from the paw of the lion, to protect us from the ravages of the bear; and thus putting our trust in God, and our own firm hearts and strong arms, we will vindicate and defend the rights we claim.

In the course of my long career, I have met with a great variety of men here, and there have been points of collision between us. Whatever of offence there has been to me, I leave here. I carry no hostile feelings away. Whatever of offence I have given, which has not been redressed, I am willing to say to Senators in this hour of parting, I offer you my apology for any thing I may have done in the Senate; and I go thus released from obligation, remembering no injury I have received, and having discharged what I deem the duty of man, to offer the only reparation at this hour for every injury I have ever inflicted.[363]

★ FACT: PRESIDENT JEFFERSON DAVIS GAVE AMPLE REASONS FOR SOUTHERN SECESSION

Later, as the ongoing outrages committed by Lincoln and the North continued to mount, President Davis made numerous other comments on secession, recording many of these in his books, in particular, the Conservative classic, *The Rise and Fall of the Confederate Government*. Less than a year after the above speech before the U.S. Senate, and with the War now in its seventh month, Davis addressed a session of the Confederate Congress at Richmond, Virginia, on November 18, 1861. This detailed report on conditions in the Confederacy at the time also includes a number of illuminating justifications for Southern secession:

> The few weeks which have elapsed since your adjournment have brought us so near the close of the year that we are now able to sum up its general results. The retrospect is such as should fill the hearts of our people with gratitude to Providence, for his kind interposition in their behalf. Abundant yields have rewarded the labor of the agriculturist, whilst the manufacturing industry of the Confederate States was never so prosperous as now. The necessities of the times have called into existence new branches of manufactures, and given a fresh impulse to the activity of those heretofore in operation. The means of the Confederate States for manufacturing the necessaries and comforts of life within themselves, increase as the conflict continues, and we are gradually becoming independent of the rest of the world for the supply of such military stores and munitions as are indispensable for war.
>
>
>
> The Confederate Capitol at Richmond, Virginia, 1862.
>
> The operations of the army, soon to be partially interrupted by the approaching winter, have afforded a protection to the country and shed a glorious luster upon its arms through the trying vicissitudes of more than one arduous campaign, which entitle our brave volunteers to our praise and gratitude.

From its commencement up to the present period the war has been enlarging its proportions and expanding its boundaries so as to include new fields. The conflict now extends from the shores of the Chesapeake to the confines of Missouri and Arizona, yet sudden calls from the remotest points for military aid have been met with promptness enough not only to avert disaster in the face of superior numbers, but also to roll back the tide of invasion from the border.

When the war commenced, the enemy were possessed of certain strategic points and strong places in the Confederate States. They greatly exceeded us in numbers, in available resources, and in the supplies necessary for war. Military establishments had long been organized, and were completed. The navy, and, for the most part, the army, once common to both, were in their possession. To meet all this we had to create not only an army in the face of war itself, but also military establishments necessary to equip and place it in the field. It ought, indeed, to be a subject of gratulation that the spirit of the volunteer, and the patriotism of the people, have enabled us, under Providence, to grapple successfully with these difficulties.

A succession of glorious victories, at Bethel, Bull Run, Manassas, Springfield, Lexington, Leesburg and Belmont, has checked *the wicked invasion which greed of gain and the unhallowed lust of power brought upon our soil*, and has proved that numbers cease to avail when directed against a people fighting for *the sacred right of self-government and the privileges of freemen*. After more than seven months of war, the enemy have not only failed to extend their occupancy of our soil, but new States and Territories have been added to our Confederacy. While, instead of their threatening march of unchecked conquest, they have been driven at more than one point to assume the defensive; and upon a fair comparison between the two belligerents as to men, military means and financial condition, the Confederate States are relatively much stronger now than when the struggle commenced.

Since your adjournment, the people of Missouri have conducted the war in the face of almost unparalleled difficulties with a spirit and success alike worthy of themselves and of the great cause in which they are struggling.

Since that time Kentucky, too, has become the theater of active hostilities. The Federal forces have not only refused to acknowledge her right to be neutral, and have insisted upon making her a party to the war, but have invaded her for the purpose of attacking the Confederate States. *Outrages of the most despotic character have been perpetrated upon her people. Some of her most eminent citizens have been seized and borne away to languish in foreign prisons, without knowing who were their accusers, or the specific charges made against them, while others have been forced to abandon their homes, their families and property and seek a refuge in distant lands.*

Finding that the Confederate States were about to be invaded through Kentucky, and that her people, after being deceived into a mistaken security, were unarmed and in danger of being subjugated by the Federal forces, our armies were marched into that State to repel the enemy and prevent their

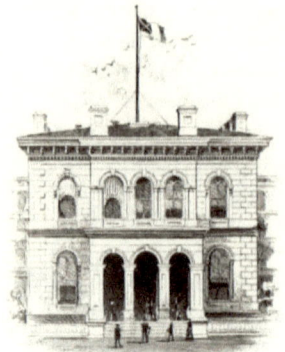

The Confederacy's Treasury Department, Richmond, Virginia.

occupation of certain strategic points which would have given them great advantages in the contest—a step which was not only justified by the necessity of self-defense on the part of the Confederate States, but also by a desire to aid the people of Kentucky. It was never intended by the Confederate Government to conquer or coerce the people of that State, but, on the contrary, it was declared by our generals that they would withdraw their troops if the Federal Government would do likewise. Proclamation was also made of our desire to respect the neutrality of Kentucky, and the intention to abide by the wishes of her people as soon as they were free to express their opinions.

These declarations were approved by me, and I should regard it as one of the best effects of the march of our troops into Kentucky if it should aid in *giving to her people liberty of choice and a free opportunity to decide their own destiny according to their own will.*

The army has been chiefly instrumental in prosecuting the great contest in which we are engaged, but the navy has also been effective in full proportion to its means. The naval officers, deprived to a great extent of an opportunity to make their professional skill available at sea, have served with commendable zeal and gallantry on shore and upon island waters, further detail of which will be found in the reports of the Secretary of the Navy and the Secretary of War.

In the transportation of the mails many difficulties have arisen, which will be found fully developed in the report of the [Confederate] Postmaster-General [John H. Reagan]. The absorption of the ordinary means of transportation for the movement of troops and military supplies, the insufficiency of the rolling stock of railroads for the accumulation of business, resulting both from military operations and the obstruction of water communication by the presence of the enemy's fleet, the failure and even refusal of contractors to comply with the terms of their agreements, the difficulties inherent in inaugurating to vast and complicated a system as that which requires postal facilities for every town and village in a Territory so extended as ours, have all combined to impede the best directed efforts of the Postmaster-General, whose zeal, industry and ability, have been taxed to the utmost extent. Some of these difficulties can only be overcome by time and an improved condition of the country upon the restoration of peace, but others may be remedied by legislation, and your attention is invited to the recommendation contained in the report of the head of that department.

The condition of the Treasury will, doubtless, be a subject of anxious inquiry on your part. I am happy to say that the financial system already adopted has worked well so far, and promises good results for the future. To the extent that treasury notes may be issued, the Government is enabled to borrow money without interest, and thus facilitate the conduct of the war. This extent is measured by the portion of the field of circulation which these notes can be made to occupy. The proportion of the field thus occupied depends again upon the amount of the debts for which they are receivable, and dues, not only to the Confederate but State Governments, but also to corporations and individuals, are payable in this medium. A large amount of it may be circulated at par.

There is every reason to believe that the Confederate treasury note is fast becoming such a medium. The provision that these notes shall be convertible into Confederate stock, bearing eight per cent, interest, at the pleasure of the holder, insures them against a depreciation below the value of that stock, and no considerable fall in that value need be feared, so long as the interest shall be punctually paid. The punctual payment of this interest has been secured by the act passed by you at the last session, imposing such a rate of taxation as must provide sufficient means for that purpose.

For the successful prosecution of this war it is indispensable that the means of transporting troops and military supplies be furnished, as far as possible in such manner as not to interrupt the commercial intercourse between our people, nor place a check upon their productive energies. To this end the means of transportation from one section of our country to the other must be carefully guarded and improved; and this should be the object of anxious care on the part of the State and Confederate Governments, so far as they have power over the subject.

We have already two main systems of through transportation from north to south. One from Richmond, along the seaboard; the other through Western Virginia to New Orleans. A third might be secured by completing a link of about forty miles between Danville, in Virginia, and Greenborough, North Carolina. The construction of this comparatively short line would give us a through route from north to south in the interior of the Confederate States, and give us access to a population and to military resources from which we are now in a great measure, debarred. We should increase greatly the safety and capacity of our means for transporting men and military supplies.

If the construction of the road should, in the judgment of Congress, as it is in mine, be indispensable for the most successful prosecution of the war, the action of the Government will not be restrained by the constitutional objection which would attach to a work for commercial purposes; and attention is invited to the practicability of securing its early completion by giving the needful aid to the company organized for its construction and administration.

If we husband our means and make a judicious use of our resources, it would be difficult to fix a limit to the period during which we could conduct a war against the adversary whom we now encounter. *The very efforts which he makes to desolate and invade us must exhaust his means*, whilst they serve to complete the circle and diversify the productions of our industrial system.

The reconstruction which he seeks to effect by arms becomes daily more and more palpably impossible. *Not only do the causes which induced us to separate still last in full force, but they have been strengthened, and whatever doubt may have lingered on the minds of any must have been completely dispelled by subsequent events.*

If, instead *a dissolution of a league*, it were indeed a rebellion in which we are engaged, we might find ample vindication for the course we have adopted in the scenes which are now being enacted in the United States. Our people now look with contemptuous astonishment on those [Yankees] with whom they have been so recently associated. They shrink with aversion from the bare idea of renewing such a connection. When they see a President making war without the assent of Congress—when they behold judges, threatened because they maintain the writ of habeas corpus, so sacred to freemen—when they see justice and law trampled under the armed heel of military authority, and upright men and innocent women dragged to distant dungeons—when they find all this tolerated and applauded by a people who had been in the full enjoyment of freedom but a few months ago, they believe that there must be some radical incompatibility between such a people and themselves. With such a people we may be content to live at peace, but our separation from them is final; for the independence we have asserted we will accept no alternative.

Confederate emissaries James M. Mason (left) and John Slidell (right), hapless victims in the infamous Trent Affair, courtesy of the Lincoln administration; yet another overt example of Yankee Liberals disregarding established law.

The nature of the hostilities which they have waged against us must be characterized as barbarous whenever it is understood. They have bombarded undefended villages, without giving notice to women and children to enable them to escape, and in one instance selected the night as the period when they might surprise them most effectually whilst asleep and unconscious of danger. Arson and rapine, the destruction of private houses and property, and injuries of the most wanton character, even upon noncombatants, have marked their forays along the borders and upon our territory. We ought to have been admonished by these things that they were disposed to make war upon us in the most cruel and relentless spirit, yet we were not prepared to see them fit out a large naval expedition with the confessed purpose not only to pillage, but to incite a servile war in our midst.

If they convert their soldiers into incendiaries and robbers, and involve us in a species of war which claims non-combatants, women and children, as its victims, they must expect to be treated as outlaws and enemies of mankind. There are certain rights of humanity which are entitled to respect even in war, and he who refuses to regard them forfeits his claim if captured, to be considered a prisoner of war, and must expect to be dealt with as an offender against all law, human and divine.

But not content with violating our rights under the law of nations at home, they have extended these injuries to us within other jurisdictions. The distinguished gentlemen [James M. Mason of Virginia and John Slidell of Louisiana], whom, with your approval at the last session, I commissioned to represent the Confederacy at certain foreign courts, have been recently seized by the [Union] captain [Charles Wilkes] of a United States ship-of-war [the USS *San Jacinto*] while on board a British mail steamer [the *Trent*] on their voyage from the neutral Spanish port of Havana to England [an event later known as "The Trent Affair"]. The United States have thus claimed a general jurisdiction over the high seas, and entering a British ship, sailing under its country's flag, violated the rights of embassy, for the most part held sacred, even among barbarians, by seizing ministers whilst under the protection and within the dominions of a neutral nation.

These gentlemen [Mason and Slidell] were as much under the jurisdiction of the British Government, upon that ship and beneath that flag, as if they had been on its soil, and a claim on the part of the United States to seize them in the streets of London would have been as well founded as that to apprehend them where they were taken. Had they been malefactors, and citizens even of the United States, they could not have been arrested on a British ship or on British soil, unless under the express provisions of a treaty, and according to the forms therein provided for the next extradition of criminals.

But rights the most sacred seem to have lost all respect in their eyes. When Mr. [Charles J.] Faulkner, a former minister of the United States to France, commissioned before the secession of Virginia, his native State, returned in good faith to Washington to settle his accounts and fulfil all the obligations into which he had entered, he was perfidiously arrested and imprisoned in New York, where he now is. The unsuspecting confidence with which he reported to his Government was abused, and his desire to fulfil his trust to them was used to his injury.

In conducting this war, we have sought no aid and proffered no alliances offensive and defensive abroad. We have asked for a recognized place in the family of nations; but, in doing so, we have demanded nothing for which we did not offer a fair equivalent. The advantages of intercourse are mutual among nations, and in seeking to establish diplomatic relations we were only endeavoring to place that intercourse under the regulation of public law. Perhaps we had the right, if we had chosen to exercise it, to ask to know whether the principle, that blockades to be binding must be effectual, so solemnly announced by the great powers of Europe at Paris, is to be generally enforced or applied only to particular parties.

When the Confederate States, at your last session, became a party to the declaration reaffirming this principle of international law, which has been recognized so long by publicists and governments, we certainly supposed that it was to be universally enforced. The customary law of nations is made up of their practice rather than their declarations, and if such declarations are only to be enforced in particular instances at the pleasure of those who make them, then the commerce of the world, so far from being placed under the regulation of a general law, will become subject to the caprice of those who execute it or suspend it at will. If such is to be the course of nations in regard to this law, it is plain that it will thus become a rule for the weak and not for the strong.

Feeling that such views must be taken by the neutral nations of the earth, I have caused the evidence to be collected which proves completely the utter inefficiency of the proclaimed blockade of our coast, and shall direct it to be laid before such governments as shall afford us the means of being heard. But although we should be benefitted by the enforcement of this law, so solemnly declared by the great powers of Europe, we are not dependent on that enforcement for the successful prosecution of the war. As long as hostilities continue the Confederate States will exhibit a steady increasing capacity to furnish their troops with food, clothing and arms.

If they should be forced to forego many of the luxuries and some of the comforts of life, they will at least have the consolation of knowing that they are thus daily becoming more and more independent of the rest of the world. If, in this process, labor in the Confederate States should be gradually diverted from those great southern staples which have given life to so much of the commerce of mankind into other channels, so as to make them rival producers, instead of profitable customers, they will not be the only or even the chief losers by this change in the direction of their industry.

Although it is true that the cotton supply from the Southern States could only be totally cut off by the subversion of our social system, yet it is plain that a long continuance of this blockade might, by a diversion of labor and investment of capital in other employments, so diminish the supplies as to bring ruin upon all those interests of foreign countries which are dependent on that staple. For every laborer who is diverted from the culture of cotton in the South, perhaps four times as many elsewhere, who have found subsistence in the various employments growing out of its use, will be forced also to change their occupation. While *the war which is waged to take from us the right of self-government* can never attain that end, it remains to be seen how far it may work a revolution in the industrial system of the world, which may carry suffering to other lands as well as to our own. In the meantime, we shall continue this struggle in humble dependence upon Providence, from whose searching scrutiny we cannot conceal the secrets of our hearts, and to whose rule we confidently submit. For the rest we shall depend upon ourselves. Liberty is always

Virginia statesman Charles J. Faulkner, illegally arrested and incarcerated in a Yankee prison by Lincoln and the U.S. government.

won where there exists the unconquerable will to be free, and we have reason to know the strength that is given by a conscious sense not only of the magnitude but of the righteousness of our cause.[364]

★ FACT: VIRGINIA GOVERNOR JOHN LETCHER COMPARED LINCOLN TO ENGLAND'S KING GEORGE III

"In remitting the Georgia Resolutions to the Virginia Legislature," on January 6, 1862, Democratic (a Conservative at the time) Virginia Governor John Letcher gave the following speech in defense of Southern secession before the Senate and House of Delegates:

> Gentlemen of the Senate and House of Delegates: I received from his Excellency Joseph E. Brown, Governor of the State of Georgia, a communication enclosing joint resolutions adopted by the Legislature of that State, and approved December 11, 1861. These resolutions relate to matters of the first importance, and they command my cordial approbation. They declare the sentiments of the Southern Confederacy, and will be enthusiastically responded to by the people of all classes.
>
> In communicating those resolutions to the General Assembly I embrace the opportunity to fill up a hiatus in the history of the State growing out of her changed relations. Virginia dissolved her connection with the Government of the United States on the 17th day of April last, having watched closely the political conduct of President Lincoln and his Cabinet from the 4th day of March preceding. *A large portion of our people believed, from the revelations of his inaugural message, that he designed to subjugate the South, and much of his policy as developed in the first six weeks of his administration, tended to confirm and strengthen this belief. The appearance of his proclamation, however, calling on Virginia and other States for volunteers, removed all doubts, and made it plain and palpable that subjugation was his object. He had revealed his purpose by the issue of his proclamation, to use Virginians, if possible, in coercing their Southern slaveholding brethren into submission to his will and obedience to his Government and authority.* Virginia, seeing that the only hope of preserving her rights and honor as a State and the liberties of her people consisted in dissolving her connection with the Government of the United States and resuming her sovereignty, adopted that course, and subsequently determined to unite her destiny with her Southern sisters. She did

Southerners accurately compared the North's tyrannical "King Abraham" to Great Britain's tyrannical King George. Both violated the laws of sovereigns and slaughtered thousands of their own people.

so; and her Convention, being at the time in session, adopted such ordinances and regulations as were necessary to protect her citizens against the machinations of enemies at home and the encroachments of enemies from abroad.

Events that have transpired since the 17th day of April last have more than confirmed the worst apprehensions of the people of Virginia, and have furnished an ample and complete justification for the secession of the State. All the wicked results apprehended when she seceded have been fearfully realized, and they now constitute an important chapter in the history of the stirring times in which we live.

Such were the considerations that influenced and determined the action of Virginia.

I now propose to show that *while President Lincoln professes to have inaugurated this war for preservation and perpetuation of the Constitution in its spirit and letter, he has violated in the most direct manner many of its most important provisions.* I propose, in the next place, to compare his conduct with the conduct of George the Third [of England], and to prove, by reference to the Declaration of Independence, that most of his acts have been identical with those denounced by our forefathers as justifiable grounds for our separation from the mother country.

The war which has been waged against us by President Lincoln is the most unnatural and at the same time, the most disgraceful that has ever occurred. We are struggling for our rights and liberties, for the protection of persons and property, and for the preservation of the honor and institutions of the South. The ruthless assault that has been made upon us and the unjustifiable attempt to submission present a most extraordinary spectacle in the eyes of the civilized world.

When a [Union] Secretary of War [Edwin M. Stanton] can quietly seat himself at his desk and coolly, calmly and deliberately commit to paper a recommendation to arm the slaves of the Southern States, place them in the field and incite them to hostility to their masters and the destruction of their families, what extreme may we not reasonably anticipate from an administration that retains such an official in its service? When an administration can go to work to destroy ports in States over which they claim to have jurisdiction, by sinking obstructions in the channels of our rivers and harbors (a policy unheard of among civilized nations), what enormity may we not be prepared to expect?

President Lincoln and his Cabinet have annulled the Constitution, have suspended the writ of habeas corpus, *and have declared martial law without constitutional warrant, but in defiance of it. Representative government has ceased to command their respect, and the direct tendency now in what remains of the late United States Government is inevitably towards consolidation and despotism. Passions and prejudice, avarice and selfishness, malignity and meanness have controlled their action and directed their efforts against us.*

Having presented these general views, I now present specifications showing in what particulars the Constitution has been violated. Some of these specifications show violations anterior to the secession of Virginia, others show violations equally palpable subsequent to her secession.

In the preamble to the Constitution of the United States our forefathers declared the purposes and objects they had in view in the formation of the Government, and those purposes and objects were *"to establish justice, insure domestic tranquillity, provide for the common defense, promote the general welfare, and secure the blessings of liberty"* to themselves and their posterity. The Government has been so administered and directed as to defeat all these purposes and objects. Justice has not been established, nor is it respected by President Lincoln and his Cabinet. Domestic tranquillity has not been insured, but domestic disturbance has been inaugurated and encouraged. The common defense has not been provided for, but Northern arms have been levelled at Southern breasts, and the welfare of our people has been disregarded. The blessings of liberty have not been secured to us, but we have found the Federal authorities exerting all their power and using all the means at their command to reduce the Southern people to abject submission to Northern numbers.

President Lincoln and his Cabinet have wilfully and deliberately proposed to violate every provision of the third section of the fourth article of the Constitution, which each one of them solemnly swore or affirmed, in the presence of Almighty God, to *"preserve, protect and defend."* That section is in these words:

> "New States may be admitted by the Congress into this Union; but no new State shall be formed or erected without the jurisdiction of any other State, nor any State formed by the junction of two or more States or parts of States, without the consent of the Legislatures of the States concerned as well as of the Congress."

They have deliberately proposed to annex certain counties in Maryland to Virginia, and thus form the new State of Kanawha [West Virginia], within the jurisdiction of Virginia, without the consent of the Legislatures of those States and of Congress. They have proposed to take the four counties lying in the Pan Handle, from Virginia and attach them to Pennsylvania, without the consent of the Legislature of the States interested and of Congress. They have proposed to join the eastern counties of Virginia to Maryland, and thus make a new State by the junction of parts of two States, without the consent of the Legislatures of these States and of Congress. These propositions present a most plain and glaring violation of the Constitution, and evidence an intensity of malignity towards Virginia and Virginians without a parallel in the history of the United States.

The first amendment to the

In 1862 Virginia Governor John Letcher avowed that the South was fighting for her constitutional "rights and liberties," and described Lincoln's War as "the most disgraceful that has ever occurred."

Abraham Lincoln: anti-First Amendment Liberal, white supremacist, and war criminal.

Constitution declares "that Congress shall make no law abridging the freedom of speech or of the press." President Lincoln and his Cabinet have wilfully disregarded the spirit of this article. Numerous instances could be cited to prove that the solemnities of an oath have not restrained them in *their efforts to abridge "the freedom of speech" and to muzzle "the press." The numberless arrests made by them in Western and Eastern Virginia, in Kentucky, in Missouri, in Maryland, in Washington City, and also in the free States, when nothing more was charged against the parties arrested than the declaration of their opinion in condemnation of the policy of President Lincoln and his Cabinet, show that freedom of speech is not tolerated by them. The notorious fact that [nearly 400] papers have been suppressed in New York, Philadelphia and elsewhere by the exercise of Executive power, fully attests a scandalous usurpation for the destruction of the independence of the press.*

The President and his Cabinet and the military officers under their direction and control, have violated the fourth article of the amendment to the Constitution which guarantees "the rights of the people to be secure in their persons, houses, papers and effects against unreasonable searches and seizures," and declares that it "shall not be violated." *This article has been habitually disregarded, and every observant man will call to mind numerous instances of the violation—the result of suspicion, merely.*

He and his Cabinet have violated, as deliberately and wilfully, the fifth article of the amendments to the Constitution, which is in these words:

> "No person shall be held to answer for a capital or otherwise infamous crime unless on a presentment or indictment of a grand jury, except in cases arising in the land or naval forces or in the militia, when in actual service or time of war or public danger; nor shall any person be subject for the same offense to be twice put in jeopardy of life or limb; nor shall be compelled in any criminal case to be a witness against himself; nor to be deprived of life, liberty or property without due process of law: nor shall private property be taken for public use without just compensation."

Without a presentment or indictment of a grand jury, they have, on mere suspicion of crime, caused men and women to be arrested and confined under strong guards, and have detained them for weeks and months. They have prostituted the telegraph to their uses, for the purpose of communicating orders for the arrest of suspected persons, repudiating all those safeguards which the law has wisely thrown around the citizen for his protection. Desolation has followed in the footsteps of the

Federal army. Neither life, liberty nor property has been respected by them. They have murdered many of the best citizens of the country, they have incarcerated others in jails and forts, and they have seized and appropriated private property to public use without just compensation to the owner.

He and his Cabinet have disregarded the injunctions of the sixth article of the amendments to the Constitution, not less flagrantly than those to which I have referred. That article declares:

> "In all criminal prosecutions the accused shall enjoy the right to a speedy and public trial by an impartial jury of the State and district wherein the crime shall have been committed, which district shall have been previously ascertained by law, and to be informed of the nature and cause of the accusation, to be confronted with the witnesses against him, to have compulsory process for obtaining witnesses in his favor, and to have the assistance of counsel for his defense."

He and his Cabinet have seized large numbers of our citizens; withdrawn them from their homes, their families and their business; cast them into loathsome prisons; refused to inform them of the cause and nature of the accusation against them; denied to them the right and opportunity of consultation with friends or counsel, and have withheld from them a speedy and public trial by an impartial jury. They would neither confront them with the witnesses against them, nor would they allow them to have compulsory process for obtaining witnesses in their favor.

The conduct of President Lincoln has been as oppressive and tyrannical toward the Confederate States as the acts of the King of Great Britain, which caused our first Revolution, were toward the colonies. The comparison cannot fail to make its impression upon the mind even of the most casual observer.

President Lincoln has plundered the public treasury, and has delivered at least forty thousand dollars to [Francis H.] Pierpoint to enable him and his traitorous associates in the Commonwealth of Virginia to overthrow the State Government, and to organize within the limits of this State a new Government. *He has thus been guilty of the unprincipled conduct of using the people's money to lavish upon traitors and encourage them to perseverance in their work of treason.*

[Letcher now quotes Thomas Jefferson's Declaration of Independence to illustrate Lincoln's similarities to England's King George III.]

"The history" of Abraham Lincoln "is a history of repeated injuries and usurpations, all having for their object the establishment of an absolute tyranny over these" Confederate States.

To this end "he has affected to render the military independent of and superior to the civil power."

He has combined with Pierpoint and other traitors in Virginia "to subject us to a jurisdiction foreign to our Constitution and unacknowledged by our laws, giving his assent to their acts of pretended legislation."

He is endeavoring to quarter "large bodies of armed troops amongst us."

"He has plundered our seas, ravaged our coasts, burned our towns and destroyed the lives of our people."

He is endeavoring to cut off "our trade with all parts of the world."

He is endeavoring to impose "taxes upon us without our consent."

He is endeavoring to deprive us, "in many cases, of the benefits of trial by jury."

"He has abdicated government here by declaring us out of his protection and waging war against us."

"He is at this time transporting large bodies of mercenaries to complete the works of death, desolation and tyranny already began with circumstances of cruelty and perfidy scarcely paralleled in the most barbarous ages, and totally unworthy the head of a civilized nation."

He has endeavored to excite domestic insurrections amongst us by proposing to put arms in the hands of our slaves, and thereby encouraging them to "an undistinguished destruction of all ages, sexes and condition."

Paraphrasing the Declaration of Independence, Letcher said of America's sixteenth president: "The history of Abraham Lincoln is a history of repeated injuries and usurpations, all having for their object the establishment of an absolute tyranny over these Confederate States."

He has violated laws human and divine to gratify his passions, glut his prejudices and to wreak his vengeance upon a people who ask only their rights, and who are struggling to preserve their liberties. Can a Government conducted on such principles endure?

In every stage of these oppressions, attempted or consummated, prior to the secession of the State, we warned President Lincoln and the Northern people of the inevitable consequences of their course, and admonished them that if justice was not accorded to us the Union must be dissolved. In every stage of these oppressions since the secession of the State we have resisted them as became a free people asserting independence. Our admonitions and resistance have been answered by repeated injury and oppression, aggravated by war and bloodshed and by the assumption and exercise of power which even an autocrat would hesitate to assume and exercise. *A President "whose character is thus marked by every act which may define a tyrant is unfit to be a ruler of a free people."*

I have thus presented:

1. The considerations that influenced and controlled the action of Virginia in separating herself from the Government of the United States and resuming her sovereignty.

2. The results which President Lincoln's policy gave us fearful reason to

apprehend, and which are now matters of history stamped indelibly upon its pages. In these I enumerate its *repeated violations of a Constitution which he had solemnly sworn to support.*

3. I have run *a parallel between the conduct of President Lincoln and George the Third, and have demonstrated that the former has shown himself not less a tyrant and usurper than the latter.*

The Constitution of the United States has had no binding efficacy upon us since the 17th day of April last. On that day we repudiated it, and declared to the world that we would not be longer bound by its provisions. From that day Virginia dates a new era. Her own Constitution, her laws and her ordinances constituted the rule of her guidance from that day forward until her union with the Confederate States was consummated. While she occupied a position as an independent State she deported herself with the grace and dignity that became "the mother of States"; after her Union with the Confederate Government she fulfilled her obligations faithfully in her new relation.

The occurrences of the past nine months have demonstrated conclusively that we cannot live together as equals under the Government of the United States; and *the habitual violation of the provisions of the Constitution, and the open disregard of the laws by President Lincoln and his officials*, render governmental association between us impossible. Mutual respect between the citizens of the Southern Confederacy and those of the North has ceased to exist. Mutual confidence has been succeeded by mutual distrust; and mutual good will by mutual aversion. *No government can be enduring which does not possess the affection and respect of the governed. It cannot be that the people of the Confederate States can again entertain a feeling of affection and respect for the Government of the United States. We have, therefore, separated from them, and now let it be understood, that the separation "is and ought to be final and irrevocable"*—that *Virginia will, under no circumstances, entertain any proposition from any quarter which may have for its object a restoration or reconstruction of the late Union on any terms and conditions whatever.*

We must be content with nothing less than the unqualified recognition of the independence of the Southern Confederacy and its nationality by the Government of the United States; and to this end we must meet the issue they have tendered to us with spirit, energy and determination, and with a firm resolve on the part of each of the Confederate States that everything shall be done that may be necessary to insure the triumph of our arms and thus secure our liberty and independence for the South.

In conclusion, I recommend that before your adjournment this day you reaffirm, by solemn vote in each house, the resolutions adopted by the General Assembly of Georgia. The Empire State of the South has spoken; let not "the Mother of States" remain silent on a subject of so much significance and importance to the Southern Confederacy. Respectfully, John Letcher.[365]

★ FACT: SOUTH CAROLINA GOVERNOR FRANCIS W. PICKENS VIGOROUSLY DEFENDED THE RIGHT OF SECESSION AS AN ASSURANCE OF "PERSONAL POLITICAL RIGHTS"

On March 28, 1861, South Carolina Governor Francis W. Pickens gave the following message to the State Convention of South Carolina:

> I herewith transmit the ordinances and resolutions of the different States that have seceded, and would call attention to the obvious propriety of providing for them, together with our own ordinance on the same subject, some suitable place of safe deposit. They are the simple, but authentic records of events well calculated to produce a profound impression upon the future destiny of our country.
>
> *Heretofore in the history of the world, the great struggle has been to secure the personal rights of individuals. In former times the power of government absorbed all individual or personal rights of citizens. But our English ancestors, by their sturdy virtues, engrafted, at different periods, such grants and restrictions upon the British Constitution as effectually secured personal rights, and as far as that branch of liberty is involved, they made it as perfect as any other country.*
>
> To secure the political rights of separate and independent communities, required a higher and broader range of political experience. The guarantees for personal rights in England was a great advance over the old feudal system of Europe; and it was then left to the separate States of America to develop a higher experience over a larger extent of territory, in those guarantees necessary to secure the local rights of separate independent communities, united under one common government.
>
> The old Constitution was intended to effect this advance in the science of Government, and *if it had been properly administered*, would have continued to develop the mighty resources and power of a wonderful people. But, under the combination of ambition with fanaticism, they [Northern Liberals] attempted to organize the great masses of the people so as to act together in a consolidated majority, and administer the common Government without regard to the sacred guarantees by which the local rights and interests of separate communities should be preserved under the absolute control of their separate Governments. This, of course, reversed the whole philosophy of our peculiar system, and if permitted to become successful, would have given us no advance over the European system of Government. In fact, it would have placed us behind them in

South Carolina Governor Francis W. Pickens insisted that the South fought "to secure the personal rights of individuals," and justified secession due to the North's repeated constitutional violations.

progress, for many of their most enlightened and powerful Governments asserted the doctrine, and acted upon it, that Governments and dynasties can be changed by Popular Sovereignty, expressed through universal suffrage, in independent communities; and they avow this as a substitute for the old theory of divine and hereditary right.

Under our old Articles of Confederation the Government had failed, and the Constitution of the United States grew out of the force of circumstances, and was adopted in order to secure, at that period, a more perfect union to enable us to resist foreign aggression. We have outgrown that state of things, and the danger lately was not from foreign aggression, but from internal corruption, and from an assumption in parts and majorities of absolute Governments over other parts, without reference to the limitations and reservations of the compact. Thus, that *Constitution ran its career, and fulfilled its destiny, under the perverted and vitiated idea that we were a consolidated people. Under prejudices fostered by designing [progressive] men, and under the worst passions inflamed by bad [left-wing] men, an absolute majority was created, who assumed that their will must necessarily be the Government, instead of the fixed principles of the Constitution, which were intended to guard the local rights and interests of the separate and independent communities which composed the Confederacy of States.*

Our State, true to the great principles upon which the Confederacy was formed, and true to those great and progressive ideas which were so identified with American Independence, was *forced to resume her original powers of Government*: and if she succeeds in engrafting the *fundamental right of a separate and independent State to withdraw from any Confederacy that may be formed*, whenever her people, in sovereign Convention assembled, shall so decide, then she will have made another advance in the science of Government, and added another guaranty to the great principle of civil liberty. And *if this principle could be secured without an appeal to arms and blood, it would show that the country has progressed in civilization and intelligence, as to be able to settle all controversies and issues involving political rights, by an appeal to reason, interest, to free discussion, to Conventions, to treaties and covenants, rather than by an appeal to brutal force.*

True, we have encountered misrepresentation and abase, and for a people so small in numbers as we are to make such an issue as we did, was full of danger and difficulty.

But no people are fit to be free, unless they are able to treat denunciation with indifference, and to meet danger with fortitude.

From peculiar circumstances, South Carolina was called on to take the first step in this march to independence. She had to encounter the first shock in the bitterness and fierce passions of our opponents. Those who had mastered the power of the Government, and were fondly gazing on the rich and ripe fruit supposed to be just within their grasp, naturally felt exasperated in disappointment, caused by this State interposing to arrest them in their lawless career of mad ambition and wild fanaticism. For a period we were surrounded with great difficulties, and threatened with danger that appeared imminent.

As far as the Executive is concerned, I always considered that the peculiar mission of this State was, by a firm and temperate course, to lay the foundation of the Confederacy of States, homogeneous in feeling and interest, with such institutions and domestic civilization as would unite them in our common destiny, with a government devoted to their peace and safety, and *with no interest to produce the slightest aggression upon other people*; but deeply interested to develop those productions that are so largely demanded in the peaceful pursuits of mankind, and entering so largely into the comforts and progressive civilization of the world.

When this State first withdrew from the Federal Union, I felt that we bore, on one side, critical relations to the Confederacy we had left, and also very delicate and peculiar relations to those Slave States which constituted the border of the Southern States; and we had still higher and more sacred duties and relations toward our sister States of the South, who were expected nobly to come to our side in the formation of a new Confederacy.

All these relations made our course quite complicated, and full of deep obligations. In administering the duties of the Executive office, I can truly say that I never for one moment lost sight of the relations our State bore to all, and it has ever been my endeavor, while sustaining her separate rights and independence, never to do anything that might show indifference to any of the great, complicated interests and relations with which she was surrounded.

When your illustrious body adjourned, you saw the State standing alone, surrounded with peril, and clouds resting upon the future. Under the kind dispensations of a superintending Providence, I am now able to present her to you under a brighter day, surrounded by other States rich in their resources, with their brave and patriotic sons standing as a guard in the portals of a new Temple, reared by our common counsels, and dedicated to the separate sovereignty of free and independent States.—Francis W. Pickens.[366]

South Carolina's Sovereignty Flag.

★ FACT: CONFEDERATE VICE PRESIDENT ALEXANDER H. STEPHENS DEFENDED SECESSION AS THE ONLY MEANS TO PRESERVE THE "BALANCE OF POWER" BETWEEN THE STATES On September 22, 1864, Confederate Vice President Alexander H. Stephens wrote a letter that is germane to our discussion. A few pertinent excerpts follow:

Easy and perfect solution to all present troubles, and those far more grievous ones which loom in prospect, and portentously threaten in the coming future, is nothing more than the simple recognition of *the fundamental principle and truth upon which all American constitutional liberty is founded*, and upon the maintenance of which alone it can be preserved—that is, *the sovereignty, the ultimate, absolute sovereignty, of the States*. This doctrine our Legislature announced to the people of the North and to the world. It is the only key-note to peace—-permanent, lasting peace—consistent with the security of the public liberty.

The old Confederation [that is, the original U.S.A. of 1781] was formed upon this principle. The old Union [1787] was afterwards formed upon this principle. *No league can ever be formed or maintained between any State, North or South, securing public liberty, upon any other principle. The whole framework of American institutions, which in so short a time had won the admiration of the world, and to which we were indebted for such an unparalleled career of prosperity and happiness, was formed upon this principle. All our present troubles sprung from a departure from this principle, from a violation of this essential law of our political organization.* In 1776 our ancestors, and the ancestors of those who are waging this unholy crusade against us, together proclaimed the great and eternal truth for the maintenance of which they jointly pledged their lives, their fortunes, and their sacred honor, that *governments are instituted amongst men, deriving their just powers from the consent of the governed, and that whenever any form of government becomes destructive of those ends for which it was formed, it is the right of the people to alter or abolish it and institute a new government, laying its foundations on such principles, and organizing its powers in such a form as to them may seem most likely to effect their safety and happiness.*

Confederate Vice President Alexander H. Stephens said that all of the problems between the Conservative South and the Liberal North could be resolved if the North would simply recognize "the fundamental principle upon which all American constitutional liberty is founded: the absolute sovereignty of the states."

It is needless here to state that by "people" and "governed," in this annunciation, is meant communities and bodies of men capable of organizing and maintaining a government, not individual members of society. The consent of the governed refers to the will of the mass of the community or State in its organized form, and expressed through its legitimate and properly constituted organs. *It was upon this principle the Colonists stood justified before the world in effecting their separation from the mother country. It was upon this principle that the original thirteen co-equal and co-sovereign States formed the Federal compact of the old Union in 1787. It is upon the same principle that the present co-equal and co-sovereign States of our Confederacy formed their new compact of Union.*

> The idea that the old Union or any Union between sovereign States, consistently with this fundamental truth, can be maintained by force is preposterous. This war springs from an attempt to do this preposterous thing. Superior power may compel a Union of some sort, but it would not be the Union of the old Constitution or of our new. It would be that sort of Union that results from despotism.
>
> The subjugation of the people of the South by the people of the North would necessarily involve the destruction of the Constitution, and the overthrow of their liberties as well as ours. The men or party at the North [Yankee Democrats, that is, Northern Conservatives], to whom you refer, who favor peace, must be brought to a full realization of this truth in all its bearings before their efforts will result in much practical good. Any peace growing out of a union of States established by force will be as ruinous to them as to us.
>
> . . . The chief aid and encouragement we can give the peace party at the North [the Peace Democrats; that is, antiwar Yankee Conservatives] is to keep before them *these great fundamental principles and truths*, which alone will lead them and us to permanent and lasting peace, with possession and enjoyment of constitutional liberty. With these principles once recognized, the future would take care of itself, and there would be no more war so long as they should be adhered to. All questions of boundaries, confederacies, and union or unions would naturally and easily adjust themselves, according to the interests of parties and the exigencies of the times. *Here lies the true law of the balance of power and the harmony of States.*—Alexander H. Stephens.[367]

★ **FACT: JEFFERSON DAVIS TOO SPOKE OF THE IMBALANCE OF POWER BETWEEN SOUTH & NORTH**
In 1850, 14 years before Stephens uttered the words above, Jefferson Davis spoke the following before the U.S. Senate, hinting at the secession of the Southern states that was sure to follow—unless the imbalance of power between the sections was addressed and corrected:

> The danger is one of our own times, and it is that sectional division of the people which has created the necessity of looking to the question of the balance of power, and which carries with it, when disturbed, the danger of disunion.[368]

★ **FACT: THE LIBERAL NORTH PURPOSEFULLY SHIFTED THE BALANCE OF POWER ONTO ITSELF**
Unfortunately, as Bledsoe notes, this danger was disregarded and even encouraged in the Liberal North, which had long desired political supremacy over its conservative Southern neighbors. In this way the South eventually fell into a "constitutional minority," one that threatened

to deprive it of "all reserved rights":

> The balance of power was overthrown. The South lost, more and more, her original equality in the Union; and the just design of the fathers was despised and trampled under foot by the Northern . . . [Liberals]. Every census showed, that her power had diminished, as her dangers had increased; and she no longer found herself in the original Union of equal sections. On the contrary, she found herself in a minority, which the Southern men of 1787 would have shunned as the plague; and threatened by a vast majority as cruel as death, and as inexorable as the grave. This was not the Union of the fathers; but the warped, and perverted Union of unjust [Liberal] rule and domination. The States of New England, never failed to threaten a dissolution of the Union, whenever, in their jealous imaginations, there seemed even a prospect that the balance of power might turn in favor of the South in only one branch of Congress. Yet the more the balance was actually turned in their favor, and the South, contrary to the design of the fathers, reduced to a hopeless minority, the more imperiously they demanded her implicit submission to Northern rule, and the more fiercely was denounced here every struggle to maintain her original equality and independence as "Southern aggression."[369]

★ FACT: THOUGH A LIBERAL, U.S. PRESIDENT WOODROW WILSON SUPPORTED THE RIGHT OF THE SOUTH TO SECEDE

Liberal South-loving U.S. President Woodrow Wilson (back row, third from left) and his cabinet.

Virginian Dr. Woodrow Wilson, though a Democrat (then Liberal), was not only proud of his Southern heritage, the highly educated president of Princeton University—who went on to become our 28th U.S. president—was also very knowledgeable about the War for Southern Independence. As such, he did not take secession and the formation of the Confederate States of America out of context, as modern South-haters so. Instead, his firm grasp of the history behind Southern secession allowed the erudite scholar to defend the right in a thorough and authoritative way, as the following writings from 1903 reveal:

> When they conceived that the time had come to put their right of withdrawal from the Union into practice, the southern statesmen showed at once, with

a manifest naturalness and sincerity, what generation they were of. They acted, with an all but unconscious instinct, upon the principles of 1788. *They conceived the unmaking of the constitution to be, not an act of revolution or of lawless change, but a simple, though it were solemn, legal transaction, like the formal abrogation of a great treaty, to be effected by the same means by which it had originally been adopted.* South Carolina, who led in the fateful business, adjourned her legislature and called a constitutional convention together: a body like that which had declared her assent to the constitution in the far year 1788. By formal ordinance of that convention the ordinance of the convention of 1788 was repealed, and the connection of the State with the Union authoritatively severed. That was her act of "secession," taken in the highest sovereign fashion known to her law and tradition. As in 1788, so now there was no submission of the action of the convention to the vote of the people for ratification. A representative convention was as sovereign in South Carolina in 1860 as in 1788. The other States followed her example as of course. Their theory of constitutional right and practice was identical with hers. Each State in its turn called a convention, as in the old days of the formation of the Union, and committed to it as of course the sovereign determination of the political connections of the commonwealth. Each convention in turn repealed the ordinance of the convention which had stood in its place seventy years before.

And then, because the old process was being reversed and a government not made but set aside, the same conventions went on to take up the task of reconstruction, that another government, more to their liking, might be set up in the place of the familiar one now rejected. They chose delegates to meet at Montgomery and frame a constitution under which a government should be established for the seceded States about to be combined in a new confederacy. When the work of the Montgomery convention was finished, they ratified and accepted it, without resort to the people or renewal of their authority. It was a critical time. Those who directed the unprecedented business were subtly aware, for all their stout theory of legal right, that the touch of revolution was upon all that they did. The work was therefore hurried forward. Hot feeling was astir. Rumors of force to be used, of armed resistance by the North, were in the air. It was imperative that the new group of States should be ready as soon as possible with a common organization through which they could act effectively and to a common purpose. The convention at Montgomery, therefore, at once chose officers for the new government as well as a constitution, and gave it an immediate temporary organization; and the sovereign conventions of the several States unhesitatingly ratified all that it did. Not until the year was out which had been fixed as the term of the provisional government was the direct action of the people asked for, except in Texas, which came to its resolution of secession while the new confederate government was in process of formation, and Virginia, which waited until it had been formed. In each of those States the ordinance of secession was submitted to the vote of the people and ratified by them. Even when the term of the provisional government had expired the voters of the new Confederacy were asked, not to ratify the constitutional arrangements upon which it had been founded, but only the choice of officers which the convention had made. They chose electors and members of Congress, merely, and affairs went on as they had been planned.

There was here no distrust of the people. No one doubted the legal validity of what had been done or deemed the method revolutionary or undemocratic. Nowhere else was there such homogeneity of opinion as in the South, nowhere else so habitual an acquiescence in conservative and established ways of action. It was not, however, a habit rooted in lethargy or indifference. Nowhere else in the world, perhaps, was there a more alert political population, a rank and file more keenly alive to points of political doctrine and practice. Politics were everywhere the favorite theme of conversation. Many a white man of the poorer class could read as little as any slave; but he heard his leaders so often upon every question of moment, whether of domestic or of foreign policy, at court, on market days, at neighborhood rallies for political discussion or religious exercise, at public barbecue and festival, that news came to him without newspapers and the principles of politics without books.

John C. Calhoun of South Carolina, a secession advocate and one of America's highest authorities on constitutional law.

Every matter of large significance or small he heard debated by the best informed men of the country-side. They gave him, first or last, no small part of what they had learned by travel, by reading, by service in the public councils. Through them he knew the characters and the motives of public men, the gossip as well as the controversies of politics, the happenings and the humors of the wide world. With such things to talk about around the fireside and at the cross-roads shop, upon his long rides from plantation to plantation and with his cronies upon every casual meeting, he had more than books could have given him.

Southern speakers felt as much put upon their mettle before audiences gathered at their neighborhood hustings in the midst of a season of controversy as before any audience gathered in the capitol at Washington. Southern voters were not likely to be made dupes of. They had elected the men who sat in the sovereign conventions which cut their connection with the Union with a full knowledge of the business they were to meet upon, and did not doubt that the conclusions of those bodies were their own authentic acts. Political method was not in dispute among them. They accounted themselves disciples of Mr. [John C.] Calhoun in respect of constitutional right and the legal remedy for abuses in the conduct of the federal government. What he had taught them was in their minds the commonplace and matter of course foundation of political theory. *They did not doubt that they had the right to secede, or that sovereign representative conventions were the proper instruments of secession.*

But many of them had doubted the policy and the occasion. Men forgot afterwards the sturdy fight made among the southern people for the preservation of the Union, by men whom all southerners loved and would upon ordinary occasion have followed right willingly; forgot *the doubtful balance of parties* and opinion there had been among them for many anxious years together. *That final breach and agitation between North and South had begun, not a single short year before, when Mr. Lincoln was nominated and the Republican party [then the Liberal party] began to gather for its triumph, but in 1848*, when the territory acquired from Mexico was to be disposed of as between North and South and southern men had insisted that *the balance between the sections*, disturbed in 1820 by the compromise concerning Missouri, should be redressed. Mr. [Stephen A.] Douglas's unpalatable doctrine of "squatter sovereignty" had deepened the mischief. He softened it as he could, to keep the southern men at his back; but the disguise of his careful phrases was stripped off by Mr. Lincoln in debate. The searching questions of a masterful opponent forced him to say that, though no law of Congress could exclude property in slaves from the Territories, the unfriendly provisions of territorial law itself might, if the settlers chose, render its tenure practically impossible. From that day the southern leaders knew that to act with a party which followed Mr. Douglas was to lose *the constitutional battle they had fought a long generation through for the balance of power between North and South.* There was steadfast love for the Union in the South as in the North. Mr. Calhoun had loved it, and it had broken his heart that he could not save it upon the principles which he conceived to be its heart and life. Men who knew the South only by some casual glimpse of southern men, some brief journey through the southern country, some transient sojourn of a single season, deemed the southern people as unstable, as easily stirred to rash action as a Gallic populace, so passionately did they seem to respond to the appeals of their orators, so eagerly did they yield themselves to the excitements of every agitation. But they were an English folk, strengthened here and there by the sober Scots-Irish strain and the earnest blood of the steadfast Huguenot. They held to their principles, their habits, their prepossessions with a simple, instinctive, undeliberate consistency which no excitement of the moment really touched or unsettled. *They had been schooled, as all the nation had, in a loyal allegiance to the Union which their own statesmen had done so much to set up and make illustrious. Whatever their old-fashioned view of the character of its constitution or of the rights of the States as members of the great partnership, no ordinary occasion, no sudden gust of passion could have torn their thoughts from those old moorings.* It had taken a long twelve years of agitation to get them in revolutionary mood, and men whom they equally loved and heeded had stood all those critical days through on the one side and on the other in determined combat, some to save, some to break the Union.

It was by appealing to their very *conservatism*, their attachment to the older models and theory of their government, that the advocates of secession had won.—Woodrow Wilson[370]

The Conservative Founding Fathers, men like John Quincy Adams, designed the U.S. government so that "all power" would be "inherent in the people."

★ FACT: THE SOUTH HAD THE RIGHT TO SECEDE BECAUSE OF THE NATURE OF OUR GOVERNMENT

The ultimate legality and justification for secession, as this book repeatedly proves, is the structure and nature of our government; and more specifically because of the relationship between the states and the government as designed, in their infinite wisdom, by the Founding Fathers. In truth, no other defense is needed. Sage perfectly summarizes these "averments of fact," which conclusively show:

1. That "all power is inherent in the people" of the state; and that the phrases: *"the sovereign and independent body-politic," "the commonwealth," "the state," and "the people,"* are all used in one and the same declaration as synonymous. And, to preclude doubt, Massachusetts [as one example] redeclares her sovereignty with still greater emphasis, as follows: "The people of this commonwealth have the sole and exclusive right of governing themselves as a free, sovereign, and independent state."

2. That no power ever goes out of the state, except by delegation; that *all power belongs to the state as much after delegation as before*; and that delegated powers must necessarily be used, for the state, by her "substitutes and agents."

3. That all the powers in the general government are delegated by, and derived from, "the sovereign and independent bodies-politic,"—that is to say, "the commonwealths" or "the states"—"the people having no political existence, and capacity for political action, except as such "bodies politic," or "states." Said Mr. [Daniel] Webster [in 1833]: "No such thing as sovereignty of government . . . is known in North America. . . . With us, all power is with the people."

4. That *the said "people," "body-politic," "commonwealth," or " state have an "inalienable and indefeasible right to institute, reform, alter, or totally change government,"* whenever they think proper.

5. That no authority can be exercised in the state but that derived from the people thereof, i.e. "the sovereign body-politic," "the commonwealth," "the state."[371]

★ **FACT: THERE ARE EIGHT PRIMARY JUSTIFICATIONS FOR SOUTHERN SECESSION**
We have covered the most salient reasons for the secession of the Southern states (there are many others listed in Appendices D and F), all which can be summed up as follows:

> First, *the destruction of the balance of power*, which was originally established between the North and the South; and which was *deemed by the authors of the Constitution to be essential to the freedom, safety, and happiness of those sections of the Union.*
>
> Secondly, the *sectional legislation*, by which the original poverty of the North was exchanged for the wealth of the South; *contrary to the great design of the Constitution, which was to establish the welfare of all sections alike, and not the welfare of one section at the expense of another.*
>
> Thirdly, *the formation of a faction, or "the party of the North pledged against the South"; in direct and open violation of the whole spirit and design of the new Union;* involving a failure of the great ends for which the Republic was ordained.
>
> Fourthly, *the utter subversion and contemptuous disregard of all the checks of the Constitution, instituted and designed by its authors for the protection of the minority against the majority; and the lawless reign of the Northern . . . [Liberals].*
>
> Fifthly, *the unjust treatment of the slavery question, by which the compacts of the Constitution made by the North in favor of the South, were grossly violated by her; while, at the same time, she insisted on the observance of all the compacts made by the South in her own favor.*
>
> Sixthly, *the sophistry and hypocrisy of the North*, by which she attempted to justify her injustice and oppression of the South.
>
> Seventhly, *the horrible abuse and slander, heaped on the South, by the writers of the North*; in consequence of which she became the most despised people on the face of the globe; whose presence her proud ally felt to be a contamination and a disgrace.
>
> Eighthly, *the contemptuous denial of the right of secession; the false statements, and the false logic by which that right was concealed from the people of the North; and the threats of extermination in case the South should dare to exercise that right.*
>
> These, it is believed, are the principal causes by which the last hope of freedom for the South in the Union was extinguished; and, consequently, she determined to withdraw from the Union. Bravely and boldly did she strike for Liberty; and, if she fell, it was because, as the London *Times* said, "she had to fight the world."[372]

7
THE PRO-SLAVERY SECESSIONISTS

IT IS TRUE THAT SOME Southerners claimed secession as the best means to continue slavery, an institution upon which they *seemingly* placed great significance. Though such individuals made up an insignificant minority, for political gain enemies of the South have overstated their popularity, power, and influence, *and* reinterpreted their sociopolitical views, all in an attempt to portray them as "racists" speaking for the "entire South."

The South has never denied that pro-slavery secessionists existed in our region in the 1860s, and even long before. What we object to is the gross perversion of their words, the ridiculous over-magnification of their numbers, and the preposterous exaggeration of their effect on the secession movement and the start of Lincoln's War; in particular by simplistic and biased South-haters with no true knowledge of Southern history.

It is true that some Southerners felt secession was a way to preserve slavery. They were not only an unpopular and tiny minority, however, but their words have been intentionally twisted by South-haters in an effort to falsely magnify the slavery issue and portray Dixie in a negative light.

Let us look at a few of Dixie's pro-slavery secessionists now, namely Iverson, Hammond, and Hunter. Afterward I will decipher the meaning underlying their words, which will help us debunk the many false charges made by the anti-South movement regarding slavery and secession.

★ **FACT: GEORGIA SENATOR ALFRED IVERSON SR. BELIEVED THAT SECESSION WAS ONE WAY TO SAVE SLAVERY**

One of the more prominent pro-slavery secessionists was Georgia Senator Alfred Iverson Sr., who made the following comments on December 5, 1860, before the U.S. Senate:

Alfred Iverson Sr.

> Sir, the Southern States now moving in this matter are not doing it without due consideration. We have looked over the whole field. We believe that the only security for the institution [slavery] to which we attach so much importance is secession and a Southern confederacy. We are satisfied, notwithstanding the disclaimers upon the part of the Black Republicans [that is, Liberal abolitionists] to the contrary, that they intend to use the Federal power, when they get possession of it, to put down and extinguish the institution of slavery in the Southern States.[373]

★ **FACT: SOUTH CAROLINA SENATOR JAMES H. HAMMOND THOUGHT THAT SLAVERY HAD A BENEFICENT & CIVILIZING EFFECT ON NATIVE AFRICANS**

South Carolina Senator James H. Hammond gave the following speech at Barnwell Court House, October 27, 1858:

> From the time that the wise and good [Spanish priest Bartolomé de] Las Casas first introduced into America the institution of African slavery—I say institution, because it is the oldest that exists, and will, I believe, survive all others that now flourish—it has had its enemies. For a long while they were chiefly men of peculiar and eccentric religions notions. Their first practical and political success arose from the convulsions of the French revolution, which lost to that empire its best colony. Next came the prohibition of the slave-trade, the excitement of the Missouri compromise in this country, and then the deliberate emancipation of the slaves in their colonies by the British Government in 1833-1834. About the time of the passage of that act the abolition agitation was revived again in this country, and Abolition societies were formed. I remember the time well, and some of you do also.
>
> And what then was the state of opinion in the South? [George] Washington had emancipated his slaves. [Thomas] Jefferson had bitterly denounced the system, and had done all that he could to destroy it. Our Clays, Marshalls, Crawfords, and many other prominent Southern men, had led off in the colonization scheme [Note: this is not accurate. The American

Colonization Society was founded in the North].[374] The inevitable effect in the South was that she believed slavery to be an evil—weakness—disgraceful—nay, a sin. She shrunk from the discussion of it. She cowered under every threat. She attempted to apologize, to excuse herself under the plea—which was true—that England had forced upon her: and in fear and trembling she awaited a doom that she deemed inevitable. But a few bold spirits took the question up: they compelled the South to investigate it anew and thoroughly, and what is the result? Why it would be difficult to find now a Southern man who feels the system to be the slightest burden on his conscience; who does not, in fact, regard it as an equal advantage to the master and the slave elevating both, as wealth, strength, and power, and as one of the main pillars and controlling influences of modern civilisation, and who is not now prepared to maintain it at every hazard. Such

James H. Hammond.

have been for us the happy results of this abolition discussion. So far our gain has been immense from this contest, savage and malignant as it has been. Nay, we have solved already the question of emancipation by this reexamination and exposition of the false theories of religion, philanthropy, and political economy which embarrassed our fathers in their day.

With our convictions and our strength, emancipation here is simply an impossibility to man, whether by persuasion, purchase, or coercion. The rock of Gibraltar does not stand so firm on its basis as our slave system. For a quarter of a century it has borne the brunt of a hurricane, as fierce and pitiless as ever raged. At the North and in Europe they cried "havoc," and let loose upon us all the dogs of war. And how stands it now? Why, in this very quarter of a century our slaves have doubled in numbers and each slave has more than doubled in value. The very negro who as a prime laborer would have brought $400 in 1828, would now, with thirty more years upon him, sell for $800. What does all this mean? Why, that we ourselves have settled this question of emancipation against all the world, in theory and in practice, and the world must accept our solution.[375]

★ **FACT: VIRGINIA SENATOR ROBERT M. T. HUNTER MAINTAINED THAT SLAVERY HAD BECOME MORE ACCEPTABLE DUE TO THE RADICAL ABOLITION MOVEMENT** The following remarks by Virginia Senator Robert M. T. Hunter are from his Charlottesville speech, given at the Breckinridge Democratic State Convention, 1860:

When I first entered the Federal councils, which was at the commencement of Mr. [Martin] Van Buren's administration, the moral and political status of the slavery question was very different from what it now is. Then the Southern men themselves, with but few exceptions, admitted slavery to be a moral evil, and palliated and excused it upon the plea of necessity. Then there were few men of any party to be found in the non-slaveholding States [the North] who did not maintain both the constitutionality and expediency of the anti-slavery resolution, now generally known as the Wilmot Proviso. Had any man at that day ventured the prediction that the Missouri restriction would ever be repealed, he would have been deemed a visionary and theorist of the wildest sort. What a revolution have we not witnessed in all this! The discussion and the contest on the slavery question have gone on ever since, so as to absorb almost entirely the American mind. In many respects the results of that discussion have not been adverse to us. Southern men no longer occupy a deprecatory attitude upon the question of negro slavery in this country. While they by no means pretend that slavery is a good condition of things, under any circumstances and in all countries, they do maintain that, under the relations that the two races stand to each other here, it is best for both that the inferior should he subjected to the superior. *The same opinion is extending even to the North, where it is entertained by many*, although not generally accepted. As evidence, too, of the growing change on this subject of the public sentiment of the world, I may refer to the course of France and Great Britain in regard to the coolie and the African apprenticeship system introduced into their colonies. That they are thus running the slave trade in another form is rarely denied. It is not to be supposed that these Governments are blind to the real nature of this coolie-trade; and the arguments by which they defend it already afford an evidence of a growing change in their opinions upon slavery in general.[376]

Robert M. T. Hunter.

★ FACT: THE REMARKS OF PRO-SLAVERY SECESSIONISTS ARE NOT WHAT THEY APPEAR TO BE

Enemies of the South like to point to secessionists Iverson, Hammond, and Hunter as examples of the "entrenched white racism" that was allegedly "endemic" to the South at the time. But a deeper look at the language used by these individuals and others like them yields a far different reality.

As I will discuss in more detail shortly, all three men are using several well-known political tactics to make their points, garner attention, and gather support for secession. Does this make their pro-slavery stance more acceptable to us from our 21st-Century perspective? Of course not. But it does make it more understandable.

With Iverson specifically, while the surface issue appears to be the "security of slavery," his real concern is over the law-breaking proclivities of Constitution-hating Northern Liberals. As for Hammond, he justifies the continuance of slavery primarily because he believes that it "elevates" the African, which, for those of us who have *thoroughly and objectively* studied the shocking savagery of many early slave-owning native African peoples, is absolutely true.[377] Hunter justifies slavery by saying that "the inferior should he subjected to the superior," the exact same argument used by Lincoln to rationalize his own racism. Said Lincoln in 1858:

> . . . there is a physical difference between the white and black races which I believe will forever forbid the two races living together on terms of social and political equality. And inasmuch as they cannot so live, while they do remain together *there must be the position of superior and inferior*, and *I as much as any other man am in favor of having the superior position assigned to the white race.*[378]

Lastly, Hunter goes on to rightly point out the hypocrisy of abolitionists, who overlook the so-called "coolie and the African apprenticeship system" used by France and Great Britain, but execrate the American South for engaging in the same practices.

★ FACT: IN HIS INFAMOUS "CORNERSTONE" SECESSION SPEECH C.S. VICE PRESIDENT ALEXANDER H. STEPHENS LINKED THE IDEA OF SECESSION WITH SLAVERY
We now pass on to the man many consider the best known "pro-slavery" secessionist of all: Georgia icon Alexander H. Stephens, from whose ancestors I myself descend. My cousin's most famous (to Yanks infamous) address is known as the "Cornerstone Speech," in which he defends both secession and slavery. It was delivered at the Athenæum in Savannah, Georgia, on March 21, 1861, with the start of the "Civil War" only three weeks away.

This address has been long and widely hailed by the anti-South movement as "proof" that the Old South was "inherently racist," that "slavery was at the root of secession," that "slavery was the cause of the American Civil War," that Dixie's economic system was based "solely on slavery," and that the South's participation in that conflict was only to "preserve slavery." One particularly Dixie-loathing Yankee misled generations of Americans by declaring that the South had "proclaimed human slavery as the corner-stone of the rebellion,"[379] as we are about to see, a falsehood of gargantuan proportions. Another radical South-hating Yankee, Thaddeus Stevens, arrogantly and ignorantly pronounced:

> All this struggle by calm and dignified and moderate "Patriots" [that is, Southern Conservatives]; all this clamor against "Radicals" [that is, Northern Liberal abolitionists]; all this cry of "the Union as it was, and the Constitution as it is"; is but a persistent effort to reestablish slavery, and to rivet anew and forever the chains of bondage on the limbs of immortal beings. May the God of Justice thwart their designs and paralyze their wicked efforts![380]

Grumpy South-hater and Yankee hero Thaddeus Stevens, another Liberal Northerner who spread the lie that the South only cared about preserving slavery.

Liberal Illinois Representative Ebon C. Ingersoll (the brother of Yankee hero and famed left-wing atheist Robert G. Ingersoll), made these comments:

> I believe Slavery is the mother of this Rebellion, that this Rebellion can be attributed to no other cause but Slavery; from that it derived its life, and gathers its strength to-day. Destroy the mother, and the child dies. Destroy the cause, and the effect will disappear.[381]

We in the South, of course, know that none of this is true. It is all, in fact, nothing but misinformation and disinformation, Liberal anti-South propaganda, masquerading as "Northern patriotism." And I will now show how and why.

★ FACT: STEPHENS' "CORNERSTONE SPEECH" WAS PURPOSEFULLY FILLED WITH HYPERBOLE & EXAGGERATION, COMMON TOOLS OF THE POLITICIAN
It is a fact, at the time, that Stephens believed blacks were ordained by God to be subordinate to whites (an idea he later rejected), and it is equally true that he declared that slavery was the "cornerstone" of the Confederate Constitution. Yet, since less than 5 percent of Southern white men owned slaves, it is obvious that the latter statement is impossibly incorrect. Why then did he make it?

With only a tiny minority of the South being interested in slavery, Stephens needed to say something that would get both his constituents' attention and their support in the terrible partisan political battles then raging with the North. The most efficient way to accomplish this was to use the tried and true tactics of exaggeration, fear-mongering, and hyperbole,[382] the same ones routinely used by politicians to this day "to influence the popular vote."[383]

★ FACT: REVEALINGLY, LINCOLN'S EMANCIPATION PROCLAMATION DID NOT END SLAVERY OR THE WAR
We must also consider the bold fact that if slavery had been the "cause of the War," as pro-North advocates continue to maintain, then why did the conflict not end with Lincoln's Emancipation Proclamation on January 1, 1863? Instead, the War dragged on for another two years, proving once and for all that the North was only fighting to install an empire, while the South was only fighting to prevent it.[384]

★ FACT: STEPHENS SHOWED THAT THE NORTH WAS AGAINST SOUTHERN SECESSION, IN PART, BECAUSE IT WOULD INTERFERE WITH THE YANKEE SLAVE TRADE
Let us keep in mind that at the time of Stephens' "Cornerstone Speech" the Confederate States of America was officially just one month old. What follows are a few pertinent excerpts from that address. We begin

with his comments on secession. The call of the Confederacy's provisional vice president to the podium was greeted with "deafening rounds of applause":

> ... We have intelligence, and virtue, and patriotism. All that is required is to cultivate and perpetuate these. Intelligence will not do without virtue. France was a nation of philosophers. These philosophers become Jacobins. They lacked that virtue, that devotion to moral principle, and that patriotism which is essential to good government. Organized upon principles of perfect justice and right—seeking amity and friendship with all other powers—I see no obstacle in the way of our upward and onward progress. Our growth, by accessions from other States, will depend greatly upon whether we present to the world, as I trust we shall, a better government than that to which neighboring States belong. If we do this, North Carolina, Tennessee, and Arkansas cannot hesitate long; neither can Virginia, Kentucky, and Missouri. They will necessarily gravitate to us by an imperious law. We made ample provision in our constitution for the admission of other States; it is more guarded, and wisely so, I think, than the old constitution on the same subject, but not too guarded to receive them as fast as it may be proper. Looking to the distant future, and, perhaps, not very far distant either, it is not beyond the range of possibility, and even probability, that all the great States of the north-west will gravitate this way, as well as Tennessee, Kentucky, Missouri, Arkansas, etc. Should they do so, our doors are wide enough to receive them, but not until they are ready to assimilate with us in principle.
>
> The process of disintegration in the old Union may be expected to go on with almost absolute certainty if we pursue the right course. We are now the nucleus of a growing power which, if we are true to ourselves, our destiny, and high mission, will become the controlling power on this continent. To what extent accessions will go on in the process of time, or where it will end, the future will determine. So far as it concerns States of the old Union, this process will be upon no such principles of reconstruction as now spoken of, but upon reorganization and new assimilation. [Loud applause.] Such are some of the glimpses of the future as I catch them.
>
> But at first we must necessarily meet with the inconveniences and difficulties and embarrassments incident to all changes of government. These will be felt in our postal affairs and changes in the channel of trade. These

Southern paragon Confederate Vice President Stephens, one of the most misunderstood, misquoted, and maligned statesmen in American history.

inconveniences, it is to be hoped, will be but temporary, and must be borne with patience and forbearance.

As to whether we shall have war with our late confederates [Northerners], or whether all matters of differences between us shall be amicably settled, I can only say that the prospect for a peaceful adjustment is better, so far as I am informed, than it has been.

The prospect of war is, at least, not so threatening as it has been. The idea of coercion, shadowed forth in President Lincoln's inaugural, seems not to be followed up thus far so vigorously as was expected. Fort Sumter, it is believed, will soon be evacuated. What course will be pursued toward Fort Pickens, and the other forts on the gulf, is not so well understood. It is to be greatly desired that all of them should be surrendered. Our object is peace, not only with the North, but with the world. All matters relating to the public property, public liabilities of the Union when we were members of it, we are ready and willing to adjust and settle upon the principles of right, equity, and good faith. War can be of no more benefit to the North than to us. Whether the intention of evacuating Fort Sumter is to be received as an evidence of a desire for a peaceful solution of our difficulties with the United States, or the result of necessity, I will not undertake to say. I would fain hope the former. Rumors are afloat, however, that it is the result of necessity. All I can say to you, therefore, on that point is, keep your armor bright and your powder dry. [Enthusiastic cheering.]

Stephens called out the North over its rank hypocrisy regarding secession, slavery, and the Constitution.

The surest way to secure peace, is to show your ability to maintain your rights. The principles and position of the present administration of the United States—the republican [Liberal] party—present some puzzling questions. While it is a fixed principle with them never to allow the increase of a foot of slave territory, they seem to be equally determined not to part with an inch "of the accursed soil [of the Southern states]." Notwithstanding their clamor against the institution, they seemed to be equally opposed to getting more, or letting go what they have got. *They were ready to fight on the accession of Texas, and are equally ready to fight now on her secession.* Why is this? How can this strange paradox be accounted for?

There seems to be but one rational solution—and that is, notwithstanding their professions of humanity, *they are disinclined to give up the* benefits they derive from slave labor. Their philanthropy yields to their interest. The idea of enforcing the laws, has but one object, and that is a collection of the taxes, raised by slave labor to swell the fund, necessary to meet their heavy appropriations. The spoils is what they are after—though they come from the labor of the slave. [Continued applause.]

... That as the admission of States by Congress under the [U.S.] constitution was an act of legislation, and in the nature of a contract or compact between the States admitted and the others admitting, why should not this contract or compact be regarded as of like character with all other civil contracts—liable to be rescinded by mutual agreement of both parties? The seceding States have rescinded it on their part, they have resumed their sovereignty. Why cannot the whole question be settled, if the north desire peace, simply by the [U.S.] Congress, in both branches, with the concurrence of the President, giving their consent to the separation, and a recognition of our independence?[385]

★ FACT: STEPHENS' "RACISM" WAS TYPICAL OF THE DAY & WAS FAR LESS SEVERE THAN LINCOLN'S RACISM

While anti-South writers *never* cite the above statements from Stephens' Cornerstone Speech (it would give away the North's integral connection to slavery), there is one that they *always* mention:

[The] corner-stone [of the Constitution of the Southern Confederacy] rests upon the great truth, that the negro is not equal to the white man; that slavery, subordination to the superior race, is his natural and normal condition.[386]

Before discussing the facts behind these words, let us compare them with those of Yankee President Abraham Lincoln, delivered publicly a few years earlier on July 17, 1858, at Springfield, Illinois:

My declarations upon this subject of negro slavery may be misrepresented, but cannot be misunderstood. I have said that *I do not understand the Declaration [of Independence] to mean that all men were created equal in all respects.* ... Certainly the negro is not our equal in color—perhaps not in many other respects.[387]

A few months later, on September 18, 1858, at Charleston, Illinois, Lincoln made the following statement:

I will say then that *I am not, nor ever have been, in favor of bringing about in any way the social and political equality of the white and black races*—that *I am not, nor ever have been, in favor of making voters or jurors of negroes, nor of qualifying them to hold office, nor to intermarry with white people*; and I will say in addition to this that *there is a physical difference between the white and black races which I believe will forever forbid the two races living together on terms of social and political equality*. And inasmuch as they cannot so live, while they do remain together *there must be the position of superior and inferior, and I as much as any other man am in favor of having the superior position assigned to the white race.*[388]

Stephens possessed the mild white racism that was endemic to American society at the time. However, it was far less severe than the entrenched bigotry found north of the Mason-Dixon Line, where Yankees like Lincoln spent their entire lives trying to deport blacks (or at least contain them in their own state) in an attempt to make the country "white from coast to coast." In this photo Stephens is pictured with a black man, something white supremacist Lincoln never did, and never would have done. Stephens, was in fact, considered a "friend of the African race," and was idolized by his own black servants, whom he treated as part of his family.

My point here is that Vice President Stephens' racism was little different than President Lincoln's in this regard. Both men were products of a 19th-Century white society that saw blacks as an "inferior race," the term Lincoln always used when referring to African-Americans.[389]

In truth, however, Lincoln's overall racism was far more severe. For example, "Honest Abe" was a leader and a lifelong member of the racist, Yankee-founded, American Colonization Society, whose central mission was "to make America white from coast to coast" by deporting as many African-Americans as possible.[390] Stephens, in contrast, never supported such efforts, carried on excellent relationships with African-Americans, and was loved and respected by every black man and woman who knew him, including his own servants—whom he treated, by long Southern tradition, like members of his own family.[391] Yet, here is what Lincoln had to say about whites and blacks: "What I would most desire would be the separation of the white and black races."[392]

Thus, if critics of the South wish to avoid being called hypocrites,

Northerner Lincoln must be denounced just as heartily as Southerner Stephens. As the "Great Emancipator" Lincoln said of "nearly all white people" living in America at the time (and he included himself in this group):

> There is a natural disgust in the minds of nearly all white people, to the idea of an indiscriminate amalgamation [mixing] of the white and black races.[393]

★ FACT: STEPHENS WAS QUOTING A YANKEE WHEN HE SAID THE CONFEDERATE CONSTITUTION WAS BUILT ON SLAVERY
As for Stephens' "slavery is the cornerstone" comment, it turns out to be far less venomous and racist than modern South-loathers claim—and in fact, as I have shown in my books on the vice president, he was widely known as a true friend of the black man.

Stephens was paraphrasing Yankee Henry Baldwin when, speaking of the new C.S. Constitution, the vice president said: "Its foundations are laid, its corner-stone rests upon the great truth that the negro is not equal to the white man."

For one thing, as noted, Stephens was engaging in hyperbole to get his point across, a common enough practice among politicians. Second, the speech we read today is not a literal translation of the original, but an "interpretation" by journalists in the audience, who introduced their own biases and mistakes into the final transcription. Third, Stephens himself repeatedly maintained that his words had been misinterpreted, and for good reason: when he said that slavery was the "cornerstone" of the C.S. Constitution, he was merely repeating the words of a Yankee judge, Associate Justice of the U.S. Supreme Court Henry Baldwin of Connecticut who, 28 years earlier, in 1833, had said:

> Slavery is the corner-stone of the [U.S.] Constitution. The foundations of the Government are laid and rest on the rights of property in slaves, and the whole structure must fall by disturbing the corner-stone.[394]

As Richard M. Johnston stated later in 1884, all Stephens did during his Cornerstone Speech was accurately point out the fact that *"on the subject of slavery there was no essential change in the new [Southern Confederate] Constitution from the old [the U.S. Constitution]."*³⁹⁵

★ FACT: THE NORTH HAS HAD MORE THAN ITS SHARE OF NOTABLE WHITE RACISTS
In 1863, just two years after Stephens' Cornerstone Speech, New York physician Dr. John H. Van Evrie came out with his popular book, *Negroes and Negro "Slavery": The First, an Inferior Race—the Latter, its Normal Condition*,³⁹⁶ in which the Yankee white supremacist argued that blacks were naturally inferior to whites, were, in fact, a different species than whites, could not stand upright like whites, could not facially express emotions like whites, would never be able to speak English like whites, that slavery was the black man's natural occupation, and that the slave trade was "beneficial," among other white racist stereotypes.³⁹⁷

Such sentiments were not shared by the majority of Southern whites!

Yet most of Van Evrie's fellow New Yorkers agreed with him,³⁹⁸ as did the rest of the Northeast; support that further fueled the massive and profitable Yankee slave business, not only in the Empire State, but throughout the entire Northeast. One of these was the mayor of New York City, Fernando Wood, who referred to the Republican [that is Liberal] Party's policy of abolition as "the bloody and brutal policy of the Administration Party." Furthermore, Wood asserted, abolition was "the crisis of the fate of the Union," for slavery was "the best possible condition to insure the happiness of the Negro race."³⁹⁹

Secessionist New York City Mayor Fernando Wood, one of millions of Victorian white Yankee racists.

If Stephens is to be quoted as a representative of the "racist South," then individuals such as Wood and Van Evrie—and there were many more like them—must be quoted as representatives of the racist North.

★ FACT: THE WORDS OF PRO-SLAVERY SECESSIONIST GEORGIA SENATOR ROBERT A. TOOMBS HAVE BEEN GROSSLY MISREPRESENTED

Another one of the South's more forceful and articulate pro-slavery secessionists was Georgia Senator Robert A. Toombs, who uttered the following words to his Yankee compatriots on January 7, 1861, before the U.S. Senate. Because this is one of the speeches most widely used by the anti-South movement to "prove" that the South only wanted to secede in order to "preserve slavery," I cite this very interesting address at length, a necessary concession in order to disprove the many Yankee myths associated with it. Lincoln's War was still four months away:

> I will now read my own demands, acting under my own convictions, and the universal judgment of my countrymen. *They are considered the demands of an extremist. To hold to a constitutional right now makes one considered as an extremist—I believe that is the appellation these traitors and villains, North and South, employ.* I accept their reproach rather than their principles. Accepting their designation of treason and rebellion, there stands before them as good a traitor, and as good a rebel as ever descended from revolutionary loins.
>
> What do the rebels demand? First, "that the people of the United States shall have an equal right to emigrate and settle in the present or any future acquired territories, with whatever property they may possess (including slaves), and be securely protected in its peaceable enjoyment until such Territory may be admitted as a State into the Union, *with or without slavery, as she may determine*, on an equality with all existing States." That is our territorial demand. We have fought for this Territory when blood was its price. We have paid for it when gold was its price. We have not proposed to exclude you, though you have contributed very little of blood or money. I refer especially to New England. *We demand only to go into those Territories upon terms of equality with you, as equals in this great Confederacy [the U.S.A.], to enjoy the common property of the whole Union, and receive the protection of the common government, until the Territory is capable of coming into the Union as a sovereign State, when it may fix its own institutions to suit itself.*
>
> The second proposition is, "that property in slaves shall be entitled to the same protection from the Government of the United States, in all of its departments, everywhere, which the Constitution confers the power upon it to extend to any other property, *provided nothing herein contained shall be construed to limit or restrain the right now belonging to every State to prohibit, abolish, or establish and protect slavery within its limits.*" *We demand of the common government to use its granted powers to protect our property as well as yours. For this protection we pay as much as you do. This very property is subject to taxation. It has been taxed by you and sold by you for taxes. The title to thousands and tens of*

thousands of slaves is derived from the United States. We claim that the Government, while the Constitution recognizes our property for the purposes of taxation, shall give it the same protection that it gives yours. Ought it not to be so? You say no. Every one of you upon the committee said no. Your Senators say no. Your House of Representatives says no. Throughout the length and breadth of your *conspiracy against the Constitution*, there is but one shout of no! This recognition of this right is the price of my allegiance. Withhold it, and you do not get my obedience. This is the philosophy of the armed men who have sprung up in this country. *Do you ask me to support a government that will tax my property; that will plunder me; that will demand my blood, and will not protect me? I would rather see the population of my native State laid six feet beneath her sod than they should support for one hour such a government. Protection is the price of obedience everywhere, in all countries. It is the only thing that makes government respectable. Deny it and you cannot have free subjects or citizens; you may have slaves.*

Robert A. Toombs of Georgia was among the tiny minority of Confederates who spoke of slavery in connection with secession. Modern pro-North writers, however, malevolently misinterpret his words while misleadingly depicting him as a "typical Southerner."

We demand, in the next place, "that persons committing crimes against slave property in one State, and fleeing to another, shall be delivered up in the same manner as persons committing crimes against other property, and that the laws of the State from which such persons flee shall be the test of criminality." That is another one of the demands of an extremist and rebel. *The Constitution of the United States, article four, section two, says:*

"A person charged in any State with treason, felony, or other crime, who shall flee from justice and be found in another State, shall, on demand of the executive authority of the State from which he fled, be delivered up to be removed to the State having jurisdiction of the crime."

But the non-slave-holding [Northern] States, treacherous to their oaths and compacts, have steadily refused, if the criminal only stole a negro, and that negro was a slave, to deliver him up. It was refused twice on the requisition of my own State as long as twenty-two years ago. It was refused by [Liberal Edward] Kent and by [Conservative John] Fairfield, Governors of Maine, and representing, I believe, each of the then Federal parties [Whig and Democratic]. We appealed then to fraternity, but we submitted; and this constitutional right has been practically a dead letter from that day to this.

The next case came up between us and the State of New York, when the present senior Senator (Mr. [William H.] Seward) was the Governor of that State; and he refused it. Why? He said it was not against the laws of New York to steal a negro, and therefore he would not comply with the demand. He made a similar refusal to Virginia. Yet these are our confederates; these are our sister States! There is the bargain; there is the compact. You have sworn to it. Both these Governors swore to it. The Senator from New York swore to it. The Governor of Ohio swore to it when he was inaugurated. *You cannot bind them by oaths. Yet they talk to us of treason*; and I suppose they expect to whip freemen into loving such brethren! They will have a good time in doing it!

It is natural we should want this provision of the Constitution carried out. The Constitution says slaves are property; the Supreme Court says so; the Constitution says so. The theft of slaves is a crime; they are a subject matter of felonious asportation. By the text and letter of the Constitution you agreed to give them up. You have sworn to do it, and you have broken your oaths. Of course, those who have done so look out for pretexts. Nobody expected them do otherwise. I do not think I ever saw a perjurer, however bald and naked, who could not invent some pretext to palliate his crime, or who could not, for fifteen shillings, hire an Old Bailey lawyer to invent some for him. Yet this requirement of the Constitution is another one of the extreme demands of an extremist and a rebel.

The next stipulation is that fugitive slaves shall be surrendered under the provisions of the fugitive-slave act of 1850, without being entitled either to a writ of *habeas corpus*, or trial by jury, or other similar obstructions of legislation, in the State to which he may flee. Here is the Constitution:

"No person held to service or labor in one State, under the laws thereof, escaping into an other, shall, in consequence of any law or regulation therein, be discharged from such service or labor, but shall be delivered up on claim of the party to whom such service or labor may be due."

This language is plain, and everybody understood it the same way for the first forty years of your government. In 1793, in Washington's time, an act was passed to carry out this provision. It was adopted unanimously in the Senate of the United States, and nearly so in the House of Representatives. *Nobody then had invented pretexts to show that the Constitution did not mean a negro slave. It was clear; it was plain. Not only the Federal courts, but all the local courts in all the States, decide that this was a constitutional obligation. How is it now? The North sought to evade it; following the instincts of their natural character, they commenced with the fraudulent fiction [that is, the unconstitutional view] that fugitives were entitled to* habeas corpus, *entitled to trial by jury in the State to which they fled. They pretended to believe that our fugitive slaves were entitled to more rights than their white citizens*; perhaps they were right, they know one another better than I do. You may charge a white man with treason, or felony, or other crime, and you do not require any trial by jury before he is given up; there is nothing to determine but that he is legally charged with a crime and that he fled, and then he is to be delivered up upon demand. White people are delivered up every day in this way; but not slaves. Slaves, black people, you say, are entitled to trial by jury; and *in this way schemes have been invented to defeat your plain constitutional obligations*.

. . . The next demand made on behalf of the South is,

> "that Congress shall pass effective laws for the punishment of all persons in any of the States who shall in any manner aid and abet invasion or insurrection in any other State, or commit any other act against the laws of nations, tending to disturb the tranquillity of the people or government of any other State."

That is a very plain principle. The Constitution of the United States now requires, and gives Congress express power, to define and punish piracies and felonies committed on the high seas, and offences against the laws of nations. *When the honorable and distinguished Senator from Illinois (Mr. [Stephen A.] Douglas) last year introduced a bill for the purpose of punishing people thus offending under that clause of the Constitution, Mr. Lincoln, in his speech at New York, which I have before me, declared that it was a "sedition bill"; his press and party hooted at it. So far from recognizing the bill as intended to carry out the Constitution of the United States, it received their jeers and jibes. The Black Republicans of Massachusetts elected the admirer and eulogist of John Brown's courage as their governor, and we may suppose he will throw no impediments in the way of John Brown's successors.* The epithet applied to the bill of the Senator from Illinois is quoted from a deliberate speech delivered by Lincoln in New York, for which, it was stated in the journals, according to some resolution passed by an association of his own party, he was paid a couple of hundred dollars. The speech should therefore have been deliberate. *Lincoln denounced that bill*. He places the stamp of his condemnation upon a measure intended to promote the peace and security of confederate States. *He is, therefore, an enemy of the human race, and deserves the execration of all mankind.*

We demand these five propositions. Are they not right? Are they not just? Take them in detail, and *show that they are not warranted by the Constitution*, by the safety of our people, by the principles of eternal justice. We will pause and consider them; but mark me, we will not let you decide the question for us.

. . . Senators, *the Constitution* is a compact. It contains all our obligations and the duties of the Federal Government. I am content and have ever been content to sustain it. While I doubt its perfection, while I do not believe it was a good compact, and while I never saw the day that I would have voted for it as a proposition *de novo* ["anew"], yet I am bound to it by oath and by that common prudence which would induce men to abide by established forms rather than to rush into unknown dangers. *I have given to it, and intend to give to it, unfaltering support and allegiance*, but I choose to put that allegiance on the true ground, not on the false idea that anybody's blood was shed for it. I say that the Constitution is the whole compact. All the obligations, all the chains that fetter the limbs of my people, are nominated in the bond, and they wisely excluded any conclusion against them, by declaring that *"the powers not granted by the Constitution to the United States, or forbidden by it to the States, be longed to the States respectively or the people."*

Big government Liberal Abraham Lincoln riding arrogantly through Richmond, Virginia, after Lee's surrender. He had only days to live. Toombs referred to him as "an enemy of the human race," one who "deserves the execration of all mankind"—a sentiment today echoed by all intelligent educated Conservative Americans.

Now I will try it by that standard; I will subject it to that test. The law of nature, the law of justice, would say—and it is so expounded by the publicists—that equal rights in the common property shall be enjoyed. Even in a monarchy the king cannot prevent the subjects from enjoying equality in the disposition of the public property. Even in a despotic government this principle is recognized. It was the blood and the money of the whole people (says the learned Grotius, and say all the publicists) which acquired the public property, and therefore it is not the property of the sovereign. *This right of equality being, then, according to justice and natural equity, a right belonging to all*

States, when did we give it up? You say Congress has a right to pass rules and regulations concerning the Territory and other property of the United States. Very well. Does that exclude those whose blood and money paid for it? Does "dispose of" mean to rob the rightful owners? You must show a better title than that, or a better sword than we have.

But, you say, try the right. I agree to it. But how? By our judgment? No, not until the last resort. What then; by yours? No, not until the same time. How then try it? *The South has always said, by the Supreme Court. But that is in our favor, and [thus] Lincoln says he will not stand that judgment.* Then each must judge for himself of the mode and manner of redress. *But you deny us that privilege, and finally reduce us to accepting your judgment.* The Senator from Kentucky comes to your aid, and says he can find no constitutional right of secession. Perhaps not; but *the Constitution is not the place to look for State rights. If that right belongs to independent States, and they did not cede it to the Federal Government, it is reserved to the States, or to the people.* Ask your new commentator where he gets the right to judge for us. Is it in the bond?

The Northern doctrine was, many years ago, that the Supreme Court was the judge. That was their doctrine in 1800. They denounced [James] Madison for the report of 1799 [see Appendix C], on the Virginia resolutions [see Appendix B]; they denounced [Thomas] Jefferson for framing the Kentucky resolutions [see Appendix B], because they were presumed to impugn the decisions of the Supreme Court of the United States; and they declared that that court was made, by the Constitution, the ultimate and supreme arbiter. That was the universal judgment—the declaration of every free State in this Union, in answer to the Virginia resolutions of 1798, or of all who did answer, even including the State of Delaware, then under Federal control.

The Supreme Court have decided that, by the Constitution, we have a right to go to the Territories and be protected there with our property. You say, we cannot decide the compact for ourselves. Well, can the Supreme Court decide it for us? Mr. Lincoln says he does not care what the Supreme Court decides, he will turn us out anyhow. He says this in his debate with the honorable member from Illinois Mr. [Stephen A.] Douglas. I have it before me. *He said he would vote against the decision of the Supreme Court.* Then you did not accept that arbiter. *You will not take my construction; you will not take the Supreme Court as an arbiter; you will not take the practice of the government; you will not take the treaties under Jefferson and Madison; you will not take the opinion of Madison upon the very question of prohibition in 1820. What, then, will you take? You will take nothing but your own judgment; that is, you will not only judge for yourselves, not only discard the court, discard our construction, discard the practice of the government, but you will drive us out, simply because you will it.* Come and do it!

You have sapped the foundations of society; you have destroyed almost all hope of peace. *In a compact where there is no common arbiter, where the parties finally decide for themselves*, the sword alone at last becomes the real, if not the constitutional, arbiter. *Your party says that you will not take the decision of the*

Supreme Court. You said so at Chicago; you said so in committee; every man of you in both Houses says so. What are you going to do? You say we shall submit to your construction. We shall do it, if you can make us; but not otherwise, or in any other manner. That is settled. You may call it secession, or you may call it revolution; but there is a big fact standing before you, ready to oppose you—that fact is, freemen with arms in their hands. The cry of the Union will not disperse them; we have passed that point; they demand equal rights; you had better heed the demand.—Robert A. Toombs[400]

Such commentary cannot be truly understood without a thorough knowledge of both American and Southern history. Thus the South-hating Liberal practice of taking pro-slavery secessionists' words literally, *and* also out of context, never fails to create confusion and animus. But this is their purpose, after all; which is why they commit these crimes to begin with: to indoctrinate the public against the South, while enshrining the North on a pedestal of righteousness.

Let us now debunk each of these outrageous anti-South lies one by one. We will begin with Toombs' speech.

★ **FACT: NORTHERN LIBERALS REVERSED THE MEANING OF LANGUAGE TO DISGUISE THEIR ANTI-AMERICAN AGENDA**
Toombs notes that he is called an "extremist," a "rebel," and a "traitor" due to his views on the Constitution and secession. But, as he rightly replies, since when is it extreme, rebellious, or treasonous "to hold to a constitutional right"? As was their practice, Victorian Liberals reversed the meaning of words and terms to conceal their anti-American schemes from the public, for it is those who ignore, denounce, and violate the Constitution who are the true extremists, rebels, and traitors.

★ **FACT: TOOMBS, DAVIS, LEE, & THE REST COULD NOT BE "TRAITORS": THEY WERE FOLLOWING THE LAW**
As this book clearly proves, the Founders placed state sovereignty above the powers of the federal government—which has *no* sovereignty. This means that individual Southerners were not responsible for secession and therefore cannot be considered "traitors." Sage explains:

How absurd it is to hold individual [Southern] citizens responsible for secession, they having no more volition or power to stop the state, than the man in the moon has to stop that orb! In Virginia, for instance, 150,000 voters, including General Lee,

Robert E. Lee, a Conservative law-abiding anti-secessionist, adored the Constitution and obeyed it to the letter, particularly when it came to its tacit guarantee of state sovereignty. How then could he be a "traitor" for leaving the Union with his home state? He could not, and he was not.

sent delegates to a convention, which duly deliberated, and ultimately voted the state out of the union. As a citizen he was compelled to obey, and finally defend the state. Opposition, after the convention had acted, would have been punishable enmity to his commonwealth, she having possession of him and his family and estate, and the fullest possible power of punishment. *It must strike every one, then, that states having seceded as bodies, and* ipso facto *carried all the citizens out of the union, Davis, Lee and others, cannot be held responsible as individuals for secession, or for the war which the said states waged against the federal government.* Regardless of the condition, position, wishes or acts of any citizen, *the state took the deliberate and solemn step of seceding from the union,* and the further step of federating with other states, which had seceded for the same causes and about the same time. The important act of secession was done in precisely the form, and with the solemnities observed by the original states, in their corporate act of "assenting to" and "ratifying" the instrument of union called the federal constitution—that is to say, a convention of each state, elected and empowered by the sovereign people thereof, after due deliberation, declared the will of that political entity or "moral person" called "the state" to be—withdrawal of the consent, and the "delegated" authority, of said state from the federal constitution. *This is secession.*[401]

. . . *Each one [Toombs, Davis, Lee, etc.] knew of the old ordinance or law of his state, "ratifying" her federal compact, and commanding him to obey her federal government, and he had long obeyed it; but a later act repealed the former, and commanded him not to obey the said government; and he knew the power to repeal to be precisely commensurate with that to enact.* Why should the citizen heed and obey the state's command, contained in her ordinance of ratification, and disobey her countermand? *And how could there be rebellion and treason in obeying the authority which had habitually commanded him, and which he had habitually obeyed—the authority of the self-governing body he belonged to?*

. . . *Whether a state, acting thus, did right or wrong, is not now the question; citizens had no choice. And furthermore, as to Mr. Davis, he did not vote for secession, and did not even favor the policy, though he had no doubt as to the right. If General Lee voted at all, he voted against secession.*[402]

★ **FACT: TOOMBS GAVE THE NORTH FIVE "DEMANDS" THAT WOULD PREVENT SECESSION, NONE OF THEM HAVING TO DO WITH PRESERVING SLAVERY**
In his speech Conservative Senator Toombs offers Northern and Southern Republicans (the Liberals of the day) five "demands" that, if fulfilled, will halt Southern secession. They are that:

1) Americans have the right to settle anywhere in the U.S. with whatever property they possess, including slaves.
2) *All* taxed personal property, including slaves, will be protected by the government.
3) Persons who commit crimes against slaves in one state and flee to another will be arrested and tried like any other criminal.
4) As private property, fugitive slaves will be surrendered without being entitled to a writ of *habeas corpus* or trial by jury.
5) Persons who aid or encourage the invasion of or insurrection in another state shall be punished.

There is nothing here that demands or even asks for the preservation of slavery. Toombs is merely asserting that those of his propositions which are already in the Constitution be upheld and those which are not be incorporated into the Constitution as amendments.[403] In discussing his second demand he actually asks that

> nothing herein contained shall be construed to limit or restrain the right now belonging to every State to *prohibit, abolish, or establish and protect slavery* within its limits.[404]

As is clear from such comments even the most ardent Southern fire-eaters, such as Toombs, saw slavery as a pro-choice issue, *not* a pro-slavery issue.

★ **FACT: THE CHIEF REASON PRO-SLAVERY MEN GAVE FOR SECESSION WAS NOT SLAVERY BUT EQUAL RIGHTS UNDER THE CONSTITUTION**
The most important motivation behind Southern secession is completely missed, ignored, or suppressed by Liberals and uninformed Conservatives; namely that *the North was constantly breaking the law by*

violating the Constitution's clauses, and in particular those concerning slavery. Conservative Southerners felt, and rightly so, that if Liberals were willing to go this far, there was nothing to prevent them from going further, perhaps to the point where they would alter the Constitution to eliminate states' rights altogether in their ongoing attempt to consolidate political power in the central government. At the opening of his address Toombs makes these comments:

> Senators, my [fellow patriotic Southern] countrymen have demanded no new government; they have demanded no new constitution. Look to their records at home and here from the beginning of this national strife until its consummation in the disruption of the empire, and *they have not demanded a single thing except that you shall abide by the Constitution of the United States; that constitutional rights shall be respected, and that justice shall be done.* Sirs, they have stood by your Constitution; they have stood by all its requirements; they have performed all its duties unselfishly, uncalculatingly, disinterestedly, until a party sprang up in this country [the Republican Party, the Liberal party of that time] which endangered their social system—a party which they arraign, and which they charge before the American people and all mankind, with having made proclamation of outlawry against four thousand millions of their property in the Territories of the United States; with having put them under *the ban of the empire* in all the States in which their institutions exist, outside the protection of Federal laws; with having aided and abetted insurrection from within and invasion from without, with the view of subverting those institutions, and desolating their homes and their firesides. For these causes they have taken up arms.
>
> . . . I have stated that the discontented States of this Union have demanded nothing but clear, distinct, unequivocal, well-acknowledged constitutional rights; rights affirmed by the highest judicial tribunals of their country; rights older than the Constitution; rights which are planted upon the immutable principles of natural justice; rights which have been affirmed by the good and the wise of all countries, and of all centuries. We demand no power to injure any man. We demand no right to injure our confederate States [to the North]. We demand no right to interfere with their institutions, either by word or deed. We have no right to disturb their peace, their

Though he was a pro-slavery secessionist, Toombs never demanded the preservation of the institution; only that the South be permitted its "well-acknowledged constitutional rights."

tranquillity, their security. We have demanded of them simply, solely—nothing else—to give us equality, security, and tranquility. Give us these, and peace restores itself. Refuse them, and take what you can get.[405]

★ FACT: ULTIMATELY THE SOUTH ONLY WANTED THE SAME RIGHTS THE NORTH HAD GIVEN HERSELF
In the end, as is plain from Toombs' speech, the South was not trying to "preserve slavery" when she seceded. She was merely asking to be treated equally under the Constitution, in the same equitable manner in which the North treated herself. This concept is called "equal rights," and it is one that is well-known to Liberals, wherever they are from.

The idea was also familiar to Victorian Southerners, for they had been experiencing unequal rights at the hands of Northerners for decades prior to Lincoln's War, with Liberal Yankees arrogantly and illegally deciding what was constitutional and what was not for *all* the states, both North and South. This is not "equal rights under the law." It is dictatorship, tyranny, and totalitarianism posing as "American patriotism."

★ FACT: DECADES OF SUFFERING AT THE HANDS OF VICIOUS YANKEE LIBERALS HELPED SPUR THE PRO-SLAVERY SECESSIONIST MOVEMENT
Pro-slavery secessionist sentiment in the conservative South only came after decades of wanton exploitation, disrespect, and over-taxation by Northern Liberals. The anger and frustration behind their words is thus understandable. In 1860 most Southerners could still recall the suffering their parents and grandparents had gone through under the hateful rule of Northern Liberals, who never missed an opportunity to humiliate, plague, encumber, goad, taunt, and punish the South. Economic, political, and social subjugation was their goal, the complete Northernization of the South, the very charge leveled at the North by Davis and other Southern officials at the start of Lincoln's War.

★ FACT: SOUTHERNERS WERE & STILL ARE STRONG ADVOCATES OF CONSTITUTIONAL GOVERNMENT
From the formation of the U.S.A. and the creation of the Articles of Confederation (our first constitution) and later the U.S. Constitution (our second), there has been a sharp line of demarcation separating the

Southern and the Northern views of the Constitution.

In the early South the Constitution and its many clauses and amendments engendered awe, respect, and obedience, even when some aspect was not particularly liked. The law is the law, and Old South Southerners, steeped in a sense of Christian submission, European etiquette, and military duty, had a natural appreciation for solemn documents like the U.S. Constitution.

In the Old North we find the opposite attitude, one personified in the North's highest leader: Abraham Lincoln, a self-professed agnostic and anti-Christian.[406] As is self-evident from tracing his political lineage, Lincoln was a political descendant of Alexander Hamilton and the early American Federalists, monarchists, and consolidationists, which is why, like modern day Liberals, he did not like the Constitution.[407]

Like Liberals today, Liberal Founding Father Alexander Hamilton had little love for the U.S. Constitution, calling it "a frail and worthless fabric."

Lincoln's own liberal compatriots called it a "scrap of paper," a "covenant with death and a league with hell,"[408] "hate's polluted rag,"[409] and "a thing of nothing, which must be changed."[410] Hamilton referred to it as "weak,"[411] "a frail and worthless fabric,"[412] while John Adams had such a low opinion of it that he assumed it would disappear within a generation.[413] A half century later radical William Lloyd Garrison burned the Constitution in the public square.[414] In our own time big government Liberal Barack Hussein Obama followed in Lincoln's footsteps, referring to the Constitution as "an imperfect document," while his anti-American followers eagerly campaigned to have the entire document thrown out, calling it "old, outdated, and useless."[415] Bledsoe writes of the Liberals of the 1860s (then the Republicans):

> For the Constitution, for the compact of 1787, for that "covenant with death and agreement with hell," they cared less than nothing; *except when it agreed with their own will, or could be made a pretext for their dark designs*.[416]

Fowler correctly noted the sentiment in the South at the time:

> Many *Southern statesmen [Conservatives]* have been under the impression, that the *Northern States [Liberals]* have very little reverence for the Constitution, and that they would be very ready to enlarge or diminish its powers, if, by so doing, they could advance their own material interests, and their own political power; that under the pretence of advancing the "general welfare," they would sacrifice the vested rights of the South; that under the pretence of promoting "the greatest good of the greatest number," they would violate sacred compacts; that from *their greed of money and their greed of political power*, they are ready to sacrifice honor and duty to self-interest, and that *they love negroes only because they hate their masters.*[417]

As a leftist, Lincoln, who began his political life as a Whig (Liberal),[418] was no different than Obama and every other progressive when it came to the Constitution. In February 1861, while meeting with a Southern peace commission at Willard's Hotel in Washington, D.C., the president-elect was asked by New York businessman William E. Dodge what he was going to do to prevent war with the South. Lincoln's response is chilling:

> When I get to the Oval Office, I shall take an oath *to the best of my ability* to preserve, protect, and defend the Constitution. This is a great and solemn duty. With the support of the people and the assistance of the Almighty I shall undertake to perform it. I have full faith that I shall perform it. *It is not the Constitution as I would like to have it*, but as it is that is to be defended.[419]

Reading between the lines it is obvious that even prior to becoming president, Lincoln was plotting to alter, and even destroy, the carefully constructed government of Jefferson, Madison, Monroe, Paine, Gerry, Mason, Henry, and the other *conservative* Founders. And a majority of his 20 million Yankee constituents were perfectly willing to go along with this overt outlawry. Should anyone be surprised that the Constitution-loving conservative South began plans to disassociate itself from the Constitution-hating liberal North the day of Lincoln's election?

★ FACT: PRO-SLAVERY SECESSIONISTS REGULARLY USED COMMONLY KNOWN SPEAKERS' TACTICS TO GAIN ATTENTION & SUPPORT

As discussed, pro-slavery secessionists, like Iverson, Stephens, and

Toombs used hyperbole and exaggeration to emphasize their point (that the South would not be bullied by the North), draw attention to themselves, and gain support from fellow Southerners. Thus much of the bluster and extravagance in their speeches must be chalked up to this widely accepted political tradition; one still very much in use by today's American politicians, both liberal and conservative.

And then as now such statements were usually rhetorical not literal. Those familiar with the entire corpus of *authentic* Southern history understand this; those who are not do not.

★ FACT: IT WAS NOT SOUTHERN ECONOMICS BUT PERSONAL FINANCES THAT MOTIVATED PRO-SLAVERY SECESSIONISTS
For the many reasons we have covered, it is impossible to accept that well educated, highly intelligent men, as all of the pro-slavery secessionists were, could possibly have believed that "slavery was essential to the South's economy." And in fact, despite the absurd claims of overly imaginative and vindictive South-haters, few if any did. None of the men cited here show any interest in this topic at all.

What they *were* interested in was their own personal finances in relation to slavery. The South's 3.5 million slaves represented some $4 billion in investment,[420] the equivalent of $120 billion today.[421] The majority of Southern slaveholders were perfectly willing, and anxious, to free their slaves under a constitutional amendment (later the Thirteenth Amendment). But they hoped to be compensated by the government. This Northern Liberals refused to consider—which only skewed the balance of power further North, making secession that much more viable and appealing to Conservative Southerners.[422]

★ FACT: CONSTITUTIONALITY & INTERFERING YANKEE LIBERALS HELPED PROPEL SOUTHERN SECESSION
Why then did this tiny minority, Southern pro-slavery secessionists, appeal to slavery as one of the main justifications for Southern secession? As noted above, for two reasons: the conservative, independent-minded, law-abiding Southerner's strict adherence to the Constitution, and his refusal to be told what to do by what he perceived as meddling, overbearing, self-righteous, South-hating Yankee Liberals. Again, in light of authentic history, the South's resistance to the idea of remaining

in the Union is entirely understandable.

★ FACT: SLAVERY WAS FAR FROM BEING THE ONLY REASON GIVEN FOR SECESSION BY PRO-SLAVERY ADVOCATES
Contrary to Yankee myth, slavery was not the only reason given by pro-slavery secessionists for leaving the Union, as the citations above clearly show. Even a cursory reading makes plain a number of other logical motivations, from the Liberal Yanks' utter disregard for the Constitution to the irreconcilable cultural differences between South and North.[423]

Either way, the men cited in this chapter were voicing their personal opinions; opinions that in no way reflected the views of the vast majority of Southerners at the time, 95 percent who did not own slaves, cared nothing for the institution, and preferred to see it disappear as soon as practicable. It was their own Southern ancestors, after all, who had started the American abolition movement and who had been trying to rid Dixie of the "peculiar institution" for centuries.[424]

President Davis never wanted to preserve slavery. Indeed, before the War even started he told his wife that one result of the conflict would be the total abolition of slavery—a fact widely and happily accepted across the abolitionist South.

★ FACT: JEFFERSON DAVIS NEVER PROMOTED SLAVERY AS A REASON FOR SECESSION
For one thing, Confederate President Jefferson Davis never specifically or solely advocated secession for the purpose of preserving slavery, and, as the most respected and highest leader in Dixie, his views were the only ones that actually mattered to most Southerners at the time. For another thing, the Southern populace, which had always been far more abolitionary in nature than Northerners, would not have supported Davis or secession if he had.

This was, in fact, true of every Southern leader at the time: ultimately all were only interested in preserving the Constitution and the unwritten rights guaranteed to the sovereign states in that compact. Woodrow Wilson commented that "their people had followed and upheld them upon that expectation, and would not willingly have followed them on any other."[425]

★ **FACT: IT IS PREPOSTEROUS TO THINK THAT MILLIONS OF AMERICANS WOULD HAVE DIED TO EITHER DESTROY OR PRESERVE SLAVERY**
What you will never read in any pro-North book is that no Southerner or Northerner was willing to die to either preserve or destroy slavery. The very idea that millions of men would jeopardize their lives, as well as their families, to tamper with an institution that was on the verge of extinction is absolutely preposterous; a laughable fantasy cooked up by those desperate to conceal the truth about the War;[426] particularly in light of the fact that in his First Inaugural Speech the North's highest leader, President Lincoln, said he had neither the legal right or the personal desire to interfere with slavery.[427]

While few people today stop to consider this fact, Union officers were perfectly aware of it. One of them, Union General Donn Piatt, once declared of his president:

> Lincoln well knew that the North was not fighting to free slaves, nor was the South fighting to preserve slavery.[428]

Confederate officers knew the truth too, of course, as we are about to see: the South would never have dreamed of seceding or fighting over anything but the preservation, not of slavery, but of the Constitution.

★ **FACT: "PRESERVING SLAVERY" WAS USED BY PRO-SLAVERY SECESSIONISTS AS A METAPHOR FOR PRESERVING CONSTITUTIONAL LAW**
It is a fact then that pro-slavery secessionists offered a number of reasons for secession, *none* of which were concerned with *preserving slavery*, but with *preserving law*—constitutional law in particular. Slavery, here a euphemism for "law," was used by them merely as a pretext to persuade fellow Southerners of the necessity of secession; another pro-law weapon in the arsenal of Southern politicians to win public favor for separation.

To interpret the words of this particular minority in any other way is to disingenuously and violently take them out of context, distorting and perverting them for the sole purpose of misleading the masses. With the information and knowledge I have provided here, however, this great crime against American history is no longer tenable.

8

BOTH SIDES SAID THAT THE WAR WAS NOT OVER SLAVERY

BEFORE PROCEEDING WITH OUR STUDY of the truth about Southern secession, it is vital to debunk one of the most patently absurd and virulent Yankee myths ever invented; namely that "the American Civil War was fought over slavery: the North in an effort to destroy it, the South in an effort to preserve it." According to this Liberal yarn, the South then seceded for the sole purpose of perpetuating the institution. But if the War did not concern slavery, then it is obvious that the South did not secede to maintain it. And that is precisely what this chapter will show.

Jefferson Davis correctly stated that slavery was only an "incident," not the cause of the War.

★ FACT: JEFFERSON DAVIS DECLARED THAT THE WAR WAS NOT ABOUT SLAVERY

In reality, the highest leaders on both sides of the Mason-Dixon Line repeatedly denounced this view. Let us begin with the most important individual of the Great War of 1861, Conservative C.S. President Jefferson Davis, who made the following comment on the subject:

The truth remains intact and incontrovertible, that the existence of African servitude was in no wise the cause of the conflict, but only an incident. In the later controversies that arose, however, its effect in operating as a lever upon the passions, prejudices, or sympathies of mankind, was so potent that *it has been spread like a thick cloud over the whole horizon of historic truth.*⁴²⁹

★ FACT: ABRAHAM LINCOLN DECLARED THAT THE WAR WAS NOT ABOUT SLAVERY

The leader of the Union, Liberal U.S. President Abraham Lincoln, also strongly spoke out against the idea that the cause of the War was connected to slavery. As we have noted several times, he made this clear from his very first day in office, when, on March 4, 1861, in his First Inaugural Address, the new U.S. commander-in-chief drove home his policies on slaves ("property") and slavery. Said Lincoln:

Apprehension seems to exist among the people of the Southern States that by the accession of a Republican administration their property and their peace and personal security are to be endangered. *There has never been any reasonable cause for such apprehension.* Indeed, the most ample evidence to the contrary has all the while existed and been open to their inspection. *It is found in nearly all the published speeches of him who now addresses you.* I do but quote from one of those speeches when I declare that *"I have no purpose, directly or indirectly, to interfere with the institution of slavery in the States where it exists. I believe I have no lawful right to do so, and I have no inclination to do so."* Those who nominated and elected me did so with full knowledge that I had made this and many similar declarations, and had *never recanted them.*⁴³⁰

Abraham Lincoln emphatically stated that the War was not about slavery, and called those who contradicted him "my enemies."

Many of his own constituents did not agree with Lincoln, and continued to claim that the War was one of abolition. Angered, in the midst of the conflict he released the following statements:

My enemies pretend I am now carrying on this war for the sole purpose of abolition. So long as I am President, it shall be carried on for the sole purpose of restoring the Union. . . . If there be those who would not save the Union unless they could at the same time destroy slavery, *I do not agree with them. My paramount object in this struggle is to save the Union, and is not either to save or to destroy slavery. If I could save the Union without freeing any slave I would do it.*[431]

Mainstream historians and the liberal media like to gloss over these important words, so let us repeat them here in order to establish the truth once and for all: if Lincoln were alive today, he would consider those who claim that his War was fought over slavery his "enemies."

If this is not clear enough, early on Lincoln's Secretary of War Simon Cameron wrote the following to Union General Benjamin F. Butler:

President Lincoln desires the right to hold slaves to be fully recognized. The war is prosecuted for the Union, hence no question concerning slavery will arise.[432]

In 1861 the U.S. Congress issued a resolution stating that the War had nothing to do with slavery.

★ FACT: THE U.S. CONGRESS DECLARED THAT THE WAR WAS NOT ABOUT SLAVERY

The U.S. Congress was of the same mind as its president, asserting that the Civil War had no relationship to slavery. On July 22, 1861, it issued the following resolution:

. . . this war is not waged upon our part in any spirit of oppression, nor for any purpose of conquest or subjugation, nor purpose of overthrowing or interfering with the rights or established institutions [for example, slavery] of those States; but to defend and maintain the supremacy of the Constitution and to preserve the Union with all the dignity, equality, and rights of the several States unimpaired; that as soon as these objects are accomplished the war ought to cease.[433]

★ FACT: ULYSSES S. GRANT SAID HE WOULD RATHER FIGHT FOR THE CONFEDERACY THAN ABOLITION

The Union's highest military officer, Ulysses S. Grant, agreed, offering this comment on the topic of slavery and the cause of the War:

The sole object of this war is to restore the union. Should I be convinced it has any other object, or that the government designs using its soldiers to execute the wishes of the Abolitionists, I pledge to you my honor as a man and a soldier, I would resign my commission and carry my sword to the other side.[434]

Grant, a slave owning Yankee Liberal who was soon to become our eighteenth president, states here that he would sooner fight for the Confederacy than fight for the Union against slavery!

★ **FACT: ROBERT E. LEE HELD THAT THE WAR WAS NOT ABOUT SLAVERY, BUT ABOUT PRESERVING THE FOUNDERS' ORIGINAL GOVERNMENT**
The Confederacy's highest military official was of the same mind. General Robert E. Lee made the following statement about the secession of the Southern states:

Union hero and slave owner General Ulysses S. Grant vowed that if he found out the Union was fighting to abolish slavery he would immediately resign and join the Confederacy.

> All the South has ever desired was that the Union as established by our forefathers should be preserved; and that the government as originally organized should be administered in purity and truth.[435]

★ **FACT: SOUTHERNERS AS A WHOLE MAINTAINED THAT THEY FOUGHT TO PRESERVE STATES' RIGHTS, NOT SLAVERY**
In 1893 Yankee author Caleb W. Loring, no friend of the South, wrote:

Confederate hero, abolitionist, and non-slave owner General Robert E. Lee affirmed that the South fought only to preserve the government of the Founding Fathers.

> In the renewed friendly relations at the dinner-table and in the lecture-room, the North of late has had the pleasure of listening to the speeches and discourses of Southern orators, soldiers, and politicians, who, while asserting their loyalty to the Union, claim that that Union was a compact between independent sovereign States, *from which each of these independent sovereign States had an undoubted right to secede; our Southern brethren, beaten in the trial of arms, persistently insist that they fought for the right.*[436]

Thousands of other similar quotes by important Confederate and Union leaders could be appended here.

★ FACT: LEE WAS AN ABOLITIONIST, GRANT WAS A SLAVE OWNER
And why, Mildred Lewis Rutherford rightly asked, if "the Union was fighting to destroy slavery" and "the Confederacy was fighting to preserve slavery," was Grant, a slaveholder and an anti-abolitionist, put in command of the Union army, while Lee, a non-slave owner and an abolitionist, was put in command of the Confederate army?[437]

★ FACT: THERE WERE MORE YANKEE SLAVE OWNING MILITARY OFFICERS THAN CONFEDERATE SLAVE OWNING MILITARY OFFICERS
The argument is even more absurd when we consider that at the start of Lincoln's War in the Spring of 1861 there were 315,000 slave owners in the Yankee military, but only 200,000 in the South's military.[438] Even Yankee Liberal Daniel Webster of New Hampshire readily acknowledged that all of the leading men of the South regarded slavery as "an evil, a blight, a scourge, and a curse," one that needed to be abolished as soon as possible.[439]

Mildred L. Rutherford, Historian General of the United Daughters of the Confederacy in the early 1900s, pointed out a singular fact never discussed by the anti-South movement. The War could not have been over slavery for one simple reason: Grant was a slave owner, Lee was not.

★ FACT: THE FOUNDERS FORMED THE U.S.A. AS A CONFEDERACY OR CONFEDERATE REPUBLIC
If Lincoln and his Liberal Northern compatriots did not wage war on the South to abolish the "peculiar institution," then why fight at all? According to "conventional wisdom," otherwise known as

Yankee (that is, Liberal) mythology, the North fought in order to "preserve the Union." But did it?

The Founders created the U.S.A. as a *confederate republic*,[440] not a *nation* (an idea they rejected),[441] or even a *democracy* (the word does not appear in any of America's founding documents),[442] all three which are different forms of government.[443] In a confederate republic the individual states are defined as "nation-states"[444] or "distinct nations" as John Jay referred to them.[445] A *republic* itself is defined as a small, weak, decentralized government, which, in our case, is supported by a *confederacy*, a union of independent states, whose power, authority, and sovereignty rests on the bedrock of the separation of powers, the right of secession, and states' rights.[446] It was for such reasons that our country was originally known as "the Confederacy" by the Founders, and her first Constitution was called "the Articles of Confederation." This is also why many Americans and foreigners once referred to our republic, the U.S.A., as "the Confederate States of America."[447]

★ FACT: THE FOUNDERS FORMED THE U.S.A. AS A VOLUNTARY FRIENDLY ASSOCIATION OF NATION-STATES
Most significantly, based on the foundation of the Declaration of Independence (which declared the secession of the American colonies from England), the U.S.A. was originally set up as a *voluntary* league of states;[448] a "friendly association" of sovereigns held together by "good faith,"[449] all with the right to accede (enter) *and* secede (leave) the Union at will. Thus Sage refers to its formation in 1776 as a "voluntary and a happy union."[450] Let us recall the statement of St. George Tucker, who, in 1803, correctly noted that:

> The Constitution of the United States, then, being that instrument by which the Federal Government hath been created, its powers defined and limited, and the duties and functions of its several departments prescribed, the Government, thus established, may be pronounced to be a Confederate Republic, *composed of several Independent and Sovereign Democratic States*, united for their common defence and security against foreign Nations, and for the purposes of harmony and mutual intercourse between each other; *each State retaining an entire liberty of exercising, as it thinks proper, all those parts of its Sovereignty which are not mentioned in the Constitution, or Act of Union, as parts that ought to be exercised in common.*
>
> In becoming a member of the Federal Alliance, established between the

American States by the Articles of Confederation, *she [that is, a state] expressly retained her Sovereignty and Independence. The constraints, put upon the exercise of that Sovereignty by those Articles, did not destroy its existence.*

The Federal Government . . . [is] the organ through which the united Republics communicate with foreign Nations, and with each other. Their submission to its operation is voluntary . . .[451]

Likewise, we have noted the words of French aristocrat Alexis de Tocqueville concerning the voluntary aspect of the U.S. government and the legal right of secession:

The [American] Union was formed by the *voluntary* agreement of States; and, in uniting together, *they have not forfeited their nationality, nor have they been reduced to the condition of one and the same people. If one of the States chose to withdraw its name from the contract, it would be difficult to disprove its right of doing so; and the Federal Government would have no means of maintaining its claims directly either by force or by right.*[452]

★ FACT: LINCOLN DID NOT PRESERVE THE UNION, HE DESTROYED IT

What then of Lincoln's pledge to "preserve the Union" by preventing the Southern states from seceding? Did he accomplish his goal?

It is clear that because a union is, by definition, a *voluntary* association between groups, whether they are groups of people or groups of states,[453] that he destroyed, or at least injured, the American Union[454]—making his title, "the Savior of Our Country," darkly ironic indeed.[455] In truth, as the Charleston *Mercury* correctly noted at the time, Lincoln transformed our "confederated republic to a national sectional despotism."[456] Empire-building at the hands of despots is the opposite of what the Founding Generation had in mind for the U.S.A. Here in the Conservative South this would make Lincoln "the Antichrist of our Country," and indeed, this is how countless thousands of Southerners describe

Why is the public unaware that our sixteenth president was a socialistic Liberal, a virulent white supremacist, an anti-Christian agnostic, and a cruel dictatorial war criminal? It is because for the past 150 years these facts have been carefully concealed by his devout but unscrupulous followers, the Lincolnites.

him to this day.

In an 1870 essay Yankee abolitionist Lysander Spooner commented on Lincoln's idea of "union," and how the president and his partners in crime, his Wall Street Boys, had perverted its authentic meaning:

> Their pretenses that they have "Saved the Country," and "preserved the Glorious Union," are frauds like all the rest of the pretenses. By them they mean simply that they have subjugated, and maintained their power over, an unwilling people. This they call "Saving the Country"; as if an enslaved and subjugated people—or as if any people kept in subjugation by the sword (as it is intended that all of us shall be hereafter)—could be said to have any country. This, too, they call "preserving our Glorious Union"; as if there could be said to be any Union, glorious or inglorious, that was not voluntary. Or as if there could be said to be any union between masters and slaves; between those who conquer, and those who are subjugated.[457]

Beautiful "Shell Road," in Mobile, Alabama, home of a number of Confederate widows after the close of Lincoln's War.

Spooner is right. A "union" held together by force is *not* truly a union, or even a country. It is a dictatorship, an empire. This is also why Lincoln was, and still is, often rightly referred to in the South not only as the "American Caesar,"[458] but as the Tyrant, Czar, King, Cambyses, Charles IX, Philip II, the Northern Nero, King John, George II, and the American Nebuchadnezzar.[459] Jefferson Davis referred to Lincoln as "His Majesty Abraham the First."[460]

★ **FACT: THE TRUTH ABOUT SECESSION IS ABSOLUTELY DEVASTATING TO LIBERAL MYTHOLOGY, WHICH IS WHY THE LEFT IGNORES, REPUDIATES, & SUPPRESSES IT**
We are slowly but surely dismantling one of the North's greatest Lincolnian myths, that "the South's secession and the War were over slavery." The anti-South movement considers this a "worn-out" topic, one they insultingly refer to as a piece of "revisionist Southern

mythology." That this is false is borne out by the fact that we have authentic history on our side. Enemies of the South have only opinion, emotion, personal beliefs, ideology, and their own mythological history—fabricated by anti-American Liberal, socialist, and communist activists posing as "historians."

However, as long as South-haters continue to promote the idea that slavery was the cause of secession and the War, it is they themselves who are responsible for keeping this issue alive. It is the traditional South that has been trying, for a century and a half, to put it to rest.

★ FACT: THE DIVERSE SOUTHERN POPULATION COULD HAVE NEVER UNITED OVER THE ISSUE OF SLAVERY
It is clear from what we have just examined alone that Lincoln's War did not spring from slavery, and that therefore the South would have never seceded over this issue. Why would the South's 95 percent non-slaving owning majority risk their lives for the 5 percent slave owning minority? To any thinking person this is illogical in the extreme. As English journalist Alistair Cooke notes, slavery alone could have never united the many different types of Southerners that existed in Victorian Dixie, from independent mountaineers, avaricious merchants, and dirt farmers, to poor whites, middle-class mulattos, and wealthy slave owning blacks.[461]

★ FACT: ABOLITION WAS NOT PART OF THE REPUBLICAN PLATFORM, OR THAT OF ANY OTHER PARTY, IN 1860
Besides, how could the War have been over slavery when abolition was not part of the platform of any of the primary political parties at the time, including Lincoln's? Indeed, as we have seen, Lincoln himself promised not to interfere with the institution in his First Inaugural Speech.[462] Lincoln's *new* Republican Party (of 1854), after all, had been formed specifically to merely stop the spread of the institution, not abolish it.[463]

★ FACT: IF THE WAR HAD BEEN OVER SLAVERY WHY DID IT CONTINUE AFTER THE FINAL EMANCIPATION PROCLAMATION WAS ISSUED IN JANUARY 1863?
And if the War had been about slavery, why did it not end with the Emancipation Proclamation? Instead, the conflict continued for another

two long years.[464]

★ FACT: LINCOLN'S WAR WAS ESSENTIALLY A BATTLE BETWEEN POWER-HUNGRY NORTHERN LIBERALS & INDEPENDENCE-LOVING SOUTHERN CONSERVATIVES

What are the facts then? Why did eleven Southern states (along with portions of Kentucky and Missouri) secede to form their own confederacy?

The South left the Union because a man hostile to everything Dixie held dear had risen to America's highest office;[465] a man—the first sectional (pro-North, anti-South) president in American history—who quite deliberately planned to impose his progressive agenda on the South, dismantle her way of life, trample on her traditions, and overturn her right to self-government.[466]

On July 17, 1858, during a speech at Springfield, Illinois, Lincoln purposefully antagonized the South, openly hinting at the invasion, violence, and oppression that was to come:

The Petersen House in Washington, D.C., where Lincoln died on April 15, 1865.

> I believe that this government cannot endure permanently half slave and half free. It will become all one thing or all the other.[467]

But Liberal Lincoln was dead wrong, for there was no national precedent for enforcing the "integrity of the Union"; and even if there had been, it had never been formally declared.[468] Thus his invasion of the South was illegal, immoral, and unconstitutional. Logically, Conservative Stephen A. Douglas countered such obtuse statements, saying:

> Why cannot this government endure, divided into Free and Slave States as our fathers made it? When this government was established by Washington, Jefferson, Madison, Jay, Hamilton, Franklin, and the other sages and patriots of that day, it was composed of Free States and Slave States, bound together by one common Constitution. We have

existed and prospered from that day to this thus divided, and have increased with a rapidity never before equalled, in wealth, the extension of territory, and all the elements of power and greatness, until we have become the first nation on the face of the globe. Why can we not thus continue to prosper? *We can, if we will live up to and execute the government upon those principles upon which our fathers established it.*[469]

Bizarrely, Lincoln himself admitted in the same speech that the U.S. had already "endured, half slave and half free, for eighty-two years."[470]

★ FACT: AMERICAN LIBERALS MAINTAIN A "POLICY OF SECRECY" WHICH THEY HAVE LONG USED TO HIDE THE TRUTH ABOUT THE WAR

Why then bring up the topic of slavery at all? Why agitate things? Because, as he always did, and as was the Liberals' customary "policy of secrecy,"[471] Lincoln was attempting to obscure the real issue: the power struggle between Northern Liberals, who demanded centralization (governmental consolidation), and Southern Conservatives, who demanded states' rights (governmental decentralization).

★ FACT: LIBERAL LINCOLN ARROGANTLY ASSUMED THAT THE SOUTH SHOULD BE AN EXACT COPY OF THE NORTH

What tyrant Lincoln could never see, acknowledge, or accept was that what was right, moral, and positive for the North, was wrong, immoral, and negative for the South, and vice versa.[472] Like the typical self-righteous progressive elitist that he was, Lincoln believed that what was best for the North was also best for everyone else.[473]

★ FACT: THE SOUTH SECEDED TO CONTINUE THE FOUNDERS' EXPERIMENT OF A VOLUNTARY UNION

Southerners, of course, saw things quite differently. In 1863 the C.S.A.'s president, Jefferson Davis, declared:

> The people of the States now confederated became convinced that the Government of the United States had fallen into the hands of a sectional majority, who would pervert that most sacred of all trusts to the destruction of the rights which it was pledged to protect. They believed that to remain longer in the Union would subject them to a continuance of a disparaging discrimination, submission to which would be inconsistent with their welfare, and intolerable to a proud people. They therefore determined to sever its bonds

and establish a new Confederacy for themselves.

The experiment instituted by our revolutionary fathers, of a voluntary Union of sovereign States for the purposes specified in a solemn compact, had been perverted by those who, feeling power and forgetting right, were determined to respect no law but their own will. The Government had ceased to answer the ends for which it was ordained and established. To save ourselves from a revolution which, in its silent but rapid progress, was about to place us under the despotism of numbers, and to preserve in spirit, as well as in form, a system of government we believed to be peculiarly fitted to our condition, and full of promise for mankind, we determined to make a new association, composed of States homogenous in interest, in policy, and in feeling.

True to our traditions of peace and our love of justice, we sent commissioners to the United States to propose a fair and amicable settlement of all questions of public debt or property which might be in dispute. But the Government at Washington [i.e., Lincoln], denying our right to self-government, refused even to listen to any proposals for a peaceful separation. Nothing was then left to do but to prepare for war.[474]

Thus, Davis asserted, the South was forced to take up arms against the North, not over slavery, but

to vindicate the political rights, the freedom, equality, and State sovereignty which were the heritage purchased by the blood of our revolutionary sires.[475]

★ **FACT: PROOF THAT THE CONFEDERATE STATES WERE FIGHTING FOR CONSTITUTIONAL LIBERTY IS THAT THEY ADOPTED THE U.S. CONSTITUTION AS THE MODEL FOR THEIR OWN**
That the South took up arms in the cause of constitutional liberty, and that document's assumed assurance of self-government and personal independence, is obvious from the facts that not only did she pattern her First National Flag on the U.S. Flag,[476] but she also adopted the U.S. Constitution as the scaffolding for the C.S. Constitution. Sage writes:

The Southern commonwealths were really fighting for constitutional liberty, which, under the circumstances, they thought seriously imperiled, and likely to be preserved by secession. Earl [John] Russell's assertion was true, that "the South fought for independence, the North for empire." The wish of the former for constitutional liberty and independence was manifested by their adopting the federal [U.S.] constitution, with scarcely a change. Secession was justifiable if there was no other mode of self-preservation, or remedy for wrongs; for self-preservation was the first law of nature to states as well as persons.[477]

★ **FACT: THE EMANCIPATION PROCLAMATION OFFERS THE GREATEST PROOF THAT THE WAR WAS NOT OVER SLAVERY**
After Lincoln's War, Southerner Lyon Gardiner Tyler, the son of America's tenth President, John Tyler,[478] put the matter this way:

> The emancipation of slaves [in 1863] by the late war is the best evidence that *the South never fought for slavery, but against a foreign dictation and a sectional will*. Within the Union slavery was probably secure for many years to come. *The war was nothing more than the outcome of a tyranny exerted for seventy-two years by the North over vital interests of the South.*[479]

Lyon G. Tyler, son of U.S. President John Tyler, accurately pointed out that Lincoln's War "was nothing more than the outcome of a tyranny exerted for seventy-two years by the North over vital interests of the South."

★ **FACT: THERE WERE A MYRIAD OF SUB-ISSUES THAT LED UP TO SECESSION & THE WAR**
Anti-South writers refuse to discuss or even acknowledge the one real cause behind both Southern secession and the War: *Northern liberalism versus Southern conservatism*.[480] Naturally, they also ignore the dozens of sub-issues that led to both. Boucher notes that "the list of issues, both national and local, spread over a wide range," and covered many decades, dating back to the creation of the U.S.A. A partial list of these other reasons includes the following:

- The tariff
- Internal improvements [today known as "corporate welfare"]
- The United States Bank
- Nullification
- Secession [movements]
- Non-importation agreements against the North
- Local development of manufactures
- Direct trade with Europe
- The growth of the abolitionist movement
- The American Colonization Society
- Abolitionist literature in the mails

- The local slave code
- Slavery in the District of Columbia
- The powers of Congress over slavery
- National political conventions
- Presidential campaigns
- General reform of the central government [states' rights versus consolidation]
- Currency questions, the regulation of state banks
- The Independent Treasury
- Antislavery petitions
- In Congress, the right of petition
- Plans for Southern unity
- Extradition of slave thieves
- Representation in the state legislature
- Reform of the method of electing presidential electors
- State aid to railroads
- The Bank of the State
- Temperance reform
- Educational reform
- Distribution of the surplus in the national treasury
- Assumption of state debts
- Public land sales
- The admission of Oregon
- The annexation of Texas
- The war with Mexico
- The proposed acquisition of Cuba
- Various programs for single state and united Southern action
- The Compromise of 1850
- The Fugitive Slave Law
- The Finality Doctrine
- The [anti-South] book *Uncle Tom's Cabin*
- Compensated emancipation
- The Kansas-Nebraska Bill
- The Kansas struggle
- Reopening of the African slave trade
- [Conservative Preston S.] Brooks' attack upon [Liberal Charles] Sumner
- The Dred Scott decision

- Unfriendly legislation by territorial legislatures
- A congressional slave code for the territories
- John Brown's raid and the sympathy expressed for him by Northern communities
- The campaign and election of 1860[481]
- The sectional character attributed to the Republican Party [then the Liberal party]
- The recommendation by sixty-eight Northern members of Congress of Hinton R. Helper's incendiary abolition book[482]
- The Personal Liberty Bills passed by the [Liberal] Legislatures of at least twelve Northern States
- The declaration of the [Liberal] Northern dominant party, that there should be no more slave territory
- The arrogant and aggressive spirit with which that party was coming into power[483]

Above all, there was the election to the presidency of the anti-South, sectional progressive Abraham Lincoln, the spark that finally lit the fire of secession. Fowler writes:

> But now, for the first time, an anti-slavery man, Mr. Lincoln, was elected president upon an anti-slavery platform [actually, an anti-slavery extension platform], *with the expectation on the part of the electors that anti-slavery men would "take possession of the Government," and would control the councils of the nation. Moreover, the Northern triumphant party, as be longing to the most numerous section, expected to hold the Government in perpetuity* . . .[484]

★ FACT: THE NORTH HAD BEEN ABUSING THE SOUTH FOR DECADES PRIOR TO 1860

What one sees here is a pattern of sectional abuse by the North upon the South, economically, politically, socially, and psychologically. Such ill-treatment did not suddenly begin in 1860, of course. Generations earlier Southerners were already complaining bitterly of the self-righteous and unjust behavior of Yankees, a frustration that was slowly but surely building into a Southern secession movement. In their dissatisfaction and suffering, Southerners "looked to the doctrines of state[s'] rights for relief."[485] In June 1798 Thomas Jefferson wrote the following remarks in a letter to fellow Virginian John Taylor:

It is true that *we are completely under the saddle of Massachusetts and Connecticut, and they ride us very hard, cruelly insulting our feelings, as well as exhausting our strength and subsistence. Their natural friends, the three other [Liberal] Eastern States, join them from a sort of family pride, and they have the art to divide certain other parts of the Union, so as to make use of them to govern the whole.* . . If we rid ourselves of the present rulers of Massachusetts and Connecticut, we break the Union, will the work stop there? Suppose the New England States alone cut off, will our nature be changed? Are there not men to the South with all the passions of men? Immediately we shall see a Pennsylvania and Virginia party arise in the residuary Confederacy, and the public mind will be distracted with the same party spirit. . . . Mr. New showed me your letter on the subject of the protest, which gives me an opportunity of observing what you said as to the effect with you of public proceedings, and that *it is not unwise now to estimate the separate map of Virginia and North Carolina, with a view to their separate existence.* . . Seeing we must have somebody to quarrel with, I had rather keep our New England associates for that purpose, than to see our bickerings transferred to others. They are circumstanced within such narrow limits, and their population so full, that their numbers will soon be in the minority; and *they are marked . . . with such perversity of character, as to constitute, from that circumstance, the natural division of our parties.*[486]

Thomas Jefferson and his personal residence, "Monticello," at Charlottesville, Virginia.

Twenty-seven years later Jefferson still had cause to be alarmed and angry at the Conservative South's treatment by Liberal Northerners. On Christmas day 1825 he wrote this letter to fellow Conservative William B. Giles concerning the "deluded" Federalists (the Liberals of the day), who were using "incorrect and corrupt views of government" to "usurp all the rights reserved to the states":

I see as you do, and with the deepest affliction, the rapid strides with which the federal branch of our Government is advancing towards the usurpation of all the rights reserved to the States, and the consolidation in itself of all power, foreign and domestic; and that, too, by constructions which, if legitimate, leave no limits to their power. Take together the decisions of the Federal Courts, the [progressive] doctrines of the

President [at the time, Liberal John Quincy Adams], and *the misconstructions of the constitutional compact* acted on by the legislation of the federal branch, and it is but too evident that *the three ruling branches of this department, are in combination to strip their colleagues, the State authorities, of the powers reserved to them; and to exercise themselves all functions, foreign and domestic.* . . . And what is our resource for the preservation of the Constitution? Reason and argument? You might as well reason and argue with the marble columns encircling them. The representatives chosen by ourselves? They are found in the combination, some from *incorrect views of government*, some from corrupt ones, sufficient, voting together, to outnumber the sound party [Conservative], and with majorities only of one, two, or three, bold enough to go forward in defiance.

Are we then to stand to our arms. . . ? No. That must be the last resource, not to be thought of until much longer and greater sufferings. If every infraction of a compact of so many parties is to be resisted at once, as a dissolution of it, none can ever be formed which would last one year. *We must have patience and longer endurance then with our brethren while under delusion*; give them time for reflection and experience of consequences; keep ourselves in a situation to profit by the chapter of accidents; and separate from our companions only when *the sole alternatives left, are the dissolution of our Union with them, or submission to a government without limitation of powers.*

Between these two evils, when we must make a choice, there can be no hesitation. But in the meanwhile, the States would be watchful to note every material usurpation on their rights; to denounce them as they occur in the most peremptory terms; to protest against them as wrongs to which our present submission shall be considered, not as acknowledgments or precedents of right, but as a temporary yielding to the lesser evil, until their accumulation shall overweigh that of separation.[487]

★ FACT: YANKEE PERSONAL LIBERTY LAWS HELPED PROMPT SOUTHERN SECESSION

One of the many related reasons given by the South for secession was the North's "Personal Liberty Laws," which former Conservative U.S. President Franklin Pierce referred to as "unconstitutional and obnoxious laws," the result, not of civil abolitionism, but of "political abolitionism."[488] A few state examples that were reported in December 1860 will illustrate his point:

MAINE: The laws of this State provide that no sheriff, deputy sheriff, coroner, constable, jailer, justice of the peace, or other officer of the State shall arrest or detain or aid in so doing, in any prison or building belonging to this State, or in any county or town, any person on account of a claim on him as a fugitive slave, under a penalty not exceeding one thousand dollars, and make it the duty of all county attorneys to repair to the place where such person is held in custody, and render him all necessary and legal assistance in making his defence against said claim.

NEW HAMPSHIRE: The law of the State declares that slaves, coming or brought into the State, by or with the consent of the master, shall be free; declares the attempt to hold any person as a slave within the State as a felony, with a penalty of imprisonment of not less than one nor more than five years; provided, that the provisions of this section shall not apply to any act lawfully done by any officer of the United States, or other person, in the execution of any legal process.

RHODE ISLAND: This state by her legislation forbids the carrying away of any person by force out of the State; forbids any judge, justice, magistrate, or court from officially aiding in the arrest of a fugitive slave under the fugitive slave law of 1793 or 1850; forbids any sheriff or other officer from arresting or detaining and person claimed as a fugitive slave; provides a penalty of $500 or imprisonment not exceeding six months, for violating the act; denies the use of her jails to the United States for the detention of fugitive slaves.

MICHIGAN: The law of this State requires State's attorneys to act as counsel for fugitive slaves; secures to persons arrested as fugitive slaves the benefits of the writ of *habeas corpus*, and trial by jury; denies use of State jails for detention of alleged fugitives; requires that identity of fugitive slaves shall be proved by two credible witnesses, or by legal evidence equivalent thereto, and provides a fine of not less than five hundred nor more than one thousand dollars, and imprisonment in State prison for five years, for forcibly seizing, or causing to be seized, any free person, with intent to have such person held in slavery.[489]

Contrary to Yankee myth, it was not that the North's Personal Liberty Laws favored blacks which upset the South. It was that they violated the highest established law in the country: the Constitution. Indeed, *all* of the Personal Liberty Laws were unconstitutional and therefore illegal. But the unscrupulous North implemented them anyway. In essence, Yankees were practicing *nullification*, which had been found unconstitutional by President Andrew Jackson decades earlier. Thus, Northern Liberals showed themselves to be hypocrites by denouncing a policy when it did not suit them (or when it aided the South) but approving of it when it did (or when it hurt the South).

★ FACT: THE SOUTH WAS NOT ANTI-BLACK, SHE WAS PRO-CONSTITUTION
The anti-South movement believes that the Old South's resistance to the

Old North's Personal Liberty Laws proves that Victorian Southerners were "racist." This is a demonstrable fiction. But the truth does not benefit progressives, so they ignore it.

In actuality, the South, the birthplace of the American abolition movement, was not anti-black, but pro-Constitution. Being innately law-abiding, Southerners chose to follow the law, whether they agreed with it or not. Northerners, on the other hand, willingly disobeyed laws if they did not agree with them, even laws officially decided by the Constitution and the Supreme Court.

★ FACT: NORTHERN LIBERALS CONVENIENTLY BELIEVED THAT THERE WAS A "HIGHER LAW" THAN THE CONSTITUTION
Though Southerners were not fond of slavery (they had been trying to rid America of the cursed institution since the 1600s), they *were* fond of the Constitution, and the Left-wing's Personal Liberty Laws went wholly against it. Until its clauses regarding slavery and blacks were changed, Southerners chose to follow the law.

Liberal Northerners, however, held that there was a "higher law" than the Constitution, the same myth used by Liberals today to justify their anti-social behavior and illegalities. And what is that "higher law"? It is "social justice," one of the most subjective terms ever invented by the mind of man, and intentionally so: the built-in ambiguity of the concept of "higher law" allows the lockstep Liberals free reign to ignore, rewrite, suppress, or nullify any law that does not agree with their destructive and intolerant ideologies.

A black Southern nanny tending a white baby, circa 1860s. As is clear from this photo, most white Southerners treated their servants as family members. They even registered them as such at the time of purchase. As strongly as they supported emancipation, however, until slavery could be safely and equitably abolished through the amendment process, Southerners chose to follow the law. This was not racism, it was constitutionalism—something alien to many Liberals and progressives.

★ **FACT: TO SOUTHERNERS THE LIBERAL YANKEE THEORY OF "HIGHER LAW" WAS YET ANOTHER JUSTIFIABLE MOTIVE FOR SECESSION**

The Liberals' stubborn allegiance to the arbitrary theory of "higher law" only reenforced what the South had long known about Northern progressives: they had nothing but disdain for the Constitution. If Northerners could not obey the Constitution regarding slavery, there was nothing to prevent them from disregarding every other clause in that compact; most seriously, those regarding the separation of powers and the assumed and reserved rights of the states (Ninth and Tenth Amendments).

The reaction of the South to the Yanks' Personal Liberty Laws was inevitable then: if Dixie could not protect her constitutional rights within the Union she would protect them outside of it.

Confederate diplomat William L. Yancey of Georgia.

★ **FACT: MOST CONFEDERATE SECESSIONISTS THEMSELVES DECLARED THAT SOUTHERN DISUNION WAS NOT BASED ON SLAVERY**

In the Confederacy's ongoing efforts to receive official recognition from Europe, on May 4, 1861, it sent commissioners William L. Yancey, Ambrose D. Mann, and Pierre A. Rost to meet with British foreign secretary Earl (John) Russell. A few days later, on May 11, Russell sent the following revealing dispatch to Lord Lyons:

> Foreign Office, May 11, 1861. My Lord:—On Saturday last I received at my house Mr. Yancey, Mr. Mann, and Judge Rost, the three gentlemen deputed by the Southern Confederacy to obtain their recognition as an independent State.
> *One of these gentlemen, speaking for the others, dilated on the causes which had induced the Southern States to secede from the Northern. The principal of these causes, he said, was not slavery, but the very high price, which, for the sake of protecting the Northern manufacturers, the South were obliged to pay for the manufactured goods which they required.* One of the first acts of the Southern Congress was to reduce these duties, and to prove their sincerity he gave as an instance that

Louisiana had given up altogether that protection on her sugar which she enjoyed by the legislation of the United States. As a proof of the riches of the South, he stated that of $350,000,000 of exports of produce to foreign countries, $270,000,000 [or 77 percent] were furnished by the Southern States.

I said that I could hold no official communication with the delegates of the Southern States. That, however, when the question of recognition came to be formally discussed, there were two points upon which inquiry must be made—first, whether the body seeking recognition could maintain its position as an independent State; secondly, in what manner it was proposed to maintain relations with foreign States.

After speaking at some length on the first of these points, and alluding to the news of the secession of Virginia and other intelligence favorable to their cause, *these gentlemen called my attention to the article in their Constitution prohibiting the slave-trade [Article 1, Section 9, Clauses 1 and 2]. I said that it was alleged very currently that if the Slave States found that they could not compete successfully with the cotton of other countries they would revive the slave-trade for the purpose of diminishing the cost of production. They said this was a suspicion unsupported by any proof. The fact was, that they had prohibited the slave-trade, and did not mean to revive it.* They pointed to the new tariff of the United States as a proof that British manufacturers would be nearly excluded from the North, and freely admitted in the South. Other observations were made, but not of very great importance.

The delegates concluded by stating that they should remain in London for the present, in the hope that the recognition of the Southern Confederacy would not be long delayed.[490]

Several months later, on August 14, 1861, Yancey, Rost, and Mann followed up with a letter to Earl Russell, again explaining the secession of the Southern states as well as reemphasizing the Confederacy's feelings regarding slavery:

> *It was from no fear that the slaves would be liberated that secession took place. The very party in power [the Republicans, the Liberals of the day] has proposed to guarantee slavery forever in the States, if the South would but remain in the Union. Mr. Lincoln's message proposes no freedom to the slave, but announces subjection of his owner to the will of the Union, in other words to the will of the North. Even after the battle of Bull Run, both branches of the Congress at Washington passed resolutions that the war is only waged in order to uphold that (Pro-Slavery) Constitution, and to enforce the laws (many of them Pro-Slavery), and out of 172 votes in the lower House they received all but two, and in the Senate all but one vote. As the [Union] army commenced its march, the commanding-general issued an order that no slaves should be received into, or allowed to follow, the camp.*

The great object of the war, therefore, as now officially announced, is not to free the slave, but to keep him in subjection to his owner, and to control his labor through the legislative channels which the Lincoln Government designs to force upon the master. The undersigned, therefore, submit with confidence that as far as the anti-slavery sentiment of England is concerned, it can have no sympathy with the North; nay, it will probably become disgusted with a canting hypocrisy which would enlist those sympathies on false pretences. The undersigned are, however, not insensible to the surmise that the Lincoln Government may, under stress of circumstances, change its policy, a policy based at present more upon a wily view of what is to be its effect in rearing up an element in the Confederate States favorable to the reconstruction of the Union than upon any honest desire to uphold a Constitution, the main provisions of which it has most shamelessly violated. But they confidently submit to your Lordship's consideration that success in producing so abrupt and violent a destruction of a system of labor which has reared up so vast a commerce between America and the great States of Europe, which, it is supposed, now gives bread to 10,000,000 of the population of those States, which, it may be safely assumed, is intimately blended with the basis of the great manufacturing and navigating prosperity that distinguishes the age, and probably not the least of the elements of this prosperity, would be visited with results disastrous to the world, as well as to the master and slave.⁴⁹¹

South-loathers seldom if ever discuss either of these two letters, authoritative information that comes straight from Confederate government officials. It would contradict their anti-South mythology and bring the entire Liberal house of cards crashing down.

Harriet Beecher Stowe: the abolitionist writer who knew nothing about Southern slavery.

★ FACT: THE SOUTHERN PEOPLE'S REACTION TO STOWE'S BOOK *UNCLE TOM'S CABIN* REVEALS THEIR TRUE FEELINGS ABOUT SLAVERY
Naturally, Harriet Beecher Stowe's 1852 novel, *Uncle Tom's Cabin*, was greeted warmly in the Liberal North, where hatred of the Conservative South and ignorance of the facts surrounding Southern slavery were at their zenith.

In the South, however, Stowe's book was another matter, and for good reason. The fictitious work had no basis in reality, for its Yankee author had never been South of the Mason-Dixon line, had never visited a Southern plantation, and had never even met a single Southern slave. A lifelong stay-at-home Yankee, she was merely parroting the ludicrous, slanderous, and deceptive claims she found in the abolition tracts of radical South-haters; simple-minded, biased, ideological, overly emotional men and women who were completely ignorant of how the "peculiar institution" was practiced in the South.[492]

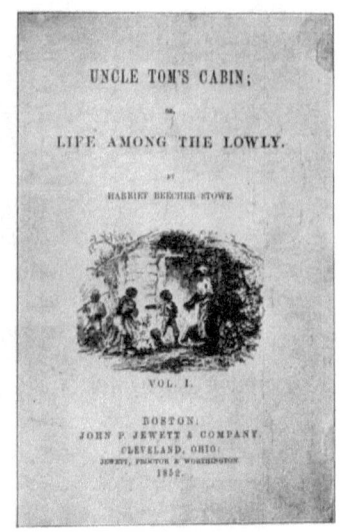

The 1852 title page from Stowe's fanciful and historically inaccurate novel, Uncle Tom's Cabin.

As such, the main result of the book "had been simply to anger the South," and Southerners quickly responded to its falsehoods, describing it "to be full of dramatic, highly colored, unreal pictures of slavery"; portraits that "would do much harm" by carrying "an erroneous picture of slavery to those only too eager to misunderstand," while serving "to confirm Southerners in the opinion that there was but hatred and misconception in the North."[493]

The South was universal in its condemnation of the badly researched poorly written novel. Not because Stowe criticized slavery in the South, but because she never mentioned that the American abolition movement had begun in the South,[494] that 25 percent of free Southern blacks were also slave owners (of both black *and* white slaves),[495] that countless thousands of Native-Americans owned slaves as well,[496] that Yankee slavery was far more severe than Southern servitude,[497] and because, in general, she intentionally portrayed Southern slavery in a deceitful and inflammatory manner, with disinformation designed to turn its readers against both the institution and the South. All of this was unnecessary. The South was *already* against slavery, and had been since the 1600s, when America's first voluntary manumission took place in the colony of Virginia.[498]

Though Stowe's book was "read with avidity in the North and abroad and taken as 'law and Gospel,'" in the South it was more correctly labeled "utterly false and pernicious," written by "a pen dipped in the gall of bitterness and overflowing with all the rage and hatred of a fiendish spirit."[499] When Northern abolitionists demanded an official Southern response to Stowe's book, they received this terse reply:

> We have no apologies, no explanations, no instructions to make or give to the enemies and detractors of the South. Throwing ourselves upon the broad basis of the Constitution, relying upon the justice of our case, we treat as traitors to our country, as infidels in the sight of God, and as the most cruel and bloody-minded persons in all the world, such frontless women as Mrs. Beecher Stowe and all her abettors and admirers.[500]

What you are reading here is not a Southern defense of slavery, as South-haters claim. It is a defense of the U.S. Constitution, which, as we have seen, the Liberal North had been ignoring and violating for decades prior to 1860. It was this long simmering flash point—that is, the two different interpretations of the Constitution, a conservative one in the South and a liberal one in the North—that finally triggered secession when the North's leading anti-South candidate, Abraham Lincoln, was elected president on November 6, 1860.

★ FACT: THE SLAVERY ISSUE WAS MERELY THE TARIFF ISSUE IN DISGUISE
Despite the 150 year effort by South-loathing Liberals and uneducated Conservatives to lay slavery at the root of both secession and the Civil War, it has not worked. Every well-read reasonably intelligent person today knows that those who initiate wars do so over money, and the power and control that goes with it. Dictatorial big government Liberal Lincoln was no different, and I have devoted an entire chapter in this book which proves it.

The idea that millions of white men and women in the North and South would risk their lives, families, homes, land, businesses, indeed, their very culture and society, to preserve or destroy slavery due to racism is ridiculous. The fact is that slavery was always about economics, not "white supremacy." Obviously—for there were both thousands of *black slave owners* and thousands of *white slaves* in early America! Indeed, the so-called "slavery issue" was nothing more than the tariff issue hidden under the Liberal guise of Northern abolitionism, and, as I have shown,

Northern abolitionism was simply "social spite,"[501] nothing more than pure "hostility towards the South."[502] Fowler was right when he said that Yankee Liberals "love negroes only because they hate their [Conservative Southern] masters."[503] Dixie-loathing Yankee Thaddeus Stevens let slip the Liberals' secret when he said of Conservative Southerners:

> . . . if their whole country must be laid waste, and made a desert, in order to save this Union from destruction, so let it be. I would rather, Sir, reduce them to a condition where their whole country is to be re-peopled by a band of freemen [freed black servants] than to see them perpetrate the destruction of this people [African-Americans] through our agency. . . . *Our object is to subdue the Rebels.*[504]

The facts behind this left-wing ruse were so well-known at one time that they were being discussed even before the start of Lincoln's War. Missouri Senator Thomas Hart Benton wrote the following in the 1850s:

> The regular inauguration of this slavery agitation dates from the year 1835; but it had commenced two years before, and in this way: nullification and disunion had commenced in 1830, upon complaint against [a] protective tariff. That, being put down in 1833 under President [Andrew] Jackson's proclamation and energetic measures, *was immediately substituted by the slavery agitation.* Mr. [John C.] Calhoun, when he went home from Congress in the spring of that year, told his friends that *"the South could never be united against the North on the tariff question—that the sugar interest of Louisiana would keep her out—and that the basis of southern union must be shifted to the slave question."* Then all the papers in his interest, and especially the one at Washington, published by Mr. Duff Green, dropped tariff agitation, and commenced upon slavery, and in two years had the agitation ripe for inauguration on the slavery question. And *in tracing this agitation to its present stage, and to comprehend its rational, it is not to be forgotten that it is a mere continuation of old tariff disunion, and preferred because more available.*[505]

Even before Lincoln's War, Southern Senator Thomas Hart Benton revealed the truth about the coming conflict: the "slavery issue" was never anything but the tariff issue in disguise.

9

WHY YANKEES HAVE NO RIGHT TO CRITICIZE THE SOUTH FOR SECEDING FROM THE UNION

IF I WERE TO PROVIDE *all* the reasons why it is both preposterous and hypocritical for South-hating Yankees to denigrate Dixie over secession, it would require an entire extra volume. For the reader's convenience, in this chapter I will merely touch on a few salient points.

★ FACT: THE AMERICAN ABOLITION MOVEMENT STARTED IN THE SOUTH
As must be patently clear to the reader by now, the anti-South movement makes a grievous error when it pins the motivation behind the Southern Secession Ordinances on slavery. The absurdity of this charge is all the more apparent when one realizes that the American abolition movement began, not in the North, as Yankee myth claims, but in the South.[506] The earliest voluntary manumission nationwide occurred in Virginia in 1655, the state which later became the first to seek a ban on both slavery and the slave trade,[507] with Virginian Thomas Jefferson leading the movement in the late 1700s and early 1800s.[508]

At one time there were more Southern organizations opposed to slavery than Northern ones,[509] and for most of the South's history practically all Southerners were abolitionists,[510] including many slaveholders themselves, one of the more famous being Mary Chesnut.[511] Of the 130 abolition societies established before 1827 by Northern abolitionist Benjamin Lundy, over 100, comprising four-fifths of the total membership, were in the South. Southern Quakers were among the first to come out against the spread of the institution. Early North Carolina, as another example, had a number of well-known "forceful" antislavery leaders, such as Benjamin Sherwood Hedrick and Daniel Reaves Goodlow. And in South Carolina the famed Quaker sisters Sarah and Angelina Grimké were just two among millions of Southerners fighting for the cause of abolition. The Southern abolition movement involved so many Southerners, so many Southern states, and covered such a large span of time, that the latter wrote an entire book on the subject.[512]

★ FACT: BOTH THE AMERICAN SLAVE TRADE & AMERICAN SLAVERY STARTED IN THE NORTH

In 1638 Boston, Massachusetts, launched the American slave trade when the 120-ton Salem vessel *Desire* brought home a shipload of African slaves from the West Indies. In 1641 Bostonians inaugurated American slavery when they became the first colony to legalize and monetize the institution.[513]

The first American slave ship, *Desire*, sailed from Massachusetts in 1638.

Slavery, in all its many forms, quickly took root in the Northeast, with major slave ports springing up in Washington, D.C., as well as such states as Rhode Island, Connecticut, Maryland, New Jersey, and Pennsylvania. During the 1700s untold numbers of Yankee slave ships traveled to the "Dark Continent" and the Caribbean, bringing back hundreds of thousands of Africans, which were sold up and down the East Coast. At the center of the Yankee slave trade was New York City, which became America's slave capital by 1800, turning it into the country's largest and most wealthy city, the financial center of the U.S.—a title it holds, thanks to Yankee slavery, to this day.[514]

★ FACT: RACIAL TOLERANCE WAS ALWAYS GREATER IN THE SOUTH THAN IN THE NORTH

One of the many well-known facts that has been thoroughly suppressed by the anti-South movement is that the people of Dixie have always been far more racially tolerant than the people of the North. Though hundreds of eyewitness accounts could be given to prove this, let us examine just one, and that from a most reputable source: French diplomat Alexis de Tocqueville, who traveled throughout the U.S. in the early 1800s. Later he recorded his observations on this topic, writing:

As described by credible eyewitnesses like Tocqueville, race relations were far friendlier in the Old South than in the Old North. The same is true of the South and the North today.

> Whosoever has inhabited the United States must have perceived that *in those parts of the Union in which the negroes are no longer slaves, they have in no wise drawn nearer to the whites. On the contrary, the prejudice of the race appears to be stronger in the States which have abolished slavery than in those where it still exists; and nowhere is it so intolerant as in those States where servitude never has been known.*
>
> . . . In the South, where slavery still exists, the negroes are less carefully kept apart; they sometimes share the labour and the recreations of the whites; the whites consent to intermix with them to a certain extent, and although the legislation treats them more harshly, *the habits of the [Southern] people are more tolerant and compassionate. In the South the master is not afraid to raise his slave to his own standing*, because he knows that he can in a moment reduce him to the dust at pleasure. *In the North the white no longer distinctly perceives the barrier which separates him from the degraded race, and he shuns the negro with the more pertinacity, since he fears lest they should some day be confounded together.*
>
> Among the Americans of the South, Nature sometimes reasserts her rights, and restores a transient equality between the blacks and the whites; but in the North pride restrains the most imperious of human passions. The American of the Northern States would perhaps allow the negress to share his licentious pleasures if the laws of his country did not declare that she may aspire to be the legitimate partner of his bed; but he recoils with horror from her who might become his wife. Thus it is, *in the United States, that the prejudice which repels the negroes seems to increase in proportion as they are emancipated, and inequality is sanctioned by the manners while it is effaced from the laws of the country.*[515]

★ FACT: ONLY 4.8 PERCENT OF INDIVIDUAL SOUTHERNERS WERE SLAVE OWNERS
Pro-North writers would have us believe that "every Southerner was once a slave owner." However, the opposite is true.

In 1860 the South had reached its highest rate of slave ownership. According to the U.S. Census that year, with a white population of 7,215,525, only 4.8 percent, or 385,000, of all white Southern men owned slaves—the exact population of modern day Wichita, Kansas. The other 95.2 percent did not. Of those who did, most owned less than five. Correcting for the mistakes of Census takers—which would include counting slave-hirers as slave owners and counting more than once those thousands of slave owners who annually moved the same slaves back and forth across multiple states—this figure, 4.8 percent, is no doubt too large. Either way, at the time Southerners themselves believed that only about 5 percent of their number owned slaves, which is slightly high, but roughly correct.[516]

★ FACT: THE CONFEDERACY BEGAN BLACK ENLISTMENT BEFORE THE UNION DID, PROVING THAT THE SOUTH WAS NOT TRYING TO PRESERVE SLAVERY
Southern black enlistment came even before the War's first major conflict, the Battle of First Manassas (First Bull Run to Yanks) on July 18, 1861. In June 1861, one year and three months before the Union officially sanctioned the recruitment of blacks in August 1862, and almost two years before Lincoln began arming blacks in March 1863, the Tennessee legislature passed a statute allowing Governor Isham G. Harris to receive into military service "all male free persons of color, between the ages of 15 and 50 . . ."[517]

The South's first all-black militia was officially formed on April 23, 1861, only nine days after the first battle of the War at Fort Sumter, South Carolina. The unit, known as the "Native Guards (colored)," was "duly and legally enrolled as a part of the militia of the State, its officers being commissioned by Thomas O. Moore, Governor and Commander-in-Chief of the State of Louisiana . . ." In contrast, the North's first all-black militia, the First South Carolina Volunteers, was not commissioned until over a year and a half later (on November 7, 1862), under Yankee Colonel Thomas Wentworth Higginson. Indeed, Lincoln did not allow official black enlistment until January 1, 1863, with the issuance of his Final Emancipation Proclamation, as that document tacitly states. Up until then he had strictly barred both blacks and Native-Americans (the former whom Lincoln and his administration referred to as "an inferior race," the latter whom they called "savages") from joining the Union military as armed soldiers. When they were, in 1863, they were forced to fight in segregated units (something the more racially tolerant Confederate military never did) and given half the pay of white Union soldiers (also something not found in the more equalitarian Southern armies).[518]

Since blacks had served officially, legally, and courageously as soldiers in all of America's conflicts up until the Civil War, Lincoln must be named as the one who injected white racism, white supremacy, and racial segregation into the U.S. military for the first time, an unfortunate situation that lasted well into the late 1940s.[519]

This rare photo is one that South-hating Liberals would rather you never see: two uniformed Confederate soldiers, Andrew Martin Chandler (left), and one of his family's African-American servants, Silas Chandler (right). Trained members of the 44th Mississippi Infantry, they are armed to the teeth and ready to defend the South at all costs. Contrary to Yankee myth, as many as 1 million Southern blacks served in the racially *integrated* Confederate military in one capacity or another; five times more than served in the racially *segregated* Union military.

Confederate Secretary of State Judah P. Benjamin announced plans for the complete abolition of slavery across the South nearly a year before the Thirteenth Amendment was ratified. His own servants offered to fight for the Confederacy if he would emancipate them; an offer, like millions of other Southern slave owners, he was only too happy to accept.

★ **FACT: THE SOUTH PLANNED ON COMPLETE ABOLITION IN JANUARY 1865, FOUR MONTHS BEFORE THE WAR ENDED & NEARLY A YEAR BEFORE THE THIRTEENTH AMENDMENT WAS ISSUED, MORE PROOF THAT THE SOUTH WAS NOT TRYING TO PRESERVE SLAVERY**

According to Yankee myth the South seceded and fought to "preserve slavery." Yet this falsehood is refuted by ten thousand facts, one of the more obvious being the following: in January 1865, nearly a year before the U.S. issued the Thirteenth Amendment (on December 6, 1865) banning slavery across the nation, Confederate Secretary of State Judah P. Benjamin ordered Confederate commissioner Duncan F. Kenner to England to announce the C.S.'s commitment to full emancipation.[520] Around the same time Benjamin himself said:

> We have 680,000 blacks capable of bearing arms, and who ought now to be in the field. Let us now say to every negro who wishes to go into the ranks on condition of being free, go and fight—*you are free. My own negroes have been to me and said, "Master, set us free and we'll fight for you."*[521]

★ **FACT: THE THIRTEENTH AMENDMENT WAS FIRST SUGGESTED BY A SOUTHERNER, NOT A NORTHERNER**

Yankee myth would have us believe that the Thirteenth Amendment was the sole product of the "abolitionist North," and that the "slave-ridden South" was completely against it.

The falseness of these beliefs is highlighted by the fact that, as just noted, the American abolition movement began in the South.[522] Thus, it should come as no surprise that the Thirteenth Amendment was first proposed by a Southern man, Missouri Senator John Brooks Henderson (originally from Virginia).[523]

★ **FACT: THE NORTH DID NOT VOTE UNANIMOUSLY ON THE THIRTEENTH AMENDMENT**

Contrary to everything we have been taught about the Thirteenth Amendment, the North was never in complete support of it and there was never a unanimous vote on it. This was true from the very beginning. On February 1, 1864, for example, the U.S. Congress put forth an early pre-Thirteenth Amendment proposition in which over one-third of the Yankee delegates voted against it (80 yeas, 46 nays). A subsequent resolution to this bill received even less support: 78 yeas, 62 nays; far less than "the two-thirds affirmative vote necessary to secure a passage through the House of the Senate Joint Resolution." Northern Liberals (Republicans at the time) considered the results "disappointing" and "discouraging."[524]

Missouri Senator John B. Henderson (of Virginia), the originator of the Thirteenth Amendment.

On June 15, 1864, a resolution to add the Thirteenth Amendment to the Constitution was again defeated by the U.S. House of Representatives (93 yeas, 65 nays, 23 not voting). Once more the votes fell short of the required two-thirds majority.[525] The proposed amendment was debated all through the month of January 1865 with no results. Finally, on January 31, 1865, the House of Representatives passed the bill. The two-thirds vote needed was finally achieved, but still without unanimous approval (119 yeas, 56 nays).[526] Why?

Not because Conservatives (at the time, the Democrats) did not want to abolish slavery, but because they rightly saw the amendment as nothing more than "social spite,"[527] a vindictive political weapon that was being used by Liberals, socialists, and radicals to weaken the Constitution and dominate and intimidate traditional Americans, particularly traditional *Southern* Americans.

Robert E. Lee's family residence "Arlington House." Virginia, Lee's home state, ratified the Thirteenth Amendment before many of the Northern states did.

★ FACT: THE SOUTHERN STATES SUPPORTED & RATIFIED THE THIRTEENTH AMENDMENT
Although you will not learn the truth from our mainstream history books, the Southern states did indeed support and ratify the Thirteenth Amendment. The amendment was, after all, proposed by a Southerner[528] in the region where the American abolition movement had gotten its start: the South.[529]

Virginia ratified the Thirteenth Amendment on February 9, 1865; Missouri on February 10, 1865; Louisiana on February 17, 1865; Tennessee on April 7, 1865; Arkansas on April 20, 1865; South Carolina on November 13, 1865; Alabama on December 2, 1865; North Carolina on December 4, 1865; Georgia on December 6, 1865; Florida on December 28, 1865; Texas on February 18, 1870; Kentucky on March 18, 1976; Mississippi on March 16, 1995.[530]

The required three-fourths of the states vote was not reached until December 6, 1865, when the amendment was officially and nationally declared in effect.[531] Revealingly, this was nearly five years after the Confederate States of America banned the slave trade in her Constitution in early 1861.[532]

★ FACT: MANY SOUTHERN STATES RATIFIED THE THIRTEENTH AMENDMENT *PRIOR* TO THE NORTHERN STATES
South-loathers do not want you to know that many of the Southern states ratified the Thirteenth Amendment *before* some of the Northern states did. Virginia, for instance, beat Ohio (which ratified on February 10, 1865); Missouri beat Indiana (which ratified on February 13, 1865); Louisiana beat Minnesota (which ratified on February 23, 1865), Wisconsin (which ratified on February 24, 1865), and Vermont (which ratified on March 9, 1865); Tennessee beat Connecticut (which ratified on May 4, 1865); and Arkansas beat New Hampshire (which ratified on July 1, 1865).

The Yankee myth that "the South was anti-Thirteenth Amendment" is now dead, and can be buried alongside the hundreds of other Liberal lies we have debunked in this book.

★ **FACT: THE CONFEDERACY BEGAN OFFICIAL EMANCIPATION IN MARCH 1865, ONE MONTH BEFORE THE WAR ENDED, PROVING THAT THE SOUTH WAS NOT TRYING TO PRESERVE SLAVERY**

While blacks fought unofficially for the South from day one, the Confederacy began official black enlistment on March 13, 1865, with congressional passage of the "Act to Increase the Military Force of the Confederate States." The initial law, also known as the "Negro Soldier Bill," only allowed for the enrollment of blacks, not their emancipation,[533] an unfortunate oversight that President Jefferson Davis quickly resolved.[534]

A few days later, on March 23, through the War Department, Davis issued General Order No. 14, which stated in part:

Davis at his Mississippi home "Beauvoir" after the War. Like every other Confederate official, he was an advocate of emancipating and enrolling slaves in the armed forces.

> . . . *No slave will be accepted as a recruit unless with his own consent* and with the approbation of his master by a written instrument *conferring, as far as he may, the rights of a freedman* . . .[535]

In other words, Southern slaves could now not only officially enlist, but they were immediately emancipated and fought under the Confederate flag as free men, on the same footing as Southern white soldiers.[536]

★ **FACT: MANY SOUTHERNERS EMANCIPATED THEIR SLAVES BEFORE OR DURING THE WAR, AGAIN PROVING THAT THE SOUTH WAS NOT TRYING TO MAINTAIN SLAVERY**

At a permanent loss of billions of dollars, thousands of white Southerners freed their servants before or during Lincoln's War. Among such men were Robert E. Lee (who was himself not a slave owner, but who freed his wife's family's servants in 1862),[537] and Nathan Bedford Forrest (who permanently shut down his slave trading business in 1859 and abolished slavery on his plantations by 1863).⁵³⁸ Forrest is particularly impressive in this regard, for though the total combined worth of his servants was in the tens of millions, he set them all free without a single penny of compensation from either the U.S. or the C.S. governments.

Southern icon Confederate General Nathan Bedford Forrest closed down his slave trading business and emancipated most of his slaves before the War. He then enlisted 45 of them in his cavalry, hand-picking seven to be his personal armed guards—hardly the actions of a white racist.

It is noteworthy that over 90 percent of Forrest's servants asked to stay on with him after they were freed,⁵³⁹ not wishing to work for anyone else; and also that he enlisted 45 of them to fight in his cavalry,⁵⁴⁰ hand-selecting seven of his most able black marksmen to serve as his personal armed guards. Of them Forrest later said: "These boys stayed with me, drove my teams, and better confederates did not live."⁵⁴¹ For these and a thousand other pro-black civil rights acts, Forrest is still called a "racist" by the ignorant, the uneducated, and the nefarious!⁵⁴²

Now, if "the South was trying to maintain the peculiar institution," as our mainstream history books tell us, why did so many of her largest slaveholders voluntarily emancipate their servants even before the start of the conflict?

★ FACT: EVERY CONFEDERATE MILITARY OFFICER & SOLDIER SUPPORTED THE IDEA OF EMANCIPATION & BLACK ENLISTMENT LONG BEFORE THE END OF THE WAR
According to Yankee myth "the South continued to be solidly against abolition right through the War, violently denouncing the idea of enlisting African Americans in the Confederate armies." Unfortunately for those making this claim, it does not match reality. Thousands of Confederate officers and soldiers—indeed, *every one of them*, it was reported—supported both abolition and black enlistment.⁵⁴³

Two of the more famous of these military men were Robert E. Lee and Patrick R. Cleburne. In January 1865, the former, a non-slave owner who hated slavery,[544] wrote out a detailed emancipation and enlistment plan, one that included the following remarks. Said General Lee:

> We should not expect slaves to fight for prospective freedom when they can secure it at once by going to the enemy, in whose service they will incur no greater risk than in ours. The reasons that induce me to *recommend the employment of negro troops* at all render the effect of the measures I have suggested upon slavery immaterial, and in my opinion the best means of securing the efficiency and fidelity of this auxiliary force would be to *accompany the measure with a well-digested plan of gradual and general emancipation. As that will be the result of the continuance of the war, and will certainly occur if the enemy succeed*, it seems to me most advisable to adopt it at once, and thereby obtain all the benefits that will accrue to our cause.[545]

A year earlier, in January 1864, the latter drew up one of the most convincing emancipation and enlistment plans. In it General Cleburne made the following remarks:

> Adequately to meet the causes which are now threatening ruin to our country, we propose . . . that we retain in service for the war all troops now in service, and that we *immediately commence training a large reserve of the most courageous of our slaves, and further that we guarantee freedom within a reasonable time to every slave in the South who shall remain true to the Confederacy in this war. As between the loss of independence and the loss of slavery, we assume that every patriot will freely give up the latter—give up the negro slave rather than be a slave himself.* If we are correct in this assumption it only remains to show how this great national sacrifice is, in all human probabilities, to change the current of success and sweep the [Yankee] invader from our country.
>
> . . . The immediate effect of *the emancipation and enrollment of negroes* on the military strength of the South would be: To enable us to have armies numerically superior to those of the North, and a reserve of any size we might think necessary; to enable us to take the offensive, move forward, and forage on the enemy. It would open to us in prospective another and almost untouched source of supply, and furnish us with the means of preventing temporary disaster, and carrying on a protracted struggle. *It would instantly remove all the vulnerability, embarrassment, and inherent weakness which result from slavery.*
>
> . . . *We can only get a sufficiency by making the negro share the danger and hardships of the war. If we arm and train him and make him fight for the country in her hour of dire distress, every consideration of principle and policy demand that we should set him and his whole race who side with us free. It is a first principle with*

mankind that he who offers his life in defense of the State should receive from her in return his freedom and his happiness, and we believe in acknowledgment of this principle. The Constitution of the Southern States has reserved to their respective governments the power to free slaves for meritorious services to the State [see Article 1, Section 8, Clause 16, and Article 4, Section 2, Clause 1 of the C.S. Constitution].[546]

It is politic besides. For many years, ever since the agitation of the subject of slavery commenced, the negro has been dreaming of freedom, and his vivid imagination has surrounded that condition with so many gratifications that it has become the paradise of his hopes. To attain it he will tempt dangers and difficulties not exceeded by the bravest soldier in the field. The hope of freedom is perhaps the only moral incentive that can be applied to him in his present condition. It would be preposterous then to expect him to fight against it with any degree of enthusiasm, therefore we must bind him to our cause by no doubtful bonds; we must leave no possible loop-hole for treachery to creep in. The slaves are dangerous now [thanks to the Yankees' anti-South propaganda, then being ruthlessly dispersed across the South], but armed, trained, and collected in an army they would be a thousand fold more dangerous: therefore *when we make soldiers of them we must make free men of them beyond all question*, and thus enlist their sympathies also. *We can do this more effectually than the North can now do, for we can give the negro not only his own freedom, but that of his wife and child, and can secure it to him in his old home.*

Confederate General Patrick R. Cleburne was publicly campaigning for abolition as early as January 1864.

. . . If, then, we touch the institution at all, we would do best to make the most of it, and *by emancipating the whole race* upon reasonable terms, and within such reasonable time as will prepare both races for the change, secure to ourselves all the advantages, and to our enemies all the disadvantages that can arise, both at home and abroad, from such a sacrifice. Satisfy the negro that if he faithfully adheres to our standard during the war *he shall receive his freedom and that of his race.* Give him as an earnest of our intentions such immediate immunities as will impress him with our sincerity and be in keeping with his new condition, *enroll a portion of his class as soldiers of the Confederacy*, and we change the race from a dreaded weakness to a position of strength.

. . . It is said [by a small minority of uninformed Southerners that] slavery is all we are fighting for, and if we give it up we give up all. *Even if this were true, which we deny, slavery is not all our enemies are fighting for. It is merely the pretense to establish sectional superiority and a more centralized form of* government, and to deprive us of our rights and liberties. We have now briefly proposed a plan which we believe will save our country. It may be imperfect, but in all human probability it would give us our independence.[547]

★ FACT: AMONG THE SOUTHERN POPULACE THERE WAS VIRTUALLY "NO OPPOSITION" TO THE IDEA OF ENLISTING BLACKS IN THE CONFEDERATE MILITARY
While anti-South partisans continue to assert that "the Old South was a racist slavocracy that would never sanction black enlistment in the Confederate armies," the facts tell a different story. On October 18, 1864, almost two years before the War ended, the following editorial, written by a Southern civilian, appeared in the Richmond (Virginia) Enquirer. It was entitled: "Using the Slaves":

> The proposition to extend the Conscript Law to the slaves of the States was first formerly advanced by the *Enquirer* in the issue of the 6th instant. Since that time, *we have received many assurances of its popular favor, and none whatever of opposition to it*. We learn that *the planters in the extreme Southern States favor the proposition, and some have signified their readiness to free five, ten, or fifteen of their slaves, if they will enter the army*. The near approach of the time when the [Confederate] Congress meets again requires that expression be given to the sentiments of the country upon this important measure. We therefore earnestly invite its discussion, and open our columns to opponents as well as friends of the proposition.
>
> The result of the late [U.S.] elections is still in doubt, and whether [Liberal] Lincoln or [Conservative Union General George B.] McClellan will be elected it is yet impossible to determine; but there is no uncertainty us to the question of carrying on the war. Whether Lincoln or McClellan be the next President, the voice, and the almost unanimous voice, of that people is for a vigorous prosecution of the war. The duty of preparing to meet that issue will be before the approaching session of the Confederate Congress; that body will have before it, for consideration, the ways and means, as well of men as of money, for carrying on the war on our part.
>
> The war-cry of the enemy—"No parley with rebellion in the field; no compromise with slavery in the readjustment"—fully informs our people that, in plain vernacular, *the whites of these [Southern] States are to be subjugated to slavery [by a Liberal-dominated Northern government], and their slaves reduced to the miserable condition of Yankee free negroes*. This is the view of the people among our enemies, and this will be the result of the war, whether ended by Lincoln or McClellan, if the people of these States permit themselves to be conquered.
>
> *The conscription of negroes should be accompanied with freedom and the privilege of remaining in the States*; this is no part of abolitionism; it is the exercise by the

master of the unquestionable right of manumission; it is remunerating those who defend our cause with the privilege of freedom. Nor should this important subject be prejudiced with questions about putting the negro on an equality with our friends, brothers, and fathers. Many of the soldiers in their childhood were fondled and nursed by faithful negro nurses, and yet no question of equality was ever raised. Many a man has manumitted slaves without ever being subjected to the suspicion of being an abolitionist.

The issues involved in this war are too exalted in their importance and character for us to permit them to be compromised by being degraded to a question of property. The liberty and freedom of ourselves and of our children, the nationality of our country, the right of enjoying any kind of property, the houses over our heads, and the very graves of our children and friends, are involved in this struggle. *Failure makes slaves of all, white and black; robs all of property, real and personal; divides our lands among our conquerors, who will plough up the very graves of our dead as fertilized ground for making money. We have in our midst a half million of fighting material [that is, black servants] which is property—shall we use that property for the common cause? Justice and sound policy demand that we make freemen of those who fight for freedom.* We conscript the master and we impress his horses, cattle, wheat, and every other property except slaves. *This very exception is an imputation that this war is for slavery and not for freedom. By conscripting the negroes we show to the world the earnestness that is in our people; we prove to our enemies that at the moment of our supposed exhaustion, in the fifth year of the war, we shall meet them with larger armies than we have before raised; and we explode the false accusation that we are fighting for slavery, or a slaveholders' Confederacy.*

In 1860, even before Lincoln's War, it was widely known that slavery was "on the verge of extinction," a relief to Southerners everywhere. Not surprisingly, when the idea of emancipation and black enlistment came up, the average white Southerner gave it his or her full support.

There are those who doubt whether sound policy would trust negroes with arms. We are not of those who entertain any fears upon that subject. Drill and discipline make valuable, soldiers of Russian serfs, and no negroes in these States are so ignorant and brutal as those serfs. *Between service with the Confederacy and with the Yankees, between living among us with all their strong local attachments, and going among strangers, who are now openly buying and selling them to recruiting officers, our slaves will find no difficulty in choosing [sides].* And, when once it is understood that *freedom and a home in the South are the privileges offered* by the Confederate authorities, while the enemy extend the beggarly hospitalities of Yankee philanthropy, not only will desertion from our ranks be infrequent, but the drafted negroes of the Yankee armies will exchange service.

This subject addresses itself to the consideration of our people, at this particular time, with great force. The prospect of four more years of war are before our people; the enemy will not even "parley" with us without unconditional surrender, the fruits of which would be the confiscation of all property, *the deportation of whole communities, the degradation of the people, and the domination and tyranny of Yankee masters*. There can be no reconstruction which does not embrace a surrender first, which will not permit confiscation afterwards, which *does not insure enslaving the white, without freeing the blacks*.

If there are any weak-kneed people who imagine they can save their property by reconstruction, let them study the Shibboleth of all parties in the United States—"No parley with rebellion in the field; no compromise with slavery in the adjustment." Unconditional surrender is first demanded before even a parley. We are to lay down our arms and submit to the kindness of the Butlers, Grants, Shermans, and Sheridans; to the fate of New Orleans, the condition of the Valley, the misery of Atlanta, and, after all that degradation, to give up all our slaves in the adjustment. If there are any reasons against extending the conscription to slaves, we should like to have them stated; but *we are decidedly of opinion that the whole country will agree to the proposition, and that at an early day the next Congress will be called upon to provide for it by law.*[548]

Due to ignorance and malice, enemies of the South have frequently used presentism to create their own fictitious version of this editorial; an effort to forward their assault on the Southern people and the Southern Confederacy. Let us take some of the more popularly misread statements here and clarify them based on the views of Conservative Southerners living in 1864, rather the views of Liberal Northerners living in 2017:

• First, according to the *Enquirer's* informal polling, the reaction from the Southern populace to the idea of black enlistment was 100 percent positive, with "none whatever in opposition to it."
• Even slave owners from the deepest part of the South, where so-called "white racism" was allegedly strongest, were ready to fully emancipate their slaves, "if they enter the Confederate army."
• One of the most unrecognized reasons for secession is given here; namely that by leaving the Union, Southern whites sincerely believed that Southern blacks would be spared the innumerable miseries of becoming "free Yankee negroes." As America's racist Black Codes and

the racist American Colonization Society both originated in the North, and as white racism was (and still is) far more severe in the North than in the South, this was no idle belief, making secession for this purpose alone entirely justifiable.

Our most racist U.S. president, Abraham Lincoln, as just one primary example, not only supported full scale black deportation,[549] but if this was not ultimately workable he was willing to try the idea of corralling African-Americans in their own all-black state.[550] "What I would most desire," said our sixteenth chief executive publicly on July 17, 1858, "would be the separation of the white and black races."[551] Few if any Victorian Southern black servants wished to be subjected to this kind of menacing Yankee prejudice, much preferring the more tolerant South—even with the many unknowns that came with personal freedom.

• The *Enquirer* recommends that blacks who are willing to serve in the Confederate military be granted full and complete freedom, as well as the opportunity to remain in the United States. This was the opposite of what Lincoln and many Northerners wanted. A onetime leader and lifelong member of the American Colonization Society,[552] Lincoln campaigned throughout his entire adult life[553] to have as many African-Americans as possible deported to (that is, "colonized" in) foreign lands, including, he hoped, Europe, the Caribbean, South America, and "their own native land," Africa.[554] On October 16, 1854, Lincoln, for instance, made this public pronouncement:

> If all earthly power were given me, I should not know what to do as to the existing institution. *My first impulse would be to free all the slaves, and send them to Liberia [Africa]—to their own native land.*[555]

• The *Enquirer* makes an important distinction between "abolition" and "manumission," the former merely being then a Yankee term for the simple termination of slavery, the latter being a Southern term for the actual freeing of a slave by his or her owner. Southern slaveholders held that it was important to personally enlist then free their slaves. Only then could their servants grasp the existential connection between "defending the Southern Cause" (self-government) and personal freedom (emancipation)—one already well-known to Southern white children.

This was not a "patriarchal" concession, as modern Liberals charge, but a mutually beneficial arrangement that gave satisfaction and pride in both freedman and former master. This was especially significant to Southern slave owners, who stood to lose billions of dollars: in 1850, for example, the average slave cost around $1,200, roughly $36,000 in today's currency—a significant investment that would be forever lost upon manumission.

When Conservative Yankee Stephen A. Douglas called for continued white supremacy during a debate with Lincoln in 1858, Liberal Lincoln agreed with him, saying he had no desire for whites and "niggers" to marry.

• The *Enquirer* does not want the subject of black Confederate enlistment to "be prejudiced with questions about putting the negro on an equality with our friends, brothers, and fathers." Is this white racism? Yes. But it was a mild form of racism that was part and parcel of American white society at the time, and was, in fact, no different than the black racism that existed in the same period. Behind closed doors, where black racism has always hidden and flourished, many Victorian African-Americans were revolted by the sight of white skin, a vestige of the native African belief that "only black skin is beautiful."556

In any case, the *Enquirer's* Southern white racism, which viewed whites as superior and blacks as inferior, was absolutely endemic to the white North in the 1860s. In September 1859, just a year before he was elected president, Lincoln himself made this statement:

> Negro equality! Fudge!! How long, in the Government of a God great enough to make and maintain this universe, shall there continue [to be] knaves to vend and fools to gulp, so low a piece of demagoguism as this?557

During his August 21, 1858, debate with Stephen A. Douglas at Ottawa, Illinois, Lincoln not only agreed with his opponent's call for continued white supremacy, he also complained that he had been misrepresented as having promoted interracial marriage. In response, he angrily denied the accusation, saying that he had never intended to "set the niggers and white people to marry together."558 As if to try and put a permanent period on this sentiment, at the same debate Lincoln said:

> . . . this is the true complexion of all I have ever said in regard to the institution of slavery and the black race. This is the whole of it, and *anything that argues me into this idea of perfect, social, and political equality with the negro, is but a specious and fantastic arrangement of words*, by which a man can prove a horse chestnut to be a chestnut horse.[559]

At the same debate, he answered Douglas' charge that he was "trying to establish racial equality" with this remark:

> *I had no thought in the world that I was doing anything to bring about a political and social equality of the black and white races.*[560]

On October 18, 1858, from Springfield, Illinois, Lincoln wrote a letter to one J. N. Brown. Impatient with those who continually questioned and misunderstood him, the exasperated president again expanded on his racial feelings:

> I do not perceive how I can express myself, more plainly, than I have done . . . I have expressly disclaimed all intention to bring about social and political equality between the white and black races . . . I say . . . that Congress, which lays the foundations of society, should . . . be strongly opposed to the incorporation of slavery among its elements. But *it does not follow that social and political equality between whites and blacks, must be incorporated* . . .[561]

• The *Enquirer* does not want to be "subjected to the suspicion of being an abolitionist." This is an anti-Yankee statement, not a true anti-abolition statement. We know this because, as has been noted several times, the American abolition movement began in the South,[562] with the first voluntary manumission occurring in Virginia in 1655.[563] Southerners from Thomas Jefferson[564] to Robert E. Lee detested slavery and fought against it at every opportunity.[565]

This statement actually reflects the widespread dislike of that small minority known as *radical* Yankee abolitionists, who cruelly and unreasonably called for *immediate, uncompensated, complete, unconditional abolition* across the South—an impossibility since this type of emancipation would have wreaked havoc not only on the South's economics, but on Southern society as a whole, both black and white.[566] Time was needed to plan out a workable emancipation that would not cripple the South. Though the North allowed itself hundreds of years to gradually emancipate its slaves, it unfairly and inhumanely refused to grant the South the same privilege.⁵⁶⁷

• The *Enquirer* does not want the war on the South to be reduced to a question of slave property. Why? Because for the South the War was never about her property in slaves, or even slavery generally. It was about personal independence and self-government, as silently promised in the U.S. Constitution, and as embodied in the ancient tradition of national law and state sovereignty. The Richmond writer himself says:

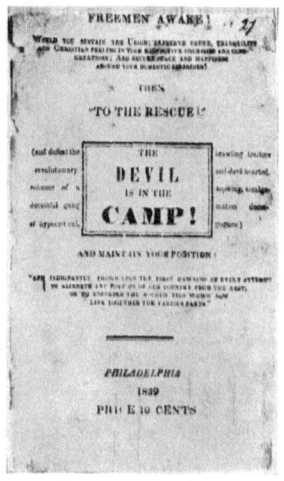

This ten-cent anti-abolition pamphlet printed in Philadelphia, Pennsylvania, in 1839, warns that "the Devil is in the Camp!," illustrating the outright contempt Yankees had for abolitionists at the time. An appeal is made here to the "Christian feelings" of fellow Northerners. "Freemen awake!" it reads, it is time to "rescue and defeat the revolutionary scheme of a deceitful gang of hypocritical, brawling traitors and dark hearted, aspiring, amalgamation demagogues." According to the pamphlet's Northern authors, abolition put the very survival of the Union at stake.

> The liberty and freedom of ourselves and of our children, the nationality of our country, the right of enjoying any kind of property, the houses over our heads, and the very graves of our children and friends, are involved in this struggle. Failure makes slaves of all, *white and black*; robs all of property, real and personal; divides our lands among our conquerors, who will plough up the very graves of our dead as fertilized ground for making money.⁵⁶⁸

• Liberals have long held that in the mid 1800s only the North cared about justice for African-Americans. Elsewhere I discuss the deep humanitarianism and Christianity of traditional Southerners, which manifested in a profound and tender racial tolerance (which included legally registering their slaves as literal family members)⁵⁶⁹ that was rare north of the Mason-Dixon Line.⁵⁷⁰ Thus the *Enquirer* specifically states that "justice" demands that the South give freedom to those slaves who are willing to fight for freedom.

• The *Enquirer* points out that by not enlisting blacks in Confederate military service, the South is creating the illusion that she is indeed fighting to "preserve slavery." "By conscripting the negroes," says the writer, "we explode the false accusation that we are fighting for slavery, or a slaveholders' Confederacy."

• The *Enquirer* notes that some questioned whether blacks could be trusted with guns and other weapons or not, an illogical view from any standpoint. Those who voiced this opinion were certainly in the minority and completely unaware of Southern reality. The majority of plantations across the South were managed and operated by slaves, most who carried arms in order to protect the owners' family and property, as well as their fellow servants.[571] As noted, Confederate General Nathan Bedford Forrest enlisted and armed 45 of his own slaves in his cavalry (along with 20 additional servants from other plantations), hand-selecting seven of them to serve as his personal guards.[572] Stonewall Jackson's army contained some 3,000 uniformed, highly trained, armed black soldiers.[573] Many other examples could be given.

Actually, it was in the North, where white racism was always more severe (and still is),[574] where there was the greatest apprehension about arming blacks. This is just one of the many reasons Lincoln would not allow blacks to officially serve as soldiers for the first two years of the War, only allowing armed service with the issuance of the Final Emancipation Proclamation on January 1, 1863.[575]

Lincoln, in fact, had long been vehemently against enlisting blacks as real soldiers. On July 21, 1862, for instance, he met with his cabinet and stated: "I am averse to arming the negroes,"[576] just one of dozens of times in which, for obviously racist reasons, he flatly refused to even entertain the idea. When hundreds of Northern blacks pressured the Union to allow them to fight, Lincoln was not interested, and had his secretary of war, Simon Cameron, give them the following brusque reply:

> This Department has no intention at present to call into the service of the Government any colored soldiers.[577]

On August 6, 1862, Lincoln's War Department sent a similar message to Wisconsin Governor Edward Salomon that read: "The President declines to receive Indians or negroes as troops."[578] Or as Cameron put it even more indelicately, the present conflict "forbids the use of savages."[579] Thus, tens of thousands of blacks (and Native-Americans) were turned away by Lincoln during the first two years of the War.

Blacks who managed to enlist in the Union army without being noticed were soon caught and "honorably discharged." White clergyman Moncure D. Conway wrote: "At Washington I found that the mere mention of a Negro made the president nervous . . ."[580] Naturally, Lincoln's racism permeated out across Yankeedom. In Cincinnati, Ohio, a black Union recruiting office was shut down by police, who told those African-Americans who had shown up to fight for Honest Abe: "This is the white man's war, and you damned niggers are not needed or wanted!"[581]

Let us compare the Yankee attitude toward conscripting blacks with the Confederate attitude. General Robert E. Lee's view was typical across the South, so I will cite a letter he wrote to Conservative Missouri Representative Ethelbert Barksdale, at Richmond, Virginia, on February 18, 1865, concerning the matter:

> Sir: I have the honor to acknowledge the receipt of your letter of the 12th instant, *with reference to the employment of negroes as [Confederate] soldiers. I think the measure, not only expedient but necessary.* The enemy will certainly use them against us, if he can get possession of them; and, as his present numerical superiority will enable him to penetrate many parts of the country, I cannot see the wisdom of the policy of holding them to await his arrival, when we may, by timely action and judicious management, use them to arrest his progress. I do not think that our white population can supply the necessities of a long war, without overtaxing its capacity, and imposing great suffering on our people; and I believe that we should provide for a protracted struggle, not merely for a battle or a campaign. In answer to your second question, I can only say that, *in my opinion, the negroes, under proper circumstances, will make efficient soldiers.* I think we could at least do as well with them as the enemy, and he attaches great importance to their assistance. *Under good officers and good instruction I do not see why they should not become soldiers. They possess all the physical qualification, and their habits of obedience constitute a good foundation for discipline. They furnish more promising material than many armies of which we read in history, which owed their efficiency to discipline alone. I think those who are employed should be freed. It would be neither just nor wise, in my opinion, to require them to remain as slaves.* The best course to pursue, it seems to me, would be to call for such as are willing to come with the consent of their owners. An impressment or draft would not be likely to bring out the best class, and this course would make the war more distasteful to them and their owners. I have no doubt that, if [the Confederate] Congress would authorise their reception into the service, and empower the President [Davis] to call upon individuals

or States for such as they are willing to contribute, with the condition of emancipation to all enrolled, a sufficient number would be forthcoming to enable us to try the experiment. If it prove successful, most of the objections to the measure would disappear; and if individuals still remained unwilling to send their negroes to the army, the force of public opinion in the States would soon bring about such legislation as would remove all obstacles. I think the matter should be left as far as possible to the people and to the States, which alone can legislate, as the necessities of this particular service may require. As to the mode of organizing them, it should be left as free from restraint as possible. Experience will suggest the best course, and it would be inexpedient to trammel the subject with provisions that might, in the end, prevent the adoption of reforms suggested by actual trial.[582]

A "government plantation" was nothing more than a Southern plantation that had been violently stolen by the U.S. government from its original owner. It was here that "freed" Southern slaves were sent by Yankees to be reenslaved and worked, sometimes literally, to death. The pay was around 2 cents an hour, with "subordination" punishable by "imprisonment in darkness on bread and water." This was the North's idea of "emancipation."

• The *Enquirer* points out something that was well-known in the South *during the War*, but which has been suppressed by modern day enemies of Dixie. Besides the fact that the North was still engaging in the slave trade at the time, Yankees were also still practicing slavery by "openly buying and selling Southern slaves to Union recruiting officers."

• Another item of interest from the *Enquirer* editor is his reference to the "freedom and a home" offered by the South to black Confederate enlistees. This is contrasted with the "beggarly hospitalities of Yankee philanthropy," which Southern blacks could expect if they joined the Union army. What is he referring to here?

This question can be answered by asking another. What happened to the thousands of blacks Lincoln refused to arm after emancipation? They were herded like cattle onto "government plantations," Southern farms whose peaceful and harmless white owners had been driven off or killed,[583] and whose land and wealth the socialistic president then redistributed to affluent Yankee businessmen.⁵⁸⁴ Here so-called "freed" black men, women, and children, were put to work doing ordinary labor, the same drudgery they had performed previously as slaves (mainly laundry, cooking, and cleaning), and from which Lincoln was allegedly trying to free them. A ten-hour work day, twenty-six days a month, was mandatory. The pay was $10 a month ($0.26 a day, or 2.6 cents an hour). "Insubordination" was punishable by "imprisonment in darkness on bread and water."⁵⁸⁵ This was Lincoln's idea of "emancipation."⁵⁸⁶

Speaking before the Confederate Congress on December 7, 1863, President Jefferson Davis commented on the Yankees' conduct toward Southern blacks; or as he put it, the "unrelenting warfare [that has] been waged by these pretended friends of human rights and liberties against the unfortunate negroes":

> Wherever the enemy have been able to gain access, they have forced into the ranks of their army every able-bodied [black] man that they could seize, and have either left the aged, the women, and the children to perish by starvation, or have gathered them into camps, where they have been wasted by a frightful mortality. Without clothing or shelter, often without food, incapable, without supervision, of taking the most ordinary precaution against disease, these helpless dependents, accustomed to have their wants supplied by the foresight of their masters, are being rapidly exterminated wherever brought in contact with the [Yankee] invaders. By the Northern man, on whose deep rooted [racial] prejudices no kindly restraining influence is exercised, they are treated with aversion and neglect. There is little hazard in predicting that, in all localities where the enemy have gained a temporary foothold, the negroes, who under our care increased six fold in number since their importation into the [Yankee] colonies of Great Britain, will have been reduced by mortality during the war to not more than one half their previous number.
>
> Information on this subject is derived not only from our own observation and from the reports of the negroes who succeeded in escaping from the enemy, but full confirmation is afforded by statements published in the Northern journals, humane persons engaged in making *appeals to the charitable for aid in preventing the ravages of disease, exposure, and starvation among the negro women and children who are crowded into* [Union] *encampments*.⁵⁸⁷

After their violent forced enlistment, most Southern blacks fled from Lincoln's armies at the first opportunity,⁵⁸⁸ back to the comfort, warmth, security, and domesticity of their homes in the South.⁵⁸⁹ The Yankee top brass was not amused. While stationed at Camden, South Carolina, one of Sherman's officers, Lieutenant Thomas J. Myers, wrote to his wife on February 26, 1865:

> The damned [Southern] niggers, as a general rule, preferred to stay at home, particularly when they found out that we [Yanks] only wanted the able bodied men (and to tell you the truth the youngest and best looking women).[590]

A favorite family pastime in the colonial North was attending slave burnings. This particular Yankee slave is being roasted to death in downtown New York City for a minor infraction of one of the state's many strict Black Codes: leering at a white woman.

Northern newspapers too were confused by the homesick Southern black's propensity for fleeing back to Dixie whenever the chance arose. In the summer of 1862 Rhode Island's *Providence Post* wrote that most Southern blacks evinced no friendliness toward the Yankees whatsoever. And neither had they attempted to flee north out of Dixie, or attack and overwhelm their white owners. In fact, the few who had crossed over into Union lines showed no urge to work or fight; only a desire to live off Northern whites, for their hearts were with the Southern Confederacy.[591] Indeed, one of the most common songs sung by Southern blacks who were stuck in the North was *I Wish I Was in Dixie's Land*.[592]

★ **FACT: YANKEES ABOLISHED SLAVERY IN THEIR REGION DUE TO UNPROFITABILITY & RACISM, THEN PUSHED THE INSTITUTION ON THE SOUTH**

It is little wonder that few Southern blacks had any interest in moving North. It was Yankees who had founded both the American slave trade and American slavery,[593] and it was Yankees who—when it was discovered that slavery was not compatible with the long Northern winters, short Northern summers, and the Northeast's rocky soil and hilly terrain—decided that people of the African race were not really compatible with those of the European race.[594] They then began pushing the entire institution southward, where it began to flourish in the flat alluvial crop lands, the year-round heat, and the more racially tolerant environment of Dixie. Thus the Yankee did not end slavery in his region because he felt shame or guilt, but because it became both economically unprofitable and racially intolerable,[595] the same argument Lincoln would use decades later when he became a black colonizationist and crusaded for the mass deportation of African-Americans.[596]

★ FACT: LINCOLN WAS NOT AN ABOLITIONIST, BUT A WHITE SUPREMACIST WHO USED BLACKS AS POLITICAL PAWNS
If Southern secession was for the sole purpose of preserving slavery, and if the North invaded the South in order to destroy the institution, one must wonder why, in his First Inaugural Address, Lincoln told America that he had no desire or legal right to disturb slavery.[597] One would also be entitled to ask why Lincoln

- supported the 1861 proslavery Corwin Amendment, which would have allowed slavery to continue in perpetuity if the Southern states would only agree to remain in the Union and pay their taxes.[598]
- came up with the idea of the "Ten Percent Plan," issued on December 8, 1863.[599] Here, a Confederate state could be "readmitted" to the Union if just 10 percent of its citizens took an oath of allegiance to the U.S. Afterward, that state could reestablish slavery if it so desired.[600] In 1864, according to Confederate Secretary of State Judah P. Benjamin, far from demanding complete and immediate abolition, Lincoln let it be known that he was willing to let the issue be decided on by a general vote in both the South and the North.[601]
- told Confederate diplomats at the February 1865 Hampton Roads Peace Conference that he had issued the Emancipation Proclamation as a "*temporary* war measure," and that as soon as the seceded states agreed to rejoin the Union they could continue practicing slavery if they wished (this, of course, showed Lincoln's complete lack of understanding of why the South had seceded in the first place).[602]
- was a leader in and a lifelong member of the American Colonization Society,[603] an organization founded in the North by Yankee racists, whose primary goal was to deport as many blacks as possible in order to make America "as white as New England."[604]
- was widely known among Southern blacks as a white racist.[605]
- detested both abolitionists and the abolition movement.[606]

- said that abolition was worse than slavery.[607]
- stalled the Emancipation Proclamation for as long as possible[608]—and then only issued it for military, political, and deportation purposes.[609]
- forced slaves to complete the construction of the Capitol dome in Washington, D.C., as well as build many other structures in and around the District.[610]
- implemented extreme racist military policies.[611]
- used profits from Northern slavery to fund his War.[612]
- often referred to blacks as "niggers."[613]
- repeatedly said he was willing to allow slavery to continue in perpetuity if the Southern states would come back into the Union.[614]
- pushed right up to the last day of his life for the deportation of all American blacks.[615]
- as a lawyer defended slave owners in court.[616]
- continually blocked black enlistment, black suffrage, and black citizenship.[617]

★ FACT: IT WOULD HAVE COST TEN TIMES LESS TO SIMPLY FREE AMERICA'S SLAVES THAN TO GO TO WAR

Even money-obsessed Lincoln understood that it would cost Americans ten times more to fight and kill each other for four years than if they would have simply ended slavery—more irrefutable proof that his War was not about the "peculiar institution."[618]

Lincoln typified the Yankee view of interracial relationships: the mixing of the races created "mulattoes," which endangered the purity of the white race. One of the best ways to avoid this "problem" was to abolish slavery then deport freed blacks ("colonization"). Another option he liked was to simply contain slavery in the South, by which he hoped to prevent a flood of "niggers" from pouring North and running over whites "like sheep."

★ FACT: LINCOLN WAS AGAINST THE SPREAD OF SLAVERY BECAUSE IT CAUSED A "MIXING OF THE RACES"

As one of its reasons for seceding, South Carolina said that Lincoln held "opinions and purposes [that] are hostile to slavery." But actually Lincoln was not against slavery as much as he was against the *spread* of slavery, and he was only against the extension of slavery because it causes a mixing of the races, which he felt dilutes and therefore "contaminates" the white race. As the prejudiced president put it during a public debate with Stephen A. Douglas in Chicago on July 10, 1858, "the inferior race bears the superior down."[619]

★ FACT: LINCOLN WANTED THE WESTERN TERRITORIES TO BE TURNED INTO "WHITES ONLY" STATES
On October 16, 1854, during a speech at Peoria, Illinois, the true white supremacist was revealed, along with the one of the real reasons he was against slavery (and its extension). Said Lincoln:

> Whether slavery shall go into Nebraska, or other new Territories, is not a matter of exclusive concern to the people who may go there. The whole nation is interested that the best use shall be made of the Territories. *We want them for homes of free white people. This cannot be, to any considerable extent, if slavery shall be planted within them.*[620]

★ FACT: LINCOLN BELIEVED THAT WHEN WHITES & BLACKS MIX TOGETHER, IT DEGRADES THE WHITE RACE
It is here that we also uncover the reason Lincoln himself was not a slave owner like Grant and tens of thousands of other Yankees.[621] It is here that we come to the very foundation of his antislavery views and of his Emancipation Proclamation: it was not so much slavery itself that bothered him. It was that the institution brought whites and blacks into close proximity with one another, the latter "degrading" the former. Thus to keep America white (one of Lincoln's stated lifelong goals), slavery would first have to be abolished (emancipation), then blacks would have to be deported to foreign lands (colonization).[622]

★ FACT: LINCOLN FOUND RACE-MIXING "DISGUSTING"
Lincoln, like the black racists, black separatists, and black colonizationists who came before and after him,[623] felt a deep repugnance toward those of other races. Speaking from his own Caucasian point of view, he summed up his feelings on the matter this way:

> *There is a natural disgust in the minds of nearly all white people, at the idea of an indiscriminate amalgamation of the white and black races . . .*[624]

★ **FACT: LINCOLN WAS AGAINST INTERRACIAL MARRIAGE & THE CREATION OF "MULATTOES"**
On June 26, 1857, at Springfield, Illinois, Lincoln lectured his Northern audience on the many benefits of "a separation of the races":

> *Judge [Stephen] Douglas is especially horrified at the thought of the mixing of blood by the white and black races: agreed for once—a thousand times agreed. There are white men enough to marry all the white women, and black men enough to marry all the black women; and so let them be married. . . . A separation of the races is the only perfect preventive of amalgamation; but as an immediate separation is impossible the next best thing is to keep them apart where they are not already together. If white and black people never get together in Kansas, they will never mix blood in Kansas. That is at least one self-evident truth. A few free colored persons may get into the free States, in any event; but their number is too insignificant to amount to much in the way of mixing blood. . . . In 1850 there were in the United States 405,751 mulattoes. Very few of these are the offspring of whites and free blacks; nearly all have sprung from the black slaves and white masters. These statistics show that slavery is the greatest source of amalgamation.*[625]

A one penny token made by Lincoln's favorite organization: the racist American Colonization Society, whose mission statement was to "make America as white as New England." Lincoln was a leader in the Illinois chapter of the ACS, a state whose legislature he convinced to finance black deportation.

By "amalgamation," Lincoln was referring to one of white Northerners' most monumental fears: miscegenation (interracial mixing, cohabitation, or marriage), something fairly common and much more widely accepted in the South. Indeed, the word miscegenation was coined by Northerners. Why? Anti-Lincoln Yankees wanted to play up on the Northern dread of "race-mixing," which they believed would be the certain result of Lincoln's Emancipation Proclamation.[626]

★ **FACT: LINCOLN HOPED TO SEND ALL AMERICAN BLACKS "BACK TO AFRICA"**
Lincoln loved the word miscegenation and used it at every opportunity. Even in his July 6, 1852, eulogy to his lifelong hero, slave owner Henry Clay, Lincoln managed to bring up the topics of miscegenation and

colonization, noting that the former could be allayed, even prevented, in the North by the latter. Sending blacks back to Africa would have an added benefit he noted: that of disseminating European-American religion and civilization, with God's blessing, among a primitive and barbaric people. Quoting slave owner Clay, Lincoln said:

> "*There is a moral fitness in the idea of returning to Africa her children*, whose ancestors have been torn from her by the ruthless hand of fraud and violence. Transplanted in a foreign land, they will carry back to their native soil the rich fruits of religion, civilization, law, and liberty. May it not be one of the great designs of the Ruler of the universe . . . thus to transform an original crime into a signal blessing to that most unfortunate portion of the globe?"[627]

Lincoln himself then added that Clay's

> suggestion of the possible ultimate redemption of the African race and African continent, was made twenty-five years ago. Every succeeding year has added strength to the hope of its realization. *May it indeed be realized.*[628]

Finally, Lincoln, who considered himself to be one of the "friends of colonization," declares his true feelings on the matter:

> If, as the friends of colonization [black deportation] hope, the present and coming generations of our countrymen shall by any means *succeed in freeing our land from the dangerous presence of slavery, and at the same time in restoring a captive people to their long-lost fatherland* with bright prospects for the future, and this too so gradually, that neither races nor individuals shall have suffered by the change, it will indeed be a glorious consummation. And if to such a consummation the efforts of Mr. Clay shall have contributed, it will be what he most ardently wished, and *none of his labors will have been more valuable to his country and his kind.*[629]

★ **FACT: LINCOLN CAMPAIGNED TO SEPARATE THE RACES**
Six years later Lincoln came out publicly for mass black deportation once again, this time during a speech he gave on July 17, 1858, before an audience at Springfield, Illinois. According to the black colonizationist's own statement:

> What I would most desire would be the separation of the white and black races.[630]

Amazingly, the man who uttered these words is still referred to as "the great friend of the black man" by the very people who should know better: scholars, professors, teachers, educators, librarians, writers, museum managers, school administrators, and researchers.

President Lincoln never stopped working on his black colonization plans, even including it in his Preliminary Emancipation Proclamation, issued on September 22, 1862.

★ FACT: EVEN AS PRESIDENT, LINCOLN CONTINUED PUSHING FOR BLACK DEPORTATION

Nine years on, now president of the United States, Lincoln was just as zealous about black colonization. In his Annual Message to Congress on December 3, 1861, he once again took the opportunity to promote the idea of deporting blacks, in this case, free blacks:

> It might be well to consider, too, whether the free colored people already in the United States could not, so far as individuals may desire, be included in such colonization.[631]

As a result of this speech, in 1861 and 1862, the U.S. Congress had $600,000 (about $15,000,000 in today's currency) set aside to aid in Lincoln's colonization plan to ship millions of blacks out of the country.[632]

A year later, in his Second Annual Message to Congress on December 1, 1862, he reemphasized his position on the issue:

> I cannot make it better known than it already is, that *I strongly favor colonization.*[633]

In this same speech Lincoln asks Congress to set aside funding for black deportation, and even suggests an amendment to the Constitution to expedite it.[634] It reads:

> Congress may appropriate money and otherwise *provide for colonizing free colored persons*, with their own consent, at any place or places *without the United States*.[635]

★ FACT: LINCOLN'S BLACK DEPORTATION PLANS INCLUDED EXILING AFRICAN-AMERICANS TO LATIN AMERICA, EUROPE, & THE CARIBBEAN

Lincoln was so adamant about expatriating American blacks that he was willing to settle them almost anyplace—as long as it was, as he said, "without the United States." This included Europe, Latin America, or the Caribbean, or anywhere else they would be accepted. As such, he funded experimental colonies in what are now Panama and Belize, as well as in Haiti.[636]

★ FACT: AFRICA WAS LINCOLN'S FAVORED CONTINENT FOR BLACK DEPORTATION

The reverse side of the ACS one cent token, showing a freed African-American man being dropped off in Liberia—as the name indicates, a country specifically founded for the deportation and colonization of "liberated" blacks.

But, being a manager in the American Colonization Society, the white founders of Liberia, he seemed to have a special interest in this particular African colony. In his public debate with Douglas on August 21, 1858, at Ottawa, Illinois, Lincoln told a supportive Yankee crowd that his remedy for America's "racial problem" would be to first emancipate all enslaved blacks, then "send them to Liberia—to their own native land."[637] This is a revealing statement, for his opponent had not asked Lincoln what he would do with blacks after they were freed. Only what he intended to do about slavery.[638] Consumed with the idea of colonization, he himself added the comment about deporting them to Liberia.

★ FACT: FEW SHOWED ANY INTEREST IN BLACK DEPORTATION, EXCEPT LINCOLN

Besides working hand-in-hand with the Yankee-founded ACS, white separatist Lincoln labored for years on his own personal emancipation-colonization plan, one that contained five clauses. The fifth stated that all emancipated blacks were to be shipped out of the U.S. and settled on foreign soil. For a variety of obvious reasons neither Congress, the border states, or most African-Americans themselves, ever showed any interest in his black deportation plan.⁶³⁹

★ FACT: PRESIDENT LINCOLN INCLUDED A DEMAND FOR BLACK DEPORTATION IN HIS PRELIMINARY EMANCIPATION PROCLAMATION, SEPTEMBER 22, 1862
Nonetheless, Lincoln went on promoting it and even included it in his September 22, 1862, Preliminary Emancipation Proclamation. Why did this racist clause not make it into his Final Emancipation Proclamation, issued on January 1, 1863, the one the public is so familiar with today? Because his advisors asked him to remove it as being potentially offensive to abolitionists, whose support he would need for his 1864 reelection campaign.⁶⁴⁰

★ FACT: A BLACK COLONY FOR DEPORTED AFRICAN-AMERICANS WAS TO BE NAMED AFTER LINCOLN
In honor of his nearly nonstop efforts to rid the nation of African-Americans, one of Lincoln's senators, Samuel Pomeroy, came up with the idea of naming a black colony in Latin America, "Linconia."⁶⁴¹

Union General Benjamin F. Butler confirmed that he met with Lincoln in April 1865, just before the president's assassination, in order to discuss black deportation.

★ FACT: LINCOLN CONTINUED TO PROMOTE BLACK COLONIZATION UNTIL THE LAST DAY OF HIS LIFE
Lincolnites and other pro-North advocates have long pretended that their canonized president eventually repudiated the idea of black colonization. But, according to one of his own Union generals, this is false.

In his memoirs Yankee General Benjamin "the Beast" Butler (like Lincoln also despised in the South for war crimes against humanity), writes that in early April 1865 Lincoln invited him to the White House to discuss his latest ideas on shipping blacks out of the U.S. This was only days before the president was killed by John Wilkes Booth at Ford's Theater in Washington, D.C.⁶⁴²

10

ECONOMICS: THE MAIN REASON THE NORTH DID NOT WANT THE SOUTH TO SECEDE

WE HAVE ESTABLISHED THAT THE South did not secede to "preserve slavery" or "destroy the Union," and that the North did not invade the South in order to "destroy slavery" or "preserve the Union." We have also seen that the South separated herself from the North for one primary reason and one primary reason only: to maintain the Constitution and government of the Founding Fathers, who created the conservative Bill of Rights to help insure the recognition and continuance of states' rights as implicitly laid down in the Ninth and Tenth Amendments.

Among these rights was the right of secession, not mentioned specifically because it is a natural right of sovereigns (that is, it exists outside and beyond the Constitution), and because it was so well-known and accepted at the time that it was not thought necessary. "Though not expressed, [it] was mutually understood," said Rawle.[643] Thus secession became the only rational solution for the South when Constitution-hating, history-ignorant, Liberal tyrant Abraham Lincoln was elected.

But what of the North? Why send 3 million soldiers to invade a constitutionally formed country because she acted on her legal right to secede, a right endorsed by many of the Founding Fathers, as well as scores of U.S. presidents and statesmen? What then was the real motivation behind Lincoln's unconstitutional and unnecessary war?

As with all large military conflicts it was the almighty dollar.

Ultra Liberal Southern slave owner Henry Clay, champion of the Left-wing's big government program, the purposefully misnamed "American System," was understandably Lincoln's favorite politician.

★ **FACT: FROM THE BEGINNING LINCOLN MADE IT CLEAR THAT HE WAS A BIG GOVERNMENT LIBERAL**

A republic confederation is America's true traditional form of nationhood, not a democratic nation—which is what we are moving toward today. While the Old North was nationalistic, liberal, and progressive, the Old South was confederate, conservative, and traditional. And so it clung to the old ways, which included the Confederacy of the Framers,[644] a group that feared not just big government, but government itself, whatever its size.[645]

In 1860, however, Liberal Lincoln openly campaigned on a platform promoting Liberal Henry Clay's anti-South, consolidating American System. This is not surprising since Clay, like Lincoln, was well-known as "a convert to theories and measures hostile to the earliest and most cherished principles of the old Republican [that is, Thomas Jefferson's Conservative] party."[646] Indeed, from his very first day as a politician, Lincoln made it clear that he stood front and center with the Hamiltonian federalists, monarchists, and socialists who preceded him, the same radicals and revolutionaries who had created the *new* Republican Party in 1854 (which has absolutely no connection to either today's Republican Party, or Jefferson's).[647] The following, for instance, is from his first speech as a candidate for the Illinois Legislature in 1832:

> Fellow citizens, I presume you all know who I am. I am humble Abraham Lincoln. I have been solicited by many friends to become a candidate for the Legislature. My politics are short and sweet, like the old woman's dance. I

am in favor of a national bank. I am in favor of the internal improvement system, and a high protective tariff. These are my sentiments and political principles. If elected, I shall be thankful; if not, it will be all the same.[648]

Those who know their political history will recognize all of the policies Lincoln mentions as left-wing. "Internal improvements," for example, was the 19th-Century term for "corporate welfare," still a favorite of Liberals the world over.

★ FACT: LINCOLN PROMISED TO COLLECT HIS TARIFFS FROM THE SECEDING SOUTHERN STATES
With Lincoln's 28 year record as an anti-South, socialistic Liberal, is it any wonder that on the day of his election to the presidency, November 6, 1860, the conservative Southern states began to urgently discuss secession and forming their own nation?[649] On December 20, just a few weeks later, the first Southern state, South Carolina, did just that. Mississippi, Florida, Alabama, Georgia, Louisiana, and Texas quickly followed, and on February 8, 1861, the new Southern Confederacy was officially formed.[650]

An unwavering left-wing warmonger, Lincoln stuck to his guns, ignoring the existence of the new confederate republic to his south. Arrogantly considering it nothing more than a pesky "rebellion" made up of "persons engaged in disorderly proceedings,"[651] in his First Inaugural Address on March 4, 1861, he promised to invade any state that did not pay his new exorbitantly high tariff rate:

> The power confided to me will be used to hold, occupy, and possess the property and places belonging to the government, and *to collect the duties and imposts*; but beyond what may be necessary for these objects, there will be no invasion . . . In doing this there needs to be no bloodshed or violence; and there shall be none, unless it be forced upon the national authority.[652]

The South refused to "pay up," and the always money-minded Lincoln went on to occupy Dixie.

It was Southerner Thomas Jefferson who said of Northerners: "They are avaricious and venal, looking always for gain."[653] Thus it was the Yankee love of money, along with Northern greed and materialism, that led to the inevitable "violence" of the so-called "Civil War."[654] For clearly, as we will discuss in more detail shortly, the South did not "force bloodshed upon the national authority," as Lincoln put it. By placing cupidity above constitutional rights, it was he himself who was responsible.

★ FACT: MOST YANKEES SAW SLAVERY AS A WHITE ECONOMIC ISSUE, NOT A BLACK CIVIL RIGHTS ISSUE

Most in the North and West supported Lincoln's unwarranted aggression: the War would be one concerned with money, not with morals, constitutional legalities, patriotism, or black civil rights. If the slavery issue were to be brought into it at all, as the New York *Times* asserted, it will not be about "conscience and religion," but about "social and industrial economy." Lincoln's party members concurred, stating that the War had nothing to do with abolition. Instead, where slavery was concerned, it was about protecting free white labor against the "degrading" effects of the "peculiar institution." A Western newspaper editor spoke for the vast majority of Lincoln devotees when he said: "I'm not against slavery because it hurts blacks, but because it hurts whites."[655]

Kentucky Liberal Cassius M. Clay agreed with Lincoln that abolition was for the benefit of whites, not blacks.

Many Southern abolitionists used the same argument. One of these, Kentucky aristocrat Cassius M. Clay (a cousin of Lincoln's idol, Henry Clay), stated that his own personal emancipation plans were created

> to seek the highest welfare of the white, whatever may be the consequences of liberation of the African.[656]

For Clay, Lincoln, and most other emancipationists, slavery was objectionable because, they believed, it hampered economic growth and competed with white labor. In 1841 Clay stood before the Kentucky legislature and said that there are many whites who would import slaves "to clear up the forests of the Green River Country" . . . . [But] [t]ake one day's ride from this capital and then go and tell them what you have seen. . . . tell them of the houses untenanted and decaying: tell them of the [white] depopulation of the country and consequent ruin of the towns and villages: tell them *the white Kentuckian has been driven out by slaves*, by the unequal competition of unpaid labor: tell them that the mass of our people are uneducated: tell them that *you have heard the children of the white Kentuckian crying for bread, whilst the children of the African was clothed, and fed, and laughed!* And then ask them if they will have blacks to fell their forests.[657]

★ FACT: FOR LINCOLN THE WAR BEGAN WITH CONCERN OVER HIS "REVENUE"

Lincoln's own words on this topic are instructive. Southern partisan Albert Taylor Bledsoe recorded the following infuriating conversation with the Yankee leader:

When asked, as President of the United States, "why not let the South go?" his simple, direct, and *honest answer revealed one secret of the wise policy of the Washington Cabinet*. "Let the South go!" said he, "where, then, shall we get our *revenue?*" *There lies the secret*. The Declaration of Independence is great; the voice of all the fathers is mighty; but then they yield us no *revenue*. The right of self government is "a most valuable, a most sacred right;" but in this particular case, it gives us no *revenue*. Hence, this "most valuable, this most sacred right" [Lincoln's description of secession in 1848] may and should shine upon every other land under heaven; but here it must "pale its ineffectual fires," and sink into utter insignificance and contempt in the August presence of the "*almighty dollar.*"[658]

Pro-North historians never discuss Lincoln's primary concern over the secession of the Southern states: the potential loss of his "revenue."

Bledsoe put the matter this way:

> The word . . . went forth from President Lincoln: *"If we let the South go, where shall we get our revenue?"* is one of the causes of the great change in question. Several books had, in 1860, been published to illustrate the subject of *"Southern Wealth and Northern Profits,"* and, upon reflection, the North concluded that, after all, she had some use for the South. She was naturally indignant at the thought of losing the bird, which had so long laid for her the golden egg.[659]

★ FACT: ORIGINALLY THE SOLE PURPOSE OF LINCOLN'S NAVAL BLOCKADE WAS ECONOMIC

On April 19, 1861, only a few weeks after his First Inaugural Address, and only four days after his illegal announcement calling for 75,000 troops to invade the South[660] (according to the Constitution, only Congress can declare war),[661] the progressive Northern president issued his infamous proclamation calling for a blockade of the Confederacy's 3,600-mile coastline.[662] The edict was, as usual, unconstitutional, for Lincoln published it without congressional approval (under international law blockades are unlawful unless war has been officially declared; it had not).[663]

Yet the contents of Lincoln's proclamation are revealing: the only purpose given is the collection of the tariff, or "the revenue," as he terms it. The opening paragraph reads:

> Whereas an insurrection against the Government of the United States has broken out in the States of South Carolina, Georgia, Alabama, Florida, Mississippi, Louisiana, and Texas, and the laws of the United States for *the collection of the revenue cannot be effectually executed* therein conformably to that provision of the Constitution which requires duties to be uniform throughout the United States . . .[664]

★ FACT: JEFFERSON DAVIS TESTIFIED THAT LINCOLN'S WAR WAS FOUGHT OVER ECONOMIC ISSUES IN THE NORTH, CONSTITUTIONAL ISSUES IN THE SOUTH

Meanwhile, two months before the start of Lincoln's War, on February 18, 1861, at Montgomery, Alabama, the president of the new Southern Confederacy, Jefferson Davis, gave his First Inaugural Address. Touching on the tariff issue, he emphasized the fact that any and all future conflicts that might occur between the South and the North would certainly be economically based. Why? Because a protective tariff raised the price of goods imported by the South.⁶⁶⁵ Speaking of the Confederate states, Davis said:

> An agricultural people, whose chief interest is the export of commodities required in every manufacturing country, our true policy is peace, and *the freest trade* which our necessities will permit. It is alike our interest and that of all those to whom we would sell, and from whom we would buy, that *there should be the fewest practicable restrictions upon the interchange of these commodities.* There can, however, be but little rivalry between ours and any manufacturing or navigating community such as the Northeastern States of the American Union.
> . . . Actuated solely by a desire to protect and preserve our own rights, and promote our own welfare, the separation of the Confederate States has been marked by no aggression upon others, and followed by no domestic convulsion. Our industrial pursuits have received no check; the cultivation of our fields has progressed as heretofore, and even should we be involved in war, there would be no considerable diminution in the production of the great staple which constitutes our exports, and in which the commercial world has an interest scarcely less than our own. This common interest of producer and consumer can only be interrupted by external force, which would obstruct shipments to foreign markets—a course of conduct which would be detrimental to manufacturing and commercial interests abroad. Should reason guide the action of the government from which we have separated, a policy so detrimental to the civilized world, the Northern States included, could not be dictated by even the strongest desire to inflict injury upon us; but, if the contrary should be proven true, a terrible responsibility will rest upon it, and the suffering of millions will bear testimony to the folly and wickedness of our aggressors.⁶⁶⁶

Davis rightly emphasized the economic nature of Southern secession and of Lincoln's War on Dixie.

Three years later, in an 1864 interview with a Northern journalist, Davis said:

> *I tried all in my power to avert this war. I saw it coming, and for twelve years I worked night and day to prevent it, but I could not. The North was mad and blind; it would not let us govern ourselves, and so the war came,* and now it must go on till the last man of this generation falls in his tracks, and his children seize his musket and

fight our battle, *unless you acknowledge our right to self-government. We are not fighting for slavery. We are fighting for Independence, and that, or extermination, we will have.*[667]

. . . [Slavery] never was an essential element. It was only a means of bringing other conflicting elements to an earlier culmination. . . . There are essential differences between the North and the South, that will, however this war may end, make them two nations.[668]

★ FACT: SOUTHERN NEWSPAPERS VIEWED THE WAR ECONOMICALLY

In Alabama an article in the November 26, 1863, issue of the Mobile *Register* pointed out, as Davis did above, that the North had already decided to conquer the South economically *prior* to Lincoln's War. Therefore, the conflict could not have been over slavery. "It was for the Constitution and our civil rights, not for the Negroes, that we fought," the writer asserted; "it was not due to slavery, but because of the abuses and injustices the South suffered at the hands of the Yankee. Yet the institution of slavery continues to be held up as the cause of the Civil War by the uninformed."[669]

★ FACT: CONFEDERATE GENERAL RICHARD TAYLOR ASSERTED THAT THE SOUTH DID NOT FIGHT FOR SLAVERY

Sixteen years later, in 1879, Confederate General Richard Taylor, son of U.S. President Zachary Taylor, wrote in his memoirs:

During all these years the conduct of the Southern people has been admirable. Submitting to the inevitable, they have shown fortitude and dignity, and rarely has one been found base enough to take wages of shame from the oppressor and maligner of his brethren. Accepting the harshest conditions and faithfully observing them, *they have struggled in all honourable ways, and for what? For their slaves? Regret for their loss has neither been felt nor expressed. But they have striven for that which brought our forefathers to Runnymede, the privilege of exercising some influence in their own government.*[670]

★ FACT: THE NORTHERN SLAVE TRADING BUSINESS WOULD HAVE DIED IF THE SOUTH HAD SECEDED

Contrary to Yankee myth, one of the main reasons the North did not want the South to secede was that it would have had a deleterious effect on the Northern slave trading business. For, as was well-known at the time, "the largest part of the federal revenues was drawn through the tariff from the pockets of slaveholders."⁶⁷¹

Indeed, the entire slave trading enterprise was owned and operated by Northern businessmen, Lincoln's "Wall Street Boys": wealthy Yankee industrialists, robber barons, and capitalists. The slave trade under their auspices thrived legally in the Northern states until 1862, when Yankee Nathaniel Gordon of New York became the first and last American slaver to be executed for engaging in the sordid enterprise. Gordon was hanged on February 21 under Lincoln's personal order.⁶⁷²

Additional proof of the flourishing Yankee slave trade right up and into the early months of the Civil War was the capture of the last American slave ship (also from New York) by the U.S. government on April 21, 1861. Named the *Nightingale*, at the time of her seizure the vessel, from the so-called "abolitionist North," had nearly 1,000 manacled Africans on board.⁶⁷³ She was doing "business as usual" up until the first few weeks of the War.⁶⁷⁴

In fact, it was the North's heavy dependence on the Yankee slave trade and the selling of its human product to the South, that helped precipitate the War: when, in early 1861, the Confederacy banned all slave trading with foreign nations, which included the U.S., the North panicked, thinking that it was about to lose one of its primary streams of wealth. (Had Union politicians taken the time to read Article 1, Section 9, Clauses 1 and 2, of the C.S. Constitution, they would have seen that the Confederacy still allowed slave trading with the U.S.)⁶⁷⁵ Frightened, the Union decided it was better to beat the South into submission than allow her to jeopardize the Yankee slave trading business,⁶⁷⁶ which had been in nonstop operation since the early 1600s.⁶⁷⁷

Like nearly every other Confederate official, Conservative General Richard Taylor, the son of U.S. President Zachary Taylor, declared that the South did not fight over slavery, but for the constitutional right of self-government.

★ FACT: LINCOLN USED PROFITS FROM THE YANKEE SLAVE TRADE TO FUND HIS WAR

Ironically, it was profits from the Yankee slave trade that helped Lincoln fund his war on the South. In 1870 Northern abolitionist Lysander Spooner put the president, his "Wall Street Boys," and their military campaign in perspective:

> *The pretence that the "abolition of slavery" was either a motive or justification for the war, is a fraud of the same character with that of "maintaining the national honor."* Who, but such usurpers, robbers, and murderers as they, ever established slavery? Or what government, except one resting upon the sword, like the one we now have [war criminal and former slave owner Ulysses S. Grant was then president of the U.S.], was ever capable of maintaining slavery? *And why did these [Northern] men abolish slavery? Not from any love of liberty in general—not as an act of justice to the black man himself, but only "as a war measure," and because they wanted his assistance, and that of his friends, in carrying on the [Civil] war they had undertaken for maintaining and intensifying that political, commercial, and industrial slavery, to which they have subjected the great body of the people, both white and black. And yet these imposters now cry out that they have abolished the chattel slavery of the black man—although that was not the motive of the war*—as if they thought they could thereby conceal, atone for, or justify that other slavery which they were fighting to perpetuate, and to render more rigorous and inexorable than it ever was before. There was no difference of principle—but only of degree—between the [chattel] slavery they boast they have abolished, and the [economic] slavery they were fighting to preserve; for all restraints upon men's natural liberty, not necessary for the simple maintenance of justice, are of the nature of slavery, and differ from each other only in degree.[678]

Leftist New Englander Lysander Spooner was revolted by Lincoln's hypocrisy and shocked at the manner in which his administration used blacks as political tools.

By subduing the South and forcing her to return to the Union, Lincoln was able to continue imposing high tariffs on his Southern neighbors which, in turn, created huge corporate profits for Yankee businessmen (which included dozens of Northern slave traders), his biggest and most important financial backers. For not only did they finance both his campaigns, but, as is clear from Spooner's observations above, they also funded the War itself.⁶⁷⁹ It was a self-serving symbiotic relationship that the wily Lincoln crafted and managed with the skill and finesse of a surgeon.

★ FACT: LINCOLN COULD NOT AFFORD TO FORFEIT THE SOUTH'S MANY NATURAL & HUMAN RESOURCES
Besides tariffs Lincoln's subjugation of the South benefitted the North financially in another way: Dixie's 3,549 miles of coastline, her innumerable port towns, inlets, rivers, immense fertile farmlands, abundant agricultural products, and her hardworking people, were all vital to Northern economic growth and stability. The South's major seaports alone—New Orleans, Louisiana; Mobile, Alabama; Pensacola, Florida; Fernandina, Florida; Savannah, South Carolina; Charleston, South Carolina; Wilmington, Delaware; New Bern, North Carolina; and Norfolk, Virginia—were worth untold billions of dollars to the North.

The Liberal North could not risk losing the massive taxes it derived from the Conservative South's lucrative seaports. This alone made Southern secession intolerable to Yankees, and, in their minds, gave them full justification for their violent and unconstitutional invasion of Dixie.

The South was so abundant in natural and manmade resources that in 1860, just prior to the start of Lincoln's War, not only was she far richer than the North,⁶⁸⁰ but her economy was the third largest of any region or country in either Europe or the Americas.⁶⁸¹ As far as wealth, the Confederate States were the fourth richest nation in the world,⁶⁸² more affluent than any European country except England. Modern Italy did not reach the level of per capita income the antebellum South possessed until the beginning of World War II.⁶⁸³

Additionally, between 1840 and 1860, the per capita income of the South grew at an average annual rate of 1.7 percent, and was a third higher than in the North. This is a sustained long-term growth rate that has been achieved by few nations.[684] And though the South possessed only 30 percent of America's population, 60 percent of America's wealthiest men were Southerners, a group that owned twice as much property as moneyed Northerners.[685]

In 1860, of the 7,000 U.S. families who possessed wealth of $111,000 or more, 4,500 of them (nearly 65 percent) lived in the South, while of the richest percentile that same year, 59 percent were Southerners.[686] So wealthy was the Confederacy that if she had been allowed to develop without interference from Lincoln, she would have become one of the world's major international powers, with a standing army many times bigger than the North's[687]—and this with a far smaller population than the North.[688]

The jealous, greedy, materialistic, commercially-minded North could not ignore such riches, power, and potential. For the Southern states, in essence, were seen by Yankees as vital elements in the creation of a nationwide domestic market that was to be controlled at the North.[689]

★ FACT: CHARLES DICKENS MAINTAINED THAT LINCOLN'S WAR WAS PURELY FOR "ECONOMIC CONTROL"

Based on economics alone then, Lincoln was not going to allow the South to secede. For the North the American "Civil War" was indeed, in great part, a conflict built around business and finance. While modern Yankee mythologists have tried hard to obscure this fact, Lincoln knew it and so did nearly everyone else, including many foreigners. In 1862 English novelist Charles Dickens exposed the truth behind America's "War Between the States":

Like other intelligent foreigners, Charles Dickens understood that the North's attack on the South was nothing but a thinly disguised attempt to gain "economic control of the United States."

> The Northern onslaught upon slavery is no more than a piece of specious humbug disguised to conceal its desire for economic control of the United States. Union means so many millions a year lost to the South; secession means loss of the same millions to

the North. *The love of money is the root of this as many, many other evils. The quarrel between the North and South is, as it stands, solely a fiscal quarrel.*[690]

The South was rich in countless resources. Therefore her "economic control" was absolutely vital to Northern interests. It is easy to see then why Lincoln and his Wall Street Boys considered Dixie the ultimate money prize, one they could not afford to lose.[691]

★ **FACT: WHEN HE ISSUED HIS CALL TO WAR, LINCOLN WAS FOCUSED ON ECONOMICS**
On July 1, 1861, in his Message to Congress, Lincoln drove the point home: the South *must* be forced to return to the Union, otherwise the North would suffer tremendous loss financially. Said the president:

> What is now combated, is the position that secession is consistent with the Constitution—is lawful, and peaceful. It is not contended that there is any express law for it; and nothing should ever be implied as law, which leads to unjust, or absurd consequences. *The nation purchased, with money, the countries out of which several of these States were formed. Is it just that they shall go off without leave, and without refunding?* The nation paid very large sums, (in the aggregate, I believe, nearly a hundred millions) to relieve Florida of the aboriginal tribes. Is it just that she shall now be off without consent, or without making any return?
>
> The nation is now in debt for money applied to the benefit of these so-called seceding States, in common with the rest. Is it just, either that creditors shall go unpaid, or the remaining States pay the whole? A part of the present national debt was contracted to pay the old debts of Texas. Is it just that she shall leave, and pay no part of this herself?
>
> Again, if one State may secede, so may another; and when all shall have seceded, *none is left to pay the debts. Is this quite just to creditors? Did we notify them of this sage view of ours, when we borrowed their money?* If we now recognize this doctrine, by allowing the seceders to go in peace, it is difficult to see what we can do, if others choose to go, or to extort terms upon which they will promise to remain.[692]

★ **FACT: LINCOLN INTENDED TO NORTHERNIZE THE SOUTH IN ORDER TO FULFILL HIS LIBERAL ECONOMIC DREAM**
If Lincoln and his Northern constituents were truly fighting to "abolish slavery," a laughable view from whatever angle one chooses to observe it, why did he once make the following comment to Interior Department official T. J. Barnett:

The entire South needs to be obliterated and replaced with new businessmen and new ideas.[693]

The answer is that from the beginning, one of Lincoln's chief goals was the Northernization of the South, to be remade into the industrial likeness of the Northeast. The purpose? To turn the Founders' confederate republic into a single "indivisible nation" that could be controlled by the Liberal elite at Washington; the dream of every rank and file American leftist, progressive, and radical.[694]

★ FACT: FOR HIS LEFT-WING APPROACH TO ECONOMICS, LINCOLN CONTINUES TO BE WORSHIPED BY LIBERALS

Why did the founder of modern communism, Russian revolutionary Karl Marx, idolize big government Liberal Abraham Lincoln? Because the two had so much in common politically. Conversely, socialist Marx had nothing but disdain for small government Conservative Jefferson Davis, and backed the Union's plan to wage a full scale war against the freedom-loving South.

Money, refunds, the tariff, revenue, credit, debts, bills, loans, taxes. Combined, these formed the major motivating factor behind the American "Civil War," implemented by the same big government Liberal who launched what would one day become the IRS; the same man who continues to be idolized by communists, socialists, Marxists, and dictators around the world: Abraham Lincoln.[695]

11

SECESSION AND THE UNITED STATES ARE SYNONYMOUS

WHY DOES THE LEFT, AND many of the less educated from the Right, continue to punish, defame, and blackwash the South for seceding from the Union in 1860 and 1861? There can be only one of two answers: ignorance or malice. For the documentation supporting the legal right of secession in America, and more particularly the right as it was practiced by the Southern states, is abundant and clear, and has been since 1776. Those who are not aware of it have not researched diligently enough, and those who are aware of it but are concealing it are dishonest and unethical.

In this book I have laid out the roots, the causes, and the many justifications for secession as history has recorded and presented them, and as traditional Southerners and true Conservatives (and even some of our more intelligent Liberals) view and interpret them. Let us close now with a few final important facts.

★ FACT: LINCOLN'S WAR DID NOT DESTROY SECESSION
The right of secession was not annulled by or because of Lincoln's War. All the bullets, bombs, and bloodshed the North unleashed could not undo nor even alter what the Founding Fathers established on July 4, 1776: a *voluntary* union with the colonial, and later states', right of ingress and egress, of entrance and exit, of accession and secession.[696]

This right did not magically disappear between Lee's surrender on April 9, 1865, and today.

In their fake version of history, uninformed Liberals and Conservatives pretend that it did, and try to back this falsehood up by declaring that "secession is now illegal." But statements by the uneducated do not make them true. Such individuals merely spout empty words; words designed to mislead, confuse, inculcate, propagandize, and betray the American public.

As we will see shortly from the writings of Supreme Court Justices Salmon P. Chase (in 1868) and Samuel Nelson (in 1870), if they would read authentic history rather than their own fictions, they would know that even immediately after the conflict, "when the Civil War might have *seemed* to the partisan to have changed the relation of the States to the Union and of the Union to the States," this relationship remained just as it had when the Founders first formulated our government.[697]

Informed anti-South advocates have come to terms with this reality. In 1893 one of them, Caleb W. Loring of Massachusetts, wrote grudgingly:

> *The superiority in men and wealth that gave the North the victory did not decide the right or wrong of secession: it may have shown its impracticability; but if the right ever existed it remains to-day.* . . . . Even Jefferson Davis, in the conclusion of his history [*The Rise and Fall of the Confederate Government*], concedes that the result of the war has shown that secession is impracticable. *It is difficult, however, to understand how might has made right, and the conquest of the richer and more populous North over the weaker South has settled forever the right or wrong of the matter.*[698]

The U.S. White House at Washington, D.C. Lincoln's War may have made secession more arduous and complex, but it did not make it illegal.

Yes, Lincoln's War made secession more difficult, but not unlawful. Thus the right of secession remains active, accessible, and legal to this day. Let us see how and why.

★ **FACT: IN AMERICA ALL POLITICAL POWER DERIVES FROM THE PEOPLE, NOT THE GOVERNMENT**

Our state Constitutions, the original 13 which were written between

1662 and 1780, "declared the State to be sovereign and independent,"[699] and here, in essence, is what they say:

> All political power is inherent in and derived from the people. All just governments are founded on their authority and instituted for their benefit, and public officers and magistrates *are their servants and agents*. The people, therefore, have at all times an inalienable and indefeasible right to institute, alter or reform their governments in such manner as shall seem to them proper.[700]

★ FACT: THE SOVEREIGNTY OF THE STATES HAS BEEN UPHELD BY BOTH EDUCATED CONSERVATIVES & LIBERALS THROUGHOUT ALL OF AMERICAN HISTORY
Those who claim that secession was not lawful in 1860, and is not lawful today, can only maintain this belief by also believing that the states have lost the sovereignty originally granted them by the people and the U.S. Constitution in 1776, in 1781, and again in 1789. As this is clearly *not* the case—for the sovereignty of the states has always been considered "indestructible" (even by many Liberals)—the charge that secession was illegal in the mid 1800s is also patently erroneous. Here is what some of the greatest political minds and committees in America have had to say on this vital topic:

> This Union must be a *voluntary* one, and not compulsory. A Union upheld by force would be a despotism.—William H. Seward, 1844

> *The States were, before the Union was.* . . . Our federal Republic forever must exist through the combination of these several free, self-existing, stubborn States.—William H. Seward, 1865

> The only parties to the Constitution, contemplated by it originally, were *the thirteen confederate States.*—Daniel Webster, 1819

> The States are united, *confederated.*—Daniel Webster, 1850

> *The States never conceived the idea of consolidating themselves into one government . . . or of . . . ceasing to be Maryland and Virginia, Massachusetts and Carolina.* . . . I hope never to see the original idea departed from.—Daniel Webster, 1852

> A Union of *co-equal sovereign States* requires, as its basis, the harmony of its members, and *their voluntary co-operation* in its organic functions.—Edward Everett, 1860

The Constitution, in all of its provisions looks to . . . *indestructible States*.—Salmon P. Chase, 1869

In fact and in theory, *the Union is an association of States, or a confederacy*. The States are the parties to the compact.—Alexander Hamilton, *The Federalist*, 1787

The States are regarded as *distinct and independent sovereigns* . . . by the constitution proposed.—James Madison, *The Federalist*, 1788

The business of the federal convention . . . comprehended the views and establishments of *thirteen independent sovereignties*.—James Wilson

Daniel Webster of New Hampshire maintained that though the states were united, they remained confederated; that is, they did not lose their independence, freedom, or sovereignty, or their status as "little republics," when they joined the Union.

The government of the United States was instituted by a number of *sovereign States* for the better security of their rights.—Roger Sherman

The *sovereignty* and jurisdiction of this State extends to all places within the boundaries thereof.—The Constitution of New York

The people of this commonwealth have the sole and exclusive right of governing themselves, as *a free, sovereign and independent State*.—The Constitution of Massachusetts

The American Flag must wave over States, not over provinces.—Rutherford B. Hayes[701]

★ **FACT: THE ABSOLUTE SOVEREIGNTY OF THE STATES IS ASSURED BY THE PRONOUNCEMENTS OF THE SUPREME COURT**

As I have pointed out, if the states are sovereign then secession is legal. Secession can only be illegal if the states are not sovereign. Are they? According to the Supreme Court they are—and have been from the beginning, and still are today. Scott writes:

> The Supreme Court of the United States, which is the "paramount and independent tribunal," to quote Mr. [Edward J.] Phelps' language, "to determine its construction," has repeatedly, in the hundred years and more following the institution of the Government under the Constitution, been called upon to interpret that charter of government in cases presented to it and properly involving its provisions, and *it has, from its first to its last decision, spoken the uniform language of statesman and of jurist, irrespective of section or party*.[702]

And what is the "uniform language of statesman and of jurist"? In 1793 Supreme Court Justice James Iredell of North Carolina, appointed by George Washington, wrote:

> Every State in the Union, in every instance where its sovereignty has not been delegated to the United States, I consider to be as completely sovereign, as the United States are in respect to the powers surrendered. The United States are sovereign as to all the powers of Government actually surrendered: *Each State in the Union is sovereign as to all the powers reserved*. It must necessarily be so, because the United States have no claim to any authority but such as the States have surrendered to them: Of course *the part not surrendered must remain as it did before*.[703]

In 1816 Supreme Court Justice Joseph Story of Massachusetts wrote:

> . . . it is perfectly clear that t*he sovereign powers vested in the state governments, by their respective constitutions, remained unaltered and unimpaired*, except so far as they were granted to the government of the United States.
>
> These deductions do not rest upon general reasoning, plain and obvious as they seem to be. *They have been positively recognized by one of the articles in amendment of the constitution, which declares, that "the powers not delegated to the United States by the constitution, nor prohibited by it to the states, are reserved to the states respectively, or to the people."*
>
> The government, then, of the United States can claim no powers which are not

Supreme Court Justice Joseph Story, another high ranking Yankee official who upheld the right of secession.

granted to it by the constitution, and the powers actually granted, must be such as are expressly given, or given by necessary implication.[704]

Chief Justice John Marshall noted that the states "are each sovereign." Thus when the people act, "they act in their states," not in "one common mass."

In 1819 Chief Justice of the Supreme Court John Marshall said:

> No political dreamer was ever wild enough to think of breaking down the lines which separate the States, and of compounding of the American people into one common mass. Of consequence, *when they act, they act in their States.*
>
> In America, the powers of sovereignty are divided between the government of the Union, and those of the States. *They are each sovereign, with respect to the objects committed to it, and neither sovereign with respect to the objects committed to the other.*[705]

In 1868 Chief Justice of the Supreme Court Salmon P. Chase said:

> Under the Articles of Confederation each State retained its sovereignty, freedom, and independence, and every power, jurisdiction, and right not expressly delegated to the United States. Under the Constitution, though the powers of the States were much restricted, still, all powers not delegated to the United States, nor prohibited to the States, are reserved to the States respectively, or to the people. And we have already had occasion to remark at this term, that *"the people of each State compose a State, having its own government, and endowed with all the functions essential to separate and independent existence,"* and that *"without the States in union, there could be no such political body as the United States."* Not only, therefore, can there be no loss of separate and independent autonomy to the States, through their union under the Constitution, but it may be not unreasonably said that the preservation of the States, and the maintenance of their governments, are as much within the design and care of the Constitution as the preservation of the Union and the maintenance of the National Government.[706]

In 1870 Associate Justice of the Supreme Court Samuel Nelson said:

> The general government, and the States, although both exist within the same territorial limits, are *separate and distinct sovereignties, acting separately and independently of each other,* within their respective spheres. The former in its appropriate sphere is supreme; but *the States within the limits of their powers not granted, or, in the language of the tenth amendment, " reserved," are as independent*

of the general government as that government within its sphere is independent of the States.⁷⁰⁷

In 1905 Supreme Court Justice David J. Brewer said:

We have in this Republic a dual system of government, National and state, each operating within the same territory and upon the same persons; and yet working without collision, because their functions are different. There are certain matters over which the National Government has absolute control and no action of the State can interfere therewith, and there are others in which the State is supreme, and in respect to them the National Government is powerless. *To preserve the even balance between these two governments and hold each in its separate sphere is the peculiar duty of all courts,* preeminently of this—a duty oftentimes of great delicacy and difficulty.⁷⁰⁸

Supreme Court Justice David J. Brewer emphasized our "dual system of government, national and state," making the "National Government powerless" over certain actions of the states.

★ **FACT: THE RIGHT OF SECESSION IS PERMANENTLY ASSURED BY THE RELATIONSHIP BETWEEN THE STATES & THE FEDERAL GOVERNMENT AS DETERMINED BY THE CONSTITUTION**

Let us enumerate a few vital facts pertaining to our government, which in turn prove that secession is permanently assured—not by the Constitution directly, but indirectly, by the relationship between the states and the federal government as laid down in the Constitution:

1. The states existed, as separate and independent sovereign states, *before* the federal Constitution.

2. They, as commonwealths, *alone* acted in establishing that constitution and the government under it.

3. The *entire existence and powers* of the said government are from and under them.

4. Each and every federal functionary is *a citizen and subject of a state*, elected by, and acting for, such state.

5. Our "united states," or "union of states"—as these phrases indicate—is a *federation [that is, confederation or confederacy] of sovereignties.*[709]

Though a Liberal (then known as a "Federalist") Alexander Hamilton acknowledged that our American union is "an association of states or a confederacy."

Among our highest authorities on these matters are the Founding Fathers Alexander Hamilton, James Madison, and John Jay, the authors of *The Federalist*, published in 1788. Sage notes of this publication that it is

universally considered to be the most authoritative of all commentaries on the federal constitution, as it was written by the very ablest of the framers, at the time that the states were in process of deciding upon it, and as it powerfully aided in overcoming the charges against, and the apprehensions concerning, the proposed system.[710]

The opinions of these astute men are worth citing. Let us begin with Hamilton:

If the new plan [that is, the U.S. Constitution] be adopted [this occurred the following year on March 4, 1789], the union will still be, in fact and in theory, an *association of states or a confederacy*. . . . Every constitution for the united states must inevitably consist of a great variety of particulars, in which *thirteen independent states are to be accommodated in their interests, or opinions of interest*. . . . Hence the necessity of making such a system as will satisfy all the parties to the compact. . . . The states are essential component parts of the union, . . . *the people of the states are the sovereigns of it.*[711]

Madison:

Each state, in ratifying the constitution, is considered as a sovereign body, independent of all others, and only to be bound by its own voluntary act. In this relation, then, the new constitution will be a *federal [that is, confederal or confederate]*, and not a national, constitution. . . . The states are regarded as distinct and independent sovereigns by the constitution proposed.[712]

Jay:

> I am in favor of the states continuing united under one federal government, vested with sufficient powers for all general and national purposes, and I am opposed to the idea of forming three or four confederacies instead of one. . . . . Some time must yet elapse before all the states will have decided on the present plan, which is characterized as a "union of states." *As for the general government, they are the agents and overseers for the people, by whom they are to be appointed.*[713]

Others from the Founding Generation were equally as definitive concerning the concept that "the states acceded to the federal system as parties to a compact, and were to act as sovereigns under the new form [confederacy]."[714] When Washington, for example, wrote to North Carolina Governor Samuel Johnston on June 19, 1789, he made note of "the political relation which is to subsist hereafter between the state of North Carolina and the states now in union." Benjamin Franklin too "considered the constitution to be a compact between sovereign states," for at the Philadelphia Convention in 1787 he proposed that "each state should have equal suffrage, to secure the sovereignties of the individual states and their authority over their own citizens."[715]

Founding Father and Yankee politician John Dickinson once described the newly formed U.S.A. as a "a confederacy of republics . . . in which the sovereignty of each state is represented with equal suffrage in one legislative body, the people of each state . . . in another, and the sovereignties and people . . . conjointly represented in a president." New York Senator Gouverneur Morris, who had been given the task of rewriting the Constitution after the Articles of Confederation had been dropped, was put in charge of changing the original words, "We, the people of the states," to " We, the people of the United States." This would make him another authority regarding the construction of our government and its relation to the states. Said Morris years later: "The constitution was a compact,

Founding Father John Jay of New York referred to the colonies or states as "distinct nations."

not between individuals, but between political societies, . . . each enjoying sovereign power, and, of course, equal rights."⁷¹⁶

Pennsylvania statesman James Wilson asserted that the object of the 1787 Philadelphia Convention was to induce the states "to confederate anew on better principles." "Let it be remembered," he went on to say, "that the business of the federal convention was not local, but general; not limited to the views and establishments of a single state, but co-extensive with the continent, and comprehending the views and establishments of thirteen independent sovereignties." Another Pennsylvanian, Tench Coxe, stated that though the federal constitution was to be adopted by the people, "yet it was to be done in their capacities as citizens of the several members of our confederacy. . . . Had the federal convention meant to exclude the idea of union, that is, of several and separate sovereignties joining in a confederacy, they would have said, 'We, the people of America,' for union necessarily involves the idea of competent states, which complete consolidation excludes. But the severalty of the states is frequently recognised in the most distinct manner, in the course of the constitution."⁷¹⁷

A signer of the Declaration of Independence, Samuel Adams was one of our most patriotic and influential Founders. At the convention of Massachusetts, he stated that "the amendment proposed by her (and afterwards adopted by the states) that 'all powers not expressly delegated by the constitution were reserved to the several states,' was 'consonant with the second article of the present confederation, that each state retains its sovereignty, freedom and independence, and every power not expressly delegated to the united states.'" Similarly, in a letter to Elbridge Gerry, Adams wrote hopefully that this amendment would be "a line drawn as clearly as may be, between the federal powers vested in Congress, and the distinct sovereignty of the several states, upon which the private and personal rights of the citizens depend."⁷¹⁸

Founding Father Samuel Adams of Massachusetts wanted a "clear line" drawn between the powers of the federal government and the sovereign powers of the "free and independent states."

Supreme Court Justice Oliver Ellsworth of Connecticut called the U.S. a "confederation," and held that it is unconstitutional to "coerce sovereign bodies."

Roger Sherman, on the committee to formulate the Declaration of Independence, as well as one of its signatories, declared that "the government of the United States was instituted by a number of sovereign states for the better security of their rights, and the advancement of their interests." Oliver Ellsworth, who later served as chief justice of the United States, referred to the U.S.A. as a "confederation," noting that "the constitution does not attempt to coerce sovereign bodies—states in their political capacity," but only provides for legal coercion of individual citizens.[719]

The president of the ratifying convention of Virginia, Edmund Pendleton, referred to the people of his state as "the fountain of all power," noting:

> If we Virginians find it to our interest to be intimately connected with the other twelve states, to establish one common government, and bind in, one ligament the strength of the thirteen states, we shall find it necessary to delegate powers proportionate to that end; for the delegation of adequate powers in this government, is no less necessary than in our state government.[720]

U.S. Chief Justice John Marshall said that even if a state "be called at the bar of the federal court," and judicial coercion be attempted, "it is not rational to suppose that the sovereign power should be dragged before a court." North Carolina statesman James Iredell believed the federal Senate "necessary to preserve completely the sovereignty of the states." In convention Massachusetts Senator Fisher Ames said "the senators represent the sovereignty of the states in the qualities of ambassadors." Theophilus Parsons of Massachusetts held that the Senate was created "to preserve the sovereignty of the states." Christopher Gore, also of Massachusetts, asserted that "the senate represents the sovereignty of the states."[721]

At the same convention Massachusetts Governor James Bowdoin said that "without a confederacy the Several states, being distinct sovereignties, would determine the disputes that might arise by the law of name, which is the right of the strongest." In arguing in favor of the U.S. Constitution another Massachusetts governor, George Cabot, said: "The senate is a representation of the sovereignty of the individual states."⁷²² According to Southern constitutional scholar Sage,

Supreme Court Justice James Iredell believed that one of the primary functions of the Senate is "to preserve completely the sovereignty of the states."

> *state sovereignty* is not a mere deduction, made by Jefferson and others, after the federal compact was formed, and expressed originally in the Resolutions of 1798 and 1799; but *is a great and indestructible fact or entity, which was recognized by all the fathers, as essential and vital to each commonwealth of the federalised states, as an integral part of such state's being.*⁷²³

★ FACT: ULTIMATELY THE QUESTION OF SECESSION IS OUTSIDE THE CONSTITUTION

On December 20, 1860, the day the first Southern state seceded, Conservative Alabama Senator James L. Pugh noted what has been clear to Southerners from the start: the legalities surrounding secession are extraconstitutional; that is, beyond the provisions of the U.S. Constitution:

> The whole theory of our Government is built upon the expectation that the States will not secede, but that all will continue to be integral parts of the confederacy. *If you ask, where is authority under the Constitution for a State to secede? I would ask, where is there any thing in the Constitution to prevent its secession?*
> ... Whether a State can or cannot secede, and what others may do towards her, or she towards them—*these are questions behind the Constitution of the United States, and, if I may say so without inconvenience, far above it. These are questions of political science and not of constitutional construction; questions upon which empires are often dismembered and dynasties overthrown.*⁷²⁴

Why does the right of secession lie outside the Constitution? Because, as we are about to see, it is "founded on God's gift of self-government to man."⁷²⁵ And *that* is why it became part of "the great Law of Nations, which govern all compacts between sovereigns."⁷²⁶

★ FACT: MADISON CALLED SECESSION, NOT A "CONSTITUTIONAL RIGHT," BUT A "NATURAL RIGHT"

President James Madison, a constitutional scholar of the first magnitude, may have referred to secession as a "last resort," and a "choice between the alternative evils," but he recognized it nonetheless, calling it "a natural not a constitutional right." In explaining his position Madison wrote that the U.S. Constitution was formed not by the Governments of the States as the Federal Government superseded by it was formed; nor by a majority of the people of the U.S. as a single Community, in the manner of a consolidated Government. *It was formed by the States, that is by the people of each State, acting in their highest sovereign capacity through Conventions representing them in that capacity, in like manner and by the same authority as the State Constitutions were formed*; with this characteristic and essential difference that the Constitution of the U.S. being a compact among the States, that is the people thereof making them the parties to the compact over one people for specified objects, cannot be revoked or changed at the will of any State within its limits as the Constitution of a State may be changed at the will of the State, that is *the people who compose the State and are the parties to its constitution and retained their powers over it*.

Though he disliked the idea of secession, Madison admitted that, if necessary, a state, being sovereign, could leave the Union and resume its powers of government.

. . . In the event of a failure of all these Constitutional resorts against usurpations and abuses of power and of an accumulation thereof rendering passive obedience and nonresistance a greater evil than resistance and revolution, *there can remain but one resort, the last of all, the appeal from the cancelled obligation of the Constitutional compact to original rights and the law of self-preservation* [that is, secession and the resumption of the powers of government which are necessary to the people for their happiness]. This is the *Ultima ratio* [the last resort] under all Governments, whether consolidated, confederated, or partaking of both those characters. *Nor can it* be doubted that in such an extremity a single State would have a right, though it would be a natural not a constitutional right to make the appeal. The same may be said indeed of particular portions of any political community whatever so oppressed as to be driven to a choice between the alternative evils.[727]

★ FACT: STATE SOVEREIGNTY & SECESSION GO HAND IN HAND
America's greatest minds have always correctly viewed secession as deriving its legality and legitimacy from the sovereignty of the states. One of these was President James Buchanan, who in 1860 commented:

> In order to justify secession as a constitutional remedy, it must be on the principle that the Federal Government is a mere voluntary association of States, to be dissolved at pleasure by any one of the contracting parties. If this be so, the confederacy [that is, the U.S.A.] is a rope of sand, to be penetrated and dissolved by the first adverse wave of public opinion in any of the States. In this manner our thirty-three States may resolve themselves into as many petty jarring and hostile republics, each one retiring from the Union without responsibility, whenever any sudden excitement might impel them to such a course. By this course a Union might be entirely broken up into fragments in a few weeks, which cost our fathers many years of toil, privation, and blood to establish.
>
> It is not pretended that any clause in the Constitution gives countenance to such a theory. It is altogether founded on inference, not from any language contained in the instrument itself, but from the sovereign character of the several States by which it was ratified. But is it beyond the power of a State, like an individual, to yield a portion of its sovereign rights to secure the remainder? In the language of Madison, who has been called the father of the Constitution, *it was formed by the States—that is, by the people in each of the States acting in their highest sovereign capacity; and formed, consequently, by the authority which formed the State Constitutions.*[728]

Conservative President Buchanan was a Victorian statesmen who saw secession and sovereignty as being integrally connected. Secession is legal, he rightly noted, "on inference" due to "the sovereign character of the several states by which the Constitution was ratified."

While secession was repugnant to him, President Buchanan admitted that there was nothing in the Constitution which allowed the federal government to prevent a state from leaving the Union. For the Constitution itself "inferred" the "sovereign character of the states."

Despite these cold hard facts, espoused by so many of our most learned thinkers, there are those today, possessing not an ounce of knowledge or experience in the field of constitutional law or American politics, who continue to claim that "secession was and is illegal." On what basis? There is none, not in the Constitution or in any other official U.S. document.[729]

Carpenters Hall, Philadelphia, Pennsylvania, where the First Continental Congress met in 1774.

★ FACT: THE INDIVIDUAL STATES, NOT THE FEDERAL GOVERNMENT, ARE THE SOLE & FINAL JUDGES OF THE LEGALITY OF SECESSION

This being true, *questions concerning the legality of secession must be thrown back on the individual states, whose sovereignty is guaranteed by the Ninth and Tenth Amendments.* This is precisely what occurred in 1860. The Southern states fell back onto what Madison called the "numerous and indefinite powers"[730] embodied in their sovereignty as independent "nation-states,"[731] "little republics,"[732] or "distinct nations,"[733] each which had *voluntarily* joined the Union. This, by inference, and more specifically by definition, gave them the right to *voluntarily* leave the Union.[734] Only a radical Liberal, socialist, or communist would think differently. Fowler writes:

> The evidence in this inquiry is *largely philological* [that is, related to language]. The common rules for interpreting language must be applied to the Constitution in order to learn what it is. *The meaning attributed to the several clauses by the Convention that formed it, and the several State Conventions which adopted it, may be safely considered as the true meaning.*
>
> Practically, the true course to be pursued by the Federal Government in the construction of the Constitution, is *never to attempt to exercise any doubtful powers. The benefit of a doubt should always accrue to the residuary powers reserved to the States, and never to the delegated powers intrusted by the Constitution to the Federal Government.*
>
> The burden of proof rests on the Federal Government. *In the last resort the parties to the constitutional compact must be the judges.*[735]

★ **FACT: OUR STATE CONSTITUTIONS GUARANTEE THE RIGHT OF SECESSION**

As I related earlier, a number of our state constitutions guarantee secession through the right to resume the powers given to them by the U.S. Constitution. The Constitution of the State of Virginia, for instance, declares that

> the powers granted under the [U.S.] Constitution, being derived from the people of the United States, *may be resumed by them, whensoever the same shall be perverted to their injury or oppression, and that every power not granted thereby remains with them and at their will.*[736]

★ **FACT: THE U.S. CONSTITUTION IS MOST ACCURATELY INTERPRETED THROUGH THE LENS OF THE STATE CONVENTIONS**

In his 1920 book, *The United States of America: A Study in International Organization*, James Brown Scott made the following pertinent comments:

> *In interpreting the Constitution it must always be borne in mind that, while the intent of the framers of that instrument is important, as showing the meaning which they ascribed to it, the greatest weight must be given to the proceedings in the State Conventions ratifying the Constitution and to the first ten amendments which are . . . in the nature of an authoritative and contemporaneous interpretation put upon the Constitution by three-fourths and more of the States in the exercise of their rights under the Constitution.* It is believed that these principles of interpretation, constituting as they do *a perfect canon of construction*, have never been better stated than by Mr. [James] Madison, who would have been supposed to be inclined to favor the views of the framers, because of his membership in the Convention and his authorship of the Notes in which their views are preserved, to the detriment of the authority of the State conventions.[737]

In regards to these remarks I quote now from a letter President Madison wrote to Thomas Ritchie on September 15, 1821:

> But, after all, whatever veneration might be entertained for the body of men who formed our Constitution, the sense of that body could never be regarded as the oracular guide in expounding the Constitution. *As the instrument came from them it was nothing more than the draft of a plan, nothing but a dead letter, until life and validity were breathed into it by the voice of the people, speaking through the several State Conventions. If we were to look, therefore, for the meaning of the*

instrument beyond the face of the instrument, we must look for it, not in the General Convention, which proposed, but in the State Conventions, which accepted and ratified the Constitution.

As a guide in expounding and applying the provisions of the Constitution, the debates and incidental decisions of the [General] Convention can have no authoritative character. However desirable it be that they should be preserved as a gratification to the laudable curiosity felt by every people to trace the origin and progress of their political Institutions, and as a source perhaps of some lights on the Science of Government, the legitimate meaning of the Instrument must be derived from the text itself; or *if a key is to be sought elsewhere, it must be not in the opinions or intentions of the Body which planned and proposed the Constitution, but in the sense attached to it by the people in their respective State Conventions where it received all the Authority which it possesses.*

I must say that the real measure of the powers meant to be granted to Congress by the Convention, as I understood and believe, is to be sought in the specifications, to be expounded indeed not with the strictness applied to an ordinary statute by a Court of Law; nor on the other hand with a latitude that under the name of means for carrying into execution a limited Government, would transform it into a Government without limits.[738]

A U.S. ironclad plying a Virginia river in the 1860s. The American "Civil War" was unnecessary, illegal, and immoral, but none of this prevented Lincoln from violating the Constitution, the South's God-given "natural rights," and the internationally recognized laws of sovereigns—which include the right of secession.

To reemphasize, according to our country's highest authorities the meanings of the rights found within the clauses and amendments of the U.S. Constitution must be gleaned, interpreted, and understood by each individual state, *not* by the Federal government. Thus Fowler writes:

When the Supreme Court or Congress, or, more comprehensively, when the General Government exercises doubtful power or powers that any of the States claim to be not delegated, but reserved, *then the States, acting in Convention or by their Legislatures, can determine whether the power in question is delegated or reserved. The States are to judge in the last resort of the constitutionality of the acts of the Federal Government. The Constitution gives to them this authority,* in giving them power to amend the Federal Constitution. If three-fourths of the States refuse to act by their Legislatures or by Convention, in the manner prescribed by the Constitution, then the aggrieved States have to choose between bearing the evil complained of, or vindicating the right of revolution [that is, secession]; just as the colonies did when they made the Declaration of Independence, and sustained it by a seven years' war against the unreasonable demands of the mother country. And as the aggrieved States have in such a case the right to determine what it is their duty to do; so in like manner the other States, acting through the forms of the Federal Government, have also the right to determine what it is their duty to do in their relations to the aggrieved States.[739]

★ FACT: THE SOUTHERN VIEW OF SECESSION IS ACCURATE, HISTORICAL, & DEMONSTRABLE

In 1860 the Southern states were certainly "aggrieved," and so they began acting upon their constitutional rights. Among these important rights were accession and secession, and nowhere have they been more accurately described than by the freedom-loving, independent minded, individualistic, law-abiding people of the South.

The Southern view of secession was superbly articulated by Senator Robert M. T. Hunter of Virginia on January 15, 1861:

> I believe that *it contravenes no provision of the Constitution, for one or more of the States to secede from the Union; not by virtue of any power conferred upon them by that instrument, but in consequence of the States never having surrendered it to the General Government*: the Constitution declares that "the powers not delegated to the United States by the Constitution are reserved to the States respectively, or the people." I apprehend that *it will be admitted that the States may exercise any or all of their reserved powers without a violation of the Constitution. If, then, they have never parted with their right to resume their original sovereignty, when, in their opinion, the Government becomes destructive of the ends for which it was instituted, it is no violation of the Constitution for them to secede*. If there is any clause in the Constitution by which they deprived themselves of this right, it has escaped my observation.[740]

After all, as John Marshall noted, "a power remains till it is given away," and the power of secession has never been "given away."[741]

★ FACT: CONSTITUTIONAL OR NOT, EACH STATE HAS THE RIGHT OF REVOLUTION, WHICH INCLUDES SECESSION
Even if, for the sake of argument, we were to accept the erroneous view that there is no constitutional or even extraconstitutional basis for secession, *each state still retains the right of revolution*, and, as Robert E. Lee himself noted, "secession is revolution."[742] On December 5, 1860, Conservative Georgia Senator Alfred Iverson Sr. made the following comments before the U.S. Senate:

> . . . each state has the right of revolution, which all admit. Whenever the burdens of the government under which it acts become so onerous that it cannot bear them, or if anticipated evil shall be so great that the State believes it would be better off—even risking the perils of secession—out of the Union than in it, then that State, in my opinion, like all people upon earth has the right to exercise the great fundamental principle of self-preservation, and go out of the Union—though, of course, at its own peril—and bear the risk of the consequences. And while no State may have the *constitutional* right to secede from the Union, *the President [James Buchanan] may not be wrong when he says the Federal Government has no power under the Constitution to compel the State to come back into the Union.* It may be a *casus omissus [a case of omission]* in the Constitution; but I should like to know where the power exists in the Constitution of the United States to authorize the Federal Government to coerce a sovereign State. *It does not exist in terms, at any rate, in the Constitution.*[743]

Robert E. Lee said that secession is "revolutionary," and indeed it is. This is why we call America's fight to secede from Great Britain the "Revolutionary War." But none of this makes secession illegal, for each state, as a sovereign "little republic," retains the permanent "right of revolution."

★ FACT: SECESSION HAS ALWAYS BEEN LEGAL, FOR WITHOUT IT THERE WOULD BE NO U.S.A.
Over the centuries thousands have defended and justified the right of secession. But one defense is so obvious that few have paid any attention to it. One of those who did was pro-South attorney and constitutional scholar Bernard J. Sage, who in 1878 wrote:

My constant aim is to show by the words of the Fathers, the truth of history, and the principles of public law and constitutional liberty—not to advocate the right of secession. It must be said, however, that *to get rid of this right, we must destroy the sovereignty of the states, for this right is elemental—an integral part of sovereignty, and not a mere power, to be granted or reserved by sovereignty. It is original, indivisible, indefeasible, and inalienable; and, as a part of sovereignty, it must ever remain above sovereignty's institutions or federal pacts.* Control it, and it is gone like a bubble—the commonwealth has lost its soul, and become provincial! And it is an utter absurdity to say, that the Declaration of Independence, did but announce a truth as old as the world, i.e., the right of revolution, or in other words, that a worm has the right to turn, or a people resist, when trodden on. No, no! *the intent was to insist upon a republican people's absolute and peaceable right, at all times, and for any cause that suited them, to change their political institutions. This is the common law of the land—fundamental and supreme—founded on God's gift of self-government to man; and [as the colonies declared]* . . . *before the federal pact was established, that [their]* . . . *"people alone, have an incontestible, inalienable, and indefensible right to institute government, and to reform, alter, or totally change the same, when"* *they think proper.* . . . *It was this very aim, that caused our republics [individual states] to form their federation [confederacy].* If they find, as is often the case with human devices, that their work is defective, and likely to bring evil and ruin, instead of safety and welfare, it is absurd to say that the some collective and corporate reason, judgment, and will, is not to be freely exercised again, on the same subject, and for the same end![744]

★ FACT: CONFEDERATE VICE PRESIDENT ALEXANDER H. STEPHENS GAVE ONE OF THE MOST EXPRESSIVE & ACCURATE JUSTIFICATIONS FOR SOUTHERN SECESSION

In his exceptional 1868 book, *A Constitutional View of the Late War Between the States*, Confederate Vice President Alexander H. Stephens provides us with what I consider among the most superb explanations and justifications for the secession of the Southern states. A brilliant constitutional scholar and Conservative Georgia politician, Stephens laid out the facts in a colloquy or formal conversation between himself and a fictional Radical Liberal Yankee he named "Judge Bynum":

Now as to the rightfulness of the State's thus resuming her Sovereign powers! In doing it she *seceded* from that Union, to which, in the language of Mr. Jefferson, as well as General Washington, she had *acceded* as a Sovereign State. She repealed her ordinance by which she ratified and agreed to the Constitution and became a party to the Compact under it. She declared herself no longer bound by that Compact, and dissolved her alliance with the other parties to it. The Constitution of the United States, and the laws passed in pursuance of it, were no longer the supreme law of the people of Georgia, any more than the treaty with France was the supreme law of both countries, after its abrogation, in 1798, by the same rightful authority which had made it in the beginning.

In answer to your question, whether she could do this without a breach of her solemn obligations, under the Compact, I give this full and direct answer: *she had a perfect right so to do, subject to no authority, but the great moral law which governs the intercourse between Independent Sovereign Powers, Peoples, or Nations. Her action was subject to the authority of that law and none other. It is the inherent right of Nations, subject to this law alone, to disregard the obligations of Compacts of all sorts, by declaring themselves no longer bound in any way by them. This, by universal consent, may be rightfully done, when there has been a breach of the Compact by the other party or parties. It was on this principle, that the United States abrogated their treaty with France, in 1798.* The justifiableness of the act depends, in every instance, upon the circumstances of the case. The general rule is, if all the other States—the Parties to the Confederation—faithfully comply with their obligations, under the Compact of Union, no State would be morally justified in withdrawing from a Union so formed, unless it were necessary for her own preservation. *Self-preservation is the first law of nature, with States or Nations, as it is with individuals.*

Conservative Confederate Vice President Alexander H. Stephens of Georgia: like most Southerners, an anti-secessionist before Lincoln's invasion; a secessionist afterward.

But in this case the breach of plighted faith was not on the part of Georgia, or those States which withdrew or attempted to withdraw from the Union. Thirteen of their Confederates had openly and avowedly disregarded their obligations under that clause of the Constitution which covenanted for the rendition of fugitives from service, to say nothing of the acts of several of them, in a like open and palpable breach of faith, in the matter of the rendition of fugitives from justice. These are facts about which there can be no dispute. Then, by universal law, as recognized by all Nations, savage as well as civilized, the Compact, thus broken by some of the Parties, was no longer binding upon the others. The breach was not made by the seceding States. Under the circumstances, and the facts of this case, therefore, the legal as well as moral right, on the part of Georgia, according to the laws of Nations and nature, to declare herself no longer bound by the Compact, and to withdraw from the Union under it, was perfect and complete. *These principles are too incontestably established to be questioned, much less denied, in the forum of reason and justice.*

Hence the broad and unqualified admission of Mr. [Daniel] Webster, that, *if the Constitution was a Compact between Sovereign States, the right to secede followed as a matter of course. This right comes not from anything in the Constitution, but from the great law of Nations, governing all Compacts between Sovereigns.* His language, you recollect, was: "where Sovereign communities are parties, there is no essential difference between a Compact, a Confederation, and a League. They all equally rest on the plighted faith of the Sovereign party. A League, or Confederacy, is but a subsisting or continuing treaty." "If, in the opinion of either party," he added, "it be violated, such party may say that he will no longer fulfil its obligations on his part, but will consider the whole League or Compact at an end, although it might be one of its stipulations that it should be perpetual."

The right of a State to secede from the Union upon this principle of the laws of Nations was fully admitted by Mr. Webster, if it be true that the Constitution is a Compact between States; and that too when, even in the opinion of any Party to it, the Compact had been broken on the other side. But in this case there is no question as to the fact of the breach on the other side.

Judge [Joseph] Story, who strove so hard to establish the position that the Government of the United States is a National Government, proper and not Federal [that is, Confederal or Confederate], is equally explicit in his admission as to the right of Secession, if it be true that the Constitution is a Compact between States. On this point there is no disagreement between him and Mr. Webster. Judge Story first states the position of Judge [St. George] Tucker, in his Commentaries on the Constitution, as follows:

> "It is a Federal Compact. *Several Sovereign and independent States may unite themselves together by a perpetual Confederation, without each ceasing to be a perfect State. They will, together, form a Federal [that is, a Confederal or Confederate] Republic.* The deliberations in common will offer no violence to each member, though they may in certain respects put some constraint on the exercise of it in virtue of voluntary engagements. The extent, modifications, and objects of the Federal authority are mere matters of discretion. So long as the separate organization of the members remains, and, from the nature of the Compact, must continue to exist, both for local and domestic, and for Federal purposes, *the Union is, in fact as well as in theory, an association of States, or a Confederacy*."

This is Story's statement of Tucker's position. It is substantially correct. He afterwards comments on it, as follows:

> "The obvious deductions, which may be, and indeed have been drawn, from *considering the Constitution as a Compact between the States, are, that it operates as a mere treaty*, or convention between

them, and *has an obligatory force upon each State no longer than it suits its pleasure*, or its consent continues; that each State has a right to judge for itself in relation to the nature, extent, and obligations of the instrument, *without being at all bound by the interpretation of the Federal Government, or by that of any other State; and that each retains the power to withdraw from the Confederacy, and to dissolve the connection, when such shall be its choice; and may suspend the operations of the Federal Government, and nullify its acts within its own territorial limits, whenever, in its own opinion, the exigency of the case may require. These conclusions may not always be avowed; but they flow naturally from the doctrines which we have under consideration.* They go to the extent of reducing the Government to a mere Confederacy during pleasure; and of thus presenting *the extraordinary spectacle of a nation existing only at the will of each of its constituent parts."*

In this, *Judge Story fully admits the right of a State to withdraw or secede from the Union*, if the Constitution be a Compact between the States as States, even without an open breach of the Compact by the Confederates. He says, *it is an obvious deduction from the fact of its being a Government founded on Compact*; too clear and logical to give room for doubt or question. *He was too thoroughly versed in the laws of nations to raise a point even on this conclusion*, if the premises as to the Constitution being a Compact between States be correct. Hence his labored argument in assault upon the premises. Hence his utmost efforts were put forth, with what success we have seen, to show that the States were never Sovereign, and that the Constitution is not a Compact between States, but that it is a social Compact between all the people of the United States in mass as one nation. However extraordinary, in the opinion of Judge Story, would be the spectacle of a nation existing only at the will of each of its constituent parts, yet just such a nation ours is, according to his own frank admission, *if it be true that the Constitution is founded upon Compact between Sovereign States, (and this, by common consent between us, is a question now no longer open for consideration.)*

Our "Nation," such as it is, is indeed a most extraordinary and wonderful spectacle! This we have abundantly seen in the course of our present investigation; and if Judge Story had more profoundly studied its nature and character, he might have been much more profoundly struck with many even more extraordinary features in it than that one to which he here specially refers.

That one has nothing in it more extraordinary than every other Federal Republic that ever existed. [Baron de] Montesquieu saw in such systems nothing more extraordinary than that under them the world had been saved from universal monarchical rule.

This right of a State to consider herself no longer bound by a Compact which, in her judgment, has been broken by her Confederates, and to secede from a Union, formed as ours was, has nothing about it, either new or novel. It is incident to all Federal

Republics. It is not derived from the Compact itself. It does not spring from it at all. It is derived from the same source that the right is derived to abrogate a treaty by either or any of the parties to it. That is seldom set forth in the treaty itself, and yet it exists, whether it be set forth or not. So, in any Federal Compact whatever, the parties may or may not expressly provide for breaches of it. But where no such provision is made, the right exists by the same laws of Nations which govern in all matters of treaties or conventions between Sovereigns. The admission of the right of Secession, under this law, on the part of the several States of our Union, by Mr. Webster and Judge Story, if it be true that the Constitution is a Compact between the States, might be considered ample authority, in answer to your question on that point; since the conclusion, to which we arrived, that it is such a Compact.

But I do not mean to let it rest barely on this.

I maintain that *such was the general understanding of the parties to the Constitution at the time it was adopted, as well as that such is its true exposition. Contemporanea Expositio est optima et fortissima in Lege*: "The best and surest mode of expounding an instrument is by referring to time when, and circumstances under which, it was made."

When Thomas Jefferson wrote the all-important Kentucky Resolutions in 1798, he was merely voicing the sentiments of the "large majority" of Americans at the time—the same conservative majority that elected him president in 1800 and again in 1804.

First, then, I maintain that it [secession] *is a necessary incident of that Sovereignty which was believed to be reserved to the States severally, in the original Constitution, but which reservation, to quiet the apprehensions of the more cautious, was immediately after inserted in express terms, by way of amendment. It was expressly reserved in the ratifications of Virginia, New York, and Rhode Island. These ratifications were received by the other States, which fixes the construction of all at the time. Moreover, the Government was formed, or to be formed, according to the very terms of the Constitution, by the Secession of nine States at least from their former Union, which was declared to be perpetual, and to which their faith was plighted in the most solemn manner, that no changes in the Articles of their Union should ever be made without the unanimous consent of its thirteen members. What is there in the history of the times or in the acts of the parties, which goes to show that the same general opinion, as to the Sovereign right to secede, did not continue to exist in reference to the present Constitution, which required no pledge as to its perpetuity?*

Secondly. It is very clear that Mr. Jefferson believed in this right. This, the Kentucky Resolutions fully establish. The large majority by which he was elected, after the fierce contest of 1800, shows that the same opinion must have been then very generally entertained. Even Mr. Hamilton must have believed that this right was incident to the system; for in his urgent appeals to Mr. Jefferson, as early as 1790, for his influence with members of Congress, in aid of the bill for the assumption of the State debts, he presented the strong reason, that if that measure should not pass, there was great danger of a Secession of the members from the creditor States, which would end in "a separation of the States." *He was then connected with the Government. He was Secretary of the Treasury. Would he have urged such an argument if he had not believed that those States had a right to withdraw?* Moreover, his letter to Mr. Gouverneur Morris, of the 27th of February, 1802, shows very clearly, taken in connection with his whole career, that he did not believe that the Government of the United States had any inherent Sovereign power whatever. He looked upon the system as radically defective in this particular. "Perhaps," says he [Hamilton] in this letter, "no man in the United States has sacrificed or done more for the present Constitution than myself; and contrary to all my anticipations of its fate, as you know from the very beginning. I am still laboring to prop the frail and worthless fabric [that is, the U.S. Constitution]. Yet I have the murmurs of its friends no less than the curses of its foes, for my reward." The worthlessness of the fabric, in his opinion, consisted, as we know, in the want of the energy of a consolidation of the Sovereignties of the several States in one single grand Republic, which he had at first insisted upon in the Federal Convention of 1787. When that failed, he did give the Federal plan agreed upon a zealous and patriotic support. He contributed greatly to its adoption by the States. But he never had confidence in its durability. He thought it would go to pieces by State disintegration. His belief and conviction of the want of power on the part of the General Government, as formed to prevent such disintegration, is shown from all that he said in the New York State Convention, when the Constitution was before that body, and what he wrote on the same subject in *The Federalist* afterwards.

But, thirdly. One of the earliest, if not the earliest, commentators on the Constitution, not as a politician, but as a jurist and publicist, was Judge [St. George] Tucker, Professor of Law in the University of William and Mary, in Virginia. In his edition of [William] Blackstone's Commentaries, there is an appendix by him to the first volume, of considerable length, devoted to the consideration of Governments generally, and particularly the Constitution of the United States. He wrote in 1803. He held that the Constitution was a Federal Compact between States. And while no more devoted friend to the Union under the Constitution perhaps ever lived, he yet was forced, from this indisputable fact, to what Story said was an obvious deduction—that is, that *the right of Secession, on the part of any one or more of the States, was a necessary incident from the very nature of the system.* His language is this:

> "The Constitution of the United States, then, being that instrument by which the Federal Government hath been created, its powers

defined and limited, and the duties and functions of its several departments prescribed, *the Government, thus established, may be pronounced to be a Confederate Republic, composed of several Independent and Sovereign Democratic States,* united for their common defence and security against foreign Nations, and for the purposes of harmony and mutual intercourse between each other; *each State retaining an entire liberty of exercising, as it thinks proper, all those parts of its Sovereignty which are not mentioned in the Constitution, or Act of Union,* as parts that ought to be exercised in common.

The 18th-Century English judge and judicial scholar William Blackstone, an early supporter of the idea of the separation of powers, which was adopted by the U.S. Founding Fathers.

"In becoming a member of the Federal Alliance, established between the American States by the Articles of Confederation, *she expressly retained her Sovereignty and Independence. The constraints, put upon the exercise of that Sovereignty by those Articles, did not destroy its existence.*

". . . The Federal Government, then, appears to be the organ through which the united Republics communicate with foreign Nations, and with each other. Their submission to its operation is *voluntary*; its councils, its engagements, its authority, are theirs, modified and united. *Its Sovereignty is an emanation from theirs, not a flame, in which they have been consumed, nor a vortex, in which they are swallowed up. Each is still a perfect State, still Sovereign, still independent, and still capable, should the occasion require, to resume the exercise of its functions, as such, in the most unlimited extent.*

". . . But, until the time shall arrive, when the occasion requires a resumption of the rights of Sovereignty by the several

States (and far be that period removed, when it shall happen), the exercise of the rights of Sovereignty by the States, individually, is wholly suspended or discontinued in the cases before mentioned; nor can that suspension ever be removed, so long as the present Constitution remains unchanged, but by the dissolution of the bonds of union; an event which no good citizen can wish, and which no good or wise administration will ever hazard."[745]

A clearer or truer exposition of this feature of the Constitution of the United States was never made in fewer words. This exposition went to the country with the sanction of his high authority, and was not gainsayed or controverted by any writer of distinction, that I am aware of, until Chancellor [James] Kent's Commentaries appeared in 1826, and Story's, in 1833. I do not mean to say that no one of that class of politicians, barely, who figured during the Administration of the elder Adams [John], denied this right; but that no jurist or publicist of eminence denied it up to that time. Chancellor Kent goes into no argument. . . . But, mean while, Mr. [William] Rawle, an eminent jurist of Pennsylvania, wrote an elaborate work upon the Constitution [*A View of the Constitution of the United States of America*], which was published in 1825. He was United States District Attorney under Washington, and had been offered, by him, the Attorney-Generalship of the United States. He was, also, a firm supporter of the Administration of the elder Adams. This shows the character of the man, and the authority with which his opinions should be received. His investigations brought him to the same conclusion to which Judge Tucker had come. That conclusion is expressed by him in the following language:

U.S. President John Adams and his personal residence "Peacefield," at Quincy, Massachusetts.

> "Having thus endeavored to delineate the general features of this peculiar and invaluable form of Government, we shall conclude with adverting to the principles of its cohesion, and to the provisions it contains for its own duration and extension.
>
> "The subject cannot, perhaps, be better introduced than by presenting, in its own words, an emphatical clause in the Constitution:

'The United States shall guarantee, to every State in the Union, a Republican form of Government; shall protect each of them against invasion; and, on application of the Legislature, or of the Executive, when the Legislature cannot be convened, against domestic violence.'

[Rawle continues:] "The Union is an association of the people of Republics; its preservation is calculated to depend on the preservation of those Republics. The principle of representation, although, certainly, the wisest and best, is not essential to the being of a Republic; but, to continue a member of the Union, it must be preserved; and, therefore, the guarantee must be so construed. *It depends on the State itself, to retain or abolish the principle of representation; because it depends on itself, whether it will continue a member of the Union. To deny this right, would be inconsistent with the principles on which all our political systems are founded; which is, that the people have, in all cases, a right to determine how they will be governed.*

"This right must be considered as an ingredient in the original composition of the General Government, which, though not expressed, was mutually understood; and the doctrine, heretofore presented to the reader, in regard to the indefeasible nature of personal allegiance, is so far qualified, in respect to allegiance to the United States. It was observed that it was competent for a State to make a Compact with its citizens, that the reciprocal obligations of protection and allegiance might cease on certain events; and it was further observed that allegiance would necessarily cease on the dissolution of the society to which it was due.

". . . *The Secession of a State from the Union depends on the will of the people of such State.* The people, alone, as we have already seen, hold the power to alter their Constitution. *The Constitution of the United States is, to a certain extent, incorporated into the Constitutions of the several States, by the act of the people. The State Legislatures have only to perform certain organical operations in respect to it. To withdraw from the Union, comes not within the general scope of their delegated authority. There must be an express provision to that effect inserted in the State Constitutions.* This is not, at present, the case with any of them, and it would, perhaps, be impolitic to confide it to them. A matter, so momentous, ought not to be intrusted to those who would have it in their power to exercise it lightly and precipitately, upon sudden dissatisfaction or causeless jealousy, perhaps against the interests and the wishes of a majority of their constituents.

"But in any manner by which a Secession is to take place, nothing is more certain than that the act should be deliberate, clear, and unequivocal. The perspicuity and solemnity of the original obligation require correspondent qualities in its dissolution. The powers of the General Government cannot be defeated or impaired by an ambiguous or implied Secession on the part of the State, although a Secession may, perhaps, be conditional. The people of the State may have some reasons to complain in respect to acts of the General Government; they may, in such cases, invest some of their own officers with the power of negotiation, and may declare an absolute Secession in case of their failure. Still, however, the Secession must in such case be distinctly and peremptorily declared to take place on that event, and in such case—as in the case of an unconditional Secession—the previous ligament with the Union would be legitimately and fairly destroyed. But, in either case, the people is the only moving power.

"Under the Articles of Confederation the concurrence of nine States was requisite for many purposes. If five States had withdrawn from that Union, it would have been dissolved. In the present Constitution there is no specification of numbers after the first formation. It was foreseen that there would be a natural tendency to increase the number of States with the increase of population then anticipated, and now so fully verified. *It was also known, though it was not avowed, that a State might withdraw itself.* The number would therefore be variable.

". . . To withdraw from the Union is a solemn, serious act. Whenever it may appear expedient to the people of a State, it must be manifested in a direct and unequivocal manner."

[Stephens continues:] Mr. Rawle came to the same logical conclusion upon the subject of Secession that Judge Tucker had come to. *He also distinctly asserts that it was known at the time, though not avowed, that a State might withdraw itself.* "It was mutually understood," he says. He was a living actor in the scenes.

Fourthly. It is upon the grounds or assumption that this was the general understanding of the nature of the Government at the time, that we can account for the triumphant success of Mr. Jefferson, in 1800, on the principles of the Virginia and Kentucky Resolutions of 1798-99, and Mr. Madison's [1799] Report, referred to before. It is in accordance with this general understanding that we can account for Mr. Hamilton's strong reason for Mr. Jefferson's co-operation in the matter just stated.

It is in accordance with the same general understanding that we can account for what I have seen it stated was the action of the Massachusetts Legislature in 1803, on the acquisition of Louisiana. That State, it is said, then declared, by solemn resolve, "That the annexation of Louisiana to the Union, transcends the Constitutional power of the Government of the United States. *It formed a new Confederacy to which the States united by the former Compact are not bound to adhere.*"[746]

Stephen then discusses the case of Massachusetts' attempt to secede in 1844 and 1845:

> The Legislature of Massachusetts, in 1844, did, without question, pass a series of Resolutions upon the annexation of Texas, of which the following is a part:
>
> > "Resolved, That the project of the annexation of Texas, unless arrested on the threshold, may drive these States into a dissolution of the Union."
>
> On the same subject, on the 22nd of February, 1845, the same body adopted another series of Resolutions, in which the following occurs:
>
> > "Resolved, and as the powers of Legislation granted in the Constitution of the United States to Congress, do not embrace the case of the admission of a foreign State, or foreign territory, by Legislation, into the Union, such an act of admission would have no binding force whatever on the people of Massachusetts."
>
> Here are authentic copies of each of these sets of Resolutions. They are not at all inconsistent with those said to have been passed on a similar subject in 1803. *These Resolutions show clearly the understanding of Massachusetts as late as 1844-1845, of the nature of the Compact of our Union. Though she did not see fit to exercise her right to secede or withdraw, she nevertheless unmistakably asserted her right to do so under circumstances then existing, by asserting that she would not be bound by the anticipated action of the General Government in the matter of the annexation of Texas.*

An 1814 political cartoon satirizing the Hartford Convention, at which Yankees planned to secede from the Union and form a "New England Confederacy." Secessionist leader Timothy Pickering of Massachusetts kneels near the bottom center praying for success. England's King George III (right) shouts encouragement from the opposite shore.

Moreover, it is in strict accordance with this general understanding that several of the Eastern States, upon the call of Massachusetts, assembled by their deputies in the well-known New England or Hartford Convention, in December, 1814. These States, it is well known, were greatly disaffected towards the Federal Administration. It was during our last war with Great Britain. They conceived their interest to be improperly sacrificed by the policy pursued in the conduct of the war. The Convention was called to devise some course to be taken by these States for a redress of their common grievances. They did nothing, however, but issue an address setting forth their grievances, and appoint a delegation to present them, with their views, to the Federal authorities at Washington; and provide for another Convention to take further action in the premises. This address went into a very full review of the nature of the Government. In it the following principles are set forth:

> "It is as much the duty of the State authorities to watch over the rights reserved, as of the United States to exercise the powers which are delegated."

Further on this language occurs:

> "But in cases of deliberate, dangerous and palpable infractions of the Constitution, affecting the Sovereignty of a State and liberties of the people, *it is not only the right, but the duty of such a State to interpose its authority for their protection in the manner best calculated to secure that end. When emergencies occur which are either beyond the reach of the judicial tribunals, or too pressing to admit of the delay incident to their forms, States which have no common umpire must be their own judges, and execute their own decisions.*"

To this document are signed, amongst others, the venerable names of Nathan Dane, George Cabot, Zephenia Swift, James Hillhouse, and Harrison G. Otis. Dane was the founder of the Professorship of Law in the Cambridge University, and was the author of the Abridgment of American Law, so often quoted by Judge Story, as well as the author of the celebrated ordinance for the government of the North-western Territory, in 1787. *That these States did intend to secede and withdraw from the Union, unless their grievances complained of were redressed, there can be no doubt, and that these eminent jurists thought then that they had a right to do so, is equally clear.*

The news, however, of the treaty of peace which had been signed at Ghent, on the 24th day, of December, 1814, was soon after received in this country, and put an end to all other proceedings under this movement of these States.

But what is remarkable in the history of that controversy is, that *in no debate in Congress were the fundamental doctrines of this address called in question,* so far as I have been able to discover. Mr. Madison, then President, made no allusion, in his message to Congress, to this movement. *Niles's Register* contains six able leading editorial articles against this Convention and its proceedings, but *in none of them is the right of the States to withdraw from the Union, if they choose to do so, questioned.* It is true, the Convention was generally odious, at the time, to the people of a large majority of the States, and has been ever since. This was from the fact that the threatened Secession was in time of war, and a war which had been undertaken mainly, at the instance of these States, in defence of their shipping and navigating interests. It is also true, that some journalists and partisans of the day did charge the movement to be treasonable. But what have not partisan journalists and public speakers, in times of excitement, charged to be treasonable! Almost every matter in the administration of Government, that does not suit their own peculiar views and notions. *This charge was not made by any of the officials of the Government, that I am aware of, and what I mean to say is, that the right of a State to withdraw from the Union was never denied or questioned, that I am aware of, by any jurist, publicist, or statesman of character and standing, until [James] Kent's Commentaries appeared, in 1826, nearly forty years after the Government had gone into operation!* From the weight of evidence, therefore, the conclusion follows, that in the opinion of the fathers generally, as well as of the great mass of the people throughout the country, the right existed. It has been stated by high authority, that "the right of Secession" is not a plant of Southern origin—it first sprung up in the North." *A more accurate statement would be that it was not sectional but continental in its origin. It was generally recognized in all parts of the Union during the earlier days of the Republic.*

French diplomat Alexis de Tocqueville recognized the "voluntary" nature of the American Union, asserting that there was no governmental authority to prevent a state from seceding.

Fifthly and lastly, *this right, so apparent to all clear and unbiased minds from all the facts connected with the history and nature of the Government, is fully and clearly recognized by all foreign writers and publicists who have made our institutions their study.* Prominent in this class stands Tocqueville, before alluded to. On this point he says:

> "However strong a Government may be, it cannot easily escape from the consequences of a principle which it has once admitted as the foundation of its Constitution. *The Union was formed by the voluntary agreement of the States; and these, in uniting together, have not forfeited their Nationality, nor have they been reduced to the condition of one and the same people. If one of the States chose to withdraw its name*

from the contract, it would be difficult to disprove its right of doing so, and the Federal Government would have no means of maintaining its claims directly, either by force or by right."[747]

★ FACT: ALL CHARGES AGAINST JEFFERSON DAVIS WERE EVENTUALLY DROPPED DUE TO THE FACTS PROVIDED HERE

The information presented in this book is why Jefferson Davis, though charged, arrested, and imprisoned for "treason" after the War, was never given a complete trial; this despite the fact that he repeatedly requested one. Unfortunately for history, he was repeatedly turned down: the U.S. government had asked three different prosecuting attorneys to try him, but all three refused, deeming the case thoroughly unwinnable.[748] Why?

A full public trial would have allowed the South's brilliant legal minds, including Davis', to prove the legality of secession *and* expose what I call "The Great Yankee Coverup"; that is, the wholesale concealment of the many illegalities of Lincoln's War—most importantly the Liberals' attempt to crush states' rights, which includes the right of secession.[749] One of the North's own lawyers stated:

If secession was illegal then Jefferson Davis was guilty of treason and should have been executed. Yet all charges against him were dropped, despite his own pleas for a full public trial. Why? This is a question no South-hater dares to answer!

> Gentleman, the Supreme Court of the United States will have to acquit that man [Davis] under the Constitution when it will be proven to the world that the North waged an unconstitutional warfare against the South.[750]

No wonder that before Davis was captured trying to reorganize his armies, President Lincoln and General Grant had ardently "wished and hoped" that he would escape unnoticed into the Southern wilderness.[751]

The reality is that it was not Conservative Constitution-loving Davis who committed treason against the U.S. It was Liberal Constitution-hating Lincoln. And it was Lincoln who, had he lived, should have been tried.[752] In 1878 Louisiana attorney Bernard J. Sage, one of the lawyers who defended Jefferson Davis against the absurd charge of "treason," rightly declared:

> It was the [constitutional] facts and principles . . . and the vital importance of them to these "stubborn," "indestructible states" [in the South] that caused [William H.] Seward, [Salmon P.] Chase, and President [Andrew] Johnson to *evade the trial of Davis*, [Robert E.] Lee, and the other confederate chiefs, *while pretending to desire it*. Reason, silent in War, longed to implead "the government" in time of peace. *Justice would have vindicated the defendants and their "lost cause"—this being the cause of institutional liberty—the cause of the American commonwealths.*[753]

In 1873 a pertinent letter appeared in the Norfolk *Virginian*. It read:

> [An] event of great historical interest, in which Judge [John H.] Clifford participated, was the solemn consultation of a small number of the ablest lawyers of the north, at Washington, a few months after the war, upon the momentous question as to whether the federal government should commence a criminal prosecution against Jefferson Davis for his participation and leadership in the war of secession. In this council, which was surrounded at the time with the utmost secrecy, and which has never yet been described, were U.S. attorney-general [James] Speed, Judge Clifford, William M. Evarts, and perhaps half a dozen others, who had been selected from the whole northern profession for their legal ability and acumen; and *the result of their deliberation was the sudden abandonment [of the idea of prosecution], in view of the insurmountable difficulties in the way of getting a final conviction, which were revealed by their patient study of the law bearing upon the case.*[754]

Cooper, Estill, and Lemmon write similarly:

> JEFFERSON DAVIS BROUGHT TO TRIAL ON THE 3ʳᴅ DAY OF DECEMBER, 1868
> Mr. Davis was brought to trial in the Circuit Court of the United States for the District of Virginia, before Chief Justice [Salmon P.] Chase of the Supreme Court of the United States and District Judge [John C.] Underwood. Several indictments for treason and for conspiring with Robert E. Lee and many others to levy war against the United States were preferred against him. He was brought to trial on all of them. A motion to quash the indictments was made by his counsel, one of the most distinguished of whom was Charles O'Connor of New York. *After argument, Chief Justice Chase announced that the Court "had failed to agree upon a decision in regard to the motion to quash the indictments against Mr. Jefferson Davis,"* and instructed the reporter of the Court to

record him as "being of opinion that the indictment should be quashed."

Judge Underwood, being of a contrary opinion, the case was certified to the Supreme Court of the United States for decision. *No further proceedings were ever taken in the cases. The Attorney-General of the United States never asked the Supreme Court for a hearing on the certificate; and, at a subsequent term of the Circuit Court of the United States for Virginia, all the indictments against Mr. Davis were dismissed. It is manifest from these proceedings that the counsel for the United States became satisfied that they could not procure a conviction of Mr. Davis before their own tribunals. He had long previously been fully vindicated by the enlightened public opinion of the world.*[755]

★ **FACT: SOUTH-HATERS NEVER ASK WHY, IF SECESSION WAS ILLEGAL, NOT ONE CONFEDERATE OFFICER WAS EXECUTED FOR TREASON AFTER THE WAR**
Davis was not the only Confederate official who escaped death because secession was lawful and Lincoln's War was not. There were some 425 Confederate general officers.[756] Not a single one was executed for "treason"—or for any other reason after the War.[757] Though this fact has been in the public domain for 150 years, the simple souls who belong to the anti-South movement have managed to ignore or suppress it.

But authentic facts are eternal and cannot be erased from history, and I stamp this one here again for all to see: during the postbellum era not a single Confederate officer was ever arrested, imprisoned, tried, and executed for treason, ironclad proof that the U.S. government secretly recognized that secession was perfectly legal before, during, and after the War.

★ **FACT: SECESSION HAS NEVER BEEN & NEVER WILL BE ILLEGAL, AND FOR A MULTITUDE OF REASONS**
In their wondrous sagacity, the Founders, as well as their conservative political descendants,
1) purposefully created the U.S.A. as a "confederate republic,"[758] our union being the former, our government being the latter.
2) rejected the idea of forming a "national government."[759]
3) declared state sovereignty (not the Union) "perpetual."[760]
4) insisted that the Union exists only at the "good pleasure" of the states; that is, the people.[761]
5) asserted that the independent sovereign "states are the soul" of the Constitution.[762]

6) said that our Union and our government were created by and rest on "public opinion"—and can thus be undone by the same.[763]
7) made secession a vital "ingredient in the original composition of the general government."[764]
8) intentionally left any mention of secession out of the Constitution since it was "mutually understood,"[765] and more importantly, because it is, by international law, an innate right of all sovereigns.[766]
9) stressed that the U.S.A. was "founded on the great principle of *voluntary* federation," this fact alone making secession legal.[767]
10) went as far as to make it unlawful for the federal government to coerce the states.[768]
11) stipulated that when one state violates constitutional law, it absolves the other states from their constitutional obligations, including their membership in the compact (Union).[769]
12) said it was up to each individual state, not the federal government, to decide upon the right of secession.[770]
13) took great care during the writing of the Declaration of Independence to emphasize the idea that "when any form of Government becomes destructive of the ends for which it was established, *it is the right of the people to alter or to abolish it*, and to institute new government."[771]

In his memoirs Union General Ulysses S. Grant declared that had the South fought for one more year, the Union would have let it go. This means that in the Spring of 1865, hypocritical Yankee Liberals were on the verge of being forced to publicly recognize secession as legal, legitimate, and constitutional—just as they saw it themselves 50 years earlier in 1815, when they were planning to secede and form a "New England Confederacy."

These 13 immortal facts of history which I have compiled, one for each of the 13 seceded Southern States, make the words "secession" and "United States of America" synonymous.

Bearing this important information in mind, it is obvious that secession is just as legal today as it was in 1776, 1799, 1815, 1832, and 1860, during our many secession movements. The only thing that could make it illegal is a constitutional amendment, and there is not now, and never has been such an amendment, and there never will be. Why? Because prohibiting secession would completely alter the nature of the U.S. government and its relationship to the states. Indeed, the government would become national, the Union would become a nation, and the states as independent sovereigns would disappear, forever "chaining" them to the national government.[772]

Thus those who claim secession is illegal either simply do not want to believe that it is legal, are ignorant of history, or they are lying.

Why suppress the truth, reinterpret the Constitution to fit an anti-American agenda, then rewrite a fictional account of secession and the War?

★ FACT: THE "SECESSION IS ILLEGAL" LIE WAS INVENTED TO JUSTIFY THE GREAT LIBERAL AGENDA: LINCOLN'S WAR
In answer to the above question: it was the Liberals' (in 1860, the Republicans) attempt to justify the unnecessary deaths of countless thousands and the needless bombing of the South into rubble for the sole purpose of installing big government (known as the "American System") at Washington, D.C.

This reveals the "secession has never been legal" argument of Liberals and unenlightened Conservatives to be the sham that it is. An erroneous notion put forth to hide the illegalities and pointless destruction of Lincoln's Liberal War against the American people and the conservatively oriented Constitution. For, just as General Grant and many others eventually conceded, if the South had won, the right of secession would have been openly acknowledged, permitted, and authorized[773]—*just as it had been before the conflict*. Case closed.

The End

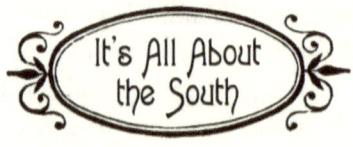

APPENDIX A

THE DAY SOUTH CAROLINA SECEDED

A Brief Description of the Moment the Palmetto State Left the Union

BY JAMES FORD RHODES, 1895

The [South Carolina secession] convention met the fourth day of its session [December 20, 1860] at twelve o'clock in St. Andrew's Hall [Charleston]. Chancellor [John A.] Inglis, Judge of Chancery, a silver-haired gentleman, a large planter and slave-holder, and a man of parts, reported the ordinance of secession. Explaining that the committee had used the utmost brevity, he read with flashing eyes the burning declaration, "We, the people of the State of South Carolina, in convention assembled, do declare and ordain . . . that the union now subsisting between South Carolina and other States under the name of 'The United States of America' is hereby dissolved." December 20, at a quarter-past one, this ordinance was unanimously passed.

It was known in the city that on this day the convention would take decisive action, and an excited throng had gathered about the hall eager for the first announcement of what its representatives, sitting in solemn and secret conclave, had done. Immediately on the declaration of the vote the door-keeper was apprised. He gave the word to the policeman nearest him. It was passed from mouth to mouth until it reached the sentinel at the tall iron gate at the entrance, and by him was proclaimed to the impatient crowd.

Cheer after cheer rent the air. In less than fifteen minutes the Charleston *Mercury* had issued an extra [issue,] giving the text of the ordinance, and the news that it had been unanimously adopted; six thousand of these were soon sold, and the whole city knew that South Carolina had, as she would wish it expressed, resumed her sovereign powers.

The chimes of St. Michael's pealed an exultant note; the bells of all the other churches were loudly rung. The gun by the post-office, christened "Old Secession," and on which a copy of the ordinance had been pasted, belched forth the thunder of celebration; the cannon in the citadel echoed the glad tidings. Houses and shops were emptied; the streets were full of people. The cares of business and of family were forgotten; all faces wore smiles; all as they walked seemed to tread in air; joy was unconfined. Old men ran shouting down the streets. When friend met friend there was the hearty grasp of the hand as one said, "Thank God, they have put her out at last!" and as the other replied, "I breathe free now."

Then they congratulated one another on the change of weather. For three days the sky had frowned and poured down rain. On this December 20 the sun had risen full and clear, and it pleased these men to say that Heaven smiled on their action. Volunteers donned their uniforms and hastened to their armories. New palmetto flags everywhere appeared. Everyone wore a blue cockade in his hat. Great enthusiasm was shown at the unfurling of a banner on which blocks of stone in an arch typified the fifteen Southern

States; these were surmounted by the statue of [John C.] Calhoun with the Constitution in his hand, and the figures of Faith and Hope; at the base of the arch were blocks broken in fragments representing the Northern States. A scroll interpreted the allegory: a "Southern republic" was "built from the ruins" of the other half of the country. The sentiment of the community was shared by the boys firing noisy crackers, and, as it grew dark, Roman-candles—a spontaneous testimony to the general joy. That day the patricians of Charleston drank champagne with their dinners.

It was decided to make the signing of the ordinance an impressive public ceremony. The governor and the legislature, who had followed the convention to Charleston, were invited to assist in the proceedings that evening. At half-past six the members of the convention came together at the place of their deliberations, and, forming in files of two with locked arms, they marched silently, lighted by the flare of bonfires, to Institute Hall, which had been selected because it was the largest assembly-room in the city. At the foot of the staircase they were joined by the State senators and representatives.

South Carolina's Coat of Arms.

The hall was packed with spectators. The galleries were filled with ladies, dressed with what elegance the last year's wardrobe afforded. But dearer now to the Southern heart than trappings and show were the bright eyes and interested, encouraging looks of those women, who little recked [understood] that they were then beginning a course of devotion and heroism which has justly won the admiration of the world. On the floor the brilliant uniforms of the officers of the new-born army made a picturesque and suggestive contrast to the conventional broad cloth of the Carolina gentlemen.

The audience had not long to wait. The cry, "The convention is coming!" drew every one's regard. Its president, leaning on the arm of the clerk, entered by a door in the rear of the hall and took his place upon the rostrum. Following him came the President of the Senate and the Speaker of the House clad in their robes of office, with the clerks of both bodies in their black silken gowns. The delegates, the senators, and the representatives made their entrance by another door and took the reserved places in the body of the hall.

A clergyman with bowed form and hair as white as snow advanced to the front of the platform with upraised hands, the whole assembly rising to their feet in reverent attitude while he invoked the blessing and favor of Almighty God on this great act of his people about to be consummated. The president of the convention, holding in his hand the parchment with the great seal of the State, read slowly and solemnly therefrom the Ordinance of Secession. As the last word "dissolved" left his lips the audience broke forth into cheers and shouts and roars that lasted until physical exhaustion made silence a necessity. The delegates sat grave and silent. They were now asked by the president to step forward and sign the ordinance. This ceremony took two hours, but the audience remained to witness it.

When Robert B. Rhett, who had been a disunionist since 1832, advanced to the rostrum, there were thunders of applause; cheers greeted Delegate [John M.] Spratt, whose vehement advocacy of the reopening of the African slave-trade singled him out for notice; and ex-Governor [William H.] Gist, who had been the official mouth-piece of the beginning of this secession movement, also inspired demonstrations of popular favor. To many of the people looking on there must have come the thought of that other signing of a Declaration of Independence, of that new era ushered in July 4, 1776; and their feeling grew stronger that now was beginning a second glorious revolution, which, if successful, would, on account of a securer basis, be more lasting.

Those who knew that [Yankee diplomat and Massachusetts Congressman] Caleb Cushing, now regarded as the envoy of a foreign power, had been solicited by a committee of the legislature to attend this ceremony, might have imagined a likeness between this invitation and the request for assistance which another representative body—the French National Assembly of 1789—had preferred to [Thomas] Jefferson; and prophetic souls, to whom came the picture of the greatest of revolutions, must have seen beyond this present pledging of faiths an era of blood. It cannot but have occurred to all that in this very hall,

The Old State House, Columbia, South Columbia, where the state's Ordinance of Secession was adopted on December 20, 1860.

eight months before, had been played the first act of the drama of secession, when the delegates from the cotton States withdrew from the national Democratic convention.

When all the signatures had been affixed to the instrument the president said, "I proclaim the State of South Carolina an independent commonwealth." And then the enthusiasm and the joy knew no bounds. Such cries of exultation, such shouts of gladness had never before been heard in Charleston. The scene in the streets was impressive, the avenues to the hall being filled with an ardent throng. Military companies marched and countermarched to the strains of martial music. The hurrahs above were taken up by the crowd below.

Before the response to the cheers over the final declaration of the president had died away, the clerk of the convention mounted a chair in the streets and, holding aloft the parchment, besought silence. When he had finished reading the ordinance to the people wild gladness reigned. Bonfires were lighted; pistols and fireworks were shot off. The liberty-pole at the head of Hayne Street was brilliantly illuminated. Patricians and plebeians, planters and poor whites of the country, rich merchants and laborers of the city mingled in a common throng and blended their voices in hailing the new era of independence.

With truth could an organ of public opinion two days later say, "The most impressive feature in the action of South Carolina is the concentrated unanimity of her people."[774]

APPENDIX B

THE KENTUCKY & VIRGINIA RESOLUTIONS

Written in Response to the Liberals' Unconstitutional Alien & Sedition Laws of 1798

BY THOMAS JEFFERSON & JAMES MADISON, 1798

KENTUCKY RESOLUTIONS, November 1798, Jefferson

1. Resolved, That the several States composing the United States of America are not united on the principle of unlimited submission to their General Government; but that, by compact, under the style and title of a Constitution for the United States and of Amendments thereto, they constituted a general government for special purposes, delegated to that Government certain definite powers, reserving each State to itself the residuary mass of right to their own self-government; and that whensoever the General Government assumes undelegated powers, its acts are unauthoritative, void, and of no force: That to this compact each State acceded as a State, and is an integral party, its co-States forming as to itself the other party: That the government created by this compact was not made the exclusive or final judge of the extent of the powers delegated to itself; since that would have made its discretion, and not the constitution, the measure of its powers; but that, as in all other cases of compact among parties having no common judge, each party has an equal right to judge for itself, as well of infractions, as of the mode and measure of redress.

2. That the Constitution of the United States having delegated to Congress a power to punish treason, counterfeiting the securities and current coin of the United States, piracies and felonies committed on the high seas, and offences against the laws of nations, and no other crimes whatever, and it being true as a general principle, and one of the amendments to the Constitution having also declared, "that the powers not delegated to the United States by the Constitution, nor prohibited by it to the States, are reserved to the States respectively or to the people"; therefore, also the same act of Congress, passed on the 14th day of July, 1798, and entitled, "An act in addition to the act entitled, 'an act for the punishment of certain crimes against the United States," as also the act passed by them on the 27th day of June, 1798, entitled "An act to punish frauds committed on the Bank of the United States'" (and all other their acts which assume to create, define, or punish crimes other than those enumerated in the Constitution), are altogether void and of no force, and that the power to create, define, and punish such other crimes is reserved, and of right appertains solely and exclusively, to the respective States, each within its own territory.

3. That it is true as a general principle, and is also expressly declared by one of the amendments to the Constitution, that "the powers not delegated to the United States by the Constitution, nor prohibited by it to the States, are reserved to the States respectively or to the people"; and that no power over the freedom of religion, freedom of speech, or freedom of the press, being delegated to the United States by the

Constitution, nor prohibited by it to the States, all lawful powers respecting the same did of right remain, and were reserved, to the States or to the people: That thus was manifested their determination to retain to themselves the right of judging how far the licentiousness of speech and of the press may be abridged without lessening their useful freedom, and how far those abuses which cannot be separated from their use should be tolerated rather than the use be destroyed; and thus, also, they guarded against all abridgment by the United States of the freedom of religious opinions and exercises, and retained to themselves the right of protecting the same, as this State, by a law passed on the general demand of its citizens, had already protected them from all human restraint or interference: And that, in addition to this general principle and express declaration, another and more special provision has been made by one of the amendments to the Constitution, which expressly declares that "Congress shall make no law respecting an establishment of religion or prohibiting the free exercise there of, or abridging the freedom of speech or of the press," thereby guarding in the same sentence, and under the same words, the freedom of religion, of speech, and of the press, insomuch that whatever violates either throws down the sanctuary which covers the others, and that libels, falsehoods, and defamation, equally with heresy and false religion, are withheld from the cognizance of federal tribunals: That therefore the act of the Congress of the United States, passed on the 14th day of July, 1798, entitled "An act in addition to the act for the punishment of certain crimes against the United States," which does abridge the freedom of the press, is not law, but is altogether void and of no effect.

Thomas Jefferson, third president of the United States and author of the 1798 Kentucky Resolutions, a major building block in the foundation of the Southern secession movement of 1860.

4. That alien friends are under the jurisdiction and protection of the laws of the State wherein they are; that no power over them has been delegated to the United States nor prohibited to the individual States distinct from their power over citizens; and it being true, as a general principle, and one of the amendments to the Constitution having also declared that "the powers not delegated to the United States by the Constitution, nor prohibited by it to the States, are reserved to the States respectively or to the people," the act of the Congress of the United States, passed on the 22nd day of June, 1798, entitled "An act concerning aliens," which assumes power over alien friends not delegated by the Constitution, is not law, but is altogether void and of no force.

5. That in addition to the general principle as well as the express declaration that powers not delegated are reserved, another and more special provision inserted in the Constitution from abundant caution has declared "that the migration or importation of such persons as any of the States now existing shall think proper to admit shall not be prohibited by the Congress prior to the year 1808": That this Commonwealth does admit the migration of alien friends described as the subject of the said act concerning

aliens; that a provision against prohibiting their migration is a provision against all acts equivalent thereto, or it would be nugatory; that to remove them when migrated is equivalent to a prohibition of their migration, and is therefore contrary to the said provision of the Constitution and void.

6. That the imprisonment of a person under the protection of the laws of this Commonwealth on his failure to obey the simple order of the President to depart out of the United States, as is undertaken by the said act, entitled "an act concerning aliens," is contrary to the Constitution, one amendment to which has provided, that "no person shall be deprived of liberty without due process of law," and that another having provided "that in all criminal prosecutions the accused shall enjoy the right to a public trial by an impartial jury, to be informed of the nature and cause of the accusation, to be confronted with the witnesses against him, to have compulsory process for obtaining witnesses in his favor, and to have the assistance of counsel for his defence," the same act undertaking to authorize the President to remove a person out of the United States who is under the protection of the law, on his own suspicion, with out accusation, without jury, without public trial, without confrontation of the witnesses against him, without having witnesses in his favor, without defence, without counsel, is contrary to these provisions also of the Constitution, is therefore not law, but utterly void and of no force. That transferring the power of judging any person, who is under the protection of the laws, from the courts to the President of the United States, as is undertaken by the same act concerning aliens, is against the article of the Constitution which provides that "the judicial power of the United States shall be vested in courts, the judges of which shall hold their offices during good behavior"; and that the said act is void for that reason also; and it is further to be noted, that this transfer of judiciary power is to that magistrate of the General Government who already possesses all the executive, and a qualified negative in all the legislative powers.

7. That the construction applied by the General Government (as is evinced by sundry of their proceedings) to those parts of the Constitution of the United States which delegates to Congress a power to lay and collect taxes, duties, imposts, and excises; to pay the debts, and provide for the common defence and general welfare of the United States, and to make all laws which shall be necessary and proper for carrying into execution the powers vested by the Constitution in the Government of the United States, or any department thereof, goes to the destruction of all the limits prescribed to their power by the Constitution. That words meant by that instrument to be subsidiary only to the execution of the limited powers ought not to bo so construed as themselves to give unlimited powers, nor a part so to be taken as to destroy the whole residue of the instrument: That the proceedings of the General Government under color of these articles will be a fit and necessary subject for revisal and correction at a time of greater tranquillity, while those specified in the preceding resolutions call for immediate redress.

8. That the preceding resolutions be transmitted to the Senators and Representatives in Congress from this Commonwealth, who are hereby enjoined to present the same to their respective houses, and to use their best endeavors to procure, at the next session of Congress, a repeal of the aforesaid unconstitutional and obnoxious acts.

9. Lastly, That the Governor of this Commonwealth be, and is hereby, authorized and requested to communicate the preceding resolutions to the legislatures of the several States, to assure them that this Commonwealth considers union for specified national purposes, and particularly for those specified in their late federal compact, to be friendly to the peace, happiness, and prosperity of all the States: that faithful to that compact, according to the plain intent and meaning in which it was understood and acceded to by the several parties, it is sincerely anxious for its preservation: that it does also believe, that to take from the States all the powers of self-government, and transfer them to a general and consolidated government, without regard to the special obligations and reservations solemnly agreed to in that compact, is not for the peace, happiness, or prosperity of these States: And that therefore this Commonwealth is determined, as it doubts not its co-States are, tamely to submit to undelegated and consequently unlimited powers in no man or body of men on earth: that if the acts before specified should stand, these conclusions would flow from them; that the General Government may place any act they think proper on the list of crimes, and punish it themselves, whether enumerated or not enumerated by the Constitution as cognizable by them; that they may transfer its cognizance to the President or any other person, who may himself be the accuser, counsel, judge, and jury, whose suspicions may be the evidence, his order the sentence, his officer the executioner, and his breast the sole record of the transaction; that a very numerous and valuable description of the inhabitants of these States, being by this precedent reduced as outlaws to the absolute dominion of one man, and the barrier of the Constitution thus swept away from us all, no rampart now remains against the passions and the power of a majority of Congress to protect from a like exportation or other more grievous punishment the minority of the same body , the legislatures, judges, governors, and counselors of the States, nor their other peaceable inhabitants who may venture to reclaim the constitutional rights and liberties of the States and people, or who for other causes, good or bad, may be obnoxious to the views, or marked by the suspicions of the President, or be thought dangerous to his or their elections or other interests, public or personal; that the friendless alien has indeed been selected as the safest subject of a first experiment; but the citizen will soon follow, or rather has already followed; for already has a sedition act marked him as its prey: that these and successive acts of the same character, *unless arrested on the threshold, may tend to drive these States into revolution and blood* and will furnish new calumnies against republican governments, and new pretexts for those who wish it to be believed that man cannot be governed but by a rod of iron: that it would be a dangerous delusion, were a confidence in the men of our choice to silence our fears for the safety of our rights: that confidence is everywhere the parent of despotism; free government is founded in jealousy and not in confidence; it is jealousy and not confidence which prescribes limited constitutions to bind down those whom we are obliged to trust with power: that our Constitution has accordingly fixed the limits to which and no further our confidence, may go; and let the honest advocate of confidence read the alien and sedition acts, and say if the Constitution has not been wise in fixing limits to the government it created, and whether we should be wise in destroying those limits? Let him say what the Government is if it be not a tyranny, which the men of our choice have conferred on the President, and the President of our choice has assented to

and accepted over the friendly strangers, to whom the mild spirit of our country and its laws had pledged hospitality and protection: that the men of our choice have more respected the bare suspicions of the President than the solid rights of innocence, the claims of justification, the sacred force of truth, and the forms and substance of law and justice in questions of power, then, let no more be heard of confidence in man, but bind him down from mischief by the chains of the Constitution. That this Commonwealth does therefore call on its co-States for an expression of their sentiments on the acts concerning aliens and for the punishment of certain crimes hereinbefore specified, plainly declaring whether these acts are or are not authorized by the federal compact? And it doubts not that their sense will be so announced as to prove their attachment unaltered to limited government, whether general or particular, and that the rights and liberties of their co-States will be exposed to no dangers by remaining embarked on a common bottom with their own; That they will concur with this Commonwealth in considering the said acts as so palpably against the Constitution, as to amount to an undisguised declaration that the compact is not meant to be the measure of the powers of the General Government, but that it will proceed in the exercise over these States of all powers whatsoever: That they will view this as seizing *the Rights of the States*, and consolidating them in the hands of the General Government with a power assumed to bind the States, (not merely in cases made federal,) but in all cases whatsoever, by laws made, not with their consent, but by others against their consent; That this would be to surrender the form of government we have chosen, and to live under one deriving its powers from its own will, and not from our authority; and that the co-States, recurring to their natural right in cases not made federal, will concur in declaring these acts void and of no force, and will each unite with this Commonwealth in requesting their repeal at the next session of Congress.

VIRGINIA RESOLUTIONS, December 1798, Madison

1. Resolved, That the General Assembly of Virginia doth unequivocally express a firm resolution to maintain and defend the Constitution of the United States and the constitution of this State against every aggression, either foreign or domestic; and that they will support the Government of the United States in all measures warranted by the former.

2. That this Assembly most solemnly declare a warm attachment to the Union of the States, to maintain which it pledges its powers; and that, for this end, it is their duty to watch over and oppose every infraction of those principles which constitute the only basis of that Union, because a faithful observance of them can alone secure its existence and the public happiness.

3. That this Assembly doth explicitly and peremptorily declare, that it views the powers of the Federal Government as resulting from the compact to which the States are parties, as limited by the plain sense and intention of the instrument constituting that compact; and that, in case of a deliberate, palpable, and dangerous exercise of other powers, not granted by the said compact, the States, who are parties thereto, have the right, and are in duty bound to interpose for arresting the progress of the evil, and for maintaining, within their respective limits, the authorities, rights, and liberties

appertaining to them.

4. That the General Assembly doth also express its deep regret that a spirit has, in sundry instances, been manifested by the Federal Government to enlarge its powers by forced constructions of the constitutional charter which defines them; and that indications have appeared of a design to expound certain general phrases (which, having been copied from the very limited grant of powers in the former Articles of Confederation, were the less liable to be misconstrued) so as to destroy the meaning and effect of the particular enumeration which necessarily explains and limits the general phrases, and so as to consolidate the States, by degrees, into one sovereignty, the obvious tendency and inevitable result of which would be to transform the present republican system of the United States into an absolute, or, at best, a mixed monarchy.

5. That the General Assembly doth particularly protest against the palpable and alarming infractions of the Constitution in the two late cases of the "alien and sedition acts," passed at the last session of Congress; the first of which exercises a power nowhere delegated to the Federal Government, and which, by uniting legislative and judicial powers to those of executive, subverts the general principles of free government, as well as the particular organization and positive provisions of the Federal Constitution; and the other of which acts exercises, in like manner, a power not delegated by the Constitution, but, on the contrary, expressly and positively forbidden by one of the amendments thereto—a power which, more than any other, ought to produce universal alarm, because it is levelled against the right of freely examining public characters and measures, and of free communication among the people thereon, which has ever been justly deemed the only effectual guardian of every other right.

James Madison, fourth president of the United States and author of the 1798 Virginia Resolutions, another important document that inspired the 1860 Southern secession movement.

6. That this State, having by its convention, which ratified the Federal Constitution, expressly declared that, among other essential rights, "the liberty of conscience and the press cannot be cancelled, abridged, restrained, or modified, by any authority of the United States," and from its extreme anxiety to guard these rights from every possible attack of sophistry and ambition, having, with other States, recommended an amendment for that purpose, which amendment was, in due time, annexed to the Constitution—it would mark a reproachful inconsistency, and criminal degeneracy if an indifference were now shown to the most palpable violation of one of the rights thus declared and secured, and to the establishment of a precedent which may be fatal to the other.

7. That the good people of this Commonwealth, having ever felt, and continuing to feel, the most sincere affection for their brethren of the other States, the truest anxiety for establishing and perpetuating the union of all, and *the most scrupulous fidelity to that Constitution*, which is the pledge of mutual friendship and the instrument of mutual happiness, the General Assembly doth solemnly appeal to the like dispositions in the other States, in confidence that they will concur with this Commonwealth in declaring, as it does hereby declare, that the acts aforesaid are unconstitutional, and that the necessary and proper measures will be taken by each for co-operating with this State in maintaining unimpaired the authorities, rights, and liberties reserved to the States respectively, or to the people.

8. That the Governor be desired to transmit a copy of the foregoing resolutions to the executive authority of each of the other States, with a request that the same may be communicated to the legislature thereof, and that a copy be furnished to each of the Senators and Representatives representing this State in the Congress of the United States.[775]

The Conservative American colonists were willing to risk their lives to establish self-government (which includes the right of secession), and ensure the constitutional protection of natural rights and personal liberty. Liberals have been trying to undo and destroy their efforts ever since.

APPENDIX C

THE VIRGINIA REPORT OF 1799

*Addressed to Virginia's House of Delegates,
In Defense of the Kentucky & Virginia Resolutions*

BY JAMES MADISON, 1799

Report of the committee to whom were referred the communications of various states relative to the resolutions of the General Assembly of this state, concerning the Alien and Sedition Laws.

Whatever room might be found in the proceedings of some of the states who have disapproved of the resolutions of the General Assembly of this commonwealth, passed on the 21st day of December, 1798, for painful remarks on the spirit and manner of those proceedings, it appears to the committee most consistent with the duty, as well as dignity of the General Assembly, to hasten an oblivion of every circumstance which might be construed into a diminution of mutual respect, confidence, and affection, among the members of the Union.

The committee have deemed it a more useful task, to revise, with a critical eye, the resolutions which have met with this disapprobation; to examine fully the several objections and arguments which have appeared against them; and to inquire whether there be any errors of fact, of principle, or of reasoning, which the candour of the General Assembly ought to acknowledge and correct.

The first of the resolutions is in the words following: *Resolved, That the General Assembly of Virginia doth unequivocally express a firm resolution to maintain and defend the Constitution of the United States, and the Constitution of this state, against every aggression, either foreign or domestic, and that they will support the government of the United States in all measures warranted by the former.*

No unfavourable comment can have been made on the sentiments here expressed. To maintain and defend the Constitution of the United States, and of their own state, against every aggression, both foreign and domestic, and to support the government of the United States in all measures warranted by their Constitution, are duties which the General Assembly ought always to feel, and to which, on such an occasion, it was evidently proper to express its sincere and firm adherence.

In their next resolution—*The General Assembly most solemnly declares a warm attachment to the union of the states, to maintain which it pledges all its powers; and that, for this end, it is its duty to watch over and oppose every infraction of those principles, which constitute the only basis of that union, because a faithful observance of them can alone secure its existence and the public happiness.*

The observation just made is equally applicable to this solemn declaration, of warm attachment to the union, and this solemn pledge to maintain it; nor can any question arise among enlightened friends of the union, as to the duty of watching over and opposing every infraction of those principles which constitute its basis, and a faithful observance of which can alone secure its existence, and the public happiness thereon depending.

The third resolution is in the words following: *That this Assembly doth explicitly and peremptorily declare, that it views the powers of the Federal Government, as resulting from the compact, to which the states are parties, as limited by the plain sense and intention of the instrument constituting that compact; as no farther valid than they are authorized by the grants enumerated in that compact; and that in case of a deliberate, palpable and dangerous exercise of other powers, not granted by the said compact, the states who are parties thereto have the right, and are in duty bound, to interpose for arresting the progress of the evil, and for maintaining within their respective limits, the authorities, rights, and liberties appertaining to them.*

On this resolution, the committee have bestowed all the attention which its importance merits; they have scanned it not merely with a strict, but with a severe eye; and they feel confidence in pronouncing, that, in its just and fair construction, it is unexceptionably true in its several positions, as well as constitutional and conclusive in its inferences.

The resolution declares, first, that "it views the powers of the Federal Government, as resulting from the compact to which the states are parties;" in other words, that the Federal powers are derived from the Constitution, and that the Constitution is a compact to which the states are parties.

Clear as the position must seem, that the federal powers are derived from the Constitution, and from that alone, the committee are not unapprised of a late doctrine, which opens another source of federal powers, not less extensive and important, than it is new and unexpected. The examination of this doctrine will be most conveniently connected with a review of a succeeding resolution. The committee satisfy themselves here with briefly remarking, that in all the contemporary discussions and comments which the Constitution underwent, it was constantly justified and recommended, on the ground, that the powers not given to the government, were

U.S. Founder and "Father of the Constitution," James Madison. In order to both clarify and defend the 1798 Kentucky and Virginia Resolutions (which had been vehemently attacked by Liberals, known as "Federalists" at the time), the following year Madison wrote the Virginia Report (of 1799). Due to its detailed, scholarly, persuasive analysis of constitutional law, 61 years later Southern secessionists found it galvanizing and inspirational.

with held from it; and that, if any doubt could have existed on this subject, under the original text of the Constitution, it is removed, as far as words could remove it, by the 12th amendment, now a part of the Constitution, which expressly declares, "that the powers not delegated to the United States, by the Constitution, nor prohibited by it to the states, are reserved to the states respectively, or to the people."

The other position involved in this branch of the resolution, namely, "that the states are parties to the Constitution or compact," is, in the judgment of the committee, equally free from objection. It is indeed true, that the term "states," is sometimes used in a vague sense, and sometimes in different senses, according to the subject to which it is applied. Thus, it sometimes means the separate sections of territory occupied by the political societies within each; sometimes the particular governments, established by those societies; sometimes those societies as organized into those particular governments; and, lastly, it means the people composing those political societies, in their highest sovereign capacity. Although it might be wished that the perfection of language admitted less diversity in the signification of the same words, yet little inconveniency is produced by it, where the true sense can be collected with certainty from the different applications. In the present instance, whatever different constructions of the term "states," in the resolution, may have been entertained, all will at least concur in that last mentioned; because, in that sense, the Constitution was submitted to the "states:" in that sense the "states" ratified it: and, in that sense of the term "states," they are consequently parties to the compact, from which the powers of the federal government result.

The next position is, that the General Assembly views the powers of the federal government, "as limited by the plain sense and intention of the instrument constituting that compact," and "as no farther valid than they are authorized by the grants therein enumerated." It does not seem possible, that any just objection can lie against either of these clauses. The first amounts merely to a declaration, that the compact ought to have the interpretation plainly intended by the parties to it; the other to a declaration, that it ought to have the execution and effect intended by them. If the powers granted, be valid, it is solely because they are granted: and, if the granted powers are valid, because granted, all other powers not granted, must not be valid.

The resolution, having taken this view of the federal compact, proceeds to infer, "that, in case of a deliberate, palpable, and dangerous exercise of other powers, not granted by the said compact, the states, who are parties thereto, have the right and are in duty bound to interpose for arresting the progress of the evil, and for maintaining within their respective limits, the authorities, rights, and liberties appertaining to them."

It appears to your committee to be a plain principle, founded in common sense, illustrated by common practice, and essential to the nature of compacts, that, where resort can be had to no tribunal superior to the authority of the parties, the parties themselves must be the rightful judges in the last resort, whether the bargain made has been pursued or violated. The Constitution of the United States was formed by the sanction of the states, given by each in its sovereign capacity. It adds to the stability and dignity, as well as to the authority of the Constitution, that it rests on this legitimate and solid foundation. The states, then, being the parties to the constitutional compact, and in their sovereign capacity, it follows of necessity, that there can be no tribunal above their authority, to decide in the last resort, whether the compact made by them be violated; and, consequently, that, as the parties to it, they must themselves decide, in the last resort, such questions as may be of sufficient magnitude to require their interposition.

It does not follow, however, that because the states, as sovereign parties to their constitutional compact, must ultimately decide whether it has been violated, that such a decision ought to be interposed, either in a hasty manner, or on doubtful and inferior occasions. Even in the case of ordinary conventions between different nations, where, by the strict rule of interpretation, a breach of a part may be deemed a breach of the whole, every part being deemed a condition of every other, part and of the whole, it is always laid down that the breach must be both wilful and material to justify an application of the rule. But in the case of an intimate and constitutional union, like that of the United States, it is evident that the interposition of the parties, in their sovereign capacity, can be called for by occasions only, deeply and essentially affecting the vital principles of their political system.

The resolution has accordingly guarded against any misapprehension of its object, by expressly requiring for such an interposition, "the case of a deliberate, palpable, and dangerous breach of the Constitution, by the exercise of powers not granted by it." It must be a case, not of a light and transient nature, but of a nature dangerous to the great purposes for which the Constitution was established. It must be a case, moreover, not obscure or doubtful in its construction, but plain and palpable. Lastly, it must be a case not resulting from a partial consideration, or hasty determination; but a case stamped with a final consideration and deliberate adherence. It is not necessary, because the resolution does not require that the question should be discussed, how far the exercise of any particular power, ungranted by the Constitution, would justify the interposition of the parties to it. As cases might easily be stated, which none would contend ought to fall within that description; cases, on the other hand, might, with equal ease, be stated, so flagrant and so fatal, as to unite every opinion in placing them within that description.

But the resolution has done more than guard against misconstruction, by expressly referring to cases of a deliberate, palpable, and dangerous nature. It specifies the object of the interposition which it contemplates, to be solely that of arresting the progress of the evil of usurpation, and of maintaining the authorities, rights, and liberties appertaining to the states, as parties to the Constitution.

From this view of the resolution, it would seem inconceivable that it can incur any just disapprobation from those who, laying aside all momentary impressions, and recollecting the genuine source and object of the Federal Constitution, shall candidly and accurately interpret the meaning of the General Assembly. If the deliberate exercise of dangerous powers, palpably withheld by the Constitution, could not justify the parties to it, in interposing even so far as to arrest the progress of the evil, and thereby to preserve the Constitution itself, as well as to provide for the safety of the parties to it, there would be an end to all relief from usurped power, and a direct subversion of the rights specified or recognised under all the state constitutions, as well as a plain denial of the fundamental principle on which our independence itself was declared.

But it is objected that the judicial authority is to be regarded as the sole expositor of the Constitution, in the last resort; and it may be asked for what reason, the declaration by the General Assembly, supposing it to be theoretically true, could be required at the present day and in so solemn a manner.

On this objection it might be observed, first, that there may be instances of usurped power, which the forms of the Constitution would never draw within the control of the judicial department; secondly, that if the decision of the judiciary be raised above the authority of the sovereign parties to the Constitution, the decisions of the other departments, not carried by the forms of the Constitution before the judiciary, must be equally authoritative and final with the decisions of that department. But the proper answer to the objection is, that the resolution of the General Assembly relates to those great and extraordinary cases, in which all the forms of the Constitution may prove ineffectual against infractions dangerous to the essential rights of the parties to it. The resolution supposes that dangerous powers, not delegated, may not only be usurped and executed by the other departments, but that the judicial department also may exercise or sanction dangerous powers beyond the grant of the Constitution; and, consequently, that the ultimate right of the parties to the Constitution, to judge whether the compact has been dangerously violated, must extend to violations by one delegated authority, as well as by another; by the judiciary, as well as by the executive, or the legislature.

However true, therefore, it may be, that the judicial department, is, in all questions submitted to it by the forms of the Constitution, to decide in the last resort, this resort must necessarily be deemed the last in relation to the authorities of the other departments of the government; not in relation to the rights of the parties to the constitutional compact, from which the judicial as well as the other departments hold their delegated trusts. On any other hypothesis, the delegation of judicial power would annul the authority delegating it; and the concurrence of this department with the others in usurped powers, might subvert forever, and beyond the possible reach of any rightful remedy, the very Constitution which all were instituted to preserve.

The truth declared in the resolution being established, the expediency of making the declaration at the present day, may safely be left to the temperate consideration and candid judgment of the American public. It will be remembered that a frequent recurrence to fundamental principles, is solemnly enjoined by most of the state constitutions, and particularly by our own, as a necessary safeguard against the danger of degeneracy to which republics are liable, as well as other governments, though in a less degree than others. And a fair comparison of the political doctrines not unfrequent at the present day, with those which characterized the epoch of our revolution, and which form the basis of our republican constitutions, will best determine whether the declaratory recurrence here made to those principles, ought to be viewed as unseasonable and improper, or as a vigilant discharge of an important duty. The authority of constitutions over governments, and of the sovereignty of the people over constitutions, are truths which are at all times necessary to be kept in mind; and at no time perhaps more necessary than at the present.

The fourth resolution stands as follows: *That the General Assembly doth also express its deep regret, that a spirit has in sundry instances, been manifested by the federal government, to enlarge its powers by forced constructions of the constitutional charter which defines them; and that indications have appeared of a design to expound certain general phrases, (which, having been* copied from the very limited grant of powers in the former articles of confederation, were the less liable to be misconstrued,) so as to destroy the meaning and effect of the particular enumeration which necessarily explains, and limits the general phrases; and so as to consolidate the states, by degrees, into one sovereignty, the obvious tendency and inevitable result of which would be, to transform the present republican system of the United States into an absolute, or, at best, a mixed monarchy.

The first question here to be considered is, whether a spirit has in sundry instances been manifested by the Federal Government to enlarge its powers by forced constructions of the constitutional charter.

The General Assembly having declared its opinion merely by regretting in general terms that forced constructions for enlarging the federal powers have taken place, it does not appear to the committee necessary to go into a specification of every instance to which the resolution may allude. The Alien and Sedition Acts being particularly named in a succeeding resolution, are of course to be understood as included in the allusion. Omitting others which have less occupied public attention, or been less extensively regarded as unconstitutional, the resolution may be presumed to refer particularly to the bank law, which from the circumstances of its passage, as well as the latitude of construction on which it is founded, strikes the attention with singular force; and the carriage tax, distinguished also by circumstances in its history having a similar tendency. Those instances, alone, if resulting from forced construction and calculated to enlarge the powers of the Federal Government, as the committee cannot but conceive to be the case, sufficiently warrant this part of the resolution. The committee have not thought it incumbent on them to extend their attention to laws which have been objected to, rather as varying the constitutional distribution of powers in the Federal Government, than as an absolute enlargement of them; because instances of this sort, however important in their principles and tendencies, do not appear to fall strictly within the text under review.

The other questions presenting themselves, are—1. Whether indications have appeared of a design to expound certain general phrases copied from the "Articles of Confederation" so as to destroy the effect of the particular enumeration explaining and limiting their meaning. 2. Whether this exposition would by degrees consolidate the states into one sovereignty. 3. Whether the tendency and result of this consolidation would be to transform the republican system of the United States into a monarchy.

1. The general phrases here meant must be those "of providing for the common defence and general welfare."

In the "Articles of Confederation," the phrases are used as follows, in Article 8: "All charges of war, and all other expenses that shall be incurred for the common defence and general welfare, and allowed by the United States in Congress assembled, shall be defrayed out of a common treasury, which shall be supplied by the several states, in proportion to the value of all land within each state, granted to, or surveyed for any person, as such land and the buildings and improvements thereon shall be estimated, according to such mode as the United States in Congress assembled shall from time to time direct and appoint."

In the existing [U.S.] Constitution, they make the following part of Section 8: "The Congress shall have power to lay and collect taxes, duties, imposts, and excises, to pay the debts, and to provide for the common defence and general welfare of the United States."

This similarity in the use of these phrases in the two great federal charters, might well be considered, as rendering their meaning less liable to be misconstrued in the latter; because it will scarcely be said, that in the former they were ever understood to be either a general grant of power, or to authorize the requisition or application of money by the old Congress to the common defence and general welfare, except in the cases afterwards enumerated, which explained and limited their meaning; and if such was the limited meaning attached to these phrases in the very instrument revised and remodelled by the present Constitution, it can never be supposed that when copied into this Constitution, a different meaning ought to be attached to them.

That, notwithstanding this remarkable security against misconstruction, a design has been indicated to expound these phrases in the Constitution, so as to destroy the effect of the particular enumeration of powers by which it explains and limits them, must have fallen under the observation of those who have attended to the course of public transactions. Not to multiply proofs on this subject, it will suffice to refer to the debates of the federal legislature, in which arguments have on different occasions been drawn, with apparent effect, from these phrases, in their indefinite meaning.

To these indications might be added, without looking farther, the official report on manufactures, by the late Secretary of the Treasury, made on the 5th of December, 1791; and the report of a committee of Congress, in January, 1797, on the promotion of agriculture. In the first of these it is expressly contended to belong "to the discretion of the national legislature to pronounce upon the objects which concern the general welfare, and for which, under that description, an appropriation of money is requisite and proper. And there seems to be no room for a doubt, that whatever concerns the general interests of learning, of agriculture, of manufactures, and of commerce, are within the sphere of the national councils, as far as regards the application of money." The latter report assumes the same latitude of power in the national councils, and applies it to the encouragement of agriculture by means of a society to be established at the seat of government. Although neither of these reports may have received the sanction of a law carrying it into effect, yet, on the other hand, the extraordinary doctrine contained in both, has passed without the slightest positive mark of disapprobation from the authority to which it was addressed.

Now, whether the phrases in question be construed to authorize every measure relating to the common defence and general welfare, as contended by some; or every measure only in which there might be an application of money, as suggested by the caution of others; the effect must substantially be the same, in destroying the import and force of the particular enumeration of powers which follow these general phrases in the Constitution. For it is evident that there is not a single power whatever, which may not have some reference to the common defence, or the general welfare; nor a power of any magnitude, which, in its exercise, does not involve or admit an application of money. The government, therefore, which possesses power in either one or other of these extents, is a government without the limitations formed by a particular enumeration of powers; and consequently, the meaning and effect of this particular enumeration is destroyed by the exposition given to these general phrases.

This conclusion will not be affected by an attempt to qualify the power over the "general welfare," by referring it to cases where the general welfare is beyond the reach of separate provisions by the individual states; and leaving to these their jurisdictions, in cases to which their separate provisions may be competent. For, as the authority of the individual states must in all cases be incompetent to general regulations operating through the whole, the authority of the United States would be extended to every object relating to the general welfare, which might, by any possibility, be provided for by the general authority. This qualifying construction, therefore, would have little, if any tendency, to circumscribe the power claimed under the latitude of the terms "general welfare."

The true and fair construction of this expression, both in the original and existing federal compacts, appears to the committee too obvious to be mistaken. In both, the Congress is authorized to provide money for the common defence and general welfare. In both, is subjoined to this authority, an enumeration of the cases to which their powers shall extend. Money cannot be applied to the general welfare otherwise than by an application of it to some particular measures, conducive to the general welfare. Whenever, therefore, money has been raised by the general authority, and is to be applied to a particular measure, a question arises whether the particular measure be within the enumerated authorities vested in Congress. If it be, the money requisite for it may be applied to it; if it be not, no such application can be made. This fair and obvious interpretation coincides with, and is enforced by the clause in the Constitution, which declares, that "no money shall be drawn from the treasury, but in consequence of appropriations by law." An appropriation of money to the general welfare would be deemed rather a mockery than an observance of this constitutional injunction.

2. Whether the exposition of the general phrases here combated would not, by degrees, consolidate the states into one sovereignty, is a question concerning which the committee can perceive little room for difference of opinion. To consolidate the states into one sovereignty, nothing more can be wanted, than to supersede their respective sovereignties in the cases reserved to them, by extending the sovereignty of the United States, to all cases of the "general welfare," that is to say, to all cases whatever.

3. That the obvious tendency and inevitable result of a consolidation of the states into one sovereignty, would be to transform the republican system of the United States into a monarchy, is a point which seems to have been sufficiently decided by the general sentiment of America. In almost every instance of discussion, relating to the consolidation in question, its certain tendency to pave the way to monarchy seems not to have been contested. The prospect of such a consolidation has formed the only topic of controversy. It would be unnecessary, therefore, for the committee to dwell long on the reasons which support the position of the General Assembly. It may not be improper, however, to remark two consequences evidently flowing from an extension of the federal powers to every subject falling within the idea of the "general welfare."

One consequence must be, to enlarge the sphere of discretion allotted to the executive magistrate. Even within the legislative limits properly defined by the Constitution, the difficulty of accommodating legal regulations to a country so great in extent, and so various in its circumstances, has been much felt; and has led to occasional investments of power in the executive, which involve perhaps as large a portion of discretion as can be deemed consistent with the nature of the executive trust. In proportion as the objects of legislative care might be multiplied, would the time allowed for each be diminished, and the difficulty of providing uniform and particular regulations for all be increased. From these sources would necessarily ensue a greater latitude to the agency of that department which is always in existence, and which could best mould regulations of a general nature, so as to suit them to the diversity of particular situations. And it is in this latitude, as a supplement to the deficiency of the laws, that the degree of executive prerogative materially consists.

The other consequence would be that of an excessive augmentation of the offices, honours, and emoluments depending on the executive will. Add to the present legitimate stock, all those of every description which a consolidation of the states would take from them, and turn over to the Federal Government, and the patronage of the executive would necessarily be as much swelled in this case, as its prerogative would be in the other.

This disproportionate increase of prerogative and patronage must, evidently, either enable the chief magistrate of the Union, by quiet means, to secure his re-election from time to time, and finally, to regulate the succession as he might please; or, by giving so transcendent an importance to the office, would render the elections to it so violent and corrupt, that the public voice itself might call for an hereditary, in place of an elective succession. Whichever of these events might follow, the transformation of the republican system of the United States into a monarchy, anticipated by the General Assembly from a consolidation of the states into one sovereignty, would be equally accomplished; and whether it would be into a mixed or an absolute monarchy, might depend on too many contingencies to admit of any certain foresight.

The resolution next in order, is contained in the following terms: *That the General Assembly doth particularly protest against the palpable and alarming infractions of the Constitution, in the two late cases of the "Alien and Sedition Acts" passed at the last session of Congress; the first of which exercises a power nowhere delegated to the Federal Government; and which, by uniting legislative and judicial powers to those of executive, subverts the general principles of a free Government, as well as the particular organization and positive provisions of the Federal Constitution; and the other of which acts exercises, in like manner, a power not delegated by the Constitution; but, on the contrary, expressly and positively forbidden by one of the amendments thereto: a power which, more than any other, ought to produce universal alarm; because it is levelled against that right of freely examining public characters and measures, and of free communication among the people thereon, which has ever been justly deemed the only effectual guardian of every other right.*

The subject of this resolution having, it is presumed, more particularly led the General Assembly into the proceedings which they communicated to the other states, and being in itself of peculiar importance, it deserves the most critical and faithful investigation; for the length of which no other apology will be necessary.

The subject divides itself into first, "The Alien Act," secondly, "The Sedition Act."

I. Of the "Alien Act," it is affirmed by the resolution. 1st: That it exercises a power nowhere delegated to the Federal Government. 2nd: That it unites legislative and judicial powers to those of the executive. 3rd: That this union of power subverts the general principles of free government. 4th: That it subverts the particular organization and positive provisions of the Federal Constitution.

In order to clear the way for a correct view of the first position, several observations will be premised.

In the first place, it is to be borne in mind, that it being a characteristic feature of the Federal Constitution, as it was originally ratified, and an amendment thereto having precisely declared, "That the powers not delegated to the United States by the Constitution, nor prohibited by it to the states, are reserved to the states respectively, or to the people," it is incumbent in this, as in every other exercise of power by the Federal Government, to prove from the Constitution, that it grants the particular power exercised.

The next observation to be made is, that much confusion and fallacy have been thrown into question, by blending the two cases of aliens, members of a hostile nation; and aliens, members of friendly nations. These two cases are so obviously and so essentially distinct, that it occasions no little surprise that the distinction should have been disregarded: and the surprise is so much the greater, as it appears that the two cases are actually distinguished by two separate acts of Congress, passed at the same session, and comprised in the same publication; the one providing for the case of "alien enemies;" the other "concerning aliens" indiscriminately; and consequently extending to aliens of every nation in peace and amity with the United States. With respect to alien enemies, no doubt has been intimated as to the federal authority over them; the Constitution having expressly delegated to Congress the power to declare war against any nation, and of course to treat it and all its members as enemies. With respect to aliens who are not enemies, but members of nations in peace and amity with the United States, the power assumed by the act of Congress is denied to be constitutional; and it is accordingly against this act, that the protest of the General Assembly is expressly and exclusively directed.

A third observation is, that were it admitted, as is contended, that the "act concerning aliens" has for its object not a penal, but a preventive justice, it would still remain to be proved that it comes within the constitutional power of the federal legislature; and if within its power, that the legislature has exercised it in a constitutional manner.

In the administration of preventive justice, the following principles have been held sacred: that some probable ground of suspicion be exhibited before some judicial authority; that it be supported by oath or affirmation; that the party may avoid being thrown into confinement, by finding pledges or sureties for his legal conduct sufficient in the judgment of some judicial authority; that he may have the benefit of a writ of *habeas corpus*, and thus obtain his release, if wrongfully confined; and that he may at any time be discharged from his recognizance, or his confinement, and restored to his former liberty and rights, on the order of the proper judicial authority, if it shall see sufficient cause.

All these principles of the only preventive justice known to American jurisprudence are violated by the Alien Act. The ground of suspicion is to be judged of, not by any judicial authority, but by the executive magistrate alone; no oath or affirmation is required; if the suspicion be held reasonable by the President, he may order the suspected alien to depart the territory of the United States, without the opportunity of avoiding the sentence, by finding pledges for his future good conduct; as the President may limit the time of departure as he pleases, the benefit of the writ of *habeas corpus* may be suspended with respect to the party, although the Constitution ordains, that it shall not be suspended, unless when the public safety may require it in case of rebellion or invasion, neither of which existed at the passage of the act; and the party being under the sentence of the President, either removed from the United States, or being punished by imprisonment, or disqualification ever to become a citizen on conviction of not obeying the order of removal, he cannot be discharged from the proceedings against him, and restored to the benefits of his former situation, although the highest judicial authority should see the most sufficient cause for it.

But, in the last place, it can never be admitted, that the removal of aliens, authorized by the act, is to be considered, not as punishment for an offence, but as a measure of precaution and prevention. If the banishment of an alien from a country into which he has been invited, as the asylum most auspicious to his happiness; a country where he may have formed the most tender of connexions, where he may have vested his entire property, and acquired property of the real and permanent, as well as the movable and temporary kind; where he enjoys under the laws a greater share of the blessings of personal security and personal liberty than he can elsewhere hope for, and where he may have nearly completed his probationary title to citizenship; if, moreover, in the execution of the sentence against him, he is to be exposed, not only to the ordinary dangers of the sea, but to the peculiar casualties incident to a crisis of war, and of unusual licentiousness on that element, and possibly to vindictive purposes which his emigration itself may have provoked; if a banishment of this sort be not a punishment, and among the severest of punishments, it will be difficult to imagine a doom to which the name can be applied. And if it be a punishment, it will remain to be inquired, whether it can be constitutionally inflicted, on mere suspicion, by the single will of the executive magistrate, on persons convicted of no personal offence against the laws of the land, nor involved in any offence against the law of nations, charged on the foreign state of which they are members.

One argument offered in justification of this power exercised over aliens is, that the admission of them into the country being of favour, not of right, the favour is at all times revocable.

To this argument it might be answered, that allowing the truth of the inference, it would be no proof of what is required. A question would still occur, whether the Constitution had vested the discretionary power of admitting aliens in the federal government, or in the state governments.

But it cannot be a true inference, that because the admission of an alien is a favour, the favour may be revoked at pleasure. A grant of land to an individual may be of favour, not of right; but the moment the grant is made, the favour becomes a right, and must be forfeited before it can be taken away. To pardon a malefactor may be favour, but the pardon is not, on that account, the less irrevocable. To admit an alien to naturalization is as much a favour, as to admit him to reside in the country; yet it cannot be pretended, that a person naturalized can be deprived of the benefit, any more than a native citizen can be disfranchised.

Again, it is said, that aliens not being parties to the Constitution, the rights and privileges which it secures cannot be at all claimed by them.

To this reasoning, also, it might be answered, that although aliens are not parties to the Constitution, it does not follow that the Constitution has vested in Congress an absolute power over them. The parties to the Constitution may have granted, or retained, or modified the power over aliens, without regard to that particular consideration.

But a more direct reply is, that it does not follow, because aliens are not parties to the Constitution, as citizens are parties to it, that whilst they actually conform to it, they have no right to its protection. Aliens are not more parties to the laws, than they are parties to the Constitution; yet, it will not be disputed, that as they owe, on one hand, a temporary obedience, they are entitled in return to their protection and advantage.

If aliens had no rights under the Constitution, they might not only be banished, but even capitally punished, without a jury or the other incidents to a fair trial. But so far has a contrary principle been carried, in every part of the United States, that except on charges of treason, an alien has, besides all the common privileges, the special one of being tried by a jury, of which one-half may be also aliens.

It is said, further, that by the law and practice of nations, aliens may be removed at discretion, for offences against the law of nations; that Congress are authorized to define and punish such offences; and that to be dangerous to the peace of society is, in aliens, one of those offences.

The distinction between alien enemies and alien friends, is a clear and conclusive answer to this argument. Alien enemies are under the law of nations, and liable to be punished for offences against it. Alien friends, except in the single case of public ministers, are under the municipal law, and must be tried and punished according to that law only.

This argument also, by referring the Alien Act to the power of Congress to define and punish offences against the law of nations, yields the point that the act is of a penal, not merely of a preventive operation. It must, in truth, be so considered. And if it be a penal act, the punishment it inflicts, must be justified by some offence that deserves it.

Offences for which aliens, within the jurisdiction of a country, are punishable, are first, offences committed by the nation of which they make a part, and in whose offences they are involved: Secondly, offences committed by themselves alone, without any charge against the nation to which they belong. The first is the case of alien enemies; the second, the case of alien friends. In the first case, the offending nation can no otherwise be punished than by war, one of the laws of which authorizes the expulsion of such of its members, as may be found within the country, against which the offence has been committed. In the second case, the offence being committed by the individual, not by his nation, and against the municipal law, not against the law of nations, the individual only, and not the nation, is punishable; and the punishment must be conducted according to the municipal law, not according to the law of nations. Under this view of the subject, the act of Congress, for the removal of alien enemies, being conformable to the law of nations, is justified by the Constitution: and the "act," for the removal of alien friends, being repugnant to the constitutional principles of municipal law, is unjustifiable.

Nor is the act of Congress, for the removal of alien friends, more agreeable to the general practice of nations, than it is within the purview of the law of nations. The general practice of nations, distinguishes between alien friends and alien enemies. The latter it has proceeded against, according to the law of nations, by expelling them as enemies. The former it has considered as under a local and temporary allegiance, and entitled to a correspondent protection. If contrary instances are to be found in barbarous countries, under undefined prerogatives, or amid revolutionary dangers, they will not be deemed fit precedents for the government of the United States, even if not beyond its constitutional authority.

It is said, that Congress may grant letters of marque and reprisal; that reprisals may be made on persons, as well as property; and that the removal of aliens may be considered as the exercise in an inferior degree, of the general power of reprisal on persons.

Without entering minutely into a question that does not seem to require it, it may be remarked, that reprisal is a seizure of foreign persons or property, with a view to obtain that justice for injuries done by one state or its members, to another state or its members, for which, a refusal of the aggressor requires such a resort to force under the law of nations. It must be considered as an abuse of words to call the removal of persons from a country, a seizure or reprisal on them: nor is the distinction to be overlooked between reprisals on persons within the country and under the faith of its laws, and on persons out of the country.

But, laying aside these considerations, it is evidently impossible to bring the Alien Act within the power of granting reprisals; since it does not allege or imply any injury received from any particular nation, for which this proceeding against its members was intended as a reparation. The proceeding is authorized against aliens of every nation; of nations charged neither with any similar proceeding against American citizens, nor with any injuries for which justice might be sought, in the mode prescribed by the act. Were it true, therefore, that good causes existed for reprisals against one or more foreign nations, and that neither persons nor property of its members, under the faith of our laws, could plead an exemption, the operation of the act ought to have been limited to the aliens among us, belonging to such nations. To license reprisals against all nations, for aggressions charged on one only, would be a measure as contrary to every principle of justice and public law, as to a wise policy, and the universal practice of nations.

It is said, that the right of removing aliens is an incident to the power of war, vested in Congress by the Constitution.

This is a former argument in a new shape only; and is answered by repeating, that the removal of alien enemies is an incident to the power of war; that the removal of alien friends, is not an incident to the power of war.

It is said, that Congress are by the Constitution to protect each state against invasion; and that the means of preventing invasion are included in the power of protection against it.

The power of war in general, having been before granted by the Constitution, this clause must either be a mere specification for greater caution and certainty, of which there are other examples in the instrument, or be the injunction of a duty, superadded to a grant of the power. Under either explanation, it cannot enlarge the powers of Congress on the subject. The power and the duty to protect each state against an invading enemy, would be the same under the general power, if this regard to greater caution had been omitted.

Invasion is an operation of war. To protect against invasion is an exercise of the power of war. A power, therefore, not incident to war, cannot be incident to a particular modification of war. And as the removal of alien friends, has appeared to be no incident to a general state of war, it cannot be incident to a partial state, or a particular modification of war.

Nor can it ever be granted, that a power to act oh a case when it actually occurs, includes a power over all the means that may tend to prevent the occurrence of the case. Such a latitude of construction would render unavailing every practicable definition of particular and limited powers. Under the idea of preventing war in general, as well as invasion in particular, not only an indiscriminate removal of all aliens might be enforced, but a thousand other things still more remote from the operations and precautions appurtenant to war, might take place. A bigoted or tyrannical nation might threaten us with war, unless certain religious or political regulations were adopted by us; yet it never could be inferred, if the regulations which would prevent war, were such as Congress had otherwise no power to make, that the power to make them would grow out of the purpose they were to answer. Congress have power to suppress insurrections, yet it would not be allowed to follow, that they might employ all the means tending to prevent them; of which a system of moral instruction for the ignorant, and of provident support for the poor, might be regarded as among the most efficacious.

One argument for the power of the general government to remove aliens, would have been passed in silence, if it had appeared under any authority inferior to that of a report, made during the last session of Congress, to the House of Representatives by a committee, and approved by the House. The doctrine on which this argument is founded, is of so new and so extraordinary a character, and strikes so radically at the political system of America, that it is proper to state it in the very words of the report.

"The act [concerning aliens] is said to be unconstitutional, because to remove aliens is a direct breach of the Constitution, which provides, by the 9th section of the 1st article, that the migration or importation of such persons as any of the states shall think proper to admit, shall not be prohibited by the Congress, prior to the year 1808."

Among the answers given to this objection to the constitutionality of the act, the following very remarkable one is extracted."

"Thirdly, that as the Constitution has given to the states no power to remove aliens, during the period of the limitation under consideration, in the meantime, on the construction assumed, there would be no authority in the country, empowered to send away dangerous aliens, which cannot be admitted."

The reasoning here used, would not in any view, be conclusive; because there are powers exercised by most other governments, which in the United States are withheld by the people, both from the general government, and from the state governments. Of this sort are many of the powers prohibited by the declarations of right prefixed to the constitutions, or by the clauses in the constitutions, in the nature of such declarations. Nay, so far is the political system of the United States distinguishable from that of other countries, by the caution with which powers are delegated and defined, that in one very important case, even of commercial regulations and revenue, the power is absolutely locked up against the hands of both governments. A tax on exports can be laid by no constitutional authority whatever. Under a system thus peculiarly guarded, there could surely be no absurdity in supposing, that alien friends, who if guilty of treasonable machinations may be punished, or if suspected on probable grounds, may be secured by pledges or imprisonment, in like manner with permanent citizens, were never meant to be subjected to banishment by any arbitrary and unusual process, either under the one government or the other.

But, it is not the inconclusiveness of the general reasoning in this passage, which chiefly calls the attention to it. It is the principle assumed by it, that the powers held by the states, are given to them by the Constitution of the United States; and the inference from this principle, that the powers supposed to be necessary which are not so given to state governments, must reside in the government of the United States.

The respect, which is felt for every portion of the constituted authorities, forbids some of the reflections which this singular paragraph might excite, and they are the more readily suppressed, as it may be presumed, with justice perhaps, as well as candour, that inadvertence may have had its share in the error. It would be an unjustifiable delicacy, nevertheless, to pass by so portentous a claim, proceeding from so high an authority, without a monitory notice of the fatal tendencies with which it would be pregnant.

Lastly, it is said, that a law on the same subject with the Alien Act, passed by this state originally in 1785, and re-enacted in 1792, is a proof that a summary removal of suspected aliens, was not heretofore regarded by the Virginia Legislature, as liable to the objections now urged against such a measure.

This charge against Virginia vanishes before the simple remark, that the law of Virginia relates to "suspicious persons being the subjects of any foreign power or state, who shall have made a declaration of war, or actually commenced hostilities, or from whom the President shall apprehend hostile designs;" whereas the act of Congress relates to aliens, being the subjects of foreign powers and states, who have neither declared war, nor commenced hostilities, nor from whom hostile designs are apprehended.

2. It is next affirmed of the Alien Act, that it unites legislative, judicial, and executive powers in the hands of the President.

However difficult it may be to mark, in every case, with clearness and certainty, the line which divides legislative power, from the other departments of power, all will agree, that the powers referred to these departments may be so general and undefined, as to be of a legislative, not of an executive or judicial nature; and may for that reason be unconstitutional. Details to a certain degree, are essential to the nature and character of a law; and on criminal subjects, it is proper, that details should leave as little as possible to the discretion of those who are to apply and to execute the law. If nothing more were required, in exercising a legislative trust, than a general conveyance of authority, without laying down any precise rules, by which the authority conveyed should be carried into effect; it would follow, that the whole power of legislation might be transferred by the legislature from itself, and proclamations might become substitutes for laws. A delegation of power in this latitude, would not be denied to be a union of the different powers.

To determine, then, whether the appropriate powers of the distinct departments are united by the act authorizing the executive to remove aliens, it must be inquired whether it contains such details, definitions and rules, as appertain to the true character of a law; especially, a law by which personal liberty is invaded, property deprived of its value to the owner, and life itself indirectly exposed to danger.

The Alien Act declares, "that it shall be lawful for the President to order all such aliens as he shall judge dangerous to the peace and safety of the United States, or shall have reasonable ground to suspect, are concerned in any treasonable, or secret machinations, against the government thereof, to depart," etc.

Could a power be well given in terms less definite, less particular, and less precise? To be dangerous to the public safety; to be suspected of secret machinations against the government: these can never be mistaken for legal rules or certain definitions. They leave everything to the President. His will is the law.

But, it is not a legislative power only, that is given to the President. He is to stand in the place of the judiciary also. His suspicion is the only evidence which is to convict: his order, the only judgment which is to be executed.

Thus, it is the President whose will is to designate the offensive conduct; it is his will that is to ascertain the individuals on whom it is charged; and it is his will, that is to cause the sentence to be executed. It is rightly affirmed, therefore, that the act unites legislative and judicial powers to those of the executive.

3. It is affirmed, that this union of power subverts the general principles of free government.

It has become an axiom in the science of government, that a separation of the legislative, executive, and judicial departments, is necessary to the preservation of public liberty. Nowhere has this axiom been better understood in theory, or more carefully pursued in practice, than in the United States.

4. It is affirmed that such a union of powers subverts the particular organization and positive provisions of the Federal Constitution.

According to the particular organization of the Constitution, its legislative powers are vested in the Congress, its executive powers in the President, and its judicial powers in a supreme and inferior tribunals. The union of any two of these powers, and still more of all three, in any one of these departments, as has been shown to be done by the Alien Act, must consequently subvert the constitutional organization of them.

That positive provisions, in the Constitution, securing to individuals the benefits of fair trial, are also violated by the union of powers in the Alien Act, necessarily results from the two facts, that the act relates to alien friends, and that alien friends being under the municipal law only, are entitled to its protection.

II. The second object against which the resolution protests, is the Sedition Act. Of this act it is affirmed, 1: That it exercises in like manner a power not delegated by the Constitution. 2: That the power, on the contrary, is expressly and positively forbidden by one of the amendments to the Constitution. 3: That this is a power, which more than any other ought to produce universal alarm; because it is levelled against that right of freely examining public characters and measures, and of free communication thereon, which has ever been justly deemed the only effectual guardian of every other right.

1. That it exercises a power not delegated by the Constitution.

Here again, it will be proper to recollect, that the Federal Government being composed of powers specifically granted, with a reservation of all others to the states or to the people, the positive authority under which the Sedition Act could be passed must be produced by those who assert its constitutionality. In what part of the Constitution, then, is this authority to be found?

Several attempts have been made to answer this question, which will be examined in their order. The committee will begin with one, which has filled them with equal astonishment and apprehension; and which, they cannot but persuade themselves, must have the same effect on all, who will consider it with coolness and impartiality, and with a reverence for our Constitution, in the true character in which it issued from the sovereign authority of the people. The committee refer to the doctrine lately advanced as a sanction to the Sedition Act, "that the common or unwritten law," a law of vast extent and complexity, and embracing almost every possible subject of legislation, both civil and criminal, makes a part of the law of these states, in their united and national capacity.

The novelty and, in the judgment of the committee, the extravagance of this pretension, would have consigned it to the silence in which they have passed by other arguments, which an extraordinary zeal for the act has drawn into the discussion: But the auspices under which this innovation presents itself, have constrained the committee to bestow on it an attention, which other considerations might have forbidden.

In executing the task, it may be of use to look back to the colonial state of this country, prior to the Revolution; to trace the effects of the Revolution which converted the colonies into independent states; to inquire into the import of the articles of confederation, the first instrument by which the union of the states was regularly established; and finally, to consult the Constitution of 1788, which is the oracle that must decide the important question.

In the state, prior to the Revolution, it is certain that the common law, under different limitations, made a part of the colonial codes. But whether it be understood that the original colonists brought the law with them, or made it their law by adoption; it is equally certain, that it was the separate law of each colony within its respective limits, and was unknown to them, as a law pervading and operating through the whole, as one society.

It could not possibly be otherwise. The common law was not the same in any two of the colonies; in some, the modifications were materially and extensively different. There was no common legislature, by which a common will could be expressed in the form of a law; nor any common magistracy, by which such a law could be carried into practice. The will of each colony, alone and separately, had its organs for these purposes.

This stage of our political history furnishes no foothold for the patrons of this new doctrine.

Did then the principle or operation of the great event which made the colonies independent states, imply or introduce the common law as a law of the Union?

The fundamental principle of the Revolution was, that the colonies were co-ordinate members with each other, and with Great Britain, of an empire, united by a common executive sovereign, but not united by any common legislative sovereign. The legislative power was maintained to be as complete in each American parliament, as in the British parliament. And the royal prerogative was in force in each colony, by virtue of its acknowledging the king for its executive magistrate, as it was in Great Britain, by virtue of a like acknowledgment there. A denial of these principles by Great Britain, and the assertion of them by America, produced the Revolution.

There was a time, indeed, when an exception to the legislative separation of the several component ana coequal parts of the empire obtained a degree of acquiescence. The British parliament was allowed to regulate the trade with foreign nations, and between the different parts of the empire. This was, however, mere practice without right, and contrary to the true theory of the Constitution. The conveniency of some regulations, in both those cases, was apparent; and as there was no legislature with power over the whole, nor any constitutional pre-eminence among the legislatures of the several parts, it was natural for the legislature of that particular part which was the eldest and the largest, to assume this function, and for the others to acquiesce in it. This tacit arrangement was the less criticised, as the regulations established by the British parliament operated in favour of that part of the empire which seemed to bear the principal share of the public burdens, and were regarded as an indemnification of its advances for the other parts. As long as this regulating power was confined to the two objects of conveniency and equity, it was not complained of, nor much inquired into. But, no sooner was it perverted to the selfish views of the party assuming it, than the injured parties began to feel and to reflect; and the moment the claim to a direct and indefinite power was ingrafted on the precedent of the regulating power, the whole charm was dissolved, and every eye opened to the usurpation. The assertion by Great Britain of a power to make laws for the other members of the empire in all cases whatsoever, ended in the discovery that she had a right to make laws for them in no cases whatsoever.

Such being the ground of our Revolution, no support nor colour can be drawn from it, for the doctrine that the common law is binding on these states as one society. The doctrine, on the contrary, is evidently repugnant to the fundamental principle of the Revolution.

The Articles of Confederation are the next source of information on this subject.

In the interval between the commencement of the Revolution and the final ratification of these articles, the nature and extent of the Union was determined by the circumstances of the crisis, rather than by any accurate delineation of the general authority. It will not be alleged, that the "common law" could have had any legitimate birth as a law of the United States during that state of things. If it came, as such, into existence at all, the charter of confederation must have been its parent.

Here again, however, its pretensions are absolutely destitute of foundation. This instrument does not contain a sentence or syllable that can be tortured into a countenance of the idea, that the parties to it were, with respect to the objects of the common law, to form one community. No such law is named or implied, or alluded to as being in force, or as brought into force by that compact. No provision is made by which such a law could be carried into operation; whilst, on the other hand, every such inference or pretext is absolutely precluded by Article 2, which declares, "that each state retains its sovereignty, freedom, arid independence, and every power, jurisdiction, and right, which is not by this confederation expressly delegated to the United States, in Congress assembled."

Thus far it appears that not a vestige of this extraordinary doctrine can be found in the origin or progress of American institutions. The evidence against it has, on the contrary, grown stronger at every step, till it has amounted to a formal and positive exclusion, by written articles of compact among the parties concerned.

Is this exclusion revoked, and the common law introduced as a national law, by the present Constitution of the United States? This is the final question to be examined.

It is readily admitted, that particular parts of the common law may have a sanction from the Constitution, so far as they are necessarily comprehended in the technical phrases which express the powers delegated to the government; and so far also, as such other parts may be adopted by Congress as necessary and proper for carrying into execution the powers expressly delegated. But, the question does not relate to either of these portions of the common law. It relates to the common law beyond these limitations.

The only part of the Constitution which seems to have been relied on in this case is the second Section of Article 3. "The judicial power shall extend to all cases in law and equity, arising under this Constitution, the laws of the United States, and treaties made or which shall be made under their authority."

It has been asked what cases, distinct from those arising under the laws and treaties of the United States, can arise under the Constitution, other than those arising under the common law; and it is inferred, that the common law is accordingly adopted or recognised by the Constitution.

Never, perhaps, was so broad a construction applied to a text so clearly unsusceptible of it. If any colour for the inference could be found, it must be in the impossibility of finding any other cases in law and equity, within the provision of the Constitution, to satisfy the expression; and rather than resort to a construction affecting so essentially the whole character of the government, it would perhaps be more rational to consider the expression as a mere pleonasm, or inadvertence. But, it is not necessary to decide on such a dilemma. The expression is fully satisfied, and its accuracy justified, by two descriptions of cases, to which the judicial authority is extended, and neither of which implies that the common law is the law of the United States. One of these descriptions comprehends the cases growing out of the restrictions on the legislative power of the states. For example, it is provided that "no state shall emit bills of credit," or "make anything but gold and silver coin a tender in payment of debts." Should this prohibition be violated, and a suit between citizens of the same state be the consequence, this would be a case arising under the Constitution, before the judicial power of the United States. A second description comprehends suits between citizens and foreigners, or citizens of different states, to be decided according to the state or foreign laws; but submitted by the Constitution to the judicial power of the United States; the judicial power being, in several instances, extended beyond the legislative power of the United States.

To this explanation of the text, the following observations may be added:

The expression, "cases in law and equity," is manifestly confined to cases of a civil nature; and would exclude cases of criminal jurisdiction. Criminal cases in law and equity would be a language unknown to the law.

The succeeding paragraph of the same section is in harmony with this construction. It is in these words: "In all cases affecting ambassadors, other public ministers, and consuls, and those in which a state shall be a party, the Supreme Court shall have original jurisdiction. In all the other cases [including cases in law and equity arising under the Constitution] the Supreme Court shall have appellate jurisdiction both as to law and fact; with such exceptions, and under such regulations, as Congress shall make."

This paragraph, by expressly giving an appellate jurisdiction, in cases of law and equity arising under the Constitution, to fact, as well as to law, clearly excludes criminal cases, where the trial by jury is secured; because the fact, in such cases, is not a subject of appeal. And, although the appeal is liable to such exceptions and regulations as Congress may adopt, yet it is not to be supposed that an exception of all criminal cases could be contemplated; as well because a discretion in Congress to make or omit the exception would be improper, as because it would have been unnecessary. The exception could as easily have been made by the Constitution itself, as referred to the Congress.

Once more, the amendment last added to the Constitution, deserves attention, as throwing light on this subject. "The judicial power of the United States shall not be construed to extend to any suit in law or equity, commenced or prosecuted against one of the United States, by citizens of another state, or by citizens or subjects of any foreign power." As it will not be pretended that any criminal proceeding could take place against a state, the terms law or equity, must be understood as appropriate to civil, in exclusion of criminal cases.

From these considerations, it is evident, that this part of the Constitution, even if it could be applied at all to the purpose for which it has been cited, would not include any cases whatever of a criminal nature; and consequently, would not authorize the inference from it, that the judicial authority extends to offences against the common law, as offences arising under the Constitution.

It is further to be considered, that even if this part of the Constitution could be strained into an application to every common law case, criminal as well as civil, it could have no effect in justifying the Sedition Act, which is an exercise of legislative, and not of judicial power: and it is the judicial power only, of which the extent is defined in this part of the Constitution.

There are two passages in the Constitution, in which a description of the law of the United States is found. The first is contained in Article 3, Section 2, in the words following: "This Constitution, the laws of the United States, and treaties made, or which shall be made under their authority." The second is contained in the second paragraph of Article 6 as follows: "This Constitution, and the laws of the United States which shall be made in pursuance thereof, and all treaties made, or which shall be made, under the authority of the United States, shall be the supreme law of the land." The first of these descriptions was meant as a guide to the judges of the United States; the second, as a guide to the judges in the several states. Both of them consists of an enumeration, which was evidently meant to be precise and complete. If the common law had been understood to be a law of the United States, it is not possible to assign a satisfactory reason why it was not expressed in the enumeration.

In aid of these objections, the difficulties and confusion inseparable from a constructive introduction of the common law, would afford powerful reasons against it.

Is it to be the common law with or without the British statutes?

If without the statutory amendments, the vices of the code would be insupportable.

If with these amendments, what period is to be fixed for limiting the British authority over our laws?

Is it to be the date of the eldest or the youngest of the colonies?

Or are the dates to be thrown together, and a medium deduced?

Or is our independence to be taken for the date?

Is, again, regard to be had to the various changes in the common law made by the local codes of America?

Is regard to be had to future, as well as past changes?

Is the law to be different in every state, as differently modified by its code; or are the modifications of any particular state to be applied to all?

And on the latter supposition, which among the state codes would form the standard?

Questions of this sort might be multiplied with as much ease, as there would be difficulty in answering them.

The consequences flowing from the proposed construction, furnish other objections equally conclusive; unless the text were peremptory in its meaning, and consistent with other parts of the instrument.

These consequences may be in relation to the legislative authority of the United States; to the executive authority; to the judicial authority; and to the governments of the several states.

If it be understood, that the common law is established by the Constitution, it follows that no part of the law can be altered by the legislature; such of the statutes already passed, as may be repugnant thereto would be nullified; particularly the "Sedition Act" itself, which boasts of being a melioration of the common law; and the whole code, with all its incongruities, barbarisms, and bloody maxims, would be inviolably saddled on the good people of the United States.

Should this consequence be rejected, and the common law be held, like other laws, liable to revision and alteration, by the authority of Congress, it then follows, that the authority of Congress is co-extensive with the objects of common law; that is to say, with every object of legislation: for to every such object does some branch or other of the common law extend. The authority of Congress would, therefore, be no longer under the limitations marked out in the Constitution. They would be authorized to legislate in all cases whatsoever.

In the next place, as the President possesses the executive powers of the Constitution, and is to see that the laws be faithfully executed, his authority also must be coextensive with every branch of the common law. The additions which this would make to his power, though not readily to be estimated, claim the most serious attention.

This is not all; it will merit the most profound consideration, how far an indefinite admission of the common law, with a latitude in construing it, equal to the construction by which it is deduced from the Constitution, might draw after it the various prerogatives making part of the unwritten law of England. The English constitution itself is nothing more than a composition of unwritten laws and maxims.

In the third place, whether the common law be admitted as of legal or of constitutional obligation, it would confer on the judicial department a discretion little short of a legislative power.

On the supposition of its having a constitutional obligation, this power in the judges would be permanent and irremediable by the legislature. On the other supposition, the power would not expire, until the legislature should have introduced a full system of statutory provisions. Let it be observed, too, that besides all the uncertainties above enumerated, and which present an immense field for judicial discretion, it would remain with the same department to decide what parts of the common law would, and what would not, be properly applicable to the circumstances of the United States.

A discretion of this sort has always been lamented as incongruous and dangerous, even in the colonial and state courts; although so much narrowed by positive provisions in the local codes on all the principal subjects embraced by the common law. Under the United States, where so few laws exist on those subjects, and where so great a lapse of time must happen before the vast chasm could be supplied, it is manifest that the power of the judges over the law would, in fact, erect them into legislators; and that, for a long time, it would be impossible for the citizens to conjecture, either what was, or would be law.

In the last place, the consequence of admitting the common law as the law of the United States, on the authority of the individual states, is as obvious as it would be fatal. As this law relates to every subject of legislation, and would be paramount to the constitutions and laws of the states, the admission of it would overwhelm the residuary sovereignty of the states, and by one constructive operation, new model the whole political fabric of the country.

From the review thus taken of the situation of the American colonies prior to their independence; of the effect of this event on their situation; of the nature and import of the articles of confederation; of the true meaning of the passage in the existing Constitution from which the common law has been deduced; of the difficulties and uncertainties incident to the doctrine; and of its vast consequences in extending the powers of the Federal Government, and in superseding the authorities of the state governments; the committee feel the utmost confidence in concluding, that the common law never was, nor, by any fair construction, ever can be, deemed a law for the American people as one community; and they indulge the strongest expectation that the same conclusion will finally be drawn, by all candid and accurate inquirers into the subject. It is indeed distressing to reflect, that it ever should have been made a question, whether the Constitution, on the whole face of which is seen so much labour to enumerate and define the several objects of federal power, could intend to introduce in the lump, in an indirect manner, and by a forced construction of a few phrases, the vast and multifarious jurisdiction involved in the common law; a law filling so many ample volumes; a law overspreading the entire field of legislation; and a law that would sap the foundation of the Constitution as a system of limited and specified powers. A severer reproach could not, in the opinion of the committee, be thrown on the Constitution, on those who framed, or on those who established it, than such a supposition would throw on them.

The argument, then, drawn from the common law, on the ground of its being adopted or recognised by the Constitution, being inapplicable to the Sedition Act, the committee will proceed to examine the other arguments which have been founded on the Constitution.

They will waste but little time on the attempt to cover the act by the preamble to the Constitution; it being contrary to every acknowledged rule of construction, to set up this part of an instrument, in opposition to the plain meaning expressed in the body of the instrument. A preamble usually contains the general motives or reasons, for the particular regulations or measures which follow it; and is always understood to be explained and limited by them. In the present instance, a contrary interpretation would have the inadmissible effect, of rendering nugatory or improper every part of the Constitution which succeeds the preamble.

The paragraph in Article 1, Section 8, which contains the power to lay and collect taxes, duties, imposts, and excise; to pay the debts, and provide for the common defence and general welfare, having been already examined, will also require no particular attention in this place. It will have been seen that in its fair and consistent meaning, it cannot enlarge the enumerated powers vested in Congress.

The part of the Constitution which seems most to be recurred to, in defence of the "Sedition Act," is the last clause of the above section, empowering Congress "to make all laws which shall be necessary and proper for carrying into execution the foregoing powers, and all other powers vested by this Constitution in the government of the United States, or in any department or officer thereof."

The plain import of this clause is, that Congress shall have all the incidental or instrumental powers necessary and proper for carrying into execution all the express powers; whether they be vested in the government of the United States, more collectively, or in the several departments or officers thereof. It is not a grant of new powers to Congress, but merely a declaration, for the removal of all uncertainty, that the means of carrying into execution, those otherwise granted, are included in the grant.

Whenever, therefore, a question arises concerning the constitutionality of a particular power, the first question is, whether the power be expressed in the Constitution. If it be, the question is decided. If it be not expressed the next inquiry must be, whether it is properly an incident to an express power, and necessary to its execution. If it be, it may be exercised by Congress. If it be not, Congress cannot exercise it.

Let the question be asked, then, whether the power over the press, exercised in the "Sedition Act," be found among the powers expressly vested in the Congress? This is not pretended.

Is there any express power, for executing which it is a necessary and proper power?

The power which has been selected, as least remote, in answer to this question, is that of "suppressing insurrections;" which is said to imply a power to prevent insurrections, by punishing whatever may lead or tend to them. But, it surely cannot, with the least plausibility, be said, that a regulation of the press, and a punishment of libels, are exercises of a power to suppress insurrections. The most that could be said, would be, that the punishment of libels, if it had the tendency ascribed to it, might prevent the occasion of passing or executing laws necessary and proper for the suppression of insurrections.

Has the Federal Government no power, then, to prevent as well as to punish resistance to laws?

They have the power, which the Constitution deemed most proper, in their hands for the purpose. The Congress has power before it happens, to pass laws for punishing it; and the executive and judiciary have power to enforce those laws when it does happen.

It must be recollected by many, and could be shown to the satisfaction of all, that the construction here put on the terms "necessary and proper," is precisely the construction which prevailed during the discussions and ratifications of the Constitution. It may be added, and cannot too often be repeated, that it is a construction absolutely necessary to maintain their consistency with the peculiar character of the government, as possessed of particular and defined powers only; not of the general and indefinite powers vested in ordinary governments. For, if the power to suppress insurrection, includes a power to punish libels; or if the power to punish, includes a power to prevent, by all the means that may have that tendency; such is the relation and influence among the most remote subjects of legislation, that a power over a very few, would carry with it a power over all. And it must be wholly immaterial, whether unlimited powers be exercised under the name of unlimited powers, or be exercised under the name of unlimited means of carrying into execution limited powers.

This branch of the subject will be closed with a reflection which must have weight with all; but more especially with those who place peculiar reliance on the judicial exposition of the Constitution, as the bulwark provided against undue extensions of the legislative power. If it be understood that the powers implied in the specified powers, have an immediate arid appropriate relation to them, as means, necessary and proper for carrying them into execution, questions on the constitutionality of laws passed for this purpose, will be of a nature sufficiently precise and determinate for judicial cognizance and control! If, on the other hand, Congress are not limited in the choice of means by any such appropriate relation of them to the specified powers; but may employ all such means as they may deem fitted to prevent, as well as to punish, crimes subjected to their authority; such as may have a tendency only to promote an object for which they are authorized to provide; every one must perceive, that questions relating to means of this sort, must be questions of mere policy and expediency, on which legislative discretion alone can decide, and from which the judicial interposition and control are completely excluded.

2. The next point which the resolution requires to be proved, is, that the power over the press exercised by the Sedition Act, is positively forbidden by one of the amendments to the Constitution.

The amendment stands in these words—"Congress shall make no law respecting an establishment of religion, or prohibiting the free exercise thereof, or abridging the freedom of speech or of the press; or the right of the people peaceably to assemble, and to petition the government for a redress of grievances."

In the attempts to vindicate the "Sedition Act," it has been contended,
1. That the "freedom of the press" is to be determined by the meaning of these terms in the common law. 2. That the article supposes the power over the press to be in Congress, and prohibits them only from abridging the freedom allowed to it by the common law.

Although it will be shown, in examining the second of these positions, that the amendment is a denial to Congress of all power over the press, it may not be useless to make the following observations on the first of them.

It is deemed to be a sound opinion, that the Sedition Act, in its definition of some of the crimes created, is an abridgment of the freedom of publication, recognised by principles of the common law in England.

The freedom of the press under the common law, is, in the defences of the Sedition Act, made to consist in an exemption from all previous restraint on printed publications, by persons authorized to inspect and prohibit them. It appears to the committee, that this idea of the freedom of the press, can never be admitted to be the American idea of it: since a law inflicting penalties on printed publications, would have a similar effect with a law authorizing a previous restraint on them. It would seem a mockery to say, that no law should be passed, preventing publications from being made, but that laws might be passed for punishing them in case they should be made.

The essential difference between the British government, and the American constitutions, will place this subject in the clearest light.

In the British government, the danger of encroachments on the rights of the people, is understood to be confined to the executive magistrate. The representatives of the people in the legislature, are not only exempt themselves, from distrust, but are considered as sufficient guardians of the rights of their constituents against the danger from the executive. Hence it is a principle, that the parliament is unlimited in its power; or, in their own language, is omnipotent. Hence, too, all the ramparts for protecting the rights of the people, such as their magna charta, their bill of rights, etc., are not reared against the parliament, but against the royal prerogative. They are merely legislative precautions against executive usurpations. Under such a government as this, an exemption of the press from previous restraint by licensers appointed by the king, is all the freedom that can be secured to it.

In the United States, the case is altogether different. The people, not the government, possess the absolute sovereignty. The legislature, no less than the executive, is under limitations of power. Encroachments are regarded as possible from the one, as well as from the other. Hence, in the United States, the great and essential rights of the people are secured against legislative, as well as against executive ambition. They are secured, not by laws paramount to prerogative, but by constitutions paramount to laws. This security of the freedom of the press requires, that it should be exempt, not only from previous restraint by the executive, as in Great Britain, but from legislative restraint also; and this exemption, to be effectual, must be an exemption not only from the previous inspection of licensers, but from the subsequent penalty of laws.

The state of the press, therefore, under the common law, cannot, in this point of view, be the standard of its freedom in the United States.

But there is another view, under which it may be necessary to consider this subject.

It may be alleged, that although the security for the freedom of the press, be different in Great Britain and in this country; being a legal security only in the former, and a constitutional security in the latter; and although there may be a further difference, in an extension of the freedom of the press here, beyond an exemption from previous restraint, to an exemption from subsequent penalties also; yet that the actual legal freedom of the press, under the common law, must determine the degree of freedom which is meant by the terms, and which is constitutionally secured against both previous and subsequent restraints.

The committee are not unaware of the difficulty of all general questions, which may turn on the proper boundary between the liberty and licentiousness of the press. They will leave it therefore for consideration only, how far the difference between the nature of the British government, and the nature of the American governments, and the practice under the latter, may show the degree of rigour in the former to be inapplicable to, and not obligatory in the latter.

The nature of governments elective, limited, and responsible, in all their branches, may well be supposed to require a greater freedom of animadversion [criticism] than might be tolerated by the genius of such a government as that of Great Britain. In the latter, it is a maxim, that the king, an hereditary, not a responsible magistrate, can do no wrong; and that the legislature, which in two-thirds of its composition, is also hereditary, not responsible, can do what it pleases. In the United States, the executive magistrates are not held to be infallible, nor the legislatures to be omnipotent; and both being elective, are both responsible. Is it not natural and necessary, under such different circumstances, that a different degree of freedom, in the use of the press, should be contemplated?

Is not such an inference favoured by what is observable in Great Britain itself? Notwithstanding the general doctrine of the common law, on the subject of the press, and the occasional punishment of those who use it with a freedom offensive to the government; it is well known, that with respect to the responsible members of the government, where the reasons operating here, become applicable there, the freedom exercised by the press, and protected by the public opinion, far exceeds the limits prescribed by the ordinary rules of law. The ministry, who are responsible to impeachment, are at all times animadverted on, by the press, with peculiar freedom; and during the elections for the House of Commons, the other responsible part of the government, the press is employed with as little reserve towards the candidates.

The practice in America must be entitled to much more respect. In every state, probably, in the Union, the press has exerted a freedom in canvassing the merits and measures of public men, of every description, which has not been confined to the strict limits of the common law. On this footing, the freedom of the press has stood; on this footing it yet stands. And it will not be a breach, either of truth or pf candour, to say, that no persons or presses are in the habit of more unrestrained animadversions on the proceedings and functionaries of the state governments, than the persons and presses most zealous in vindicating the act of Congress for punishing similar animadversions on the government of the United States.

The last remark will not be understood as claiming for the state governments an immunity greater than, they have heretofore enjoyed. Some degree of abuse is inseparable from the proper use of everything; and in no instance is this more true, than in that of the press. It has accordingly been decided by the practice of the states, that it is better to leave a few of its noxious branches to their luxuriant growth, than by pruning them away, to injure the vigour of those yielding the proper fruits. And can the wisdom of this policy be doubted by any who reflect, that to the press alone, chequered as it is with abuses, the world is indebted for all the triumphs which have been gained by reason and humanity, over error and oppression; who reflect, that to the same beneficent source, the United States owe much of the lights which conducted them to the rank of a free and independent nation; and which have improved their political system into a shape so auspicious to their happiness. Had "Sedition Acts," forbidding every publication that might bring the constituted agents into contempt or disrepute, or that might excite the hatred of the people against the authors of unjust or pernicious measures, been uniformly enforced against the press, might not the United States have been languishing at this day, under the infirmities of a sickly confederation? Might they not possibly be miserable colonies, groaning under a foreign yoke?

To these observations, one fact will be added, which demonstrates that the common law cannot be admitted as the universal expositor of American terms, which may be the same with those contained in that law. The freedom of conscience, and of religion, are found in the same instruments which assert the freedom of the press. It will never be admitted, that the meaning of the former, in the common law of England, is to limit their meaning in the United States.

Whatever weight may be allowed to these considerations, the committee do not, however, by any means intend to rest the question on them. They contend that the article of amendment, instead of supposing in Congress a power that might be exercised over the press, provided its freedom was not abridged, was meant as a positive denial to Congress, of any power whatever on the subject.

To demonstrate that this was the true object of the article, it will be sufficient to recall the circumstances which led to it, and to refer to the explanation accompanying the article.

When the Constitution was under the discussions which preceded its ratification, it is well known, that great apprehensions were expressed by many, lest the omission of some positive exception from the powers delegated, of certain rights, and of the freedom of the press particularly, might expose them to the danger of being drawn by construction within some of the powers vested in Congress; more especially of the power to make all laws necessary and proper for carrying their other powers into execution. In reply to this objection, it was invariably urged to be a fundamental and characteristic principle of the Constitution, that all powers not given by it, were reserved; that no powers were given beyond those enumerated in the Constitution, and such as were fairly incident to them; that the power over the rights in question, and particularly over the press, was neither among the enumerated powers, nor incident to any of them; and consequently that an exercise of any such power, would be a manifest usurpation. It is painful to remark, how much the arguments now employed in behalf of the Sedition Act, are at variance with the reasoning which then justified the Constitution, and invited its ratification.

From this posture of the subject, resulted the interesting question in so many of the conventions, whether the doubts and dangers ascribed to the Constitution, should be removed by any amendments previous to the ratification, or be postponed, in confidence that as far as they might be proper, they would be introduced in the form provided by the Constitution. The latter course was adopted; and in most of the states, the ratifications were followed by propositions and instructions for rendering the Constitution more explicit, and more safe to the rights not meant to be delegated by it. Among those rights, the freedom of the press, in most instances, is particularly and emphatically mentioned. The firm and very pointed manner, in which it is asserted in the proceedings of the convention of this state, will be hereafter seen.

In pursuance of the wishes thus expressed, the first Congress that assembled under the Constitution, proposed certain amendments which have since, by the necessary ratifications, been made a part of it; among which amendments, is the article containing, among other prohibitions on the Congress, an express declaration that they should make no law abridging the freedom of the press.

Without tracing farther the evidence on this subject, it would seem scarcely possible to doubt, that no power whatever over the press was supposed to be delegated by the Constitution, as it originally stood; and that the amendment was intended as a positive and absolute reservation of it.

But the evidence is still stronger. The proposition of amendment is made by Congress, is introduced in the following terms: *"The conventions of a number of the states having at the time of their adopting the Constitution expressed a desire, in order to prevent misconstructions or abuse of its powers, that further declaratory and restrictive clauses should be added; and as extending the ground of public confidence in the government, will best ensure the beneficent ends of its institutions."*

Here is the most satisfactory and authentic proof, that the several amendments proposed, were to be considered as either declaratory or restrictive; and whether the one or the other, as corresponding with the desire expressed by a number of the states, and as extending the ground of public confidence in the government.

Under any other construction of the amendment relating to the press, than that it declared the press to be wholly exempt from the power of Congress, the amendment could neither be said to correspond with the desire expressed by a number of the states, nor be calculated to extend the ground of public confidence in the government.

Nay more; the construction employed to justify the "Sedition Act," would exhibit a phenomenon, without a parallel in the political world. It would exhibit a number of respectable states, as denying first that any power over the press was delegated by the Constitution; as proposing next, that an amendment to it, should explicitly declare that no such power was delegated; and finally, as concurring in an amendment actually recognising or delegating such a power.

Is then the federal government, it will be asked, destitute of every authority for restraining the licentiousness of the press, and for shielding itself against the libellous attacks which may be made on those who administer it?

The Constitution alone can answer this question. If no such power be expressly delegated, and it be not both necessary and proper to carry into execution an express power; above all, if it be expressly forbidden by a declaratory amendment to the Constitution, the answer must be, that the federal government is destitute of all such authority.

And might it not be asked in turn, whether it is not more probable, under all the circumstances which have been reviewed, that the authority should be withheld by the Constitution, than that it should be left to a vague and violent construction; whilst so much pains were bestowed in enumerating other powers, and so many less important powers are included in the enumeration?

Might it not be likewise asked, whether the anxious circumspection which dictated so many peculiar limitations on the general authority, would be unlikely to exempt the press altogether from that authority? The peculiar magnitude of some of the powers necessarily committed to the federal government; the peculiar duration required for the functions of some of its departments; the peculiar distance of the seat of its proceedings from the great body of its constituents; and the peculiar difficulty of circulating an adequate knowledge of them through any other channel; will not these considerations, some or other of which produced other exceptions from the powers of ordinary governments, all together, account for the policy of binding the hand of the federal government, from touching the channel which alone can give efficacy to its responsibility to its constituents; and of leaving those who administer it, to a remedy for their injured reputations, under the same laws, and in the same tribunals, which protect their lives, their liberties, and their properties?

But the question does not turn either on the wisdom of the Constitution, or on the policy which gave rise to its particular organization. It turns on the actual meaning of the instrument; by which it has appeared, that a power over the press is clearly excluded, from the number of powers delegated to the federal government.

3. And in the opinion of the committee, well may it be said, as the resolution concludes with saying, that the unconstitutional power exercised over the press by the "Sedition Act," ought "more than any other, to produce universal alarm; because it is levelled against that right of freely examining public characters and measures, and of free communication among the people thereon, which has ever been justly deemed the only effectual guardian of every other right."

Without scrutinizing minutely into all the provisions of the "Sedition Act," it will be sufficient to cite so much of Section 2, as follows: *"And be it further enacted, that if any person shall write, print, utter, or publish, or shall cause or procure to be written, printed, uttered or published, or shall knowingly and willingly assist or aid in writing, printing, uttering or publishing any false, scandalous and malicious writing or writings against the government of the United States, or either house of the Congress of the United States, or the President of the United States, with an intent to defame the said government, or either house of the said Congress, or the President, or to bring them, or either of them, into contempt or disrepute; or to excite against them, or either, or any of them, the hatred of the good people of the United States, etc. Then such person being thereof convicted before any court of the United States, having jurisdiction thereof, shall be punished by a fine not exceeding two thousand dollars, and by imprisonment not exceeding two years."*

On this part of the act, the following observations present themselves:

1. The Constitution supposes that the President, the Congress, and each of its houses may not discharge their trusts, either from defect of judgment or other causes. Hence, they are all made responsible to their constituents, at the returning periods of

election; and the President, who is singly entrusted with very great powers, is, as a further guard, subjected to an intermediate impeachment.

2. Should it happen, as the Constitution supposes it may happen, that either of these branches of the government may not have duly discharged its trust, it is natural and proper that, according to the cause and degree of their faults, they should be brought into contempt or disrepute, and incur the hatred of the people.

3. Whether it has, in any case, happened that the proceedings of either, or all of those branches, evince such a violation of duty as to justify a contempt, a disrepute or hatred among the people, can only be determined by a free examination thereof, and a free communication among the people thereon.

4. Whenever it may have actually happened, that proceedings of this sort are chargeable on all or either of the branches of the government, it is the duty as well as right of intelligent and faithful citizens, to discuss and promulge them freely, as well to control them by the censorship of the public opinion, as to promote a remedy according to the rules of the Constitution. And it cannot be avoided, that those who are to apply the remedy must feel, in some degree, a contempt or hatred against the transgressing party.

5. As the act was passed on July 14, 1798, and is to be in force until March 3, 1801, it was of course, that during its continuance, two elections of the entire House of Representatives, an election of a part of the Senate, and an election of a President, were to take place.

6. That consequently, during all these elections, intended by the Constitution to preserve the purity; or to purge the faults of the administration, the great remedial rights of the people were to be exercised, and the responsibility of their public agents to be screened, under the penalties of this act.

May it not be asked of every intelligent friend to the liberties of his country, whether the power exercised in such an act as this, ought not to produce great and universal alarm? Whether a rigid execution of such an act, in time past, would not have repressed that information and communication among the people, which is indispensable to the just exercise of their electoral rights? And whether such an act, if made perpetual, and enforced with rigour, would not, in time to come, either destroy our free system of government, or prepare a convulsion that might prove equally fatal to it?

In answer to such questions, it has been pleaded that the writings and publications forbidden by the act, are those only which are false and malicious, and intended to defame; and merit is claimed for the privilege allowed to authors to justify, by proving the truth of their publications, and for the limitations to which the sentence of fine and imprisonment is subjected.

To those who concurred in the act, under the extraordinary belief that the option lay between the passing of such an act, and leaving in force the common law of libels, which punishes truth equally with falsehood, and submits the fine and imprisonment to the indefinite discretion of the court; the merit of good intentions ought surely not to be refused. A like merit may perhaps be due for the discontinuance of the corporal punishment, which the common law also leaves to the discretion of the court. This merit of intention, however, would have been greater, if the several mitigations had not been limited to so short a period; and the apparent inconsistency would have been avoided between justifying the act at one time, by contrasting it with the rigors of the common law, otherwise in force, and at another time by appealing to the nature of the crisis, as requiring the temporary rigour exerted by the act.

But, whatever may have been the meritorious intentions of all or any who contributed to the Sedition Act, a very few reflections will prove, that its baneful tendency is little diminished by the privilege of giving in evidence the truth of the matter contained in political writings.

In the first place, where simple and naked facts alone are in question, there is sufficient difficulty in some cases, and sufficient trouble and vexation in all, of meeting a prosecution from the government, with the full and formal proof necessary in a court of law.

But in the next place, it must be obvious to the plainest minds, that opinions, and inferences, and conjectural observations, are not only in many cases inseparable from the facts, but may often be more the objects of the prosecution than the facts themselves; or may even be altogether abstracted from particular facts; and that opinions and inferences, and conjectural observations, cannot be subjects of that kind of proof which appertains to facts, before a court of law.

Again: It is no less obvious, that the intent to defame or bring into contempt or disrepute, or hatred, which is made a condition of the offence created by the act, cannot prevent its pernicious influence on the freedom of the press. For, omitting the inquiry, how far the malice of the intent is an inference of the law from the mere publication, it is manifestly impossible to punish the intent to bring those who administer the government into disrepute or contempt, without striking at the right of freely discussing public characters and measures: because those who engage in such discussions, must expect and intend to excite these unfavourable sentiments, so far as they may be thought to be deserved. To prohibit, therefore, the intent to excite those unfavourable sentiments against those who administer the government, is equivalent to a prohibition of the actual excitement of them; and to prohibit the actual excitement of them, is equivalent to a prohibition of discussions having that tendency and effect; which, again, is equivalent to a protection of those who administer the government, if they should at any time deserve the contempt or hatred of the people, against being exposed to it, by free animadversions on their characters and conduct. Nor can there be a doubt, if those in public trust be shielded by penal laws from such strictures of the press, as may expose them to contempt or disrepute, or hatred, where they may deserve it, in exact proportion as they may deserve to be exposed, will be the certainty and criminality of the intent to expose them, and the vigilance of prosecuting and punishing it; nor a doubt, that a government thus intrenched in penal statutes, against the just and natural effects of a culpable administration, will easily evade the responsibility, which is essential to a faithful discharge of its duty.

Let it be recollected, lastly, that the right of electing the members of the government, constitutes more particularly the essence of a free and responsible government. The value and efficacy of this right, depends on the knowledge of the comparative merits and demerits of the candidates for public trust; and on the equal freedom, consequently, of examining and discussing these merits and demerits of the candidates respectively. It has been seen, that a number of important elections will take place whilst the act is in force, although it should not be continued beyond the term to which it is limited. Should there happen, then, as is extremely probable in relation to some or other of the branches of the government, to be competitions between those who are, and those who are not, members of the government, what will be the situations of the competitors? Not equal; because the characters of the former will be covered by the "Sedition Act" from animadversions exposing them to disrepute among the people; whilst the latter may be exposed to the contempt and hatred of the people, without a violation of the act. What will be the situation of the people? Not free; because they will be compelled to make their election between competitors, whose pretensions they are not permitted, by the act, equally to examine, to discuss, and to ascertain. And from both these situations, will not those in power derive an undue advantage for continuing them selves in it; which by impairing the right of election, endangers the blessings of the government founded on it?

It is with justice, therefore, that the General Assembly have affirmed in the resolution, as well that the right of freely examining public characters and measures, and free communication thereon, is the only effectual guardian of every other right as that this particular right is levelled at, by the power exercised in the "Sedition Act."

The resolution next in order is as follows: *That this state having by its convention, which ratified the federal Constitution, expressly declared, that among other essential rights, "the liberty of conscience and of the press cannot be cancelled, abridged, restrained or modified by any authority of the United States," and from its extreme anxiety to guard these rights from every possible attack of sophistry and ambition, having, with other states, recommended an amendment for that purpose, which amendment was, in due time, annexed to the Constitution, it would mark a reproachful inconsistency, and criminal degeneracy, if an indifference were now shown to the most palpable violation of one of the rights thus declared and secured; and the establishment of a precedent, which may be fatal to the other.*

To place this resolution in its just light, it will be necessary to recur to the act of ratification by Virginia, which stands in the ensuing form:

We, the delegates of the people of Virginia, duly elected in pursuance of a recommendation from the General Assembly, and now met in convention, having fully and freely investigated and discussed the proceedings of the federal convention, and being prepared as well as the most mature deliberation hath enabled us to decide thereon, do, in the name and in behalf of the people of Virginia, declare and make known, that the powers granted under the Constitution, being derived from the people of the United States, may be resumed by them, whensoever the same shall be perverted to their injury or oppression; and that every power not granted thereby, remains with them, and at their will. That, therefore, no right of any denomination can be cancelled, abridged, restrained, or modified, by the Congress, by the Senate, or House of Representatives, acting in any capacity, by the President, or any department or officer of the United States, except in those instances in which power is given by the Constitution for those purposes; and that, among oilier essential rights, the liberty of conscience and of the press, cannot be cancelled, abridged, restrained, or modified, by any authority of the United States.

Here is an express and solemn declaration by the convention of the state, that they ratified the Constitution in the sense, that no right of any denomination can be cancelled, abridged, restrained, or modified by the government of the United States or any part of it; except in those in stances in which power is given by the Constitution; and in the sense particularly, "that among other essential rights, the liberty of conscience and freedom of the press cannot be cancelled, abridged, restrained, or modified, by any authority of the United States."

Words could not well express, in a fuller or more forcible manner, the understanding of the convention, that the liberty of conscience and the freedom of the press, were equally and completely exempted from all authority whatever of the United States.

Under an anxiety to guard more effectually these rights against every possible danger, the convention, after ratifying the Constitution, proceeded to prefix to certain amendments proposed by them, a declaration of rights, in which are two articles providing, the one for the liberty of conscience, the other for the freedom of speech and of the press.

Similar recommendations having proceeded from a number of other states, and Congress, as has been seen, having in consequence thereof, and with a view to extend the ground of public confidence, proposed, among other declaratory and restrictive clauses, a clause expressly securing the liberty of conscience and of the press; and Virginia having concurred in the ratifications which made them a part of the Constitution, it will remain with a candid public to decide, whether it would not mark an inconsistency and degeneracy, if an indifference were now shown to a palpable violation of one of those rights, the freedom of the press; and to a precedent therein, which may be fatal to the other, the free exercise of religion.

That the precedent established by the violation of the former of these rights, may, as is affirmed by the resolution, be fatal to the latter, appears to be demonstrable, by a comparison of the grounds on which they respectively rest; and from the scope of reasoning, by which the power over the former has been vindicated.

First. Both of these rights, the liberty of conscience and of the press, rest equally on the original ground of not being delegated by the Constitution, and consequently withheld from the government. Any construction, therefore, that would attack this original security for the one, must have the like effect on the other.

Secondly. They are both equally secured by the supplement to the Constitution; being both included in the same amendment, made at the same time, and by the same authority. Any construction or argument, then, which would turn the amendment into a grant or acknowledgment of power with respect to the press, might be equally applied to the free dom of religion.

Thirdly. If it be admitted that the extent of the freedom of the press, secured by the amendment, is to be measured by the common law on this subject, the same authority may be resorted to, for the standard which is to fix the extent of the "free exercise of religion." It cannot be necessary to say what this standard would be; whether the common law be taken solely as the unwritten, or as varied by the written law of England.

Fourthly. If the words and phrases in the amendment, are to be considered as chosen with a studied discrimination, which yields an argument for a power over the press, under the limitation that its freedom be not abridged, the same argument results from the same consideration, for a power over the exercise of religion, under the limitation that its freedom be not prohibited.

For, if Congress may regulate the freedom of the press, provided they do not abridge it, because it is said only "they shall not abridge it," and is not said, "they shall make no law respecting it," the analogy of reasoning is conclusive, that Congress may regulate and even abridge the free exercise of religion, provided they do not prohibit it, because it is said only "they shall not prohibit it," and is not said, "they shall make no law respecting, or no law abridging it."

The General Assembly were governed by the clearest reason, then, in considering the "Sedition Act," which legislates on the freedom of the press, as establishing a precedent that may be fatal to the liberty of conscience; and it will be the duty of all, in proportion as they value the security of the latter, to take the alarm at every encroachment on the former.

The two concluding resolutions only remain to be examined. They are in the words following:

That the good people of this commonwealth, having ever felt and continuing to feel the most sincere affection for their brethren of the other states; the truest anxiety for establishing and perpetuating the union of all; and the most scrupulous fidelity to that Constitution, which is the pledge of mutual friendship, and the instrument of mutual happiness; the General Assembly doth solemnly appeal to the like dispositions in the other states, in confidence that they will concur with this commonwealth in declaring, as it does hereby declare, that the acts aforesaid are unconstitutional; and, that the necessary and proper measures will be taken by each, for co-operating with this state, in maintaining unimpaired the authorities, rights, and liberties reserved to the states respectively, or to the people.

That the governor be desired to transmit a copy of the foregoing resolutions to the executive authority of each of the other states, with a request that the same may be communicated to the legislature thereof; and that a copy be furnished to each of the senators and representatives representing this state in the Congress of the United States.

The fairness and regularity of the course of proceeding here pursued, have not protected it against objections even from sources too respectable to be disregarded.

It has been said, that it belongs to the judiciary of the United States, and not the state legislatures, to declare the meaning of the Federal Constitution.

But a declaration that proceedings of the Federal Government are not warranted by the Constitution, is a novelty neither among the citizens, nor among the legislatures of the states; nor are the citizens or the legislature of Virginia, singular in the example of it.

Nor can the declarations of either, whether affirming or denying the constitutionality of measures of the Federal Government, or whether made before or after judicial decisions thereon, be deemed, in any point of view, an assumption of the office of the judge. The declarations, in such cases, are expressions of opinion, unaccompanied with any other effect than what they may produce on opinion, by exciting reflection. The expositions of the judiciary, on the other hand, are carried into immediate effect by force. The former may lead to a change in the legislative expression of the general will; possibly to a change in the opinion of the judiciary; the latter enforces the general will, whilst that will and that opinion continue unchanged.

And if there be no impropriety in declaring the unconstitutionality of proceedings in the Federal Government, where can be the impropriety of communicating the declaration to other states, and inviting their concurrence in a like declaration? What is allowable for one, must be allowable for all; and a free communication among the states, where the Constitution imposes no restraint, is as allowable among the state governments as among other public bodies or private citizens. This consideration derives a weight, that cannot be denied to it, from the relation of the state legislatures to the federal legislature, as the immediate constituents of one of its branches.

The legislatures of the states have a right also to originate amendments to the Constitution, by a concurrence of two-thirds of the whole number, in applications to Congress for the purpose. When new states are to be formed by a junction of two or more states, or parts of states, the legislatures of the states concerned are, as well as Congress, to concur in the measure. The states have a right also to enter into agreements or compacts, with the consent of Congress. In all such cases, a communication among them results from the object which is common to them.

It is lastly to be seen, whether the confidence expressed by the resolution, that the necessary and proper measures would be taken by the other states for co-operating with Virginia in maintaining the rights reserved to the states, or to the people, be in any degree liable to the objections which have been raised against it.

If it be liable to objection, it must be because either the object or the means are objectionable.

The object being to maintain what the Constitution has ordained, is in itself a laudable object.

The means are expressed in the terms "the necessary and proper measures." A proper object was to be pursued, by means both necessary and proper.

To find an objection, then, it must be shown that some meaning was annexed to these general terms, which was not proper; and, for this purpose, either that the means used by the General Assembly were an example of improper means, or that there were no proper means to which the terms could refer.

In the example given by the state, of declaring the Alien and Sedition Acts to be unconstitutional, and of communicating the declaration to the other states, no trace of improper means has appeared. And if the other states had concurred in making a like declaration, supported, too, by the numerous applications flowing immediately from the people, it can scarcely be doubted, that these simple means would have been as sufficient, as they are unexceptionable.

It is no less certain that other means might have been employed, which are strictly within the limits of the Constitution. The legislatures of the states might have made a direct representation to Congress, with a view to obtain a rescinding of the two offensive acts; or, they might have represented to their respective senators in Congress their wish, that two-thirds thereof would propose an explanatory amendment to the Constitution; or two-thirds of themselves, if such had been their option, might, by an application to Congress, have obtained a convention for the same object.

These several means, though not equally eligible in themselves, nor probably, to the states, were all constitutionally open for consideration. And if the General Assembly, after declaring the two acts to be unconstitutional, the first and most obvious proceeding on the subject, did not undertake to point out to the other states a choice among the farther measures that might become necessary and proper, the reserve will not be misconstrued by liberal minds into any culpable imputation.

These observations appear to form a satisfactory reply to every objection which is not founded on a misconception of the terms employed in the resolutions. There is one other, however, which may be of too much importance not to be added. It cannot be forgotten, that among the arguments addressed to those who apprehended danger to liberty from the establishment of the General Government over so great a country, the appeal was emphatically made to the intermediate existence of the state governments, between the people and that government, to the vigilance with which they would descry the first symptoms of usurpation, and to the promptitude with which they would sound the alarm to the public. This argument was probably not without its effect; and if it was a proper one then, to recommend the establishment of the Constitution, it must be a proper one now, to assist in its interpretation.

The only part of the two concluding resolutions that remains to be noticed, is the repetition in the first, of that warm affection to the union and its members, and of that scrupulous fidelity to the Constitution, which have been invariably felt by the people of this state. As the proceedings were introduced with these sentiments, they could not be more properly closed than in the same manner. Should there be any so far misled as to call in question the sincerity of these professions, whatever regret may be excited by the error, the General Assembly cannot descend into a discussion of it. Those, who have listened to the suggestion, can only be left to their own recollection of the part which this state has borne in the establishment of our national independence, in the establishment of our national Constitution, and in maintaining under it the authority and laws of the Union, without a single exception of internal resistance or commotion. By recurring to these facts, they will be able to convince themselves, that the representatives of the people of Virginia, must be above the necessity of opposing any other shield to attacks on their national patriotism, than their own consciousness, and, the justice of an enlightened public; who will perceive in the resolutions themselves, the strongest evidence of attachment both to the Constitution and to the Union, since it is only by maintaining the different governments and departments within their respective limits, that the blessings of either can be perpetuated.

The extensive view of the subject thus taken by the committee, has led them to report to the House, as the result of the whole, the following resolution:

Resolved, That the General Assembly, having carefully and respectfully attended to the proceedings of a number of the states, in answer to its resolutions of December 21, 1798, and having accurately and fully re-examined and reconsidered the latter, finds it to be its indispensable duty to adhere to the same, as founded in truth, as consonant with the Constitution, and as conducive to its preservation; and more especially to be its duty to renew, as it does hereby renew, its protest against "The Alien and Sedition Acts," as palpable and alarming infractions of the Constitution.[776]

APPENDIX D

THE GROWTH OF SECTIONAL ANTAGONISM

A Chart Showing the Development of Issues That Led to Southern Secession

BY OSCAR H. COOPER, HARRY F. ESTILL, & LEONARD LEMMON, 1908

ANDREW JACKSON ADMINISTRATION: 1829-1837
- The New President
- Changes in Office
    - Jackson's policy
    - Policy of later presidents
- The National Bank
    - First United States banks
    - Jackson's opposition
    - Removal of deposits
    - Final action of Congress
- Tariff Development
    - The first tariff
    - Positions of New England and the South
    - Tariff of 1816
    - Change of sentiment
    - Tariff of 1824
    - Tariff of 1828
- Nullification
    - The Hayne-Webster debate
    - Tariff of 1832
    - Action of South Carolina
    - Action of the president
    - The Calhoun-Webster debate
    - Compromise tariff
- Indian Uprisings
    - The Sacs and the Foxes
    - The Seminoles
- The Abolition Crusade
    - The pioneers
    - Various opinions
    - Deeds of violence
    - Action of Congress

- Railways and New States
    - First railway in the United States
    - Steam engines
    - First locomotive
    - Increase of railways
    - Two new states
- The Whig Party
    - Opposition to Jackson
    - Rise of Whigs
    - Presidential election

MARTIN VAN BUREN ADMINISTRATION: 1837-1841
- The New President
- Financial Panic
    - Cause
    - Results
- The Sub-Treasury
    - The president's views
    - Sub-treasury system
- Slavery
    - The abolitionists
    - Feeling, North and South
- Scientific Progress

WILLIAM H. HARRISON & JOHN TYLER ADMINISTRATIONS: 1841-1845
- Harrison's Election and Death
- President Tyler
    - Services and character
- The National Bank Controversy
    - Repeal of Sub-treasury law
    - Passage of Bank bills
    - President's vetoes
    - Results
- The Ashburton Treaty [named after Alexander Baring, 1st Baron of Ashburton]
    - Trouble with Great Britain
    - Settlement of the dispute
- The Tariff Legislation
    - The Tariff of 1842
- The Dorr Rebellion [named after Thomas W. Dorr]
    - Suffrage in Rhode Island
    - Uprising of Dorr
    - New constitution
- The Mormons

- Founder of the sect [Joseph Smith]
- Troubles in Illinois
- Settlement in Utah
• The Telegraph
    - The first experiment
    - Spread of telegraph lines
• Texas
    - The Texas revolution
    - The Republic of Texas
    - The state of Texas
    - Presidential election
    - Annexation
• Florida and Iowa admitted

JAMES K. POLK ADMINISTRATION: 1845-1849
• The New President
• The Oregon Boundary
    - Claims of England and of U.S.
    - Boundary settled
• The Oregon Trail
    - First explorations
    - Trading expeditions
    - First settlement
    - Rivalry of English
    - [Marcus] Whitman's achievements
• Beginning of the Mexican War
    - Disputed boundary of Texas
    - Orders to General [Zachary] Taylor
    - First engagement
• Battles in Texas
    - Palo Alto
    - Resaca de la Palma
• Taylor's Invasion
    - Capture of Monterey
    - Battle of Buena Vista
• General [Winfield] Scott's Invasion of Mexico
    - Vera Cruz
    - March to the capital
    - Fall of the city
• Conquest of California
    - The Mexican province
    - [John C.] Frémont's campaign
    - Commodore [John D.] Sloat

- New Mexico Taken
    [Stephen W.] Kearney's campaign
- Treaty of Peace
    New State
- Gold in California
    The discovery of gold
    The "gold fever"
    Increase in population

ZACHARY TAYLOR & MILLARD FILLMORE ADMINISTRATIONS: 1849-1853
- The Presidents
    The services of Taylor
    Death of Taylor
    Services of Fillmore
- The Problem of the Administration
    Military government of California
    Movements toward statehood
    The old controversy
- Conflicting Opinions
- Compromise of 1850
    The "Omnibus Bill"
    Debate on the bill
- The Fugitive-Slave Agitation
    The Fugitive-Slave Law
    Resistance by individuals
    Nullification by states
    "Underground Railway"
    Views of Northern statesmen
- Railroad Development
    The Erie Railroad
    Increase of railroads

FRANKLIN PIERCE ADMINISTRATION: 1853-1857
- The New President
- The Kansas-Nebraska Bill
    First settlers of the plains
    [Stephen A.] Douglas' bill
    Opposition to the bill
    Its passage
- The Struggle for Kansas
    Emigrant societies
    Immigration to Kansas
    Conflicts

- The Republican Party of 1854 (the Liberal party at the time; not related to the Republican Party of Thomas Jefferson or Ronald Reagan)
    - First principles
    - Composition of the party
- Our First World's Fair
- Treaty with Japan
    - Gadsden Purchase [named after James Gadsden]

JAMES BUCHANAN ADMINISTRATION: 1857-1861
- The New President
- The Dred Scott Decision
    - Origin of the suit
    - Appeals and final decision
    - Results of the decision
- Mormon Insurrection
- Panic of 1857
    - Cause
    - New tariff law
- Lincoln-Douglas Debates
    - Position of Douglas on Missouri Compromise
    - His position on the Kansas question
    - Canvass for Illinois senatorship
    - Debates of the candidates
- New States
- Mineral Discoveries
    - Gold in Colorado
    - Coal
    - Silver
    - Oil wells
- Scientific Progress
    - Maps of winds and sea currents
    - Bed of Atlantic Ocean explored
- John Brown's Raid
    - Brown's plan
    - Seizure of U.S. arsenal
    - Capture and execution
    - Feeling in North and South
- Presidential Campaign of 1860
    - Democratic Convention at Charleston [the Democratic Party was the Conservative party at the time]
    - First split in Democratic party
    - Constitutional party
    - Republicans [Liberals]

Second split in Democratic party
Position of the parties on slavery
- The Election
  The Abolitionists [radical Liberals]
  Vote of the sections
  Popular vote and electoral vote
  Effect of the election
- Buchanan's Message
  Northern nullification
  Anti-slavery agitation
  Secession
- Efforts at Compromise
  [John J.] Crittenden's proposition
  Peace Congress
- Secession
  Action of Legislature of South Carolina
  Convention of South Carolina
  Action of other Southern states
- Federal Property
  Action of Seceded states
  South Carolina's commissioners
- Right of Secession
  Historic view
  Legal view
- Reasons for Secession
  Violations of Constitution by Northern states
  Centralizing tendencies of North
  Sectional feeling
  Success of Republican party
- Cause of the War
  The South's desire
  Growth of coercion sentiment
- The Confederate States
  Organization
  Constitution
  Sketch of President Davis
  Sketch of Vice-President Stephens
- End of Buchanan's Administration
  Divisions in the cabinet
  Reception of South Carolina commissioners
  Affairs at Charleston Harbor[777]

APPENDIX E

SECESSION A LEGAL RIGHT

A Brief Statement of the Lawful Ground for the Right of Secession

BY OSCAR H. COOPER, HARRY F. ESTILL, & LEONARD LEMMON, 1908

- The states were "free, sovereign, and independent," and were so recognized by each other and by England in the Treaty of Paris prior to the adoption of the Constitution.
- The Constitution was formed as a compact or agreement between these "free, sovereign, and independent" states.
- The general government of the United States provided in the Constitution was created to promote the general welfare of the states.
- Its powers were given to it by the states and were specified by the Constitution; all other powers were reserved to the states.
- In case of violation of the Constitution by any member of the Union, the other members were released from obligation to maintain the Union.
- Secession, or withdrawal from the compact, was a final and peaceable mode of redress.
- Such were the teachings of many of the fathers and founders of the United States.
- The people of the Southern states held steadfastly to these teachings and believed sincerely and implicitly that the states had the legal right to withdraw from the Union.[778]

Confederate Monument, Columbia, South Carolina.

APPENDIX F

REASONS FOR SECESSION

A Brief Southern Justification for Leaving the Union

BY OSCAR H. COOPER, HARRY F. ESTILL, & LEONARD LEMMON, 1908

It is an error to suppose that the Southern states rushed hastily and blindly into secession. The grave questions involved in a course so decisive as that of seceding from the Union were discussed with intense earnestness throughout the South. *The states, at last concluding that their constitutional rights could not be saved in the Union, deliberately withdrew.* Their reasons for this course may be summed up as follows:

1. *Fourteen Northern states,* by passing "Personal Liberty Laws," *had nullified the Constitution* (see **Article 4, Section 2, Clauses 2 and 3,** of the Constitution), and *they had also violated Federal laws passed in pursuance of the Constitution.* These violations of the Constitution by the Northern states not only absolved the Southern states from further obligation to the constitutional compact, but *they also showed that the Constitution could not be enforced and the government maintained with these states.*

2. *The North had abandoned the historic and legal view of a Union under the terms of the Constitution. It had come to hold that the Constitution was not a compact between the states, but the supreme law over the states, and that not only was the Union not created by the states, but that the states had been created by the Union.* These ideas were held by the Republican party [then the Liberal party], which was just coming into power. This party was pledged to disregard certain decisions of the Supreme Court and to attack slavery.

3. *Sectional feeling* between the North and South existed to some extent in Colonial days, being apparent even in the convention that formed the Constitution. *This feeling became stronger as the conflict of interests between the agricultural and manufacturing communities began to find expression in tariff legislation*; but it was the growth of abolitionism *[and its corresponding disregard for the Constitution]* that transformed sectional feeling into sectional fury. Although the Republican [Liberal] party denounced the John Brown Raid, still the Abolitionists [radical Liberals]

at the North glorified John Brown, fanatic as he was, whose mad plot sent a thrill of horror into every Southern home. Slavery and slaveholders were denounced, in public and in private, by the press, from pulpit and rostrum, in story, essay, and poem. *This persistent [malicious] and powerful crusade inevitably incensed and embittered the South beyond endurance. Among the masses of the people, North and South, sectional antipathy supplanted the friendlier feeling of earlier times. Thus differences in ideas, sentiment, and institutions had made two different peoples, almost two different countries, of the North and the South. A separation was felt to be the only logical outcome.*

4. Lincoln had declared that "the country cannot exist half slave and half free." *To the South this meant that Lincoln and the great [Liberal] party which had elected him would undermine the constitutional rights of the states wherever and whenever it was practicable to do so [particularly] in the interest of abolition. The question with every Southerner then was, What is best for the South to do in view of all the circumstances? Can the rights of the states be preserved best in the Union or out of the Union? The question was answered by her acts; she withdrew from the Union.*[779]

APPENDIX G

AVERMENTS OF FACT

Or, Why Jefferson Davis Was Not a "Traitor"

BY BERNARD JANIN SAGE, 1878

THE REPUBLIC
1. The state is people thereof: they are the state.
2. No other organization of self-governing people exists.
3. Such societies alone are "the people of the united states."
4. "All political power is inherent" in such societies.
5. So the state constitutions declare or imply.
6. Hence each state is sovereign, i.e. has the "all-power."
7. It is a completely organized, self-governing body.
8. The people are not sovereign as individuals.
9. Sovereignty is only predicable of the organized people.
10. Societal organization was completed, in forming the state.
11. Hence, the alleged national society was impossible.
12. All the states have agreed that each is sovereign.
13. That is to say, each has the right of self-government.
14. The voting citizens hold and wield the governing power.
15. The voter's authority is an endowment by the state.
16. With it the voters express the sovereign will.
17. Such state is the republic, or self-governing people.
18. It is the only possible dwelling of sovereign mind.
19. Making constitutions and governing, are functional acts.
20. The state's mind is intact after, as before such action.

THE REPUBLIC OF REPUBLICS
21. The states in union are the republic of republics.
22. If nation there be, they are the integers—not fractions.
23. Hamilton called them the "essential component parts."
24. Joel Barlow called the states in union federalised states.
25. The Fathers all similarly characterised the system.
26. It answers to Montesquieu's "republic of republics."
27. Its members are moral or corporate, not natural persons.
28. The general sovereignty is that of the states allied.
29. They severally delegate "powers," not sovereignty.

30. Their constitution only contains delegations.
31. The convention of 1787 called it a "delegation" and a "trust."
32. So Washington wrote, by their "unanimous order."
33. The constitution itself fully sustains the averment.
34. All not delegated are reserved—kept out of the pact.
35. These delegations cannot belong to "trustees" or "agents."
36. Such powers must belong to the delegating states.
37. Hence, the federal government cannot be sovereign.
38. Hence, too, each ratifying and delegating state is so.
39. Each state ratified by exerting her mind and will.
40. This alone subjected her people to the constitution.
41. Hence, 13 states "ordained and established" the compact.

CITIZENSHIP AND ALLEGIANCE
42. Citizens remained "citizens of different states."
43. So the federal compact declares and implies.
44. The state alone has authority to govern her citizens.
45. The federal powers they obey, are delegated by her.
46. Protection and allegiance are reciprocal obligations.
47. Protection is due from the society to the member.
48. Allegiance is due from the said citizen to society.
49. The tie of allegiance, then, is the social compact.
50. By this compact, the will of all wholly governs each.
51. This is the sole cohesive force of a republic.
52. All citizens are members and subjects of states.
53. The transfer of citizenship would dissolve the state.
54. Citizenship or allegiance was never transferred.
55. President Andrew Jackson greatly erred in saying it was.

TREASON
56. Treason is a citizen's breach of allegiance to his sovereign.
57. The society is the sovereign, and object of the crime ["secession"].
58. "Treason against the U.S." is "levying war" against them.
59. It is not "levying war against" the nation or government.
60. Nor is it "levying war against" the union or association.
61. But it is "levying war against" the described "states."
62. A co-action of state wills established and defined the crime.
63. The power to try and to punish it, is delegated by each state.
64. Obviously the crime is against the guilty citizen's state.
65. Davis and Lee were true to their respective states.
66. Hence they were patriots and not traitors.[780]

NOTES

1. F. Moore, TRR, Vol. 7, p. 306.
2. Seabrook, TQJD, p. 53.
3. Woods, p. 47.
4. On Lincoln's socialistic, Marxist, and communist thoughts, ideas, and tendencies, see e.g., Seabrook, LW, passim; McCarty, passim; Browder, passim; Benson and Kennedy, passim.
5. See J. W. Jones, TDMV, pp. 144, 200-201, 273.
6. See Seabrook, TAHSR, passim. See also, Pollard, LC, p. 178; J. H. Franklin, pp. 101, 111, 130, 149; Nicolay and Hay, ALCW, Vol. 1, p. 627.
7. See e.g., Seabrook, TQJD, pp. 30, 38, 76.
8. See e.g., J. Davis, RFCG, Vol. 1, pp. 55, 422; Vol. 2, pp. 4, 161, 454, 610. Besides using the term "Civil War" himself, President Davis cites numerous other individuals who used it as well.
9. See e.g., *Confederate Veteran*, March 1912, Vol. 20, No. 3, p. 122.
10. Minutes of the Eighth Annual Meeting, July 1898, p. 87.
11. Sage, p. 36.
12. Mish, s.v. "secession."
13. There are Northerners who believe that secession is purely a Southern word, and Southerners who hold that secession is a Northern word. Both are incorrect, for both regions used it from the founding of the U.S.A. Northerners who employed the word in their writings and speeches include U.S. presidents like John Quincy Adams, Franklin Pierce, and James Buchanan, lawyers like Caleb W. Loring, newspapermen like Horace Greeley, governors such as Samuel J. Tilden, and academics like William Rawle. The list of Southerners who regularly used the word secession in their writings and speeches is even longer, and includes Southern presidents and vice presidents, statesmen, attorneys, Confederate generals and soldiers, governors, and writers. In this group we have Jefferson Davis, Alexander H. Stephens, Robert A. Toombs, Nathaniel Macon, Woodrow Wilson, Albert T. Bledsoe, Robert E. Lee, Maxcy Gregg, Robert B. Rhett, John Letcher, Francis W. Pickens, Alfred Iverson Sr., Bernard J. Sage, and George E. Pickett, to name but a few. A number of the South's orders of disunion themselves contained the word secede or secession, and indeed were each entitled "Ordinance of Secession."
14. Mish, s.v. "secession."
15. Traupman, s.v. "secedo."
16. Mish, s.v. "secede."
17. Oxford Dictionary, s.v. "Secede."
18. Seabrook, LW, p. 306.
19. Seabrook, LW, p. 306.
20. Steel, page 3.
21. Calvert, Vol. 8, pp. 1-5. Emphasis added.
22. Jensen, NN, p. 25; Lancaster and Plumb, p. 197.
23. F. Moore, AE, Vol. 2, p. 204. Emphasis added.
24. The problems that arose from the Articles of Confederation dealt mainly with the issue of the balance of power between the states and the central government. By the mid 1780s, many, mainly Federalists (the Liberals of the day), came to believe that the Articles had formulated a central government that was too weak. It would need more power, they argued. But how much more? It was this issue that was addressed at the Constitutional Convention (May 25 to September 17, 1787) in Philadelphia, Pennsylvania. Unfortunately for the Antifederalists (the Conservatives of the day), instead of merely re-weighing the delicate balance of powers, the convention members decided to create an entirely new government. In the process, the original confederate government was diluted and the Articles of Confederation were largely abandoned. Antifederalists resisted. Federalists pushed and, to a great degree, got their way. With the ratification of the new Constitution in 1789, the U.S. Confederacy became a confederate republic, a compromise on the original pure confederacy. See Stephens, ACV, Vol. 1, pp. 504-505. As a political entity the U.S. Confederacy had lasted a mere eight years, from 1781 to 1789. However, because the new

government contained various important aspects carried over from the Confederacy, Americans would continue to refer to the U.S. as "the Confederacy" for many generations to come. See Jensen, NN, pp. 348, 421, passim; Collier and Collier, passim.

25. Napolitano, pp. 25, 63.
26. Calvert, Vol. 8, p. 37. Emphasis added.
27. Bronowski and Mazlish, p. 213.
28. Calvert, Vol. 8, p. 33. Emphasis added.
29. Findlay and Findlay, pp. 168-169. See also, pp. 215-217.
30. Greeley, HSSER, p. 17. Emphasis added.
31. Findlay and Findlay, p. 213.
32. Findlay and Findlay, p. 212.
33. Bledsoe, p. 131. Emphasis added.
34. J. C. Hamilton, Vol. 4, p. 113. Emphasis added.
35. F. Moore, AE, Vol. 1, p. 188. Emphasis added.
36. Fowler, pp. 253-254. Emphasis added.
37. Bledsoe, p. 154. Emphasis added.
38. Sage, p. 71.
39. Fowler, p. 261.
40. Fowler, p. 241. Emphasis added.
41. Fowler, p. 239. Emphasis added.
42. Fowler, p. 242. Emphasis added.
43. Scott, p. 332. Emphasis added.
44. Fowler, pp. 247-248. Emphasis added.
45. Fowler, p. 243.
46. Rogers, p. 3. Emphasis added.
47. Fowler, p. 45.
48. Rogers, pp. 3-4. Emphasis added.
49. Fowler, p. 45.
50. E. P. Powell, p. 128. Emphasis added.
51. Stephens, ACV, Vol. 1, pp. 504-505. Emphasis added.
52. Fowler, p. 68. Emphasis added.
53. Ashe, pp. 6, 53, 63, 75; Woods, p. 64.
54. G. E. Pickett, p. 34.
55. Rawle, pp. 289-290. Emphasis added.
56. Rawle, pp. 289, 295. Emphasis added.
57. Calhoun and Webster, p. 52. Emphasis added.
58. Story, Vol. 1, pp. 287-289. Emphasis added.
59. McHenry, pp. xliii-xliv. Emphasis added.
60. Quincy, pp. 109-110. Emphasis added.
61. Upshur, p. 131. Emphasis added.
62. Rogers, p. 10.
63. Rogers, p. 10.
64. Johnston, Vol. 6, p. 54.
65. Fowler, pp. 249-251.
66. Johnston, Vol. 6, pp. 54-56. For Tucker's remarks on this topic, see Tucker, Vol. 1, pp. 170-187.
67. Rogers, pp. 10-11. Emphasis added.
68. Rogers, p. 11. Emphasis added.
69. Rogers, p. 12. Emphasis added.
70. Nicolay and Hay, ALAH, Vol. 9, p. 184.
71. A. C. Gordon, p. 111. Emphasis added.
72. F. Moore, AE, Vol. 2, p. 321. Emphasis added.
73. F. Moore, AE, Vol. 2, p. 327.
74. Collier and Collier, p. 4.
75. Fowler, pp. 249-251.

76. Spaeth and Smith, p. 12.
77. Spaeth and Smith, p. 12.
78. Findlay and Findlay, p. 6.
79. Findlay and Findlay, p. 190.
80. Ashe, p. 54.
81. Tocqueville, Vol. 2, p. 426. Emphasis added.
82. Fowler, p. 251. Emphasis added.
83. Bledsoe, p. 155. Emphasis added.
84. Rawle, pp. 289, 290.
85. Stephens, ACV, Vol. 1, p. 514.
86. Smelser, TDR, p. 78.
87. Cooper, Estill, and Lemmon, p. 340. Emphasis added.
88. Johnston, Vol. 6, p. 102. Emphasis added.
89. Seabrook, TQJD, p. 42.
90. T. J. Randolph, p. 284. Emphasis added.
91. J. Davis, RFCG, Vol. 1, p. 173. Emphasis added.
92. J. Davis, RFCG, Vol. 2, p. 623.
93. J. Davis, RFCG, Vol. 1, p. 173. Emphasis added.
94. Sage, Appendix I, p. 2.
95. Nicolay and Hay, ALCW, Vol. 2, p. 60.
96. Forman, p. 354. Emphasis added.
97. Foley, p. 894. Emphasis added.
98. Foley, p. 513. Emphasis added.
99. Fowler, pp. 214-215. Emphasis added.
100. See e.g., Bledsoe, pp. 1-4.
101. Fowler, p. 217. Emphasis added.
102. Fowler, pp. 215-216. Emphasis added.
103. Fowler, p. 216. Emphasis added.
104. Collier and Collier, p. 4.
105. Foley, pp. 212, 797.
106. Hamilton, Madison, and Jay, p. 21.
107. H. A. Washington, p. 174.
108. Ashe, p. 21.
109. Burns and Peltason, p. 41.
110. Collier and Collier, p. 4.
111. Ashe, pp. 17, 25.
112. Rouse, pp. 78-79. Emphasis added.
113. Collier and Collier, p. 4.
114. Rosenbaum and Brinkley, s.v. "Antifederalists."
115. Rowland, Vol. 1, p. 509.
116. See e.g., Foley, pp. 399, 900.
117. Garland, p. 103.
118. Henry, p. 16. The question of loyalty to state or nation was debated as early as 1787, at the Constitutional Convention in Philadelphia. Collier and Collier, p. 264. While most Northerners pledged their allegiance to the nation, well into the 1800s most Southerners chose to give their allegiance to their home states. This tradition lives on across Dixie to this day.
119. Rouse, p. 56.
120. Rouse, p. 56. Emphasis added.
121. Rouse, pp. 56-58.
122. Fowler, pp. 243-244.
123. Fowler, p. 243. Emphasis added.
124. Fowler, pp. 249-251.
125. Beach, Vol. 3, s.v. "Calhoun, John Caldwell."
126. See Seabrook, C101, passim.

127. Henry, SC, pp. 12-13.
128. Sage, p. 90. Emphasis added.
129. The word "federal" is a shortening, abbreviation, or corruption of the word "confederal," which means "confederacy." See Seabrook, AL, pp. 15-21.
130. Stephens, ACV, Vol. 1, p. 503.
131. Sage, pp. 104-105. Emphasis added.
132. Sage, pp. 120, 174.
133. Ashe, p. 21.
134. Rouse, p. 320. Emphasis added.
135. Sage, pp. 214, 215, 221.
136. Fowler, p. 249. Emphasis added.
137. Stephens, ACV, Vol. 1, p. 297.
138. Beach, Vol. 3, s.v. "Calhoun, John Caldwell."
139. See Seabrook, C101, passim.
140. E. McPherson, TPHOTUSADTGR, p. 106. Emphasis added.
141. Pollard, LC, p. 175. Emphasis added.
142. Pollard, LC, p. 181. Emphasis added.
143. See Stonebraker, pp. 67-68.
144. J. B. Scott, pp. 84-85. Emphasis added. See also pp. 86-87.
145. Bateman, p. 179. Emphasis added.
146. Fowler, pp. 244-246. Emphasis added.
147. Fowler, pp. 249-251.
148. Seabrook, CFF, pp. 44-45.
149. Bergh, Vol. 1, p. 167. Emphasis added.
150. Bergh, Vol. 1, pp. 167-168. Emphasis added.
151. Fowler, pp. 238-239. Emphasis added.
152. Fowler, p. 240. Emphasis added.
153. Fowler, pp. 240-241.
154. Bledsoe, pp. 137, 138-139, 140. Emphasis added.
155. The twenty-seven amendments to the Constitution are: (Bill of Rights, first ten Amendments) First Amendment: freedom of religion, press, expression, assembly, petition (1791); Second Amendment: right to bear arms (1791); Third Amendment: quartering of soldiers (1791); Fourth Amendment: search and seizure (1791); Fifth Amendment: grand jury, double jeopardy, self-incrimination, due process (1791); Sixth Amendment: criminal prosecutions, jury trial, right to confront and to counsel (1791); Seventh Amendment: common law suits, trial by jury in civil cases (1791); Eighth Amendment: excessive bail or fines, cruel and unusual punishment (1791); Ninth Amendment: non-enumerated rights, construction of Constitution (1791); Tenth Amendment: states' rights (rights reserved to states), i.e., powers of the states and people (1791); Eleventh Amendment: suits against a state, judicial limits (1795); Twelfth Amendment: election of president and vice president (1804); Thirteenth Amendment: abolition of slavery (1865); Fourteenth Amendment: privileges and immunities, due process, equal protection, apportionment of representatives, Civil War disqualification and debt (1868); Fifteenth Amendment: rights not to be denied on account of race (1870); Sixteenth Amendment: status of income tax clarified (1913); Seventeenth Amendment: senators elected by popular vote (1913); Eighteenth Amendment: Prohibition, liquor abolished (1919); Nineteenth Amendment: women given the vote (1920); Twentieth Amendment: presidential term and succession (1933); Twenty-First Amendment: Eighteenth Amendment repealed (1933); Twenty-Second Amendment: two-term limit on president (1951); Twenty-Third Amendment: presidential vote for District of Columbia (1961); Twenty-Fourth Amendment: poll taxes barred (1964); Twenty-Fifth Amendment: presidential disability and succession (1967); Twenty-Sixth Amendment: voting age set to eighteen years (1971); Twenty-Seventh Amendment: compensation of members of Congress (1992). See K. L. Hall, s.v. "Constitutional Amendments."
156. Cooper, Estill, and Lemmon, p. 340.
157. Bledsoe, pp. 193-194.
158. C. Johnson, pp. 115-117.
159. For plotting with Alexander Hamilton against administration policy, Pickering was dismissed by Adams, the first and only secretary of state to be terminated in this manner. DeGregorio, s.v. "John Adams" (p. 28).

160. DeGregorio, s.v. "James Monroe" (p. 78).
161. C. King, Vol. 4, pp. 364-366. Emphasis added.
162. C. Adams, p. 15.
163. DeGregorio, s.v. "James Madison" (p. 66).
164. Smelser, TDR, p. 78.
165. H. Adams, p. 351.
166. H. Adams, p. 338. Emphasis added.
167. Faulkner, pp. 181-182, 210.
168. During America's early history, in fact, Massachusetts threatened to secede from the Union on four different occasions, all without any violent resistance from any other state. Pollard, LC, p. 85.
169. DeGregorio, s.v. "Woodrow Wilson" (p. 411).
170. Pollard, LC, p. 96.
171. J. Davis, RFCG, Vol. 1, p. 54. Emphasis added.
172. E. McPherson, TPHOTUSADTGR, pp. 49-50. Emphasis added.
173. Rogers, p. 13. Emphasis added.
174. Buchanan was born in Pennsylvania.
175. On vacating the presidential chair for the last time, Buchanan told Lincoln: "My dear sir, if you are as happy on entering the White House as I on leaving it, you are a very happy man indeed." C. O'Brien, SLUSP, p. 83.
176. Rogers, p. 13.
177. E. McPherson, TPHOTUSADTGR, pp. 51-52. Emphasis added.
178. Loring, p. 5. Emphasis added.
179. Rogers, pp. 13-14. Emphasis added.
180. Rogers, p. 14. Emphasis added.
181. F. Moore, TRR, Vol. 7, p. 306. Emphasis added.
182. Nicolay and Hay, ALCW, Vol. 2, p. 55.
183. Nicolay and Hay, ALCW, Vol. 2, p. 61.
184. The height of irony is that while Lincoln referred to his critics as snakes, he was one himself. According to the ancient science of Chinese astrology, Lincoln was born under the sign of the "Snake." Chinese astrologers tell us that when angered, Snakes are fueled by a hatred that knows no bounds; yet they keep their antagonistic feelings well-hidden. Instead, using their devious calculating minds, they seek to totally destroy their enemies; but only when the time is just right. The Snake's vindictive spirit is second only to its lust for power, intrigue, and the limelight. Lau, pp. 119, 121. Besides being vengeful and power-hungry, Snakes are also known to be stealthy, secretive, stingy, jealous, possessive, stubborn, dishonest, lethargic, and procrastinating. At their worst, Snakes not only engage in bizarre and antisocial behavior, but they can also become criminals. Wu, p. 148. Whether one accepts Chinese astrology as valid or not, I know of no better description of our sixteenth president—as my books on Lincoln show.
185. Bledsoe, p. 188.
186. As we will see, states like Tennessee actually referred to their secession ordinances as a "Declaration of Independence."
187. Seabrook, AL, p. 53.
188. L. Johnson, pp. 123-128.
189. Nicolay and Hay, ALCW, Vol. 1, p. 142.
190. Woodworth, p. xi; Zinn, p. 129; Encyc. Brit., s.v. "Lincoln, Abraham"; Hendelson, s.v. "Lincoln, Abraham."
191. C. Johnson, pp. 119-120. Lincoln later "painfully" admitted that he was "not a military man." Nicolay and Hay, ALCW, Vol. 2, p. 218.
192. Findlay and Findlay, pp. 84-85.
193. Rogers, p. 15.
194. See Seabrook, AL, pp. 293-318.
195. Rawle, pp. 9, 93, 296-297.
196. J. Davis, RFCG, Vol. 1, p. 145.
197. Loring, p. 9.
198. Beach, Vol. 3, s.v. "Calhoun, John Caldwell."
199. Sage, pp. 71-72. Emphasis added.

200. Seabrook, TQJD, p. 51. Emphasis added.
201. Pierson, pp. 45-46.
202. F. T. Reid, Vol. 3, p. 519.
203. Pierson, p. 46.
204. Rawle, pp. 9, 93, 296-297.
205. Calvert, Vol. 8, p. 5.
206. Greeley, HSSER, p. 17.
207. Fowler, pp. 249-251.
208. Findlay and Findlay, pp. 168-169. See also, pp. 215-217.
209. W. C. Davis, HD, pp. 79-80.
210. Seabrook, L, pp. 763, 877.
211. W. B. Garrison, LNOK, pp. 193-197.
212. Nicolay and Hay, ALCW, Vol. 2, p. 283.
213. Nicolay and Hay, ALCW, Vol. 2, pp. 285-287.
214. See F. Moore, TRR, Vol. 7, p. 306.
215. See e.g., Nicolay and Hay, ALCW, Vol. 2, pp. 55, 61.
216. Seabrook, LW, p. 101.
217. Seabrook, ARB, p. 301.
218. Loring, pp. 2-3. Emphasis added.
219. W. Wilson, Vol. 4, p. 284. Emphasis added.
220. Sage, Appendix I, p. 1.
221. Sage, Appendix I, p. 2.
222. Bledsoe, pp. 125-126. Emphasis added.
223. See e.g., E. McPherson, TPHOTUSADTGR, p. 392.
224. Entire books have been devoted to promoting this Yankee myth, one of the more angry, fact-free, unhistorical, and anti-Southern ones being the 1886 work entitled, *The Great Conspiracy*, by South-hating author John Alexander Logan.
225. E. McPherson, TPHOTUSADTGR, p. 29.
226. See the harshly anti-South work by William P. Rogers, passim.
227. W. Wilson, Vol. 4, p. 289.
228. Boucher, p. 143.
229. J. W. Jones, PRAALOGREL, p.137. Emphasis added.
230. Index to Reports of Committees, 1874-1875, p. 213.
231. E. McPherson, TPHOTUSADTGR, p. 2.
232. E. McPherson, TPHOTUSADTGR, pp. 3-8.
233. E. McPherson, TPHOTUSADTGR, p. 8.
234. E. McPherson, TPHOTUSADTGR, p. 4.
235. E. McPherson, TPHOTUSADTGR, p. 4.
236. E. McPherson, TPHOTUSADTGR, p. 5.
237. E. McPherson, TPHOTUSADTGR, p. 12.
238. See Seabrook, EYWTATCWIW, pp. 33-37.
239. Seabrook, AL, p. 58.
240. Index to Reports of Committees, p. 214.
241. Victor, TCHOTSR, Vol. 1, p. 194.
242. Stephens, ACV, Vol. 1, p. 144. Emphasis added.
243. Fowler, pp. 49, 243. Emphasis added.
244. W. Wilson, Vol. 4, pp. 271, 273, 274-275. Emphasis added.
245. Barnhardt, pp. 127-128. Emphasis added.
246. Toryism has been defined differently by different people at different times and in different countries. While today Toryism is normally associated with conservatism, in Stephens' day it was more closely allied with authoritarianism, tyranny, and despotism.
247. Pollard, EFTS, pp. 7-44. Emphasis added.
248. Cooper, Estill, and Lemmon, p. 340.
249. Hart and Channing, p. 3.

250. Hart and Channing, pp. 9-10. Emphasis added.
251. Hart and Channing, pp. 10-11. Emphasis added.
252. Hart and Channing, pp. 11-12. Emphasis added.
253. Hart and Channing, pp. 12-13. Emphasis added.
254. Hart and Channing, pp. 13-14. Emphasis added.
255. Hart and Channing, pp. 15-16. Emphasis added.
256. Hart and Channing, pp. 17-18. Emphasis added.
257. Hart and Channing, pp. 18-19. Emphasis added.
258. Hart and Channing, pp. 19-20. Emphasis added.
259. Hart and Channing, pp. 20-21. Emphasis added.
260. Victor, THCIVILPAMOTSR, Vol. 2, pp. 522-523.
261. Loring, pp. 514-516. Emphasis added.
262. Seabrook, EYWTAASIW, pp. 230-250.
263. Seabrook, EYWTAAAATCWIW, pp. 121-122.
264. Seabrook, TGYC, p. 148.
265. Seabrook, EYWTAASIW, pp. 236-237.
266. Seabrook, EYWTAASIW, pp. 427-428, 430.
267. Seabrook, EYWTAAAATCWIW, p. 280.
268. Tilley, FTHLO, p. 10.
269. Seabrook, ALWAL, p. 70.
270. Seabrook, ALWAL, p. 71. Emphasis added.
271. Boucher, p. 135. Emphasis added.
272. Boucher, p. 136. Emphasis added.
273. Boucher, pp. 136-137. Emphasis added.
274. Seabrook, TQJD, p. 51. Emphasis added.
275. E. McPherson, TPHOTUSADTGR, p. 38. This is a paraphrasal of Toombs' words and sentiments.
276. Seabrook, EYWTAASIW, pp. 549-645.
277. See *Journal of the Convention of the People of South Carolina*, passim.
278. Johnston, Vol. 6, p. 57.
279. E. McPherson, TPHOTUSADTGR, p. 390.
280. See Boucher, p. 93.
281. Johnston, Vol. 6, pp. 68-69. Emphasis added.
282. Seabrook, LW, p. 17. Emphasis added.
283. Seabrook, TQJD, p. 80. Emphasis added.
284. Seabrook, AL, pp. 127-128.
285. Seabrook, NBFATKKK, pp. 44, 108; Catton, Vol. 2, p. 443.
286. Seabrook, LW, p. 17. Emphasis added.
287. Coleman, Vol. 1, pp. 224-249.
288. The Crittenden-Johnson Resolution is not to be confused with the Crittenden Resolutions, or Crittenden Compromise, as it is also called. See e.g., Fowler, pp. 229-230.
289. E. McPherson, TPHOTUSADTGR, p. 16.
290. Stedman and Hutchinson, Vol. 6, p. 46.
291. See Seabrook, TGYC, passim.
292. For more on this topic, see Seabrook, ALWAL, passim.
293. Seabrook, ALWAL, pp. 77-79, 84.
294. For more on Yankee white racism, see Seabrook, EYWTAASIW, passim; Seabrook, S101, passim; Seabrook, NBFATKKK, passim; Seabrook, EYWTAAAIW, passim.
295. Seabrook, AL, p. 250.
296. W. B. Garrison, LNOK, p. 186; DiLorenzo, LU, p. 28.
297. Nicolay and Hay, ALCW, Vol. 1, p. 556.
298. Seabrook, TCOTCSOAE, p. 65.
299. For more on Yankee white racism, see Seabrook, EYWTAASIW, passim; Seabrook, S101, passim; Seabrook, NBFATKKK, passim; Seabrook, EYWTAAAIW, passim.
300. Seabrook, TUAL, p. 81.

301. Nicolay and Hay, ALCW, Vol. 1, p. 241.
302. Garraty and McCaughey, p. 254.
303. Bledsoe, p. 146.
304. There were hated even by many Yankees who professed to be racially tolerant and empathetic to the plight of the African-American. One of these was the famed poet Walt Whitman, who, like most Northerners, detested slavery in principle but in practice opposed civil rights for free blacks. As such he often denounced abolitionists, not only for their fanaticism, but also for consistently breaking the law. Kaplan, pp. 132, 133.
305. See Seabrook, AL, pp. 268-270.
306. Cooper, Estill, and Lemmon, p. 290. Emphasis added.
307. Boucher, pp. 106-107. Emphasis added.
308. Bledsoe, pp. 151-152. Emphasis added.
309. E. McPherson, TPHOTUSADTGR, p. 56. Emphasis added.
310. Johnston, Vol. 6, p. 110.
311. Faulkner, p. 353.
312. Faulkner, p. 353.
313. *Debow's Commercial Review of the South and West*, February 1847, Vol. 3, No. 11, p. 98. Emphasis added.
314. Faulkner, p. 353.
315. Mann, p. 295.
316. *Congressional Globe*, 35th Congress, 1st Session (December 7, 1857 to June 14, 1858), p. 441. Emphasis added.
317. Muzzey, TUSOA, Vol. 1, p. 524.
318. Muzzey, TUSOA, Vol. 1, p. 524.
319. Seabrook, EYWTATCWIW, pp. 24, 120.
320. Fowler, p. 99. Emphasis added.
321. W. Wilson, Vol. 4, pp. 189-192. Emphasis added.
322. For more on the original U.S. Confederacy, see Jensen, NN, passim; AC, passim.
323. Simpson, p. 72.
324. Sage, Appendix F, p. 3.
325. Sage, Appendix F, p. 3. Emphasis added.
326. Seabrook, EYWTATCWIW, p. 47.
327. Seabrook, EYWTATCWIW, p. 48.
328. Sage, p. 73.
329. Rozwenc, pp. 10-11.
330. McWhiney and Jamieson, pp. 171-172.
331. *The American Annual Cyclopedia (of 1861)*, Vol. 1, p. 648.
332. Fowler, p. 240. Emphasis added.
333. Johnston, Vol. 6, pp. 83-85. Emphasis added.
334. Fowler, pp. 233-235. Emphasis added.
335. Seabrook, EYWTAAAATCWIW, p. 159.
336. Seabrook, EYWTAAAATCWIW, p. 159.
337. Fowler, p. 238.
338. Seabrook, EYWTAAAATCWIW, pp. 159-160.
339. See Seabrook, EYWTAASIW, pp. 647-685.
340. Seabrook, EYWTAAAATCWIW, p. 160.
341. Seabrook, EYWTAASIW, pp. 615-616. Emphasis added.
342. Johnston, Vol. 6, p. 60. Emphasis added.
343. Johnston, Vol. 6, p. 60.
344. See Seabrook, LW, passim.
345. Calvert, Vol. 8, p. 5.
346. Garraty and McCaughey, p. 244; Faust, s.v. "slavery."
347. Napolitano, p. 75.
348. Channing, p. 165.
349. McElroy, pp. 444-447.

350. Seabrook, AL, p. 66.
351. Seabrook, AL, p. 66.
352. W. Wilson, Vol. 4, pp. 208-209.
353. Hart and Channing, pp. 3-9. Emphasis added.
354. Seabrook, EYWTATCWIW, p. 87.
355. See Seabrook, ARB, passim.
356. *Journal of the Convention of the People of South Carolina*, p. 337.
357. Seabrook, EYWTAASIW, pp. 802-804. Emphasis added.
358. Seabrook, LW, p. 32.
359. Seabrook, EYWTATCWIW, p. 82.
360. E. McPherson, TPHOTUSADTGR, p. 17. Emphasis added.
361. E. McPherson, TPHOTUSADTGR, p, 20. Emphasis added.
362. *Journal of the Convention of the People of South Carolina*, pp. 467-476. Emphasis added.
363. Pollard, EFTS, pp. 72-76. Emphasis added.
364. Victor, THCIVILPAMOTSR, Vol. 2, pp. 430-433. Emphasis added.
365. Rogers, pp. 524-528. Emphasis added.
366. Rogers, pp. 61-62. Emphasis added.
367. E. McPherson, TPHOTUSADTGR, pp. 430-431. Emphasis added.
368. Bledsoe, p. 241.
369. Bledsoe, pp. 237-238. Emphasis added.
370. W. Wilson, Vol. 4, pp. 270-278. Emphasis added.
371. Sage, pp. 67-68. Emphasis added.
372. Bledsoe, pp. 256-257. Emphasis added.
373. Johnston, Vol. 6, p. 81.
374. See Seabrook, AL, p. 250.
375. E. McPherson, TPHOTUSADTGR, pp. 25-26.
376. E. McPherson, TPHOTUSADTGR, p. 26. Emphasis added.
377. See Seabrook, EYWTAASIW, pp. 62-119.
378. Seabrook, TGYC, p. 147. Emphasis added.
379. E. McPherson, TPHOTUSADTGR, p. 478.
380. Logan, p. 561.
381. Logan, p. 589.
382. Seabrook, EYWTAASIW, pp. 262-263.
383. Johnston, Vol. 6, p. 58.
384. Seabrook, TAHSR, pp. 193-194.
385. Seabrook, TAHSR, pp. 202-204. Emphasis added.
386. Seabrook, TGYC, p. 147.
387. Seabrook, TGYC, p. 147. Emphasis added.
388. Seabrook, TGYC, p. 147. Emphasis added.
389. See e.g., Nicolay and Hay, ALCW, Vol. 1, pp. 289, 370, 457, 458, 469, 539; Basler, ALSW, pp. 400, 402, 403-404; Stern, pp. 492-493; Holzer, pp. 189, 251.
390. Seabrook, EYWTAASIW, pp. 732, 745-746, 769-771.
391. Seabrook, TQAHS, pp. 13-15, 362-406.
392. Lincoln made this statement in a public speech July 17, 1858, less than two years before being elected president. Seabrook, TUAL, p. 91.
393. Seabrook, TGYC, p. 148. Emphasis added.
394. Seabrook, TGYC, p. 148. See also Fowler, p. 267.
395. Seabrook, TGYC, p. 148.
396. See Van Evrie, passim.
397. Seabrook, EYWTAASIW, pp. 214-215.
398. Among them was Lincoln's future secretary of state, William H. Seward of New York, who, on September 4, 1860, said during a speech at Detroit, Michigan: "The great fact is now fully realized that the African race here is a foreign and feeble element, like the Indians, incapable of assimilation . . . a pitiful exotic, unwisely and unnecessarily transplanted into our fields . . ." Munford, p. 167.

399. Logan, pp. 585-586.
400. Johnston, Vol. 6, pp. 91-104. Emphasis added.
401. Sage, pp. 37-38. Emphasis added.
402. Sage, p. 36. Emphasis added.
403. Burgess, Vol. 1, pp. 96-97.
404. Johnston, Vol. 6, p. 93. Emphasis added.
405. Johnston, Vol. 6, pp. 89-91. Emphasis added.
406. Seabrook, AL, pp. 495-518.
407. Modern socialists also dislike the Declaration of Independence, in this case because it promotes the "bourgeois" idea of "private property and its logical corollaries, competitive industry and individual liberty." Hillquit, SITAP, p. 79.
408. Rutherford, TOH, p. ix.
409. Bledsoe, p. 152.
410. J. G. Randall, p. 79.
411. J. H. Moore, p. 163.
412. Bryan, LAS, p. 279.
413. Faulkner, p. 136.
414. Rutherford, TOH, p. 28.
415. Seabrook, AL, pp. 27, 68.
416. Bledsoe, p. 152. Emphasis added.
417. Fowler, p. 238. Emphasis added.
418. Macy, p. 247; Faulkner, p. 346; F. Curtis, Vol. 1, p. 271.
419. Seabrook, AL, pp. 67-68. Emphasis added.
420. Johnston, Vol. 6, p. 89.
421. I arrive at this sum by taking the South's 3.5 million servants and valuing them at about $1,200 a piece, which equals $4 billion. In 1860 the purchasing power of $4 billion was roughly $120 billion. Note that $1.00 in 1860 was roughly the modern equivalent of $30.00.
422. To his credit, in the beginning Lincoln supported compensating Southern slave owners. But he soon gave up the idea when he saw that it would cost him abolitionist votes in the 1864 election.
423. See, for example, Iverson's complete speech. Johnston, Vol. 6, pp. 76-86.
424. Seabrook, EYWTAASIW, pp. 549-645.
425. W. Wilson, Vol. 4, p. 209.
426. Seabrook, LW, p. 23.
427. Seabrook, LW, p. 17.
428. Seabrook, LW, p. 239.
429. Seabrook, LW, pp. 16-17. Emphasis added.
430. Seabrook, LW, p. 17. Emphasis added.
431. Seabrook, LW, p. 17. Emphasis added.
432. Seabrook, LW, p. 18. Emphasis added.
433. Seabrook, LW, p. 18. Emphasis added.
434. Seabrook, LW, p. 18. Emphasis added.
435. Seabrook, CFF, p. 184. Emphasis added.
436. Loring, p. 1. Emphasis added.
437. Rutherford, TOH, pp. 13-14.
438. Tilley, FTHLO, p. 10.
439. Seabrook, CFF, pp. 24, 278-284, 303. See also Muzzey, Vol. 1, p. 521.
440. Beach, Vol. 3, s.v. "Calhoun, John Caldwell."
441. Fowler, p. 249.
442. Seabrook, ALWAL, pp. 109-112.
443. It was America's antipathy toward democracy that prompted English novelist Rudyard Kipling to criticize the U.S.A. in the late 1800s. R. Miller, p. 173.
444. Collier and Collier, p. 4.
445. Hamilton, Madison, and Jay, p. 21.
446. Seabrook, AL, p. 42.

447. Seabrook, C101, passim.
448. Rawle, pp. 9, 93, 296-297.
449. Rozwenc, pp. 10-11.
450. Sage, p. 73.
451. Seabrook, AL, p. 90. Emphasis added.
452. Tocqueville, Vol. 2, p. 426. Emphasis added.
453. J. Davis, RFCG, Vol. 1, p. 439.
454. C. Adams, p. 49.
455. W. B. Garrison, CWC, p. 220.
456. T. D. Morris, p. 202.
457. Spooner, NT, No. 6, p. 55. Emphasis added.
458. See C. Adams, p. 36.
459. M. Davis, p. 80.
460. Cooper, JDA, p. 551.
461. A. Cooke, ACA, p. 206.
462. See Nicolay and Hay, ALCW, Vol. 2, p. 1; Beard and Beard, Vol. 2, pp. 39-40.
463. Seabrook, ALWAL, pp. 77-78, 84.
464. See Stonebraker, p. 250.
465. J. M. McPherson, BCF, p. 254.
466. C. Adams, p. 89.
467. Lincoln and Douglas, p. 74. Emphasis added.
468. Johnston, Vol. 6, p. 66.
469. Lincoln and Douglas, pp. 186-187. Emphasis added.
470. Lincoln and Douglas, p. 74.
471. Seabrook, LW, p. 90.
472. Simpson, pp. 74, 76.
473. To this day many Southerners believe this sentiment is still very much alive across the North—and with good reason. The ongoing disrespect shown for the traditional South, toward her history, heroes, culture, icons, traditions, monuments, and society, as daily displayed in print, TV, radio, film, and on the Internet certainly substantiates this view.
474. F. Moore, TRR, Vol. 4, p. 201. Emphasis added.
475. ORA, Ser. 2, Vol. 3, p. 153. Emphasis added.
476. See Seabrook, CFF, passim.
477. Sage, p. 24. Emphasis added.
478. To his great credit, Virginian John Tyler (1790-1862), America's tenth president, was the only man of that office, former or future, to either join the Confederacy or serve in the Confederate government. Though he did not fight in Lincoln's "Civil War" (being too old at the time), he served as a member of the Provisional Congress of the Confederacy. He was later elected to the Confederate House of Representatives, but passed away before taking his seat. Tyler was an example of the overt anti-South bias that has long permeated the U.S. government: because of his devotion to the Confederate Cause, Northerners in his day regarded him as a traitor, his death in 1862 was ignored in Washington, and an official U.S. memorial was not placed over his grave until 1915, fifty-three years after he died. DeGregorio, s.v. "John Tyler" (pp. 158-159). In total, six men who would become U.S. presidents fought in the War for Southern Independence; unfortunately for history, all got it wrong by siding with liberal tyrant Lincoln and the North: Benjamin Harrison, James A. Garfield, Ulysses S. Grant, Rutherford B. Hayes, Chester A. Arthur, and William McKinley.
479. Tyler, LTT, Vol. 2, p. 567. Emphasis added.
480. See Seabrook, LW, passim.
481. Boucher, p. 83.
482. See Helper, passim.
483. Fowler, p. 232.
484. Fowler, p. 232. Emphasis added.
485. Fowler, p. 51.
486. Fowler, pp. 51-52. Emphasis added.
487. Rayner, pp. 499-500. Emphasis added.

488. E. McPherson, TPHOTUSADTGR, p. 391.
489. E. McPherson, TPHOTUSADTGR, pp. 44-46.
490. E. McPherson, TPHOTUSADTGR, p. 27. Emphasis added.
491. E. McPherson, TPHOTUSADTGR, p. 27. Emphasis added.
492. Seabrook, EYWTATCWIW, pp. 102, 106, 151.
493. Boucher, p. 90.
494. Seabrook, EYWTAASIW, pp. 549-645.
495. Seabrook, EYWTATCWIW, p. 82.
496. Seabrook, EYWTAASIW, pp. 57-59, 111-112, 248-250, 375, 377-380.
497. Seabrook, EYWTAASIW, pp. 420-444.
498. Seabrook, AL, p. 192.
499. Boucher, p. 89.
500. Boucher, p. 90. Emphasis added.
501. Boucher, p. 106.
502. W. Wilson, Vol. 4, pp. 189-192. Emphasis added.
503. Fowler, p. 238. Emphasis added.
504. Logan, p. 358. Emphasis added.
505. E. McPherson, TPHOTUSADTGR, p. 390. Emphasis added.
506. Seabrook, EYWTAASIW, pp. 549-645.
507. Seabrook, EYWTAASIW, p. 549.
508. Seabrook, EYWTAASIW, pp. 556, 558-566.
509. Shenkman, p. 121.
510. Seabrook, EYWTAASIW, p. 549.
511. Seabrook, EYWTATCWIW, p. 100.
512. Seabrook, EYWTAASIW, p. 571.
513. Seabrook, EYWTAASIW, pp. 182-183.
514. Seabrook, EYWTAASIW, pp. 167-228.
515. Seabrook, EYWTAASIW, pp. 658, 659. Emphasis added.
516. Seabrook, EYWTAAAATCWIW, p. 203.
517. Seabrook, EYWTAAAATCWIW, p. 278.
518. Seabrook, EYWTAAAATCWIW, pp. 278-279.
519. Seabrook, EYWTAAAATCWIW, p. 279.
520. Seabrook, EYWTAASIW, p. 575.
521. Seabrook, EYWTAASIW, p. 783. Emphasis added.
522. Seabrook, EYWTAASIW, pp. 549-645.
523. Seabrook, EYWTAASIW, p. 862.
524. Logan, pp. 553-554.
525. Logan, p. 590.
526. Logan, pp. 607-614.
527. Boucher, p. 106.
528. Seabrook, EYWTAASIW, p. 862.
529. Seabrook, EYWTAASIW, pp. 549-645.
530. Logan, p. 614.
531. Seabrook, EYWTAAAATCWIW, pp. 118, 119, 158, 186, 190, 311, 312, 317, 325, 328, 331, 361, 378.
532. Seabrook, TCOTCSOAE, pp. 65-66.
533. E. McPherson, TPHOTUSADTGR, pp. 611-612.
534. Seabrook, EYWTAASIW, p. 787.
535. ORA, Ser. 4, Vol. 3, p. 1161. Emphasis added.
536. Seabrook, EYWTAASIW, p. 787.
537. Seabrook, TQREL, p. 110.
538. Seabrook, NBFAAA, pp. 35-36.
539. Seabrook, NBFAAA, pp. 48-49.
540. Seabrook, NBFAAA, p. 44.

541. Seabrook, NBFAAA, p. 44.
542. For the truth about Forrest, see any of my nine books on him, in particular *A Rebel Born*.
543. Seabrook, EYWTAASIW, p. 800.
544. Seabrook, LW, p. 169.
545. Seabrook, TQREL, p. 226. Emphasis added.
546. Seabrook, TCOTCSOAE, pp. 62, 114.
547. Seabrook, EYWTAASIW, pp. 802-804. Emphasis added.
548. E. McPherson, TPHOTUSADTGR, p. 429. Emphasis added.
549. Seabrook, AL, pp. 241-262.
550. Seabrook, TUAL, p. 81.
551. Seabrook, TUAL, p. 91.
552. Seabrook, AL, p. 250.
553. Seabrook, AL, pp. 256-257.
554. Seabrook, AL, p. 254.
555. Seabrook, AL, p. 412. Emphasis added.
556. Seabrook, AL, p. 243.
557. Benson and Kennedy, p. 261; Sinkler, p. 47; Gould, p. 35; Basler, TCWOAL, Vol. 3, p. 399.
558. Nicolay and Hay, ALCW, Vol. 1, p. 292.
559. Bryan, p. 291. Emphasis added.
560. Lincoln and Douglas, p. 95. Emphasis added.
561. Nicolay and Hay, ALCW, Vol. 5, pp. 87, 89. Emphasis added.
562. Seabrook, EYWTAASIW, pp. 549-645.
563. Seabrook, EYWTAASIW, p. 549.
564. Seabrook, EYWTAASIW, pp. 558-566.
565. Seabrook, LW, p. 169.
566. Seabrook, EYWTAASIW, pp. 236, 551, 570, 591, 599, 602, 607.
567. Seabrook, EYWTAAAATCWIW, pp. 159-160.
568. E. McPherson, TPHOTUSADTGR, p. 429. Emphasis added.
569. Seabrook, EYWTAAAATCWIW, p. 125.
570. Seabrook, EYWTAASIW, pp. 658, 659.
571. Seabrook, EYWTAASIW, pp. 309, 317, 385, 482.
572. Seabrook, NBFAAA, p. 44.
573. Seabrook, EYWTATCWIW, p. 159.
574. To this day more hate crimes are committed in the North than in the South, and the head of the modern KKK (the National Knights of the Ku Klux Klan) lives, not in the South, but in the North (New York), one of the fastest growing regions for KKK membership in the U.S. Seabrook, EYWTAAAATCWIW, p. 71.
575. Seabrook, AL, p. 354.
576. Tyler, PH, p. 12.
577. ORA, Ser. 3, Vol. 1, p. 133. Emphasis added.
578. Cornish, p. 73; D. Brown, pp. 179-180.
579. ORA, Ser. 3, Vol. 1, p. 184.
580. Conway, p. 108.
581. R. M. Reid, p. 2; Barney, pp. 127-128. My paraphrasal.
582. E. McPherson, TPHOTUSADTGR, p. 611. Emphasis added.
583. Pollard, SHW, Vol. 2, p. 198; L. Johnson, p. 135. For official reference to Lincoln's "government plantations," see, for example, ORA, Ser. 1, Vol. 26, Pt. 1, p. 764. See also Nicolay and Hay, ALCW, Vol. 2, pp. 471-472.
584. Seabrook, CFF, p. 288.
585. ORA, Ser. 1, Vol. 15, p. 595. See also pp. 593-594.
586. Seabrook, AL, p. 353.
587. F. Moore, TRR, Vol. 8, pp. 278-279. Emphasis added.
588. Wiley, SN, pp. 12-14.
589. Gragg, p. 85.
590. H. C. Dean, p. 83.

591. Barrow, Segars, and Rosenburg, BC, p. 15.
592. Seabrook, EYWTAASIW, p. 399.
593. Seabrook, EYWTAASIW, pp. 167-250.
594. In *Uncle Tom's Cabin* Stowe takes note of the hypocrisy among Yankee abolitionists. In one scene, for example, she has a Southerner say to a Northerner who is both an "abolitionist" and a black colonizationist: "You loathe them [slaves] as you would a snake or a toad, yet you are indignant at their wrongs. You would not have them abused; but you don't want to have anything to do with them yourselves. You would send them to Africa, out of your sight and smell, and then send a missionary or two to do up all the self-denial of elevating them compendiously." Stowe, p. 196.
595. Seabrook, EYWTAASIW, pp. 236-237.
596. Seabrook, EYWTAASIW, pp. 734-780.
597. E. P. Powell, p. 128.
598. Seabrook, GTBTAY, p. 48; Nicolay and Hay, ALCW, Vol. 2, p. 6; Beard and Beard, Vol. 2, p. 65; DiLorenzo, LU, pp. 24, 25.
599. W. S. Powell, p. 144. See Nicolay and Hay, ALCW, Vol. 2, pp. 442-444.
600. See Current, LNK, pp. 223, 239, 240, 241.
601. Harwell, p. 307.
602. Seabrook, AL, pp. 144-145.
603. W. B. Garrison, LNOK, p. 186; DiLorenzo, LU, p. 28.
604. Seabrook, EYWTAASIW, pp. 732, 745-746, 769-771.
605. C. Adams, p. 135; DiLorenzo, TGC, p. 255; Johannsen, p. 55.
606. Nicolay and Hay, ALCW, Vol. 3, p. 33.
607. Nicolay and Hay, CWAL, Vol. 1, p. 15.
608. McKissack and McKissack, pp. 134, 135.
609. Seabrook, L, p. 647.
610. De Angelis, pp. 12-18; Lott, p. 65; J. J. Holland, passim.
611. Garrison, LNOK, p. 176; J. M. McPherson, BCF, pp. 788-789.
612. See Spooner, NT, No. 6, p. 54; Pollard, LC, p. 154; Graham, BM, passim.
613. See Nicolay and Hay, CWAL, Vol. 11, pp. 105-106; Nicolay and Hay, ALCW, Vol. 1, p. 483; Holzer, pp. 22-23, 67, 318, 361.
614. Current, LNK, pp. 242-246; W. C. Davis, AHD, p. 164; Garrison, LNOK, p. 181; Weintraub, p. 73.
615. B. F. Butler, p. 903. See also W. P. Pickett, pp. 326-327.
616. Current, LNK, pp. 218-219; W. B. Garrison, LNOK, pp. 35-37; Greenberg and Waugh, p. 355.
617. M. Davis, p. 83. See also Seabrook, AL, passim.
618. Rutland, p. 226; C. Johnson, p. 200.
619. Nicolay and Hay, ALCW, Vol. 1, p. 257. Lincoln is here quoting his opponent Stephen A. Douglas, but is agreeing with him, as his words before and after this statement confirm.
620. Nicolay and Hay, ALCW, Vol. 1, p. 197. Emphasis added.
621. See Tilley, FTHLO, p. 10.
622. Catton, Vol. 1, p. 86.
623. America's history of black racism and black racial separatism is nearly as long as that of whites. Former Northern slave, Frederick Douglass, for example, once said "I saw in every white man an enemy . . ." Douglass, NLFD, p. 109. Black racism toward Caucasians was particularly strong during the 1800s: many African-Americans at this time were revolted by the sight of white skin, a vestige of the native African belief that "only black skin is beautiful." Blassingame, p. 25. Early American black nationalism, some of which grew out of a revulsion toward white racism, was expedited by a black Massachusetts Quaker named Paul Cuffe, who financed the emigration of nearly forty other blacks to Sierra Leone in 1815. Garry and McCaughey, p. 145. In 1877, a number of blacks actually sought out the American Colonization Society (a Northern white supremacist organization to which Lincoln belonged), asking for help in resettling them in Liberia. Adams and Sanders, p. 228. In the 1920s, a black-sponsored "Back to Africa" movement emerged. Its founder, Jamaican-born black nationalist Marcus Garvey, promoted the ideas of black pride, economic independence from whites, and the establishment of a black-only state in Africa. Unfortunately for supporters of the Back to Africa movement, Garvey was later convicted of fraud, imprisoned, and eventually deported. Rosenbaum, s.v. "Garvey, Marcus Moziah." Even earlier, in the 19th Century, African-American abolitionist Martin Delany advocated a separation of the races, with an emphasis on black separatism

specifically. Rosenbaum, s.v. "Delaney, Martin Robinson." Delany and Garvey were not the first, nor the last, American blacks to push for black separatism. The idea continues today among numerous African-American groups, many with extreme racist ideologies. Rosenbaum and Brinkley, s.v. "Back to Africa"; "Colonization." Like Lincoln and most other 19th-Century white Northerners, the majority of today's black racists are against interracial marriage and for racial separation. Needless to say, white separatist Lincoln, a lifelong champion of the idea of American apartheid and a former chapter leader of the American Colonization Society in Illinois, would have fully supported the Back to Africa movement. See Seabrook, L, pp. 584-633.

624. Nicolay and Hay, ALCW, Vol. 1, p. 231. Emphasis added.
625. Nicolay and Hay, ALCW, Vol. 1, p. 234. Emphasis added. Actually, Lincoln was wrong: later scientific studies, such as those done by Edward Byron Reuter, revealed that the percentage of mulattos went up only *after* slavery ended. Reuter, pp. 120-122. Thus there was almost no connection between slavery and "amalgamation" (race mixing), as Lincoln derogatorily referred to it. See Fogel and Engerman, pp. 130-136.
626. Wilson and Ferris, s.v. "Miscegenation."
627. Nicolay and Hay, ALCW, Vol. 1, p. 175. Emphasis added.
628. Nicolay and Hay, ALCW, Vol. 1, pp. 175-176. Emphasis added.
629. Nicolay and Hay, ALCW, Vol. 1, p. 176.
630. Seabrook, TUAL, p. 91.
631. E. McPherson, TPHOTUSADTGR, 134.
632. Nicolay and Hay, ALAH, Vol. 6, p. 356. See also pp. 357-358.
633. Nicolay and Hay, ALCW, Vol. 2, p. 274. Emphasis added.
634. Cornish, p. 95.
635. Nicolay and Hay, ALCW, Vol. 2, p. 271. Emphasis added.
636. Lincoln's colonization experiments in Panama, Belize, and Haiti all failed miserably, with death rates of over 50 percent in some cases. C. Johnson, p. 182.
637. Nicolay and Hay, ALCW, Vol. 1, p. 288.
638. See Holzer, p. 49.
639. Current, LNK, pp. 221-222.
640. Seabrook, AL, p. 257.
641. DiLorenzo, RL, p. 18.
642. Seabrook, AL, pp. 255-257.
643. Rawle, p. 289.
644. Ashe, pp. 21-22.
645. Burns and Peltason, p. 31.
646. Seabrook, ALWAL, p. 52.
647. For a detailed discussion on the switching of American party platforms, see Seabrook, ALWAL, passim.
648. F. T. Miller, p. 112.
649. Harwell, p. 3.
650. Denney, p. 25. The other four states of the Confederacy, Virginia, Arkansas, North Carolina, and Tennessee, would secede later, after the Battle of Fort Sumter and Lincoln's call for troops in April 1861.
651. Pollard, LC, p. 176.
652. Nicolay and Hay, ALAH, Vol. 3, pp. 333-334.
653. Oglesby, p. 34.
654. Thornton and Ekelund, p. xiv.
655. Foner, FSFLFM, p. 62. My paraphrasal.
656. Greeley, WCMC, p. 174.
657. Greeley, WCMC, pp. 73-74. Emphasis added.
658. Bledsoe, pp. 143-144. Emphasis added.
659. Bledsoe, pp. 150-151. Emphasis added.
660. Nicolay and Hay, ALCW, Vol. 2, p. 34.
661. Findlay and Findlay, pp. 84-85; Napolitano, pp. 14-15.
662. Nicolay and Hay, ALCW, Vol. 2, pp. 35-36.

663. As the president, not Congress, had "declared war," it was not an official declaration, and was therefore illegal. See K. L. Hall, s.v. "Lincoln, Abraham"; "Civil War"; W. B. Garrison, CWC, p. 13; W. B. Garrison, CWTFB, p. 254.
664. Nicolay and Hay, ALCW, Vol. 2, p. 35. Emphasis added.
665. Northerners favored a protective tariff because they believed it helped protect Yankee businesses from foreign competition. Weintraub, p. 55. One of the most notorious governmental taxes was the Tariff of Abominations of 1828, which was placed on imported manufactured goods. Proposed by President John Quincy Adams of Massachusetts, he hoped the exorbitantly high duty would secure domestic industry which, at the time, was headquartered in the North. DeGregorio, s.v. "John Quincy Adams" (pp. 99-100). Obviously, Southerners were not happy. Vice President John C. Calhoun of South Carolina—who saw the tax as a direct attack on the South—rightly called the Tariff of Abominations, "unconstitutional, oppressive, and unjust." Tocqueville, Vol. 2, p. 450.
666. J. Davis, RFCG, Vol. 1, pp. 233, 235. Emphasis added.
667. Seabrook, TQJD, p. 80.
668. F. Moore, TRR, Vol. 11, pp. 83, 84. Emphasis added.
669. See Durden, p. 43. My paraphrasal.
670. R. Taylor, p. 238.
671. Boucher, p. 91.
672. Seabrook, AL, pp. 177-178.
673. Farrow, Lang, and Frank, pp. 131-132.
674. Kennedy, pp. 104-105.
675. Seabrook, TCOTCSOAE, p. 65.
676. Stonebraker, p. 81.
677. See Seabrook, EYWTAASIW, passim.
678. Spooner, NT, No. 6, pp. 56-57. Emphasis added.
679. Also see Pollard, LC, p. 154.
680. Pollard, LC, pp. 131-132.
681. Kennedy and Kennedy, SWR, p. 21.
682. Fogel, p. 87.
683. Fogel and Engerman, p. 249.
684. Fogel, pp. 87-88. Sadly, Lincoln's War destroyed much of the South's wealth. As just one example, it took Dixie another 100 years (into the 1960s) to reduce her income gap to the level she had enjoyed in 1860. Fogel, p. 89.
685. Current, TC, s.v. "Plantation."
686. Fogel, p. 436.
687. Fogel, pp. 414-415.
688. Collier and Collier, p. 71.
689. Hacker, p. 593.
690. "American Disunion," Charles Dickens, *All the Year Round*, December 21, 1861, p. 299. Emphasis added.
691. Ashe, p. 24.
692. Nicolay and Hay, ALCW, Vol. 2, p. 63. Emphasis added.
693. Seabrook, LW, p. 82.
694. Seabrook, ALWAL, pp. 85, 98.
695. For a detailed examination of Lincoln's liberal background and politics, see Seabrook, ALWAL, passim; Seabrook, LW, passim; Seabrook, AL, passim; Seabrook, EYWTATCWIW, passim.
696. Fowler, pp. 249-251.
697. Scott, p. 334.
698. Loring, p. iii. Emphasis added.
699. Johnston, Vol. 6, p. 50.
700. F. T. Reid, Vol. 3, p. 516. Emphasis added.
701. Sage, from the front matter.
702. Scott, p. 333. Emphasis added.
703. Scott, p. 333. Emphasis added.

704. Scott, p. 334. Emphasis added.
705. Scott, p. 334. Emphasis added.
706. Scott, pp. 334-335. Emphasis added.
707. Scott, p. 335. Emphasis added.
708. Scott, p. 335. Emphasis added.
709. Sage, p. 43. Emphasis added.
710. Sage, p. 44.
711. Sage, p. 44. Emphasis added.
712. Sage, p. 45. Emphasis added.
713. Sage, p. 45. Emphasis added.
714. Sage, p. 46.
715. Sage, p. 46.
716. Sage, pp. 46-47.
717. Sage, p. 47.
718. Sage, p. 48.
719. Sage, pp. 48-49.
720. Sage, p. 49.
721. Sage, p. 49.
722. Sage, pp. 49-50.
723. Sage, p. 51. Emphasis added.
724. Fowler, p. 217. Emphasis added.
725. Sage, Appendix I, p. 5.
726. Stephens, ACV, Vol. 1, p. 497.
727. Scott, pp. 336, 337. Emphasis added.
728. Fowler, p. 218. Emphasis added.
729. Rawle, p. 289.
730. Fowler, p. 216.
731. Collier and Collier, p. 4.
732. Foley, pp. 212, 797.
733. Hamilton, Madison, and Jay, p. 21.
734. Rawle, pp. 9, 93, 296-297.
735. Fowler, p. 260. Emphasis added.
736. J. Davis, RFCG, Vol. 1, p. 173.
737. Scott, p. 331. Emphasis added.
738. Scott, pp. 331-332. Emphasis added.
739. Fowler, pp. 268-269. Emphasis added.
740. Fowler, p. 219. Emphasis added.
741. Bledsoe, p. 126.
742. J. W. Jones, PRAALOGREL, p. 137.
743. Johnston, Vol. 6, pp. 78-79. Emphasis added.
744. Sage, Appendix I, p. 5. Emphasis added.
745. For the complete text, see Tucker, Vol. 1, pp. 170-187.
746. Stephens, ACV, Vol. 1, pp. 495-510. Emphasis added.
747. Stephens, ACV, Vol. 1, pp. 511-515. Emphasis added.
748. C. Adams, p. 186. After his capture on May 10, 1865, near Irwinville, Georgia, Davis was imprisoned at Fort Monroe, Virginia, for "treason" where, for two long years he was chained, treated inhumanely, and suffered numerous indignities in a cold, dark, damp cell. He became ill on several occasions and nearly lost his life. To the great relief of his family and supporters, President Davis survived the ordeal, and on May 14, 1867, he was "released on bond." This was an intelligent move on the part of the U.S. government, as a trial would have certainly uncovered the unlawfulness of both the North's war on the South and Davis' imprisonment. Sobel, s.v. "Davis, Jefferson." Also hoping to prove that secession was legal, numerous other Confederates demanded that they be tried for "treason" by the U.S. government. All were turned down—for obvious reasons. C. Johnson, p. 201.
749. See my book, *The Great Yankee Coverup*.

750. Stonebraker, p. 75.
751. Sandburg, SOL, pp. 412-414.
752. Seabrook, EYWTATCWIW, pp. 113-114.
753. Sage, p. 448. Emphasis added.
754. Sage, p. v. Emphasis added.
755. Copper, Estill, and Lemmon, pp. 420-421. Emphasis added.
756. W. B. Garrison, CWTAFB, p. 152.
757. R. Miller, p. 336.
758. Stephens, ACV, Vol. 1, p. 504.
759. Fowler, p. 249.
760. Bledsoe, pp. 137, 138-139, 140.
761. Calhoun and Webster, p. 52.
762. Sage, pp. 120, 174.
763. Rogers, p. 13.
764. Rawle, p. 290.
765. Rawle, pp. 289-290.
766. Sage, Appendix I, p. 5.
767. Seabrook, TQJD, p. 51.
768. Rogers, p. 13.
769. Hart and Channing, p. 6; Cooper, Estill, and Lemmon, pp. 342-343.
770. Rogers, pp. 10-11.
771. Dunning, Vol. 3, p. 95.
772. Sage, p. 448. Let us remind ourselves that the U.S.A. is a psephocracy (government by ballot-elected representatives), or more technically, a confederate representative democratic republic. In other words, the U.S.A. is not solely a confederacy, a democracy, a representative democracy, or a republic. It has features of all four, which is what makes our country and our Constitution politically unique.
773. Seabrook, ARB, p. 301.
774. Rhodes, pp. 189-203.
775. E. McPherson, TPHOTUSADTPOR, pp. 254-257. Emphasis added.
776. J. W. Randolph, pp. 189-233. Emphasis added.
777. Cooper, Estill, and Lemmon, pp. 350-354.
778. Cooper, Estill, and Lemmon, p. 341.
779. Cooper, Estill, and Lemmon, pp. 342-343. Emphasis added.
780. Sage, pp. 58-60.

BIBLIOGRAPHY

Note: My pro-South readers are to be advised that the majority of the books listed here are anti-South in nature (some extremely so), and were written primarily by liberal elitist, socialist, communist, and Marxist authors who loathe the South, and typically the United States and the U.S. Constitution as well. Despite this, as a scholar I find these titles indispensable, for *an honest evaluation of Lincoln's War is not possible without studying both the Southern and the Northern versions*—an attitude, unfortunately, completely lacking among pro-North historians (who read and study only their own ahistorical version). Still, it must be said that the material contained in these often mean-spirited works is largely the result of a century and a half of Yankee myth, falsehoods, cherry-picking, slander, sophistry, editorializing, anti-South propaganda, outright lies, and junk research, as modern pro-North writers merely copy one another's errors without ever looking at the original 19th-Century sources. This type of literature, filled as it is with both misinformation and disinformation, is called "scholarly" and "objective" by pro-North advocates. In the process, the mistakes and lies in these fact-free, fault-ridden, South-shaming, historically inaccurate works have been magnified over the years, and the North's version of the "Civil War" has come to be accepted as the only legitimate one. Indeed, it is now the only one known by most people. That over 95 percent of the titles in my bibliography fall into the anti-South category is simply a reflection of the enormous power and influence that the pro-North movement—our nation's cultural ruling class—has long held over America's education system, libraries, publishing houses, and media (paper and electronic). My books serve as a small rampart against the overwhelming tide of anti-South Fascists, Liberals, cultural Marxists, and political elites, all who are working hard to obliterate Southern culture and guarantee that you will never learn the Truth about Lincoln and his War on the Constitution and the American people.

Abbott, John Stevens Cabot. *The Life of General Ulysses S. Grant*. Boston, MA: B. B. Russell, 1868.

Abernathy, Thomas P. *The South in the New Nation, 1789-1819*. Baton Rouge, LA: Louisiana State University Press, 1961.

Adams, Charles. *When in the Course of Human Events: Arguing the Case for Southern Secession*. Lanham, MD: Rowman and Littlefield, 2000.

Adams, Henry (ed.). *Documents Relating to New-England Federalism, 1800-1815*. Boston, MA: Little, Brown, and Co., 1877.

Adams, Nehemiah, Rev. *A South-side View of Slavery: Three Months at the South, in 1854*. Boston, MA: T. R. Marvin, 1855.

Alderman, Edwin Anderson, and Joel Chandler Harris (eds.). *Library of Southern Literature*. 12 vols. 1907. New Orleans, LA: The Martin and Hoyt Co., 1910 ed.

Alexander, William T. *History of the Colored Race in America*. Kansas City, MO: Palmetto Publishing, Co., 1800.

Ames, Herman Vandenberg (ed.). *State Documents on Federal Relations: The States and the United States - No. 6: Slavery and the Union*. Philadelphia, PA: University of Pennsylvania, 1906.

Andrews, Sidney. *The South Since the War: As Shown by Fourteen Weeks of Travel and Observation in Georgia and the Carolinas*. Boston, MA: Ticknor and Fields, 1866.

Ashe, Captain Samuel A'Court. *A Southern View of the Invasion of the Southern States and War of 1861-1865*. 1935. Crawfordville, GA: Ruffin Flag Co., 1938 ed.

Ashworth, John. *Slavery, Capitalism, and Politics in the Antebellum Republic*. 2 vols. New York, NY: Cambridge University Press, 2007.

Astor, Gerald. *The Right to Fight: A History of African Americans in the Military*. Cambridge, MA: Da Capo, 2001.

Barnes, Gilbert H., and Dwight L. Dumond (eds.). *Letters of Theodore Dwight Weld, Angelina Grimké Weld and Sarah Grimké, 1822-1844*. 2 vols. New York, NY: D. Appleton-Century Co., 1934.

Barney, William L. *Flawed Victory: A New Perspective on the Civil War*. New York, NY: Praeger Publishers, 1975.

Barnhardt, Luther Wesley. *The Secession Conventions of the Cotton South*. Madison, WI: University of Wisconsin, 1922.

Barrow, Charles Kelly, J. H. Segars, and R. B. Rosenburg (eds.). *Black Confederates*. 1995. Gretna, LA: Pelican Publishing Co., 2001 ed.

Basler, Roy Prentice (ed.). *Abraham Lincoln: His Speeches and Writings*. 1946. New York, NY: Da Capo Press, 2001 ed.

—— (ed.). *The Collected Works of Abraham Lincoln*. 9 vols. New Brunswick, NJ: Rutgers University Press, 1953.

Bateman, William O. *Political and Constitutional Law of the United States of America*. St. Louis, MO: G. I. Jones and Co., 1876.

Baxter, Maurice G. *Henry Clay and the American System*. Lexington, KY: University Press of Kentucky, 2004.

Beach, Frederick Converse (ed.). *The Encyclopedia Americana: A Universal Reference Library*. 16 vols. New York, NY: Scientific American Compiling Co., 1903-1905.

Beard, Charles A., and Birl E. Schultz. *Documents on the State-Wide Initiative, Referendum and Recall*. New York, NY: Macmillan, 1912.

Beard, Charles A., and Mary R. Beard. *The Rise of American Civilization*. 1927. New York, NY: MacMillan, 1930 ed.

Benson, Al, Jr., and Walter Donald Kennedy. *Lincoln's Marxists*. Gretna, LA: Pelican, 2011.

Benton, Thomas Hart. *Thirty Years View; or A History of the Working of the American Government for Thirty Years, From 1820 to 1850*. 2 vols. New York, NY: D. Appleton and Co., 1854.

Bergh, Albert Ellery (ed.). *The Writings of Thomas Jefferson*. 20 vols. Washington, D.C.: Thomas Jefferson Memorial Association of the U.S., 1905.

Bernhard, Winfred E. A. (ed.). *Political Parties in American History - Vol. 1. 1789-1828*. New York, NY: G. P. Putnams' Sons, 1973.

Berry, Wendell. *The Unsettling of America: Culture and Agriculture*. San Francisco, CA: Sierra Club Books, 1996.

Berwanger, Eugene H. *The Frontier Against Slavery: Western Anti-Negro Prejudice and the Slavery Extension Controversy*. 1967. Urbana, IL: University of Illinois Press, 1971 ed.

Blackerby, Hubert R. *Blacks in Blue and Gray*. New Orleans, LA: Portals Press, 1979.

Blackstone, William. *Commentaries on the Laws of England*. 4 vols. London, UK: T. Cadell, 1794.

Blassingame, John W. *The Slave Community: Plantation Life in the Antebellum South*. 1972. New York, NY: Oxford University Press, 1974 ed.

Bledsoe, Albert Taylor. *Is Davis a Traitor; or Was Secession a Constitutional Right Previous to the War of 1861?* Richmond, VA: The Hermitage Press, 1907.

Bottomore, T. B., and Maximilien Rubel (eds.). *Karl Marx: Selected Writings in Sociology and Social Philosophy*. 1956. New York, NY: McGraw-Hill, 1964 ed.

Boucher, Chauncey Samuel. *South Carolina and the South on the Eve of Secession, 1852 to 1860*. (From *Washington University Studies*, "Humanistic Series," Vol. 6, No. 2.) St. Louis, MO: Washington University, 1919.

Boyd, James P. *Parties, Problems, and Leaders of 1896: An Impartial Presentation of Living National Questions*. Chicago, IL: Publishers' Union, 1896.

Bronowski, Jacob, and Bruce Mazlish. *The Western Intellectual Tradition: From Leonardo to Hegel*. 1960. New York, NY: Harper and Row, 1975 ed.

Browder, Earl. *Lincoln and the Communists*. New York, NY: Workers Library Publishers, Inc., 1936.

Brown, Dee. *Bury My Heart at Wounded Knee: An Indian History of the American West*. 1970. New York, NY: Owl Books, 1991 ed.

Bryan, William Jennings. *The First Battle: A Story of the Campaign of 1896*. Chicago, IL: W. B. Conkey Co., 1896.

Burgess, John William. *The Civil War and the Constitution: 1859-1865*. 2 vols. New York, NY: Charles Scriber's Sons, 1906.

Burns, James MacGregor. *The Vineyard of Liberty*. New York, NY: Alfred A. Knopf, 1982.

Burns, James MacGregor, and Jack Walter Peltason. *Government by the People: The Dynamics of American National, State, and Local Government.* 1952. Englewood Cliffs, NJ: Prentice-Hall, 1964 ed.

Butler, Benjamin Franklin. *Butler's Book (Autobiography and Personal Reminiscences of Major-General Benjamin F. Butler: A Review of His Legal, Political, and Military Career).* Boston, MA: A. M. Thayer and Co., 1892.

Butler, Lindley S., and Alan D. Watson (eds.). *The North Carolina Experience: An Interpretive and Documentary History.* Chapel Hill, NC: University of North Carolina Press, 1984.

Calhoun, John C., and Daniel Webster. *Speeches of John C. Calhoun and Daniel Webster, in the Senate of the United States, on the Enforcing Bill.* Boston, MA: Beals, Homer and Co., 1833.

Calvert, Thomas H. *The Federal Statutes Annotated.* 10 vols. Northport, NY: Edward Thompson, 1905.

Capers, Henry D. *The Life and Times of C. G. Memminger.* Richmond, VA: Everett Waddey, 1893.

Catton, Bruce. *The Coming Fury* (Vol. 1). 1961. New York, NY: Washington Square Press, 1967 ed.

———. *Terrible Swift Sword* (Vol. 2). 1963. New York, NY: Pocket Books, 1967 ed.

———. *A Stillness at Appomattox* (Vol. 3). 1953. New York, NY: Pocket Books, 1966 ed.

Chadwick, French Ensor. *Causes of the Civil War, 1859-1861.* New York, NY: Harper and Brothers, 1906.

Channing, Steven A. *Confederate Ordeal: The Southern Home Front.* 1984. Morristown, NJ: Time-Life Books, 1989 ed.

Chesnut, Mary. *A Diary From Dixie: As Written by Mary Boykin Chesnut, Wife of James Chesnut, Jr., United States Senator from South Carolina, 1859-1861, and afterward an Aide to Jefferson Davis and a Brigadier-General in the Confederate Army.* New York, NY: D. Appleton and Co., 1905 ed.

Cleveland, Henry (ed.). *Alexander H. Stephens in Public and Private; With Letters and Speeches, Before, During, and Since the War.* Philadelphia, PA: National Publishing Co., 1866.

Coleman, Mrs. Chapman. *The Life of John J. Crittenden: With Selections From His Correspondence and Speeches.* 2 vols. Philadelphia, PA: J. B. Lippincott and Co., 1873.

Collier, Christopher, and James Lincoln Collier. *Decision in Philadelphia: The Constitutional Convention of 1787.* 1986. New York, NY: Ballantine, 1987 ed.

Confederate War Journal, Vol. 1, No. 1, April 1893. New York, NY: War Journal Publishing Co., 1893.

Conway, Moncure Daniel. *Testimonies Concerning Slavery.* London, UK: Chapman and Hall, 1865.

Cooke, Alistair. *Alistair Cooke's America.* 1973. New York, NY: Alfred A. Knopf, 1984 ed.

Cooke, John Esten. *A Life of General Robert E. Lee.* New York, NY: D. Appleton and Co., 1871.

Cooley, Henry S. *A Study of Slavery in New Jersey.* Baltimore, MD: Johns Hopkins University Press, 1896.

Cooper, Oscar H., Harry F. Estill, and Leonard Lemmon. *History of Our Country: A Text-Book for Schools* (Texas edition). 1895. Boston, MA: Ginn and Co., 1908 ed.

Cooper, William J., Jr. *Jefferson Davis, American.* New York, NY: Vintage, 2000.

Cornish, Dudley Taylor. *The Sable Arm: Black Troops in the Union Army, 1861-1865.* 1956. Lawrence, KS: University Press of Kansas, 1987 ed.

Countryman, Edward. *The American Revolution.* 1985. New York, NY: Hill and Wang, 1993 ed.

Cummins, Joseph. *Anything For a Vote: Dirty Tricks, Cheap Shots, and October Surprises in U.S. Presidential Campaigns.* Philadelphia, PA: Quirk, 2007.

Current, Richard N. *The Lincoln Nobody Knows.* 1958. New York, NY: Hill and Wang, 1963 ed.

———. (ed.) *The Confederacy (Information Now Encyclopedia).* 1993. New York, NY: Macmillan, 1998 ed.

Curry, Leonard P. *Blueprint for Modern America: Nonmilitary Legislation of the First Civil War Congress.* Nashville, TN: Vanderbilt University Press, 1968.

Curti, Merle, Willard Thorpe, and Carlos Baker (eds.). *American Issues: The Social Record.* 1941. Chicago, IL: J. B. Lippincott, 1960 ed.

Curtin, Philip D. *The Atlantic Slave Trade: A Census.* Madison, WI: The University of Wisconsin Press, 1969.

———. *The Rise and Fall of the Plantation Complex: Essays in Atlantic History.* 1990. Cambridge, UK: Cambridge University Press, 1999 ed.

Curtis, Francis. *The Republican Party: A History of Its Fifty Years' Existence and a Record of Its Measures and Leaders, 1854-1904.* 2 vols. New York, NY: G. P. Putnam's Sons, 1904.

Curtis, George Ticknor. *Life of James Buchanan: Fifteenth President of the United States.* 2 vols. New York, NY: Harper and Brothers, 1883.

———. *Constitutional History of the United States: From Their Declaration of Independence to the Close of Their Civil War.* 2 vols. New York, NY: Harper and Brothers, 1896.
Curtis, William Eleroy. *Abraham Lincoln.* Philadelphia, PA: J. B. Lippincott Co., 1902.
Dabney, Robert Lewis. *A Defense of Virginia and the South.* Dahlonega, GA: Confederate Reprint Co., 1999.
Davis, Jefferson. *The Rise and Fall of the Confederate Government.* 2 vols. New York, NY: D. Appleton and Co., 1881.
Davis, Michael. *The Image of Lincoln in the South.* Knoxville, TN: University of Tennessee Press, 1971.
Davis, Varina. *Jefferson Davis: Ex-President of the Confederate States of America - A Memoir by His Wife.* 2 vols. New York, NY: Belford Co., 1890.
Davis, William C. *An Honorable Defeat: The Last Days of the Confederate Government.* New York, NY: Harcourt, 2001.
Dawson, Sarah Morgan. *A Confederate Girl's Diary.* London, UK: William Heinemann, 1913.
De Angelis, Gina. *It Happened in Washington, D.C.* Guilford, CT: Globe Pequot Press, 2004.
Dean, Henry Clay. *Crimes of the Civil War, and Curse of the Funding System.* Baltimore, MD: William T. Smithson, 1869.
Dean, Vera Micheles. *The Nature of the Non-Western World.* 1957. New York, NY: Mentor, 1962 ed.
De Forest, John William. *A Volunteer's Adventures: A Union Captain's Record of the Civil War.* 1946. North Haven, CT: Archon, 1970 ed.
DeGregorio, William A. *The Complete Book of U.S. Presidents.* 1984. New York, NY: Barricade, 1993 ed.
DiLorenzo, Thomas J. "The Great Centralizer: Abraham Lincoln and the War Between the States." *The Independent Review,* Vol. 3, No. 2, Fall 1998, pp. 243-271.
———. *The Real Lincoln: A New Look at Abraham Lincoln, His Agenda, and an Unnecessary War.* Three Rivers, MI: Three Rivers Press, 2003.
———. *Lincoln Unmasked: What You're Not Supposed to Know About Dishonest Abe.* New York, NY: Crown Forum, 2006.
———. *Hamilton's Curse: How Jefferson's Archenemy Betrayed the American Revolution—and What It Means for America Today.* New York, NY: Crown Forum, 2008.
Denney, Robert E. *The Civil War Years: A Day-by-Day Chronicle of the Life of a Nation.* 1992. New York, NY: Sterling Publishing, 1994 ed.
Denson, John V. (ed.). *Reassessing the Presidency: The Rise of the Executive State and the Decline of Freedom.* Auburn, AL: Mises Institute, 2001.
Doubleday's Encyclopedia. 1931. New York, NY: Doubleday, Doran and Co., 1939 ed.
Douglas, Henry Kyd. *I Rode With Stonewall: The War Experiences of the Youngest Member of Jackson's Staff.* 1940. Chapel Hill, NC: University of North Carolina Press, 1968 ed.
Douglass, Frederick. *Narrative of the Life of Frederick Douglass: An American Slave.* 1845. New York, NY: Signet, 1997 ed.
———. *The Life and Times of Frederick Douglass, From 1817 to 1882.* London, UK: Christian Age Office, 1882.
Dunning, William Archibald. *A History of Political Theories.* 3 vols. New York, NY: Macmillan, 1922.
Durant, Will, and Ariel Durant. *The Age of Reason Begins: A History of European Civilization in the Period of Shakespeare, Bacon, Montaigne, Rembrandt, Galileo, and Descartes, 1558-1648.* New York, NY: Simon and Schuster, 1961.
Durden, Robert F. *The Gray and the Black: The Confederate Debate on Emancipation.* Baton Rouge, LA: Louisiana State University Press, 1972.
Early, Jubal A. *A Memoir of the Last Year of the War for Independence in the Confederate States of America.* Lynchburg, VA: Charles W. Button, 1867.
Encyclopedia Britannica: A New Survey of Universal Knowledge. 1768. Chicago, IL/London, UK: Encyclopedia Britannica, 1955 ed.
Evans, Clement Anselm (ed.). *Confederate Military History.* 12 vols. Atlanta, GA: Confederate Publishing Co., 1899.
Farrow, Anne, Joel Lang, and Jennifer Frank. *Complicity: How the North Promoted, Prolonged, and Profited From Slavery.* New York, NY: Ballantine, 2005.
Faulkner, Harold Underwood. *American Political and Social History.* 1937. New York, NY: Appleton-Century-Crofts, 1948 ed.

Faust, Patricia L. (ed.). *Historical Times Illustrated Encyclopedia of the Civil War*. New York, NY: Harper and Row, 1986.

Fogel, Robert William. *Without Consent or Contract: The Rise and Fall of American Slavery*. New York, NY: W. W. Norton, 1989.

Fogel, Robert William, and Stanley L. Engerman. *Time On the Cross: The Economics of American Negro Slavery*. Boston, MA: Little, Brown, and Co., 1974.

Foley, John P. (ed.). *The Jeffersonian Cyclopedia*. New York, NY: Funk and Wagnalls, 1900.

Foner, Eric. *Free Soil, Free Labor, Free Men: The Ideology of the Republican Party Before the Civil War*. New York, NY: Oxford University Press, 1970.

———. *Reconstruction: America's Unfinished Revolution, 1863-1877*. 1988. New York, NY: Harper and Row, 1989 ed.

Ford, Paul Leicester (ed.). *The Works of Thomas Jefferson*. 12 vols. New York, NY: G. P. Putnam's Sons, 1904.

Ford, Worthington Chauncey (ed.). *A Cycle of Adams Letters*. 2 vols. Boston, MA: Houghton Mifflin, 1920.

Forman, S. E. *The Life and Writings of Thomas Jefferson*. Indianapolis, IN: Bowen-Merrill, 1900.

Fowler, William Chauncey. *The Sectional Controversy; or Passages in the Political History of the United States, Including the Causes of the War Between the Sections*. New York, NY: Charles Scribner, 1864.

Franklin, John Hope. *Reconstruction After the Civil War*. Chicago, IL: University of Chicago Press, 1961.

Garland, Hugh A. *The Life of John Randolph of Roanoke*. New York, NY: D. Appleton and Co., 1874.

Garraty, John A. (ed.). *Historical Viewpoints: Notable Articles From American Heritage - Vol. 1: To 1877*. 1970. New York, NY: Harper and Row, 1979 ed.

Garraty, John A., and Robert A. McCaughey. *A Short History of the American Nation*. 1966. New York, NY: Harper Collins, 1989 ed.

Garrison, Webb B. *Civil War Trivia and Fact Book*. Nashville, TN: Rutledge Hill Press, 1992.

———. *The Lincoln No One Knows: The Mysterious Man Who Ran the Civil War*. Nashville, TN: Rutledge Hill Press, 1993.

———. *Civil War Curiosities: Strange Stories, Oddities, Events, and Coincidences*. Nashville, TN: Rutledge Hill Press, 1994.

———. *The Amazing Civil War*. Nashville, TN: Rutledge Hill Press, 1998.

Goodwyn, Lawrence. *The Populist Movement: A Short History of the Agrarian Revolt in America*. 1976. Oxford, UK: Oxford University Press, 1978 ed.

Gordon, Armistead Churchill. *Figures From American History: Jefferson Davis*. New York, NY: Charles Scribner's Sons, 1918.

Gould, Stephen Jay. *The Mismeasure of Man*. New York, NY: W. W. Norton and Co., 1981.

Gragg, Rod. *The Illustrated Confederate Reader: Extraordinary Eyewitness Accounts by the Civil War's Southern Soldiers and Civilians*. New York, NY: Gramercy Books, 1989.

Graham, John Remington. *A Constitutional History of Secession*. Gretna, LA: Pelican Publishing Co., 2003.

———. *Blood Money: The Civil War and the Federal Reserve*. Gretna, LA: Pelican Publishing Co., 2006.

Greeley, Horace (ed.). *The Writings of Cassius Marcellus Clay*. New York, NY: Harper and Brothers, 1848.

———. *A History of the Struggle for Slavery Extension or Restriction in the United States From the Declaration of Independence to the Present Day*. New York, NY: Dix, Edwards and Co., 1856.

———. *The American Conflict: A History of the Great Rebellion in the United States, 1861-1865*. 2 vols. Hartford, CT: O. D. Case and Co., 1867.

Greenberg, Martin H., and Charles G. Waugh (eds.). *The Price of Freedom: Slavery and the Civil War - Vol. 1: The Demise of Slavery*. Nashville, TN: Cumberland House, 2000.

Greene, Lorenzo Johnston. *The Negro in Colonial New England, 1620-1776*. New York, NY: Columbia University Press, 1942.

Greenhow, Rose O'Neal. *My Imprisonment and the First Year of Abolition Rule at Washington*. London, UK: Richard Bentley, 1863.

Grob, Gerald N., and Robert N. Beck (eds.). 2 vols. *American Ideas: Source Readings in the Intellectual History of the United States*. New York, NY: The Free Press, 1963.

Hacker, Louis Morton. *The Shaping of the American Tradition*. New York, NY: Columbia University Press, 1947.

Hall, Kermit L. (ed.) *The Oxford Companion to the Supreme Court of the United States.* New York, NY: Oxford University Press, 1992.

Hall, Walter Phelps, Robert Greenhalgh Albion, and Jennie Barnes Pope. *A History of England and the Empire-Commonwealth.* 1937. Waltham, MA: Blaisdell, 1965 ed.

Hamer, Philip May. *The Secession Movement in South Carolina, 1847-1852.* Allentown, PA: H. Ray Haas and Co., 1918.

Hamilton, Alexander, James Madison, and John Jay. *The Federalist: A Collection of Essays by Alexander Hamilton, James Madison, and John Jay.* New York, NY: The Co-operative Publication Society, 1901.

Hamilton, John C. (ed.). *The Works of Alexander Hamilton; Comprising His Correspondence, and His Political and Official Writings.* 12 vols. New York, NY: John C. Hamilton, 1850.

Hamilton, Neil A. *Rebels and Renegades: A Chronology of Social and Political Dissent in the United States.* New York, NY: Routledge, 2002.

Handlin, Oscar (ed.). *Readings in American History - Vol. 1: From Settlement to Reconstruction.* 1957. New York, NY: Alfred A. Knopf, 1970 ed.

Hart, Albert Bushnell, and Edward Channing (eds.). *Ordinances of Secession and Other Documents* (from *American Historical Leaflets: Colonial and Constitutional*, No. 12, November 1893). New York, NY: A. Lovell and Co., 1893.

Hartzell, Josiah. *The Genesis of the Republican Party.* Canton, OH: n.p., 1890.

Harwell, Richard B. (ed.). *The Confederate Reader: How the South Saw the War.* 1957. Mineola, NY: Dover, 1989 ed.

Helper, Hinton Rowan. *The Impending Crisis of the South: How to Meet It.* New York, NY: A. B. Burdick, 1860.

Hendelson, William H. (ed.) *Funk and Wagnalls New Encyclopedia.* New York, NY: Funk and Wagnalls, 1973 ed.

Henderson, George Francis Robert. *Stonewall Jackson and the American Civil War.* 2 vols. London, UK: Longmans, Green, and Co., 1919.

Henry, Robert Selph (ed.). *The Story of the Confederacy.* 1931. New York, NY: Konecky and Konecky, 1999 ed.

Hildreth, Richard. *The White Slave: Another Picture of Slave Life in America.* Boston, MA: Adamant Media Corp., 2001.

Hill, Kenneth L. *An Essential Guide to American Politics and the American Political System.* Bloomington, IN: Author House, 2012.

Hillquit, Morris. *History of Socialism in the United States.* 1903. New York, NY: Funk and Wagnalls, 1910 ed.

——. *Socialism in Theory and Practice.* New York, NY: Macmillan, 1909.

Hillquit, Morris, and John A. Ryan. *Socialism: Promise or Menace?* New York, NY: Macmillan, 1914.

Hoffman, Michael A., II. *They Were White and They Were Slaves: The Untold History of the Enslavement of Whites in Early America.* Dresden, NY: Wiswell Ruffin House, 1993.

Hofstadter, Richard. *The American Political Tradition, and the Men Who Made It.* New York, NY: Alfred A. Knopf, 1948.

——. (ed.) *Great Issues in American History: From Reconstruction to the Present Day, 1864-1969.* 1958. New York, NY: Vintage, 1969 ed.

Holland, Jesse J. *Black Men Built the Capitol: Discovering African-American History in and Around Washington, D.C.* Guilford, CT: The Globe Pequot Press, 2007.

Holland, Josiah Gilbert. *The Life of Abraham Lincoln.* Springfield, MA: Gurdon Bill, 1866.

Holland, Rupert Sargent (ed.). *Letters and Diary of Laura M. Towne: Written From the Sea Islands of South Carolina, 1862-1884.* Cambridge, MA: Riverside Press, 1912.

Holzer, Harold (ed.). *The Lincoln-Douglas Debates: The First Complete, Unexpurgated Text.* 1993. Bronx, NY: Fordham University Press, 2004 ed.

Index to Reports of Committees of the House of Representatives for the Second Session of the Forty-Third Congress, 1874-1875. Washington, D.C.: Government Printing Office, 1875.

Jensen, Merrill. *The New Nation: A History of the United States During the Confederation, 1781-1789.* New York, NY: Vintage, 1950.

——. *The Articles of Confederation: An Interpretation of the Social-Constitutional History of the American*

Revolution, 1774-1781. Madison, WI: University of Wisconsin Press, 1959.

Johannsen, Robert Walter. *Lincoln, the South, and Slavery: The Political Dimension*. Baton Rouge, LA: Louisiana State University Press, 1991.

Johnson, Clint. *The Politically Incorrect Guide to the South (and Why It Will Rise Again)*. Washington, D.C.: Regnery, 2006.

Johnson, Ludwell H. *North Against South: The American Iliad, 1848-1877*. 1978. Columbia, SC: Foundation for American Education, 1993 ed.

Johnson, Michael, and James L. Roark. *Black Masters: A Free Family of Color in the Old South*. New York, NY: W.W. Norton, 1984.

Johnson, Oliver. *William Lloyd Garrison and His Times*. 1879. Boston, MA: Houghton Mifflin and Co., 1881 ed.

Johnston, Alexander (ed.). *Representative American Orations to Illustrate American Political History*. 8 vols. London, UK: T. Fisher Unwin, 1885.

Johnstone, Huger William. *Truth of War Conspiracy, 1861*. Idylwild, GA: H. W. Johnstone, 1921.

Jones, John William. *Personal Reminiscences, Anecdotes, and Letters of Gen. Robert E. Lee*. New York, NY: D. Appleton and Co., 1875.

———. *The Davis Memorial Volume; Or Our Dead President, Jefferson Davis and the World's Tribute to His Memory*. Richmond, VA: B. F. Johnson, 1889.

Journal of the Convention of the People of South Carolina, Held in 1860, 1861, and 1862, Together With the Ordinances, Reports, Resolutions, etc. Columbia, SC: The South Carolina Convention, 1862.

Kaplan, Justin. *Walt Whitman: A Life*. New York, NY: Simon and Schuster, 1980.

Kennedy, James Ronald, and Walter Donald Kennedy. *The South Was Right!* Gretna, LA: Pelican Publishing Co., 1994.

Kennedy, Walter Donald. *Myths of American Slavery*. Gretna, LA: Pelican Publishing Co., 2003.

Kettell, Thomas Prentice. *History of the Great Rebellion*. Hartford, CT: L. Stebbins, 1865.

Kinder, Hermann, and Werner Hilgemann. *The Anchor Atlas of World History: From the French Revolution to the American Bicentennial*. 2 vols. Garden City, NY: Anchor, 1978.

King, Charles R. (ed.). *The Life and Correspondence of Rufus King*. 6 vols. New York, NY: G. P. Putnam's Sons, 1897.

King, Edward. *The Great South: A Record of Journeys*. Hartford, CT: American Publishing Co., 1875.

Lancaster, Bruce, and J. H. Plumb. *The American Heritage Book of the Revolution*. 1958. New York, NY: Dell, 1975 ed.

Lapsley, Arthur Brooks (ed.). *The Writings of Abraham Lincoln*. 8 vols. New York, NY: The Lamb Publishing Co., 1906.

Lau, Theodora. *The Handbook of Chinese Horoscopes*. 1979. New York, NY: Harper and Row, 1988 ed.

Lincoln, Abraham. *The Autobiography of Abraham Lincoln* (selected from the *Complete Works of Abraham Lincoln*, 1894, by John G. Nicolay and John Hay). New York, NY: Francis D. Tandy Co., 1905.

Lincoln, Abraham, and Stephen A. Douglas. *Political Debates Between Abraham Lincoln and Stephen A. Douglas*. Cleveland, OH: Burrows Brothers Co., 1894.

Lind, Michael (ed.). *Hamilton's Republic: Readings in the American Democratic Nationalist Tradition*. New York, NY: Free Press, 1997.

Logan, John Alexander. *The Great Conspiracy: Its Origin and History*. New York, NY: A. R. Hart and Co., 1886.

Loring, Caleb William. *Nullification, Secession, Webster's Argument, and the Kentucky and Virginia Resolutions Considered in Reference to the Constitution and Historically*. New York, NY: G.P. Putnam's Sons, 1893.

Lossing, Benson John. *A Common-School History of the United States: From the Earliest Period to the Present Time*. New York, NY: Sheldon and Co., 1870.

Lott, Stanley K. *The Truth About American Slavery*. 2004. Clearwater, SC: Eastern Digital Resources, 2005 ed.

Lowry, Don. *Dark and Cruel War: The Decisive Months of the Civil War, September-December 1864*. New York, NY: Hippocrene, 1993.

Machan, Tibor R. (ed.). *The Libertarian Reader*. Totowa, NJ: Rowman and Littlefield, 1982.

Mackay, Alexander. *The Western World; or, Travels in the United States in 1846-47*. 3 vols. London, UK: Richard Bentley, 1850.

Macy, Jesse. *Political Parties in the United States, 1846-1861*. London, UK: Macmillan 1900.
Madison, James. *Letters and Other Writings of James Madison, Fourth President of the United States*. 4 vols. Philadelphia, PA: J. B. Lippincott and Co., 1865.
Magliocca, Gerard N. *The Tragedy of William Jennings Bryan: Constitutional Law and the Politics of Backlash*. New Haven, CT: Yale University Press, 2011.
Mann, Mary Tyler Peabody. *Life of Horace Mann*. Boston, MA: Walker, Fuller, and Co., 1865.
Martin, Michael, and Leonard Gelber. *Dictionary of American History*. Lanham, MD: Rowman and Littlefield, 1978.
McCarty, Burke (ed.). *Little Sermons in Socialism by Abraham Lincoln*. Chicago, IL: The Chicago Daily Socialist, 1910.
McElroy, Robert. *Jefferson Davis: The Unreal and the Real*. 1937. New York, NY: Smithmark, 1995 ed.
McGehee, Jacob Owen. *Causes That Led to the War Between the States*. Atlanta, GA: A. B. Caldwell, 1915.
McGuire, Hunter, and George L. Christian. *The Confederate Cause and Conduct in the War Between the States*. Richmond, VA: L. H. Jenkins, 1907.
McHenry, George. *The Cotton Trade: Its Bearing Upon the Prosperity of Great Britain and Commerce of the American Republics, Considered in Connection with the System of Negro Slavery in the Confederate States*. London, UK: Saunders, Otley, and Co., 1863.
McIlwaine, Shields. *Memphis Down in Dixie*. New York, NY: E. P. Dutton, 1848.
McKay, John P., Bennett D. Hill, and John Buckler. *A History of Western Society - Vol. 1: From Antiquity to the Enlightenment*. Boston, MA: Houghton Mifflin, 1987.
——. *A History of Western Society - Vol. 2: Since 1500*. Boston, MA: Houghton Mifflin, 1988.
McKissack, Patricia C., and Frederick McKissack. *Sojourner Truth: Ain't I a Woman?* New York: NY: Scholastic, 1992.
McManus, Edgar J. *A History of Negro Slavery in New York*. Syracuse, NY: Syracuse University Press, 1966.
——. *Black Bondage in the North*. Syracuse, NY: Syracuse University Press, 1973.
McPherson, Edward. *The Political History of the United States of America, During the Great Rebellion (From November 6, 1860, to July 4, 1864)*. Washington, D.C.: Philp and Solomons, 1865.
——. *The Political History of the United States of America, During the Period of Reconstruction, (From April 15, 1865, to July 15, 1870,) Including a Classified Summary of the Legislation of the Thirty-ninth, Fortieth, and Forty-first Congresses*. Washington, D.C.: Philp and Solomons, 1871.
McPherson, James M. *Abraham Lincoln and the Second American Revolution*. New York, NY: Oxford University Press, 1991.
——. *Battle Cry of Freedom: The Civil War Era*. Oxford, UK: Oxford University Press, 2003.
McWhiney, Grady, and Perry D. Jamieson. *Attack and Die: Civil War Military Tactics and the Southern Heritage*. Tuscaloosa, AL: University of Alabama Press, 1982.
Melish, Joanne Pope. *Disowning Slavery: Gradual Emancipation and 'Race' in New England 1780-1860*. Ithaca, NY: Cornell University Press, 1998.
Meltzer, Milton. *Slavery: A World History*. 2 vols. in 1. 1971. New York, NY: Da Capo Press, 1993 ed.
Meriwether, Elizabeth Avery (pseudonym, "George Edmonds"). *Facts and Falsehoods Concerning the War on the South, 1861-1865*. Memphis, TN: A. R. Taylor and Co., 1904.
Miller, Francis Trevelyan. *Portrait Life of Lincoln*. Springfield, MA: Patriot Publishing Co., 1910.
Miller, John Chester. *The Wolf By the Ears: Thomas Jefferson and Slavery*. 1977. Charlottesville, VA: University Press of Virginia, 1994 ed.
Miller, Marion Mills (ed.). *Great Debates in American History*. 14 vols. New York, NY: Current Literature, 1913.
Miller, Nathan. *Star-Spangled Men: America's Ten Worst Presidents*. New York, NY: Touchstone, 1998.
Miller, Russell. *The Adventures of Arthur Conan Doyle: A Biography*. New York, NY: Thomas Dunne Books, 2008.
Min, Pyong Gap (ed.). *Encyclopedia of Racism in the United States*. 3 vols. Westport, CT: Greenwood Press, 2005.
Minor, Charles Landon Carter. *The Real Lincoln: From the Testimony of His Contemporaries*. Richmond, VA: Everett Waddey Co., 1904.
Minutes of the Eighth Annual Meeting and Reunion of the United Confederate Veterans, Atlanta, GA, July 20-23, 1898. New Orleans, LA: United Confederate Veterans, 1907.

Minutes of the Ninth Annual Meeting and Reunion of the United Confederate Veterans, Charleston, SC, May 10-13, 1899. New Orleans, LA: United Confederate Veterans, 1907.

Minutes of the Twelfth Annual Meeting and Reunion of the United Confederate Veterans, Dallas, TX, April 22-25, 1902. New Orleans, LA: United Confederate Veterans, 1907.

Mirabello, Mark. *Handbook for Rebels and Outlaws*. Oxford, UK: Mandrake of Oxford, 2009.

Mish, Frederick C. (ed.). *Webster's Ninth New Collegiate Dictionary*. 1984. Springfield, MA: Merriam-Webster.

Moore, Frank. *American Eloquence: A Collection of Speeches and Addresses, by the Most Eminent Orators of America*. 2 vols. New York, NY: D. Appleton and Co., 1858.

———. (ed.). *The Rebellion Record: A Diary of American Events*. 12 vols. New York, NY: G. P. Putnam, 1861.

Moore, George Henry. *Notes on the History of Slavery in Massachusetts*. New York, NY: D. Appleton and Co., 1866.

Moore, John Henry. *A Study in States Rights*. New York, NY: Neale Publishing Co., 1911.

Morgan, Edmund S. *The Birth of the Republic, 1763-1789*. 1956. Chicago, IL: University of Chicago Press, 1967 ed.

Morris, Thomas D. *Free Men All: The Personal Liberty Laws of the North, 1780-1861*. Baltimore, MD: Johns Hopkins University Press, 1974.

Munford, Beverley Bland. *Virginia's Attitude Toward Slavery and Secession*. Richmond, VA: self-published, 1909.

Muzzey, David Saville. *The United States of America: Vol. 1, To the Civil War*. Boston, MA: Ginn and Co., 1922.

———. *The American Adventure: Vol. 2, From the Civil War*. 1924. New York, NY: Harper and Brothers, 1927 ed.

Napolitano, Andrew P. *The Constitution in Exile: How the Federal Government has Seized Power by Rewriting the Supreme Law of the Land*. Nashville, TN: Nelson Current, 2006.

Nicolay, John G., and John Hay (eds.). *Abraham Lincoln: A History*. 10 vols. New York, NY: The Century Co., 1890.

———. *Complete Works of Abraham Lincoln*. 12 vols. 1894. New York, NY: Francis D. Tandy Co., 1905 ed.

———. *Abraham Lincoln: Complete Works*. 12 vols. 1894. New York, NY: The Century Co., 1907 ed.

O'Brien, Cormac. *Secret Lives of the U.S. Presidents: What Your Teachers Never Told You About the Men of the White House*. Philadelphia, PA: Quirk, 2004.

———. *Secret Lives of the Civil War: What Your Teachers Never Told You About the War Between the States*. Philadelphia, PA: Quirk, 2007.

Oglesby, Thaddeus K. *Some Truths of History: A Vindication of the South Against the Encyclopedia Britannica and Other Maligners*. Atlanta, GA: Byrd Printing, 1903.

Oliver, Edmund Henry. *Roman Economic Conditions to the Close of the Republic*. Toronto, CAN: University of Toronto Library, 1907.

Olmsted, Frederick Law. *A Journey in the Seaboard Slave States, With Remarks on Their Economy*. New York, NY: Dix and Edwards, 1856.

———. *A Journey Through Texas; or a Saddle-Trip on the Western Frontier*. New York, NY: Dix and Edwards, 1857.

———. *A Journey in the Back Country*. New York, NY: Mason Brothers, 1860.

———. *The Cotton Kingdom: A Traveler's Observations on Cotton and Slavery in the American Slave States*. 2 vols. London, UK: Sampson Low, Son, and Co., 1862.

ORA (full title: *The War of the Rebellion: A Compilation of the Official Records of the Union and Confederate Armies*). 70 vols. Washington, DC: Government Printing Office, 1880.

ORN (full title: *Official Records of the Union and Confederate Navies in the War of the Rebellion*). 30 vols. Washington, DC: Government Printing Office, 1894.

Owsley, Frank Lawrence. *King Cotton Diplomacy: Foreign Relations of the Confederate States of America*. 1931. Chicago, IL: University of Chicago Press, 1959 ed.

Oxford English Dictionary. 1928. Oxford, UK: Oxford University Press, 1979 ed.

Perman, Michael. *Pursuit of Unity: A Political History of the American South*. Chapel Hill, NC: University of North Carolina Press, 2009.

Pickett, George E. *The Heart of a Soldier: As Revealed in the Intimate Letters of General George E. Pickett, CSA*. 1908. New York, NY: Seth Moyle, 1913 ed.
Pickett, William Passmore. *The Negro Problem: Abraham Lincoln's Solution*. New York, NY: G. P. Putnam's Sons, 1909.
Pierson, William Whatley. *Texas Versus White: A Study in Legal History*. Durham, NC: self-published, 1916.
Pike, James Shepherd. *The Prostrate State: South Carolina Under Negro Government*. New York, NY: D. Appleton and Co., 1874.
Pollard, Edward Alfred. *Echoes From the South: Comprising the Most Important Speeches, Proclamations, and Public Acts Emanating From the South During the Late War*. New York, NY: E. B. Treat, 1866.
——. *Southern History of the War*. 2 vols. in 1. New York, NY: Charles B. Richardson, 1866.
——. *The Lost Cause*. 1867. Chicago, IL: E. B. Treat, 1890 ed.
——. *The Lost Cause Regained*. New York, NY: E. B. Treat and Co., 1867.
——. *Life of Jefferson Davis, With a Secret History of the Southern Confederacy, Gathered "Behind the Scenes in Richmond."* Philadelphia, PA: National Publishing Co., 1869.
Potter, David M. *The Impending Crisis: 1848-1861*. New York, NY: Harper and Row, 1976.
Powell, Edward Payson. *Nullification and Secession in the United States: A History of the Six Attempts During the First Century of the Republic*. New York, NY: G. P. Putnam's Sons, 1897.
Powell, William S. *North Carolina: A History*. 1977. Chapel Hill, NC: University of North Carolina Press, 1988 ed.
Quincy, Josiah. *Memoir of the Life of John Quincy Adams*. Boston, MA: Crosby, Nichols, Lee and Co., 1860.
Randall, James Garfield. *Lincoln: The Liberal Statesman*. New York, NY: Dodd, Mead and Co., 1947.
Randolph, J. W. *The Virginia Report of 1799-1800, Touching the Alien and Sedition Laws; Together With the Virginia Resolutions of December 21, 1798, the Debate and Proceedings Thereon in the House of Delegates of Virginia, and Several Other Documents Illustrative of the Report and Resolutions*. Richmond, VA: self-published, 1850.
Randolph, Thomas Jefferson (ed.). *Memoir, Correspondence, and Miscellanies, from the Papers of Thomas Jefferson*. 4 vols. Charlottesville, VA: F. Carr and Co., 1829.
Raum, Green Berry. *History of Illinois Republicanism: Embracing a History of the Republican Party in the State to the Present Time*. Chicago, IL: Rollins Publishing Co., 1900.
Rawle, William. *A View of the Constitution of the United States of America*. Philadelphia, PA: H. C. Carey and I. Lea, 1825.
Rayner, B. L. *Sketches of the Life, Writings, and Opinions of Thomas Jefferson*. New York, NY: A. Francis and W. Boardman, 1832.
Reid, Frank T. (ed.). *The Southern Law Review, and Chart of the Southern Law Review Union* (Vol. 3, No. 1, January 1874). Nashville, TN: Frank T. Reid and Co., 1874.
Reid, Richard M. *Freedom for Themselves: North Carolina's Black Soldiers in the Era of the Civil War*. Chapel Hill, NC: University of North Carolina Press, 2008.
Reid, Whitelaw. *After the War: A Southern Tour - May 1, 1865, to May 1, 1866*. Cincinnati, OH: Moore, Wilstach and Baldwin, 1866.
Remsburg, John B. *Abraham Lincoln: Was He a Christian?* New York, NY: The Truth Seeker Co., 1893.
Reports of Committees of the Senate of the United States (for the Thirty-eighth Congress). Washington, D.C.: Government Printing Office, 1864.
Report of the Joint Committee on Reconstruction (at the First Session, Thirty-ninth Congress). Washington, D.C.: Government Printing Office, 1866.
Reports of Committees of the Senate of the United States (for the Second Session of the Forty-second Congress). Washington, D.C.: Government Printing Office, 1872.
Report of the Joint Select Committee to Inquire into the Condition of Affairs in the Late Insurrectionary States. Washington, D.C.: Government Printing Office, 1872.
Reuter, Edward Byron. *The Mulatto in the United States*. Boston, MA: Gorham Press, 1918.
Rhodes, James Ford. *History of the United States from the Compromise of 1850 to the Final Restoration of Home Rule at the South in 1877*. 7 vols. 1895. New York, NY: Macmillan Co., 1907 ed.
Rogers, William P. *The Three Secession Movements in the United States: Samuel J. Tilden, the Democratic*

Candidate for Presidency; the Advisor, Aider and Abettor of the Great Secession Movement of 1860; and One of the Authors of the Infamous Resolution of 1864; His Claims as a Statesman and Reformer Considered. Boston, MA: John Wilson and Son, 1876.

Rosenbaum, Robert A. (ed). *The New American Desk Encyclopedia.* 1977. New York, NY: Signet, 1989 ed.

Rosenbaum, Robert A., and Douglas Brinkley (eds.). *The Penguin Encyclopedia of American History.* New York, NY: Viking, 2003.

Rouse, Adelaide Louise (ed.). *National Documents: State Papers So Arranged as to Illustrate the Growth of Our Country From 1606 to the Present Day.* New York, NY: Unit Book Publishing Co., 1906.

Rove, Karl. *The Triumph of William McKinley: Why the Election of 1896 Still Matters.* New York, NY: Simon and Schuster, 2015.

Rowland, Dunbar (ed.). *Jefferson Davis, Constitutionalist: His Letters, Papers, and Speeches.* 10 vols. Jackson, MS: Mississippi Department of Archives and History, 1923.

Rozwenc, Edwin Charles (ed.). *The Causes of the American Civil War.* 1961. Lexington, MA: D. C. Heath and Co., 1972 ed.

Rubenzer, Steven J., and Thomas R. Faschingbauer. *Personality, Character, and Leadership in the White House: Psychologists Assess the Presidents.* Dulles, VA: Brassey's, 2004.

Ruffin, Edmund. *The Diary of Edmund Ruffin: Toward Independence: October 1856-April 1861.* Baton Rouge, LA: Louisiana State University Press, 1972.

Rutherford, Mildred Lewis. *Four Addresses.* Birmingham, AL: The Mildred Rutherford Historical Circle, 1916.

——. *A True Estimate of Abraham Lincoln and Vindication of the South.* N.p., n.d.

——. *Truths of History: A Historical Perspective of the Civil War From the Southern Viewpoint.* Confederate Reprint Co., 1920.

——. *The South Must Have Her Rightful Place In History.* Athens, GA, 1923.

Rutland, Robert Allen. *The Birth of the Bill of Rights, 1776-1791.* 1955. Boston, MA: Northeastern University Press, 1991 ed.

Sachsman, David B., S. Kittrell Rushing, and Roy Morris, Jr. (eds.). *Words at War: The Civil War and American Journalism.* West Lafayette, IN: Purdue University Press, 2008.

Sage, Bernard Janin. *The Republic of Republics: A Retrospect of our Century of Federal Liberty.* Philadelphia, PA: self-published, 1878.

Salley, Alexander Samuel, Jr. *South Carolina Troops in Confederate Service.* 2 vols. Columbia, SC: R. L. Bryan, 1913 and 1914.

Samuel, Bunford. *Secession and Constitutional Liberty: In Which is Shown the Right of a Nation to Secede From a Compact of Federation and That Such Right is Necessary to Constitutional Liberty and a Surety of Union.* 2 vols. New York, NY: Neale Publishing, 1920.

Sandburg, Carl. *Abraham Lincoln: The War Years.* 4 vols. New York, NY: Harcourt, Brace and World, 1939.

——. *Storm Over the Land: A Profile of the Civil War.* 1939. Old Saybrook, CT: Konecky and Konecky, 1942 ed.

Sargent, F. W. *England, the United States, and the Southern Confederacy.* London, UK: Sampson Low, Son, and Co., 1863.

Scharf, John Thomas. *History of the Confederate Navy, From Its Organization to the Surrender of Its Last Vessel.* Albany, NY: Joseph McDonough, 1894.

Scott, James Brown. *The United States of America: A Study in International Organization.* New York, NY: Oxford University Press, 1920.

Seabrook, Lochlainn. *Abraham Lincoln: The Southern View.* 2007. Franklin, TN: Sea Raven Press, 2013 ed.

——. *A Rebel Born: A Defense of Nathan Bedford Forrest.* 2010. Franklin, TN: Sea Raven Press, 2011 ed.

——. *Everything You Were Taught About the Civil War is Wrong, Ask a Southerner!* 2010. Franklin, TN: Sea Raven Press, revised 2014 ed.

——. *The Quotable Jefferson Davis: Selections From the Writings and Speeches of the Confederacy's First President.* Franklin, TN: Sea Raven Press, 2011.

——. *The Quotable Robert E. Lee: Selections From the Writings and Speeches of the South's Most Beloved Civil War*

General. Franklin, TN: Sea Raven Press, 2011 Sesquicentennial Civil War Edition.
——. *Lincolnology: The Real Abraham Lincoln Revealed In His Own Words*. Franklin, TN: Sea Raven Press, 2011.
——. *The Unquotable Abraham Lincoln: The President's Quotes They Don't Want You To Know!* Franklin, TN: Sea Raven Press, 2011.
——. *The Constitution of the Confederate States of America Explained: A Clause-by-Clause Study of the South's Magna Carta*. Spring Hill, TN: Sea Raven Press, 2012 Sesquicentennial Civil War Edition.
——. *The Great Impersonator: 99 Reasons to Dislike Abraham Lincoln*. Spring Hill, TN: Sea Raven Press, 2012.
——. *The Old Rebel: Robert E. Lee As He Was Seen By His Contemporaries*. Spring Hill, TN: Sea Raven Press, 2012 Sesquicentennial Civil War Edition.
——. *The Quotable Stonewall Jackson: Selections From the Writings and Speeches of the South's Most Famous General*. Spring Hill, TN: Sea Raven Press, 2012 Sesquicentennial Civil War Edition.
——. *The Alexander H. Stephens Reader: Excerpts From the Works of a Confederate Founding Father*. Spring Hill, TN: Sea Raven Press, 2013.
——. *The Quotable Alexander H. Stephens: Selections From the Writings and Speeches of the Confederacy's First Vice President*. Spring Hill, TN: Sea Raven Press, 2013 Sesquicentennial Civil War Edition.
——. *Give This Book to a Yankee! A Southern Guide to the Civil War for Northerners*. Spring Hill, TN: Sea Raven Press, 2014.
——. *Everything You Were Taught About American Slavery War is Wrong, Ask a Southerner!* Spring Hill, TN: Sea Raven Press, 2015.
——. *Confederacy 101: Amazing Facts You Never Knew About America's Oldest Political Tradition*. Spring Hill, TN: Sea Raven Press, 2015.
——. *The Great Yankee Coverup: What the North Doesn't Want You to Know About Lincoln's War!* Spring Hill, TN: Sea Raven Press, 2015.
——. *Slavery 101: Amazing Facts You Never Knew About America's "Peculiar Institution."* Spring Hill, TN: Sea Raven Press, 2015.
——. *Confederate Flag Facts: What Every American Should Know About Dixie's Southern Cross*. Spring Hill, TN: Sea Raven Press, 2016.
——. *Nathan Bedford Forrest and the Ku Klux Klan: Yankee Myth, Confederate Fact*. Spring Hill, TN: Sea Raven Press, 2016.
——. *Everything You Were Taught About African-Americans and the Civil War is Wrong, Ask a Southerner!* Spring Hill, TN: Sea Raven Press, 2016.
——. *Nathan Bedford Forrest and the Ku Klux Klan: Yankee Myth, Confederate Fact*. Spring Hill, TN: Sea Raven Press, 2016.
——. *Lincoln's War: The Real Cause, the Real Winner, the Real Loser*. Spring Hill, TN: Sea Raven Press, 2016.
——. *The Unholy Crusade: Lincoln's Legacy of Destruction in the American South*. Spring Hill, TN: Sea Raven Press, 2017.
——. *Abraham Lincoln Was a Liberal, Jefferson Davis Was a Conservative: The Missing Key to Understanding the American Civil War*. Spring Hill, TN: Sea Raven Press, 2017.
——. *The Ultimate Civil War Quiz Book: Test Your Knowledge of America's Most Misunderstood Conflict*. Spring Hill, TN: Sea Raven Press, 2017.
Shenkman, Richard. *Legends, Lies and Cherished Myths of American History*. New York, NY: Perennial, 1988.
Shenkman, Richard, and Kurt Edward Reiger. *One-Night Stands with American History: Odd, Amusing, and Little-Known Incidents*. 1980. New York, NY: Perennial, 2003 ed.
Simpson, Lewis P. (ed.). *I'll Take My Stand: The South and the Agrarian Tradition*. 1930. Baton Rouge, LA: University of Louisiana Press, 1977 ed.
Sinkler, George. *The Racial Attitudes of American Presidents from Abraham Lincoln to Theodore Roosevelt*. New York, NY: Doubleday, 1972.
Smelser, Marshall. *American Colonial and Revolutionary History*. 1950. New York, NY: Barnes and Noble, 1966 ed.
——. *The Democratic Republic, 1801-1815*. New York, NY: Harper and Row, 1968.
Smith, Emma Peters, David Saville Muzzey, and Minnie Lloyd. *World History: The Struggle for Civilization*. Boston, MA: Ginn and Co., 1946.

Sobel, Robert (ed.). *Biographical Directory of the United States Executive Branch, 1774-1898*. Westport, CT: Greenwood Press, 1990.

Sorrel, Gilbert Moxley. *Recollections of a Confederate Staff Officer*. New York, NY: Neale Publishing Co., 1905.

South Carolina Convention. *Declaration of the Immediate Causes Which Induce and Justify the Secession of South Carolina From the Federal Union; and the Ordinance of Secession*. Charleston, SC: self-published, 1860.

Spaeth, Harold J., and Edward Conrad Smith. *The Constitution of the United States*. 1936. New York, NY: HarperCollins, 1991 ed.

Sparks, Jared (ed.). *The Works of Benjamin Franklin*. 10 vols. Chicago, IL: Townsend Mac Coun, 1882.

Speer, Albert. *Inside the Third Reich*. 1969. New York, NY: Avon, 1971 ed.

Spence, James. *On the Recognition of the Southern Confederation*. Ithaca, NY: Cornell University Library, 1862.

Spooner, Lysander. *No Treason* (only Numbers 1, 2, and 6 were published). Boston, MA: Lysander Spooner, 1867-1870.

Stedman, Edmund Clarence, and Ellen Mackay Hutchinson (eds.). *A Library of American Literature: From the Earliest Settlement to the Present Time*. 10 vols. New York, NY: Charles L. Webster and Co., 1888.

Steel, Samuel Augustus. *The South Was Right*. Columbia, SC: R. L. Bryan Co., 1914.

Stephens, Alexander Hamilton. *Speech of Mr. Stephens, of Georgia, on the War and Taxation*. Washington, D.C.: J and G. Gideon, 1848.

———. *Recollections of Alexander H. Stephens: His Diary Kept When a Prisoner at Fort Warren, Boston Harbour, 1865*. New York, NY: Doubleday, Page, and Co., 1910.

———. *A Constitutional View of the Late War Between the States; Its Causes, Character, Conduct and Results*. 2 vols. Philadelphia, PA: National Publishing, Co., 1868.

Stern, Philip Van Doren (ed.). *The Life and Writings of Abraham Lincoln*. 1940. New York, NY: Modern Library, 2000 ed.

Stonebraker, J. Clarence. *The Unwritten South: Cause, Progress and Results of the Civil War - Relics of Hidden Truth After Forty Years*. Seventh ed., n.p., 1908.

Story, Joseph. *Commentaries on the Constitution of the United States*. 3 vols. Boston, MA: Hilliard, Gray, and Co., 1833.

Stovall, Pleasant A. *Robert A. Toombs: Statesman, Speaker, Soldier, Sage*. New York, NY: Cassell Publishing Co., 1892.

Stowe, Harriet Beecher. *Uncle Tom's Cabin: A Tale of Life Among the Lowly*. London, UK: George Routledge and Co., 1852.

Taylor, Richard. *Destruction and Reconstruction: Personal Experiences of the Late War in the United States*. New York, NY: D. Appleton, 1879.

Taylor, Susie King. *Reminiscences of My Life in Camp With the 33rd United States Colored Troops Late 1st S. C. Volunteers*. Boston, MA: Susie King Taylor, 1902.

Taylor, Walter Herron. *General Lee: His Campaigns in Virginia, 1861-1865, With Personal Reminiscences*. Norfolk, VA: Nusbaum Book and News Co., 1906.

Tenney, William Jewett. *The Military and Naval History of the Rebellion in the United States*. New York, NY: D. Appleton and Co., 1865.

Thatcher, Marshall P. *A Hundred Battles in the West: St. Louis to Atlanta, 1861-1865*. Detroit, MI: Marshall P. Thatcher, 1884.

The American Annual Cyclopedia and Register of Important Events of the Year 1861. New York, NY: D. Appleton and Co., 1868.

The American Annual Cyclopedia and Register of Important Events of the Year 1862. New York, NY: D. Appleton and Co., 1869.

The American Annual Cyclopedia and Register of Important Events of the Year 1863. New York, NY: D. Appleton and Co., 1864.

The Collegiate Encyclopedia. 1963. New York, NY: Grolier, 1970 ed.

The Congressional Globe, Containing Sketches of the Debates and Proceedings of the First Session of the Twenty-Eighth Congress (Vol. 13). Washington, D.C.: The Globe, 1844.

The Great Issue to be Decided in November Next: Shall the Constitution and the Union Stand or Fall, Shall

Sectionalism Triumph? Washington, D.C.: National Democratic Executive Committee, 1860.

The National Almanac and Annual Record for the Year 1863. Philadelphia, PA: George W. Childs, 1863.

Thompson, Holland. *The New South: A Chronicle of Social and Industrial Evolution.* New Haven, CT: Yale University Press, 1920.

Thornton, Gordon. *The Southern Nation: The New Rise of the Old South.* Gretna, LA: Pelican Publishing Co., 2000.

Thornton, John. *Africa and Africans in the Making of the Atlantic World, 1400-1800.* 1992. Cambridge, UK: Cambridge University Press, 1999 ed.

Thornton, Mark, and Robert B. Ekelund, Jr. *Tariffs, Blockades, and Inflation: The Economics of the Civil War.* Wilmington, DE: Scholarly Resources, 2004.

Thorpe, Francis Newton. *The Constitutional History of the United States.* 3 vols. Chicago, IL: Callaghan and Co., 1901.

Tilley, John Shipley. *Lincoln Takes Command.* 1941. Nashville, TN: Bill Coats Limited, 1991 ed.

——. *Facts the Historians Leave Out: A Confederate Primer.* 1951. Nashville, TN: Bill Coats Limited, 1999 ed.

Tocqueville, Alexis de. *Democracy in America.* 2 vols. 1836. New York, NY: D. Appleton and Co., 1904 ed.

Traupman, John C. *The New College Latin and English Dictionary.* 1966. New York, NY: Bantam, 1988 ed.

Tucker, St. George. *Blackstone's Commentaries: With Notes of Reference, to the Constitution and Laws, of the Federal Government of the United States; and of the Commonwealth of Virginia.* 5 vols. Philadelphia, PA: Birch and Small, 1803.

Turner, Edward Raymond. *The Negro in Pennsylvania: Slavery, Servitude, Freedom, 1639-1861.* Washington, D.C.: American Historical Association, 1911.

Tyler, Lyon Gardiner. *The Letters and Times of the Tylers.* 3 vols. Williamsburg, VA: N.P., 1896.

——. *Propaganda in History.* Richmond, VA: Richmond Press, 1920.

——. *The Gray Book: A Confederate Catechism.* Columbia, TN: Gray Book Committee, SCV, 1935.

Unger, Irwin. *These United States: The Questions of Our Past - Vol. 2: Since 1865.* 1978. Englewood Cliffs, NJ: Prentice Hall, 1992 ed.

Upshur, Abel Parker. *A Brief Enquiry Into the True Nature and Character of Our Federal Government.* Philadelphia, PA: John Campbell, 1863.

Vallandigham, Clement Laird. *Speeches, Arguments, Addresses, and Letters of Clement L. Vallandigham.* New York, NY: J. Walter and Co., 1864.

Van Evrie, John H. *Negroes and Negro "Slavery": The First, an Inferior Race—the Latter, its Normal Condition.* Baltimore, MD: self-published, 1853.

Victor, Orville James. *The History, Civil, Political and Military, of the Southern Rebellion, From its Incipient Stages to its Close.* 3 vols. New York, NY: James D. Torrey, 1861.

——. *The Comprehensive History of the Southern Rebellion and the War for the Union.* 3 vols. New York, NY: James D. Torrey, 1862.

Washington, Booker T. *Up From Slavery: An Autobiography.* 1901. Garden City, NY: Doubleday, Page and Co., 1919 ed.

Washington, Henry Augustine. *The Writings of Thomas Jefferson.* 9 vols. New York, NY: H. W. Derby, 1861.

Weintraub, Max. *The Blue Book of American History.* New York, NY: Regents Publishing Co., 1960.

Welles, Gideon. *Diary of Gideon Welles, Secretary of the Navy Under Lincoln and Johnson* (Vol. 1). Boston, MA: Houghton Mifflin, 1911.

Wells, H. G. *The Outline of History: Being a Plain History of Life and Mankind.* 2 vols. 1920. Garden City, NY: Garden City Books, 1961 ed.

White, Henry Alexander. *The Making of South Carolina.* New York, NY: Silver, Burdett and Co., 1906.

White, Melvin Johnson. *The Secession Movement in the United States, 1847-1852.* Madison, WI: University of Wisconsin, 1910.

Wiley, Bell Irvin. *Southern Negroes: 1861-1865.* 1938. New Haven, CT: Yale University Press, 1969 ed.

——. *The Life of Johnny Reb: The Common Soldier of the Confederacy.* 1943. Baton Rouge, LA: Louisiana State University Press, 1978 ed.

———. *The Plain People of the Confederacy*. 1943. Columbia, SC: University of South Carolina, 2000 ed.
———. *The Life of Billy Yank: The Common Soldier of the Union*. 1952. Baton Rouge, LA: Louisiana State University Press, 2001 ed.
Wilkens, J. Steven. *America: The First 350 Years*. Monroe, LA: Covenant Publications, 1998.
Wilson, Charles Reagan, and William Ferris. *Encyclopedia of Southern Culture* (Vol. 1). New York, NY: Anchor, 1989.
Wilson, Clyde N. *Why the South Will Survive: Fifteen Southerners Look at Their Region a Half Century After I'll Take My Stand*. Athens, GA: University of Georgia Press, 1981.
Wilson, Woodrow. *A History of the American People*. 5 vols. New York, NY: Harper and Brothers, 1903.
Woods, Thomas E., Jr. *The Politically Incorrect Guide to American History*. Washington, D.C.: Regnery, 2004.
Woodworth, Steven E. *Jefferson Davis and His Generals: The Failure of Confederate Command in the West*. Lawrence, KS: University Press of Kansas, 1990.
Wright, John D. *The Language of the Civil War*. Westport, CT: Oryx, 2001.
Wu, Shelly. *Chinese Astrology: Exploring the Eastern Zodiac*. Franklin, Lakes, NJ: Career Press, 2005.
Zavodnyik, Peter. *The Age of Strict Construction: A History of the Growth of Federal Power, 1789-1861*. Washington, D.C.: Catholic University of America Press, 2007.
Zinn, Howard. *A People's History of the United States: 1492-Present*. 1980. New York, NY: HarperCollins, 1995.

INDEX

Adams, John, 29, 34, 56, 71, 239, 341
Adams, John Q., 38, 39, 86, 213, 260
Adams, Samuel, 56, 58, 324
Adams, Shelby L., 451
Ames, Fisher, 325
Anderson, Loni, 451
Arthur, King, 450
Ashby, Turner, 187
Ashe, Samuel A., 47
Atkins, Chet, 451
Baldwin, Henry, 226
Baring, Alexander, 400
Barksdale, Ethelbert, 289
Barlow, Joel, 408
Barnett, T. J., 143, 313
Bartlett, Josiah, 56
Bateman, William O., 64
Bayard, James A., 144
Beauregard, Pierre G. T., 450
Benjamin, Judah P., 274, 293
Benton, Thomas H., 268
Bernstein, Leonard, 451
Bigler, William, 98, 144
Black, Jeremiah S., 75
Blackstone, William, 41, 339
Bledsoe, Albert T., 28, 69, 88, 208, 239, 305, 306
Bolling, Edith, 451
Boone, Daniel, 450
Boone, Pat, 451
Booth, John Wilkes, 300
Boucher, Chauncey S., 256
Bowdoin, James, 325
Braxton, Carter, 56
Breckinridge, John C., 63, 99, 450
Brewer, David J., 321
Brooke, Edward W., 451
Brooks, Preston S., 257, 451
Browder, Earl, 101
Brown, J. N., 286
Brown, John, 162, 231, 258, 403, 407
Brown, Joseph E., 197
Buchanan, James, 45, 73, 75, 86, 89, 328, 333, 403, 404
Buchanan, Patrick J., 167, 451
Buford, Abraham, 450
Burke, Edmund, 21, 86
Burnett, L. W., 79
Burr, Aaron, 71
Butler, Andrew P., 451
Butler, Benjamin F., 246, 283, 300
Cabell, Edward C., 130
Cabot, George, 326, 345
Calhoun, John C., 37, 141, 189, 211, 212, 268, 354, 399
Cameron, Simon, 246, 288
Campbell, Joseph, 449
Carroll, Charles (of Carrollton), 56
Carson, Martha, 451
Carter, Theodrick, 450
Cash, Johnny, 451
Caudill, Benjamin E., 449
Chandler, Andrew M., 273
Chandler, Silas, 273
Chase, Salmon P., 56, 83, 316, 318, 320, 348
Chase, Samuel, 56
Cheairs, Nathaniel F., 451
Chesnut, Mary, 270, 451
Clark, Abraham, 56
Clark, William, 450
Clay, Cassius M., 304
Clay, Henry, 147, 296, 297, 302, 304
Cleburne, Patrick R., 176, 279, 280
Clifford, John H., 348
Clingman, Thomas L., 141, 142
Clinton, George, 78
Clymer, George, 56

Cobb, Howell, 92
Cobb, Thomas R. R., 108, 111
Coleridge, Samuel T., 68
Combs, Bertram T., 451
Conway, Moncure D., 289
Cooke, Alistair, 252
Coolidge, Calvin, 16
Cooper, Oscar H., 48, 348
Cornplanter, Chief, 65
Coxe, Tench, 324
Crandall, Prudence, 148
Crawford, Cindy, 451
Crawford, William, 49
Crittenden, John J., 144, 145, 404
Crockett, Davy, 450
Cruise, Tom, 451
Curtis, George T., 28
Cushing, Caleb, 355
Cyrus, Billy R., 451
Cyrus, Miley, 451
Dana, Charles A., 116
Dane, Nathan, 345
Dargan, Edmund S., 178
Davis, Jefferson, 11, 13, 21, 31, 44, 49, 50, 55, 73, 81, 82, 85, 90, 91, 139, 142, 146, 147, 155, 167, 187, 189, 190, 197, 208, 235, 238, 242, 244, 251, 254, 255, 277, 289, 291, 306-308, 314, 316, 347, 348, 404, 409, 449, 450
Dickens, Charles, 312, 313
Dickinson, John, 323
Diogenes, 149
Dodge, William E., 240
Dodson, Jacob, 288
Dorr, Thomas W., 400
Douglas, Stephen A., 148, 162, 212, 231, 233, 253, 285, 286, 295, 296, 299, 402, 403
Duvall, Robert, 451
Edward I, King, 450
Ellery, William, 56
Ellsworth, Oliver, 60, 325
Estill, Harry F., 48, 348

Evarts, William M., 348
Everett, Edward, 317
Fairfield, John, 230
Faulkner, Charles J., 195, 196
Faulkner, Harold U., 154
Fillmore, Millard, 402
Fitch, John, 98
Florence, Thomas B., 150
Floyd, William, 56
Foote, Shelby, 449
Forbes, Christopher, 451
Forrest, Nathan B., 13, 87, 90, 187, 277, 288, 449, 450
Forster, William E., 156
Fowler, William C., 28, 29, 31, 32, 60, 64, 67, 94, 156, 161, 240, 258, 268, 329, 331
Franklin, Benjamin, 56, 80, 253, 323
Frémont, John C., 401
Gadsden, James, 403
Garlington, Albert C., 43
Garrison, William L., 148, 163, 239
Gayheart, Rebecca, 451
George III, King, 12, 53-55, 57, 99, 198, 201, 344
Gerry, Elbridge, 56, 240, 324
Giles, William B., 259
Gist, States R., 450
Gist, William H., 355
Golovin, Ivan, 68
Goodlow, Daniel R., 270
Gordon, George W., 450
Gordon, John B., 187
Gordon, Nathaniel, 309
Gore, Christopher, 325
Grant, Ulysses S., 85, 86, 246, 248, 283, 295, 310, 347, 351
Grattan, Thomas C., 47
Graves, Robert, 449
Greeley, Horace, 44, 86
Green, Duff, 268
Gregg, Maxcy, 177
Griffith, Andy, 451
Grimké, Angelina, 270
Grimké, Sarah, 270

Grotius, 232
Guaraldi, Vince, 451
Gwinnett, Button, 56
Hall, Lyman, 56
Hamilton, Alexander, 26, 28, 29, 31, 58, 60, 61, 78, 91, 239, 253, 302, 318, 322, 339, 343, 408
Hamlin, Hannibal, 120
Hammond, James H., 216, 219
Harding, William G., 450
Harllee, William W., 43
Harris, Isham G., 92, 272
Harrison, Benjamin, 56
Harrison, William H., 40, 400
Hart, John, 56
Hayes, Rutherford B., 318
Hayne, Robert Y., 82, 399
Hedrick, Benjamin S., 270
Helper, Hinton R., 162, 258
Henderson, John B., 274
Hendricks, Thomas A., 42
Henry, Patrick, 59, 65, 240
Hewes, Joseph, 56
Heyward, Thomas, Jr., 56
Higginson, Thomas W., 272
Hillhouse, James, 345
Homer, 104
Hood, John B., 450
Hooper, William, 56
Hopkins, Stephen, 56
Hopkinson, Francis, 56
Hunter, Robert M. T., 130, 217, 219, 332
Huntington, Samuel, 56, 65
Ingersoll, Ebon C., 220
Ingersoll, Robert G., 220
Inglis, John A., 353
Iredell, James, 319, 325
Iverson, Alfred, Sr., 160, 216, 219, 240, 333
Jackson, Andrew, 29, 43, 112, 141, 189, 261, 268, 399, 400, 409, 451
Jackson, Henry R., 450
Jackson, Stonewall, 187, 288, 450
James, Frank, 451
James, Jesse, 451
Jamison, David F., 43, 159
Jay, John, 249, 253, 322
Jefferson, Thomas, 21, 23, 29, 32-34, 42, 44, 49, 51, 54-56, 66, 70-72, 81, 86, 90, 91, 158, 160, 163, 187, 201, 216, 233, 240, 253, 258, 269, 286, 302, 303, 326, 329, 334, 338, 343, 355, 356, 403, 451
Jent, Elias, Sr., 450
Jesus, 162, 450
John, Elton, 451
Johnson, Andrew, 144, 145, 348
Johnson, Samuel, 21
Johnston, Alexander, 41
Johnston, Joseph E., 13
Johnston, Richard M., 227
Johnston, Samuel, 323
Judd, Ashley, 451
Judd, Naomi, 451
Judd, Wynonna, 451
Kearney, Stephen W., 402
Keitt, Laurence M., 177
Kennedy, John P., 144
Kenner, Duncan F., 274
Kent, Edward, 230
Kent, James, 341, 346
Kent, William, 42
Keough, Riley, 451
King, Rufus, 70, 71
Las Casas, Bartolomé de, 216
Lee, Fitzhugh, 451
Lee, Francis Lightfoot, 56
Lee, Richard Henry, 56
Lee, Robert E., 54, 87, 90, 187, 234, 248, 276-278, 286, 289, 316, 333, 348, 409, 450
Lee, Stephen D., 450
Lee, William H. F., 451
Lemmon, Leonard, 48, 348
Letcher, John, 197, 199, 201, 203
Lewis, Francis, 56
Lewis, Meriwether, 450

Lincoln, Abraham, 11, 14, 22, 27, 36, 43, 44, 47, 51, 53, 58, 59, 61-63, 66, 70, 73, 78-81, 83-86, 90, 92, 96-99, 106, 108, 111, 120, 126, 132, 141-147, 150, 152-154, 157, 167, 169, 175, 190, 194, 196-202, 212, 215, 219, 221, 223-226, 228, 231, 233, 238-240, 243, 245, 248, 250-252, 254, 255, 258, 264, 265, 267, 268, 272, 273, 277, 281, 284-286, 288, 290, 291, 293, 294, 296, 297, 299-304, 306, 309-316, 331, 347, 351, 403, 407
Livingston, Philip, 56
Locke, John, 24
Lodge, Henry C., 77, 78
Longstreet, James, 13, 187, 450
Loring, Caleb W., 86, 247, 316
Lovejoy, Elijah, 148
Loveless, Patty, 451
Lundy, Benjamin, 270
Lynch, Thomas, Jr., 56
Lyons, Lord, 263
Mackay, Alexander, 48
Macon, Nathaniel, 53
Madison, James, 25, 31, 34, 41, 42, 45, 51, 53, 63, 65, 69, 74, 75, 86, 91, 233, 240, 253, 318, 322, 327-330, 343, 346, 364
Manigault, Arthur M., 450
Manigault, Joseph, 450
Mann, Ambrose D., 263, 264
Mann, Horace, 154
Marshall, John, 320, 325, 332
Marvin, Lee, 451
Marx, Karl, 86, 112, 314
Mason, George, 78, 240
Mason, James M., 194, 195
Maury, Abram P., 451
McClellan, George B., 281
McGavock, Caroline E., 451
McGavock, David H., 451
McGavock, Emily, 451

McGavock, Francis, 451
McGavock, James R., 451
McGavock, John W., 451
McGavock, Lysander, 451
McGavock, Randal W., 451
McGrath, Andrew G., 43
McGraw, Tim, 451
McKean, Thomas, 56
Memminger, Christopher G., 43, 170
Meriwether, Elizabeth A., 451
Meriwether, Minor, 451
Middleton, Arthur, 56
Monroe, James, 240
Montesquieu, Baron de, 61, 337, 408
Moore, Thomas O., 272
Morgan, John H., 187, 450
Morley, John, 86
Morris, Gouverneur, 35, 80, 323, 339
Morris, Lewis, 56
Morris, Robert, 56
Morton, John, 56
Morton, John W., 451
Mosby, John S., 187, 450
Myers, Thomas J., 292
Napoleon I, 93
Nelson, Samuel, 316, 320
Nelson, Thomas, Jr., 56
Nugent, Ted, 451
Obama, Barack H., 239, 240
Otis, Harrison G., 345
Owsley, Frank L., 158
O'Connor, Charles, 348
Paca, William, 56
Paine, Robert T., 56
Paine, Thomas, 240
Parsons, Theophilus, 325
Parton, Dolly, 451
Patterson, William, 58
Pendleton, Edmund, 325
Penn, John, 56
Pericles, 104
Pettus, Edmund W., 450
Phelps, Edward J., 319
Piatt, Donn, 243
Pickens, Francis W., 43, 204

Pickering, Timothy, 71, 72, 344
Pickett, George E., 36
Pierce, Franklin, 44, 86, 138, 260, 402
Pierpoint, Francis H., 201
Pillow, Gideon J., 450
Pinckney, Charles C., 158
Plato, 149
Polk, James K., 86, 401, 451
Polk, Leonidas, 450
Polk, Lucius E., 451
Pollard, Edward A., 62
Pomeroy, Samuel, 300
Porter, David, 103
Presley, Elvis, 451
Presley, Lisa Marie, 451
Price, Rodman M., 79
Pugh, James L., 326
Quincy, Josiah, 39
Randolph, Edmund J., 80, 81, 451
Randolph, George W., 451
Randolph, John, 55
Rawle, William, 36, 37, 48, 86, 341-343, 350
Read, George, 56
Reagan, John H., 192
Reagan, Ronald, 403, 451
Reuter, Edward B., 296
Reynolds, Burt, 451
Rhett, Robert B., 155, 178, 355
Ritchie, Thomas, 330
Robbins, Hargus, 451
Robert the Bruce, King, 450
Rodney, Caesar, 56
Rogers, William P., 43
Ross, George, 56
Rost, Pierre A., 263, 264
Rucker, Edmund W., 450
Rush, Benjamin, 56
Russell, (Earl) John, 263, 264
Rutherford, Mildred L., 248
Rutledge, Edward, 56
Sage, Bernard J., 17, 48, 50, 82, 213, 234, 249, 255, 322, 326, 333, 348, 399, 405, 406, 408

Salomon, Edward, 288
Schenck, Robert C., 30, 31
Scott, Dred, 147, 157, 165, 257, 403
Scott, George C., 451
Scott, James B., 319, 330
Scott, Winfield, 401
Scruggs, Earl, 451
Seabrook, John L., 450
Seabrook, Lochlainn, 449-451, 453
Seger, Bob, 451
Seward, William H., 42, 144, 146, 230, 317, 348
Seymour, Thomas H., 44
Sheridan, Philip H., 283
Sherman, Roger, 56, 65, 318, 325
Sherman, William T., 283, 292
Skaggs, Ricky, 451
Slidell, John, 194, 195
Sloat, John D., 401
Smith, James, 56
Smith, Joseph, 401
Snead, Thomas L., 130
Speed, James, 348
Spooner, Lysander, 251, 310, 311
Spratt, John M., 355
Stanton, Edwin M., 198
Steel, Samuel A., 22
Stephens, Alexander H., 11, 13, 48, 90, 93, 96, 103, 106, 147, 206-208, 219, 221-223, 225-227, 240, 334, 404, 450
Stevens, Thaddeus, 220, 268
Stewart, Alexander P., 450
Stockton, Richard, 56
Stone, Thomas, 56
Story, Joseph, 38, 319, 336-339, 341, 345
Stowe, Harriet B., 265, 267
Stuart, Jeb, 187, 450
Sumner, Charles, 257
Swift, Zephenia, 345
Taylor, George, 56
Taylor, J., 163
Taylor, John, 258
Taylor, Richard, 13, 308, 450

Taylor, Sarah K., 450
Taylor, Zachary, 308, 401, 402, 450
Thackeray, William M., 21
Thornton, Matthew, 56
Tilden, Samuel J., 42, 43
Tocqueville, Alexis de, 47, 164, 250, 271, 346
Toombs, Robert A., 49, 99, 100, 102, 109, 111, 140, 228, 232, 234-237, 241
Tucker, St. George, 34, 41, 47, 61, 249, 336, 339, 341, 343
Tyler, John, 39, 86, 256, 400
Tyler, Lyon G., 256
Tynes, Ellen B., 451
Underwood, John C., 348
Upshur, Abel P., 39
Van Buren, Martin, 40, 218, 400
Van Evrie, John H., 227
Vance, Robert B., 451
Vance, Zebulon, 451
Vattel, Emer de, 26
Venable, Charles S., 450
Walton, George, 56
Washington, George, 12, 26, 28, 29, 36, 38, 60, 61, 65, 68, 71, 78, 91, 216, 231, 253, 319, 323, 334, 341, 409
Washington, John A., 450
Washington, Thornton A., 450
Webster, Daniel, 31, 162, 213, 248, 317, 336, 338, 399
Webster, Noah, 21
Weld, Theodore, 148
Whipple, William, 56
Whitman, Marcus, 401
Wilkes, Charles, 195
Williams, William, 56, 65
Wilson, Henry, 144
Wilson, James, 56, 66, 80, 318, 324
Wilson, Woodrow, 73, 86, 87, 95, 157, 167, 209, 242, 451
Winder, Charles S., 451
Winder, John H., 450
Witherspoon, John, 56

Witherspoon, Reese, 451
Wolcott, Oliver, 56, 65
Wolseley, Garnet J., 87
Womack, John B., 450
Womack, Lee Ann, 451
Wood, Fernando, 78, 227
Wythe, George, 56
Yancey, William L., 263, 264
Zollicoffer, Felix K., 451

MEET THE AUTHOR

"ASKING THE PATRIOTIC SOUTH TO STOP HONORING HER CONFEDERATE ANCESTORS IS LIKE ASKING THE SUN NOT TO SHINE." — COLONEL LOCHLAINN SEABROOK

LOCHLAINN SEABROOK, a neo-Victorian and world acclaimed man of letters, is a Kentucky Colonel and the winner of the prestigious Jefferson Davis Historical Gold Medal for his "masterpiece," *A Rebel Born: A Defense of Nathan Bedford Forrest*. A classic littérateur and an unreconstructed Southern historian, he is an award-winning author, Civil War scholar, Bible authority, and a traditional Southern Agrarian of Scottish, English, Irish, Dutch, Welsh, German, and Italian extraction.

A child prodigy, Seabrook is today a true Renaissance Man whose occupational titles also include encyclopedist, lexicographer, musician, artist, graphic designer, genealogist, photographer, and award-winning poet. Also a songwriter and a screenwriter, he has a 40 year background in historical nonfiction writing and is a member of the Sons of Confederate Veterans, the Civil War Trust, and the National Grange.

Known to his many fans as the "voice of the traditional South," due to similarities in their writing styles, ideas, and literary works, Seabrook is also often referred to as the "new Shelby Foote," the "Southern Joseph Campbell," and the "American Robert Graves" (his English cousin). Seabrook coined the terms "South-shaming" and "Lincolnian liberalism," and holds the world's record for writing the most books on Nathan Bedford Forrest: nine. In addition, Seabrook is the first Civil War scholar to connect the early American nickname for the U.S., "The Confederate States of America," with the Southern Confederacy that arose eight decades later, and the first to note that in 1860 the party platforms of the two major political parties were the opposite of what they are today (Victorian Democrats were conservatives, Victorian Republicans were liberals).

The grandson of an Appalachian coal-mining family, Seabrook is a seventh-generation Kentuckian, co-chair of the Jent/Gent Family Committee (Kentucky), founder and director of the Blakeney Family Tree Project, and a board member of the Friends of Colonel Benjamin E. Caudill. Seabrook's literary works have been endorsed by leading authorities, museum curators, award-winning historians, bestselling authors, celebrities, noted scientists, well regarded educators, TV show hosts and producers, renowned military artists, esteemed Southern organizations, and distinguished academicians from around the world.

Above, Colonel Lochlainn Seabrook, "the voice of the traditional South," award-winning Civil War scholar and unreconstructed Southern historian. America's most popular and prolific pro-South author, his many books have introduced hundreds of thousands to the truth about the War for Southern Independence. He coined the phrase "South-shaming" and holds the world's record for writing the most books on Nathan Bedford Forrest: nine.

Seabrook has authored over 50 popular adult books on the American Civil War, American and international slavery, the U.S. Confederacy (1781), the Southern Confederacy (1861), religion, theology, thealogy, Jesus, the Bible, the Apocrypha, the Law of Attraction, alternative health, spirituality, ghost stories, the paranormal, ufology, social issues, and cross-cultural studies of the family and marriage. His Confederate biographies, pro-South studies, genealogical monographs, family histories, military encyclopedias, self-help guides, and etymological dictionaries have received wide acclaim.

Seabrook's eight children's books include a Southern guide to the Civil War, a biography of Nathan Bedford Forrest, a dictionary of religion and myth, a rewriting of the King Arthur legend (which reinstates the original pre-Christian motifs), two bedtime stories for preschoolers, a naturalist's guidebook to owls, a worldwide look at the family, and an examination of the Near-Death Experience.

Of blue-blooded Southern stock through his Kentucky, Tennessee, Virginia, West Virginia, and North Carolina ancestors, he is a direct descendant of European royalty via his 6th great-grandfather, the Earl of Oxford, after which London's famous Harley Street is named. Among his celebrated male Celtic ancestors is Robert the Bruce, King of Scotland, Seabrook's 22nd great-grandfather. The 21st great-grandson of Edward I "Longshanks" Plantagenet), King of England, Seabrook is a thirteenth-generation Southerner through his descent from the colonists of Jamestown, Virginia (1607).

(Photo © Lochlainn Seabrook)

The 2nd, 3rd, and 4th great-grandson of dozens of Confederate soldiers, one of his closest connections to Lincoln's War is through his 3rd great-grandfather, Elias Jent, Sr., who fought for the Confederacy in the Thirteenth Cavalry Kentucky under Seabrook's 2nd cousin, Colonel Benjamin E. Caudill. The Thirteenth, also known as "Caudill's Army," fought in numerous conflicts, including the Battles of Saltville, Gladsville, Mill Cliff, Poor Fork, Whitesburg, and Leatherwood.

Seabrook is a direct descendant of the families of Alexander H. Stephens, John Singleton Mosby, William Giles Harding, and Edmund Winchester Rucker, and is related to the following Confederates and other 18th- and 19th-Century luminaries: Robert E. Lee, Stephen Dill Lee, Stonewall Jackson, Nathan Bedford Forrest, James Longstreet, John Hunt Morgan, Jeb Stuart, Pierre G. T. Beauregard (approved the Confederate Battle Flag design), George W. Gordon, John Bell Hood, Alexander Peter Stewart, Arthur M. Manigault, Joseph Manigault, Charles Scott Venable, Thornton A. Washington, John A. Washington, Abraham Buford, Edmund W. Pettus, Theodrick "Tod" Carter, John B. Womack, John H. Winder, Gideon J. Pillow, States Rights Gist, Henry R. Jackson, John Lawton Seabrook, John C. Breckinridge, Leonidas Polk, Zachary Taylor, Sarah Knox Taylor (first wife of Jefferson Davis), Richard Taylor, Davy Crockett, Daniel Boone, Meriwether Lewis (of the Lewis and Clark Expedition)

Andrew Jackson, James K. Polk, Abram Poindexter Maury (founder of Franklin, TN), Zebulon Vance, Thomas Jefferson, Edmund Jennings Randolph, George Wythe Randolph (grandson of Jefferson), Felix K. Zollicoffer, Fitzhugh Lee, Nathaniel F. Cheairs, Jesse James, Frank James, Robert Brank Vance, Charles Sidney Winder, John W. McGavock, Caroline E. (Winder) McGavock, David Harding McGavock, Lysander McGavock, James Randal McGavock, Randal William McGavock, Francis McGavock, Emily McGavock, William Henry F. Lee, Lucius E. Polk, Minor Meriwether (husband of noted pro-South author Elizabeth Avery Meriwether), Ellen Bourne Tynes (wife of Forrest's chief of artillery, Captain John W. Morton), South Carolina Senators Preston Smith Brooks and Andrew Pickens Butler, and famed South Carolina diarist Mary Chesnut.

Seabrook's modern day cousins include: Patrick J. Buchanan (conservative author), Cindy Crawford (model), Shelby Lee Adams (Letcher Co., Kentucky, photographer), Bertram Thomas Combs (Kentucky's 50th governor), Edith Bolling (wife of President Woodrow Wilson), and actors Andy Griffith, Riley Keough, George C. Scott, Robert Duvall, Reese Witherspoon, Lee Marvin, Rebecca Gayheart, and Tom Cruise.

Seabrook's screenplay, *A Rebel Born*, based on his book of the same name, has been signed with acclaimed filmmaker Christopher Forbes (of Forbes Film). It is now in pre-production, and is set for release in 2017 as a full-length feature film. This will be the first movie ever made of Nathan Bedford Forrest's life story, and as a historically accurate project written from the Southern perspective, is destined to be one of the most talked about Civil War films of all time.

Born with music in his blood, Seabrook is an award-winning, multi-genre, BMI-Nashville songwriter and lyricist who has composed some 3,000 songs (250 albums), and whose original music has been heard in film (*A Rebel Born, Cowgirls 'n Angels, Confederate Cavalry, Billy the Kid: Showdown in Lincoln County, Vengeance Without Mercy, Last Step, County Line, The Mark*) and on TV and radio worldwide. A musician, producer, multi-instrumentalist, and renown performer—whose keyboard work has been variously compared to pianists from Hargus Robbins and Vince Guaraldi to Elton John and Leonard Bernstein—Seabrook has opened for groups such as the Earl Scruggs Review, Ted Nugent, and Bob Seger, and has performed privately for such public figures as President Ronald Reagan, Burt Reynolds, Loni Anderson, and Senator Edward W. Brooke. Seabrook's cousins in the music business include: Johnny Cash, Elvis Presley, Lisa Marie Presley, Billy Ray and Miley Cyrus, Patty Loveless, Tim McGraw, Lee Ann Womack, Dolly Parton, Pat Boone, Naomi, Wynonna, and Ashley Judd, Ricky Skaggs, the Sunshine Sisters, Martha Carson, and Chet Atkins.

Seabrook lives with his wife and family in historic Middle Tennessee, the heart of Forrest country and the Confederacy, where his conservative Southern ancestors fought valiantly against Liberal Lincoln and the progressive North in defense of Jeffersonianism, constitutional government, and personal liberty.

LochlainnSeabrook.com

LOCHLAINN SEABROOK ∽ 453

If you enjoyed this book you will be interested in Colonel Seabrook's other popular related titles:

☞ EVERYTHING YOU WERE TAUGHT ABOUT THE CIVIL WAR IS WRONG, ASK A SOUTHERNER!
☞ EVERYTHING YOU WERE TAUGHT ABOUT AMERICAN SLAVERY IS WRONG, ASK A SOUTHERNER!
☞ CONFEDERATE FLAG FACTS: WHAT EVERY AMERICAN SHOULD KNOW ABOUT DIXIE'S SOUTHERN CROSS
☞ ABRAHAM LINCOLN WAS A LIBERAL, JEFFERSON DAVIS WAS A CONSERVATIVE

Available from Sea Raven Press and wherever fine books are sold

ALL OF OUR BOOK COVERS ARE AVAILABLE AS 11" X 17" POSTERS, SUITABLE FOR FRAMING

SeaRavenPress.com • NathanBedfordForrestBooks.com

www.ingramcontent.com/pod-product-compliance
Lightning Source LLC
Chambersburg PA
CBHW030515230426
43665CB00010B/625